The Dyirbal language of North Queensland

CAMBRIDGE STUDIES IN LINGUISTICS

General Editors · W. SIDNEY ALLEN · EUGENIE J. A. HENDERSON · FRED W. HOUSEHOLDER · JOHN LYONS · R. B. LE PAGE · F. R. PALMER · J. L. M. TRIM

THE DYIRBAL LANGUAGE
OF NORTH QUEENSLAND

R.M.W. DIXON

Professor of Linguistics
in the School of General Studies,
Australian National University

CAMBRIDGE
at the University Press : 1972

Published by the Syndics of the Cambridge University Press
Bentley House, 200 Euston Road, London NW1 2DB
American Branch: 32 East 57th Street, New York, N.Y.10022

© Cambridge University Press 1972

Library of Congress Catalogue Card Number: 78–190415

ISBN: 0 521 08510 1

Printed in Great Britain
at the University Printing House, Cambridge
(Brooke Crutchley, University Printer)

This study is dedicated to the surviving speakers of the Dyirbal, Giramay and Mamu dialects. For more than ten thousand years they lived in harmony with each other and with their environment. One hundred years ago many of them were shot and poisoned by European invaders. Those allowed to survive have been barely tolerated tenants on their own lands, and have had their beliefs, habits and language held up to ridicule and scorn. In the last decade they have seen their remaining forests taken and cleared by an American company, with the destruction of sites whose remembered antiquity is many thousands of years older than the furthest event in the shallow history of their desecrators.

The survivors of the three tribes have stood up to these adversities with dignity and humour, fortified by their amusement at the blindness of the invader to the richness of the environment, and of the life of the people he believes himself to be supplanting.

They continue to look forward to the day when they may again be allowed to live in peaceful possession of some of their own lands, and may be accorded a respect which they have been denied, but which they have been forcibly made to accord to others.

Contents

        6.7.1   *-ru*   266
        6.7.2   *-bu*   268
        6.7.3   *-bi*   268

7   PHONOLOGY   269
    7.1   Systems of phonological features   269

    7.2   Word structures
            7.2.1   Segments   272
            7.2.2   Stress   274

    7.3   Phonic realisations of phonological systems   276

    7.4   Statistical support for phonological description
            7.4.1   Probabilities of occurrence   279
            7.4.2   Statistical association   281

    7.5   Special phonological processes
            7.5.1   Insertion and assimilation   283
            7.5.2   Elision and conflation   287

    7.6   A morphophonological rule   288

    7.7   *r* and *l*   289

    7.8   Word order   291

8   SEMANTICS   292
    8.1   Guwal-Dyalŋuy correspondences   292

    8.2   Verb semantics
            8.2.1   Nuclear and non-nuclear verbs   293
            8.2.2   Syntactic possibilities   296
            8.2.3   Verb types and their syntactic properties 299

    8.3   Adverbal semantics   301

    8.4   Noun semantics   302
            8.4.1   Generic terms in Guwal   303
            8.4.2   Guwal-Dyalŋuy correspondences: taxonomic
                        grouping   304
            8.4.3   Metaphoric naming   305
            8.4.4   Semantic basis of noun class membership   306
            8.4.5   Loan concepts   311

List of Maps and Plates

Acknowledgements

It is impossible adequately to express the writer's gratitude to the informants, particularly Chloe Grant (*marḍi* or *miḍabunḍal*) and George Watson (*muyiḍa*, *ɲiyiḍa* or *banganḍala*). It is their intelligence, and their unfailing interest, patience and willingness to work long hours to suit the writer's convenience, that has made this description possible. Amongst other informants who contributed to the variety of facts presented below are the late Paddy Biran (*garanba*), Tommy Springcart (*ḍumbulu*), the late Jimmie Murray (*giriɲḍaɲ*), Jack Murray (*yangaɲ*) Mosley Digman (*badibadi*), Joe Kinjun (*giɲḍubayil*), the late Joe Chalum (*ḍalam*), Spider Henry (*ḍinbala*), the late Jinnie Watson (*dunma* or *wargabaṟan*), Rose Runaway (*ḍarmay*), Mary Ann Murray (*miɲaḍaŋgay*) and Lorna (*ḍubula*).

The Australian Institute of Aboriginal Studies wholly supported a year's field work in North Queensland from September 1963 to September 1964, provided a grant for continuing work on field material in 1965, partly financed a field trip in March and April 1967, and wholly financed a field trip in December 1970. The writer is most grateful for the constant encouragement, cooperation and help provided by the Institute, and its principal F. D. McCarthy, throughout this period.

The Central Research Fund of the University of London generously provided the balance of finance for the 1967 field trip.

A special word of thanks is due to the late Lindsay Cowan, Mrs Cowan and family of Murray Upper, for their continued hospitality and friendship throughout the eight and a half years of the project; and to Mr and Mrs Ernie Grant, of Tully, in 1967, and Mr and Mrs George Henry, of Bellenden, in 1970. Others who helped the project include Mrs Graham Haydon, Jack Doolan, the late Douglas Seaton, and Mr and Mrs G. J. W. Gaynor. The Director of the Queensland Department of Native Affairs (now: Department of Aboriginal and Island Affairs), and the various Superintendents and Managers of the Palm Island Aboriginal Settlement were most cooperative.

Many of the ideas of chapter 1 (and some of those in other parts of the book) evolved during discussions with Kenneth Hale and Geoffrey

O'Grady; the writer owes a tremendous debt to each of them. In
addition, Hale allowed his unpublished materials on Walbiri, Lardil,
Dyabugay, Yidin, Wik Munkan, Yanyula and Wik Meʔn to be drawn
on. A number of other linguists made available unpublished material
on Australian languages; particular thanks are due to J. G. Breen
(Waḻuwara), Luise Hercus (Arabana), Heather Hinch (Maung), J. Earl
Hughes (Nunggubuyu), Sandra Keen (Yukulta), Christine Kilham and
Barbara Sayers (Wik Munkan), Jean Kirton (Yanyula), Terry Klokeid
and Ephraim Bani (Mabuiag), Christine Furby (Garawa), Charles
Osborne (Tiwi), Eirlys Richards and Joyce Hudson (Walmatjari),
Margaret Sharpe (Alawa), Judith Stokes (Aniṉḏilyaugwa), Peter Sutton
(Biria and Gugu-Baḏun), N. B. Tindale (Bulway), and Colin Yallop
(Alyawara dialect of Arandic). The data quoted from Dyangun,
Mbabaɽam, Muluridyi, Nyawigi, Olgolo, Wagaman, Wargamay, Waruṇu,
and some of that from Yidin, is from the writer's own field notes.

   A. Capell has, since 1962, advised and shaped the writer's plans and
given unstinting help in many ways. Thanks are also due, for linguistic
help and advice, to La Mont West, Jnr, and Stephen Wurm. M. A. K.
Halliday, John Lyons, T. S. T. Henderson and Erik Fudge read earlier
drafts of this description and contributed a good deal of welcome
comment. Warren Cowgill gave much useful advice during the writing
of the main draft. John Haiman and Luise Hercus provided valuable
criticism and correction of the final version.

   The writer taught aspects of the grammar of Dyirbal at University
College London in 1965/6, in 1967, and again in 1970, and at Harvard
University in 1968. In all cases, the reactions and suggestions of
students were most welcome. The Harvard class – consisting of Kenneth
Hale, Ives Goddard, Michael Silverstein, Rudolph de Rijk and John
Nicholls – was the most stimulating group the writer has ever confronted;
several important new insights into the underlying grammatical
patterning of Dyirbal emerged during that semester.

   The writer's wife dislikes typical 'acknowledgements to wife'
exusions. Amongst other things, she made a thorough study of the
literature on the area and, much to their surprise, questioned aborigines
on the details of several secret and half-forgotten practices. Partly as
a result of this they continue to view her with awe, and to consider
her the major investigator, with the writer merely a slave deputed to
deal with the dull chores of grammatical detail. So be it.

Preface

What follows is a revision of the sections on grammar and phonology
of the writer's London PhD thesis [Dixon, 1968 *a*]. The main points
of the semantics section have already been summarised in print [Dixon,
1971]. Further work on the lexicon, and its semantic structure, with
particular reference to the special 'mother-in-law language' (2.5, 8.1),
is proceeding, with a view to the eventual publication of a comprehensive
dictionary-thesaurus of Dyirbal.

Since the grammatical natures of Australian languages are not widely
known, it has seemed worthwhile, in chapter 1, to give a brief survey
of some of the recurring characteristics of languages across the continent.
In addition, some references to points of similarity in the grammars of
other languages are included, in smaller type, throughout the description
of Dyirbal.

The grammar is written at two distinct 'levels'. The 'facts' of the
grammar – affixes, their syntactic effect, types of construction, and so
on – are described in chapters 3, 4 and 6. Chapter 5 interprets some
of these facts, setting up explanatory generalisations and describing
the 'deep' grammar of Dyirbal in terms of a number of syntactic
relations and a number of transformational rules. It has seemed desirable
to (at least partially) separate facts from interpretations in the case of
a language like Dyirbal that has not previously been described in any
way. The correctness of chapters 3, 4 and 6 cannot seriously be in
dispute. Chapter 5, however, is far more open to argument. A quite
different set of generalisations, with greater explanatory power, might
well be providable instead of those given here. As linguistic theory
progresses chapter 5 is rather likely to stand in need of revision; this
is unlikely to be true for chapters 3, 4 and 6.

The writer believes that syntax is, for a number of reasons, more
interesting and more fundamental than morphology and is better
presented first. Chapter 3 mentions the word classes of Dyirbal and
gives inflectional paradigms that are needed for following the account
of syntax in chapter 4. Chapter 5 attempts a 'deep' interpretation of

some of the facts of chapter 4. Chapter 6 discusses the non-inflectional morphology, and gives further detail on some of the inflections. The phonological description needs to refer to morphological and syntactic points – one criterion in setting up a phonological description involves maximum simplicity of morphophonological rules – and is placed after the grammatical chapters.

The grammatical description, and particularly chapter 5, is loosely based on the transformational generative model [Chomsky, 1957, 1965 et al.]. The presentation of grammatical facts, in chapters 3, 4 and 6, has been influenced in part by the grammar-writing tradition associated with Franz Boas, Edward Sapir and their pupils [Boas, 1911; Voegelin, 1952; et al.].

Informality has been aimed at throughout the exposition, in order to ensure maximum readability. Traditional terms – case names 'dative', 'genitive', and so on – have been used wherever possible, in preference to difficult, unusual or neologised terms. Excessive symbolisation has been avoided. In particular no attempt has been made to write a completely formal (transformational) grammar. The transformational rules that are given have considerable explanatory power (and are by no means obvious, from the information given in the factual chapters). A full set of phrase structure rules, and necessary additional trans-formational rules, can be constructed – by any reader who is interested in doing so – on the basis of the facts given in chapters 3, 4 and 6.

The description is built around 'word' and 'sentence'; suffixes, modifying words, and so on, are added by grammatical processes. Functional relations – subject-verb, verb-object, etc – are dealt with in terms of 'deep syntactic relations'. Word order in Dyirbal simple sentences is extraordinarily free – words can occur in any order in a sentence (irrespective of phrase membership); order constraints only really enter with repeated iteration involving more than one indirect object.

Dyirbal has very strong topic patterning – that is, grammatical patterning that involves several sentences in sequence in a text. This has been described in a fairly ad hoc way, in the absence of any established grammatical technique for handling it.

Phonology is regarded as an interpretative component, whose primitives are systems of phonological features. A phonological feature has a range of phonic realisation, RELATIVE TO the realisations of the other features in its system. It should be noted that the phonological description is less complete than the grammar, with no attempt being made to deal with intonation or sentence stress.

Informants' judgements of acceptability merged 'grammaticalness' and 'meaningfulness' (in the sense of Chomsky, 1957: 15). Thus, sentences that were grammatically illformed were rightly rejected; and, for instance, the perfectly grammatical *bala miḍa baŋgul yaṟaŋgu wamban* 'the man is building the mia mia' was also at one time rejected, on the grounds that men do not build huts. The non-acceptability of *bala miḍa baŋgul yaṟaŋgu wamban* is a cultural and not a linguistic matter. We have not, as a rule, attempted below to deal with selectional restrictions, of this or other types.

Canberra, September 1971

Abbreviations and Conventions

The three dialects of the Dyirbal language (2.2) are normally referred to by single letters:

D   Dyirbal dialect
G   Giramay dialect
M   Mamu dialect

D always refers to the Dyirbal dialect of the Dyirbal language and never to the complete Dyirbal language.

Three deep syntactic relations are referred to by single letters:

S   subject of an intransitive verb, for instance *bayi yaṟa* 'the man' in *bayi yaṟa ḍiŋgaliɲu* 'the man runs'; *balan guda* 'the dog' in *balan guda yanu* 'the dog goes'

A   subject (or agent) of a transitive verb, for instance *baŋgul yaṟaŋgu* 'the man' in *balan guda baŋgul yaṟaŋgu balgan* 'the man hit the dog'

O   object of a transitive verb, for instance *balan guda* 'the dog' in *balan guda baŋgul yaṟaŋgu balgan* 'the man hit the dog'

Three abbreviated names for grammatical classes are employed:

NP   noun phrase, consisting of a head noun, a noun marker, any number of adjectives, and so on

VC   verb complex, consisting of one or more verbs and/or adverbals, agreeing in surface transitivity and final inflection, together with locational adjuncts, and so on

VP   verb phrase, an immediate constituent of a sentence, consisting of either an intransitive verb complex, or a transitive verb complex together with an NP whose words are in ergative case

Examples quoted from Dyirbal texts are referred to by text and line number. Page numbers are also given in the case of those texts set out in full at the end of the book. Tapes and transcripts of other texts have been deposited with the Australian Institute of Aboriginal Studies (see p. 368).

Dyirbal sentences are sometimes provided with an interlinear gloss, and also an English translation of the complete sentence. In the interlinear gloss, lexical items are given in lower case and grammatical elements of all types in small capitals.

Dyirbal NPs do not obligatorily choose for definiteness or number; the main tense system involves a contrast between future and non-future (= present or past). Thus a sentence *balan ḍugumbil miyandaɲu*, quoted in isolation, could equally well be rendered at least eight different ways in English 'the/a woman/women laughs/laughed'. In English translations of Dyirbal examples articles are generally omitted, and singular or plural, past or present forms are used fairly arbitrarily, or as the context demands. Both grammatically and lexically, English translations give only a rough and partial indication of the meanings of Dyirbal sentences. Nothing concerning the structure of Dyirbal should be inferred from an examination of the translations.

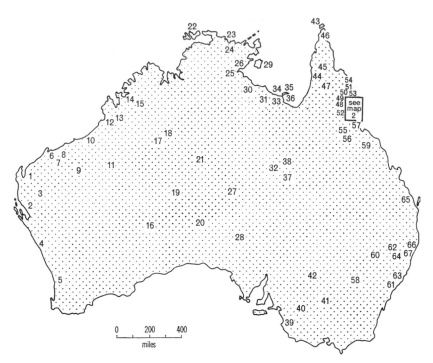

MAP 1. Australia, showing approximate locations of languages referred to

Key

Alawa 25	Gugu-Yimidir 54	Muluridyi 50	Walmatjari 18
Anewan 62	Gulŋay *see* map 2	Nanda 4	Waḷuwara 32
Aniṇḍilyaugwa 29	Gumbaiŋgar 67	Narrinyeri 39	Wanman 11
Arabana 28	Guṇu 42	Ngadyan *see* map 2	Wargamay *see* map 2
Aranda 27	Gunwinggu 24	Ngaḷuma 6	Waruŋu *see* map 2
Awabakal 61	Guŋgay *see* map 2	Ngarinjin 15	Wembawemba 41
Bailko 9	Ilba 56	Nuŋgubuyu 26	Weṛgaia 40
Bandjalang 66	Inggarda 2	Nyangumarda 10	Western Desert 16
Bandyin *see* map 2	Kalkatuŋu 38	Nyawigi 57	West Torres 43
Biria 59	Kamilaruy 60	Nyigina 13	Wik Meʔn 44
Bulway *see* map 2	Kattaŋ 63	Olgolo 47	Wik Munkan 45
Dyabugay 53	Kayardilt 36	Ooldean 20	Wiradhari 58
Dyangun 49	Kurama 7	Pitjantjatjara 19	Worora 14
Dyirbal *see* map 2	Kutjale 55	Pittapitta 37	Yanggal 34
Dyiru *see* map 2	Lardil 35	Talandji 1	Yanyula 30
Gabi 65	Mabuiag 43	Thangatti 64	Yaraikana 46
Garadjari 12	Madyay *see* map 2	Thargari 3	Yidin *see* map 2
Garawa 31	Mamu *see* map 2	Tiwi 22	Yintjipaṇṭi 8
Giramay *see* map 2	Maung 23	Wadjuk 5	Yirgay 53
Gugu-Baḍun 52	Mbabaṛam *see*	Wagaman 48	Yukulta 33
Gugu-Yaḷanji 51	map 2	Walbiri 21	Yulbaridja 17

[xxiv]

I *Australian languages*

This chapter surveys, rather briefly, some of the recurring linguistic features of languages across the continent. It does not purport to be a complete 'Handbook of Australian languages' and does not attempt to list the many individual variations from the basic pattern.

Further details on some of the points mentioned below will be found in the surveys by Schmidt, Ray [1925], Capell and Wurm. Schmidt [1912, 1919] draws some intelligent conclusions from the rather scanty and inaccurate published material then available. Capell [1956] gives a great deal of important information, much of it based on his own field work; but even in 1956 far less was known about Australian languages than today and some of Capell's data is, for instance, phonetically suspect. Wurm's [forthcoming] readable survey essentially repeats and expands some of Capell's ideas, and includes a lexicographic classification of Australian languages (see 10.1).

1.1 General

There were perhaps 600 aboriginal tribes in Australia at the time of the European invasion at the end of the eighteenth century [Tindale, 1940]. Each tribe spoke a distinct dialect, which usually had considerable lexical and grammatical similarities to neighbouring dialects. The existence of extensive dialect chains makes it difficult to put an exact figure on the number of distinct aboriginal languages; recent guesses have been that there were about 200 [Wurm, 1965; O'Grady et al., 1966].

On the basis of the similarities summarised below it has for some time seemed likely that at least the majority of Australian languages are genetically related. But, although there have been two excellent essays at phonological reconstruction over smallish areas – Hale's [1964] work on languages at the north of the Cape York Peninsula, and O'Grady's [1966] on the Pilbara region – as yet little has been done towards reconstructing proto-Australian (but see Dixon [forthcoming-b]). However, the writer is confident that progress will be made when more, reliable data is available on a variety of languages, and once there are linguists who have had a thorough training in the methods of historical linguistics working on comparative Australian.

The most divergent languages are found in and around Arnhem Land, although even these have a fair number of features in common with languages in other parts of the continent. From the small amount of data published it seems that Anewan, formerly spoken on the New England tableland, was also somewhat aberrant [Mathews, 1903a; Buchanan, 1900].

Tasmanian languages were, at one time, thought to be quite un-Australian. It now seems quite likely that Tasmanian languages are related to those on the mainland; and that it may in time be possible to prove the relationship. Tasmanian languages are not included in the present survey.

1.2 Phonology

Voicing is not normally phonologically significant. There is generally a nasal corresponding to each stop. For stops and nasals there are either 4, 5 or 6 contrasting 'places of articulation'. The maximal pattern is (with labels following O'Grady, 1966):

	lamino-	lamino-palatal/	apico-	apico-domal	dorso-
bilabial	dental	alveolar	alveolar	(retroflex)	velar
b	ḍ	ḏ	d	ḍ	g
m	ṇ	ɲ	n	ṇ	ŋ

The bilabials, the dorso-velars, and the sounds articulated with the tip of the tongue – apico-alveolars and apico-domals – are phonetically similar to sounds found in many other languages. The laminals are rather different from sounds occurring in other languages. In the case of lamino-dentals, the teeth are slightly apart, and the blade of the tongue touches both teeth, with the tip of the tongue somewhere in the region of the lower teeth ridge. For lamino-palatal/alveolars, the blade of the tongue touches the hard palate, or the alveolar ridge, or often both, with the tongue tip usually touching the teeth.

Many languages show the maximal stop-nasal pattern. There are two types of deviation: (1) languages in an area that very approximately coincides with the present state of Queensland have no retroflex series; (2) some languages have a single laminal series, with lamino-dental and lamino-alveopalatal sounds as allophonic variants. The distribution of these languages is mapped in Dixon [forthcoming-b], where data is presented which suggests that proto-Australian had a single laminal series. Many present-day languages that involve a laminal contrast show this only in a certain structural position, or before certain vowels.

In all cases bilabial, velar and all kinds of laminal stops and nasals can occur initially as well as intervocalically. However, in many cases apico-alveolars and/or apico-domals (where these occur) can function only intervocalically and not initially.

Languages east of the Gulf of Carpentaria usually have a single, apico-alveolar lateral, *l*. West of the Gulf the common pattern is for there to be one lateral corresponding to each stop-nasal series excepting bilabial and velar; but there are languages missing laterals in some series.

Australian consonant systems generally also include two semi-vowels, *w* and *y*, which can normally begin words; a semi-retroflex continuant, *ɻ*; and a flap *r*. Most languages allow some laterals and *ɻ* to occur word-initially, but only in relatively few words. *r* cannot normally occur initially.

A three-vowel system – *u, i, a* – is the norm. Vowel length is sometimes significant and sometimes not. Vowels do not as a rule occur word-initially.

Words can usually end in a vowel, or in a consonant other than a stop. Consonant clusters occur only intervocalically. All or almost all languages allow clusters of homorganic nasal plus stop, and of *r* or lateral plus stop. Most languages allow non-homorganic nasal-plus-stop clusters, and clusters involving *r* or lateral followed by a nasal, in addition to nasal-nasal clusters. Probably a minority of languages allow other types of two-member clusters, such as lateral, *ɻ* or *r* followed by *w*, or stop followed by stop. A small number of languages – mostly in Queensland – allow three-member clusters: *r, ɻ* or lateral; nasal; and stop.

In some languages every lexical root must consist of at least two syllables. Other languages allow monosyllabic roots but require that fully inflected words be disyllabic or longer. Most commonly, major stress falls on the first syllable of a word (although it appears that in some cases stress may fall on a later syllable, and may depend upon vowel length – Capell, 1956: 8). In some languages there is limited vowel harmony [Hale, mimeo-c; Capell, 1967: 99–101; Chadwick, 1968: 25–30].

Phonological systems which differ from the pattern described above
– for instance, in having fricatives, or vowel systems with more than
three members, or allowing words to begin with consonant clusters or
end with stops – can usually be shown to have, in fairly recent times,
developed out of norm systems [Hale, 1964; Dixon, 1970a, b].

A slightly fuller description of the phonologies of Australian languages, with
some exemplification, is in Dixon [forthcoming-b].

1.3   Word classes

Each lexical item belongs to just one part of speech, although there
are wide derivational possibilities (these are always clearly marked
morphologically). Thus noun and verb classes are distinguished both
in terms of inflectional possibilities and of mutually exclusive membership. Adjectives take the same basic set of inflections as nouns and, in
languages that have no noun classes (genders), it is sometimes difficult
to formulate syntactic criteria to distinguish adjective and noun.
Pronouns inflect rather differently from nouns. Amongst other parts
of speech there is usually a class of particles that do not inflect and
which provide logical or modal-type qualification of a sentence.

1.4   Syntax

The most common situation is for nouns to inflect according to a
nominative-ergative pattern, while pronouns at least superficially follow
a nominative-accusative pattern. That is, nouns have a single case
(nominative) marking intransitive subject and transitive object functions,
and another case (ergative) for transitive subject function. Pronouns,
on the other hand, have one case marking transitive and intransitive
subject and another for transitive object.

In a few languages pronouns inflect in a nominative-ergative pattern,
like nouns. There are also some languages where both pronouns and
nouns follow a nominative-accusative pattern.

Walbiri is an example of a language in which both nouns and pronouns inflect
in a nominative-ergative pattern [Hale, 1970: 776–9]. Hale [1970: 759] reports
that languages in which both nouns and pronouns follow a nominative-
accusative pattern are 'found in two widely separated areas: the Wellesley
Islands and adjacent mainland in North Qld. (e.g. Lardil, of Mornington
Island; Kayardilt, of Bentinck Island; and Yanggal of Forsythe Island); and
the northwest coast of Western Australia (e.g. Ngaḷuma of the Roebourne

area, and Yintjipaṇṭi of the Fortescue River area)'; see also von Brandenstein [1967].

Word order is in many cases extraordinarily free; in many languages every word in a phrase is inflected for case, and words can and do occur in any order in a sentence. In other cases there is both less inflection and less freedom – thus, in Gumbaiŋgar, nouns are always inflected but the inflection may be omitted from an adjective when it immediately precedes the noun it qualifies [Smythe, 1948/9: 68]. There is probably in all languages an underlying 'norm' word order – in this the verb is usually sentence-final.

Very little work has been published on relative clauses, complements and the like; it is thus not at present possible to make any generalisations about these or related phenomena in Australian languages (but see Dixon, 1969).

1.5   Pronoun

The standard Australian pronoun system involves a distinction between singular, dual and plural forms in each person. A very few languages appear to have a two-term system, lacking dual. There are rather more exceptions in the other direction, where the addition of trial (or paucal) forms makes for a four-term system.

The only languages known to the writer to lack duals are Maung, spoken on Goulburn Island, N.T., and Dyabugay, spoken just to the north of Dyirbal in the Cairns rain forest region. Languages involving trial pronouns include Aniṇḍilyaugwa and Nunggubuyu, from Eastern Arnhem Land; Worora [Love, 1931/2], Ngarinjin [Coate and Oates, 1970] and other languages from the Kimberleys; some languages of Victoria [Mathews 1902, 1903*b*, 1904; Hercus, 1966]; and Arabana in South Australia.

Perhaps slightly more than half the languages of the continent show an inclusive/exclusive distinction in first person non-singular pronouns. In some languages there are different non-singular pronouns depending on whether the two or more persons referred to belong to the same or different alternate generation levels, and/or whether they are related through male or female kinsmen, and so on.

O'Grady et al. [1966: 104] report that in all 'languages in Western Australia which are located south of the 22nd parallel of latitude, the inclusive/exclusive distinction of the nonsingular first person pronouns, marked in the languages to the north, is lacking'. Languages in other parts of the continent that lack an inclusive/exclusive distinction include Kalkatungu [Blake, 1969: 39] and

Pittapitta [Roth, 1897] in north-west-central Queensland, and all the languages to the south of Gugu-Yalanji (which itself has the distinction – R. Hershberger, 1964*a*) in the Cairns rain forest region and its hinterland. Hale [mimeo-a] discusses kinship-determined pronouns in Lardil, Aranda and other languages; see also O'Grady et al. [1966: 88, 130] and Strehlow [1944: 90 ff].

Pronominal forms show a striking similarity over the whole continent. We will use *Ḏ* and *Ṉ* for segments that are realised as lamino-dental *d̪* and *n̪* in languages having two laminal series, and as laminal *ḏ* and *ɲ* in languages with a single laminal series. Similarly, *Ḏ* and *Ṉ* will be used for segments that are realised as lamino-palatal/alveolar *ḏ* and *ɲ* in double-laminal languages and as laminal *ḏ* and *ɲ* in languages with a single series.

The following forms usually function as transitive (and often also intransitive) subject:

[1] *First person singular:* ŋaḎu ~ ŋaḎa ~ ŋayu ~ ŋaya. Forms with a stop and forms with a semi-vowel each occur in a variety of languages with wide geographical distribution; the same is true of forms ending in -*a* and those ending in -*u*.

[2] *First person dual (inclusive):* ŋali occurs in an exceptionally large number of languages.

[3] *First person plural (exclusive):* forms generally begin with ŋan- and end in a variety of ways.

If there is no inclusive/exclusive distinction the dual and plural first person forms are generally ŋali and ŋan-. Where the distinction is made the inclusive plural form is often built on a root ŋaṈ- or ŋaḎ-, while the ŋan- form has exclusive reference. However in Gugu-Yalanji [R. Hershberger, 1964*a*: 56] at least, the inclusive first person plural pronoun is ŋana. Where there is an inclusive/exclusive distinction the first person dual exclusive pronoun is not uncommonly formed by augmentation of the inclusive root ŋali.

[4] *Second person singular:* There are a fair number of different forms occurring here and they are perhaps unlikely all to be genetically related. Initial parts are ŋind- ~ ŋund- ~ Ṉind- ~ Ṉund- ~ yind- ~ yund-. The ending is almost always -*a* or -*u*, added to one of the six initial segments.

[5] *Second person dual:* forms Ṉu(m)palu ~ Ṉu(m)pala occur widely.

[6] *Second person plural:* Ṉura ~ yura occur in most western languages, and in some languages in other parts of the continent.

Examples of actual pronominal forms in a number of languages are given in Dixon [forthcoming-b]; see also Schmidt [1912].

In some eastern languages the first and second person singular pronouns have three different forms, corresponding to the functions intransitive subject, transitive subject and transitive object. Thus Gabi, in south Queensland, has forms [Mathew 1910: 208]:

	first person singular	second person singular
intransitive subject	*ŋay*	*ŋin*
transitive subject	*ŋayḍu*	*ŋindu*
transitive object	*ŋana*	*ŋina*

Only very rarely are there different forms for each of the three functional slots in the case of non-singular pronouns in any language.

Gumbaiŋgar has one form for each of the three functional slots in the case of all first and second person pronouns except first person dual inclusive and second person singular – in these two cases one form functions as both transitive and intransitive subject [Smythe, 1948/9: 38]. See also Blake and Breen [1971] on Pittapitta.

The transitive object form of pronouns is typically derived from the unmarked subject form by the addition of -*Ṇa* (examples are in Dixon, forthcoming-b).

Possessive pronouns are commonly formed by adding an affix to the unmarked 'subject' form. A number of affixes are in competition, each occurring in a variety of languages with wide geographical distribution; amongst the most common are -*gu*, -*ŋu*, -*ŋa* and -*mba*.

Languages whose possessive pronouns involve -*gu* include Wiradhari [Gunther. 1892: 67–8], and Western Desert [Douglas 1964: 73] in some incorporated forms. Aranda, in which all words end in -*a*, has -*ga* [Strehlow, 1944: 91–2]. Note that Yulbaridja has -*guṛaŋu* [O'Grady et al., 1966: 151]. -*ŋu* occurs in Waḷuwara (on singular first and second person pronouns) and Nanda [O'Grady et al., 1966: 122]. -*ŋa* is found in Gugu-Yalanji [R. Hershberger, 1964a: 56] and on non-singular pronouns in Pittapitta [Roth, 1897: 6] and Yanyula. -*mba* occurs in Pitjantjatjara [Trudinger, 1943: 210], and in Awabakal [Threlkeld, 1892: 17; H. Hale, 1846: 488–90]. Non-singular possessive pronouns in Waḷuwara involve -*ma*.

In a number of languages there are dative pronominal forms, obtained by adding an affix that is usually -*gu* to the subject form or to some underlying root. Some languages also have other pronominal inflections – allative, ablative, locative – often patterned on the noun paradigm; however, many languages lack these peripheral cases as far as pronouns are concerned.

Dative -*gu* is found in, for example, Walbiri, Awabakal [H. Hale, 1846: 488–90], Wanman, Yulbaridja and Bailko [O'Grady et al., 1966: 137, 151, 88].

In the West Torres Straits language dative pronouns involve suffix -*ka*, and
are derived from the unmarked (intransitive subject) forms of singular pronouns,
but from the possessive forms of dual and plurals [Ray, 1907a: 23; Klokeid,
personal communication].

Third person pronouns are often set off morphologically and syntactically from the first and second person forms. In some languages
third person pronouns inflect on the pattern of nouns, rather than of
other pronouns (for instance, Gumbaiŋgar – Smythe, 1948/9: 38).
Third person pronouns often carry a demonstrative meaning, and
sometimes involve an obligatory specification of the proximity of the
object referred to.

In Thargari there are 'near', 'far' and 'remote' forms of the third person
singular pronoun [Klokeid, 1969: 17]. For the Western Desert language third
person pronouns occur in four forms 'near', 'mid-distant', 'distant' and 'not
visible' [Douglas, 1964: 47/8]. Roth [1897: 2] describes a slightly different
system for Pittapitta: there are three third person forms, indicating (a) proximity
to the speaker's front or side; (b) proximity to speaker's back; and (c) remote-
ness anywhere from speaker.
   Third person pronouns do not commonly distinguish sex, although this
does happen (for the singular pronoun) in a few languages – for instance,
Yanyula and Alawa [Sharpe, forthcoming]. Aniŋḍilyaugwa distinguishes sex
for almost all pronominal person and number combinations.

There does not appear to be any third person singular pronoun form
which occurs in a fair number of languages with wide geographical
distribution. There are, however, frequently encountered regional
forms. Thus *ŋuℵa* is found in many languages in Western Australia
[O'Grady et al., 1966]; *ɲulu ~ ɲula* are found in a variety of languages
in the eastern half of the continent.

Languages in which *ɲulu* is found include Gugu-Yalanji [R. Hershberger,
1964a: 56] and Garawa; *ɲula* occurs in Bandjalang [Cunningham, 1969: 92/3]
and Waruŋu, immediately to the west of Dyirbal.

Third person dual and plural pronouns are more frequently derived
from the singular form than is the case for first and second person
forms. There are, however, forms *bula*, third person dual, and *Ṭana*,
third person plural, that recur in a wide variety of languages in all
parts of the continent. *bula* is a somewhat ubiquitous form – in many
languages it functions as a simple number adjective 'two' instead of
or in addition to being third person dual pronoun; cf. 1.11, below.
Ṭana can also occur as an adjective 'all'.

In some languages, predominantly in the central and western north but also in New South Wales and Victoria, reduced forms of pronouns are incorporated as affixes into the verb, or into the auxiliary.

For a full discussion of this see Capell [1956] and also Wurm [1969].

1.6 Noun and adjective

In the great majority of Australian languages noun and adjective inflect in the same way for case. There is typically a system of from about four to eight cases.

The few languages that lack case inflections are all in or near Arnhem Land: for instance, Gunwinggu [Oates, 1964], Maung, Nunggubuyu. In most of these languages verb prefixes provide some identification of subject and object.

In most languages intransitive subject and transitive object functions are marked by nominative case. This is almost always realised by zero inflection. In a fairly small number of languages -*Ṇa* can be used to mark transitive object function on common nouns and adjectives; in a rather larger number of languages -*Ṇa* occurs just with proper nouns, to indicate transitive object (and, in a few cases, intransitive subject).

Some of the languages which involve -*Ṇa* inflection on nouns are listed in Dixon [forthcoming-b]. This affix is plainly cognate with pronominal -*Ṇa*, mentioned above.

There are two common ergative inflections, marking transitive subject:

[1] the inflection is commonly -*gu* or -*ŋgu* on nouns ending in a vowel, but is often a homorganic stop followed by -*u* when the stem ends in a nasal. There may also be allomorphic variants, in the case of stems ending in a vowel, that depend on the length of the stem.

Some examples: Waḷuwara has simply -*gu*, with no alternants (this being derived, by regular sound change, from -*ŋgu*). Wembawemba has -*gu* after a vowel, -*u* after a consonant [Hercus, 1969: 46]. Kalkatungu has -(*ŋ*)*gu* on a disyllabic root ending with a vowel, with assimilation when the root ends in a consonant [Blake, 1969: 33].

[2] inflection -*lu* (with variant -*ḷu* in some languages).

For instance, Aranda, in which all stem-final vowels have been neutralised to a central -*a*, has ergative inflection -*la* [Strehlow, 1944: 74]. Note that Arabana has -*ru*, a development from -*lu*.

In a number of languages both -(*ŋ*)*gu* and -*lu* ~ -*ḷu* occur, as allomorphic

variants of the ergative case. Thus in Walbiri -*ŋgu* is used with disyllabic
stems and -*lu* with those of three or more syllables. In Pitjantjatjara
-*lu* occurs with proper nouns ending in a vowel and -*ŋgu* with common
nouns and adjectives ending in a vowel; proper nouns, common nouns
and adjectives that end in a consonant take a homorganic stop plus
-*u* in the ergative inflection [Trudinger, 1943: 206/7].

Ergative case inflections are one of the most complex and most fascinating
areas of Australian comparative grammar. A full discussion would be out of
place here but one or two further examples may be given. Thargari has some
similarities to Walbiri: ergative inflection is -*gu* (a development from -*ŋgu*)
with a disyllabic stem ending in a vowel, but -*du* (with assimilation, etc.) on
all other stems [Klokeid, 1969: 25]. It is tempting to speculate whether the
-*du* might be related to an original -*lu*. Gumbaiŋgar makes an interesting
comparison – oversimplifying slightly, ergative is -*du* after a vowel, a homorganic stop plus -*u* after a nasal, and just -*u* after *l* [Smythe, 1948/9: 29–31].
If Gumbaiŋgar -*du* inflection were related to an original -*lu* it would seem that
-*lu* can be assimilated to a stem-final consonant in the same way as can -(*ŋ*)*gu*.
The situation is even more complex in Walmatjari; here the ergative inflection
is:
  -*ḷu* after a stem of three or more syllables ending in a vowel;
  -*ŋu* on a disyllabic stem ending in a vowel;
  -*u* on a stem ending in a lateral or *r*;
  -*du* after a stem ending in a bilabial or apico-alveolar nasal or stop;
  -*ḍu* after a stem ending in an apico-domal nasal or stop; and
  -*ḍu* after a stem ending in a dorso-velar or lamino-palatal/alveolar nasal or
    stop.
The final three alternants specify a stop after a stem ending in a nasal or a stop;
note the rather limited assimilation here. Alternant -*ḷu* is presumably related
to the -*lu* ~ -*ḷu* occurring in other languages; -*ŋu* may be related to the ergative
inflection -(*ŋ*)*gu* in other languages; it then remains to decide whether the
alternants involving a stop relate to -*ḷu*, or to -*ŋu*, or whether they are historically
independent of both.

Virtually every language has a locative – 'at', 'on', 'in' – inflection
of nouns and adjectives. In the great majority of cases this is exactly
the same as the ergative inflection except that the final vowel of the
locative is -*a*, as against -*u* for the ergative case. The often complex
alternations encountered in the case of the ergative are exactly repeated
for the locative.

Thus Waḷuwara has -*ga* for locative inflection. Gumbaiŋgar has -*da* after a
vowel, a homorganic stop plus -*a* after a nasal, and just -*a* after *l* [Smythe,
1948/9: 29–31]. And similarly, repeating the alternations sketched above, for
Thargari [Klokeid, 1969: 28], Walbiri and Walmatjari. Different dialects of
the Pitjantjatjara/Western Desert language vary slightly in their ergative and
locative inflections – sometimes the two cases are out of step. Thus, for the

dialect Trudinger [1943: 206/7] describes, proper nouns ending in a vowel have ergative *-lu* and locative *-la*, and common nouns ending in a vowel have ergative *-ŋgu* and locative *-ŋga*. However, in the dialects described by Douglas [1964] and Glass and Hackett [1970: 34], proper nouns ending in a vowel take *-lu* and *-la* but common nouns ending in a vowel have ergative *-lu* and locative *-ŋga*.

In Wembawemba there has evidently been a semantic shift: inflections *-ga* after stem-final vowels and *-a* after consonants signal what Hercus [1969: 46–8] refers to as the 'general oblique' case with a basic meaning 'movement towards'; this contrasts with two locative cases *-(g)al* 'on' and *-(g)ada* 'in'.

In some languages phonological change has clearly neutralised an original contrast between ergative and locative. Thus in Aranda – a language which has changed in such a way that now every word ends in the same central vowel, written *a* – both ergative and locative inflections are *-la* [Strehlow, 1944: 202]. In Wik-Munkan, ergative and locative fall together and here the form *-ŋ* probably goes back to *-(ŋ)gu* and *-(ŋ)ga* respectively.

Languages in which the locative inflection appears not to be morphologically similar to the ergative include Kalkatungu [Blake, 1969: 33] and Arabana.

Some languages in the eastern part of the continent have been said to have a special 'instrumental' case. However, a separate instrumental case is lacking in most languages. Commonly, instrumental coincides with ergative – that is, both an actor, and the implement he uses, receive the same inflection. For some languages instrumental coincides not with ergative but with locative.

Instrumental coincides with locative in Waḷuwara (both are shown as *-ga*). Lardil nouns inflect according to a nominative-accusative pattern so that there is no ergative inflection; the instrumental is based on the future locative. In Aranda, ergative, locative and instrumental all fall together as *-la*. Some early and not altogether reliable grammars distinguished a quite separate instrumental – for example, in Yaraikana [Ray, 1907b: 272] and in Wiradhari [Gunther, 1892: 57].

One of the features which characterises languages of the continent is the affix *-gu*, that commonly appears with both nouns and verbs. Nominal *-gu*, which can be called the 'dative' case inflection, occurs in a wide variety of languages and marks the indirect object, or some additional object that is 'implicated' in the event described by the sentence.

See Capell [1956: 77–8]. A full syntactic and semantic discussion of *-gu* will be found in §5.3.3-4 below.

Some languages have – in addition to locative – separate allative and ablative inflections; other languages lack these and show the difference between 'rest' and 'motion towards'/'motion away from' by other means. It is not uncommon for dative and allative to fall together. Where there are separate allative and ablative inflections there is wide variation of forms between different languages (however, ablative does have the form *-ŋu(ɽu)* in a fair number of languages).

The only other case affix with wide occurrence is genitive. There is more variation of forms from language to language than in the case of the dative, but cases *-gu* and *-ŋu* do recur fairly frequently. (Occasionally, genitive and dative fall together, e.g. Gugu-Yimidir [Roth, 1901*a*: 16, 28].) In all or almost all languages possessive nouns and pronouns can be declined like adjectives: thus in *the man's son hit you*, *man* might take genitive inflection PLUS ergative inflection. In most cases a further inflection can go straight on to the genitive form; sometimes a special affix must be added after genitive and before the further case inflection.

There are just a few languages with different sets of case inflections, depending on whether the noun is singular, dual or plural; that is, a single affix carries an indication both of case and of number (for instance, Narrinyeri – Taplin, 1880; also Teichelmann and Schürmann, 1840: 5). There are some languages whose noun and pronoun inflections show tense as well as case – these are located in the Gulf country, or else due south of the Gulf, as far down as New South Wales.

In Lardil, for instance, each case has both a future and a non-future form (although there is some neutralisation: for instance, there are non-future accusative and non-future locative inflections, but a single inflection for future accusative-locative). The classic example of nouns inflecting for tense is Pittapitta [Roth, 1897]. See also Capell [1956: 59] on Guṇu.

It is normal for there to be a fair number of stem-forming affixes that precede case inflections; there is, however, considerable variation in form and meaning from language to language. The most common are dual and plural markers; the dual affix is often *guṈara* – see 1.11. Many languages also have comitative and privative derivational affixes, that serve to form adjectival stems from noun roots. Thus from noun *papa* 'water' in Bailko can be formed *papaŋaṇi* 'having water' and *papapati* 'without water' [O'Grady et al., 1966: 87]. Comitative and privative affixes appear to have quite different forms in almost every language. There is one further affix that has a fair distribution amongst east coast languages: *-gan*, serving to derive the feminine form of a noun.

-gan occurs, with a greater or lesser degree of productivity, in Gumbaiŋgar [Smythe, 1948/9: 22–3], Kattaŋ [Holmer, 1966: 40–1] and Gabi [Mathew,

1910: 200]. Capell [1956: 39] mentions that there are four noun classes in Bandjalang, shown by the affix chosen by a qualifying adjective; in the case of the feminine class the affix is *-gan* (see also Cunningham, 1969: 91; Livingstone, 1892).

A number of Australian languages, predominantly in the north, show a system of noun or gender classes. These can be marked either by class prefixes or suffixes to the noun, or by concord with verbal affixes. It is likely that noun classes, where they do occur, are a fairly recent development.

For a full discussion see Dixon [1968 *c*]; also Capell [1956].

1.7 Verb

Just as the major parts of speech – noun, verb and adjective – have mutually exclusive membership, so the transitive and intransitive subclasses of verb are mutually exclusive. That is, each verbal root is clearly marked for transitivity, in terms of the case inflections of the noun phrases that can occur with it. In the case of incorporating languages the marking extends to the number and type of obligatory pronominal affixes. And just as there are wide possibilities of derivation between the major parts of speech, so there are a number of ways in which a transitive stem can be derived from an intransitive verb root, and vice versa; these are always clearly marked morphologically.

For almost all Australian languages a number of distinct verbal conjugations must be recognised. The number of conjugations mentioned in the literature varies from two to about seven; in many cases, though, only some of these are productive, the remainder being small closed classes of what can be regarded as irregular verbs. Two conjugational subtypes can be identified between languages of wide geographical separation [Hale, 1970: 760].

The first type is characterised by the occurrence of a liquid – *l* or sometimes *ɽ* – in its paradigm; depending on the analysis appropriate to the language, the liquid will be recognised either as the final segment of the verb roots belonging to this conjugation, or else as the initial segment of some of the affixial allomorphs. The second type can be recognised through the occurrence of either *y* or zero in place of the liquid. Verbs in the first conjugation are predominantly transitive, and in the second intransitive; there are nearly always some exceptions – one or two transitive verbs that belong to the second conjugation, and usually a slightly larger number of intransitive verbs in the first conjugation.

For instance, Klokeid recognises five conjugations for Thargari [1969: 30–5]. Two are open classes and correspond to the types mentioned above: what is called the '-Ru' conjugation – with predominantly transitive members – is clearly the first type; Klokeid's '-a' conjugation – all of whose listed members, bar one, are intransitive – is the second type. The other three conjugations cover the irregular verbs of the language; they are closed classes with from two to fourteen members.

Of the six Nyangumarda conjugations recognised in O'Grady's classic study [1970], three have open membership, while the other three, which contain only five verbs in all, could be said to deal with the irregularities. Conjugation I, more than 90 % of whose members are intransitive, is clearly of our second type; conjugations II and III, both predominantly transitive, appear to be subvarieties of the first (liquid) type.

Hale [mimeo-b] recognises three conjugations for Walbiri. Two – which each have slightly different paradigms for monosyllabic and polysyllabic verbs – are open classes, and clearly correspond to the two conjugational types. Hale's third conjugation has just three monomorphemic members.

There are two conjugations in Gugu-Yalanji – verbs belonging to the first conjugation can be assigned roots ending in -*l*, and those of the second roots ending in -*ay* or -*i*. The -*l* conjugation is predominantly transitive and the -*y/i* conjugation predominantly intransitive. (Cf R. Hershberger, 1964*b*.)

4.4.2, below, contrasts verbal forms in the Giramay dialect of Dyirbal with those in the contiguous language Wargamay. Giramay and Wargamay are conjugationally similar; a difference is that whereas verbs in Giramay can be assigned roots that end in -*l* (conjugation 1) or -*y* (conjugation 2), roots in Wargamay (although distributed between two conjugations in an identical manner) cannot be assigned this final consonant. Thus there are cognate transitive roots Giramay *walmbil* and Wargamay *walmbi* 'raise up'; and the morphologically and syntactically identical forms Giramay *walmbilaygu* and Wargamay *walmbilagu* segment as *walmbil-ay-gu* and as *walmbi-la-gu* respectively (-*ay* ~ -*la* is a 'reserve passive' affix; -*gu* is 'purposive' inflection).

In most Australian languages the verb is morphologically and morphophonologically the most complex part of speech. However, there appears, on the surface at least, to be a little less interlanguage similarity as regards verb affixes than there is for nouns and pronouns.

A number of languages have three tense inflections – past, present and future. There are, however, languages with two-term tense systems: either past/non-past or future/non-future. There are also languages with more than three tenses – in these cases remote past may be distinguished from immediate past, and so on. In some languages verbal inflections can also mark aspect (covering perfect/imperfect and also such concepts as habitual, iterative, durative, etc.) and mood. The interrelation of tense, aspect and mood can result in extremely complex paradigms.

Lardil has a two-term tense system: future/non-future. In contrast, Gunwinggu distinguishes only past and non-past; there is an obligatory aspect choice within past, resulting in three inflections – non-past, past completive and past continuous [Oates, 1964: 46]. In Mabuiag, a dialect of the West Torres Straits language, Klokeid [1970: 3] recognises distinct inflections, in the declarative mood, for remote past, near past, yesterday, last night, immediate past/present, immediate future/present, near future, and remote future; he notes that fewer, if any, tense distinctions are made in the negative, imperative and other moods, and in the imperfective and other aspects. Compare with Wiradhari which appears to have ten pure tenses [H. Hale, 1846: 494]. Nyangumarda [O'Grady, 1970] and Aranda [Strehlow, 1944] provide examples of complex paradigms, involving the intersection of tense, aspect and other systems.

There are languages in which information regarding tense is shown not by inflection of a verb, but by an additional 'auxiliary' element in the sentence. Thus in Ngarinjin the auxiliary, which follows the verb, carries number, tense, mood and aspect [Coate and Oates, 1970: 54]. There are ten auxiliary roots, and each verb always occurs with a particular auxiliary (the ten classes into which auxiliaries divide verbs are thus a similar phenomenon to noun or gender classes).

Gunwinggu is similar to Ngarinjin, but here the auxiliaries appear to have been incorporated into the verb as suffixes [Oates, 1964: 36–41]. See also Sharpe [forthcoming] on Alawa. In Walbiri, tense, mood and aspect are represented discontinuously in a sentence, by elements in an auxiliary word and by suffixes to the verb word; unlike in Ngarinjin and Gunwinggu, the Walbiri auxiliary does not establish verb classes [Hale, mimeo-b].

Imperative verbs in Australian languages generally have rather wide syntactic possibilities. They can be used with second, third and sometimes first person subjects.

Imperatives are formed by the addition of an affix to the verb root; this affix almost always ends in *-a*. Where there are two main conjugations, the imperative affix for the second – predominantly intransitive – conjugation is often *-ya*; for the first – predominantly transitive – conjugation affixes *-ga* or *-la* are commonly encountered [Hale, mimeo-b; O'Grady, 1970: 852]. A number of languages have imperative inflections that give some information about the number of the subject or object.

In Gumbaingar there are two imperative inflections, according as the object of the verb is singular (*-a ~ -i*) or plural (*-ili*) [Smythe, 1948/9: 43]. In Wembawemba there are distinct inflections depending on whether the subject is singular or plural [Hercus, 1969: 65]. Similarly, the language spoken around

Adelaide, as described by Teichelmann and Schürmann [1840: 17], has an imperative paradigm that distinguishes person (second/third) and number (singular/dual/plural) of the subject. Compare with Pittapitta [Roth, 1897: 11, 21–2].

It is not unusual to find, besides a simple imperative, a continuative imperative 'keep on doing'.

In Pitjantjatjara the simple imperative has conjugationally-determined allo-morphs *-wa ~ ø ~ -ra ~ -la*, whereas the continuative imperative is *-nma ~ -ma ~ -ŋama ~ -nama* [Douglas, 1964: 40; Trudinger, 1943: 217]. Other languages with continuative imperatives include West Torres [Ray, 1907*b*: 35] and Nanda [O'Grady et al., 1966: 124]. In Mbabaṟam, the imperative affix *-g* can occur either directly on to a verb root, or following the affix *-ṟu ~ -nu* which indicates that the action was 'initiated in the past'; in the latter case *-ṟug ~ -nug* has the effect of a continuative imperative.

One of the most common and important verbal inflections is purposive *-gu*; this appears to be related to the dative inflection on nouns, mentioned in the last section [Capell, 1956: 77/8; Mathew, 1910: 207]. Purposive – which occurs in place of a tense inflection – indicates the desire to, or necessity of, doing something. The *-gu* inflection on verbs is in some published grammars called 'immediate future'; it seems likely that in many cases 'purposive' would be a semantically more apt label.

There are other similarities between inflections on nouns and verbs – see in particular the rather striking list given by Ray [1907*a*: 10] for West Torres.

Australian grammars typically feature a number of derivational affixes: (1) reflexive, which when added to a transitive verbal stem derives a form that functions as an intransitive stem; (2) reciprocal, with similar function; (3) causative, deriving a transitive from an intransitive stem; (4) intransitive verbaliser – added to a noun or adjective stem this derives an intransitive verbal stem; (5) transitive verbaliser – also to a noun or adjective stem. (In some languages the contrast between (1) and (2) is effectively neutralised, with a single affix having both reflexive and reciprocal functions.)

There is considerable variation in the forms of these affixes from language to language; however, the transitive verbaliser fairly often is or includes *-ma-*, while the intransitive verbaliser and sometimes either the reflexive or reciprocal (or both) often are or include *-ri-*.

In some languages, such as Gumbaiŋgar, there is no reflexive form of the verb 'and reflex action is expressed by the emphatic form of the personal pronoun object' [Smythe, 1948/9: 74].

It is not uncommon in Australian languages for loan words (particularly from English) to be taken always into the noun or adjective class, never into the verb class. Thus 'work' may be taken over as an adjective, but be used as a verb through the addition of an intransitive verbaliser affix.

In Australian languages there are as a rule rather few compound nouns. For some languages the same situation prevails for verbs – the great majority are monomorphemic. There are, however, languages that are highly productive as regards verb compounding. For instance, O'Grady [1970: 849] states that, in Nyangumarda, 'by dictionary count, simple, i.e. monomorphemic, verbs number barely one hundred, while complex verbs are many times more numerous; by text count, the scales are tipped the other way: simple verbs far outnumber complex'.

Other languages that have a set of productive prefixes, yielding a considerable number of compound verbs, include Gumbaiŋgar [Smythe, 1948/9: 46–7], Gabi [Mathew, 1910: 216–17] and West Torres [Ray, 1907a: 28–32].

1.8 Interrogatives

There is almost always an interrogative ('who') corresponding to the pronoun class, and another ('what') for the noun class. The most common form for the pronominal interrogative is *ŋana*, although *waɲ(u)* and *wara* are both encountered in a fair number of languages. There are two widely occurring 'what' forms: *miN̯a* and *ŋani*.

Yukulta is the only language known in which one form, *ŋaka*, covers both 'who' and 'what'.
There is a long discussion of interrogatives in Schmidt [1912], although it must always be borne in mind that Schmidt was working with published materials that were uneven in quality and in almost all cases phonetically unreliable.

Australian languages generally also have interrogative forms 'how many' and 'when'. There is generally an interrogative root from which '(at) where', 'to where' and 'from where' can be formed, by adding appropriate case inflections. English 'why' would be translated by the dative of 'what' (i.e. 'for what'). Some languages also have interrogative verbs: 'do what/do how'.

1.9   Particles and clitics

Most languages have a score or so elements that modify the meaning
of a sentence, or have a coordinative or subordinative function. These
can take the form of non-inflecting particles – that have the status of
separate phonological words – or of enclitics – syllabic elements which
cannot take primary stress but which can be added to a noun, verb or
other word after the inflectional ending. Some languages express modal
and logical modification through a mixture of particles and clitics.

Certain types of sentence modification recur from language to
language – 'doubt', 'assertion of the definite truth of a sentence',
'probability', and so on; there is little similarity between the forms of
the clitics/particles through which the meanings are expressed. An
exception is the interrogative modifier, which converts a declarative
sentence into a polar question, and typically has the form *-ma* ~ *-ba* ~ -
mba.

Languages with an interrogative clitic include Pitjantjatjara with *-mba* [Tru-
dinger, 1943: 222], Pittapitta with *-ba* [Roth, 1897: 28] and Aranda with *-ma*
[Strehlow, 1944: 19].

1.10   Interjections

Each language has a few dozen interjections; these appear, at least in
form, to be fairly language-particular. Thus, 'no' is commonly quite
different between contiguous languages, and even between dialects of
one language; tribes are not infrequently named after their word for
'no' [Ray, 1925; Watson, 1944: 4].

There are, however, at least three interjections that do recur in
languages over a wide geographical spread:

[1] a form similar to *gawu* ~ *gabu* is frequently a hortative 'come
here!'.

[2] *yuwuy* usually means 'alright' or something similar; in some
cases it has the more straightforward meaning 'yes'. It is possible that
the form *yu*, 'yes', occurring in a number of languages in or near
Arnhem Land, is related to *yuwuy*.

[3] *yagay* – often with the second syllable lengthened and stressed
as the word is shouted out – expresses sudden emotion, although there
is considerable variation in the type of emotion, from language to
language.

For the language around Adelaide, Teichelmann and Schürmann [1840: 23] describe "yakka" as an interjection expressing 'aversion and disagreeableness'. Strehlow [1944: 214] gives a full discussion of *yagay* in Aranda, mentioning that it can be a cry of warning, or of joy mingled with grief. *yagay* appears in Hercus's [1969: 302] Weṟgaia vocabulary glossed 'oh, is that so – exclamation of surprise and regret; uttered on hearing of an unexpected death'.

1.11 Lexicon

A feature of Australian languages is their apparently high rate of vocabulary replacement. On the death of a member of a tribe, with a certain proper name, the common noun on which the name was based was likely to be proscribed; it would normally have been replaced by a noun borrowed from a neighbouring language. It is perhaps this phenomenon that is responsible for the rather small number of lexical cognates that have so far been recognised between Australian languages. (A fuller discussion of lexical replacement and its implications is in 10.1, below.)

Fifty or so lexical items that occur in a wide range of languages, with almost identical forms in each, have been assembled by Capell and called 'Common Australian vocabulary' [Capell 1956: 80–94, 1962a: 10–14; Wurm, forthcoming]. There is certainly a further set of items that recur with slight formal variations in different languages (evidence of phonological change). O'Grady and the writer are currently working on reconstruction of items of the second type.

Amongst the most widely attested lexical items are *bula(y)* and *guṉara*, both occurring as the number 'two'. In some languages *bula(y)* is the lexical item 'two' while *guṉara* functions as a dual affix; in others the reverse is true.

In a great many Australian languages there is a special 'avoidance vocabulary' that has to be used either in the presence of, or when talking about, anyone who is in a tabooed kinship relation to the speaker. This is often referred to as a 'mother-in-law language', since mother-in-law is a prime example of a relation who must be avoided in the case of a male ego. In some cases there are only a few score items that definitely belong to the avoidance vocabulary; other languages have several hundred avoidance items so that in the presence of a taboo relative conversation is carried on using ONLY lexical items of the mother-in-law style.

Hale reports, from his own field work, that Walbiri is an example of a language with a restricted number of avoidance words; Yanyula and Wik Meʔn, on the other hand, have many hundreds of lexical items in the mother-in-law style,

rather like Dyirbal (2.5, 8.1, below). Thomson [1935] discusses avoidance
language in North Queensland.

Hale [1971] discusses *tjiliwiri*, a language used by Walbiri men in connection
with initiation rituals; this involves, rather roughly, replacing a grammatical
or lexical item by its antonym. Hale [mimeo-c] has also discussed Demin, a
secret language of the Lardil that is related to the everyday speech but differs
phonologically, as well as lexically from it. Capell [1962*b*] surveys the literature
on special forms of language associated with social distinction, throughout the
continent.

1.12   The development of Australian languages

Comparative work in Australia is at too early a stage to permit a sure
reconstruction of the stages through which the languages have passed.
It is, however, tempting to speculate. Suppose it is eventually shown
(and it is by no means certain that it can be) that all the languages of
Australia, including the divergent tongues in and around Arnhem Land,
are genetically related. It would then be probable that proto-Australian
was at the isolating end of the agglutinative type. That is, it would
have had some case inflections, and some affixes of other kinds, but
much less morphological complexity than most present-day languages;
verb morphology, in particular, may have been relatively simple. Most
languages have moved some distance further from the isolating and
towards the inflectional pole. Pronominal forms have been incorporated
into verbs, either as prefixes or suffixes; generic terms have become
gender markers on nouns or verbs; verbs have taken on complex tense
inflections and aspect affixes; and nouns have gained affixes such as
'dual' and 'plural'. There are some languages, however, which have
lost their original case inflections and now use word order to show
syntactic function. The latter type – all spoken in Arnhem Land or
the vicinity – have thus moved in the opposite direction from the
majority of Australian languages, at least as far as noun morphology
is concerned.

Only detailed descriptions of individual languages, and careful
comparison, will provide support or otherwise for the comments in
the last paragraph. It may, however, be impossible fully to recapture
the history of these languages. Recent archaeological work has suggested
that aborigines have been in Australia for 25,000 or more years – something like five times as long as the postulated age of the Indo-European
language family. During this period, the languages must have undergone
many geographical and other movements. A tribe may have split into

two, the parts moved in different directions, one of them merged with a further tribe (when numbers were, say, reduced due to famine) and this new tribe may later have split, and so on. Each language may, by grammatical and lexical diffusion, have influenced and been influenced by many others at every stage of its development. It may well be impossible to reconstruct all the complex changes that have occurred however much we investigate those languages that are still spoken, and however linguistically acute we are in our comparison of them.

Almost every point in the grammar of an Australian language is similar to something in the grammar of some other language; this is exemplified by the comparative notes included in the description of Dyirbal. But these similarities seem almost random, and do not in the present state of our knowledge point to any general genetic subgrouping of the languages.

The outlook is, however, far from gloomy. Good linguists are being attracted to the field and progress, on both synchronic and diachronic fronts, has been encouraging in recent years. It is likely that whatever can be reconstructed of the pre-history of Australian languages – and it may be considerable – will be, in the coming decades.

2 Dyirbal: the language and its speakers

2.1 Linguistic type

Dyirbal is a typical Australian language. It is entirely suffixing, largely agglutinative, and has extraordinarily free word order.

Phonologically it is rather simple, having the smallest number of phonemes of any Australian language. In addition to four stop-nasal series – bilabial, apico-alveolar, dorso-velar and laminal – there is a single lateral, a semi-retroflex continuant, a trill and two semi-vowels. Dyirbal has the usual three-vowel system, length not being significant. Roots and inflected words begin with a consonant and have at least two syllables; intervocalically there are two and three-member consonant clusters. The first syllables of roots, and of most affixes, bear stress.

There are clearly defined classes of (first and second person) pronoun, noun, adjective, verb, adverbal, time qualifier, particle and interjection. There are four noun classes (genders), marked not in the form of a noun but by a 'noun marker' that normally accompanies a noun; noun markers also have some of the functions fulfilled by third person pronouns in other languages. A noun marker indicates the class of a noun, agrees with it in case, and also indicates whether the referent of the noun is visible or invisible; here or there; up hill, down hill, up river, down river or across river; and whether a long, short or medium distance up or down.

Pronouns distinguish singular, dual and plural in both first and second person; there is no inclusive/exclusive distinction, and no incorporation of pronominal affixes into the verb. While nouns and noun markers inflect in a nominative-ergative pattern, pronouns (at least superficially) follow a nominative-accusative paradigm.

There is a four-term case system for pronouns and a nine-term one for nouns, noun markers and adjectives. A pronoun, noun, noun marker or adjective in genitive case can take a further inflection, provided a catalytic affix '-ɟin' is inserted immediately after the genitive. There are about twenty stem-forming affixes that can precede case inflections with nouns and adjectives.

Verbs and adverbals take a variety of aspectual and derivational affixes; the tense system has two members – future and non-future. There is a clear division into transitive and intransitive verbs (and similarly for adverbals). Two conjugation subclasses correlate statistically with, but do not coincide with, transitive and intransitive subclasses; there is one irregular verb, *yanu*, 'go'. There is no copula, nor any verb 'have' or 'become'. The language has wide and much-used possibilities of verbalisation (that apply to all nouns and adjectives, and to certain nominal expressions) and nominalisation (that apply to all verbs and adverbals).

Sentence modification is achieved partly through a set of about a dozen non-inflecting particles, and partly through three clitics, that are added to the end of the first word of a sentence. There is no separate class of locational words, as there is of time qualifiers. Locational information is largely dealt with through the complex 'noun marker' system; there are also some locational adjectives.

Dyirbal texts contain strong topic patterning: a topic may be stated, and then commented upon by a string of a score or so sentences, without repetition of the topic form. Topic patterning exploits the common Australian 'implicative relation' realised by *-gu*; this can occur with nouns, as a dative case inflection, indicating 'indirect object', and with verbs, instead of a tense inflection, indicating 'result' or 'purpose'.

2.2 Dialects

The name 'Dyirbal language', as used here, covers the 'languages' of three separate tribes: Mamu, Dyirbal and Giramay. These are grammatically almost identical, and have over 70% common vocabulary, so that it is convenient to give a single, overall description of their grammar and phonology. The 'language' of each tribe is referred to below as a 'dialect' of the Dyirbal language. Examples are given for the Dyirbal dialect, unless otherwise stated, dialectal variations being fully detailed throughout. We use the letters M, D and G to refer to the three dialects; note that D always refers to the Dyirbal dialect, and never to the full Dyirbal language.

The tribe speaking Dyirbal is called the Dyirbalŋan (or sometimes, by speakers of languages to the north, Dyirbaldyi), that speaking Giramay the Giramaygan. The tribe speaking Mamu consists of five 'hordes': Waɽibara, Dulgubara, Bagiɽgabara, Dyiɽibara and Mandubara, there being no name for the complete tribe. The members of a tribe normally marry only within the tribe (and according to section membership; for the tribe speaking Mamu, horde membership is quite independent of section membership).

Two hordes were recognised within the Dyirbalŋan tribe – Yabulumbara, living at the foot of the range in the south-eastern part of the territory, and Gambilbara, living in the higher country around the upper reaches of the Tully River.

Three other tribes also spoke dialects of what we are referring to as the Dyirbal language. They are the Malanbara, speaking Gulŋay; the Dyirubagala, speaking Dyiru; and the Ngadyandyi, speaking Ngadyan. Gulŋay and Dyiru are geographically and linguistically between Mamu and Dyirbal; the one or two surviving members of each tribe speak a blend of their original dialect and Dyirbal (Dyirbal is nowadays the dominant dialect of the region). Sufficient information could not be obtained on Gulŋay and Dyiru to include them in this study. What was obtained on Gulŋay revealed nothing that was not either in Dyirbal or Mamu or both; a brief summary is in 10.2.2.

Ngadyan is the most northerly and possibly the most divergent dialect of the language. It has undergone a phonological change whereby a sequence of (short) vowel plus syllable-final *l*, *y* or *ɽ* has been replaced by a long vowel. Ngadyan's grammar is basically similar to that of Mamu but there are some differences of affixes etc. A discussion of some of these divergent features is in 10.2.2.

The traditional tribal territories of the six tribes are indicated in map 2; in the case of Mamu the approximate locations of the five hordes are shown. Five of the six dialects were spoken in rain forest country; Giramaygan comprised a narrow strip of rain forest on the coast, from the Murray River to Cardwell, and a much larger stretch of more open country on top of the range.

Evidence presented in chapter 10 suggests that the six tribes speaking dialects of what we call the Dyirbal language are all descended from a single ancestor tribe. As the original tribe's numbers increased, it would have split into two groups, each of which became a tribe in its own right; and so on. It is likely that the original tribe lived in the southern part of the territory now occupied by the six tribes.

Our use of the name Dyirbal – which properly describes the dialect of just one tribe – as a cover term for these six closely-related dialects would be

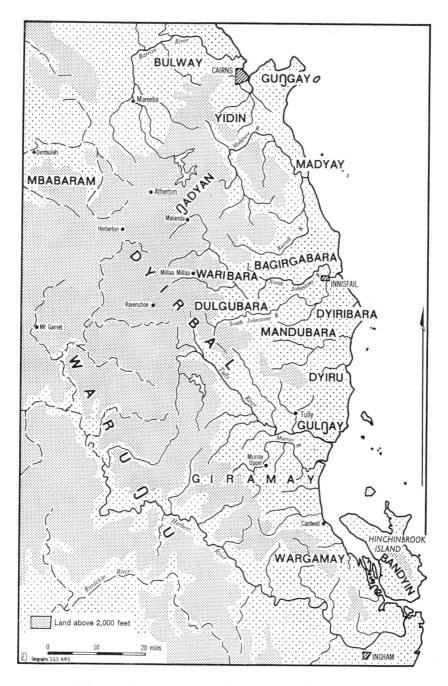

MAP 2. Language map of the Cairns rain forest region.

regarded by speakers of these languages as quite illicit. Speakers are aware of
the dialect similarities (especially qua differences between the six dialects and
other, contiguous, languages) but are also keen to emphasise the differences.
Each will maintain that his own dialect is the 'correct' way of speaking. The
aborigines do not have any overall label for the complex of six similar dialects.

We use Dyirbal as a name for the complete language since (1) both geographically and linguistically Dyirbal is a central dialect; (2) its speakers put
up the most resistance to the perils of European invasion (a group still lived
in the bush until the nineteen-thirties, more than fifty years after settlement);
as a result Dyirbal has this century emerged as the dominant dialect – it has
the most speakers and the survivors of other tribes (like Gulŋay and Dyiru)
mix their own dialect with Dyirbal. The writer is most proficient in the
Dyirbal dialect; the grammar is of this dialect, with full reference to the
grammatical differences shown by Mamu and Giramay.

2.3   Surrounding languages

The language most similar to Dyirbal is Wargamay (tribal name
Wargamaygan) spoken immediately to the south of the Giramay
dialect. Giramay and Wargamay share 60% vocabulary on the basis
of a 220-word list. There are some grammatical similarities – for
instance, the pronoun systems are identical. There are also considerable
differences – Wargamay has nothing corresponding to the four noun
classes of Dyirbal. It is difficult to decide whether the similarities
between Wargamay and the Dyirbal dialects are due to close genetic
relationship (over and above the weak genetic relationship that is
believed to link all Australian languages) or due to the diffusion of
structural features between the dialects during the thousands of years
that they have undoubtedly been in contact. A fuller discussion is in
10.2.1.

Waruŋu, spoken over the dividing range to the west of Dyirbal, is
considered by the Dyirbalŋan to be a much harder language to master
than Wargamay. Waruŋu and Dyirbal share 46% vocabulary but are,
grammatically, quite different; there is certainly no close genetic
relationship. Waruŋu appears to have considerable similarities with
languages from the centre and far west of Queensland, and may be
genetically related to them.

Mbabaṛam, to the north-west of Dyirbal, is – at least on the surface
– highly aberrant. Words can be monosyllabic and can begin with a
vowel or a consonant cluster; the final syllable can be stressed; there
are altogether seven vowels. It can be shown that Mbabaṛam has
evolved from a language of a normal Australian type, through regular

phonological change [Dixon, 1970*b*; a fuller treatment is forthcoming]. Mbabaṛam has clearly borrowed some vocabulary from Dyirbal in recent times, but otherwise the languages are quite dissimilar.

North of Mamu and east of Ngadyan are spoken Yidin, Guŋgay and Madyay; the tribal names are Yidindyi, Guŋganydyi and Madyanydyi. These are similar enough to each other to be regarded as dialects of one language; we will refer to this as the Yidin language. Yidin is, like Dyirbal, spoken exclusively in rain forest (Wargamay, Waruŋu and Mbabaṛam all occupied drier, more open country). But Yidin has only 27% vocabulary in common with the Ngadyan dialect and is grammatically much more different from Dyirbal than is Waruŋu. Amongst the surviving speakers of Yidin and Dyirbal the writer met no one who knew anything of the other language. In contrast, most speakers of Giramay could get by in Wargamay and vice versa; all Waruŋu were fairly proficient at Dyirbal and some Dyirbalŋan (especially from the north-western Gambilbara horde) knew Waruŋu. This is not necessarily a true reflection of the situation a hundred years ago but it does emphasise how different Dyirbal and Yidin are. Chapter 10 tentatively concludes that the Dyirbal tribes have come into contact with Yidin only relatively recently, as a result of tribal split, and movement northwards.

2.4 Cultural background

Dyirbal is spoken in a region that is predominantly rain forest, bounded on the east by the Coral Sea and extending to the coastal range and tableland beyond it in the west. There are many short rivers, waterfalls and swamps.

Many of the trees and vines bear fruit that can be made edible by complex treatment, which often takes several days and involves a variety of processes. As an example, Roth's [1901*b*: 10] description of the preparation of *miraɲ* 'black bean' (Castanospermum australe) cannot be bettered: 'after the beans have been gathered, the nuts are removed, and placed in heaps in the ground-ovens. After covering with leaves and sand, a fire is lit on top, with the result that the nuts are practically steamed, a process occupying from a few hours up to a whole day. When removed, they are sliced up very fine with a snail-shell knife, and put in dilly-bags in a running stream for quite a couple of days, when they are ready. If not sliced up very fine, the bitter taste remains.' Of the thirty or forty common fruit and vegetables six or seven would always at least be cooked (these by and large were the staples); the remainder could be eaten raw.

Wallabies, bandicoots, porcupines (echidnas), scrub-turkeys, eels, and so on would be speared or trapped, and the meat broiled, baked or grilled (boiling was unknown in this region). Scrub-hen and scrub-turkey eggs would be dug from the high mounds of earth they are covered with after being laid, and then fried in their shells. Grubs, cut out of rotten wood, would be eaten raw or roasted. Honey from native bees was perhaps the greatest delicacy (Roth, 1901 *b*, gives considerable information on this and other points).

Human flesh is also eaten. Anyone who has persistently broken the social code may be killed by some of the senior men of the tribe, his flesh eaten and his blood offered to younger men to drink. No particular ritual seems to be attached to human killing but it is always done deliberately, after considerable discussion of the crime of the wrong-doer; there is no evidence that anyone was killed just for the sake of being eaten.

Some men attain the status of *gubi* ('wise man' or 'doctor'). They generally have a thorough knowledge of their environment and of the customs and beliefs of the tribe. A gubi also attempts to cure illness through a mixture of genuine medicine and trickery (the latter often being effective in terms of the psychological relief it brings); in this area sweat from the armpits is believed to have healing properties. A necessary prerequisite for being a gubi is that one has drunk the blood of a cannibalistic victim; however knowledgeable any man, he cannot be a gubi unless he has tasted human blood.

The last known cannibalism was in 1940, when an aboriginal man was delibe-rately killed for excessive sexual misconduct. The gubi who was prime mover was arrested and spent about a dozen years in jail, but has now returned to the tribal territory. He was probably the most knowledgeable of the informants the writer used.

The people moved camp quite frequently in the dry season, building low sleeping huts as they were needed. During the heavy rainfall of the wet season they would return to larger, more permanent huts (that might last for several years). Fighting corroborees, involving several tribes, would be held at regular intervals [Roth, Bulletin 11, 1908]; these provided a regulated outlet for aggressiveness as well as an occasion for social intercourse.

Dyirbal mythology explains geological formations, the origins of fire and water, and of animals as altered human beings. Certain spirits are held to cause storms and mist, others to assist at initiation ceremonies, and so on. Singing corroborees involve dances that mimic animal behaviour etc., and often interrelate with myths.

It appears that beneath the veneer of fantasy some myths may provide accurate histories of events in the distant past of the people. There is, for instance, a Ngadyan myth that explains the origin of the three volcanic crater lakes Yidyam (Lake Eacham), Barany (Lake Barrine) and Ngimun (Lake Euramoo). It is said that two newly-initiated men broke a taboo and so angered the rainbow serpent, major spirit of the area (as of most of Australia – see Elkin, 1954: 220). As a result 'the camping-place began to change, the earth under the camp roaring like thunder. The wind started to blow down, as if a cyclone were coming. The camping-place began to twist and crack. While this was happening there was in the sky a red cloud, of a hue never seen before. The people tried to run from side to side but were swallowed by a crack which opened in the ground...'

This is a plausible description of a volcanic eruption. After telling the myth, in 1964, the storyteller remarked that when this happened the country round the lakes was 'not jungle – just open scrub'. In 1968, a dated pollen diagram from the organic sediments of Lake Euramoo by Peter Kershaw [1970] showed, rather surprisingly, that the rain forest in that area is only about 7,600 years old. The formation of the three volcanic lakes took place at least 10,000 years ago.

All this points to the story of the volcanic eruptions, and of the spread of rain forest, having been handed down from generation to generation for something like ten millennia. This is perfectly possible: recent archaeological work suggests that aborigines have been in Australia for at least 25,000 years, and the Dyirbal could well have been in more or less their present territory for 10,000 years or more. (There is further discussion of all this in chapter 10.)

Further evidence is contained in the myth of Giṛugar, a legendary man who came from the south, visiting each mountain, lake and island and giving it a name. The storyteller remarked that in Giṛugar's day it was possible to WALK across to the islands (Palm Island, Hinchinbrook Island, and so on). In fact geographers believe that sea level was sufficiently low for it to have been possible to walk to all the islands in the Coral Sea at the end of the last ice age, eight to ten thousand years ago.

The Dyirbalŋan (or 'Tully River Blacks') have often been quoted by anthropologists as a people who were unaware of the connection between sexual intercourse and conception. This is due entirely to Roth's [Bulletin 5, 1903] account of some of the myth-type 'explanations' of childbirth. It is, in fact, clear that the Dyirbalŋan were quite aware of the cause of conception – there is, for instance, a verb *bulmbiɲu* 'to be the male progenitor of' that has clear reference to a particular act of copulation that induced a conception. The explanations Roth quoted could be compared to the 'stork motif' in European society (a fuller rebuttal of the 'virgin birth' viewpoint is in Dixon, 1968*b*).

Some spirits are 'used' as social regulators – for instance, frightening children so that they will not leave the camp at night, go off by themselves, or bathe in deep and dangerous pools (these are said to be the abode of the rainbow-serpent). The gubi appear to have a measure of control over these beliefs.

The ear is held to be 'the seat of intelligence' [cf. Roth, Bulletin 5, 1903: 19] and language ability regarded as one measure of intelligence. Extreme insults will accuse a person of being unable to hear correctly.

The intelligence of aborigines takes a quite different form from, say, that of Europeans. They pay great attention to shape, location and direction, time being to some extent regarded as an extension of location. There are few words for numbers in aboriginal languages, complex reference to part of the palm of the hand being the usual method of counting [Roth, Bulletin 11, 1908]. Australian aborigines have highly developed sign languages, and spoken language tends to be heavily augmented by gesture.

Vagueness is held to be a severe fault; all descriptions should be as specific as possible (see 6.6). This has often been misrepresented as a failure of the aborigines to develop generic thinking. In fact the languages do contain those generic terms that are likely to be needed; and implicit generic classification clearly underlies the semantic organisation of the language (see chapter 8).

The aborigines' concept of 'possession' is radically different from any European concept, and it is necessary to know something of it in order to understand the structure of the language (for instance, the proleptic construction – 6.1.5). An (edible or material) thing will belong to some person BY RIGHT; although it could be exchanged for something else, or for some favour, it is unlikely to be given away spontaneously. If food is brought home a relative will receive a portion that he has a right to; even before the meat is cut up and distributed, some part (but not necessarily any particular part) BELONGS to the relative. Nowadays, if an aborigine spends his money on some foodstuff in the local store, he is TAKING that which is his (the money being looked upon as an overt token that a part of the goods in the store belongs to the aborigine).

Each tribe is divided into four sections, each of which has its distinctive totems. These are:

section	main totem
ḍigungara	black eel – *ḍaban*
guṟguru	meat hawk – *guṟuŋgul*
gurgila	large eel – *mubaṟay*
garbawuṟu	eagle hawk – *guriḍala*

Males are referred to by the name of their section; females are referred to through a feminine form of the section name, involving affix *-gan* (for instance, *gurgilayŋgan*).

Marriage rules, which are strictly but not inflexibly enforced, depend on section membership:

a man who is:	must marry a woman who is:	and their offspring are:
ḍigungara	*guṟguru*	*gurgila*
guṟguru	*ḍigungara*	*garbawuṟu*
gurgila	*garbawuṟu*	*ḍigungara*
garbawuṟu	*gurgila*	*guṟguru*

There is in addition a prohibition on marrying first cousins. While ego's mother's sister's and father's brother's children will be in ego's own section and thus obviously not available for marriage, his cross-cousins (father's sister's and mother's brother's children) will be members of the section from which ego must choose his wife. Cross-cousins of the opposite sex are thus subject to a special taboo.

A great deal of accurate (although not always complete) information about the life, habits and environment of the Dyirbalŋan is in Roth's eighteen bulletins, *North Queensland Ethnography* [1901–10]; consult the sections on 'lower Tully' (Malanbara, speaking Gulŋay) and 'Atherton' (Dyirbal) peoples.

2.5 'Mother-in-law language'

Each speaker had at his disposal two separate languages: a Dyalŋuy, or 'mother-in-law language', which was used in the presence of certain 'taboo' relatives; and a Guwal, or everyday language, which was used in all other circumstances. Each dialect had a Guwal and a Dyalŋuy.

The 'everyday language' is called *guwal* in the Dyirbal and Giramay dialects, and *ŋirma* in the Mamu dialect.

No man or woman would closely approach or look at a taboo relative, still less speak directly to them. The avoidance language, Dyalŋuy, had to be used whenever a taboo relative was within earshot. The taboo was symmetrical – if X was taboo to Y so was Y to X.

Taboo relatives were:

[1] a parent-in-law of the opposite sex; and, by the symmetry rule, a child-in-law of the opposite sex.

[2] a cross-cousin of the opposite sex – that is, father's sister's or mother's brother's child.

Category [2] covers just those relatives who are of the section from which ego must draw a spouse, but who must be avoided on the grounds that they are too close kin. Thus, the rules for using Dyalŋuy, together with the section system, precisely indicate who is sexually available for any person.

Dyalŋuy HAD TO be used in the presence of a parent-in-law, child-in-law or cross cousin of the opposite sex. It should also be used – although the necessity was not so strong – with a parent-in-law of the same sex. It could be used more or less optionally with a cross-cousin or child-in-law of the same sex. It would not be used in any other circumstances. Thus, a male ego must use Dyalŋuy in the presence of his mother-in-law and she must use it back; he should use it with his father-in-law but father-in-law can choose whether he replies in Dyalŋuy or in Guwal. The male ego must also use Dyalŋuy in the presence of a female cross-cousin and she must use it back; in the case of a male cross-cousin both ego and the cousin can choose whether to use Dyalŋuy or Guwal.

Dyalŋuy has not been actively spoken since about 1930 (2.6), and nothing is known for certain about the way it was learnt. Children were promised in marriage at an early age, thus acquiring a full set of taboo relatives; Dyalŋuy was probably learnt in the same way as Guwal, perhaps a year or two behind it.

Each Dyalŋuy has identical phonology, and almost exactly the same grammar, as its Guwal. However, it has an entirely different vocabulary; there is not a single lexical item common to the Dyalŋuy and Guwal of a tribe. A Dyalŋuy has only a quarter or less as many lexical items

PLATE 1 Chloe Grant (*marḍi* or *miḍabunḍal*), main informant for the Dyirbal and Giramay dialects. In the left background is Mamie Grant, Chloe's daughter-in-law, whose mother was Mbabaṛam and father Waruŋu. (1964)

PLATE 2 George Watson (*muyiḍa*, *ɲiyiḍa*, or *bangaṇḍala*), main informant
for the Mamu dialect. (1964)

PLATE 3 From left: Rosie Runaway (*ḍarmay*), who speaks Giramay and Dyirbal dialects; the writer; Chloe Grant. Note Rosie Runaway's small stature (the writer is 6 ft 3 in). (1963)

PLATE 4 The family of Joe Kinjun, last of the Malanpara tribe, at their camp on the banks of the Tully River. Joe Kinjun's head and left shoulder are visible, centre, behind his son. Joe Chalum, from the Dyirbal tribe, is furthest from the camera. (1963)

as a Guwal. A single Dyalŋuy term will correspond to a number of Guwal words. Thus there are six or more names for types of grub in Guwal, but no generic term; Dyalŋuy has just one (generic) name. Similarly, there are in Guwal separate verbs *ḍuran* 'wipe or rub', *yiḍin* 'massage (by a doctor)', *baŋgan* 'paint or draw with the finger' and *ɲamban* 'paint with the flat of the hand', but only a single Dyalŋuy verb *ḍurmbayban* 'rub' corresponding to all four Guwal items.

It appears that each Dyalŋuy has the minimum number of lexical items compatible with it being possible to say in Dyalŋuy everything that can be said in Guwal; Dyalŋuy uses every possible syntactic and semantic trick in order to make do with the minimum vocabulary. There is effectively a single underlying semantic system, realised at two levels of generality – the Guwal level (the normal semantic level for natural languages) and the rather more abstract Dyalŋuy level. Investigation of Guwal–Dyalŋuy word correspondences is extremely revealing – in many cases the correspondences give direct information about the semantic structure of the language. This is discussed in chapter 8, and more fully in Dixon [1971].

We have said that there is no lexical item common to the Guwal and Dyalŋuy of a particular tribe. However, what is a Guwal form for one tribe often turns up in the Dyalŋuy of a neighbouring people.

Thus, the words for 'sun' are:

	Guwal	Dyalŋuy
Yidin	*buɲan*	*gaṟi:man*
Ngadyan	*gari*	*buɲan*
Mamu	*gari*	*gambulu*

Dyirbal Guwal has *nudin* 'sever', *gunban* 'cut (a piece out)' and Dyirbal Dyalŋuy has just *ḍalŋgan* corresponding to both Guwal verbs. Mamu Guwal has just *gunban* (whose range of meaning covers both *nudin* and *gunban* in Dyirbal Guwal) and Mamu Dyalŋuy has *ḍalŋgan*. Ngadyan Guwal has *gunban* again and Ngadyan Dyalŋuy has *nudin*. Thus *nudin* is a Guwal verb 'cut' in Dyirbal, does not occur in Guwal or Dyalŋuy for Mamu, but is the Dyalŋuy verb 'cut' in Ngadyan.

Extensive Dyalŋuy data were obtained for the Mamu and Dyirbal dialects (but could not be obtained for Giramay). Surprisingly, although Mamu and Dyirbal Guwals have 87% common vocabulary, their Dyalŋuys have only 50% in common. Further, a Mamu Dyalŋuy word is often the same as a Guwal term from a language to the north, while a Dyirbal Dyalŋuy word may occur in a Guwal from the south.

It is suggested, in chapter 10, that, at the time the original Dyirbal-
Mamu tribe split into two separate tribes, the Dyalŋuy vocabulary was
very much smaller than it is now. The two Dyalŋuys then augmented
their vocabularies more or less independently of each other, and from
different sources.

The grammar and phonology, in chapters 3–7, are valid for both
Guwal and Dyalŋuy of each dialect; all examples involve Guwal
lexical items unless the contrary is specified.

2.6   Recent history of the tribes

White settlement expanded into the territory of the six tribes in 1864,
with the foundation of Cardwell. Over the next twenty years Europeans
took over the most accessible parts of the territory, and began felling
the forest in order to create pasture for their cattle, or for the growing
of crops. There was no settlement of any size until Tully, with its
sugar mill, in 1924. In particular, there were no mineral finds, and the
territory was spared invasion by tens of thousands of European miners,
followed by an equal number of Chinese fossickers, that was responsible
for the almost instant elimination of tribes such as Mbabaṛam.

But, sparse as the settlement was, speakers of Dyirbal were not
kindly treated. Tribes were probably reduced to less than 20% of
their pre-contact numbers within twenty years of the European
invasion (it is likely that each tribe originally had about 500 members).
European diseases to which the aborigines had no immunity, such as
measles and influenza, were responsible for many deaths, but the
major factor in the decline of numbers was wholesale murder by the
settlers. Christy Palmerston – who is portrayed as a friend of the
aborigines in white histories of the area [Bolton, 1963: 60, 94] – ambushed
the Mamu tribe, gathered together for a corroboree, and shot out all
the adult men but for a handful who managed to escape. Poisoned
flour was a favourite trick – aborigines would be found dead all along
the path from the white man's hut to their own camp. The late Lindsay
Cowan told the writer that when he arrived in the Tully district in the
early twenties he was informed that there were no 'bad aborigines'
there – they'd all been shot.

It did not end with simple slaughter. The early settlers, by a species
of mental cruelty, assured the aborigines that their customs were
childish, and that their lingo – which was assumed to consist of at most

a couple of hundred words – was unworthy of the name 'language'. One white man, whom we can call Lachlan, was enraged whenever he saw aborigines pursuing any of their traditional ceremonies (such as initiation) and would immediately slaughter the participants. Lachlan was once on top of the Herbert gorge and saw an aborigine defecating below; he shot him 'to teach them all a lesson'. It was also put about that aboriginal men were sexually inferior. Women would be appropriated at whim by the settlers and, if an aboriginal husband complained, he was likely to be sent to the semi-penal settlement on Palm Island on the grounds that he was a trouble-maker. It is interesting to note that only two half-castes grew up in the Tully region in the first quarter of this century; many were born but all others were killed soon after birth, by their white fathers.

After the initial massacres, survivors of the Giramay tribe and of the southern horde of the Dyirbal formed a joint community with headquarters near an old fighting ground on the upper reaches of the Murray River (in the white settlement of Murray Upper). A policeman's report in 1898 suggested that a reserve be established 'at the Bora ground about fourteen miles NW of Cardwell' [Holmes, 1898], but nothing was done. Today, the aborigines live as barely tolerated squatters on their own lands, and often have to work in exchange for the privilege of living on a particular settler's property.

That they survived at all seems incredible. They were aided partly by the Europeans' blindness – it was thought that most tribal practices and ceremonies had vanished when in fact many were still being secretly practised. Partly by their philosophical humour – for instance, Lachlan was called by the name *gubarngubar*, the term for 'scrub-itch', a parasitic red mite that causes severe itching and irritation. The damage that Lachlan did and the extent to which he is still, fifty years after his death, feared is demonstrated by the fact that aborigines would not use his white name when talking about him with the writer, if there was any chance of being overheard by a white man. It is in view of this that he is here referred to by a pseudonym.

Perhaps the main factor in the survival of the Dyirbalŋan has been a solid hope that one day the white man would be driven out, and the tribe would once more be able to resume peaceful occupation of its traditional lands. There is probably rather less chance now, than there was at the time of the policeman's recommendation in 1898, that a few acres might be set aside for the tribe's exclusive use (quite apart from the further question of whether they be granted title to any of their tribal territory). In the last decade the situation has further deteriorated. The remaining aborigines had thirty or more years ago come to terms with the settlers, and were accorded a measure of freedom in revisiting traditional sites, and so on, provided their men worked on the settlers' farms. Then, in 1963, the state government invited an American company completely to clear a large tract of land between the Tully and Murray Rivers, and to use the land to a maximum for grazing cattle. Thus, as the final and cruellest blow in their hundred years of contact with the white man, aborigines have seen their traditional camps – after which they were named and which they consider part of themselves, and whose associations may in some cases extend back ten millennia – razed to the ground.

Incidentally, this has also resulted in the thoughtless destruction of a good number of rare rain forest trees, whose dietary and medicinal properties are known only to the aborigines.

The original way of life has gradually broken down. Dyalŋuy ceased to be used about 1930; since then Guwal has been used, whether or not a taboo relation is in the vicinity. The last initiated man, with a full set of tribal scars, is now about 50. The last fighting corroboree was held in the mid-fifties: it was broken up by the police on the third day. Singing corroborees were still held from time to time in the sixties, with the approval and attendance of the white settlers. Marriages are still arranged according to the section system and the gubi is still listened to and respected. Although there has been no cannibalism for thirty years, the threat of being killed still makes many young men hesitate before breaking the moral code.

It is interesting to note that the main gubi, who has as little as possible to do with white people, is looked upon by them as a harmless old man, with little knowledge or influence. On the other hand, a number of particularly simple-minded old aborigines, of Uncle Tom temperament, are feted and displayed to tourists as leaders of their people.

The Dyirbalŋan have long been dependent on the white man's bread and beef. They will still hunt and eat wallabies, eels, scrub-hen eggs, and particularly fish (and even the odd Lumholtz tree-kangaroo, if they happen to encounter him) but they have quite abandoned their traditional vegetables, which involved such complex and lengthy preparation.

There were, in 1963, two or three very old people living in Murray Upper who knew only a few words of English. Those between fifty and seventy were as a rule reasonably fluent in English but would only use it in the presence of a white man. Some of the younger people maintained Dyirbal or Giramay as a first language while others had switched to English. Almost all the children (who are sometimes forbidden to speak their own language in the local school, to which they were admitted about 1950) are most at home in English. There are, however, a few families in which the children are growing up to speak Dyirbal or Giramay at least as strongly as English. In 1970 there may have been, in the Murray Upper region, two dozen fluent speakers of Dyirbal and eight or ten of Giramay. There are probably another six or ten Dyirbalŋan (survivors of the northern horde) in the Mount Garnet/Ravenshoe/Herberton area.

The other tribes have all fared worse. Bandyin, spoken on Hinchinbrook Island, is extinct (it seems from the vocabulary that survived to have been half-way between Giramay and Wargamay); it was helped on its way by the traditional beating of the island from end to end by a cordon of settlers in the early days. Dyiru and Gulŋay are both down to their last one or two speakers (and their language is inextricably mingled with Dyirbal). Ngadyan has at most six speakers and Mamu not many more. None of the survivors of these tribes speak their own language more than a part of the time, even among their own people. Nowhere outside the Murray Upper region are any children learning anything but English.

2.7 Outline of phonology

A full description of the phonology is in chapter 7. Here we merely explain the phonemic orthography in which the examples are written:

> *b* is a bilabial stop; *d* is an apico-alveolar stop; *ḍ* is a lamino-alveopalatal stop; *g* is basically a dorso-velar stop but normally involves double articulation, the front of the tongue also touching the alveolar ridge;
>
> *m*, *n*, *ɲ* and *ŋ* are a corresponding series of nasals;
>
> *l* is an alveolar lateral, *r* is generally an alveolar trill, and *ɾ* generally a semi-retroflex continuant;
>
> *w* and *y* are bilabial-velar and palatal semi-vowels;

u, *i* and *a* are close back rounded, close front unrounded and open vowels.

Stress is normally predictable, and is then not marked. It occurs on the first syllables of roots and affixes; final syllables are never stressed. The norm pattern is for the first and all odd syllables of a word to be stressed, and for the second and all even syllables to be unstressed; there is, in fact, evidence that the language has changed and is changing so that there is just one (or at any rate as few as possible) unstressed syllables between each pair of stressed ones (10.3.4).

In many cases affixes have variant forms according as they are added to stems having the norm stress pattern, or to stems that deviate from it. Thus, the instrumentive/accompanitive affix to verbs is *-mal* following a single unstressed syllable, but *-mbal* when directly following a stressed syllable or after a sequence of two unstressed syllables (4.9). The ergative inflection on nouns is *-ŋgu* on a stem of two syllables ending in a vowel, but *-gu* on to a longer stem ending in a vowel (3.2.1).

The sign / is used in transcribed texts to separate impressionistically recognised 'intonation groups'; any utterance could end at any place marked by /.

3 Word classes

For Dyirbal the following word classes, with mutually exclusive membership, can be set up:

$$\left.\begin{array}{l}\text{noun} \\ \text{adjective}\end{array}\right\} \text{nominal}$$

pronoun

$$\left.\begin{array}{l}\text{verb} \\ \text{adverbal}\end{array}\right\} \text{verbal}$$

time qualifier

particle

interjection

Noun, adjective, verb, adverbal and time qualifier are open classes (the adverbal class is rather limited – a lexicon of three thousand words contained only about two dozen adverbals); adverbals modify verbs exactly as adjectives modify nouns.

There are also 'noun markers' and 'verb markers' (3.2.2, 3.4.5, 6.5); these are, however, more in the nature of 'secondary categories' [Jespersen, 1924] and are not here treated as word classes.

This chapter first outlines the semantic content of each major word class; it then deals with the nominal inflections of nouns, adjectives and noun markers, the rather different inflections of pronouns, the tense inflections of verbs and adverbals, and the inflections of time qualifiers.

Particles show little or no inflection; like time qualifiers they qualify a complete sentence – 4.15. Interjections are listed in 4.17.

3.1 Semantic content of the open word classes

NOUNS include terms referring to flora and fauna; to parts of the bodies of humans and of other animals, parts of trees, and so on; to mineral and other environmental phenomena ('stone', 'earth', 'water', 'fire' and so on); to geographical formations ('mountain', 'forest'),

[39]

meteorological phenomena ('wind', 'cloud') and celestial bodies; to noises ('whistle', 'bang'), song-styles and language; to artefacts ('boomerang', 'dilly bag', 'cooking frame') and institutionalised parts of the environment ('camping site', 'fighting ground', 'track'); to age/sex groups ('baby', 'girl past puberty', 'newly-initiated man'); to relations ('father's elder brother', 'maternal grandmother'); to particular people and places (proper names) and to spirits. Other abstract concepts are expressed primarily through verbs and adjectives, which can yield derived nouns.

As with all languages, concentrations of specific terms are encountered in areas that are important to the life and culture of the people. For instance, there is a name for each stage in the complex preparation of *miraɲ* 'black bean' (2.4). At the opposite extreme, there are a considerable number of generic terms, many referring to flora and fauna ('snake', 'bird', 'tree' and so on); chapter 8 discusses the semantics of these generic terms.

As in other Australian languages [O'Grady, 1960], a single term may cover anything that ACTUALLY IS or POTENTIALLY COULD BE a certain thing. In the G[iramay] dialect *yugu* is the term both for 'fire' and for 'wood/tree' (D[yirbal] and M[amu] however have *buni* for 'fire', reserving *yugu* just for 'wood/tree'). *miraɲ* is the name both for a tree and for the nut that it bears; *nuba* is the term both for a bark water-bag, and also for the tree from whose bark the bag is normally made.

ADJECTIVES specify value ('good', 'bad'); age ('new'); human propensities ('greedy', 'worried', 'ashamed', 'angry', and so on); physiological states (for instance 'fast asleep', 'almost asleep', 'can't get to sleep'), speed ('fast', 'slow'), physical properties ('heavy', 'sweet', 'hot'); states resulting from actions ('split', 'covered' and also, for instance, 'finished'); dimensions ('big', 'long', 'deep'); and position and posture ('inside', 'on top', 'near', 'lying on one side doubled up'). There are cardinal number adjectives 'one', 'two', 'three', 'many' and 'very many', and a full set of derived ordinals (6.7). There are only abstract colour terms for 'black' and 'white', common nouns being used adjectivally to describe other colours – for instance, *gari* 'sun' and *guŋgu* 'red clay' for shades of red.

VERBS refer to simple motion ('go', 'cross river'), to simple rest ('stand', 'float'), and to what can be called 'induced motion' ('pull', 'throw') and 'induced rest' ('hold'); to actions that affect the object ('pierce', 'rub', 'burn'); to transfer of possession ('give', 'send'); to actions of seeing, hearing and of ignoring; to all types of language activity ('speak', 'ask', 'sing'); to bodily functions ('eat', 'cough', 'smell'); to mental activities such as dreaming, planning and liking; and to the cessation of an action or state ('fall', 'break').

As in the case of nouns, a single verb may cover both actions that ACTUALLY HAVE and actions that POTENTIALLY COULD HAVE a certain result [O'Grady, 1960]; and see 4.8.1. For instance, the two English verbs 'sleep' and 'lie down' would both be translated by *bungil* (the Dyirbaḷŋan as a rule only lie down in order to sleep). In order to state unambiguously that someone was sleeping, either an adjective or else the noun *ḏagun* 'a sleep, a night-time' would have to be brought in. Again, *balgal* can be glossed, in different instances of use, as 'hit with a long rigid object, that is not let go of' or as 'kill'. *baygul* can refer either to an action of shaking something, or of bashing something on something else – its meaning can be described 'put in motion in a trajectory, not letting go of' (whether there is any ACTUAL impact with some other object is irrelevant here, with this action there is always a POTENTIALITY of impact).

A final example of the lack of an actual/potential distinction concerns *buṟal*, which can refer to both looking (with the potentiality of seeing a particular thing) and actual seeing; similarly *ŋambal* means both 'listen' and 'hear'. Note also that the reflexive of *ŋambal* refers to thinking (literally 'listen to oneself'); similarly, the reflexive of *miḏul* 'take no notice' means 'wait' (literally 'take no notice of oneself').

ADVERBALS provide semantic qualification of a verb, referring to the start or finish of an action, or to whether something is done slowly or fast, well or badly, done again or done too much, and so on.

A fuller account of the rather complex semantics of adverbals, verbs and nouns is in chapter 8. Dyirbal verb semantics is also dealt with in some detail in Dixon [1971].

TIME QUALIFIERS refer to various time distances in the past and future. As in other Australian languages there is no word 'today', only 'earlier on today' and 'later on today'. Some locational qualifiers have a secondary time sense, with 'downhill' corresponding to 'future time'. There are also qualifiers referring to temporal appropriacy ('too soon'), as yet unfulfilled expectation ('not yet'), and permutation ('meanwhile').

3.2 Nominals: nouns and adjectives

3.2.1 Case inflections. Nouns and adjectives show identical case inflections; for five of the nine cases, inflections vary with the phonological ending of the stem. All possibilities are exemplified in Table 3.1.

TABLE 3.1 *Case inflections of nouns and adjectives*

	nominative	ergative = instrumental	simple genitive	locative
'man'	*yaɽa*	*yaɽaŋgu*	*yaɽaɲu*	*yaɽaŋga*
'rainbow'	*yamani*	*yamanigu*	*yamaniɲu*	*yamaniga*
'(any) snake'	*wadam*	*wadambu*	*wadamu*	*wadamba*
'possum'	*midin*	*midindu*	*midinu*	*midinda*
'small lizard'	*biɲɖiriɲ*	*biɲɖiriɲɖu*	*biɲɖiriɲu*	*biɲɖiriɲɖa*
'brown snake'	*walguy*	*walguyɖu*	*walguyɲu*	*walguyɖa*
'woman'	*ɖugumbil*	*ɖugumbiɽu*	*ɖugumbilɲu*	*ɖugumbiɽa*
'native bee'	*gubur*	*guburu*	*guburɲu*	*gubuɽa*
'black guana'	*gugaɽ*	*gugaɽu*	*gugaɽɲu*	*gugaɽa*

The rules for forming cases are as follows:

[1] NOMINATIVE (used as intransitive subject and transitive object) is simply the noun or adjective stem;

[2] ERGATIVE (transitive subject) involves the addition of:

    (i) *-ŋgu* to a disyllabic stem ending in a vowel,

    (ii) *-gu* to a trisyllabic or longer stem ending in a vowel,

    (iii) a homorganic stop plus *-u* to a stem ending in a nasal or *-y*,

    (iv) *-ɽu*, together with the deletion of the stem-final consonant, when the stem ends in *-l*, *-r* or *-ɽ*;

[3] INSTRUMENTAL is identical with the ergative (there are strong syntactic reasons for distinguishing two cases – 4.9.1);

[4] SIMPLE GENITIVE involves the addition of *-u* for stems ending in a nasal, and the addition of *-ɲu* for all other stems;

[5] LOCATIVE differs from ergative only in having final *-a* in place of *-u*.
Case affixes that involve no allomorphic variation are:

[6] GENERAL GENITIVE: *-mi*;

[7] DATIVE: *-gu*;

[8] ALLATIVE: *-gu* (allative is identical to dative for nouns and adjectives; the two cases do, however, have entirely different inflections in the case of noun and verb markers (3.2.2, 3.4.5) and there are also considerable syntactic reasons for distinguishing dative and allative – 6.1.5);

[9] ABLATIVE: *-ɲunu*.

The contrast between simple and general genitive is discussed in 4.11. Very roughly, simple genitive indicates that some object is, or is soon to be, actually in a person's possession; general genitive – which occurs much less frequently – indicates that the person used to own the object, or that he still owns it but does not actually have it in his possession at the present time. Genitives are only used to describe alienable possession.

There is evidence that the simple genitive inflection should be regarded as *-ŋu* on all stems, and that in the case of a stem ending in a nasal the affix-initial nasal is deleted, when it precedes an unstressed vowel, by a late phonological rule. For instance, the form *bálamáŋganɲúɳḍinda* was observed – *bálamáŋgan* is here in genitive inflection, and then the catalytic affix *-ɲḍin-* is added before the final locative inflection; in this case affix-initial *ŋ* is retained immediately before a stressed vowel. Final syllables are never stressed, so that an affix-initial nasal is always deleted when the genitive inflection is word-final.

The nine cases fall naturally into three groups:

(i) those that mark syntactic relations: nominative, ergative, instrumental, dative;

(ii) the two genitives;

(iii) those that give information about motion or its absence: allative ('to'), locative ('at'), and ablative ('from').

The genitives are set off from the rest since they alone can be followed by a further case inflection (4.11). In 5.5.2 we relate genitive inflections on nouns and pronouns to the inflections of verbs in relative clauses, and suggest that possessive phrases are a special kind of relative clause.

Dyirbal cases follow the typical Australian pattern, described in 1.6. Ergative inflection involves just *-(ŋ)gu* with no trace of the alternative inflection *-lu* that occurs as well as or instead of *-(ŋ)gu* in many languages, including Dyirbal's northerly neighbours Mbabaṛam and Yidiṇ. Two genitives are not common, but they have been reported for Gugu-Yimidir, spoken two hundred miles to the north of Dyirbal (4.11.2).

Proper and some common nouns (usually, just those referring to humans) can take the affix *-ɲa*, but only when they are in transitive object function. For these nouns there are alternative dative and locative inflections, either with or without *-ɲa* (note that no ergative, instrumental, genitive, allative or ablative forms can involve *-ɲa*). For instance, in the case of the man's name *burbula* we have alternatives:

NOMINATIVE (INTRANSITIVE SUBJECT FUNCTION): *búrbula* only
NOMINATIVE (TRANSITIVE OBJECT FUNCTION): *búrbula* or *búrbulaɲa*
DATIVE: *búrbulagu* or
 búrbulaɲángu

LOCATIVE: *búrbulaga* or
                                                   búrbulaɲáŋga

Note that, following *-ɲa*, dative inflection is *-ngu* and locative *-ŋga*.

-ɲa behaves quite differently from the regular case inflections in that it can be followed by derivational and other affixes (6.1.1); the other case inflections – with the exception of the genitives – cannot be followed by any other affix, of any kind.

Nominal *-ɲa* is clearly related to, and can better be understood by comparison with, pronominal inflection *-na ~ -ɲa* (6.2). *-Na* occurs in many Australian languages, and behaves in much the same way that it does in Dyirbal – see 1.5, 1.6 and Dixon [forthcoming-b].
Further discussion of Dyirbal case inflections and their functions is in 6.1.5.

3.2.2 Noun markers. Dyirbal has four noun classes. There is nothing in the phonological form of a noun to show its class; but a noun is normally accompanied by a 'noun marker' that shows its class, agrees with it in case, and also yields information on the location of the referent of that occurrence of the noun.

Thus we have *bayi yaṛa* 'man', *bayi yamani* 'rainbow', *balan ḍugumbil* 'woman', *balam miraɲ* 'black bean', *bala ḍawun* 'dilly bag' and *bala gubur* 'native bee'. The full paradigm for noun markers along dimensions of case and class is shown in Table 3.2.

TABLE 3.2   *Noun markers along dimensions of case and class*

	nominative	ergative = instrumental	dative	simple genitive
Class I	*bayi*	*baŋgul*	*bagul*	*baɲul*
Class II	*balan*	*baŋgun*	*bagun*	*baɲun*
Class III	*balam*	*baŋgum*	*bagum*	..
Class IV	*bala*	*baŋgu*	*bagu*	*baɲu*

Noun markers do not appear in general genitive, locative, allative or ablative forms (see the discussion of verb markers – 3.4.5). Class III covers just fruit and vegetables; not unnaturally, there is no possessive form of the class III marker (there is a form *baɲum* but it is a verb marker 'from there' – 3.4.5).

The only class IV nouns that do not have inanimate reference are names of bees. Elicitation produced *bala giṛɲḍal baɲu guburɲu* 'the honey belonging to the native bee', involving the genitive form of the class IV marker; *baɲu* can also occur in the possessive forms of pseudo-pronouns *balagara* and *balamaŋgan* − 3.3.2.

A noun marker can be analysed into three parts: first, a root such as *bala-*; second, a case inflection:

> nominative: zero
> ergative/instrumental: *-ŋgu-*⎤
> dative: *-gu-*   ⎬ together with deletion of
> simple genitive: *-ŋu-*⎦   the *-la-* of *bala-*

third, a mark of the class of the noun:

> class I: *-l*   class III: *-m*
> class II: *-n*   class IV: zero

Nominative class I form is exceptional, being *bayi* when **balal* would be expected.

The reasons for recognising the first part of a marker to be *bala-*, with deletion of *-la-* for non-nominative cases, rather than postulating that the first part is *ba-*, with nominative adding *-la-*, are given in 6.5.1; it should be noted that forms such as ergative *balaŋgul* do occur, albeit infrequently.

There are in fact three possibilities for the first element in a noun marker:

> *bala-* indicating that the referent of the noun is visible and THERE;
> *yala-* indicating that the referent is visible and HERE;
> *ŋala-* indicating that the referent is NOT VISIBLE.

The locational origin is normally the position of the speaker. *ŋala-* forms are used to refer to something that can be heard and not seen, and when describing something that is remembered from the past.

Many Australian languages have obligatory specification of proximity − 1.5. Reference to visibility is also not uncommon, occurring in, for instance, the Western Desert language (1.5) and in the West Torres language [Ray 1907*a*: 12].

The paradigm for *ŋala-* noun markers is identical to that for *bala-* forms, with initial *b-* replaced by *ŋ-* in each case. The 'visible and here' paradigm is more complex; *yala-* is the first segment for non-nominative forms, while the suppletive form *giɲa-* is used in the nominative (shown in Table 3.3).

TABLE 3.3   *Noun markers: the 'visible and here' paradigm*

	nominative	ergative = instrumental	dative	simple genitive
Class I	*giyi*	*yaŋgul*	*yagul*	*yaɲul*
Class II	*giɲan*	*yaŋgun*	*yagun*	*yaɲun*
Class III	*giɲam*	*yaŋgum*	*yagum*	..
Class IV	*giɲa*	*yaŋgu*	*yagu*	*yaɲu*

Again, the class I nominative form is irregular. In G the nominative forms are *ɲiyi*, *ɲiɲan*, *ɲiɲam* and *ɲiɲa* respectively (*ɲiɲa*- forms, unlike the *giɲa*- markers in D and M, can occur in locative case – 6.5.3).
    Thus:

(1) *bayi yaɽa miyandaɲu*   man there is laughing
(2) *giyi yaɽa miyandaɲu*   man here (this man) is laughing
(3) *ŋayi yaɽa miyandaɲu*   man is heard, but not seen, laughing

as against:

(4) *balan ḍugumbil baŋgul yaɽaŋgu bayan*   man there is singing to woman there
(5) *balan ḍugumbil yaŋgul yaɽaŋgu bayan*   man here is singing to woman there
(6) *balan ḍugumbil ŋaŋgul yaɽaŋgu bayan*   man is heard, but not seen, singing to woman there

Of the nominative noun markers, *bala-* and *giɲa-* forms are both extremely common, while *ŋala-* forms are relatively infrequent. *bala-* is the unmarked initial, and is used when no specification of visibility/ proximity is intended. *giɲa-* has a strong demonstrative meaning and (unlike *bala-* and *ŋala-*) can be used deictically:

(7) *giɲan ḍugumbil*   this is the woman

Of non-nominative markers, *bala-* forms occur perhaps ten times as frequently as those involving *yala-*, which are in turn several times more common than those involving *ŋala-*. *yala-* forms lack the demonstrative force of *giɲa-* markers.
    A *giɲa-* marker can occur in an NP with a *bala-* marker – see (101) in 4.5.1. In contrast, NPs involving both *bala-* and *yala-* forms have not been encountered.

The comments of the last two paragraphs suggest that the inclusion of *giɲa*- and *yala*- forms in one paradigm is probably incorrect. Instead, we could construct a full *yala*- paradigm, exactly like those with *bala*- and *ŋala*-, and a separate short paradigm for *giɲa*- forms, which occur in nominative case only. We could then say that nominative *yala*- forms ARE NOT USED, demonstrative markers based on *giɲa*- always being preferred. Thus:

*(8) *yayi yaṯa miyandaɲu*

is not an acceptable Dyirbal sentence; (2) is used instead. However, in some dialects *giɲa*- markers do not occur with certain affixes that can follow *bala*- and *ŋala*- forms, and IN THESE CASES nominative *yala*- markers do occur – thus *yayiɲaŋga* 'for fear of this class I thing', in which nominative *yayi* is followed by -*ɲa*- and then the locative inflection (see 6.1.5); and *yalanambila* 'with this class II thing' in which nominative *yalan* is followed by -*ɲa*- and then the derivational affix -*bila* (6.1.1). These examples support the claim that nominative markers based on the root *yala*- are 'suppressed' by *giɲa*- forms; they reappear in contexts in which *giɲa* forms do not appear.

> *ban*, *bam*, *ŋan* and *ŋam* occur as free variants of *balan*, *balam*, *ŋalan* and *ŋalam* respectively.

This is clearly a further extension of the principle of deleting the final -*la*- of *bala*- and *ŋala*-; note that the class IV nominative markers – *bala* and *ŋala* – cannot be reduced. There are only six monosyllabic words in Dyirbal, the four given here and two interjections *ŋa* 'yes' and *ŋu* 'alright' – 4.17.

A further noun marker, in D and M only, is based on the root *gila*; this occurs in nominative, ergative/instrumental, dative and simple genitive, but has a defective paradigm – 6.5.2.

Forms *bala*, *giɲa* and so on occur in a number of other Australian languages; comparative notes are included in 6.5.1, 6.5.3.

Almost all nouns have fixed class membership; the exceptions are a handful of (kinship and human age-group) words like *ḍaḍa* 'baby', *bimu* 'father's elder brother or sister' that can take class I or class II markers depending on the sex of the referent. Nouns referring to men, kangaroos and possums, most snakes and fishes, a few birds, most insects, the moon, storms, boomerangs and money come under class I; women, anything to do with fire or water, bandicoots, a few snakes and fishes, most birds, snails, grasshoppers and crickets, the sun and stars, and shields under class II; all wild fruit and vegetable food, and the trees that bear them, under class III; trees (without edible fruit), grass, sand, mud, stones, bees and honey, meat, wind, tomahawks, noises and language under class IV. An explanation of the semantic basis of noun class membership is in 8.4.4.

3.2.3 Bound forms *bayḍi*, etc. To any noun marker or demonstrative noun marker (whatever its case, noun class, and locational specification) can be optionally added:

[1] One of a set of twelve bound forms further specifying the location of the noun's referent:

bayḍi	short distance downhill	*dayi*	short distance uphill
bayḍa	medium distance downhill	*daya*	medium distance uphill
bayḍu	long distance downhill	*dayu*	long distance uphill
balbala	medium distance downriver	*dawala*	medium distance upriver
balbulu	long distance downriver	*dawulu*	long distance upriver
	guya	across the river	
	bawal	long way (in any direction)	

In M only there is a thirteenth form – *ŋaru* 'behind'.

'River' is the marked feature in the system 'river versus hill' (essentially, whether or not involving 'water'); the unmarked feature is more correctly specified 'not river' – it most often refers to 'hill' but also to 'cliff', 'tree', etc. However, for brevity *dayi* will continue to be glossed 'uphill' below; and so on.

and/or [2] one of a similar set of bound forms:

gala up (vertically)
gali down (vertically)
galu out in front (with reference to the way either actor or speaker is facing)

There are thus forms *balandaya, bagungalu, baŋuldayigala, giɲanbayḍi, baŋgundawala, bayimbawal* (the *-m-* is a predictable phonological intrusion – 7.5.1) and so on. A form of set [1] always precedes one of set [2].

In M, unlike in D, a noun marker can be followed by a form from set [1] OR one from set [2], but NOT forms from both sets.

In addition, any of these bound forms may be augmented by a suffix *-ru* in D and G or *-gu* in M (*bawal* by *-aru* or *-agu*) – 6.7.1. This intensifies the form. Thus *bayindayi yaṛa* 'man a short way uphill', *bayindayiru yaṛa* 'man a little nearer uphill'; *bayimbawal yaṛa* 'man out there', *bayimbawalaru* 'man further out there'.

3.2.4 Interrogative members. *miɲa* DM, *waɲa* G 'what (is that non-human object)?' ranges over the subclass of nouns whose members do not have human referents (for those with human referents see 3.3.3). There is an interrogative member of the adjective class: *miɲaɲ* 'how many', this effectively ranges over the subclass of number adjectives, 6.7. Both *miɲa/waɲa* and *miɲaɲ* inflect for case exactly like a noun or adjective – 3.2.1.

In D and G there is a quasi-interrogative noun *ŋambiya* 'what's it called?', that is inserted in a discourse – in the appropriate case inflection – whenever the speaker cannot immediately recall the word he wants, and needs a moment to think; it is not normally used to ask anything of another person. A typical example of the use of *ŋambiya* is in the last line of text xxxib – page 387. *ŋambiya* does not occur in M. It is interesting to note that D is spoken considerably faster than M (this was mentioned by speakers of both dialects, and had already been noticed by the writer); it may be that in the context of his slower and more measured speech a M speaker has no need for a 'thinking space device' such as *ŋambiya*.

There is a set of interrogative forms corresponding to noun markers (note that again the class I nominative form is irregular):

	nominative	ergative = instrumental	dative	simple genitive
Class I	*wuɲḍiɲ*	*wuɲḍaŋgul*	*wuɲḍagul*	*wuɲḍaɲul*
Class II	*wuɲḍan*	*wuɲḍaŋgun*	*wuɲḍagun*	*wuɲḍaɲun*
Class III	*wuɲḍam*	*wuɲḍaŋgum*	*wuɲḍagum*	..
Class IV	*wuɲḍa*	*wuɲḍaŋgu*	*wuɲḍagu*	..

These forms enquire about the location of the referent of a noun:

(9) *wuɲḍiɲ yaɽa miyandaɲu*   where is the man that is laughing?

The bound forms *bayḍi* etc., and *gali* etc., can NOT be added to an interrogative marker.

It is conceivable that a class IV genitive interrogative noun marker (presumably *wuɲḍaɲu*) could be used in some sentence like 'where is the bee whose honey this is?'. Such a form was never heard, and would be impossibly difficult to elicit.

3.3 Pronouns

3.3.1 Case inflections. There is a class of six pronouns (seven in M) whose possibilities of case inflection, qua syntactic function, differ from those for nouns and adjectives. Superficially, pronouns in D and

M follow a 'nominative-accusative' pattern, with one pronominal form functioning as transitive or intransitive subject, and another as transitive object. There is, however, a great deal of syntactic evidence for the view that both nouns and pronouns follow an underlying nominative-ergative pattern; this is discussed in 5.2. For the time being, pronominal inflections will be described in terms of syntactic function.

TABLE 3.4 *The pronoun paradigm for the three dialects*

	intransitive subject [S]	transitive subject [A]	transitive object [O]	dative	simple genitive	reference
G	*ŋayba*	*ŋaḏa*	*ŋaɲa*	*ŋaygungu*	*ŋaygu*	speaker
DM	*ŋaḏa*		*ŋayguna*	*ŋaygungu*	*ŋaygu*	
G	*ŋali*	*ŋaliɲa*	*ŋaliɲangu*	*ŋaliɲu*		speaker and
D	*ŋaliḏi*	*ŋaliḏina*	*ŋaliḏingu*	*ŋaliḏinu*		one other
M	*ŋali*	*ŋalina*	*ŋalingu*	*ŋaliɲu*		person
G	*ŋana*	*ŋanaɲa*	*ŋanaɲangu*	*ŋanaɲu*		speaker and
D	*ŋanaḏi*	*ŋanaḏina*	*ŋanaḏingu*	*ŋanaḏinu*		more than one
M	*ŋana*	*ŋanana*	*ŋanangu*	*ŋanaɲu*		other person
G	*ŋinba*	*ŋinda*	*ŋina*	*ŋinungu*	*ŋinu*	addressee
DM	*ŋinda*		*ŋinuna*	*ŋinungu*	*ŋinu*	
G	*ɲubilaḏi*	*ɲubilaḏina*	*ɲubilaḏingu*	*ɲubilaḏinu*		two persons, at
D	*ɲubalaḏi*	*ɲubaladina*	*ɲubaladingu*	*ɲubaladinu*		least one an
M	*ɲubala*	*ɲubalana*	*ɲubalangu*	*ɲubalanu*		addressee (neither the speaker)
G	*ɲura*	*ɲuraɲa*	*ɲuraɲangu*	*ɲuraɲu*		more than two
D	*ɲuraḏi*	*ɲuraḏina*	*ɲuraḏingu*	*ɲuraḏinu*		persons, at least
M	*ɲuray*	*ɲurana*	*ɲurangu*	*ɲurayɲu*		one an addressee (none the speaker)

There is a seventh member of this class in M only:

	ŋanaymba	*ŋanaymbana*	*ŋanaymbangu*	*ŋanaymbanu*		speaker and spouse

Dative and simple genitive inflections on pronouns are morphologically and syntactically compatible with the corresponding inflections on nouns and adjectives. Pronouns do not occur in general genitive, locative, allative or ablative inflection. A genitive pronoun can, like a genitive noun, take the catalytic affix -(η)din- and then any further case inflection (including, in this case, locative, allative or ablative). The full pronoun paradigm for the three dialects is shown in Table 3.4.

The forms given against a dialect are the most usual for that dialect; however, forms without the -di can occur in D (and *ɲubila* does occur in G) and appear to be syntactically and semantically identical with the -di forms; similarly, -di forms do occur in M and, to a lesser extent, in G. Alternant forms *ɲubaldina* and *ɲubiladinangu* have been observed used instead of *ɲubaladina* and *ɲubiladingu* respectively. A morphological analysis of this paradigm is provided in 6.2.

Normal labels 'first person' and 'second person', 'singular', 'dual' and 'plural' will be used below to refer to pronouns.

Dyirbal pronouns are typically Australian – see 1.5. The -di, that occurs especially strongly in the D dialect, appears to be an idiosyncrasy; it is possible (although there is no real evidence) that it is related to the -(η)din that must be suffixed to a simple genitive noun or pronoun before any further inflection is added. G has a special idiosyncrasy (that is not shared by any surrounding language) in that the second vowel of the second person dual form is -i-. The 'self and spouse' pronoun, in M, has not been reported for any other language in this area.

3.3.2 *balagara, balamaŋgan.*

It will be noticed that there are no third person pronouns in Dyirbal. *bayi, balan, balam* and *bala* are not properly regardable as third person (singular) pronouns since they normally ACCOMPANY a noun (although either noun or marker can occur alone); in any case they inflect like nouns, quite differently from pronouns.

However there are forms *bálagára* and *bálamáŋgan* (in D and M but not in G) that have some similarities to third person dual and plural pronouns in other languages. They function rather differently from *bayi*, etc.; they do, however, inflect like nominals. (And see 3.3.3 for interrogative versions of *balagara* and *balamaŋgan* – NOT formed on the basis of the interrogative version of *bala*.)

gara 'one of a pair' and *maŋgan* 'one of many' are normally noun suffixes (6.1.1), for example:

(10) *bayi burbulagara miyandaɲu* two people laughed, one of whom was burbula

(11) *bayi burbulamaŋgan miyandaɲu* many people (i.e. more than two) laughed, one being burbula

In *balagara* and *balamaŋgan*, *-gara* and *-maŋgan* appear to be suffixes to the noun marker *bala* (this would be one of the few instances of a noun marker taking nominal suffixes – 6.5.6). For case inflections we get:

either [1] *bala* inflecting as usual, and *-gara* or *-maŋgan* remaining unchanged;

or [2] *bala* remaining unchanged and the whole form inflecting like a nominal;

or [3] both [1] and [2] at once.

The different possibilities appear to be in free variation:

	nominative	ergative	dative	genitive
[1]	*balagara*	*baŋgugara*	*bagugara*	*baŋugara*
[2]		*balagaragu*	*balagaragu*	*balagaraŋu*
[3]		*baŋgugaragu*	*bagugaragu*	*baŋugaraŋu*

and similarly for *balamaŋgan*; there are no locative, allative or ablative forms. The justification for regarding *-gara* and *-maŋgan* as suffixes is that the ergative forms are *balagaragu* and *baŋgugaragu* (that is, as for a stem of more than two syllables) rather than **balagaraŋgu* and **baŋgugaraŋgu* (which would indicate a stem of two syllables – 3.2.1).

Forms *giɲagara*, *giɲamaŋgan*, *ŋalagara* and *ŋalamaŋgan* are also attested.

yala- substitutes for *giɲa-* in non-nominative forms; in fact, possibility [2] – which would involve *giɲa* occurring in an ergative form, **giɲagaragu* – is not acceptable in this case, the ergative correspondents of *giɲagara* being just *yaŋgugara* and *yaŋgugaragu*.

A *balagara/balamaŋgan* form can occur either by itself, or else with a noun, that will be accompanied by a noun marker in the usual way. Thus:

(12) *balagara miyandaɲu*   two (people) are laughing
(13) *balagara bayi yaṟa miyandaɲu*   two men there are laughing

There are no forms *balagara* or *balamaŋgan* in G; in translating from D to G adjectives *bulay* 'two' and *ḍana* 'all, many' are used; for example, the G for (13) is *bayi yaṟa bulay miyandaɲu* and the translation of *giɲamaŋgan giyi yaṟa* would be *giyi yaṟa ḍana*.

G thus shows similarities to other Australian languages, for which third person dual and plural pronouns *bula* and *Ḏana* have been reported (1.5 – for instance, Gugu-Yalanji has both *bula* and *Ḏana* [R. Hershberger, 1964*a*], while Talandji, Inggarda, and Ooldean have *Ḏana* [O'Grady *et al.*, 1966: 105, 115, 140]). In some of these languages, as in Giramay, *bula* and *Ḏana* inflect in the same way as nouns, and quite differently from first and second person pronouns.

3.3.3 Interrogative member. *waɲa* 'who' ranges over the class of pronouns and the subclass of nouns that have human referents; its case inflections are similar in some ways to those of pronouns and in other ways to those of nouns (see 5.8.4, 6.6):

	intransitive subject [S]	transitive subject [A]	transitive object [O]	dative	genitive
DM	*waɲa*	*waɳḏu*	*waɲuna*	*waɲungu*	*waɲuɲu*
G	*waɲuɲa*	*waɳḏu*	*waɲuɲa*	*waɲungu*	*waɲuɲu*

Note that, in G, the S and O forms fall together; D and M have different forms for all three syntactic functions. This is in marked contrast to the way in which the three dialects deal with first person pronouns: G has different forms for all three functions, while S and A forms fall together in D and M.

Note also that *waɲa*, which is in D and M the interrogative pronoun root, is in G the interrogative noun 'what' – 3.2.4.

The distinction between (quoting D forms) *waɲa* – with human reference – and *miɲa* – with exclusively non-human reference – is, apart from *-ɲa*, the only occurrence in the grammar of Dyirbal of the category 'human'; *-ɲa* is usually but not exclusively affixed to words referring to humans (6.1.1).

The interrogative correspondent of *bala* is *wuɲḏa* (3.2.4); thus we might expect the interrogative versions of *balagara* and *balamaŋgan* to be **wuɲḏagara* and **wuɲḏamaŋgan*. In fact they are *waɲagara* 'which two people' and *waɲamaŋgan* 'which lot of people', emphasising the semi-pronominal nature of *balagara* and *balamaŋgan*, and the fact that it is unwise to regard *bala* in these compounds as (syntactically) the class IV noun marker.

To say, for instance, 'where are those two women?' one has to use *wuɲḏan balagara*; **wuɲḏangara* and **balan wuɲḏagara* are quite unacceptable.

3.4 Verbals: verbs and adverbals

3.4.1 Transitivity. Just as an adjective, modifying a noun, will inflect in exactly the same way as the noun, so an adverbal, modifying a verb, inflects in exactly the same way as the verb. With verb root *buybal* 'hide' and adverbal root *ŋuymal* 'do it properly' we get verb complexes *buyban ŋuyman* 'hide it properly', *buybaɲ ŋuymaɲ* 'will hide it properly', *buybayiriɲu ŋuymayiriɲu* 'hide oneself properly' and so on.

Each verb or adverbal root is either strictly transitive or else strictly intransitive: we thus have transitive and intransitive subclasses of each of the classes verb and adverbal.

The terms 'transitive' and 'intransitive' are here used in a non-normal way, to refer to constructions that are basically nominative-ergative (rather than nominative-accusative) – see 5.2, 5.3.

3.4.2 Conjugations. There are two patterns of verbal inflection in Dyirbal, depending on whether the stem (as set up) ends in *-l* or in *-y*. Thus each verbal root falls into one of two conjugational subclasses.

There is some correlation between conjugational subclasses and transitivity. That is:

> of transitive verbal roots
>> about 90% are *-l* forms, the remainder *-y* forms
> of intransitive verbal roots
>> about 80% are *-y* forms, the remainder *-l* forms

Dyirbal conjugations are clearly related to the two major conjugation types, which recur in many Australian languages (1.7). In Dyirbal, it is most economical and revealing to consider each verb root, and each verbal-stem-forming affix, as ending in either *-l* or *-y*, according to the inflectional pattern of the resulting form. Stem-final *-l* and *-y* are retained before some affixes, but assimilated or lost before others.

It is probable that at one time all transitive roots were in the *-l*, and all intransitive roots in the *-y*, conjugation. Some verbs may have changed transitivity while maintaining the same conjugational association – one piece of evidence supporting this is given in the discussion of reflexives, 4.9.3. In addition, loan items may sometimes have had a meaning suggesting a certain transitivity, but a form suggesting a conjugational placement that went against the normal correlation.

Verbs in the *-l* conjugation end in *-al*, *-ul*, or *-il*, those in the *-y* conjugation in *-iy* or *-ay*, NEVER in *-uy*. No reason is known for the absence of *-uy* roots. Note that, in the analysis of Henry and Ruth Hershberger, Gugu-Yalanji verbs in the second conjugation are assigned roots ending in *-ay* or *-iy*, never in *-uy* – 1.7. (We could have omitted the *-y* from underlying verb forms *-iy* in

Dyirbal, thus producing a description that corresponded exactly with the Hershbergers' for Gugu-Yalanji; in fact we postulate a rule that deletes -*y* following -*i*- in certain circumstances – 7.5.2.)

3.4.3 Tense. Dyirbal has a two-term tense system, with an unmarked term referring to past or present time, and a marked term for reference to future time.

Either past or present time can be unambiguously shown by inclusion of an appropriate time qualifier – 4.14, 6.4. Past time can also be indicated, in all dialects, by special use of a relative clause verbal inflection – 4.10. See also 4.5.5 for -*ŋura*, which can be used in a way that suggests an 'immediate future' tense.

Interestingly, Yidin, Wargamay and Nyawigi – languages to the north and south of Dyirbal – also have a two-term tense system, but of the opposite kind: past/non-past.

The full paradigm for tense inflection is:

	-*l* stem	-*y* stem
stem	*balgal* 'hit'	*baniy* 'come'
unmarked tense	*balgan* 'hits/hit'	*baniɲu* 'comes/came'
future tense	DM *balgaɲ* 'will hit'	DM *baniɲ* 'will come'
	G *balgalḏay*	G *baninḏay*

The 'future' inflection can also carry a generic meaning, similar to that of the English present tense (e.g. 'he shoots horses').

There is one irregular verb, *yanu* 'go'. Roughly, this behaves like an -*l* root *yanul* for all forms but positive imperatives – where the root is *yana(l)* – except that the unmarked tense form is *yanu* and not *yanun*. For a full account see 6.3.3.

3.4.4 Interrogative and deictic verbs. There are two interrogative forms – transitive *wiyamal* and intransitive *wiyamay* – ranging over the classes of verbs and adverbals. Used by itself one of these forms means 'do what?'; used with a verb it becomes an adverbal interrogative 'do how?'. Thus:

(14) *bayi yaṟa wiyamaɲu* what was man doing?
(15) *ŋinda bayi yaṟa wiyaman* what did you do to man?
(16) *bayi yaṟa wiyamaɲu mabin* how did man cross river?
(17) *ŋinda bayi yaṟa wiyaman balgan* how did you hit man?

When used adverbially, *wiyamal/wiyamay* can be enquiring about the way in which the action was accomplished, or about the instrument used, or about the degree of success achieved. Thus a reply to (16) could be:

(18) *bayi yaṟa yuŋaraṉu mabin*   man swam across river

and to (17) might be:

(19) *ŋaḍa bayi yaṟa baŋgu yuguŋgu balgan*   I hit man with stick

while a reply to either (16) or (17) might involve *garḍa* 'alright':

(20) *garḍabi bayi yaṟa mabin*   man crossed river properly

(21) *garḍabi ŋaḍa bayi yaṟa balgan*   I hit man properly

(see 6.7.3 for the affix *-bi*)

    There are two deictic adverbals – transitive *yalamal* and intransitive
yalamay – that function very much like *wiyamal* and *wiyamay*; they
mean 'it is done like this' and usually either refer to a mime accompanying the utterance or else introduce quoted speech:

(22) *ŋaḍa bayi yaṟa yalaman balgan*   I hit man like this (with accom-
        panying mime)

(23) *ŋaḍa ŋinuna yalaman ŋanban/wuṉḍiṉ bayi yaṟa miyandaṉu*   I asked
        you this way 'Where is the man who is laughing?'

    In narrative, *yalamal/yalamay* can often be used alone – that is,
without any verb such as *ŋanban* 'ask', *buwaṉu* 'tell', *wurbaṉu* 'say' –
to introduce reported speech; an example is in line 80 of text xv (p. 382).
However, in elicitation, informants always insisted on inserting the
appropriate verb – when a version of (23) that did not include *ŋanban*
was suggested, it was emphasised that the sentence could only be
acceptable if *ŋanban* were to be inserted – indicating that the absence
of a verb of saying is due to discourse ellipsis.

    The interrogative and deictic verbs in M are *wiyabal* and *wiyabay*,
yalabal and *yalabay*.

The deictic verb forms are clearly historically related to the noun marker
root *yala-*, referring to something 'visible and here, i.e. THIS THING'. The
-mal/-bal element of the transitive deictic may be genetically related to transitive
verbalising suffix *-mal ~ -(m)bal*, 4.7. Within the terms of the present, synchronic analysis of Dyirbal, however, deictic verbs are not morphologically
analysable.
    There are just a few other transitive/intransitive pairs that have the same
form bar the final consonant – 9.2.1.

3.4.5 Verb markers. A verb can be accompanied by one of a set of
eight verb markers, that have some morphological correspondence with
noun markers (3.2.2); they provide locational qualification for the
verb. They are:

ALLATIVE OF PLACE	*balu* 'to there (towards a place)'	*yalu* 'to here (towards a place)'
ALLATIVE OF DIRECTION	*bali* 'to there (in a direction)'	*yali* 'to here (in a direction)'
ABLATIVE	*baɲum* 'from there'	*yaɲum* 'from here'
LOCATIVE	*balay* '(at) there'	*yalay* '(at) here'

Just as in the case of noun markers, to any verb marker can be added one of the twelve bound forms *bayḍi* etc., and/or one of the three bound forms *gali* etc., any of which may be augmented by *-ru* (3.2.3).

In D and G there are also verb markers with initial *ŋa-*, referring to something remembered from the past. Forms *ŋalu*, *ŋaɲum* and *ŋalay* are attested but not, in this sense, *ŋali (the form *ŋali* is pre-empted by the first person dual pronoun – see 3.3.1).

There are also markers based on the root *gila* – see 6.5.2.

3.4.6 Locational nominals.

A verb may also be accompanied by a noun in allative, ablative or locative inflection, optionally accompanied by an adjective in the same inflection. Thus we have, from *bala miḍa* 'camp', *miḍagu* 'to the camp', *miḍaɲunu* 'from the camp', *miḍaŋga* 'at the camp'. An allative or locative (but not an ablative) form may be augmented by *-ru*, with an implication of motion: *miḍaŋgaru* could be, for example, '[going] along by the side of the camp' or 'through the camp'.

In summary, a verb may be modified by [1] a verb marker, or [2] a locational – that is, allative, ablative or locative – nominal, or [3] both. If both occur they must agree in case – 4.3.

A noun in nominative, ergative, instrumental, (simple) genitive or dative case is normally accompanied by a noun marker, that indicates its class. A noun in allative, locative or ablative inflection cannot be accompanied by a noun marker; it can co-occur with a verb marker (that does not show class). A comparative study of the morphology of noun and verb markers is in 6.5.

A noun in allative, locative or ablative inflection could be regarded as an ad hoc place name; in these circumstances, noun class is clearly irrelevant. The Dyirbalŋan have a multiplicity of place names – for every bend in a river and dip in a ridge – often in terms of the type of tree that grows there, the rock formation, etc. It is frequently difficult to distinguish between an institutionalised place name, and simple reference to a particular object at some locality.

One set of verbs, concerned with motion – for example *baniy* 'come', *mabil* 'cross river' – can only select an allative or ablative verb-marker-and/or-locational-nominal. Another set, concerned with position – for example, *ɲinay* 'stay, sit', *ḍanay* 'stand' – can only select locative forms. Some other verbs – such as *buṛal* 'look' – can occur with either motion or position qualification.

For these selections, a locational nominal augmented by *-ru* behaves either as a rest or as a motion form. Thus *yanu miḍaŋgaru* 'go through the camp', and *ɲinaɲu miḍaŋgaru* 'sit just outside the camp'.

3.4.7 Interrogative verb markers. There is a set of interrogative forms corresponding to verb markers:

ALLATIVE OF PLACE	*wuɲḍaru* 'to which place?'
ALLATIVE OF DIRECTION	*wuɲḍari* 'in which direction?'
ABLATIVE	*wuɲḍaɲum* 'where from?'
LOCATIVE	*wuɲḍay* 'where (at)?'

The bound forms *bayḍi*, *gali* etc. cannot be added to interrogative verb markers; and locational nominals cannot occur with them.

3.5 Time qualifiers

Time qualifiers are recognised as a distinct class on the following grounds:

[1] SYNTACTICALLY. A time qualifier will normally come first in a sentence, and provides information about the complete event referred to by the sentence – 4.14.

    [2] MORPHOLOGICALLY. Time qualifiers have two inflections:

        (a) *-(ŋ)gu* 'time until'. For instance, *gilu* 'later on today', *giluŋgu* M, *gilugu* D 'until later on today'.

        (b) *-mu* 'time since'. Thus, *gubila* 'a few years ago', *gubilamu* 'since a few years ago'.

These have some similarity to allative and ablative inflections on nouns, but also important differences; a full account is in 6.4.

    There is an interrogative time word DM *miɲay*, G *miɲi* 'when'. This can take the two inflections; thus DM *miɲayŋgu*, G *miɲiŋgu* 'how long until' and DM *miɲaymu*, G *miɲimu* 'how long since'.

For instance, *miɲaymu giɲam* would normally be understood 'how old is the food (i.e. how many days old)?', whereas *miɲaymu giyi* would be taken as 'how old is the boy or man (i.e. how many years old)?'.

4 Syntax

In Dyirbal, syntactic relations are marked by case inflections and not by word order; word order is remarkably free. There is a statistically most frequent order (7.8) and this is as a rule followed in the examples below (some of the simpler examples are made up, but all have been thoroughly checked with speakers). It should be borne in mind that in almost all cases the words could be arranged in ANY order.

4.1 Simple sentences

4.1.1 Involving nominals: nominative-ergative construction.
There are two types of simple sentence in Dyirbal – transitive and intransitive. If only nominals are involved, then the words in an NP functioning as intransitive subject [S] or transitive object [O] receive nominative inflection, and the words in an NP functioning as transitive subject [A], ergative inflection:

(24) *bayi yaṛa baniɲu*   man is coming
(25) *balan ḍugumbil baniɲu*   woman is coming
(26) *balan ḍugumbil baŋgul yaṛaŋgu balgan*   man is hitting woman
(27) *bayi yaṛa baŋgun ḍugumbiṛu balgan*   woman is hitting man

It should be noted that the exemplificatory sentences given in this and other chapters are always grammatically correct, but are usually as 'wooden' as their English equivalents. Informants often suggested substituting 'his wife' for 'woman', giving a reason for the action, and generally making the sentences more interesting (see Samarin, 1967: 37). We have kept them simple so as to be able to illustrate the grammatical points without burdening the reader with lexical detail. Some idea of sentences that are likely to occur (which also involve considerably more ellipsis than we have allowed in the examples) can be gained from study of the texts (pp. 368–97).

4.1.2 Involving pronouns: nominative-accusative construction.
However, simple sentences (in D and M) involving pronouns exhibit a different type of construction:

(28) *ŋaḍa baniɲu*   I'm coming
(29) *ɲinda baniɲu*   You're coming
(30) *ŋaḍa ɲinuna balgan*   I'm hitting you
(31) *ɲinda ŋayguna balgan*   You're hitting me

These sentences exhibit a typical nominative-accusative construction, suggesting – on the basis solely of (28–31), taking no account of (24–7) – that forms *ŋaḍa* and *ɲinda* be named 'nominative', and forms *ŋayguna* and *ɲinuna* 'accusative'.

Only in D and M simple sentences involving pronouns can the 'nominative-accusative' construction be recognised. In G the singular pronouns have different case inflections for all three syntactic functions.

   The majority of Australian languages behave exactly like Dyirbal, with nouns following a nominative-ergative pattern and pronouns (superficially at least) a nominative-accusative pattern – see 1.4.

In 5.2.2 we give syntactic reasons suggesting that pronouns, like nouns, follow an underlying nominative-ergative pattern. Throughout the grammar 'nominative' is used to mean a case in a nominative-ergative system (that is, referring to transitive object and intransitive subject); we do not recognise an 'accusative' case for Dyirbal.

   Sentences can mix nouns and pronouns quite freely, without any possibility of ambiguity. Thus:

(32) *ŋaḍa bayi yaɽa balgan*   I am hitting man
(33) *ŋayguna baŋgul yaɽaŋgu balgan*   Man is hitting me

4.2   Noun phrases

4.2.1   Non-pronominal noun phrases.
If it does not contain a pronoun, a N[oun] P[hrase] will as a rule contain a noun and noun marker, and can also contain any number of adjectives (although in texts few NPs involve more than one adjective). The marker most often precedes and adjectives follow the noun. However, it is perfectly normal for NPs in Dyirbal to contain only a marker, or only a noun, or only an adjective, or else just noun and adjective, or marker and adjective. If there is no noun the unmarked reference of a class I marker will be to a man or men, and of a class II marker to a woman or women (but a class II marker without a noun might, in a suitably marked situational context, refer to a turtle say, or the sun; and so on):

(34) *bayi baniɲu*   [man] is coming

(35) *bulgan baniɲu*   big [something] is coming
(36) *bayi bulgan baniɲu*   big [man] is coming
(37) *bayi yaɽa bulgan baniɲu*   big man is coming

Sentences such as (34–6) occur freely in Dyirbal speech. However, informants
– while agreeing that such sentences were used – insisted that (37) was more
correct than (35) and (36). This suggests that a noun and noun marker should
be taken to underlie every non-pronominal NP, forms (34–36) being accounted
for in terms of 'discourse ellipsis'.

Superficially at least, noun and adjective appear to have:
[1] the same syntactic possibilities – each can be the only word in an
NP; each can be verbalised in the same ways (4.7.1); and so on.
[2] the same inflectional morphology.
They can best be distinguished in terms of surface grammar on the
grounds that an adjective can usually occur in an NP with a noun
marker belonging to any of the four classes, whereas a noun is limited
to occurrence with markers of just one class (or at most two – 3.2.2).
Noun and adjective can also be distinguished semantically.

Dyirbal distinguishes between what we can call 'alienable' and
'inalienable' possession. Alienable possession (including kinship
relation) is shown through genitive inflection of the words of the
possessor NP–4.11. Inalienable possession is shown simply by apposition.

In addition to a head noun, usually accompanied by a marker showing
its class, an NP can contain a second 'modifier' noun that cannot be
accompanied by a marker. In this case the referent of the modifying
noun is inalienably possessed by the referent of the head (as being
'a part of' it). Both nouns take case inflection appropriate to the
syntactic function of the NP:

(38) *bala mambu baŋgul yaɽaŋgu balgan*   man is hitting a back
(39) *balan ɖugumbil mambu baŋgul yaɽaŋgu balgan*   man is hitting
woman's back

Dyirbal discourse is extraordinarily elliptical, and it would be perfectly normal
to omit *ɖugumbil* from (39), producing:

(40) *balan mambu baŋgul yaɽaŋgu balgan* man is hitting her back

In (40) *balan* is the sole realisation of the NP head, *mambu* being a non-head
modifying noun. (40) can be distinguished from (38) – which involves no statement of inalienable possession, and in which *mambu* is the head of its NP –
through the different noun markers; (38) involves a class IV marker, corresponding to *mambu*, whereas (40) involves a class II marker, corresponding to the
omitted possessor noun.

Only in the case of inalienable possession can a Dyirbal NP contain two nouns, without any affixes besides case inflection. In particular, it is impossible to have an NP such as:

*(41) *bayi yaṟa balan ḍugumbil baniɲu* [man and woman are coming]

One would either have to subordinate one participant by suffixing noun and marker with *-bila* 'with' (6.1.1):

(42) *bayi yaṟa balanambila ḍugumbilbila baniɲu* man is coming with woman

Or else use the affix *-gara* 'one of a pair' (6.1.1), which should be affixed to both nouns:

(43) *bayi yaṟagara balan ḍugumbilgara baniɲu* man, being one of a pair, and woman, being the other of the pair, are coming

-gara, in one of its functions, can thus be regarded as a phrasal co-ordinator (*-gara* is used when there are two NPs to be coordinated, *-maŋgan* when there are more than two).

Dyirbal has a number of lexical and grammatical devices for referring to two people, depending on their kinship relation – for instance, *ɲaybiṟ* 'man and wife', and see the discussion of *-ḍir* and related affixes in 6.1.3. Sentences such as (42) and (43) seldom need to be used; on hearing such a sentence a Dyirbalŋan would be likely to infer that the man and woman had no right to be together, and were doing something quite illicit.

A Dyirbal sentence can contain both an ergative NP and an instrumental NP:

(44) *balan ḍugumbil baŋgul yaṟaŋgu baŋgu yuguŋgu balgan* man is hitting woman with stick

By discourse ellipsis, either or both words in the ergative and/or the instrumental NP may be omitted. Thus one might hear:

(45) *balan ḍugumbil baŋgul yuguŋgu balgan* he is hitting woman with stick

Since ergative and instrumental inflections are identical, it might be thought that *baŋgul* qualified *yuguŋgu* in (45). That they do in fact belong to different NPs is evident from an examination of noun class – *yugu* is class IV whereas *baŋgul* is a class I marker, obviously referring to a deleted agent noun.

Ergative and instrumental NPs behave differently in a number of ways – for instance, the *-ɲay* transformation changes the case of an ergative NP, but leaves an instrumental untouched – 4.9.1.

4.2.2 Pronominal noun phrases. An NP can contain a pronoun, instead of noun-plus-marker, as head; the rest of the phrase can then be as described above. For instance, inalienable possession:

(46) *ŋayguna mambu baŋgul yaṟaŋgu balgan*   man is hitting my back

Dual and plural first person pronouns are not marked as inclusive or exclusive. The dual first person pronoun can be accompanied by a second person singular pronoun (to show inclusion) or a noun-plus-marker (to show exclusion):

(47) *ŋali ŋinda baniɲu*   you and I are coming
(48) *ŋali bayi yaṟa baniɲu*   man and I are coming

Similarly in the case of the first person plural pronoun.

A pronominal NP can also contain a noun marker. For instance (see 4.16 for the interrogative clitic *-ma*):

(49) *ŋindama bayi baniɲu*   did you come?

A reply to (49) would be likely to involve the demonstrative marker *giyi*:

(50) *ŋaḍa giyi baniɲu*   I'm the one that came.

giyi qualifies *ŋaḍa* in (50); note that it can also qualify *ŋayguna*, in a transitive object NP:

(51) *ŋayguna giyi baŋgul yaṟaŋgu balgan*   I'm the one the man is hitting

A pronominal NP can also involve a noun in addition to a marker:

(52) *ŋinda/bayi yaṟa/bani*   you, man, come here!

A pronoun can be qualified by an adjective. For instance, within a transitive subject NP:

(53) *ŋinda wuygiŋgu/bam*   *miraɲ*   *babi*
     you-A old-ERG   THERE-NOM-III bean-NOM peel-IMP
     you, old [person], slice the beans!

In text xxv, line 87 (p. 394) there occurs an NP involving a pronoun, a noun marker, and an adjective – *ŋindama bayi garḍa* 'are you alright?'.

These examples lead us to conclude that a pronominal NP has all the possibilities of a non-pronominal NP, together with the inclusion of one or two pronouns.

We have so far dealt with NPs involving two nominal cases – nominative and ergative; and (leaving aside G) two pronominal cases, which we can call SA (*ŋaḍa, ŋinda, ŋali*, etc.) and O (*ŋayguna, ŋinuna, ŋalina*, etc.). These co-occur within an NP as follows:

NP with function:	noun, adjectives and noun markers are in case:	pronouns are in case:	examples
S	nominative	SA	(48–50, 52)
A	ergative	SA	(53)
O	nominative	O	(46, 51)

4.3 Verb complexes

Each verb or adverbal root has a fixed transitivity. There are derivational affixes that change transitivity – for instance, a transitive root (say, *buybal* 'hide'), plus reflexive yields an intransitive stem (*buybayiriy* 'hide oneself'); similarly, an intransitive root (*baniy* 'come') plus the comitative affix, yields a transitive stem (*banimal* 'bring'). We use the term 'surface transitivity' to refer to the transitivity of a stem, after all derivational processes have applied.

A simple sentence can be analysed into a nominative NP (that is, the topic – 4.4.3, 4.5.2) and a V[erb] P[hrase]. If the sentence is transitive, the VP will consist of an ergative NP and a transitive V[erb] C[omplex]; if intransitive, the VP will be just an intransitive VC.

A VC can contain any number of verbs or adverbals, provided that: [1] they agree in surface transitivity; and [2] they agree in tense or other final inflection (6.3.1). Thus in M, for example (*wayṇḍil* is an intransitive root 'motion upwards, other than upriver'):

(54) *balan maraba wariṇu*   birds are flying
(55) *balan maraba wariṇu wayṇḍin*   birds are flying up

VCs can also contain verb markers and/or locational nominals, subject to certain selectional restrictions (3.4.6). Thus:

(56) *bayi yaṟa ṇinaṇu balay*   man sat there
(57) *bayi yaṟa ṇinaṇu dibanda*   man sat on (or by) stone
(58) *bayi yaṟa ṇinaṇu balay dibanda*   man sat there on (or by) stone
(59) *bayi yaṟa ṇinaṇu balay dibanda bulganda*   man sat there on (or by) big stone

Sentences such as:

(60) *bayi yaṛa ɲinaɲu balay bulganda* man sat there on (or by) big [thing]

also occur; however these are, on informants' testimonies, elliptical versions of 'correct' sentences such as (59). That is, in underlying structure an adjective always qualifies a noun – see comments in 4.2.1.

4.4 Implicated phrases

4.4.1 Implicated noun phrases.

A simple sentence can be extended by what we can call an 'implicated' NP; the words in such an NP are in dative case (3.2.1, 3.2.2, 3.3.1):

(61) *balan ḍugumbil baŋgul yaṛaŋgu mundan* man took woman
(62) *balan ḍugumbil baŋgul yaṛaŋgu mundan bagum miraŋgu* man took woman to beans

This involves a third situational object ('beans') in the situational event (which already involves 'man', 'woman' and 'taking'). In contrast to allative, which indicates just 'motion towards', a dative NP indicates the expectation of implication of the beans (as goal) in some imminent action involving the woman (as actor). Similarly, with an implicated pronominal NP:

(63) *balan ḍugumbil baŋgul yaṛaŋgu mundan ŋaygungu* man took woman to me (sc. for her to do something to or for me)

The possibilities for word inclusion in an implicated NP are exactly the same as those for an NP whose words are in nominative or ergative case.

A simple sentence can, infrequently but unexceptionally, be extended by more than one implicated NP – 4.5.4.

4.4.2 -ŋay constructions.

Any transitive simple sentence, such as:

(64) *bayi bargan baŋgul yaṛaŋgu ḍurgaɲu* man is spearing wallaby
(65) *balan ḍugumbil baŋgul yaṛaŋgu balgan* man is hitting woman

can be transformed into a -ŋay form:

(66) *bayi yaṛa baŋgul bargandu ḍurganaɲu* man is spearing wallaby
(67) *bayi yaṛa baŋgun ḍugumbiṛu balgalŋaɲu* man is hitting woman

Here, ergative is substituted for the nominative inflection of the NP in O function, and nominative for the ergative inflection of the A NP. The verbal stems are put into -ŋay form. This involves:

for an -*l* stem: the addition of -*ŋay*;
for a -*y* stem: the deletion of stem-final -*y*, and addition of -*nay*.

However, a sentence can also be transformed into a -*ŋay* form in
which dative is substituted for the nominative inflection of the NP in
O function:

(68) *bayi yaṛa bagul bargangu ḍurganaɲu*   man is spearing wallaby
(69) *bayi yaṛa bagun ḍugumbilgu balgalɲaɲu*   man is hitting woman

(64), (66) and (68), and (65), (67) and (69), have the same cognitive
meanings. In (64–5) the O NP is 'topic' whereas in (66–9) the A NP
is topic, giving the sentences different statuses qua discourse patterning
– see 4.5. Sentences (64–5) show the preferred, unmarked construction
(they are referred to as 'simple sentences' below); -*ŋay* constructions
normally only occur non-initially in a discourse, as demanded by the
structure of the discourse – 4.5.

The difference between (66–7) and (68–9) is felt by speakers of
Dyirbal to be a crucial and important one; it cannot be brought out
through English glosses, but is explained in terms of the 'deep syntax'
of Dyirbal in 5.4. Roughly, in (66–7) the actor, goal and action make
up an event; (68–9) imply something more – that the actor is positively
implicating the goal in the event. The difference is essentially one of
topic.

Similarly, involving pronouns, we have:

(70) *ŋaḍa ɲinuna balgan*   I am hitting you
(71) *ŋaḍa ɲinungu balgalɲaɲu*   I am hitting you

(70) is a simple sentence corresponding to (65). (71) corresponds to (69) – the
NP that was previously in O case is now in dative inflection, and the NP that
was previously in A case is now in S case (although the change is not observable
here, since in D the first person singular pronoun is *ŋaḍa* in both A and S
functions). There appears to be no pronominal sentence corresponding to
(67) – it would be **ŋaḍa ɲinda balgalɲaɲu*, in terms of the rules explained in
chapter 5; such a sentence is totally unacceptable. A fuller discussion of the
behaviour of pronouns under the -*ŋay* transformation (in terms of which the
discussion of this paragraph will be more intelligible) is in 5.2, 5.8.2. This
behaviour is part of the evidence suggesting that pronouns have a nominative-
ergative underlying pattern.

Constructions similar to the Dyirbal -*ŋay* type have not been reported for
languages in other parts of Australia; this may, however, be a reflection of the
relatively little attention that has been paid to syntax in studies of other languages.
Of the languages surrounding Dyirbal only Wargamay appears to have a
construction of this type.

The actual shape of the *-ŋay* affix varies from dialect to dialect. After an
-l root the affix is always *-ŋay* in M, either *-ŋay* or *-ay* in D, and usually *-ay*
in G. That is, the *-ŋ-* is sometimes omitted in D and is very frequently omitted
in G. Bringing Wargamay [W] into the comparison we get the following forms
of the verb 'lift up, waken', in purposive inflection (4.4.3). Listing the dialects
in a roughly north-to-south order:

> M   *walmbilŋaygu*
> D   *walmbil(ŋ)aygu*
> G   *walmbilaygu*
> W   *walmbilagu*

Thus the W form differs from the G only in having no diphthongal *-y-* in the
penultimate syllable; on the surface, the W form appears to differ from the
G no more than the G does from the M.

In D, G and M it is most appropriate to set up *walmbil* as the verb root, thus
showing that it belongs to the first conjugation (3.4.2); the *-l* is retained before
many affixes. W has two conjugations, exactly corresponding to those in
Dyirbal, and the root of *walmbilagu* again belongs to the first. But there is no
ustification in W for setting up verb roots with a final consonant; instead, all
roots must be regarded as ending in a vowel and conjugation membership
must be stated in some other way. Thus the G and W forms, although similar
on the surface, have rather different analyses. In G the root is *walmbil*, the
transformation marker has underlying form *-ŋay* but becomes *-ay* by a dialect
rule which deletes the *-ŋ*, and the purposive inflection is *-gu*. In W the root is
walmbi-, the transformation marker has underlying form *-la*, and the purposive
inflection is again *-gu*. (And see 1.7.)

4.4.3 Implicated verb complexes.

Any NP whose words are in
nominative case (in a simple sentence, any S or O NP – but not an
A NP) can be identified as a 'topic' NP. Two consecutive sentences in
discourse are said to have a 'common topic' if they contain the same
topic NP, with the same situational referent: this NP will generally
only occur with the first sentence, not being repeated with the second
one. Thus from:

(72) *bayi yaṛa walmaɲu*   man got up
(73) *bayi yaṛa wayɲḍin*   man went uphill

is formed:

(74) *bayi yaṛa walmaɲu wayɲḍin*   man got up [and then] went uphill

A common topic may be recognised in more than two (sometimes up
to twenty or so) consecutive sentences; such a sequence of sentences
will be referred to as a 'topic chain'.

The second or succeeding VC in any topic chain may be marked as 'implicated' by each verbal form in it receiving 'purposive inflection' [Capell, 1956:77] in place of a tense inflection. The purposive inflection is:

for an -*l* stem: -*i*

for a -*y* stem: -*gu*

(In the case of an -*iy* stem a phonological rule deletes stem-final -*y*, 7.5.2)

The common 'implicative nature' of implicated NPs and implicated VCs is discussed in 5.3.3–4.

The action referred to by an implicated VC is only possible by virtue of an event, referred to by a previous sentence of the discourse, having taken place: EITHER the event has been performed as a necessary preliminary to the intended 'implicated' action; OR the implicated action is a natural (but perhaps unplanned) consequence of the event. Thus:

(75) *bayi yaṟa walmaɲu wayɳḍili*   man got up in order to go uphill

(76) *ŋaḍa ḍiŋgaliɲu*   I am running

(77) *ŋaḍa biliɲu*   I am climbing [a tree]

(78) *ŋaḍa ḍiŋgaliɲu biligu*   I am running [to a tree] to climb [it]

(79) *balan ḍugumbil baŋgul yaṟaŋgu balgan*   man hits woman

(80) *balan ḍugumbil baḍiɲu*   woman falls down

(81) *balan ḍugumbil baŋgul yaṟaŋgu balgan baḍigu*   man hits woman, causing her to fall down

(82) *bayi yaṟa wayɳḍin yalu*   man came uphill towards here

(83) *bayi yaṟa baŋgun dunduŋgu manḍan*   bird points out man's presence (i.e. by making a noise, indicating that there is something large moving in the vicinity)

(84) *bayi yaṟa wayɳḍin yalu baŋgun dunduŋgu manḍali*   man came uphill towards here, resulting in bird's pointing out his presence

See text xxv, line 49 (p. 391) for a similar example.

(85) *balam miraɲ baŋgul yaṟaŋgu dimbaɲu*   man brought beans

(86) *ŋinda balam miraɲ babin*   you scraped beans

(87) *balam miraɲ baŋgul yaṟaŋgu dimbaɲu ŋinda babili*   man brought beans so that you should scrape them

It is in fact possible for the FIRST sentence in a topic chain to have an implicated VC, although this happens relatively infrequently. In such a case the necessary 'implicating' earlier event has taken place but has not been referred to in the discourse:

(88) *balan ḍugumbil miyandaygu* woman wants to laugh (i.e. something has happened to make her want to laugh, and she will have
to restrain herself to avoid doing so)
(89) *bayi yaṟa yanuli* man has to go out (for some reason)

The next section discusses discourse structuring and topic chains
in more detail, and deals with the discourse function of -*ŋay* constructions. In fact any verbal stem can receive a purposive inflection
so that we can have, in addition to (65), (67) and (69):

(90) *balan ḍugumbil baŋgul yaṟaŋgu balgali* something happened to
enable or force the man to hit the woman
(91) *bayi yaṟa bagun ḍugumbilgu balgalŋaygu* ⟨as (90)⟩

However we can NOT have:

*(92) *bayi yaṟa baŋgun ḍugumbiṟu balgalŋaygu*

as we do have (67). Sentences of types (65), (67), (69), (90) and (91)
occur freely in texts; type (92) does not. Informants stated that (65),
(67), (90) and (91) were frequent and correct; that (69) was rather
unusual but quite correct; and that (92) was really lacking in any sense.
It appears that in view of the deep (i.e. semantic) import of an implicated
phrase it makes no sense to have a sentence whose VC is in -*ŋay* form
and implicated, but whose 'goal' NP is not in the dative inflection
(i.e. is not implicated); see 5.4.7.

On extra-linguistic grounds (90) is hardly a sensible sentence. If a sentence
includes a VC in purposive inflection it is implied that the topic of the sentence
was somehow responsible for the event taking place (5.3.4) – often, that the
topic desired it. Thus (91) is totally acceptable – the man gave the woman
a beating that in his opinion she deserved. However, the unmarked interpretation
of (90) is that the woman voluntarily allowed herself to be hit, an unlikely
circumstance that caused informants to be unhappy about this sentence. With
a more suitable verb the difficulty – which does not affect the grammar, although
it sheds considerable light on the grammatical difference between (90) and
(91) – would not arise. For instance:

(93) *balan ḍugumbil baŋgul yaṟaŋgu bayali* woman had to be sung to by man
(94) *bayi yaṟa bagun ḍugumbilgu bayalŋaygu* man had to sing to woman

would be equally acceptable.

4.5 Discourse structuring

4.5.1 Minimal sentences. Besides transitive and intransitive sentence types (4.1) and sentences transformationally derived from these (4.4.2), quasi-elliptical versions of these sentences occur quite normally in Dyirbal. But there is one requirement that any sentence must satisfy: it must contain a topic NP (that is, an NP whose words are in nominative case).

Thus we can have a transitive sentence where the 'actor' is left unspecified (cf. (26), (31)):

(95) *balan ḑugumbil balgan*   woman is being hit [by someone]
(96) *ŋayguna balgan*   I am being hit [by someone]

or a *-ŋay* sentence in which the 'goal' is left unspecified (cf. (67), (69), (71)):

(97) *bayi yaṛa balgalŋaṇu*   man is hitting [someone]
(98) *ŋaḑa balgalŋaṇu*   I am hitting [someone]

Sentences (95–8) were judged perfectly acceptable by informants. We can explain their grammaticality either by saying that all non-nominative NPs are to be marked in the grammar as optional, or else by including an optional rule that deletes them. In contrast, many sentences that contain no verb at all are heard; these often have just a nominative and a dative NP:

(99) *bayi yaṛa bagul bargangu*   man [is going out] to concern himself
      with wallaby

or even:

(100) *bayi bargangu* ⟨as (99)⟩

Informants would not accept sentences like this as good Dyirbal (although they agreed that they occurred) but insisted that a verb was needed. We can distinguish between the general acceptability of (95–8), and the relative unacceptability of (99–100), by saying that the latter involve discourse ellipsis, the former grammatical ellipsis.

Amongst the many similarities between Dyirbal and its southerly neighbour Wargamay can be counted the occurrence of sentences that include an implicative NP but no verb. The Norwegian zoologist Carl Lumholtz lived for a year in 1882/3 amongst what must have been the Wargamaygan tribe. In *Among Cannibals* [1889: 308] Lumholtz remarks: 'The suffix *go* literally means "with regard to", and is usually added to nouns to give them a verbal meaning, but it is also sometimes added to verbs. The question *Wainta*

Morbora? – that is, "Where is Morbora?" – can be answered by saying only *títyengo* (he has gone hunting *títyen*) (wallaby), (literally, with respect to wallaby); or, for example, *mittago* he is at home (literally, with regard to the hut). *Mottaigo* means "he is eating" (literally, with regard to eating). "Throw him into the water", is expressed simply by *ngallogo*. As is evident, this is a very convenient suffix, as it saves a number of moods and tenses...' Of the words Lumholtz cites *ḍiḍingu* and *ŋalugu* are clearly in dative case; *miḍagu* could be either dative or allative; *muḍagu* (or possibly *muḍaygu*) is the verb 'eat' in purposive inflection.

Other sentences consist of just a topic NP; usually this will include a demonstrative noun marker (101), a possessive phrase (102 – 4.11); an adjective (103), some suffix to the head noun (104–5), or a modifier noun with a suitable suffix (106–7):

(101) *giyi bayi yaṛa*   the man's here
(102) *ŋaygu bayi yaṛa*   he's my man (said by father, friend or wife)
(103) *bayi yaṛa bulgan*   the man is big
(104) *bayi yaṛabaḍun*   he's a real man (implying, for instance, he's a sensible fellow, not silly)
(105) *giyi landanbara*   this man comes from London
(106) *bayi yaṛa yuguŋaŋgay*   the man has no sticks
(107) *bayi muraynbila wabalaŋaru*   the black man is like a white man (looks like, or behaves like)

The affixes *-baḍun* 'really, very', *-bara* 'belonging to', *-ŋaŋgay* 'without' and *-ŋaru* 'like a' are discussed in 6.1.1. It should be noted that (101–7) are perfectly correct sentences at every level, and involve no ellipsis of any kind; see also (319) below.

4.5.2 Topic chains. We can consider any text (conversation, monologue, etc.) in Dyirbal to be underlain by a sequence of simple sentences. If a number of consecutive sentences in such a sequence have a common NP, with common referent, then they will form a topic chain: this entails each sentence being transformed into a form in which the common NP is topic NP (i.e. is in nominative case). This NP may only be stated once, at the beginning of the topic chain; optionally all or part of it may be repeated later in the chain (commonly, just the noun marker may be repeated). Thus it is quite usual to encounter a chain of a dozen sentences all 'commenting' on a single topic occurrence.

Two topic chains may run through a text in 'leapfrog' fashion – an example is in text xxv, lines 108–15 (p. 396).

For instance, the description of a fight preceding a cannibalistic killing involved the following typical topic chain:

(108) *bayi walmaɲu burbula/gubiŋgu baɽan/baḏigu/baɲum bayi/balbali-yaraɲu walmaygu/ɽudu baɽan bariŋgu/bugabili/* Burbula stood up; the gubi punched him, causing him to fall down. And then he began to turn over in order to get up. The hollow in the back of his neck was hit [by the gubi] with a tomahawk; and as a result he died.

This text-fragment (reference XXIV: 39) has been altered by the substitution of the word gubi for the name of the protagonist; this is to comply with a promise made to the storyteller.

Underlying (108) are (*baɲum* here has time reference, 'and then'):

(109) *bayi burbula walmaɲu* Burbula stood up

(110) *bayi burbula [baŋgul] gubiŋgu baɽan* the gubi punched Burbula

(111) *bayi burbula baḏigu* Burbula was caused to fall down

(112) *baɲum bayi burbula balbaliyaraɲu* Then Burbula began to turn over

(113) *bayi burbula walmaygu* in order that Burbula should stand up

(114) *bayi burbula ɽudu [baŋgul gubiŋgu baŋgu] bariŋgu baɽan* Burbula was hit in the hollow at the back of his neck by a tomahawk [wielded by the gubi]

(115) *bayi burbula bugabili* Burbula was caused to die

The implicated VCs in (111), (113) and (115) should be particularly noted: implicated VCs are typically encountered non-initially in topic chains.

(108) exemplifies topic 'elaboration' and 'reversion'. (109–13) concern Burbula, as 'situational theme'; in (114) the theme is narrowed to that part of Burbula's body that is hit – *ɽudu*, the top of the vertical depression between the two muscles at the nape of the neck; in (115) the theme naturally reverts to Burbula. The topic is shown by *bayi burbula* in (109), and by *bayi* in (112); and the topic elaboration (the theme narrowing) by *ɽudu* in (114), understood as a noun modifying the head *burbula* (an example of inalienable possession – 4.2.1). There are no a priori reasons for the topic of (115) being understood as *bayi burbula* rather than as *bayi burbula ɽudu*; but, extra-linguistically, it makes no sense to talk of (just) the hollow in the back of someone's neck dying. The elaboration is thus understood to be dropped in (115), the topic reverting to just *bayi burbula*.

If one simple sentence immediately precedes a second simple sentence in the sequence underlying a Dyirbal text, then the unmarked situational realisation of their sequential ordering is that the event referred to by the second sentence happens after the event referred to by the first sentence. Event ordering that is not one-to-one with simple sentence ordering may be marked by special time words (4.14 – *magul*). *baɲum*, in (112), is here a time qualifier that merely emphasises the normal one-to-one simple-sentence-to-event correspondence.

An SA pronominal form, such as *ŋaḍa*, can be the topic for a chain of intransitive simple sentences:

(116) *ŋaḍa ɲinaɲu/baɲum walmaɲu/wayɲḍili* I sat down, and then got up to go up the hill

An SA pronoun can also run through a sequence of transitive simple sentences:

(117) *ŋaḍa bayi yaɽa balgan/walmbin/baygun/ḍilwan* I hit the man; lifted [him] up; threw [him] down; [and] kicked [him]

(118) *ŋaḍa bala yugu yuban/balan ḍugumbil ḍilwan* I put down the stick; [and] kicked the woman

(For pronoun sequences intransitive-transitive and transitive-intransitive, and sequences involving O pronouns, see 5.2.2.)

It should be noted that it is impossible to gap [Ross, 1970] in Dyirbal; that is, it is impossible to omit the verb in one of two or more coordinated clauses that have the same verb, and different but comparable subject and object (in English, for instance, one can say 'Mary bought pears and John apples', omitting 'buy' in the second clause). A verb must always be included, in each Dyirbal clause, unless it is a minimal sentence of a type described in 4.5.1.

4.5.3 Favourite constructions. Given the two simple sentences (4.4.1):

(119) *balan ḍugumbil baŋgul yaɽaŋgu mundan bagum miraŋgu* man took woman to beans

(120) *balam miraɲ baŋgun ḍugumbiɽu babin* woman scraped beans

where the same 'woman' and 'beans' are referred to in the two sentences; then (120) can be -*ŋay*-transformed (4.4.2) into:

(121) *balan ḍugumbil bagum miraŋgu babilɲaɲu* ⟨as (120)⟩

Now (119) and (121) have identical topic NP – *balan ḍugumbil* – and identical implicated NP – *bagum miraŋgu*; from (119) and (121) we obtain the common discourse construction:

(122) *balan ḏugumbil baŋgul yaṛaŋgu mundan bagum miraŋgu babilŋaɲu*
       man took woman to scrape beans

which is underlain by (119) and (120).

   Similarly we can have:

(123) *balan ḏugumbil yanu bagum miraŋgu babilŋaɲu*   woman went to
       scrape beans

underlain by:

(124) *balan ḏugumbil yanu bagum miraŋgu*   woman went to beans
and (120).

   In both (122) and (123) the second VC could be implicated:

(125) *balan ḏugumbil baŋgul yaṛaŋgu mundan bagum miraŋgu babilŋaygu*
       man took woman to scrape beans

(126) *balan ḏugumbil yanu bagum miraŋgu babilŋaygu*   woman went to
       scrape beans

   (122–3) and (125–6) exemplify the 'favourite' discourse construction
in Dyirbal. This is underlain by two simple sentences, the first either
transitive or intransitive and the second transitive. The S or O NP of
the first sentence is identified with the A NP of the second, and the
implicated NP of the first with the O NP of the second. Constructions
of this type occur very frequently in texts – those in which the second
VC is implicated, as in (125–6), are commoner than those in which it
is not, as in (122–3).

   There are parallel constructions involving pronouns:

(127) *ŋaḏa yanu bagum miraŋgu babilŋaygu*   I went to scrape beans
(128) *ŋaḏa balan ḏugumbil mundan bagum miraŋgu babilŋaygu*   I took
       woman to scrape beans
(129) *ŋayguna baŋgul yaṛaŋgu mundan bagum miraŋgu babilŋaygu*   man
       took me to scrape beans

Note: (127) and (129) would only normally be said by a woman.

4.5.4   Iteration. Implicated NPs can be the basis for an iterative
extension of the favourite construction. We can have:

(130) *balan   ḏugumbil   baŋgul   yaṛaŋgu wawun*
       THERE-NOM-II woman-NOM THERE-ERG-I man-ERG fetch-PRES/PAST
       nayinbagu   walmbilŋaygu
       girl-PL-DAT get up-ŋay-PURP
       man fetched woman to get the girls up

underlain by:

(131) *balan ḍugumbil baŋgul yaɽaŋgu wawun bagun nayinbagu* man
    fetched woman to girls
and

(132) *balan nayinba baŋgun ḍugumbiɽu walmbili* woman got girls up

And we can also have:

(133) *balan   ḍugumbil   baŋgul   yaɽaŋgu wawun*
    THERE-NOM-II woman-NOM THERE-ERG-I man-ERG fetch-PRES/PAST
    nayinbagu walmbilŋaygu   bagum   wuḍugu
    girl-PL-DAT get up-*ŋay*-PURP THERE-DAT-III fruit-DAT
    burbilŋaygu
    pick-*ŋay*-PURP
    man fetched woman to get the girls up to pick fruit

underlain by (131),

(134) *balan nayinba baŋgun ḍugumbiɽu walmbili bagum wuḍugu* woman
    got girls up for fruit
and

(135) *balam wuḍu baŋgun nayinbagu burbili* girls picked fruit

Just as the O NP and implicative NP of (131) are identified with the
A NP and O NP respectively of (134), so the O NP and implicative NP
of (134) are identified with the A NP and O NP respectively of (135).

   (130) is built around the topic NP *balan ḍugumbil*. In exactly the
same way the addition in (133) is built around the implicated NP
bagun nayinbagu; a similar further addition could be built on to *bagum
wuḍugu*; and so on. A further example is:

(136) *ŋaḍa bayi   yaɽa   gigan   bagun*
    I-SA THERE-NOM-I man-NOM tell-PRES/PAST THERE-DAT-II
    ḍugumbilgu wawulŋaygu   ŋinungu   mundalŋaygu
    woman-DAT fetch-*ŋay*-PURP you(sg)-DAT bring-*ŋay*-PURP
    bagu   miḍagu   wambalŋaygu
    THERE-DAT-IV house-DAT build-*ŋay*-PURP
    I told the man to fetch the woman to bring you to build the house

   A simple sentence may be extended by more than one implicated
NP. For example:

(137) *balan   ḍugumbil   baŋgul   yaṛaŋgu gigan*
THERE-NOM-II woman-NOM THERE-ERG-I man-ERG tell-PRES/PAST
bagun   bunigu   bagun   nayinbagu
THERE-DAT-II fire-DAT THERE-DAT-II girl-PL-DAT
man told woman [to concern herself] with fire and girls

On the basis of this we can have a (non-iterative) 'double favourite construction' built upon a single topic. For example:

(138) *balan   ḍugumbil   baŋgul   yaṛaŋgu gigan*
THERE-NOM-II woman-NOM THERE-ERG-I man-ERG tell-PRES/PAST
bagun   bunigu mabalŋaygu   bagun   nayinbagu
THERE-DAT-II fire-DAT light-*ŋay*-PURP THERE-DAT-II girl-PL-DAT
ḍaymbalŋaygu
find-*ŋay*-PURP
man told woman to light fire and find girls

This is underlain by (137), and

(139) *balan buni baŋgun ḍugumbiṛu mabali*   woman lit fire

and

(140) *balan nayinba baŋgun ḍugumbiṛu ḍaymbali*   woman found girls

(133) and (138) are potentially ambiguous: they could be interpreted as either iterative favourite constructions, or as non-iterative double favourite constructions. In some cases, such as (138), situational possibilities resolve the ambiguity (fire could not find girls). In the case of (133), however, there is ambiguity at all levels: between underlying (131), (134) and (135), and 'man fetched woman to get girls up and pick fruit' with underlying:

(141) *balan ḍugumbil baŋgul yaṛaŋgu wawun bagun nayinbagu bagum
       wuḍugu*   man fetched woman to girls and fruit
(142) *balan nayinba baŋgun ḍugumbiṛu walmbili*   woman got girls up

and

(143) *balam wuḍu baŋgun ḍugumbiṛu burbili*   woman picked fruit

Word order is quite free for a sentence of the complexity of (130); restrictions on order come in with iterative favourite constructions. VCs and implicated NPs must occur in their iterative order (although a VC may occur before or after or in the middle of its associated implicated NP, and so on – see 7.8). Thus:

(144) *balan ḍugumbil baŋgul yaṟaŋgu gigan bagun nayinbagu ḍaymbal-ŋaygu bagun bunigu mabalŋaygu*

is, unlike (138), ambiguous. One interpretation is the same as that for (138); the other is 'man told woman to find girls so that they should light fire'.

Note that of the two kinds of favourite construction – with the second verb in tense inflection, or in purposive form – only the type involving purposive inflection can be iteratively extended.

4.5.5 -ŋura constructions. If a discourse contains two successive underlying sentences, such that the A NP, in ergative inflection, in the first is identical with the NP in nominative inflection in the second, then the verbs of the second sentence are given inflection -ŋura in place of any tense ending (verbs delete stem-final -y or -l before adding -ŋura).

Thus from:

(145) *bala yugu baŋgul yaṟangu madan*   man threw stick
(146) *bala yaṟa wayṇḍin*   man went uphill

we get:

(147) *bala yugu baŋgul yaṟaŋgu madan bayi yaṟa wayṇḍiŋura*   man threw stick and then he [immediately] went uphill

Besides its crucial syntactic role, -ŋura also indicates that the event of its simple sentence follows immediately after the event of the preceding simple sentence (that is, without any other events involving the common referent intervening). Thus (147) was glossed by one informant as 'the man threw the stick (i.e. kept on throwing it) until he went uphill'; and by another as 'the man threw the stick away so that he could climb up (i.e. unencumbered)'.

The nominative NP of the second sentence in a -ŋura construction is optionally deleted. Thus we have either (147) or:

(148) *bala yugu baŋgul yaṟaŋgu madan wayṇḍiŋura*   ⟨as (147)⟩

Sentences like (148), in which the *bayi yaṟa* is omitted, seem commoner than those like (147), although both types are quite correct.

Similarly with a pronoun, in D and M:

(149) *ŋaḍa bala yugu madan (ŋaḍa) wayṇḍiŋura*   I threw stick and then (I) [immediately] went uphill

and in G (which has wider pronominal possibilities, and *-ŋara* instead of *-ŋura*):

(150) *ŋaḏa bala yugu madan (ŋayba) wayɲḏiŋara* ⟨as (149)⟩

A fuller discussion of the behaviour of pronouns in the *-ŋura* construction is in 5.2.2. This behaviour forms another part of the evidence suggesting that pronouns have a nominative-ergative underlying pattern.

It should be noticed that, when an ergative NP in one sentence is identical with a nominative NP in the next sentence, then the *-ŋura* construction is normally obligatory. That is, we can NOT have:

*(151) *bala yugu baŋgul yaṛaŋgu madan (bayi yaṛa) wayɲḏin*

(or at least, if (151) did occur, it would have to refer to two quite different men).

We have said that, for a *-ŋura* construction, the identical NP in the second sentence must be in nominative case. It can be:

[1] an S NP in a simple sentence, as in (147–50);

or [2] an O NP in a simple sentence, for instance:

(152) *balan   ḏugumbil   baŋgul   yaṛaŋgu balgan* /
THERE-NOM-II woman-NOM THERE-ERG-I man-ERG hit-PRES/PAST
(bayi   yaṛa)   baŋgul   gambaṛu biḏiŋura
THERE-NOM-I man-NOM THERE-ERG-I rain-ERG punch-*ŋura*
man hit woman until rain started falling on him (i.e. until it started to rain)

or [3] an A NP in a *-ŋay* construction:

(153) *bala   yugu   baŋgul   yaṛaŋgu nudin* /
THERE-NOM-IV tree-NOM THERE-ERG-I man-ERG cut-PRES/PAST
(bayi   yaṛa)   bagul   ɲalŋgagu bunḏulŋaŋura
THERE-NOM-I man-NOM THERE-DAT-I child-DAT spank-*ŋay-ŋura*
man cut tree [until he stopped to] spank boy

(153) is a perfectly grammatical sentence in Dyirbal. However, informants expressed a mild preference for a version in which an intransitive verb in *-ŋura* form (for instance, *yanuŋura*) immediately precedes *bagul ɲalŋgagu*.

The underlying sentences here are:

(154) *bala yugu baŋgul yaṛaŋgu nudin*   man cut tree
(155) *bayi ɲalŋga baŋgul yaṛaŋgu bunḏun*   man spanked boy

From (155) is obtained the *-ŋay*-transform:

(156) *bayi yaṟa bagul ɲalŋgagu bunḍulŋaɲu*

and from (154) and (156) the *-ŋura* construction (153).

(A further example of a *-ŋay* plus *-ŋura* construction is in text xv, line 34, page 374.)

    -ŋura thus serves to 'introduce' a non-topic NP of one underlying sentence, as topic NP of the next (and succeeding) sentences, providing a syntactic link between consecutive topic chains; and also indicating that one event immediately follows another.

    In direct speech *-ŋura* is sometimes used in the first sentence of a discourse, just to indicate immediacy:

(157) *ŋaḍa yanuɲura*   I'll go before I do anything else

(157) is one of those sentences that informants agree occur, but which they are not really happy to call fully grammatical. This demonstrates the primacy of the syntactic function of *-ŋura* – to mark the fact that an ergative NP in one sentence becomes topic of the next sentence.

    There are two kinds of ergative NP: an A NP in a simple sentence, and an O NP in a *-ŋay* construction. All the examples we have given in this section have involved the first type of ergative NP; in fact, a *-ŋura* construction could hardly involve an ergative NP of the second type, since if an O NP in a sentence were identical to a nominative NP in the next sentence, a simple topic chain would be formed, without recourse to *-ŋay* or *-ŋura* complexities.

    Compare (157) with (3.4.3):

(158) *ŋaḍa yanuɲ*   I'll go (not necessarily at once)

and also, with implicated VC:

(159) *ŋaḍa yanuli*   I have to go

4.5.6. Summary. We can now consider all types of sequences of two simple sentences, when some NP in the first sentence is identical with some NP in the second. We use the following symbolism:

[1] x,y,z denote NPs, where the same letter repeated indicates an 'identical NP';

[2] I denotes an intransitive VC; the S NP is written before it – xI;

[3] T denotes a transitive VC; the O NP is written before and the A NP after – xTy.

There are altogether eleven possibilities:

xI – xI	xI – xTy	xI – yTx	xTy – xI
yTx – xI	xTy – xTy	xTy – xTz	xTy – zTy
xTy – yTx	xTy – zTx	xTy – yTz	

The syntactic ways of linking together these eleven types are as follows:
(i) simple topic chain, no transformations needed (4.5.2):

$$xI - xI, \ xI - xTy, \ xTy - xI, \ xTy - xTy, \ xTy - xTz$$

For these five types the identical NP is nominative in each simple sentence of the pair.
(ii) favourite construction, involving *-ŋay* transformation (4.5.3):

$$xI - yTx, \ xTy - yTx, \ xTy - zTx$$

For these three types, the identical NP is in nominative case in the first sentence of each pair, and in ergative in the second. The *-ŋay* transformation changes the case of the identical NP in the second sentence from ergative to nominative; a topic chain can then be formed as in (i).
(iii) *-ŋura* construction (4.5.5):

$$yTx - xI, \ xTy - yTz$$

As, for instance, in (147) and (152) above.
(iv) *-ŋay* transformation and *-ŋura* construction (4.5.5):

$$xTy - zTy$$

As in (153) and text xv, line 34 (p. 374).

Thus, Dyirbal has syntactic means to link ANY two sentences which have one NP in common, whatever the function of this NP in the two sentences. The linking makes the sentences form part of a topic chain – under (i) and (ii) – or serves syntactically to link successive topic chains – under (iii) and (iv).

With the rich syntactic possibilities described above a speaker of Dyirbal need, theoretically, never 'plan ahead' in choosing which construction to use in a particular sentence. Whatever surface form he chooses for a particular sentence, he will always be able to link a following sentence to it. However, speakers of Dyirbal – as of all other languages – often do plan ahead. An alternative to the *-ŋay* plus *-ŋura* treatment of a pair xTy – zTy would be to put both sentences into *-ŋay* form. Thus (154) and (155) could yield a topic chain:

(160) *bayi yaṛa bagu yugugu nudilŋaɲu baŋum bagul ɲalŋgagu bunḍulŋaɲu*   man cut tree, and spanked boy

(Here the speaker anticipated the nature of the identity between (154) and (155) when choosing a surface structure for (154).) (153) and (160) have roughly the same meaning but there are differences: (153) implies that the man continued to cut the tree right up to the time he spanked the child;

(160) states that he did cut the tree, and then spanked the child, but leaves open the question as to whether he did anything else in between.

A -*ŋay* sentence would only normally occur discourse initial if a speaker were 'planning ahead'. The norm use of both -*ŋay* and -*ŋura* constructions is syntactically to relate a sentence, that is non-initial in discourse, to the immediately preceding sentence.

4.6 Nominalisations of verbals

There are three ways in which a verbal can be nominalised. [1] The commonest is by adding -*muŋa* to the verbal stem. The resulting form functions, and takes inflections, exactly like a nominal.

For instance, from intransitive root *ḏanay* 'stand' can be derived *ḏanaymuŋa* '[someone who] habitually stands (a lot)'.
This functions like an adjective:

(161) *ŋaḏa balan ḏugumbil ḏanaymuŋa buṛan*   I saw the woman
        who is always standing around
and

(162) *ŋayguna baŋgun ḏugumbiṛu ḏanaymuŋagu buṛan*   the woman who
        is always standing around saw me

Here *ḏanaymuŋa* modifies *balan ḏugumbil*, the syntactic relation between them being the same as that between *ḏanaŋu* and the topic NP *balan ḏugumbil*, in the simple sentence:

(163) *balan ḏugumbil ḏanaŋu*   woman is standing

We will refer to such deverbal nominals as 'participles'.

Similarly, the syntactic relation between a transitive participle, and the noun it modifies, is the same as that between the corresponding verb and the topic NP in a simple sentence. From *ŋaṛnḏay* 'watch, stare' we get *ŋaṛnḏaymuŋa* '[someone who] is always being watched', as in:

(164) *ŋayguna baŋgul yaṛaŋgu ŋaṛnḏaymuŋagu biḏin*   the man who is
        always watched punched me

Here the syntactic relation between *bayi yaṛa* and *ŋaṛnḏaymuŋa* is the same as that between *bayi yaṛa* and *ŋaṛnḏaŋu* in the simple sentence:

(165) *bayi yaṛa baŋgun ḏugumbiṛu ŋaṛnḏaŋu*   woman watches man

If we wish to have a participle which describes some person as the habitual agent of some action (rather than as the habitual object, as in the last example), the -*ŋay* form of the verb must be used. Thus:
ŋaṛnḏanaymuŋa '[someone who] always watches', and:

(166) *ŋayguna baŋgul yaɽaŋgu ŋaɽɲḍanaymuŋagu biḍin*   man who always
        watches punched me

The relation between *bayi yaɽa* and *ŋaɽɲḍanaymuŋa* in (166) is the
same as that between *bayi yaɽa* and *ŋaɽɲḍanaɲu* in the *-ŋay*
construction:

(167) *bayi yaɽa bagun ḍugumbilgu ŋaɽɲḍanaɲu*   man watches woman

that is, it is the same as the syntactic relation between *bayi yaɽa* and
ŋaɽɲḍaɲu in the simple sentence:

(168) *balan ḍugumbil baŋgul yaɽaŋgu ŋaɽɲḍaɲu*   man watches woman

In summary, a participle that involves just a verb root plus *-muŋa*
has the same syntactic relation to the noun it modifies as the verb does
to an NP in S or O function to it; a participle that involves a root plus
-ŋay plus *-muŋa* has the same syntactic relation to the noun it modifies
as the verb does to an NP in A function to it. Participles are thus
formed on a nominative-ergative principle.

Now it is an extra-linguistic fact that one may often want to refer
to someone as being the habitual subject of an intransitive action –
someone who habitually stands, or sits, or runs, or coughs. Similarly,
someone may frequently be the habitual agent of a transitive action
– he may frequently hit, or spear, or cook. However, it would be rather
unusual to find someone who was, as it were, a confirmed victim – the
habitual object of a transitive action. In fact, it would be difficult to
find another example to go besides (166), which involved a verb of
a rather special type (referring to sense perception rather than to an
action which 'affected' the object).

Thus from *balgal* 'hit with a long rigid object, held in the hand;
kill' we can derive the participle *balgalŋaymuŋa* 'habitual murderer'.
This is a fairly well used form – either with serious intent or in joking
fashion. However, very little sense could be attached to *balgalmuŋa*
'someone who is habitually killed'. Similar comments apply in the
case of the great majority of transitive verb roots; there simply would
not be any use for 'habitual object' participles.

In view of this, participles of the form *balgalŋaymuŋa* are frequently
shortened by the omission of *-ŋay-*. *balgalmuŋa*, as actually used, is
thus a free variant of *balgalŋaymuŋa* 'murderer'. Generally, in the
case of verbs where the 'habitual object' sense is clearly unlikely, the
'habitual agent' form will more frequently occur without *-ŋay* than

with it; that is, *balgalmuɲa* will be encountered more frequently than *balgalɲaymuɲa*.

This might lead a casual observer to conclude that the formation of participles followed a nominative-accusative pattern, against the predominant 'nominative-ergative pattern' in the rest of the grammar. But consideration of verbs like *ɲaɽɲḍay*, and the fact that informants regard *balgalmuɲa* as a shortened form of *balgalɲaymuɲa*, indicates that participles conform to the nominative-ergative principle.

A participle such as *balgal(ɲay)muɲa* indicates a person who habitually undertakes a certain type of action, i.e. killing; it gives no information about the object of the action. There is a further type of participle that includes information about the object; it simply compounds object and verb, in that order. Thus, from *bunḍul* 'hit with a long flexible object, e.g. spank with the flat of the hand' we get *bunḍulmuɲa* '[someone who] habitually spanks', and *ḍugumbilbunḍulmuɲa* '[someone who] habitually spanks women', as in:

(169) *bayi yaɽa ḍugumbilbunḍulmuɲa baniɲu*   the man who habitually spanks women is coming

Note that, by discourse ellipsis, *bayi yaɽa* might be omitted from (169), producing:

(170) *ḍugumbilbunḍulmuɲa baniɲu*   woman-spanker is coming

Compare with:

(171) *balan ḍugumbil bunḍulmuɲa baniɲu*   the woman who habitually spanks is coming

in which *ḍugumbil* is head of the NP. Discourse ellipsis might well omit the *balan*, producing:

(172) *ḍugumbil bunḍulmuɲa baniɲu*   spanking woman is coming

The two sentences (170) and (172) might easily be confused; their stress patterns are identical.

However, confusion would never arise if the participles were, say, in ergative case. Thus:

(173) *ɲayguna baŋgul yaɽaŋgu ḍugumbilbunḍulmuɲagu mundan*   the woman-spanking man took me

(174) *ɲayguna baŋgun ḍugumbiɽu bunḍulmuɲagu mundan*   the spanking woman took me

With discourse ellipsis omitting *baŋgul yaṟaŋgu* in (173) and *baŋgun* in (174) we would get:

(175) *ŋayguna ḍugumbilbunḍulmuŋagu mundan*   woman-spanker took me
(176) *ŋayguna ḍugumbiṟu bunḍulmuŋagu mundan*   spanking woman took me

The fact that *ḍugumbil* is in ergative inflection in (176) indicates that it is a free word, the head of the A NP; the fact that there is no inflection on *ḍugumbil* in (175) indicates that it is the first morpheme in a compound participle.

The difference between sentences of the form (175) and (176) is brought out most effectively with the verb *wadil* 'swive (i.e. have sexual intercourse with)'. Compare:

(177) *ŋayguna baŋgul yaṟaŋgu wadilmuŋagu balgan*
(178) *ŋayguna baŋgul yaṟawadilmuŋagu balgan*

The first of these indicates 'I was hit by a man who habitually swives [women]' (a fuller specification would have been:

(179) *ŋayguna baŋgul yaṟaŋgu ḍugumbilwadilmuŋagu balgan*)

In contrast, (178) can only mean 'I was hit by the man-swiving man – that is, by a homosexual'. (Homosexuality was unknown to the Dyirbalŋan before white contact, and the reaction of informants was that (178) was nonsensical – or, that if such a man did exist, he should be killed.)

A participle may refer to something inanimate. Thus, from transitive *gimbil* 'blow (as of wind)', we may form *gimbilŋaymuŋa* 'that which blows a lot'; this can modify *bala gulubu* 'wind':

(180) *bala gulubu gimbilŋaymuŋa*   the wind which blows a lot

or, the shorter form:

(181) *bala gulubu gimbilmuŋa*   ⟨as (180)⟩

Just as a verb complex may contain a verb and an adverbal, so may a noun be modified by a participial verb and a participial adverbal – for instance, corresponding to simple sentence:

(182) *balam   wuḍu   baŋgul   yaṟaŋgu   ḍaŋgaɲu*
      THERE-NOM-III food-NOM THERE-ERG-I man-ERG eat-PRES/PAST
      ganbin
      do badly-PRES/PAST
      man eats food sloppily

we can have:

(183) *bayi yaṟa ḍaŋganaymuŋa ganbilmuŋa baniɲu*   man who is a sloppy eater is coming

Note that *-ŋay* can optionally be omitted from *ḍaŋganaymuɲa*; it would almost always be omitted from the adverbial participle, as in (183), on the principle that it would be unnecessarily redundant to include *-ŋay* twice.

We have thus far described participles involving *-muɲa*. There are two other types:

[2] a verbal stem by itself can function as a participle. This appears to be a little less strong than a *-muɲa* form. Thus:

> *ḍanay* '[someone who] habitually stands'
> *ḍanaymuɲa* '[someone who] habitually stands a lot'

A transitive simple stem participle MUST be compounded with an object noun. Thus we can have:

(184) *ŋayguna baŋgul yaṟabalgaṟu buṟan*   he, who habitually murders men, saw me

but not:

*(185) *ŋayguna baŋgul yaṟaŋgu balgaṟu buṟan*

In M both stem and stem-plus-*muɲa* forms are common; in D, while both do occur, stem-plus-*muɲa* forms are far more frequent, and are preferred.

[3] there are also participles involving a verbal root and suffix *-ginay*, e.g. *ḍanayginay*. This may be a dialectal form only: *-ginay* appears to have been the most common participial type in the Gulŋay dialect; it occurs in M but is less used than the *-muɲa* type; it is not used at all in D.

Participial *-ginay* is almost certainly related to the nominal affix *-ginay* 'full of, covered with' – 6.1.1. There is a number adjective *muɲa* 'many' (6.1.7) which may or may not be historically related to participial *-muɲa*.

Note that participles can modify pronouns, just as they do nouns:

(186) *balan ḍugumbil ŋaḍa ḍanayḍu balgan*   whilst standing (as I habitually do), I hit woman

4.7 Verbalisations

4.7.1 Of nominals. Any noun or adjective may be verbalised in two

distinct ways:

>   [1] it may be transformed into an intransitive verbal stem by the addition of *-bil*;
>
>   or [2] it may be transformed into a transitive verbal stem by the addition of: *-mal* to a stem of two syllables; *-(m)bal* to a stem of more than two syllables.

Thus from noun *waṛu* 'bend' we can derive transitive verbal stem *waṛumal* 'make bendy'; from the reduplicated form *waṛuwaṛu* 'many bends' is derived *waṛuwaṛubal* 'make very bendy'.

We can have:

(187) *bayi yaṛa bulganbin*   the man has become big (i.e. has grown big recently)

as well as (4.5.1):

(188) *bayi yaṛa bulgan*   the man is big

The difference between (187) and (188) lies entirely in the active/stative contrast (in the traditional sense) between verbal form *bulganbil* in (187) and nominal form *bulgan* in (188) – see 5.9.

A typical verbalisation involves adjective *wuygi* 'no good':

(189) *ŋaḍa wuygibin*   I feel ill

Verbalised adjectives are encountered more often than verbalised nouns, but any noun can be (transitively or intransitively) verbalised:

(190) *bala   mila   wumabin*
      THERE-NOM-IV clearing-NOM undergrowth-INTR VBLSR-PRES/PAST
      the thick scrub is growing back into the clearing

(191) *ŋaygu daman barŋanbin*   my son has become a youth (i.e. has passed through puberty)

As another example, *ḍugumbilbil* 'become a woman' literally implies change of sex (the process of growing up to womanhood would be described through the term for 'adolescent girl', as in (191)). There is a Dyirbalŋan hermaphrodite – although nominally a man, he is said to have underdeveloped genitals, and has rather pronounced breasts; as he has grown older his feminine characteristics have become more noticeable. It is said of him, in a semi-joking way: *bayi ḍugumbilbin*.

A verbalised noun or adjective indicates some quite definite change of state, often a surprising one. For instance, if a boy grew a beard in the normal way, this would be described (for *-bila* see 6.1.1):

(192) *bayi ɲumbulbila*   literally: he is (now) with beard i.e. he now has a beard

The sentence

(193) *bayi ɲumbulbin*

implies an abnormal growth – say, a beard appearing at the age of eight.

A verbalised nominal can make up a complete VC:

(194) *bayi yaṟa guyibin*   man is dead/man died
(195) *ŋaḍa bayi yaṟa guyiman*   I killed man (i.e. caused him to be dead)

Most frequently, though, a verbalised nominal occurs with a verb-root form, as in (199) and (202):

(196) *ŋaḍa bayi yaṟa baŋgaɲ*   I will paint man
(197) *bayi yaṟa gulgiṟi*   man is pretty (i.e. with paint)
(198) *bayi yaṟa gulgiṟibiɲ*   man will become pretty (i.e. when painted)
(199) *ŋaḍa bayi yaṟa gulgiṟimbaɲ baŋgaɲ*   I will paint the man prettily
(200) *bala gama ḍigil*   the gama-style song is good
(201) *bala gama baŋgul yaṟaŋgu bayan*   man sings gama-style song
(202) *bala gama baŋgul yaṟaŋgu ḍigilman bayan*   man sings gama-style song well

Verb forms can also be derived from participles. For instance *bayi ḍanayḍanaybin* 'he has started standing about' was encountered. Here a verbal root is first nominalised, and then the resultant nominal is verbalised. Whereas verb *ḍanaɲu* refers to an actual act of standing, for some time (note: NOT 'coming into standing position'), *ḍanaybin* implies that the subject has the habit of standing around, and that he has recently acquired this habit.

Most Australian languages have affixes that verbalise nominals. The transitive verbaliser is frequently similar in form to Dyirbal *-mal* ~ *-(m)bal* – see 1.7. For instance, Gumbaiŋgar has transitive verbaliser *-mbei* ~ *-ndei* (and intransitive *-ei* ~ *-yei* ~ *-wei*) [Smythe, 1948/9: 16]; and in Bailko there is transitiviser *-ma* and intransitiviser *-ya* [O'Grady et al., 1966: 87].

4.7.2 Of verb markers and locational nominals.
Allative and locative verb markers and locational nominals can be verbalised, to *-bil* and to *-mal* ~ *-(m)bal* forms; ablative markers and nominals cannot as a rule be verbalised. Verb markers can be nominalised whether or not they are augmented by bound forms (3.2.3, 3.4.5). Thus we can have *yalubin*, *yaluguyabin*, *balubawalmban*, *balidayigalabin*, *miḍagubin*, *miḍaŋgabin*, and so on; but not *baɲumbin*, *miḍaɲunubin*. For instance:

(203) *bayi yaṟa ɲinaɲu balay miḍaŋga*   man is sitting (or staying) in the camp there
(204) *bayi yaṟa ɲinaɲu balay miḍaŋgabin*   ⟨as (203)⟩

(205) *bayi yaṛa ɲinaɲu balaybin miḍaŋga*   ⟨as (203)⟩
(206) *bayi yaṛa ɲinaɲu balaybin miḍaŋgabin*   ⟨as (203)⟩

The difference between these four sentences is significant, but cannot easily be brought out through English glosses – see the discussion of bracketing in Dixon [1971]. Roughly, (203) implies a simple act of sitting; if either *balay* or *miḍaŋga* is verbalised, stress is placed on the fact that the man rested 'at that place' – it is implied that he has been sitting there for a considerable time; if both are verbalised – as in (206) – the emphasis is even stronger. Further examples are:

(207) *bayi yaṛa yanu balu*   man is going to that place
(208) *bayi yaṛa yanu balubin*   ⟨as (207)⟩
(209) *balan ḍugumbil baŋgul yaṛaŋgu buṛan baludayi*   man looks, towards a place a short distance uphill, at woman
(210) *balan ḍugumbil baŋgul yaṛaŋgu buṛan baludayimban*   ⟨as (209)⟩

Verbalisation extends to interrogative locational forms. For instance, a conversation included (for *aɲḍa* see 4.15.2):

(211) *aɲḍa baŋum wuɲḍarumban bayi ḍaban budin*   and then [after it was cooked] where did you take the eel to?

We stated that ablative nominals cannot usually be verbalised. In fact, forms involving verb markers *baŋum*, *yaŋum* and *gilaŋum* (6.5.2), and those in which a noun is suffixed by *-ŋunu*, never can be. But there is a further set of forms, built on an allative verb marker and involving affix *-ŋunu*. For instance, there is:

        besides *yaŋumgalu*,   also *yalugaluŋunu*
   and besides *gilaŋumgalu*, also *gilarugaluŋunu*

The forms in the second column imply an indefinacy of origin. Whereas *gilaŋumgalu* could be glossed 'from somewhere out there', *gilarugaluŋunu* implies 'from anywhere' with the additional implication that there was almost random movement, with tracks doubling back on themselves. Forms in the first column cannot be verbalised, but those in the second column can be: *yalugaluŋunubin*, *gilarugaluŋunubin*.

4.7.3 Of time qualifiers. Time qualifiers in 'time until' inflection can be verbalised. Thus:

(212) *ŋaḍa miḍuyiriɲu gilugu*   I'm waiting until later on
(213) *ŋaḍa miḍuyiriɲu gilugubin*   ⟨as (212)⟩

The 'time until' inflection is sometimes omitted before a verbaliser; there is never any possibility of confusion. Thus:

(214) *ŋaḍa miḍuyiriɲu gilubin*   ⟨as (212)⟩

As a further example, when an informant was describing how he had been lent something only overnight, he said *ŋulgagumbali budili* 'to carry it until tomorrow'; here *ŋulgagu* 'until tomorrow' has the transitiviser *-mbal*, and the whole form is in purposive inflection, agreeing with *budili*.

4.7.4 Of particles. Some, but not all, particles can be verbalised; all examples obtained involve the transitive verbaliser. There is some discussion in 4.15.3.

Processes of nominalisation and verbalisation are used fairly extensively in Guwal. In Dyalŋuy they are used to excess; there are many instances of a derived form in Dyalŋuy corresponding to a root form in Guwal – see 9.2.

4.8 Reflexive and reciprocal constructions

4.8.1 Reflexives. A reflexive verbal form can be derived from any transitive root as follows:

[1] from an *-l* root: delete root-final *-l* and in M and G – add *-ríy*; in D – add *-yiríy*, when next but one after a stressed syllable; add *-ríy* in all other cases (i.e. when following a stressed syllable, or after two or more unstressed syllables);

[2] from a *-y* root, in all dialects
add *-máriy*, to a root of two syllables;
add *-(m)báriy*, to a root of more than two syllables.

We thus have:

	reflexive form	
transitive root	in M and G	in D
búybal 'hide'	*búybaríy*	*búybayiríy*
ŋúnbiṛal 'try'	*ŋúnbiṛaríy*	*ŋúnbiṛaríy*
múnumádal 'chuck it in'	*múnumádaríy*	*múnumádayiríy*
gúniy 'search'	*gúnimáriy*	
gúnigúniy 'repeatedly search'	*gúnigúnibáriy*	

guniguniy is the reduplicated form of *guniy* – 6.3.4; *munumadal* is a compound verb from *munu* 'arse' and *madal* 'throw', meaning 'give up some task' – the form in G is *muyumadal*, corresponding to G *muyu* 'arse'.

A reflexive form functions like an intransitive stem; that is, it can co-occur in a VC with an intransitive, but not with a transitive, verb.

Reflexive forms sometimes carry a reflexive meaning:

(215) *bala yugu baŋgul yaṟaŋgu buyban*   man hides stick
(216) *bayi yaṟa buybayiriɲu*   man hides himself
(217) *balan ḍugumbil baŋgul yaṟaŋgu ɲamban*   man hears woman
(218) *bayi yaṟa ɲambayiriɲu*   man thinks

In other cases, the reflexive affix appears just to derive an intransitive from a transitive stem, without carrying any reflexive meaning:

(219) *balam wuḍu baŋgul yaṟaŋgu ḍaŋgaɲu*   man eats fruit
(220) *bayi yaṟa ḍaŋgaymariɲu bagum wuḍugu*   ⟨as (219)⟩
(221) *ŋaḍa bayi guya wagaɲu*   I am spearing fish
(222) *ŋaḍa wagaymariɲu bagul guyagu*   ⟨as (221)⟩

We will refer to sentences such as (220) and (222) as 'false reflexives'.

It appears that all verbs can form both true reflexives (if such forms would be semantically plausible) and false reflexives.

A true reflexive sentence must always involve verbal affix *-riy* (or alternant); it can optionally include the nominal affix *-ḍilu*, one of whose functions is to indicate reflexivity (see 6.1.1). *-ḍilu* is particularly useful to distinguish a true from a false reflexive. For instance, (220) might well be shortened by the omission of *bagum wuḍugu* and of *yaṟa*:

(223) *bayi ḍaŋgaymariɲu*   he eats

Since people do not eat themselves, the unmarked interpretation of (223) would be that it is a false reflexive, referring to the eating of a regular meal. If one did want to refer to a man chewing his finger, say (as a contemplative accompaniment, not in hunger), one would be sure to include *-ḍilu*:

(224) *bayinḍilu ḍaŋgaymariɲu*   he eats himself

Consider a further pair of true and false reflexives, involving the same verb, *walmbil* 'waken, get up':

(225) *ŋaḍa walmbiyiriɲu*   I am getting up
(226) *ŋaḍa walmbiyiriɲu bagul yaṟagu*   I get (or will get) man up

The true reflexive (225) can be extended by an implicative NP, in the same way that an intransitive simple sentence can be:

(227) *ŋaḍa walmbiyiriɲu bagul yaṟagu*   I am getting up to be concerned with man (e.g. to see man)

(227) could be distinguished from the false reflexive (226) by the inclusion of *-ḍilu*:

(228) *ŋaḍaḍilu walmbiyiriɲu bagul yaɽagu* ⟨as (227)⟩

A false reflexive is very like a *-ŋay* construction. It appears to have much the same syntactic purpose – to put an A NP (which is in ergative inflection in the underlying simple sentence) into nominative case, so that it can be incorporated into a topic-chain. The examples of false reflexives given above have involved nominative substituting for the ergative inflection of the A NP, and dative substituting for the nominative case of the O NP. There are also reflexive sentences similar to the other type of *-ŋay* construction, in which the O NP is put into ergative, not dative, case:

(229) *balabawal yugu baŋgul nudin*   he's cutting trees out there
(230) *bayi nudiyiriɲu yuguŋgu baŋgubawal* ⟨as (229)⟩

False reflexives are, in fact, syntactically identical with *-ŋay* constructions; they differ from them in meaning. A verb in *-ŋay* form, plus unmarked tense inflection, refers to an ACTUAL action; one in reflexive form, plus unmarked tense inflection, refers to the POTENTIALITY of some action taking place (see the discussion of actual/potential in 3.1). Thus:

(231) *bayi yaɽa ḍabandu wagaymariɲu*   man is spearing eels

refers to a man who has gone out on an eel-spearing expedition, but is not actually spearing any at the moment. He may have already found some eels, and have speared them all, and now be looking for more; or he may not yet have found any at all. In contrast:

(232) *bayi yaɽa ḍabandu waganaɲu*   man is spearing eels

means that he has just found some eels, and is at present spearing them.

Similarly, *bayi wugayiriɲu bagum ḍigagu* means 'he gives out cigarettes' – the Dyirbal verb has an 'habituative' meaning in this instance, exactly like 'gives' in the English gloss. In contrast, *bayi wugalŋaɲu bagum ḍigagu* would mean 'he is (now) giving out cigarettes'.

The casual listener to Dyirbal conversation might conclude that some verbs 'prefer' *-ŋay* constructions, while others occur more commonly in false reflexive form. In fact, all verbs can occur in both types of construction and are governed by considerations of 'actual' and 'potential' meaning, as described above. The impression of 'preferences' is a result of the contrasting natures

of different types of action. For instance, on a spearing expedition one spends
a great deal of time (sometimes, all the time!) looking for eels, and a relatively
short time actually trying to spear them – thus *wagay* 'spear' is heard much more
frequently in false reflexive than in *-ŋay* form. In contrast, if one goes out to
cut a tree down, one spends virtually all the time actually hacking away at it
– it is not surprising that *nudil* 'cut' is heard much more frequently in *-ŋay*
than in false reflexive form.

The following sentence, which was given spontaneously by an informant,
includes both false reflexive and *-ŋay* forms of the same verb:

(233) *ŋaḍa bayi buṛan ḍaŋgaymariɲu guyagu ḍaŋganaɲu*

Verbal inflection *-ɲu* marks a relative clause – 4.10. The literal translation of
(233) is 'I saw him, who is potentially eating fish, who is [in fact] actually
eating it'. That is, *ḍaŋgaymariɲu* implies that the man referred to has caught
or acquired some fish and that he is either about to eat it or has eaten it;
ḍaŋganaɲu is then more specific, and states that the man was actually eating
fish at the time I saw him. As the informant explained it in English: 'he is
having a feed of fish, when I saw him he was still eating it'.

We can have reflexive-plus-*ɲura* constructions, exactly like the *-ŋay*-
plus-*ɲura* type (4.5.5):

(234) *balan ḍugumbil baŋgul yaṛaŋgu balgan (bayi yaṛa) buybayiriɲura*
      man hit woman and then immediately hid himself

Participles can be formed from reflexive verbs. For example:

[1] *nagay* is a transitive verb 'break the bank of a river, make a
landslide'; *bala ḍaŋgil* is 'riverbank'. A part of a bank that is always
breaking down might be referred to as *bala ḍaŋgil nagaymarimuɲa*.

[2] *ŋambal* is the verb 'hear, listen'. Anyone who thinks a lot, or
anyone who listens intently to others, can be described as *ŋambayirimuɲa*
– in the first meaning the participle is derived from a true reflexive, in
the second from a false reflexive. Thus, of a man who is far from home
and is always thinking of returning, we might say:

(235) *bayi yaṛa ŋambayirimuɲa bayi banagaɲ*   man is always thinking
      that he will return home

4.8.2. Reciprocals. A reciprocal verbal form, that also functions like
an intransitive stem, can be derived from any transitive root by:
[1] reduplicating the root (verb reduplication in Dyirbal involves
repeating the first two syllables – 6.3.4); and [2] adding *-(n)bariy*.

The topic NP of a reciprocal sentence must have more than one
(animate, usually human) referent:

(236) *balagara bayi yaṛa ḍurgayḍurgaybariɲu*   the two men are spearing
      each other

(237) *balagara ɲunḍalɲunḍalnbariɲu*   the two people are kissing
(238) *balagara ḍaymbalḍaymbalbariɲu buɽbiŋga*   the two people met each other half-way

A reciprocal sentence implies that one person was subject for one instance of an action and the other object; and that their roles were reversed in a further instance. Thus:

(239) *bayi yaɽa baŋgun ḍugumbiɽu baɽan*   woman punched man
(240) *balan ḍugumbil baŋgul yaɽaŋgu baɽan*   man punched woman

are together equivalent to (for *-gara* see 4.2.1, 6.1.1):

(241) *bayi yaɽagara balan ḍugumbilgara baɽalbaɽalnbariɲu*   man and woman punched each other

Almost all Australian languages have reflexive and reciprocal verbal affixes – reflexive often involves *-ri*, see 1.7. Compare with Thargari, which has reflexive *-ri* and reciprocal with main allomorph *-dbari* [Klokeid 1969; 35–7].

4.9   Instrumental and comitative constructions

4.9.1.   Instrumental NPs.   A sentence can include a further NP, whose words are in instrumental inflection:

(242) *balan   ḍugumbil   baŋgul   yaɽaŋgu baŋgu*
THERE-NOM-II woman-NOM THERE-ERG-I man-ERG THERE-INST-IV
yuguŋgu   balgan
stick-INST hit-PRES/PAST
man is hitting woman with stick

(243) *bayi   ḍaban   baŋgul   yaɽaŋgu baŋgul*
THERE-NOM-I eel-NOM THERE-ERG-I man-ERG THERE-INST-I
ḍirgaŋgu   ḍurgaɲu
spear-INST spear-PRES/PAST
man is spearing eel with multi-prong spear

(244) *balam   ḍuguɽ   baŋgugaragu   baŋgu*
THERE-NOM-III yam-NOM two people-ERG THERE-INST-IV
gaḍindu   bagan
yamstick-INST dig-PRES/PAST
the two [women] are digging yams with a yamstick

An instrumental NP specifies some thing, other than subject and object, which is necessary for the proper performance of the action.

The instrument is often an implement or weapon or body part (e.g. hand) that is used; with a verb of giving, an instrumental NP can describe that which is given:

(245) *bayi*   *yaṛa*   *baŋgun*   *ḍugumbiṛu* *baŋgum*
        THERE-NOM-I man-NOM THERE-ERG-II woman-ERG THERE-INST-III
        miraṇḍu   *wugan*
        bean-INST give-PRES/PAST
        woman is giving man beans

(a full account of the varied syntactic possibilities of verbs of giving is in 8.2.3).

It appears that no sentence can involve more than one instrumental NP. Thus we cannot have *ŋaḍa balan ḍugumbil wuḍuŋgu wugan malaŋgu 'I gave the woman food, with my hand' – here both *wuḍu* 'food' and *mala* 'hand' are in instrumental case. Instead, *ŋaḍa balan ḍugumbil wuḍuŋgu wugan malaŋga* (with *mala* in locative case) is preferred.

On the surface, an instrumental NP appears difficult to distinguish from an ergative NP, marking transitive actor [A]; both involve a head noun, a noun marker, and optional adjectives, and the case inflections are identical. In fact, the two types of NP behave quite differently.

The -*ŋay* transformation substitutes nominative for the ergative case of an A NP; it leaves an instrumental NP unchanged:

(246) *bayi yaṛa bagul ḍabangu baŋgul ḍirgaŋgu ḍurganaṇu* ⟨as (243)⟩
(247) *balagara bagum ḍuguṛgu baŋgu gaḍindu bagalŋaṇu* ⟨as (244)⟩

(246–7) are -*ŋay* constructions in which the O NP is in dative case; instrumental NPs also remain unchanged in the other type of -*ŋay* transform, in which the O NP goes into ergative case:

(248) *bayi yaṛa baŋgun ḍugumbiṛu baŋgu yuguŋgu balgalŋaṇu* ⟨as (242)⟩

In exactly the same way, the reflexive transformation leaves an instrumental NP unchanged:

(249) *bayi yaṛa bagul ḍabangu baŋgul ḍirgaŋgu ḍurgaymariṇu*   man is (trying to) spear eels with a multi-prong spear

We mentioned that each verbal root is strictly transitive or strictly intransitive. A transitive simple sentence will normally involve an ergative NP; a simple sentence whose verbs are intransitive cannot include an ergative NP. Instrumental NPs, however, can occur in transitive and also in intransitive simple sentences. For instance, with intransitive verbs *ɽubiy*, 'eat meat' (the instrumental NP describing that which is eaten), and *gibay* 'scrape, shave':

(250) *bayi yaɽa baŋgu ḏalguɽu ɽubiɲu*   man ate meat
(251) *bayi   yaɽa   ɲumbul   barmbaŋgu gibaɲu*
    THERE-NOM-I man-NOM beard-NOM stone-INST scrape-PRES/PAST
    man shaved his beard with a sharp stone

And see (261) below.

Instrumental NPs occur far more commonly with transitive than with intransitive verbs; the reasons for this involve the semantic natures of the verbs.
    Instrumental NPs can also occur with intransitively verbalised adjectives. For instance:

(252) *bayi yaya wawaɲuṇḏindu waguligu gubibin*   Yaya became a gubi by drinking Wawa's blood

For the genitive-plus-instrumental inflection of *wawa* see 4.11.1. Note that the relation between Wawa and his blood (*waguli*) is here described by the construction for alienable possession, his blood having been drained from him in order to be drunk. In this sentence, the nonsense words *yaya* and *wawa* have been substituted for the names of the killer and his victim; as given to the writer this sentence described an actual event. See 2.4.

4.9.2 Instrumentive VCs. An event which involves an object, an actor, and an instrument can be described in two ways. Either by a simple sentence involving an instrumental NP, as in (242); or by a construction in which the verbs are in instrumentive form:

(253) *bala   yugu   baŋgul   yaɽaŋgu balgalman*
    THERE-NOM-I stick-NOM THERE-ERG-I man-ERG hit-INST-PRES/PAST
    bagun   ḏugumbilgu
    THERE-DAT-II woman-DAT
    man is hitting woman with stick

Constructions like (253) could be regarded as transformationally derived from simple sentences like (242); three changes are involved:
    [1] nominative replaces the instrumental inflection of the instrumental NP;
    [2] dative replaces the nominative inflection of the O NP;
    [3] the verbal stems are put into instrumentive form by the addition of: *-mal*, next but one after a stressed syllable; *-mbal*, in all other cases (that is, after a stressed syllable, or after a sequence of two unstressed syllables).

In M only, the instrumentive affix on to a *-y* stem is *-ŋay* followed by *-mal ~ -mbal*. Thus the instrumentive form of *ɲugay* 'grind' is *ɲugaymal* in D but *ɲuganaymbal* in M.

A full discussion of the syntax of (242) and (253) is in 5.7.

Instrumentive constructions are very common in Dyirbal discourse; for example:

(254) *bala bari baŋgul yaɽaŋgu maŋan nudilmali bagu yugugu*   man picks up axe to cut down tree with it

corresponding to simple sentences:

(255) *bala bari baŋgul yaɽaŋgu maŋan*   man picks up axe
(256) *bala yugu baŋgul yaɽaŋgu baŋgu bariŋgu nudin*   man cuts tree with axe

4.9.3 Comitative VCs. The addition of *–mal* (next but one after a stressed syllable) or *-mbal* (in all other cases) to an intransitive verbal stem produces a form that functions as a transitive stem, marking what we can call a comitative construction (see also 8.2.2):

(257) *bayi yaɽa ɲinaɲu*   man is sitting down OR settling down
(258) *balan ḍugumbil baŋgul yaɽaŋgu ɲinayman*   man is sitting down with the woman OR is married to the woman
(259) *bayi yaɽa ḍanaɲu*   man is standing
(260) *bala yugu baŋgul yaɽaŋgu ḍanayman*   man is standing with some wood (i.e. EITHER standing on a block of wood, OR leaning against a tree, OR standing under a tree, OR standing holding a stick)

The comitative affix on intransitive stems is thus phonologically identical to the instrumentive affix on transitive stems. There is some syntactico-semantic similarity; for instance, *ɽubiy* 'eat meat' has comitative form *ɽubimal*:

(261) *bala ḍalguɽ baŋgul yaɽaŋgu ɽubiman*   man ate meat

There is a degree of congruence between (242)–(253), and (250)–(261); in (253) the instrumental NP has become topic of an instrumentive verb, and in (261) the instrumental NP has become topic of a comitative verb.

Comitative verbs appear to have considerably wider semantic possibilities than instrumentive forms (see (257–60), for instance), and it is for this reason that we have NOT identified comitative with instrumentive, as a single suffix.

A further comitative example:

(262) *bayi   baŋgu   yuguŋgu   balbalimban*
THERE-NOM-I THERE-ERG-IV wood-ERG roll-COMIT-PRES/PAST
balay   dalbiŋga   bungin
THERE-LOC topside-LOC lie-PRES/PAST
the log rolled with him [when he] was lying there on top [of it]

And see *yubalnbarimali* in text xv, line 76 (page 381).

Comitative constructions can occur in conjunction with other types of construction. For example:

[1] *-ŋay* plus comitative (on to a transitive root). A *-ŋay* verbal stem functions intransitively; thus *-m(b)al* signals a comitative, not an instrumentive, construction:

(263) *balam ḍubula baŋgun ḍugumbiṟu ɲugaɲu*   woman is grinding wild flour

(264) *balan ḍugumbil ɲuganaɲu (bagum ḍubulagu)*   ⟨as (263)⟩

(265) *bayi ɲalŋga baŋgun ḍugumbiṟu ɲuganaymban (bagum ḍubulagu)* woman has a boy [sitting beside her] as she is grinding (wild flour)

Contrast (265) with the instrumentive construction involving *ɲugay*; in D:

(266) *bayi muɡay baŋgun ḍugumbiṟu ɲugayman*   woman is using grinding-stone to grind

(Note that in M the verb form would be *ɲuganaymban* in both (265) and (266).)

[2] reflexive plus comitative (on to a transitive root). For example (cf. (216)):

(267) *balan ḍugumbil baŋgul yaṟaŋgu buybayirimban*   man hides with woman

(268) *bala waya baŋgul yaṟaŋgu ḍurgaymariman*   man is spearing [fish] with the piece of wire

(269) *ŋaḍa balan   ḍugumbil   yanuman   bagul*
I-SA THERE-NOM-II woman-NOM go-COMIT-PRES/PAST THERE-DAT-I
guyagu   ḍurgaymariman
fish-DAT spear-REFL-COMIT-PRES/PAST
I took the woman with me to spear fish

4   D D L

[3] comitative plus reflexive (on to an intransitive stem). For example (cf. (258)):

(270) *bayi yaṟa ɲinaymariɲu bagun ḍugumbilgu*   man is sitting with woman OR is married to woman

(271) *balamaŋgan bayi yaṟa ɲinaymariɲu*   all the men are sitting down (i.e. with each other)

[4] comitative plus reflexive plus comitative (on to an intransitive stem). A comitative plus reflexive construction must involve at least two people or things; a comitative plus reflexive plus comitative construction must involve at least three people or things – generally, two people accompanied by a third person or thing:

(272) *bayi yaṟa baŋgugara ɲinaymariman*   two people are sitting down with man

Verbalised nominals can occur in comitative form. For example (cf. (194)):

(273) *bala bari baŋgul yaṟaŋgu guyibilmban*   man died with the toma-hawk [in his arms]

Another example is:

(274) *bayi   baŋgul   mundan*
      THERE-NOM-I THERE-ERG-I take-PRES/PAST
      bulganbilmban   /   yiɲḍagayulgira
      big-INTR VBLSR-COMIT-PRES/PAST not yet-SAME-CLITIC
      bayi   ɲalŋgaɲunu
      THERE-NOM-I child-OUT OF
      he took him with him just as if he [the taken] were a big man; but he was only a boy yet

A nominal plus transitive verbaliser *-mal ~ -(m)bal* appears not to be able to be followed by the instrumentive affix; this is almost certainly to prevent phonological infelicity (that is, a succession of two identical affixes). In fact, a reflexive suffix *-riy* intervenes, the third affix then being comitative rather than instrumentive (cf. (199)):

(275) *ŋaḍa bala   magira   bagul   yaṟagu*
      I-SA THERE-NOM-IV yellow clay-NOM THERE-DAT-I man-DAT
      baŋgaymali   gulgiṟimbarimali
      paint-INST-PURP pretty-TR VBLSR-REFL-COMIT-PURP
      I painted man prettily with yellow clay

Note that it is not possible to have a comitative affix followed by *-ŋay*. There is in fact a general rule that *-ŋay* must occur next to the verb root, with no other affix intervening – 6.3.1. (In the case of verbalised nominals, *-ŋay* must come immediately after the verbaliser *-mal* ∼ *-(m)bal*.)

It has been mentioned that the great majority of transitive roots belong to the *-l* conjugation, with just a few being *-y*-forms (3.4.2). The fact that the reflexive affix for an *-l* stem is *-(yi)riy*, while for a *-y* stem it is *-mariy* ∼ *-(m)bariy*, may be taken to suggest that *-y* stems, which are at present transitive, were originally intransitive. The reflexive suffix can only be added to an intransitive root if the root is first made transitive, and this can only be done in one way – through the comitative affix; thus we have *ɲinay* 'sit' and *ɲinaymariy*, and so on. It may be that, as an originally-intransitive stem took on a transitive role, it still put *-mal* before a reflexive affix; this *-mal* could no longer be regarded as the comitative affix and would be simply a part of *-mariy*, the allomorph of the reflexive suffix used with *-y* stems. The alternation between reflexive *-mariy* and *-(m)bariy* does not exactly parallel that between comitative *-mal* and *-mbal*, but it is similar enough to provide support for this hypothesis. (Note also the alternation *-nbal* ∼ *-galiy* in 6.3.2).

4.10   Relative clauses

If the topic NP of any sentence has the same referent as any NP – or locative noun – of a second sentence, then the (rest of the) first sentence can be embedded as relative clause on to the NP or locative noun of the second sentence. A relative clause is marked by its verbs and adverbals taking a special ending, in place of a tense inflection; the ending depends upon the NP it qualifies.

relative clause to an NP/ noun in inflection:	has verbal marking:	
nominative	*-ŋu*	with deletion of stem-final *-l* or *-y*
ergative	*-ŋuru*	
instrumental	*-ŋuru*	
dative	*-ŋugu*	
locative	*-ŋura*	

The verbal inflections can be analysed into [1] relative clause marking *-ŋu*, and [2] case ending, agreeing with that of the qualified NP/noun. Nominative and dative follow the usual rules (3.2.1); ergative/instrumental and locative, however, have special forms *-ru* and *-ra*, that occur only after a relative clause marker.

Note that the relation between ergative/instrumental and locative – that they differ only in the final vowel being *-u* in the first case and *-a* in the second – is maintained; this relation is a feature of Dyirbal (3.2.1, 3.3.1) and of the majority of Australian languages (1.6).

[1] relative clause to topic (nominative) NP

(276) *ŋaḍa balan ḍugumbil ɲinaɲu buɽan*   I am watching the woman
    who is sitting down

which is derived from (277) as matrix sentence and (278) as constituent
sentence:

(277) *ŋaḍa balan ḍugumbil buɽan*   I am watching woman
(278) *balan ḍugumbil ɲinaɲu*   woman is sitting down

Similarly, from (278) as matrix and (277) as constituent sentence:

(279) *balan ḍugumbil ŋaḍa buɽaɲu ɲinaɲu*   the woman whom I am
    watching is sitting down

Further examples are:

(280) *ŋayguna baŋgul yaɽaŋgu balgaɲu baŋgun ḍugumbiɽu buɽan*   woman
    saw me being hit by man
(281) *ŋaḍa baniɲu baɲumbalbulu ɲinaɲ*   I, who have come from a long
    way downriver, will sit down

   -ɲay, reflexive, reciprocal, instrumentive and comitative constructions
can operate freely as either matrix or constituent sentences. (282) is an
example of a relative clause involving an instrumentive verb:

(282) *ŋaḍa bala   yugu   baŋgul   yaɽaŋgu bagul*
    I-SA THERE-NOM-IV stick-NOM THERE-ERG-I man-ERG THERE-DAT-II
    ḍugumbilgu balgalmaɲu   ɲiman
    woman-DAT hit-INST-REL-NOM hold-PRES/PAST
    I caught hold of the stick the man was beating the woman with

   The 'common NP' of a constituent sentence must be in nominative
case for the sentence to be embedded on to the 'common NP' of the
matrix sentence. Thus the *-ɲay* transformation has to be applied to
a simple sentence, in which the common NP is in ergative case, ahead
of the embedding transformation. With matrix sentence:

(283) *bayi yaɽa banagaɲu*   man is returning

and constituent sentence:

(284) *bayi yuɽi baŋgul yaɽaŋgu bagan*   man speared kangaroo

(284) is *-ɲay*-transformed:

(285) *bayi yaɽa bagalɲaɲu bagul yuɽigu*   ⟨as (284)⟩

and then embedded into (283):

(286) *bayi yaṛa bagalɲaɲu bagul yuṛigu banagaɲu*   man who speared
   kangaroo is returning

   [2] relative clause to ergative NP
From:

(287) *bayi yaṛa baŋgun ḍugumbiṛu buṛan*   woman saw man

and:

(288) *balan ḍugumbil wayɲḍin*   woman went uphill

we get:

(289) *bayi yaṛa baŋgun ḍugumbiṛu wayɲḍiɲuru buṛan*   as woman was
   going uphill she saw man

Similarly, in M:

(290) *baŋgu   yuguŋgu gunbaɲuru   baŋgul   yaṛaŋgu*
   THERE-ERG-IV tree-ERG cut-REL-ERG THERE-ERG-I man-ERG
   ɲayguna biriḍu   balgan
   I-O   PARTICLE-EMPH hit-PRES/PAST
   the tree which the man had cut nearly fell on me (i.e. it could
   have fallen on me but luckily it didn't)

(for particle *biri* see 4.15.3).
And:

(291) *balan   ḍugumbil   baŋgul   yaṛaŋgu baŋgun*
   THERE-NOM-II woman-NOM THERE-ERG-I man-ERG THERE-ERG-II
   ɲalŋgaŋgu ḍilwalɲaɲuru   buṛan
   child-ERG kick-*ɲay*-REL-ERG see-PRES/PAST
   man who had kicked child saw woman

   [3] relative clause to instrumental NP

(292) *balan   ḍugumbil   baŋgul   yaṛaŋgu balgan*
   THERE-NOM-II woman-NOM THERE-ERG-I man-ERG hit-PRES/PAST
   yuguŋgu   ɲaḍa maŋgaɲuru
   stick-INST I-SA pick up-REL-INST
   man hit woman with stick that I picked up (sc: and handed to
   him)

(293) *bayi yaṛa bagun ḍugumbilgu balgalɲaɲu yuguŋgu ɲaḍa maŋgaɲuru*
   ⟨as (292)⟩

Note that a relative clause can itself contain an instrumental NP; this
remains unaffected by the relative clause transformation:

(294) *ŋinda   yuguŋgu   balgalŋuru   ŋayguna baŋgul*
     you-SA stick-INST hit-REL-ERG I-O   THERE-ERG-I
     yaṛaŋgu   ḍilwan
     man-ERG kick-PRES/PAST
     the man, whom you hit with a stick, kicked me

(295) *balan   ḍugumbil   ŋinungu gaḍindu*
     THERE-NOM-II woman-NOM you-DAT yamstick-INST
     balgalŋaŋu   baḍiŋu
     hit-*ŋay*-REL-NOM fell-PRES/PAST
     the woman, who hit you with a yamstick, fell down

   [4] relative clause to implicated (dative) NP

(296) *balan   ḍugumbil   baniŋ*
     THERE-NOM-II woman-NOM come-FUT
     yagulbayḍi   yaṛagu   miyandaŋugu
     HERE-DAT-I-DOWN-HILL-SHORT WAY man-DAT laugh-REL-DAT
     buṛalŋaygu
     see-*ŋay*-PURP
     woman will come to see men laughing just down here

(297) *balam   miraŋ   baŋgul   yaṛaŋgu budin*
     THERE-NOM-III bean-NOM THERE-ERG-I man-ERG take-PRES/PAST
     bagun   ḍugumbilgu ŋaḍa balgalŋugu
     THERE-DAT-II woman-DAT I-SA hit-REL-DAT
     man is taking beans to woman I hit

   [5] relative clause to locative noun

(298) *bayi   yaṛa   ɲinaɲu   buniŋga ɲaduŋura*
     THERE-NOM-I man-NOM sit-PRES/PAST fire-LOC light-REL-LOC
     ḍugumbiṛu
     woman-ERG
     man is sitting by fire woman made

(299) *ŋaḍa ɲinaɲu   yuguŋga yaṛaŋgu nudiŋura*
     I-SA sit-PRES/PAST tree-LOC man-ERG cut-REL-LOC
     I am sitting on the tree the man felled

Nouns in allative and ablative inflection cannot be qualified by
relative clauses. Relative clauses have been recorded qualifying a
genitive noun (the case ending on the verb agrees with the case which
follows the genitive inflection on the noun).

Word sequence is very free for most sentences including relative clauses. The preferred position for a relative clause is immediately following the NP it qualifies, irrespective of wherever this NP happens, in this instance, to come in the matrix sentence; the preferred position is likely to be used for, say, sentences like (280), that include two ergative NPs, in order to avoid ambiguity.

In M, but not in D and G, there is a second type of relative clause, with verbal marking *-mi* in place of *-ŋu*. *-mi* relative clauses have exactly the same syntax as the *-ŋu* type. Verbal endings are:

relative clause to an NP/ noun in inflection:	has verbal marking:
nominative	*-mi*
ergative	*-miru*
instrumental	*-miru*
dative	*-migu*
locative	*-mira*

There is a difference in that *-ŋu* endings replace tense inflections, whereas *-mi* endings follow the unmarked tense inflection. Thus:

	relative clause to nominative NP	
root	*-mi* type	*-ŋu* type
ɲinay 'sit'	*ɲinaɲumi*	*ɲinaŋu*
balgal 'hit'	*balganmi*	*balgaŋu*

The difference between the two kinds of relative clause in M is one of aspect. *-mi* refers to an action that is completed, while *-ŋu* refers to something that is still going on. Compare (300) and (301), which both involve a relative clause to an implicative NP, and (302) and (303), which both involve a relative clause to an ergative NP:

(300) *ŋaḍa yanu bagul yaɾagu ŋinda yuguŋgu balganmigu* I went to the man whom you had hit with a stick

(301) *ŋaḍa yanu bagul yaɾagu ŋinda yuguŋgu balgaŋugu* I went to the man whom you were hitting with a stick

(302) *bayi ɲalŋga baŋgun ḍugumbiɾu miyandaɲumiru bunḍun* woman, who had finished laughing, spanked boy

(303) *bayi ɲalŋga baŋgun ḍugumbiɾu miyandaŋuru bunḍun* woman spanked boy while laughing

An M sentence can consist of just a topic NP qualified by a relative clause of the *-mi* type. In this case the relative clause is functioning like a simple sentence in perfective aspect:

(304) *ŋaḍa babilyaɲumi bagum miraŋgu*   I've scraped the beans

Further examples of *-mi* relative clauses are in text xv, lines 3 and 66 (pp. 369, 380); text xxv, line 29 (p. 390) includes a place name involving *-mi*.

D and G have only one type of relative clause, whose semantic range covers *-mi* and *-ŋu* clauses in M. A relative clause in D or G can refer to any time but will normally refer to a time not later than the time referred to by the matrix sentence. Thus (280), for example, could mean 'woman is watching me, who had been hit by man', 'woman is watching man hit me', 'woman saw man hitting me', 'woman saw me, who had been hit by man'.

Note:

(305) *ŋinda gilu   bani   ŋaygu   wuḍugu wugaŋugu*
      you-SA later today come-IMP I-GEN-NOM food-DAT give-REL-DAT
      budilŋaygu
      carry-*ŋay*-PURP
      you come later on, to take some of the food that will have been given me by then

Here *wugaŋugu* refers to future time, but to a time anterior to that referred to by imperative *bani* (together with time qualifier *gilu* 'later on today').

A sentence in D can consist of just a topic NP, qualified by a relative clause. In this case the relative clause normally implies the completion of the action:

(306) *ŋaḍa babilyaɲu bagum miraŋgu*   I've scraped the beans

Thus, in this instance, a *-ŋu* relative clause in D is roughly equivalent to a *-mi* clause in M.

There are two main ways in which relative clauses differ from participles: [1] a participle can, at most, involve a verb and its object, whereas a relative clause can include any number of peripheral constituents, such as instrumental and implicative NPs, verb markers and locational nominals, time qualifier and particles (see (402)), and so on; [2] a relative clause refers to some actual event (with, in M, an obligatory aspect specification), whereas a participle indicates that some person is habitually involved in actions of a certain type. (And cf. the distinction *'-tor/*-tér in Indo-European – Benveniste, 1948: 62.)

4.11 Possessive phrases

4.11.1 Involving simple genitive inflection. A topic NP can be qualified by a possessive NP, all of whose words are in the simple genitive case (3.2.1, 3.2.2, 3.3.1). The possibilities for inclusion in a possessive NP are as described generally for NPs in 4.2, except that a possessive NP cannot include a second (inalienably possessed) noun. The head of the topic NP is alienably possessed (i.e. NOT as 'a part of') by the head of the possessive NP:

(307) *bayi waŋal baŋul yaṟaŋu baŋgun ḍugumbiṟu buṟan*   woman saw man's boomerang

(308) *ŋinda ŋaygu bayi galbin balgan*   you hit my son

A further form can be derived from any genitive nominal, noun marker or pronoun, by the addition of -(*ɲ*)*ḍin*. Thus:

yaṟaŋuɲḍin	from *yaṟaŋu* 'man's'
ŋaygudin	from *ŋaygu* 'my'
baŋuldin	from *baŋul* noun marker (often 'his')
balagaraŋuɲḍin	from *balagaraŋu* 'the two people's'

In G -*ŋiɲ* occurs instead of -*ŋu*(*ɲ*)*ḍin*; thus *yaṟaŋiɲ* in place of *yaṟa-ŋuɲḍin*, etc. (See 6.2 for the optional omission of genitive inflection before -*ḍin* in the case of non-singular pronouns.)

Possessives can be declined in most Australian languages; it is not uncommon for a catalytic affix to be inserted before any further inflection – 1.6. Notice that in Narrinyeri [Taplin, 1880: 10, 12] the catalytic affix is -*yin*, rather similar to Dyirbal -*ḍin*.

-*ḍin* possessive forms inflect exactly like nominals, and it is these forms, with the appropriate case inflections, that are used in possessive qualification of non-topic NPs. For instance, an ergative NP can be qualified by a possessive NP, all of whose words are in genitive plus -*ḍin* plus ergative form; an implicated NP can be qualified by a possessive NP whose words are in genitive plus -*ḍin* plus dative inflection; similarly for an instrumental NP. For example:

(309) *balan ḍugumbil ŋayguḍindu baŋgul galbindu balgan*   my son hit woman

(310) *ŋayguna baŋgul   gubiŋgu gigan   bagul*
      I-O   THERE-ERG-I gubi-ERG tell-PRES/PAST THERE-DAT-I
      waŋalgu   baŋuldjingu   yaṛaŋuṇḍingu
      boomerang-DAT THERE-GEN-I-*ḍin*-DAT man-GEN-*ḍin*-DAT
      wugalŋaygu
      give-*ŋay*-PURP
      gubi told me to give the man his (i.e. the man's) boomerangs

In addition, any locational nominal may be qualified by a -*ḍin* possessive phrase, with the appropriate locational inflection (3.2.1, 3.4.6, 4.3):

(311) *balan ḍugumbil ɲinaɲu ŋayguḍinda miḍaŋga*   woman is sitting in my camp

(312) *balan ḍugumbil yanu ŋayguḍingu miḍagu*   woman is going to my camp

(313) *balan ḍugumbil baniɲu ŋayguḍinɲunu miḍaɲunu*   woman is coming from my camp

Sometimes, if there is no possibility of ambiguity, a possessive phrase in genitive case, with or without affix -*ḍin*, but WITHOUT ANY FURTHER CASE INFLECTION, may modify a non-topic NP. For instance:

(314) *balan ḍugumbil ŋaygu baŋgul galbindu balgan*   ⟨as (309)⟩
(315) *balan ḍugumbil ɲinaɲu ŋaygu miḍaŋga*   ⟨as (311)⟩
(316) *balan ḍugumbil baniɲu ŋayguḍin miḍaɲunu*   ⟨as (313)⟩

Informants insist that (314–16) are bona fide alternatives to (309), (311) and (313), and that they are in no way deviant.

A genitive-plus-*ḍin* form cannot take a further genitive inflection; 'the possessor of a possessor' is put in the same form as 'the possessor', with word order and/or considerations of sense indicating the syntactic relations involved:

(317) *ŋaygu bulguɲu bala gaḍin*   my wife's yamstick
(318) *bayi yaṛa ŋayguḍindu yabuɲuṇḍindu baŋgun gudaŋgu baḍan*   my mother's dog bit the man

Possessive qualification of topic NPs most commonly involves simple genitive forms (e.g. *ŋaygu, yaṛaɲu*) although -*ḍin* or -*ḍi* forms (the final -*n* may be omitted if -*ḍin* is word final) can be used instead.

The writer is unsure of the difference between *ŋaygu* forms and *ŋayguḍin* forms. Two hypotheses have suggested themselves:
    [1] That properly *ŋaygu* is a qualifier 'my', whereas *ŋayguḍin* is a head in

its own right 'that which belongs to me'. This could at best be a tendency, since forms of both types apparently occur with both meanings. However, it does seem that if an NP does just consist of a genitive form (with no 'possessed' head stated) then this will more often be a genitive plus *-ḏin* form.

[2] That *ŋaygu* forms are preferred in S function, and *ŋayguḏin* forms in O function. Again, if this is the correct underlying principle, there is considerable deviation from it, both forms being encountered in both functions.

A fragment of a secretly recorded conversation illustrates NP possibilities. A speaker asks to whom a large tin standing some way away belongs (text reference IX: 92):

(319) speaker 1: *giɲabawal   waɲuɲu   ḏugi*
              THIS-NOM-IV-LONG WAY who-POSS big-NOM
              ḏanaɲu
              stand-PRES/PAST
              whose big thing is that standing over there?
    speaker 2: *ŋaygu ḏanaɲu*   it's my thing standing [there]
    speaker 3: *giɲagiɲa ḏanaɲu ḏugi*   that big thing is just standing
              there (i.e. unclaimed)
    speaker 2: *ŋaygu bala*   the thing is mine

The tin has no set name in Dyirbal, and there is no head noun in any of the NPs of (319).

The freedom of word order in Dyirbal can be illustrated from:

(320) *bayi   waɲal   baɲul   yaṟaɲu   bulganu*
      THERE-NOM-I boomerang-NOM THERE-GEN-I man-GEN big-GEN
      baŋgun   ḏugumbiṟu   buṟan
      THERE-ERG-II woman-ERG see-PRES/PAST
      woman saw big man's boomerang
and:

(321) *bayi yaṟaɲu ḏugumbiṟu buṟan waɲal baŋgun baɲul bulganu* ⟨as
     (320)⟩

In (320) the words are in their 'norm' (statistically most frequent) relative orders – 7.8. (321) is quite typical of word orders in occurring sentences and was accepted without question by informants.

After his first spell of field work the author wrote that Dyirbal had a remarkably free word order, and 'made up' (321) to illustrate the possibilities. A well-known linguist took exception to this, categorically denied that freedom of word order of this magnitude was possible in any language, and accused the writer of exaggerating. (321) was put to informants at the next opportunity,

and they castigated the writer for asking a trivial and unnecessary question –
'you know that's alright!'. This anecdote is included to show that the lot of
a linguistic field-worker is not always an easy one.

As mentioned in 4.5.1, a topic NP involving a possessive phrase can
constitute a complete sentence:

(322) *ŋaygu balan guda*   the dog is mine (= it's my dog)

In this case the 'possessed' is head of the NP and topic of the sentence.
To refer to the 'possessor' as topic, a quite different construction is
used, involving nominal affix *-bila* 'with':

(323) *ŋaḍa balanambila gudabila*   I have a dog

Further details will be found in the discussion of *-bila* in 6.1.1.

The contrast between (322) and (323) is reminiscent of the distinction made
by Indo-Europeanists between 'belonging' and 'possession' [Watkins, 1967].

The proleptic construction, which involves possessive phrases, is
discussed in 6.1.5.

4.11.2 Involving general genitive inflection. The difference
between the two kinds of genitive inflection is that the simple genitive,
-ŋu, indicates a relation of present possession, whereas the general
genitive, *-mi*, indicates a past owner. There is sometimes, in the use
of *-mi*, an indication that the object referred to still belongs to the
past owner – although it is not currently in his possession – and that
he might return to reclaim his property; in other instances, *-mi* does
not carry this implication. Genitives *-ŋu* and *-mi* thus involve an
aspectual-type contrast, rather like the contrast between *-ŋu* and *-mi*
relative clauses in M (see 5.5.2).

Amongst the uses of the general genitive are:

[1] to describe something that is (perhaps temporarily) abandoned
by its owner. Thus, on encountering some huts built by the neighbouring
tribe, but not at present inhabited by them, a speaker might describe
them: *dulgubarami bala miḍa*.

[2] to describe something lost by its owner:

(324) *baŋulḍin waybalami ŋaḍa ḍiga maŋgan*   I picked up the cigarettes
      of the white man (sc.: that he dropped and lost)

Note that since there is no general genitive inflection of noun markers,
a simple genitive marker accompanies a noun in either simple or general

genitive inflection. Here *baɲulɖin* accompanies – and agrees in case and class with – *waybalami*.

[3] to describe something given by its owner (particularly European-type giving, involving a white man – cf. 2.4):

(325) *ɲayguna yaɽaŋgu   minban   margindu*
       I-o   man-ERG shoot-PRES/PAST gun-INST
       waybalamigu
       white man-GENL GEN-INST
       man shot me with gun from the white man (i.e. that the white man gave or sold him)

[4] to describe something that belonged to someone else, who is now dead. For instance *bayi waɲal ɲumami* might – amongst other interpretations – refer to a boomerang that used to belong to the speaker's (dead) father. Anything which is very old, so that its origin is forgotten, may be described as *ɖuɖabami* 'belonging to *ɖuɖaba*, the mythical first man and creator'.

[5] *-mi* sometimes appears to have a function and meaning similar to that of the ablative *-ŋunu*. The similarities and differences can be seen in:

(326) *ɲaɖa baniɲu yaɽami*   I came from men
(327) *ɲaɖa baniɲu yaɽaŋunu* I came from men

(327) implies that the speaker is returning from a short visit to a group of strangers; (326), on the other hand, states that the speaker was at one time a member of the group, he was 'owned by them'.

[6] other uses of *-mi* that have been noted include: *bala guwalmi buri* 'a name that belonged to the language'; and an idiom-like sentence in D by which a woman can describe her husband's leaving her:

(328) *yumalmi   ɲaygu   wiru   yanu*
       body-GENL GEN-NOM I-GEN-NOM husband-NOM go-PRES/PAST
       ɖagunda
       night-LOC

The literal meaning of (328) is probably 'my husband, who belonged to my body, left in the night'.

-mi genitives are considerably less common than *-ɲu* forms; they appear to inflect like nominals – as do simple genitives – but do not require a catalytic affix:

[1] -*mi* plus instrumental – (325) and:

(329) *ŋayguna baŋgul   waŋaṟu   yaṟamigu*
I-O   THERE-INST-I boomerang-INST man-GENL GEN-INST
minban
hit-PRES/PAST
I was hit by the boomerang that belonged to the man

[2] -*mi* plus dative (text reference XXIV: 4):

(330) *ŋaḍa manigu   wayṇḍiŋura |*
I-SA   money-DAT motion up-*ŋura*
yaŋundaygudayi   buliḍimanmigu
HERE-FROM-DAT-UP-HILL-SHORT WAY policeman-GENL GEN-DAT
budilŋaygu |
take-*ŋay*-PURP
I'll go up [to town] immediately to draw money from the policeman up there

See 6.5.4 for an explanation of *yaŋundaygu*.

General genitives in allative and locative inflection are also attested.
Note that a general genitive can NOT be followed by ablative inflection.

-*ŋu* and -*mi* genitives can occur together in the same NP, at least in a proleptic construction (6.1.5):

(331) *balam wuga ḍiga ŋaygu waybalami*   give me a cigarette from [that packet]
the white man [gave you]!

See also (328).

Gugu-Yimidir is said by Roth to have two genitives, that appear rather
similar to -*ŋu* and -*mi* in Dyirbal: [1] when the article possessed is not in its
real lawful owner's possession, -*ga*; [2] when the article possessed is in its
real lawful owner's possession,...the lawful owner being represented by a
noun: -*we* after a vowel, -*be* or -*e* after a consonant. Note that the -*gu* inflection
in Gugu-Yimidir covers inalienable as well as alienable possession [Roth,
1901*a*: 16]. For further discussion of this point see Haviland [forthcoming].

4.12 Imperative constructions

4.12.1 Positive imperatives.
A positive imperative form can be
obtained from any verbal stem by deleting the final -*l* or -*y*. Every
construction has an imperative version, in which the S or A NP is
either not specified (the unmarked reference is to a second person) or
else has a pronominal as head:

(332) *ŋinda bani*   you come!

(333) *ŋinda giyi bani*   you, that man, come!

(334) *ŋali yana*   let's you and I go!

(335) *bani*   [you] come!

(336) *ŋinda bayi yaṟa balga*   you hit the man!

(337) *ŋinda bagul yaṟagu balgalŋa*   you hit the man!

(338) *balan ḏugumbil ɲinayma*   [you] sit down with the woman OR marry the woman!

(339) *buybayiri*   [you] hide yourself!

(340) *ɲubalaḏi wugalwugalnbari*   you two share it! (literally: give to each other)

And see (393) below for a conjunction of two imperative sentences in which *ŋaḏa* 'I' is the head of one A NP, and *ŋinda* 'you' the head of the other A NP.

Dyirbal is unusual amongst Australian languages (although not amongst languages in other parts of the world) in that its imperative forms involve DELETION of the stem-final consonant, rather than the ADDITION of an affix. No surrounding language has such simple imperatives (although the use of a bare stem as imperative is encountered in a few other Australian languages – for instance, in Aranda [Strehlow, 1944]). Wargamay, to the south of Dyirbal, has imperatives involving *-ga* on to a stem in the *-y* conjugation, and zero on to one from the *-l* conjugation. Mbabaṟam has *-g* on all verbs (this is plainly historically derived from *-ga*). Yidiɲ, to the north, has *-n*, *r*, or zero, depending on conjugation. Gugu-Yalanji, north of Yidiɲ, has *-ga* alternating with zero [R. Hershberger, 1964*b*: 37–8].

4.12.2 Negative imperatives. Negative imperatives are formed by [1] the inclusion of a special particle that can occur anywhere in sequence before the verb (the norm position is immediately preceding it), and [2] a special verbal ending. The details vary from dialect to dialect:

> M – particle *ŋaru*; verbal inflection *-m* replacing stem-final *-l* or *-y*.
> D – particle *galga*; verbal inflection *-m* replacing stem-final *-l* or *-y*.
> G – particle *ŋaru*; verbal inflection *-mu*, with the deletion of stem-final *-y* but the retention of *-l*

Thus:

(341) M   *ŋinda ŋaru wurbam* ⎫
      D   *ŋinda galga wurbam* ⎬ don't you speak!
      G   *ŋinba ŋaru wurbamu* ⎭

(342) M   *ŋinda bayi yaɽa ŋaru balgam* ⎫
       D   *ŋinda bayi yaɽa galga balgam* ⎬ don't you hit the man!
       G   *ŋinda bayi yaɽa ŋaru balgalmu* ⎭

Note that the imperative particle in D, *galga*, is similar in form to the transitive root *galgal* 'leave it', which occurs in all three dialects. Thus, we have positive imperative:

(343) *bala yugu galga balay*   leave the stick there!

and, in D, negative imperative:

(344) *bala yugu galga galgam balay*   don't leave the stick there!

There are semantic as well as phonological similarities between *galgal* 'leave it' and the negative imperative particle *galga* in D (for instance, some varieties of English have a negative command 'leave off doing it!'). It is interesting to note that in Kattaŋ the negative imperative particle is *waɳa*, and there is a root *waɳa* 'leave, stop, leave off' [Holmer, 1966: 78, 1967: 67].

The way in which imperatives are formed in Walbiri sheds considerable light on the situation in Dyirbal and Kattaŋ. In Walbiri (private communication from Kenneth Hale) a negative form – saying what not to do – is usually accompanied by a positive imperative – saying what to do instead; thus 'don't spear the kangaroo, leave it!' (literally = 'leave the kangaroo without spearing it') or 'don't spear the kangaroo, sit!' (literally = 'sit without spearing the kangaroo'). The positive imperative that accompanies a negative command usually involves *yampi* 'leave it', *ɲina* 'sit' or one of a small number of similar verbs. (See also Douglas [1964].) It is possible that a similar situation prevailed at one time in Dyirbal and Kattaŋ; thus (342) in D may originally have been:

*(345) *ŋinda bayi yaɽa balgam/galga*   don't you hit the man, leave him!

in which the negative imperative was marked solely by verbal ending *-m* (which would have been an entirely sufficient marking). Gradually, *galga* may have become an institutionalised part of the negative imperative and moved further forward in the sentence (nowadays, it MUST precede the verb). Note that in Walbiri the construction is still productive; thus with a negative imperative involving 'leave' the positive verb might be 'take' – 'don't leave it, take it!' In Dyirbal, however, *galga* is an established particle, with no verbal overtones, and is used with all verbs, including *galgal* – see (344).

4.13   Other constructions

4.13.1   *-bila*. In place of a tense inflection (or etc.) a verbal stem can take the affix *-bila*; the morphological details are:

   to an *-l* stem – *-bila* is added in D and G, *-ba* in M;
   to a *-y* stem – *-mbila* is added in D, *-mba* in M, *-nbila* in G, with
           the stem-final vowel being deleted in each case.

Roughly, a *-bila* VC indicates that the event referred to by this sentence MIGHT take place, and that this would have unpleasant and undesirable consequences. A *-bila* form would not be used if the consequences could be in any way pleasant. Sentences including *-bila* VCs are often (but not exclusively) used semantically to qualify imperative sentences:

(346) *ŋinda   balan   buni   muymba   baŋgun*
     you-SA THERE-NOM-II fire-NOM put out-IMP THERE-ERG-II
     dambundu   buṛalbila
     dambun-ERG see-*bila*
     you put out the fire lest the Dambun spirit sees it (i.e. and comes to torment us)

and (text reference XXXIC: 28):

(347) *galga   ɲaḍum | ɲaṛa   buṛalbila/ḍigubinagu*
     PARTICLE light-NEG IMP light-NOM see-*bila* ḍigubina-ERG
     ŋanaḍina marbambila
     we(pl)-O frighten-*bila*
     don't light [the fire], lest [Dyigubina spirit] sees the light, and Dyigubina might [come and] frighten us all

See also text XXXIb, lines 4, 5, 12 and 22 (pp. 383–5).

A *-bila* form can occur with a further *-gu* inflection; for instance (text reference XXXIa: 10):

(348) *buni   ɲaḍu   bagul   yugubaragu   banimbilagu*
     fire-NOM light-IMP THERE-DAT-I *yugubara*-DAT come-*bila*-?
     make a fire against Yugubara's coming (i.e. a fire will keep away the unpleasant Yugubara spirit)

and:

(349) *ŋaḍa bala   yugu   madan   waŋgagambilagu*
     I-SA THERE-NOM-IV stick-NOM throw-PRES/PAST step over-*bila*-?
     I chucked away the stick [that was lying across the path] otherwise I would have had to step over it

-gu appears to be the only inflection that can occur after *-bila*. The syntactic status of *-bila* sentences is unclear; to regard them as relative clauses – with the *-gu* a dative inflection – would give a tidy analysis for (348), but would not do at all in the case of (347). It is rather more likely that *-gu* in (348–9) is the purposive verbal inflection; if so, it is being used in a most peculiar way. (See also Appendix A.)

4.13.2 *-ga.* There is a further, rather obscure, verbal ending that occurs in M but not in D or G. Like *-mi* (also only in M) this is added after the unmarked tense inflection, but in this case *-u* is first added to forms ending in *-n*. Thus:

root	*-ga* form
ɲinay 'sit'	*ɲinaɲúga*
bálgal 'kill'	*bálganúga*

-ga indicates that something is irretrievably done, and that there can be no going back:

(350) *bayi yaɽa wayṇḍinuga*   he's already gone uphill (sc. don't wait here, there's no chance of him coming back for you, all you can do is follow him up)

(351) *ŋaḍa wuganuga   / yimbaŋga   / galga*
I-SA give-PRES/PAST-*ga* nothing-LOC PARTICLE
miḍuyirim
take no notice-REFL-NEG IMP
I've given [it all away and it's impossible to retrieve any to give you a share]; there's nothing; don't wait!

(352) *bayi yaɽa buwaɲuga*   man's been told (this might be said to someone who was hoping a certain person would not be told of the addressee's crime; the implication is that now he has been told there is nothing the addressee can do but stop worrying and wait for his punishment)

The difference between *-ga* and *-mi* forms in M can be seen from:

(353) *bayi bulganaɲumi*   he's swallowed [it]
(354) *bayi bulganaɲuga*   he's swallowed [it]

(353) is perfective and implies that he has finished swallowing it; it does, however, leave open the possibility that he has later spewed it up, or that he might do so. (354), on the other hand, is used to describe something that is swallowed and kept down.

Examples of *-ga* are in text xv, line 8 (p. 370), and text xxv, line 31 (p. 390).

4.14 Time qualification

Only complete simple sentences – not their constituent phrases – receive time qualification in Dyirbal. In fact every simple sentence that is not marked as in a particular grammatical relation to another sentence (e.g. by a relative, purposive, or *-ŋura* ending) or specially marked in some other way (e.g. by an imperative, or *-bila* ending) receives an obligatory time qualification: this is realised by tense inflections of the verbs and adverbs in the VC (3.4.3).

A simple sentence that has tense qualification can optionally receive additional time qualification by the inclusion of one of a set of 'time qualifiers'; these can go anywhere in sequence but their norm position is at the beginning of the sentence (preceding even a particle – 4.15.3). A time qualifier can also be included in a relative clause – see (402) below.

Time words include:

> *buluru* 'very many years ago' (the time of mythical creators)
> *bandagay* 'many years ago' (of the order of 100 years or so ago)
> *gubila* 'some time ago' (any time from about a month to about 50 years)
> *ŋudaŋga* DM, *ɽugulu* G 'the other day' (up to a month or so ago)
> *ŋumbuŋga* DM, *ɽugulmba* G 'yesterday'
> *ḍaṇḍaru* DG, *gala* M 'earlier on today'
> *ḍaṇḍa* 'now'
> *gilu* 'later on today'
> *ŋulga* 'tomorrow'
> *ḍada* 'in a few days time'
> *baray* 'next week'

The morphology of time words is dealt with in 3.5, 6.4. As mentioned in 4.7.3, 'time until' inflected forms can be verbalised.

There are two words having the form of noun or verb markers (normally providing locational qualification for a phrase) that can be employed with transferred meaning as time qualifiers for simple sentences. They are *baŋum* 'and then' and *yaŋgunbayḍigu* D, *yaŋgubayḍigu* M 'next week' (cf. *yaŋgungagaɽagabundu* 'next month' which, like *yaŋgu(n)bayḍigu*, is apparently in 'time until' inflection – from *balan gagaɽa* 'moon', *-gabun* 'another'). Note also that the time qualifier *gala* 'earlier on today' in M is identical with the bound form *gala* 'vertically up' (3.2.3). Clearly, 'past time' is correlated with 'up' and 'future time' with 'down' in the Dyirbalŋan worldview. (The examples given appear to be the only locational forms that can have time meaning.)

The words listed above provide 'point' or 'durational' time speci-fication. Another word, *magul* 'meanwhile', explicitly permutes the

time sequence of events referred to by simple sentences qua the sequence
in which the simple sentences appear underlying a discourse (4.5.2):

(355) *gilu bayi yaṛa bagun ḍugumbilgu balgalŋaygu magul wurbaṇu*   man
        has to beat woman later on today, but meanwhile he's talking

(356) *bayi yaṛa baniṇu gaḍilmbaṇu bungili magul ḍugumbilgu balgalŋaygu*
        man came and pretended to be sleeping, but meanwhile hit
        woman

(357) *bayi ṇalŋga wulaṇu/bayi ŋuma yanu gunimarigu/magul balan yabu
        duŋgaraṇu*   child got lost; father went out searching; meanwhile
        mother cried

magul is used in text xv, line 73 (p. 381).
    Two further sentence words give 'appropriate' time qualification:
    [1] *waway* 'too soon' (i.e. sooner than appropriate):

(358) *waway bayi yaṛa yanu*   man went too soon

waway is also used in text xv, line 73 (p. 381).
Note that *gulu* 'not' cannot normally be included in a sentence with
waway although the negative imperative particle *galga* can be.
    [2] *yiṇḍa* 'not yet (although expected)':

(359) *yiṇḍa bayi yaṛa baniṇu*   man has not yet come

Note that *yiṇḍa* can be used with *gulu* 'not':

(360) *yiṇḍa bayi yaṛa gulu baniṇu*   man has not yet come

The difference between these two sentences is that (359) implies that
the man has started out, but has not yet arrived; (360) implies that he
has not yet begun his journey.

yiṇḍa is used in text xxv, line 91 (p. 395).

4.15 Particles

4.15.1 Imperative particles. In G there are two 'exhortative'
particles that occur initially with imperative constructions: *gaḍi* 'try
(to do it)' and *gawu* 'come on':

(361) *gaḍi ŋinda ḍurga*   you try and spear [it]

gaḍi but not *gawu* occurs in D and M. There is a form *gaḍiḍan* – 6.1.6.

A form similar to G *gawu* occurs in many Australian languages, often listed as
an interjection – 1.10.

4.15.2 *aɲḍa.* There is one particle that is phonologically quite anomalous: *aɲḍa*, serving to mark a topic, an action, or a quality as 'new'. This is the only word of any kind in Dyirbal that does not have (and cannot have) an initial consonant; it is possible but by no means certain that it is a loan item from English 'and'.

aɲḍa is syntactically very important; it has three main functions:

[1] if *aɲḍa* occurs sentence initial it introduces a new topic – see text xv, lines 4,5 etc. (p. 369);

[2] if *aɲḍa* occurs immediately before a VC head it introduces a new type of action involving an established topic – see text xv, lines 66, 43 etc. (pp. 380, 375);

[3] if *aɲḍa* occurs immediately before or immediately after an adjective it indicates that the topic has entered into a new state (referred to by the adjective). Compare:

(362) *bayi yaṛa bulgan aɲḍa*
(363) *bayi yaṛa bulgan*

In (363) the referent of the noun is simply described as being big; in (362) the implication is that the increase in size is recent (say, the man was much smaller last time the speaker saw him).

aɲḍa, with an adjective, effectively compares the topic with some earlier stage of itself; in contrast, comparative affix *-baṛa* compares the topic with some other person or thing (6.1.1).

Examples of the adjectival use of *aɲḍa* are in text xv, lines 9, 65, etc. (pp. 370, 379).

4.15.3 Other particles. These particles, most of which do not inflect in any way, provide modal, logical or similar qualification for a complete sentence. They are (with examples from texts or informants, non-normalised):

[1] *gulu* 'not' – a straightforward simple negative (in all but imperative sentences):

(364) *bayi yaṛa gulu baniɲu*   man did not come
(365) *balan ḍugumbil baŋgul yaṛaŋgu gulu balgan*   man did not hit woman

In D *gulu* cannot normally appear in a sentence unless there is a verb (*gulu* must then precede the verb). Thus, although we can say both:

(366) *ŋaygu galbin ḍami*   my son is fat

(367) *ŋaygu galbin ḍamibin*   my son has become fat

there is only a negative version of the second sentence:

(368) *ŋaygu galbin gulu ḍamibin*   my son has not become fat

we cannot have:

*(369) *ŋaygu galbin gulu ḍami*

In M, *gulu* can occur in a sentence involving just an NP, and it then precedes the NP, e.g. *gulu ŋaygu galbin ḍami* 'my son is not fat' (and see 5.9).

[2] *galga* D, *ŋaru* MG 'don't' – the particle in negative imperative sentences – 4.12.2.

[3] *wara* indicates that an event concerned the wrong person or thing as referent of the topic NP:

(370) *bala yugu wara nudin*   wrong tree was cut down

(371) *bayi wara miyandaɲu*   he's the wrong person to laugh (he might be joining in the laughter although he has not heard the joke)

wara is contained in a place-name, mentioned in text xxv, line 29 (p. 390).

[4] *mugu* indicates that it was impossible to avoid doing something that is, in fact, quite unsatisfactory:

(372) *ŋaḍa bayi mugu wugan*   I had to give it to him (although I didn't want to)

(373) *ŋaḍa bala miḍa mugu wamban*   I built the house anyhow (i.e. not well) (but had to finish it because, say, a storm was coming)

(374) *bayi mugu buwaymariɲu*   he had to talk (he didn't want to, but someone made him)

(375) *bala baŋgul yaɽaŋgu mugu banan*   man couldn't help breaking it (and didn't mean to)

(376) *ŋaḍa mugu ḍaŋgaɲu*   I ate [for example, raw or mildewed food] (since it was impossible to cook it, or get fresher food)

(377) *ŋaḍa mugu galgan*   I had to leave [something] (for example, because I couldn't carry it)

The implications of *mugu* are brought out by one informant's comment: 'putting *mugu* in makes it "that's alright"'; see also (415) below.

[5] *yamba* indicates possibility: that the event might occur, be occurring or have occurred:

(378) *bayi yaɽa yamba baniɲu*   man might be coming

[6] *baṇḍul* D, *yuwur* M indicates that the event is always happening:

(379) *baŋgul balgan balan baṇḍul* he's always hitting her

[7] *gana* appears to indicate that an action was performed to a partial extent:

(380) *bayi yaṟa gana ŋambayiriɲu* man half-listened OR man began to realize

[8] *yanda* indicates that the actor tried to perform a certain action, but did not succeed:

(381) *bayi yaṟa yanda baniɲu* man couldn't get through (to here)

[9] *ŋaṟa* indicates that the actor couldn't do something:

(382) *bayi ŋaṟa guninaɲu* he couldn't find it

The difference, if any, between *yanda* and *ŋaṟa* is not understood by the writer.

[10] *ɲurma* indicates that the actor has intended or had tried to perform an action (but has not done so). It often occurs with an implicated VC. For example (text reference XVIII: 18):

(383) *ɲurma ɲaliḍina baŋgul bulgaygu* he had intended to swallow us two (said of the rainbow-serpent, in a myth)
(384) *ɲurma balan ḍugumbil baŋgul wugan* he tried to give it to her (but it got bent, say, and was then unsuitable as a gift)

see also (414–15).

[11] *biya* D, *biri* MG indicates that an event could well have happened but in fact didn't:

(385) *biri ŋayguna baŋgun buwaɲu* she could have told me but she didn't
(386) *biri baŋgul galgaɲu* it's a wonder he didn't leave [her]
(387) *ɲinda biri buṟan* you could have seen [it] (i.e. if you'd looked properly)
(388) *biri ŋaḍa budiɲu* I didn't take any (although I had the opportunity)
(389) *biya ɲinda balay baḍiɲu/ŋaḍabu baḍiɲu* you didn't fall over there (although you might well have), only I did

The affix *-bu* 'only' is explained in 6.7.2. In M the emphasised form *biriḍu* is common (for *-ḍu* see 6.1.1); (290) is a good illustration of the use of *biriḍu*.

[12] *ḍamu* DG, *yurmu* M 'just' (i.e. only this event, with nothing else following on from it);

(390) *ḍamu ŋaḍa bala nudin*   I only tried to cut that

and (text reference XXI: 43):

(391) *gaḍi buṛali ḍamu bani*   go on, come just [for your head] to be looked at [for lice] (i.e. we won't do anything else to you)

The forms *ḍamuru* – involving the affix *-ru* 'again', 6.7.1 – *ḍamuḍilu* – with emphatic *-ḍilu* emphasising that ONLY this event took place – and *ḍamuruḍilu* also occur.

[13] *ŋuri* indicates that an event happens to redress a balance, for example as revenge; or as a gift from A to B in return for an earlier gift from B to A; or someone taking his turn at doing something:

(392) *baŋgun ŋuri ŋaygu wugan/waŋal*   she gave me a boomerang in exchange

(393) *ŋuri   ŋaḍa wargiɲ | wuga   ŋuri   ŋinda*
PARTICLE I-SA boomerang-NOM give-IMP PARTICLE you-SA
ŋaygu   yara   wuga
I-GEN-NOM fishing line-NOM give-IMP
I'll exchange my boomerang for your fishing line

There is also a form *ŋurigabun* (for the nominal affix *-gabun* 'another' see 6.1.1) which can indicate something like 'revenge for an action that was itself revenge'. In text XXV, for example, an old man has two sons and two daughters; the daughters each have a son, grandsons to the old man. The two women kill their brothers and the old man changes into a rainbow-serpent and swallows them, getting even. The women speak to each other inside his stomach (line 64):

(394) *ŋa/ bayi   ŋalingu | ŋuri*
yes THERE-NOM-I we(du)-DAT PARTICLE
yes, that was his turn over us

Then the grandsons decide to burn the old man, as revenge for his swallowing their mothers. One says to the other (lines 79/80):

(395) *ŋali | ḍidugu   yanuli | bagul   ɲaḍulmali*
we(du)-SA *ḍidu*-DAT go-PURP THERE-DAT-I burn-INST-PURP
ŋurigabun
PARTICLE-ANOTHER

let us go for some dyidu wood, to get even again by burning
him with it

ɲuri is also used in text xv, line 20 (p. 372).

[14] *yama* D, *yaḍa* M indicates that an action was performed gently
or slowly (often: TOO gently or slowly):

(396) *yama bayi miyandaɲu*   he laughed softly
(397) *yama ŋaḍa bayi yaɽa balgan*   I just touched the man (i.e. didn't
hit him hard enough)
(398) *bala miḍa yama wambaɲu*   the house was made in such a way
that it has lots of holes in it (i.e. the filling-in material was
plaited too loosely over the frame)
(399) *bayi yama yanu*   he went on tip-toe
(400) *yaḍa baŋgul ŋayguna buwaɲu*   he whispered to me

As regards place in word order:

[i] *gulu, galga/ŋaru, wara* and *mugu* normally immediately precede
the verb; they can come anywhere in front of the verb, never
after it;

[ii] *yamba, banḍul/yuwur* and *yanda* normally immediately precede
the verb; they can come anywhere before or after it;

[iii] *ŋaɽa, ŋurma, biya/biri* and *yama/yaḍa* normally occur sentence-
initial (immediately following a time qualifier if there is one)
but can come anywhere before the verb, never after it;

[iv] *ḍamu/yurmu* normally occurs sentence-initial (after a time word),
but can come anywhere before or after the verb;

[v] *ɲuri* occurs in all positions in word order; the D informant
consistently stated that the norm position was sentence-initial,
while the M informant consistently maintained that the norm
position was immediately after the topic NP.

gana normally occurs immediately before the verb; it is not known
whether it can occur after it.

Some particles can be (at least transitively) verbalised:

(401) *bala baŋgul mugumban bulgaɲu*   he couldn't help but just swallow
it down

Other particles (for instance, *yamba*) cannot be verbalised.

It should be noted that particle and time qualification can be given
to, for instance, a relative clause:

(402) *bayi yaṛa yamba ḍaṇḍaru bungiṇu baniṇu*   man, who might have been lying down earlier on today, is coming

See 6.1.4 for an account of *-gayul* 'the same', which can behave rather like a particle; some nominal affixes – for instance *-gara* and *-maŋgan*, in their coordinating function – have some syntactic similarities to particles – 6.1.1.

4.16 Clitics

An interrogative sentence in Dyirbal contains one or more of:

[1] a noun or pronominal interrogative (3.2.4, 3.3.3) in place of an NP head;

[2] *miṇaṇ* 'how many' (3.2.4) in place of a modifying number adjective in an NP;

[3] a verbal interrogative, as well as or in place of a VC head (3.4.4);

[4] an interrogative noun marker, in place of a noun marker (3.2.4);

[5] an interrogative verb marker, in place of a verb marker or locational nominal (3.4.7);

[6] the time interrogative (3.5) in place of a time qualifier;

[7] simply questioning (rising) intonation, very much as in English;

[8] the interrogative clitic *-ma*.

[1–6] involve wh-questions; [7–8] are polar interrogatives.

-ma is one of three sentence clitics (whose vowels cannot receive major stress) that can be added to the end of the first word of a sentence (whatever this is) and that qualify a complete sentence; the other clitics are *-gira* and (in M only) *-riga*.

-ma questions whether the event referred to by the sentence actually took (or will take) place:

(403) *ŋindama balan ḍugumbil balgan*   did you hit the woman?

or, equally well:

(404) *balanma ḍugumbil ŋinda balgan*   ⟨as (403)⟩

-ma can be used together with an interrogative word, for example:

(405) *waṇḍu ŋinuna balgan*   who hit you?
(406) *waṇḍuma ŋinuna balgan*   who hit you? (the flavour of this Dyirbal sentence is brought out in the informant's gloss 'Who the hell hit you?')

-ma is used in text xxv, line 87 (p. 394).

An interrogative clitic *-ma*, or *-mba*, or *-ba*, occurs in many Australian languages
– 1.9.

   In M, *-riga*, attached to the first word of a sentence, indicates that
the statement of the sentence is definitely true; *-gira* that the statement
SHOULD be correct but that there does remain an element of doubt:

(407) *ŋaḍariga ŋamiṛbin*   I'm very hungry indeed
(408) *ŋaḍa ŋamiṛbin*   I'm hungry

and (text reference XXIV: 57):

(409) *buliḍimandu ŋanban/waŋḍu balgan/yayaŋguriga balgan*   policeman
      asked [him] 'Who killed [Wawa]?'; [he answered:] 'Yaya
      definitely killed him'

(Here *yaya* has been substituted for the person's name, which occurred
in the text; the sentence describes a real event.) When a word in a
sentence is not heard properly, and questioned, the original sentence
is often repeated exactly but for *-riga* attached to that word.
   Examples of *-gira*:

(410) *gilugira gambaṛu biḍili*   it's bound to rain later on today
as against:

(411) *gilu gambaṛu biḍili*   it'll rain later on (with far less certainty than
      (410))
Also:

(412) *bayingira balaru waymbaɲu*   he must be walking about out there
      somewhere

   In D there is no clitic *-riga*, and D *-gira* appears to provide much
the same qualification as M *-riga*, i.e. definiteness:

(413) *ḍaṇḍarugira ban buni baŋgul nudin*   he DID cut that wood today

When asked how to say 'I was going to do it, but in the end I didn't
do it' the informant gave:

(414) *ŋurmagira ŋaḍa yalamali/ yimba ŋaḍa galgan*

and when asked to repeat this said:

(415) *ŋaḍagira ŋurma bala yalamali/ yimba ŋaḍa mugu galgan*
See also (649).

4.17 Interjections

Interjections in Dyirbal have no syntactic function, and most often make up a complete utterance, or else begin an utterance. They include:

> *yimba* DM, *maya* G 'no', 'nothing', 'no more'
> *ŋa* 'yes'
> *ɲu* 'alright'
> *yuwuy* 'that's right'
> *darḍi* DM, *ḍarḍi* G 'it's a good job (that a certain thing has happened)'
> *yagay*, an exclamation to accompany some decisive action, e.g. when hunting, or when bitten by a snake
> *yaburi*, an exclamation of terror
> *mali*, an exclamation of joy when food or drink is coming
> *guguwuy* 'wait there'
> *guguṛgay* 'good job'
> *ḍuru* 'I don't know' D only
> *ŋaɲum* 'I don't know' D and M

(The difference between *ḍuru* and *ŋaɲum* in D may be that *ḍuru* tends to function as the introducer of a sentence, whereas *ŋaɲum* more often occurs in isolation, making up a complete utterance.)

An interjection may commonly be repeated several times, e.g. *ŋa ŋa*, *darḍi darḍi*, *yagay yagay yagay*.

yagay and *yuwuy*, at least, recur in many other Australian languages – 1.10.

yimba/maya are set off from the other interjections on the following grounds:

[1] *yimba* and *maya* can occur with some affixes; the other interjections never do so (there is one exception – *ḍuruḍilu*). The following have been noted:

  (i) locative inflection *yimbaŋga*, *mayaŋga* 'concerning nothing' – see (351)

  (ii) intensifiers *-ḍilu* and *-ban* (6.1.6); thus *yimbaḍilu*, *mayaḍilu*, *mayaḍiluban*

[2] there is a special word in Dyalŋuy corresponding to Guwal *yimba/maya*; it is *ḍilbu* in D and M, *ḍagin* in G. The other interjections exist in the same form in Dyalŋuy.

5 Deep syntax

Chapters 3, 4 and 6 present the basic 'facts' of the grammar of Dyirbal. This chapter attempts to interpret, generalise from, and explain the basic facts; the discussion is thus at a higher level of abstraction, and is more speculative and arguable, than chapters 3, 4 and 6.

5.1 Points to be explained

In the last chapter we mentioned that certain types of sentence were possible but that other, similar types were impossible; that certain combinations of processes were acceptable while others were unacceptable; and that certain inflections which appeared to be rather different in function were identical in form. In no case did we attempt anything more than a limited and ad hoc explanation of these facts. Before we embark on an investigation of the underlying syntactic nature of Dyirbal, it will be useful to list some of the points from chapter 4 that appear to be in need of explanation:

[1] The fact that word order is quite free, except in the case of some particles, and when there is multiple embedding. It should be noted that it is the order of WORDS in sentences that is free, not just the order of phrases (4.5.4, 4.15.3, 7.8).

[2] The apparent conflict between the nominative-accusative paradigm of pronouns, and the nominative-ergative syntax of nouns, adjectives, and noun markers (3.2.1, 3.3.1, 4.1).

[3] Case inflections on pronouns – in particular, the difference between the inflections on singular pronouns in G, and in D and M (3.3.1).

[4] The affix *-ɲa* on nouns – this can occur on a noun in a nominative NP in O function, but not in one in S function (3.2.1).

[5] The fact that dative and locative forms can involve *-ɲa*, but that ergative, instrumental, genitive, allative and ablative forms cannot (3.2.1).

[6] The two types of *-ŋay* construction – the O NP being in ergative inflection in one, but in dative in the other (4.4.2).

[7] The fact that there is only one type of -*ŋay* construction if the head of the O NP is a pronoun; it must then be in dative inflection. (There is thus no pronominal correspondent of a -*ŋay* construction in which the O noun is in ergative inflection – for instance **ŋaḍa ŋinda balgalŋaṇu* is impossible.) (4.4.2).

[8] The unacceptability of -*ŋay* constructions of the type **(92), which involve an O NP in ergative inflection and a verb in purposive inflection; this is somewhat surprising in the light of the acceptability of (65), (67), (69), (90) and (91) (4.4.3).

[9] The phenomenon of topic-chaining, including topic elaboration and reversion (4.5).

[10] Iteration, involving repeated application of the favourite construction (4.5.4).

[11] The -*ŋura* construction, serving to link together successive topic-chains (4.5.5).

[12] The fact that transitive roots in -*ŋay*, reflexive or reciprocal form function intransitively (for instance: they can occur in VCs with intransitive, but not with transitive, roots) (4.9.3, 4.8).

[13] Similarly, the fact that an intransitive root in comitative form functions transitively (4.9.3).

[14] The acceptability of minimal sentences, which contain no verb (4.5.1).

[15] The behaviour of *giṇa*- forms, which occur only in nominative case and function rather differently from other noun marker forms (3.2.2, 4.5.1).

[16] The syntax of participles (4.6).

[17] The similarities of form between certain nominal affixes, and certain verbal affixes (cf. 1.7):

	nominal	verbal
[a]	simple genitive -*ŋu*	relative clause -*ŋu*
[b]	general genitive -*mi*	relative clause -*mi* (M only)
[c]	dative -*gu*	purposive -*gu* ∼ -*i*
[d]	derivational affix -*bila* 'with'	apprehensional -*bila*
[e]	transitive verbaliser -*mal* ∼ -*(m)bal*	instrumentive/comitative -*mal* ∼ -*mbal*

Discussion of [a] and [b] is in 3.2.1, 3.2.2, 3.3.1, 4.11 and 4.10; of

[c] in 3.2.1, 3.2.2, 3.3.1, and 4.4; of [d] in 6.1.1 and 4.13.1 and of [e] in 4.7 and 4.9.

[18] The formal identity of dative and allative inflections on nouns and adjectives, as opposed to the non-identity of these inflections in the case of noun markers and verb markers (3.2.1, 3.2.2, 3.4.5).

[19] The similarity between ergative and locative inflections – morphophonological alternations are the same in each case, the sole difference being that ergative always ends in *-u* and locative in *-a* (3.2.1, 4.10).

[20] The fact that the *-ŋura* inflection on verbs (4.5.5) is identical to the inflection of the verb in a relative clause to a locative noun: *-ŋu + -ra* (4.10).

[21] The formal identity of ergative and instrumental nominal inflections (3.2.1, 3.2.2).

[22] The occurrence of instrumental NPs in both transitive and intransitive sentences (4.9.1).

[23] The fact that the *-ŋay* transformation changes the case of an NP in ergative case, but leaves untouched an instrumental NP (4.9.1).

[24] The two different types of instrumental construction – one involving an instrumental NP and the other an instrumentive VC. Thus (242) and (253), for instance, are synonymous. The way in which one of these constructions was informally described as derived from the other – in 4.9.2 – appears to involve quite *ad hoc* case permutations, etc.

[25] The formal identity of instrumentive and comitative verbal inflections, and the congruence between (242)–(253) and (250)–(261) despite further examples of non-congruence (4.9.2, 4.9.3).

[26] The fact that imperative sentences appear to have some nominative-accusative characteristics – the NP in S or A function can be unspecified (4.12.1).

[27] The fact that locative and allative verb markers and nominals can be verbalised, but not ablative forms (4.7).

[28] The syntax of *aɲɖa* (4.15.2).

[29] The difference in meaning between *-ŋay* and false reflexive forms (4.8.1).

This is not intended as an exhaustive list of points, but rather a sample of some of the more important facts that are suggestive of further, detailed investigation. They are presented in something of the spirit in which standard manuals of 'field phonemics' suggest that, after the phonetic facts of a language are obtained, 'suspicious pairs' should be circled, and their phonological contrastiveness investigated in some detail. Just as some sounds, which one would guess might fall together, sometimes turn out to belong to different phonemes, so some of the syntactic phenomena listed above may not be relatable to each other. For instance, we ARE able to relate together nominal and verbal *-ŋu*, *-mi* and *-gu*, from point [17], but we cannot find any evidence connecting nominal *-bila* with verbal *-bila*; we conclude, at least in the light of our present understanding of Dyirbal, that the formal identity between the *-bila* affixes is coincidental. Similarly, we are not at present able to offer any explanation of points [5], [18–20] and [27–9].

The analogy to phonemics should not be taken to imply that there was any 'procedure' attached to our investigation of Dyirbal syntax. Some of the generalisations of this chapter were formulated before the full range of syntactic facts had been uncovered; indeed, a major part of the information given in the last chapter was obtained during the testing of putative hypotheses concerning the deep syntax of Dyirbal.

5.2   Dyirbal as a nominative-ergative language

5.2.1   A universal hypothesis. All languages appear to have transitive and intransitive sentences, and thus to involve the three syntactic functions 'transitive subject [A]', 'transitive object [O]' and 'intransitive subject [S]'. It appears that there are two basic syntactic types:

[1] nominative-accusative languages, in which S is syntactically identified with A; and

[2] nominative-ergative languages, in which S is syntactically identified with O.

For instance, most of the languages of Europe and of Africa have a nominative-accusative syntax. Nominative-ergative languages are less numerous, but there are a number of well-attested examples – Eskimo, Basque, Chinook and so on. (See also Allen [1951], W. K. Matthews [1953] and Milner [1962].)

It has been suggested that some languages are of a mixed type – showing, for instance, some nominative-ergative characteristics within a basically nominative-accusative syntax. In each such case, when the language has been investigated in more detail and depth, it has become apparent that it is not in fact of a mixed type. Thus G. H. Matthews [1960, 1965: 142ff] mentions that 'the Siouan languages have often been cited as languages which exhibit the ergative relation'; he demonstrates that 'the ergative, in itself, is not a fundamental relation in Hidatsa [a Siouan language], but rather an automatic result of a fundamental distinction between two types of verb phrase, and a general causative construction'.

Halliday [1967–8] has recently suggested that English involves a mixture of nominative-accusative and nominative-ergative patterning. It is easy to show that English is, in fact, pure nominative-accusative in syntax – in the same way that Matthews showed this for Hidatsa – and that what appears to Halliday to be evidence for a nominative-ergative character is the result of transformational changes on a nominative-accusative base. Some of Halliday's examples are causative versions of underlying intransitive constructions – 'he marched the prisoners', which is related to 'the prisoners marched'. The causative transformation is attested for a large number of languages and appears to have some kind of universal status; it is thus quite natural to posit a causative transformation in English. Languages that are morphologically rich often have a special affix that marks a verb as causative – this is the case in Swahili and Turkish, for example; it is quite natural that English, with its rather limited morphological resources, should mark causatives entirely through word order. Halliday's other examples involve the phenomenon of bringing a non-subject NP to the front of a sentence – as in 'the clothes washed [well]', derived from '[someone] washed the clothes'. This can only be done in the presence of a manner adverbal, modal, or other qualifier; the process applies not only to object NPs but also, in appropriate circumstances, to instrumental NPs, locative NPs, and perhaps others [Dixon, 1970c]. Halliday pays no attention to the formulation of strong hypotheses concerning linguistic universals, and is thus happy to accept that English is syntactically 'mixed'. It is, in fact, his failure to set up any 'deep structure' that will deal with the underlying semantic relations, and his insistence on setting up systems which will directly generate 'surface structures', that lead him to suggest that English is part accusative, part ergative in character.

The facts concerning known languages suggest the postulation of a 'universal hypothesis':

Each natural language is either strictly nominative-accusative, or strictly nominative-ergative in syntax.

or, putting the same claim in different words:

In any language, the syntactic function in an intransitive construction (S) is syntactically identified with one and only one of the functions in a transitive construction (that is, either with A or with O).

It appears on the surface that there are two constructional patterns in Dyirbal – the nominal nominative-ergative type, and the pronominal nominative-accusative type (4.1). Dyirbal thus initially appears to be a language of mixed type, and to constitute an exception to the universal

5

hypothesis. In fact we shall show that there is only one UNDERLYING constructional pattern – the nominative-ergative type – that applies to all sentences, whether involving nouns or pronouns or both. A detailed investigation of its syntactic functioning thus reveals Dyirbal to be a 'pure' nominative-ergative language.

5.2.2 Syntactic identification in Dyirbal. Let us first recapitulate the formation of topic-chains from simple sentences involving nouns:

[1] A simple topic-chain involves the identification of the topic NP in one simple sentence with the topic NP in the next; that is, we may have S NP identified with O NP, O with S, S with S, or O with O. Thus from:

(416) *bayi yaṛa baniɲu*   man came here
(417) *bayi yaṛa baŋgun ḍugumbiṛu balgan*   woman hit man

where the *bayi yaṛa* in (416) and (417) have the same referent, can be derived:

(418) *bayi yaṛa baniɲu baŋgun ḍugumbiṛu balgan*   man came here and was hit by woman

And from (417), (416) can be derived:

(419) *bayi yaṛa baŋgun ḍugumbiṛu balgan baniɲu*   man was hit by woman and came here

Similarly in the case of two intransitive sentences with the same S NP, or two transitive sentences with the same O NP.

[2] If we have two simple sentences such that the topic (S or O) NP of the first is identical with the A NP of the second, then the *-ŋay* transformation must be applied to the second sentence before it can be joined to the first in a topic-chain. Thus, from (416) and:

(420) *balan ḍugumbil baŋgul yaṛaŋgu balgan*   man hit woman

can be derived the favourite construction:

(421) *bayi yaṛa baniɲu bagun ḍugumbilgu balgalŋaɲu*   man came here and hit woman

Similarly when the first sentence is transitive, with *bayi yaṛa* the O NP.

[3] If we have two simple sentences such that the A NP – in ergative

inflection – of the first is identical with the topic NP of the second, then they can be joined in a *-ŋura* construction. Thus from (420) and (416) can be derived:

(422) *balan ḏugumbil baŋgul yaṟaŋgu balgan (bayi yaṟa) baniŋura*   man hit woman and then immediately came here

We can now turn to sentences involving pronouns. [1] Consider:

(423) *ŋaḏa baniŋu*   I came here
(424) *ŋayguna baŋgun ḏugumbiṟu balgan*   woman hit me

which exactly correspond to (416–17), with 'I' replacing 'man'. Note that although *bayi yaṟa* is in nominative case in both (416) and (417), the pronoun takes the form *ŋaḏa* in (423) and *ŋayguna* in (424). Now a topic-chain can be formed from (423–4) exactly as it can from (416–17):

(425) *ŋaḏa baniŋu baŋgun ḏugumbiṟu balgan*   I came here and was hit by woman

Similarly, from (424), (423):

(426) *ŋayguna baŋgun ḏugumbiṟu balgan baniŋu*   I was hit by woman and came here

It will be seen that the pronominal S NP in (423) is syntactically identified with the pronominal O NP in (424), even though the pronoun has a different form in the two NPs. The form of the pronominal topic in such a topic-chain is the form it takes in the first underlying simple sentence – thus in (425), with underlying sequence (423), (424), the form is *ŋaḏa* from (423); in (426), with underlying sequence (424), (423), it is *ŋayguna* from (424).

[2] Consider now two simple sentences, involving pronouns, such that the S NP of the first is identical with the A NP of the second. For instance, (423) and:

(427) *ŋaḏa balan ḏugumbil balgan*   I hit woman

which exactly correspond to (416) and (420), again with 'I' replacing 'man'. Note that the pronoun is in the same form in (423) and (427), contrasting with the situation in the nominal sentences – 'man' is in nominative inflection in (416) but in ergative in (420).

However, despite the identity of form of the pronouns in (423) and (427), a topic-chain can NOT be formed from these two sentences by simple coordination. That is, (428) is NOT a permissible Dyirbal sentence:

*(428) *ŋaḍa baniɲu balan ḍugumbil balgan*

Instead, (423) and (427) must be joined by a favourite construction, exactly as in the case of (416) and (420):

(429) *ŋaḍa baniɲu bagun ḍugumbilgu balgalŋaɲu*   I came here and hit woman

A favourite construction must also be used to join two sentences, when the 'identical NP' is in O function in the first and in A function in the second, whether this identical NP is nominal or pronominal. Thus, from:

(430) *ŋayguna baŋgul gubiŋgu mundan*   the gubi took me

and (427), is derived:

(431) *ŋayguna baŋgul gubiŋgu mundan bagun ḍugumbilgu balgalŋaɲu* the gubi took me and I hit woman

[3] Similarly, a topic-chain cannot be formed from (427) and (423) by simple coordination. (432) is, like (428), quite ungrammatical:

*(432) *ŋaḍa balan ḍugumbil balgan baniɲu*

That is, (428) and (432) are ungrammatical in the sense in which *ŋaḍa* is taken to be in syntactic function to the second verb. An informant mentioned that (428) could mean 'I came here and someone hit the woman – not me'; (432) can, of course, mean 'I hit the woman and she came here'.

Instead, (427) and (423) must be joined by a *-ŋura* construction, exactly as in the case of (420) and (416):

(433) *ŋaḍa balan ḍugumbil balgan (ŋaḍa) baniŋura*   I hit woman and then immediately came here

Thus in FORM pronouns show a nominative-accusative patterning but in FUNCTION they exhibit a nominative-ergative patterning, exactly as do nominals. S and O pronouns have different forms but are syntactically identified, exactly as are S and O nouns (that have the same form). S and A pronouns have identical forms in D and M but can NOT simply be identified, exactly as S and A nouns (with different forms) can NOT simply be identified.

This is further borne out by the verbal inflections in relative clauses.

It was mentioned in 4.10 that a relative clause to a topic NP has verbal inflection *-ŋu*, and a relative clause to an A NP (which is in ergative case) has verbal inflection *-ŋuru*. Thus we have, with pronouns:

(434) *ŋaḍa wayṇḍiŋu miyandaɲu*   I laughed as I went uphill
(435) *ŋayguna wayṇḍiŋu baŋgul yaɽaŋgu buɽan*   man saw me going uphill
(436) *ŋaḍa wayṇḍiŋuru balan ḍugumbil buɽan*   I saw woman as I was going uphill

but not:

*(437) *ŋaḍa wayṇḍiŋuru miyandaɲu*

And

(438) *ŋaḍa wayṇḍiŋu balan ḍugumbil buɽan*

could only mean 'I saw woman as SHE was going uphill'.
    Similarly with possessive phrases – 4.11.
    With interrogative pronominal NPs we have (3.3.3):

(439) *waɲa bayi baniɲu*   who [= which man] came here?
(440) *ban ḍugumbil waṇḍu balgan*   who hit the woman?
(441) *waɲuna baŋgun ḍugumbiɽu balgan*   who did the woman hit?

Then, from (439), (441):

(442) *waɲa bayi baniɲu baŋgun ḍugumbiɽu balgan*   who came here and was hit by the woman?

From (439) and (440):

(443) *waɲa bayi baniɲu bagun ḍugumbilgu balgalɲaɲu*   who came here and hit the woman?

From (441) and (439):

(444) *waɲuna baŋgun ḍugumbiɽu balgan bayi baniɲu*   who was hit by the woman and then came here?

From (440) and (439):

(445) *waṇḍu ban ḍugumbil balgan bayi baniɲura*   who hit the woman, and then immediately came here?

Note: These sentences were originally constructed without the *bayi* in (439), (442–5); however, informants suggested that they would be better with a *bayi* in. It appears that an interrogative form does not usually function, by itself, as the topic for a series of sentences.

We thus have a general rule: irrespective of realisational identities or differences, the unmarked syntactic identification between simple sentences is always of an S NP with an O NP (or S with S, or O with O) and NEVER of an S or O NP with an A NP. To identify an S or O NP with an A NP – as in (421), (429), (431), (422), (433) – particular marked syntactic means (a favourite or a -*ŋura* construction) have to be employed.

This rule was in fact anticipated in the summary (4.5.6) of ways of generating a discourse from types of sentence-pairs – these ways do NOT depend on whether the NPs involved are nominal, pronominal or pronominal interrogative.

From our discussion above it thus appears coincidental that identical forms mark functions S and A in the case of all pronouns in D and M, and for non-singular pronouns in G. The case inflections of pronouns are discussed and explained in 5.8.2.

There is one respect in which pronouns seem to have slightly wider syntactic possibilities than nouns. We mentioned in 4.5.2 that an SA pronoun can run through a sequence of intransitive simple sentences, and also through a sequence of transitive simple sentences – as in (117–18). That is, we can identify an A pronominal NP in one sentence with an A pronominal NP in the next (but, as mentioned above, we cannot directly identify O or S with A, or vice versa). However, we can also have a -*ŋay* plus -*ŋura* construction joining two pronominal A NPs, as in (153), or else a 'planning ahead' construction, similar to (160).

It should be noted that utterances have been observed that appear to involve an A NP, whose head noun is in ergative case, joining two sentences, as:

(446) *bala yugu baŋgul yaṛaŋgu nudin/bayi ɲalŋga bunḍun*   tree was cut by man, and child was spanked [by man]

However, this can be accounted for by saying that (446) involves two quite separate sentences, but that the actor is left 'unspecified' (cf. 4.5.1) in *bayi ɲalŋga bunḍun* 'the child was spanked'; in this case the unmarked interpretation would be likely to be that 'the man', who is the actor of *bala yugu baŋgul yaṛaŋgu nudin*, is also the actor for *bayi ɲalŋga bunḍun*. Sequences such as (446) have been encountered relatively infrequently. However, sentences – like (117–18) – joined by *ŋaḍa* are much more frequent and it may be inappropriate to account for them in the same way. Note also that in the 'norm' word order, a non-pronominal NP in ergative inflection comes after any (nominative) topic NP; but an NP involving a pronoun in SA form – whether it marks function S or A in this particular instance – will precede any other NP (7.8).

We began by noticing that, very much as in the case of Hidatsa, Dyirbal appeared on the surface to be a language of mixed syntactic type, and to constitute an exception to the hypothesis that all languages are either strictly nominative-accusative or strictly nominative-ergative. Matthews showed that in Hidatsa the underlying syntactic pattern was nominative-accusative, the apparent ergativity being explainable in terms of a general causative relation. We have shown the opposite for Dyirbal – that the underlying syntax is nominative-ergative, with the apparent accusative nature being the result of special rules for assigning pronominal inflections (5.8.2). Thus, in each case, detailed investigation of apparent exceptions shows that these languages do, in fact, conform to the universal hypothesis.

It was mentioned, in 1.4, that the majority of Australian languages have nouns inflecting in a nominative-ergative pattern, and pronouns following a nominative-accusative paradigm, as in Dyirbal. It is likely that it will be possible to show, by methods similar to those used for Dyirbal, that in each case the underlying syntax is of the nominative-ergative type. It is interesting to note that some languages (for example, Walbiri) have both pronouns and nouns inflecting in a nominative-ergative pattern.

It is something of an oversimplification to say that pronouns often follow a nominative-accusative pattern. In G, for instance, singular pronouns have different forms for each of the three basic syntactic functions, S, A and O; a similar situation prevails in most languages of the eastern seaboard, and for some elsewhere. And in Pittapitta [Roth, 1897], for instance, pronouns show different forms for S, A and O in all persons and numbers. It would be more accurate to say that pronouns often appear on the surface NOT to follow a nominative-ergative pattern, but DO follow such a pattern in their syntactic behaviour.

There are, according to Hale [1970] two groups of languages in which both pronouns and nouns inflect in a nominative-accusative way: one in the north-west, and one centred on the Wellesley Islands in the Gulf of Carpentaria. Hale mentions [1970: 759] that 'it is possible to show that the northwestern languages are only superficially accusative, that they have developed an accusative system of case marking...in quite recent times'.

The best-known representative of the Wellesley Islands group of languages is Lardil. Lardil shows many divergences from the common Australian pattern, sketched in chapter 1, and it is clear that if it is related to other Australian languages (as does in fact seem likely) then it has undergone some rather sweeping syntactic and other changes. It is quite natural to suppose that these have included changes that altered the inflectional system from a nominative-ergative to a nominative-accusative type. It is interesting to note that the object of an imperative sentence is, if a noun, in nominative case (which is the case used to mark transitive and intransitive subject, in non-imperative sentences) and not accusative (which is the case a transitive object must be in, in a non-imperative sentence). Imperative constructions typically preserve archaic patterns (Whitney, 1889: 215; Watkins, 1963, 1970; Kuryłowicz, 1964: 137), and the fact that Lardil imperatives have nominative-ergative overtones suggests that Lardil may have evolved from a language that was of the nominative-ergative type. However, a great deal of descriptive and historical work would have to be done in order to confirm or disprove this hypothesis.

There is thus a good deal of evidence SUGGESTING that proto-Australian (the postulated ancestor language from which all modern languages are descended) had a nominative-ergative type syntax.

Hale [1970] has, somewhat surprisingly, postulated that proto-Australian was of the nominative-accusative type. He is thus suggesting that Lardil and the two or three other languages in the Wellesley Islands group, that have undergone a number of drastic changes of various sorts, retain the original syntactic pattern; and that the two hundred or so other Australian languages, that have probably undergone considerably milder changes of other sorts, have completely changed their syntactic type. As we have already mentioned, Hale believes that the north-western group of nominative-accusative languages have developed an accusative system rather recently; he must thus be suggesting that this group evolved from an ancestor that was of nominative-accusative type, through some intermediate stages in which the syntactic pattern was nominative-ergative.

A full discussion of Hale's proposals, which were meant to be quite tentative and suggestive, would be out of place here. We will, however, mention two fundamental points on which his discussion is misleading:

[1] Hale states that nominative-accusative languages ALWAYS have a voice distinction (i.e. a passive transformation), whereas nominative-ergative languages NEVER do. In fact, having discounted the north-western languages, he is dealing with a single group of 'true accusative languages' – Lardil and its neighbours – which do have a distinction of voice. He fails to mention that Dyirbal has, through the *-ŋay* transformation, a voice distinction; the same is true of Wargamay, to the south of Dyirbal (and see 4.4.2).

[2] Largely to explain this correlation between case and voice, Hale suggests that ergative languages have an underlying accusative structure, but that their transitive sentences are obligatorily in passive form. As evidence to support this suggestion Hale implies that the ergative inflection in ergative languages is frequently cognate with the inflection on the passive agent in accusative languages. In fact, Hale illustrates his discussion with 'artificial examples, using reconstructible morphemes' – that is, the examples are not sentences in any known Australian language. Uncontroversially, he uses *-ŋgu* for the ergative inflection (cf. 1.6). He also uses *-ŋgu* for passive agent in sentences said to be typical of accusative languages, and mentions that 'the striking similarity between passive and ergative surface structures is, of course, exaggerated in the artificial examples because I have used phonologically identical suffixes to represent the ergative ending in B and the agentive ending in A. However, this is not totally devoid of historical reality – in some Australian accusative languages, e.g. Kurama-Yintjipaṇṭi of the Northwest, the agentive

ending in passives is clearly descended from *-ŋgu ~ -lu*, which is the predominant source for the ergative inflection' [1970: 761]. But this is irrelevant,
since Hale has already stated that Kurama-Yintjipanṭi have changed from
ergative to accusative type in quite recent times. It is surely only relevant
to consider passive agentive inflection in languages of the Wellesley Islands
group. In Lardil this inflection is, in non-future sentences, identical to the
genitive inflection, i.e. *-ŋan ~ -kan*; and in future sentences, it is identical to
the non-future accusative i.e. *-n ~ -in* (Hale 1970: 777 and private communication). It is thus not remotely similar to the common ergative inflections
-ŋgu and *-lu*.

We have, in this section, resolved point [2] from 5.1.

5.3   Underlying syntactic relations

5.3.1   The rule S → NP + VP as a linguistic universal. In most
transformational-generative grammars written in recent years the first
(or an early) PS rule is of the form S→NP+VP. It has furthermore
been informally suggested that a rule of this form might be a substantive
linguistic universal; that is, it would feature in the grammar of every
language.

It seems reasonable to assume that there should be some fairly
definite semantic common factor associated with the occurrence of a
substantive universal in particular grammars; in other words, that
a substantive universal should have some universal semantic interpretation.

In Dyirbal every sentence must contain a topic NP. This demands
a first PS rule (using Σ for 'sentence', since S is already pre-empted
for referring to intransitive subject function):

(i) $\Sigma \rightarrow NP + VP$

followed by:

(ii) $VP \rightarrow \begin{Bmatrix} VC_{intr} \\ (NP) + VC_{tr} \end{Bmatrix}$

where the NP of (i) refers to an S or O topic NP, and the NP of (ii)
to an A NP. VC_{intr} and VC_{tr} refer to intransitive and transitive verb
complex respectively.

Now although (i) is in the same form as the first rule in grammars of
other languages, the semantic interpretation of the rule is quite different
in the case of nominative-ergative languages (like Dyirbal) and

nominative-accusative languages (such as English and Latin). This can be seen by subscribing functional labels to the NPs involved:

(iii) FOR NOM-ACC LANGUAGES: $\Sigma \rightarrow \text{NP}_{\text{S or A}} + \text{VP}$
(iv) FOR NOM-ERG LANGUAGES: $\Sigma \rightarrow \text{NP}_{\text{S or O}} + \text{VP}$

Thus, rule (i) occurring in the grammars of nominative-ergative and nominative-accusative languages can NOT be regarded as 'the same rule', in any significant sense in which 'the same' includes 'sameness' of semantic interpretation. That is, the rule $\Sigma \rightarrow \text{NP} + \text{VP}$ cannot be considered a substantive universal.

5.3.2   Universal syntactic relations. However, it appears to be a universal fact that all languages have intransitive and transitive sentences; that is, they have sentence types involving (in the discussion below we leave aside all consideration of the order in which phrases occur in sentences):

(v) $[\text{NP}_{\text{S}}, \text{VC}_{\text{Intr}}]$
(vi) $[\text{NP}_{\text{O}}, \text{VC}_{\text{tr}}, \text{NP}_{\text{A}}]$

We can refer to (v) and (vi) as underlying universal syntactic relations.

These can be represented in several equivalent ways, so long as appropriate conventions are stated. Thus, they could be written just in terms of class labels:

(vii) [NP, VC]
(viii) [NP, VC, NP]

where it is understood that the NP in the binary deep relation (vii) has (universal) syntactic function S, and that the first and second NPs in the ternary relation (viii) have functions O and A respectively.

Alternatively, the relations (v) and (vi) could be expressed just in terms of functional labels S, O and A, and verb subclass labels TR and INTR:

(ix) [S, INTR]
(x)   [O, TR, A]

where it is understood that S, O and A are all realised by the class NP, and so on. There are many other, entirely equivalent, ways of writing (v) and (vi).

Note that in the case of (vii) and (viii) the convention must specify that the three functives in (viii) are ordered. In the functional-label representation, on the other hand, the convention need not specify ordering: O, A and TR can be regarded as an unordered set in (x).

There seems to be no linguistic advantage involved in choosing one of these equivalent methods of representation over the others. We will use the class-label representation below, simply because it is most like contemporary TG conventions.

In addition to the universal deep relations, (v) and (vi), we have the universal hypothesis, discussed in 5.2.1, which claims that each natural language is either strictly nominative-accusative, or strictly nominative-ergative. Taking these in turn:

[1] To say that a language is nominative-accusative is to claim that it syntactically 'identifies' functions S and A. That is, S and A behave identically under a number of syntactic transformations, etc. This can be shown:

(xi)

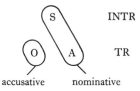

When we say that a language is of the 'nominative-accusative' type we are making a claim about the syntax of the language, and are not necessarily implying anything about its morphology (this, despite the morphological overtones of the name 'nominative-accusative').

Now in many nominative-accusative languages, S and A are marked by the same case inflection – which is referred to as 'nominative' – and O by a different inflection – called 'accusative'. This is the situation in Latin. Case specifications can then be incorporated into the diagram:

(xii)

S   INTR

O A   TR

accusative   nominative

In nominative-accusative languages that lack case inflections, and instead show syntactic function by word order, S and A may occur at the same relative position in a sentence, and O at a different position.

English is basically of this type. Information about position can also be incorporated into the diagram:

(xiii)

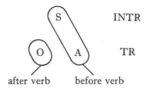

       after verb   before verb

[2] To say that a language is nominative-ergative is to claim that it syntactically 'identifies' functions S and O:

(xiv)

If this syntactic identification is reflected in case marking, the inflection that shows functions S and O is referred to as 'nominative case', and that of A 'ergative case':

(xv)

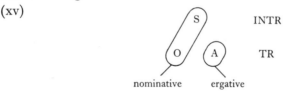

      nominative   ergative

Similarly, nominative-ergative languages that lack case inflection may have S and O occurring in the same relative position in word order, and A in some different position.

It should be noted that a language MAY have nominative-accusative syntax without there being any morphological or word-order congruity between S and A; similarly, in the case of a nominative-ergative syntax, there being no necessary morphological or word-order congruity between S and O. Dyirbal, for instance, has a nominative-ergative syntax (that is, S is identified with O, for transformational operations) but S and O pronouns are always morphologically distinct. There could well be a language with three quite different case inflections (for NPs of all types), marking S, O and A. Yet the language could still conform to the universal hypothesis, in that it could SYNTACTICALLY identify either S with A or S with O.

The discussion above takes no account of a third linguistic type mentioned by Sapir [1917: 86], involving a distinction between pronominal forms of type [A], marking transitive object and INACTIVE intransitive subject, and those of type [B], marking transitive subject and ACTIVE transitive object; Sapir quotes Dakota as an example of a language of this type. (Sapir's examples are also mentioned by Fillmore [1968: 31–5].) It should be noted that Sapir's classification appears to be based primarily on morphological, rather than syntactic, criteria; it is possible that detailed investigation of Dakota would show that SYNTACTICALLY it does conform to the universal hypothesis.

The syntactic type of a language can be shown by appropriate bracketing within the universal deep relations. Thus, having stated that all languages involve (v) and (vi), we can write (v) and:

(xvi) $[[\text{NP}_\text{O}, \text{VC}_\text{TR}], \text{NP}_\text{A}]$

for nominative-accusative languages; as against (v) and

(xvii) $[\text{NP}_\text{O}, [\text{VC}_\text{TR}, \text{NP}_\text{A}]]$

for nominative-ergative languages, with the convention that the 'outermost NP' in the ternary deep relation (that is, the NP outside the inner bracketing) is syntactically identified with the NP in the binary deep relation.

Instead of a universal rule $\text{S} \rightarrow \text{NP} + \text{VP}$, with universal semantic interpretation, we thus have (1) two universal sentence-types (v) and (vi) that have universal semantic interpretation; and (2) a formal universal: there must be syntactic identification of one of the nominal functions in (vi) with the nominal function in (v), leading to a binary first phrase structure rule.

In recent years there have been arguments as to whether the primary constituency 'cut' of a sentence is into three main parts – subject, predicate and object – or into only two parts – subject and predicate (which includes object). (For the first view see Halliday, 1961; Longacre, 1964, amongst others; for the second view see Bloch and Trager, 1942; Chomsky, 1965, amongst others.) It can be seen that there is some truth in both positions: transitive sentences do have – by (1) from the last paragraph – a basically ternary structure (from the point of view of universal semantic interpretation); but – by (2) – they have a basically binary structure from the point of view of the underlying syntax of the language they belong to.

5.3.3   Implicative relation – implicated NPs.
A good deal of the syntax of Dyirbal can be directly explained in terms of the bracketed underlying relations (v) and (xvii). Two instances of the deep relations can be joined in a topic-chain if their outermost NPs are identical. The

-ŋay transformation can be explained as a device for 'lifting' an A NP from the inner brackets of (xvii) and making it the outermost NP – 5.4.2. Relative clauses are accounted for through an NP in one instance of a deep relation 'including' a further instance of a deep relation – 5.5.1; and *-ŋura* constructions in terms of a VP in one instance of a deep relation 'including' a complete topic-chain – 5.6. Possessive and instrumental phrases can be accounted for as special instances of relative clauses – 5.5.2, 5.7.2 – and instrumentive and comitative VCs as special instances of *-ŋura* constructions – 5.7.3–5. Cases can be assigned quite naturally: the outermost NP in an instance of a deep relation will be nominative, and any other NP ergative.

There is one case, marking a syntactic relation, that cannot obviously be accounted for in terms of universal relations (v) and (vi). This is dative, marking what we have called an 'implicated NP' – 4.4.1.

To account for dative NPs, we can postulate a third type of deep relation in Dyirbal, called an 'implicative deep relation', that involves two NPs. This can be represented:

(xviii) [NP →– NP]

with the proviso that the NP at the base of the arrow (the 'implicating NP') must be the outermost NP in some instance of one of the two universal deep relations; that is, it must be a 'topic NP'. The NP at the head of the arrow (the 'implicated NP') is put into dative case.

Thus (cf. (61–2) in 4.4.1):

(447) *balan ḍugumbil baŋgul yaṟaŋgu mundan*   man took woman

is an instance of the ternary deep relation:

(xix) [*balan ḍugumbil*, [*mundal, bayi yaṟa*]]

(We are here leaving aside tense, and other secondary categories.)
When an implicative NP is added:

(448) *balan ḍugumbil baŋgul yaṟaŋgu mundan bagum miraŋgu*   man took woman to [concern herself with] beans

we say that underlying (448) are (xix) and:

(xx) [*balan ḍugumbil* →– *balam miraɲ*]

Implicated NPs are the basis for the syntactic iteration that was described in 4.5.4. Consider (cf. (136)):

(449) *ŋaḍa bayi yaṛa gigan bagun ḍugumbilgu wawulŋaygu ŋinungu mundalŋaygu bagu miḍagu wambalŋaygu*   I told the man to fetch the woman to bring you to build the house

Underlying (449) are the following instances of deep relations:

(xxi)   [*bayi yaṛa,* [*gigal, ŋaḍa*]]   I told man
(xxii)   [*bayi yaṛa →— balan ḍugumbil*]   man implicates woman
(xxiii) [*balan ḍugumbil,* [*wawul, bayi yaṛa*]]   man fetched woman
(xxiv)   [*balan ḍugumbil →— ŋinda*]   woman implicates you
(xxv)   [*ŋinda,* [*mundal, balan ḍugumbil*]]   woman brought you
(xxvi)   [*ŋinda →— bala miḍa*]   you implicate house
(xxvii) [*bala miḍa,* [*wambal, ŋinda*]]   you built house

We see that *bayi yaṛa* 'man' is topic of (xxi) and of the whole sentence (449). In (xxii) *bayi yaṛa* implicates *balan ḍugumbil* 'woman', which is in turn topic of (xxiii). We then have *balan ḍugumbil* implicating *ŋinda* 'you', which is in turn topic of (xxv). Finally, *ŋinda* implicates *bala miḍa* 'house', which is topic of the last deep relation (xxvii).

It will be seen that:

> *bayi yaṛa*   is to *balan ḍugumbil*
> as *balan ḍugumbil* is to *ŋinda*
> as *ŋinda*   is to *bala miḍa*

This suggests calling *balan ḍugumbil, ŋinda* and *bala miḍa* 'secondary topics' (more precisely: first, second and third secondary topics, respectively) of the sentence (449). The iterable favourite construction in Dyirbal can now be described: a topic [/nth secondary topic] has S or O function [/O function] in an instance of a deep relation; it then implicates a first [/n + 1th] secondary topic, and has A function in an instance of a deep relation in which the implicated secondary topic has O function.

Our postulating that an implicated NP is implicated by a topic NP, rather than by a VP, for instance, can be supported in several ways. One is that it provides a good basis for explaining the iterable favourite construction (in the paragraphs above). We say that a topic NP 'implicates' a secondary topic NP; literally, it is likely further to implicate it as 'goal' in a transitive relation in which the topic is 'actor' (although of course it may not go this far – that is, a sentence may be like (448), not being extended by a *-ŋay* VC to a form like (122)). Dyirbal is a very topic-orientated language: a topic-chain may extend for a score or so deep relations, without repetition of the initial realisation of the topic NP; it thus seems intuitively satisfactory to recognise that a topic NP is always the implicator in an implicative deep relation.

An alternative to the postulation of a third 'deep relation' would be to build implicated NPs into the two universal deep relations. We would then have:

(xxviii) $[NP_S, VC_{intr}, (NP_{implic})]$

and:

(xxix) $[NP_O, VC_{tr}, NP_A, (NP_{implic})]$

with some appropriate bracketing within the transitive relation. The disadvantages of this approach are:

[1] The two deep relations we would then have would confuse obligatory functions – S, A, O, TR and INTR – with IMPLIC, which would be optional.

[2] This would involve IMPLIC being included in BOTH deep relations, with the possible implication that it had a slightly different meaning within each relation; in fact the relation between a topic (or secondary topic) NP and an implicated NP is independent of whether the implicator NP belongs to a binary or ternary deep relation.

[3] The basic deep relations are believed to be universal; the implicative relation probably is not – this fundamental difference would be obscured.

[4] In any case a third relation would have to be postulated to account for implicated VPs, whose common factor of 'implicativeness' with implicated NPs would now be obscured (see 5.3.4).

5.3.4 Implicative relation – implicated VCs. We have still to consider implicated VCs. An implicated VC typically occurs non-initially in discourse, usually non-initially in a topic-chain. From the examples in 4.4.3 it will be seen that the action referred to by an implicated NP happens BY VIRTUE OF something referred to by an earlier segment of the topic-chain. Consider (based on text xv, line 52, p. 377):

(450) *bala   barmba   baŋgul   maŋgan   /*
THERE-NOM-IV quartz-NOM THERE-ERG-I pick up-PRES/PAST
bayguli   dibanda | bulabili
bash-PURP rock-LOC two-INTR VBLSR-PURP
the quartz was picked up by him, and bashed on a rock, so that it split into two

Here the picking up of the stone by the actor was a necessary preliminary to his bashing it on the rock; and the bashing caused the stone to split into two.

The purposive inflection of verbals in an implicated VC is plainly the realisation of some syntactic relation holding between the implicated VC and something earlier in the topic chain in which it occurs. We will postulate that this is the same underlying relation as that used to explain implicative NPs. There remains the question of WHAT implicates a VC. There are two main candidates:

[1] We could say that a VC is implicated by the immediately preceding VC in the topic-chain. Thus, in (450) we would have, in addition to the instances of universal deep relations:

(xxx) [*maŋgal →⎯ baygul*]
(xxxi) [*baygul →⎯ bulabil*]

[2] We could say that a VC is implicated by the topic NP (or, in an embedded sentence, the secondary topic NP). Thus we would write:

(xxxii) [*bala barmba →⎯ baygul*]

implying that it is the topic, by virtue of its past history in the topic-chain (here, the fact that the stone has been picked up by the man) that makes possible, or implicates, the action of 'bashing' in the chain of events. Similarly:

(xxxiii) [*bala barmba →⎯ bulabil*]

indicates that it is the history of the topic at this stage of the chain (the fact that it has been bashed on a rock) that is responsible for the action 'breaking into two' entering the chain of events.

However, an implicated VC can occur in the first sentence of a topic-chain, producing a perfectly grammatical sentence. For instance (cf (88–9) in 4.4.3):

(451) *balan ḍugumbil miyandaygu*   woman wants to laugh (i.e. something has happened to make her want to laugh, and she will have to restrain herself to avoid doing so)
(452) *bayi yaṛa yanuli*   man has to go for some reason

If we insisted that VC implicates VC, some non-purposive VC would have to be generated for (451–2), and then deleted. It is plainly more satisfactory to say that the topic NP in each sentence, by virtue of the extra-textual history of its referent, implicates the VC.

Further evidence is provided by the informant's reactions to (cf. (90–1) in 4.4.3 and the discussion there):

(453) *balan ḍugumbil baŋgul yaṛaŋgu balgali*
(454) *bayi yaṛa bagun ḍugumbilgu balgalŋaygu*

These have a degree of synonymy – both refer to 'a man hitting a woman'. However, the unmarked interpretation of (453) is that the woman voluntarily allowed herself to be hit; in (454) it is that the man hits her, probably against her wishes. It seems that if the FIRST sentence in a topic-chain includes a VC in purposive inflection, then the topic is somehow responsible (as 'implicator') for the action happening.

We thus say that it is a topic (or secondary topic) – and the topic's past history: either its textual history in the topic-chain, or the extra-textual history of its referent, or a mixture of both – that 'implicates' a VC.

We have concluded that (1) a dative NP is to be regarded as 'implicated' by a topic (or secondary topic) NP; and (2) a purposive VC is to be regarded as 'implicated' by a topic (or secondary topic) NP. The grounds for saying that the implicative relation is 'the same' in the two cases are:

[1] In each case the implicator is either a topic or secondary topic; there seems to be a syntactico-semantic common factor of 'implication' involved, the difference between the two subtypes of implicative relation being exactly what would be expected with the implicated phrase nominal, in the one case, and verbal, in the other.

[2] There is plainly a close syntactic connection between implicated NPs and implicated VCs. It is true that a sentence can involve an implicated NP but no implicated VC, and vice versa. However, we mentioned in 4.4.3 that if the VC in a *-ŋay* construction is in purposive inflection then the O NP MUST be in dative inflection; thus *(92), for instance, is ungrammatical. Further, all VCs beyond the first in an iterative chain must be in purposive form; this clearly correlates with the fact that all NPs in an iterative chain, beyond those in the first sentence, must be in dative case.

[3] There is phonological similarity. The dative inflection on implicated NPs simply involves the addition of *-gu* to a stem; the purposive inflection on implicated VCs involves the addition of *-gu* to a *-y* stem, and *-i* to an *-l* stem.

It is worth noting that in Wargamay, the language most similar to Dyirbal (and in many other Australian languages), there is no *-i* alternant, purposive inflection involving the addition of *-gu* to a stem of either conjugation.

[4] An implicative relation, commonly marked by *-gu* inflection on both nouns and verbs, has been noted (by other investigators) in many other Australian languages – see Capell [1956: 77] for a general survey.

What is particularly revealing is that the identity between nominal and verbal *-gu* has been commented on in some of the grammars that have been written by people with a native-speaker command of a language. For instance, John Mathew, who was brought up amongst the Gabi and had an excellent command of the language, remarks 'the termination *-gō* is used both with nouns and verbs, thus *dhurī-gō bam-gō yan-gō*, "to-the-scrub for-eggs going". It sometimes means "motion to", sometimes "purpose", being, in the latter case, equivalent to English "for"...' [Mathew 1910: 207].

See also Ray [1907a: 10], and the quotation from Lumholtz in 4.5.1.

In conclusion, we have suggested that, in addition to the universal syntactic relations, (v) and (vi), we must recognise a third deep relation for Dyirbal:

(xxxiv) $[X \rightarrowtail Y]$

where X is an NP that also functions as outermost NP in an instance of one of the two universal relations; and Y is either an NP or a VC. It is likely that the implicative deep relation, (xxxiv), will be needed to account for the underlying syntax of most or all other Australian languages.

In the next sections we attempt a transformational grammar explanation of Dyirbal syntax. It is clear that one of the main requirements on such a treatment be that it show and explain the similarity between implicated NPs and implicated VCs.

In this section we have discussed point [17c] from 5.1.

5.4   Tree representation of topic-chains

5.4.1   Motivation. We shall now give tree representations (so-called P-markers) for Dyirbal sentences – see Chomsky [1965], McCawley [1968]. These will incorporate generalisations that show and explain syntactic functions, and the ways in which simple sentences can be transformed, related together in topic-chains, and so on.

In English, syntactic function is shown by word order; in Dyirbal, word order is remarkably free, syntactic function being shown by case inflection. Tree representations normally provided for English sentences involve a rigid left-to-right ordering of the branches. Now Staal [1967] has argued that in the case of languages with free word order (his example is Sanskrit), it is appropriate to use 'wild trees', that do not involve ordering of branches but are defined as 'configurations of points such that there is one point at the top and each other point is connected with one and only one point above it' [1967: 14]. He thus has a first PS rule S = {NP, VP}, and so on. However, 'wild trees' have at least one considerable drawback – if a certain node dominates two nodes that have the same label, then it will be impossible to distinguish between these latter two; the tree will be ambiguous. That is, in the case of a wild tree involving:

(xxxv)

for instance, it would be impossible to compare the two instances of B between two examples of the same structure. This could only be done by introducing intermediate labels between A and B, for instance:

(xxxvi)

But the introduction of these labels would be exactly equivalent to the introduction of a left-to-right ordering convention, with D corresponding to 'to the left of C' and E to 'to the right of C'. We shall, in fact, want to work in terms of configurations such as (xxxv) (and we shall employ ordered trees).

Staal's wild trees were presumably intended to generate the words of a sentence in any order. However, what they would in fact do is generate the words in any order within a phrase, and phrases in any order within a sentence. We have seen that in Dyirbal words can occur in any order within a sentence, irrespective of phrase membership (cf. (321)). Thus, even if wild trees were used for Dyirbal we would still need a 'scrambling rule' that mixed the words from different phrases.

It is sometimes denied that any language has such a thing as free word order. In fact Dyirbal is an example of a living language with an order that is totally free, with the exception of certain particles and cases of multiple embedding. That is, any order of words CAN occur (although, of course, every possible order does not occur with equal frequency). But despite this, speakers are definitely aware of a norm word order, to which they will more closely adhere in elicitation than in conversation.

It might be thought that, if ordered trees are appropriate for English, then unordered trees, that involve case specification from the deepest stage on, would be suitable for Dyirbal. (xxxv) would be unambiguous if the two occurrences of B were marked by different cases. This would be a possible procedure, but it would be unbearably long-winded and clumsy – the many operations that trees can undergo would each have to be specified for a multiplicity of case alterations. It is considerably simpler and more revealing to state underlying syntactic relations in terms of configurations in ordered trees (the ordering being chosen just to show these relations). Transformational operations then change the configurations in various ways. Cases are assigned by a late rule, in terms of the positions of NPs in the final configurations, after the transformations have applied.

Syntactic functions will be specified within trees in terms of domination, and of relative (left-to-right) ordering. There are a considerable number of ways in which the nodes can be ordered, such that there is sufficient relative ordering for unambiguous identification of syntactic functions. There are no syntactic reasons for choosing one of these ways over the others; we have in fact chosen the order that corresponds most nearly to the underlying 'norm word order' in Dyirbal surface structure (see 7.8). For instance, topic NPs are typically sentence-initial; we adopt the convention that the topic NP is the leftmost NP dominated by Σ.

The ordering we have imposed upon trees does not correspond IN EVERY PARTICULAR to the norm order of words in sentences – for instance, we are not able to show within a tree that a pronominal A NP is likely to precede a topic NP. The correspondence could only be made exact through destroying some important syntactic generalisation shown through trees. (Specification of the exact order in which the phonological realisations of grammatical categories occur is held to be a phonological matter, in the same way that specification of morphological alternations is usually held to be a phonological matter, and so on.)

Thus, the output from the syntactic and phonological components is a sentence in 'norm' word order. We could then postulate a 'scrambling rule' that re-arranges the words in any order. However, it is likely that considerations of discourse structuring ('given' and 'new', or 'focus', or 'theme' or whatever – see Chomsky [1971], Halliday [1967–8], Dixon [1965], etc.) play some part in determining the actual order of words in a discourse. A discourse-generating component would thus act on the output from the language-general syntactic and phonological components, forming a specific discourse appropriate to some PARTICULAR extralinguistic situation.

We have in this section taken account of point [1] from 5.1.

5.4.2   Transitivity; *-ŋay* and reflexive transformations. We can
represent an intransitive simple sentence, [NP, VC], by:

(xxxvii)

and a transitive simple sentence, [NP, [VC, NP]], by
(xxxviii)

where the NP dominated by Σ in (xxxviii) is in O function, and that
dominated by VP is in A function. (Again, we are leaving aside secondary
categories such as tense.)

The leftmost mode dominated by Σ is in each case the topic NP.

We mentioned (4.3) that a VC can involve any number of verbs
and/or adverbals provided that they agree in surface transitivity (and
in final inflection). The requirement on agreement in transitivity is in
the nature of a surface structure constraint. A verb in -*ŋay* form is
surface intransitive (as mentioned in 4.9.3). This can be seen from:

[1] The fact that a -*ŋay* form can occur in a VC with an intransitive
verb, but not with a transitive verb. Thus, in text xv, line 10 (p. 370)
we have:

(455) *aɲḍa   ban   yibiḍaran   baligayul*
  PARTICLE THERE-NOM-II woman-DUAL THERE-TO(DIRECTION)-SAME
  bandalŋaɲu   marin
  follow-*ŋay*-PRES/PAST follow-PRES/PAST
  the two women followed the same route

where the VC involves the intransitive root *maril* 'follow', and the
-*ŋay* form of transitive *baṇḍal* 'follow'.

[2] In G there are different forms of the singular pronouns for
functions S, O and A. Thus, in G:

(456) *ŋaḍa bayi yaṟa banḍan*   I followed man

but

(457) *ŋayba baŋgul yaṟaŋgu bandalŋaɲu*   I followed man

It will be seen that the S form of the pronoun is used with the -*ŋay*
verbal form.

Now:

(458) *balan ḍugumbil baŋgul yaṟaŋgu balgan*   man hit woman

has tree representation:
(xxxix)

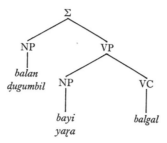

Let us consider *-ŋay* constructions in which the O NP is in ergative inflection (leaving aside, for the time being, those in which the O NP is in dative case). In providing a tree representation for:

(459) *bayi yaṟa baŋgun ḍugumbiṟu balgalŋaɲu*   man hit woman

we have to show: [1] that *bayi yaṟa* is now topic of the sentence; and [2] that the VC is now 'intransitive'.

This is achieved if we represent (459) as:
(xl)

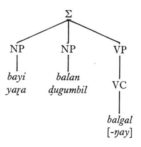

That is, the *-ŋay* transformation lifts the A NP (*bayi yaṟa* in this case), and attaches it to Σ, to the left of any other node dominated by Σ; it also attaches the feature [*-ŋay*] to the VC. By our convention that the leftmost constituent is topic, the A NP is now identified as topic. And we can define transitivity:

  [1] a VC exhaustively dominated by a VP is 'intransitive'; and
  [2] a VC directly dominated by a VP that also directly dominates an NP is 'transitive'.

Now *balgal* [*-ŋay*] in (xl) is, like the VC in (xxxvii), intransitive.

  The *-ŋay* rule can now be written (see also 5.11.2):

(α) -*ŋay* TRANSFORMATION

$$X \;_\Sigma[\quad NP \quad _{VP}[NP \quad VC]_{VP} \quad X \quad]_\Sigma \, X$$

I	∅	2	3	4	5	6 where X is a variable
⇒ I	3	2	∅	4	5	6

$$[\text{-}\eta ay]$$

Cases are assigned, AFTER all transformations have been applied, by the following convention:

(β) CASE MARKING

    (i) the leftmost NP immediately dominated by Σ (i.e. the topic NP) is in nominative case:

    (ii) all other NPs are in ergative case.

Thus *bayi yaṛa* – dominated by VP – in (xxxix) is given ergative inflection, as is *balan ḍugumbil* in (xl), the second leftmost NP dominated by Σ.

    Verbs in reflexive and reciprocal form (4.8.1, 4.8.2) are also surface intransitive. In the case of a true reflexive:

(460) *bayi yaṛa buybayiriɲu*   man hid himself

we have an underlying ternary deep relation. The tree representation for (460) is thus, at the deepest level:

(xli)

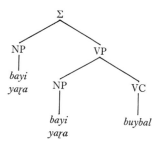

If the A and O NPs have identical referent, the reflexive transformation applies. This deletes the A NP, and marks the VC as reflexive:

(γ) REFLEXIVE TRANSFORMATION

$$X \qquad _\Sigma[NP \quad _{VP}[NP \quad VC]_{VP} \quad X]_\Sigma \qquad X$$

I	2	3	4	5	6
⇒ I	2	∅	4	5	6

$$[\text{refl}]$$

IF the referent of 2 is identical to or included within the referent of 3

The condition in (γ) is formulated to allow for such exceptional, but apparently possible, sentences as (cf. (223)):

(461) *bayi   yaṛa   mala   ḏaŋgaymariɲu*
THERE-NOM-I man-NOM hand-NOM eat-REFL-PRES/PAST
man chewed his finger

which is plainly derived from:

(xlii) $_\Sigma$[*bayi yaṛa mala*$_\text{VP}$[*bayi yaṛa, ḏaŋgay*]$_\text{VP}$]$_\Sigma$

Applying rule (γ) to (xli) we obtain:
(xliii)

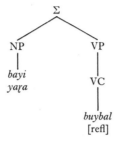

The VC in (xliii) is now intransitive, and the NP receives the same case inflection as does the topic in an intransitive simple sentence. The correctness of this specification can be verified from an examination of pronominal forms used in G. If there were no reflexive rule:
(xliv)

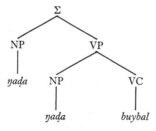

would presumably be realised by G.

*(462) *ŋaḏa ŋaɲa buyban*   I hid me

on the analogy of:

(463) *ŋaḏa bala yugu buyban*   I hid stick

and:

(464) *ŋaɲa baŋgul yaṛaŋgu buyban*   man hid me

However, having applied the reflexive rule (γ) to (xliv) we obtain:
(xlv)

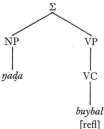

which is realised by:

(465) *ŋayba buybariɲu*

False reflexives involve a rule identical to (α), with the reflexive affix in place of *-ŋay*; we are unable to give any syntactic representation of, or explanation for, the semantic difference (involving actual and potential actions) between *-ŋay* forms and false reflexives (4.8.1).

Reciprocals are discussed in 5.10.1.

5.4.3 Simple topic-chains. Any two sentences that have a common topic NP can be conjoined; all or part of all occurrences of the topic NP after the first can be deleted (4.5.2). Thus, from:

(466) *bayi yaṛa baŋgul gubiŋgu mundan*   the gubi brought man
(467) *bayi yaṛa baŋgun ḍugumbiṛu balgan*   woman hit man

can be formed:

(468) *bayi yaṛa baŋgul gubiŋgu mundan (bayi) (yaṛa) baŋgun ḍugumbiṛu balgan*   man was brought here by the gubi and (he) was hit by woman

This can be described as a simple coordination of Σ's:
(xlvi)

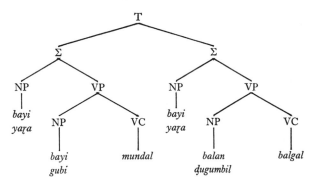

We now have T[opic-chain] as initial symbol, and a first PS rule that
rewrites it as a string of Σ's

In order to exclude Σ-coordinations that would not be bona fide
topic-chains, a constraint is needed, that must be satisfied by any tree:

CONSTRAINT I: The leftmost NPs in the Σ's of a topic-chain coordination
must have common reference. That is, in:

$$_T[_\Sigma[NP\ X]_\Sigma\ _\Sigma[NP\ X]_\Sigma\ldots_\Sigma[NP\ X]_\Sigma]_T$$

$$\text{I}\quad 2\quad\ \ \ 3\ \ 4\qquad\ \ 2n\text{-}1\ \ 2n\quad\text{where n}\geqslant 2$$

the head nouns of 1, 3, ..., 2n-1 must have the same referent. Then,
all or part of that portion of each 2i-1 (i $\geqslant$ 2), that is also included in
2i-3, can optionally be deleted.

The last sentence allows for topic 'elaboration' and 'reversion' –
4.5.2. In (108) the topics of successive parts of the chain were *bayi
burbula*, and *bayi burbula ɽudu* 'the hollow at the back of Burbula's
neck'; these have identical referents of the head nouns. Only the part
of a topic NP that is included in the previous topic NP can be deleted;
thus the elaboration, *ɽudu*, has to be stated in (114).

Constraint I is to be satisfied after transformations have been applied.
Thus, in the case of a coordination:
(xlvii)

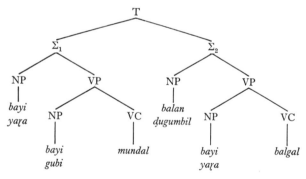

the constraint is not met. However, the *-ŋay* transformation can be
applied to Σ_2, producing:
(xlviii)

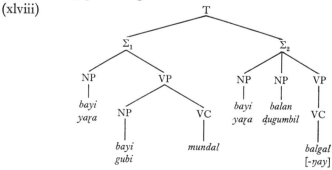

which now satisfies the constraint. The realisation of (xlviii) is:

(469) *bayi yaṟa baŋgul gubiŋgu mundan (bayi) (yaṟa) baŋgun ḍugumbiṟu*
  balgalŋaɲu man was brought here by the gubi and (he) hit
  woman

The subscripts to the Σ's in (xlvii) and (xlviii) etc. are included for ease of
reference; they have no syntactic status.

Note that the PS rules would also generate trees such as:
xlix)

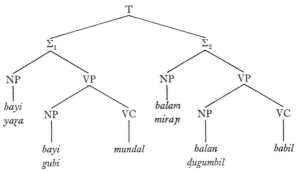

which does not and could not satisfy the constraint. (xlix) is thus
rejected as an 'illicit tree' at the stage of derivation at which constraint
1 is applied.

It should be noted that there is no overt mark of coordination within
a topic-chain (such as English 'and'). Instead, *aɲḍa* can, but need not
always, precede the first occurrence of the topic NP, to mark the
introduction of a new topic-chain (4.15.2).

5.4.4 Topic-chain involving implication.
Consider a favourite
construction, such as:

(470) *balan ḍugumbil baŋgul yaṟaŋgu wawun bagun nayinbagu walmbil-*
  ŋaygu man fetched woman to get girls up

(470) can be the basis for an iterative chain – see 4.5.5. (Note that only
a favourite construction in which the second VC is implicated can be
iteratively extended.) The main Σ, which includes the topic NP, is
plainly *balan ḍugumbil baŋgul yaṟaŋgu wawun; bagun nayinbagu*
wawulŋaygu could be regarded as a complement to the main Σ. We can
in turn have a complement to this complement, and so on – see (133).

This suggests a 'deep' tree representation for (470):

(1)

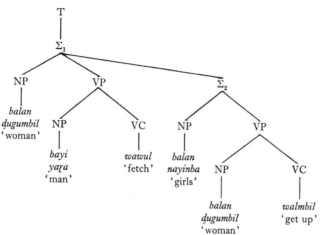

We shall find, in fact, that representations such as (1) are a satisfactory basis for an explanation of implicated NPs and VCs, types of -*ŋay* construction, and iteration generally.

To deal with (1) the second PS rule must be:

(1i) $\Sigma \rightarrow NP + VP \; (+\Sigma)$

This will generate a wide variety of sentences, in many of which the NPs in Σ_2 will be quite different from those in Σ_1. In order to filter out illicit trees, a constraint is needed:

CONSTRAINT II: If Σ_2 is directly dominated by Σ_1, the leftmost NP in Σ_2 and the leftmost NP in Σ_1 must have head nouns with identical reference. That is, in:

$$X \quad {}_\Sigma[NP \quad X \quad {}_\Sigma[NP \quad X]_\Sigma]_\Sigma \quad X$$
$$1 \qquad 2 \qquad 3 \qquad 4 \qquad 5 \qquad 6$$

the head nouns of 2 and 4 must have the same referent.

If constraint II is satisfied, rule (δ-i) must immediately be applied, deleting the leftmost NP from the lower Σ. Thus:

(δ-i) LOWER TOPIC DELETION

$$X \quad {}_\Sigma[NP \quad X \quad {}_\Sigma[NP \quad X]_\Sigma]_\Sigma \quad X$$
$$1 \qquad 2 \qquad 3 \qquad 4 \qquad 5 \qquad 6$$
$$\Rightarrow \quad 1 \qquad 2 \qquad 3 \qquad \emptyset \qquad 5 \qquad 6$$

We can now modify the case marking convention as follows:

(β') CASE MARKING
  (i) the leftmost NP immediately dominated by a Σ, that is itself immediately dominated by T, is in nominative case;
  (ii) the leftmost NP immediately dominated by a Σ, that is itself immediately dominated by Σ, is in dative case;
  (iii) all other NPs are in ergative case.

And add a convention regarding the marking of VCs:

(ϵ) VERB MARKING
  (i) a VC whose lowest dominating Σ is itself directly dominated by Σ is placed in purposive inflection (and does not receive any tense inflection);
  (ii) a VC whose lowest dominating Σ is directly dominated by T (with the T not dominated by any other node) is placed in tense inflection corresponding to the tense feature on the T.

It will be noted that constraints I and II are very similar. In the first case the topic NPs of coordinated sentences must have common reference; in the second case the topic NP of an embedded sentence must have common reference with the topic of the matrix sentence.

Conventions (β') and (ϵ) give a similar account of implicated NPs and implicated VCs. The topic NP of a lower sentence (after all transformations have applied) is marked as dative; the VC of a lower sentence is marked as purposive. Thus the common 'implicative nature' of dative NPs and purposive VCs is explained in terms of their occurrence in a lower sentence. It was suggested in 5.3.4 that in each case it is the topic NP which is the 'implicator'. This is compatible with the representation provided here, in which Σ_2 is directly dominated by Σ_1 (whose only obligatory constituent is the topic NP – see 5.4.6), and then strongly related, by constraint II, to Σ_1's topic.

Constraint II, like constraint I, applies after the *-ŋay* transformation; the case marking convention applies after the constraints. We thus have ordering:

  1. (α) *-ŋay* transformation – optional
  2. constraints I and II
  3. (δ-i) lower topic deletion (obligatory if constraint II is satisfied)
  4. (β') case and (ϵ) verb marking

We can now apply these rules, constraints and conventions to the generation of crucial sentences, discussed in chapter 4.

Firstly, consider:
(lii)

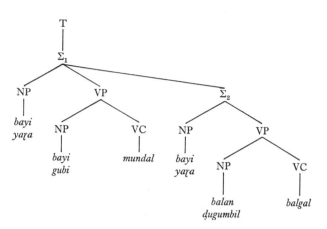

This immediately satisfies constraint II. Rule (δ-i) now applies, obligatorily deleting the topic of the lower sentence:
(liii)

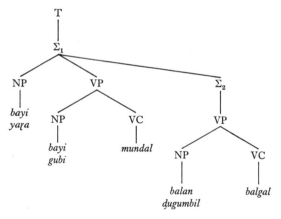

The case convention (β') now marks *bayi yaṛa* as nominative, and both *bayi gubi* and *balan ḍugumbil* as ergative; note that there is no NP immediately dominated by Σ_2. Convention (ϵ) marks *balgal* as purposive; *mundal* is given an appropriate tense inflection. (liii) is thus realised as:

(471) *bayi yaṛa baŋgul gubiŋgu mundan baŋgun ḍugumbiṛu balgali* man was brought by the gubi to be hit by the woman

The tree representation of (471) can be compared with that of (468). The parts of (468) are coordinated together in (xlvi), simply as events involving a common topic. In contrast, (lii–liii) clearly show that in (471) the man was brought here IN ORDER THAT he should be hit by the woman.

Constraint I mentioned that the repeated topic in (xlvi) could be deleted, or could be retained in whole or in part. Rule (δ-i) states that the repeated topic in a lower sentence must obligatorily be deleted. That is, according to rule (δ-i), it would be ungrammatical to insert *bayi yaṛa* after *mundan* in (471). A check of Dyirbal texts bears out this principle – a topic NP can be repeated before a VP in tense inflection, but not before a purposive VP. In (108), in 4.5.2, for instance, it can be seen that *bayi* of the topic NP is repeated before *balbaliyaraɲu*, in unmarked tense inflection, NOT before a verb in purposive inflection.

5.4.5   Iteration. Secondly, let us return to (l), the tree representation of the favourite construction (470). As it stands (l) does not satisfy constraint II; the topic NP of Σ_1 is *balan ḍugumbil* whereas that of Σ_2 is *balan nayinba*. However, we can apply the *-ŋay* transformation in the cycle on Σ_2, deriving:

(liv)

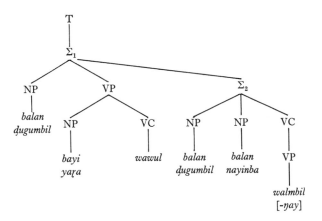

The tree now satisfies constraint II. Transformation (δ-i) must be applied, deleting the leftmost NP in Σ_2, and producing:

(lv)

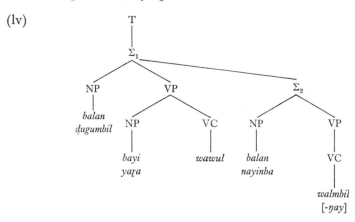

Cases are now assigned to (lv) by convention (β′). *balan ḍugumbil*, the leftmost NP of the highest Σ, is put in nominative inflection; *balan nayinba*, the leftmost NP of the lower Σ, is put in dative inflection; *bayi yaṛa* is given ergative inflection. By convention (ε), *walmbilŋay*, the VC of the lower Σ, is given purposive inflection; *wawul* is given the appropriate tense inflection. Thus (470) results.

Thirdly, we can consider an iterative construction, involving multiple application of the favourite construction. Consider (cf. (449) in 5.3.3, and (136) in 4.5.4):

(472) *ŋaḍa bayi yaṛa gigan bagun ḍugumbilgu wawulŋaygu ŋinungu mundalŋaygu bagu miḍagu wambalŋaygu*   I told the man to fetch the woman to bring you to build the house

The tree representation underlying (472) would be:

(lvi)

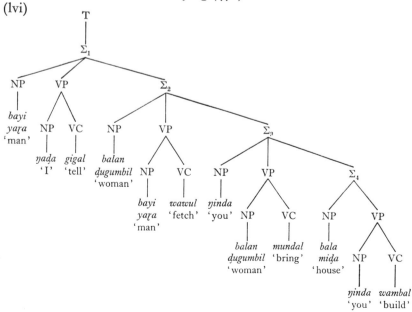

Now each pair of Σ must satisfy constraint II – that is, the constraint must be satisfied by (Σ_1, Σ_2), by (Σ_2, Σ_3), and by (Σ_3, Σ_4). In (lvi) none of the pairs satisfy the constraint – in each case the leftmost NP of a lower sentence is NOT identical with the leftmost NP of the next higher sentence.

We first apply the *-ŋay* transformation three times – in the cycles on Σ_4, Σ_3 and Σ_2. This produces:

(lvii)

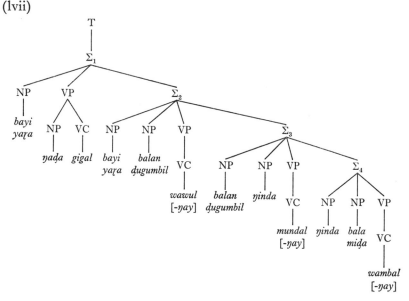

We now apply constraint II, starting with the topmost Σ. Constraint II holds for Σ_1 and Σ_2; the leftmost NP in each Σ is *bayi yaṛa*. Transformation (δ-i) is at once applied, deleting the leftmost NP in Σ_2, and producing:

(lviii)

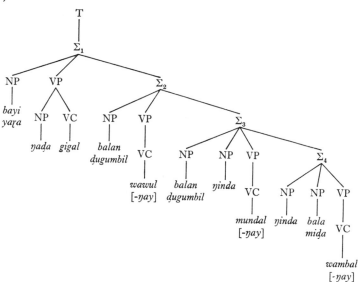

Constraint II is now applied to Σ_2 and Σ_3; it is satisfied, since *balan ḍugumbil* is the leftmost NP in each Σ. Transformation (δ-i) must now be applied, deleting *balan ḍugumbil* in Σ_3:

(lix)

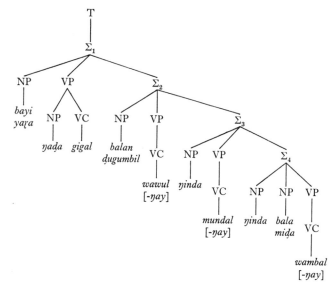

Finally, constraint II is applied to Σ_3 and Σ_4; it is satisfied, since *ŋinda* is the leftmost NP in each Σ. Rule (δ-i) now deletes *ŋinda* in Σ_4, producing:

(lx)

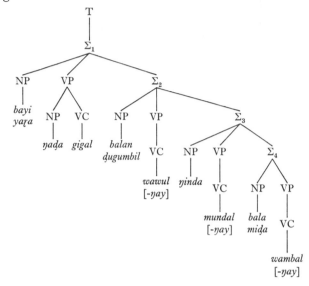

Cases are now assigned to the NPs and VCs of (lx) by conventions (β') and (ϵ). *bayi yaṛa* is placed in nominative case. *balan ḍugumbil*, *ŋinda* and *bala miḍa* are all given dative inflection – each of these phrases is the leftmost NP immediately dominated by a Σ that is itself immediately dominated by a further Σ. The remaining NP, *ŋaḍa*, is placed in ergative case (for an explanation of pronominal inflections see 5.8.2). *wawulŋay*, *mundalŋay* and *wambalŋay* are given purposive inflection, by convention (ϵ). We thus generate (472).

Note that the *-ŋay* transformations were, as is customary [Chomsky, 1965], applied to (lvi) in cycles starting with the LOWEST Σ. However, pairs of Σ's are checked to see if constraint II is satisfied, starting with the TOPMOST (or leftmost) Σ. The lower topic deletion rule, (δ-i), can be regarded as an intrinsic part of the constraint; it is only AFTER rule (δ-i) has applied to Σ_1 and Σ_2 that Σ_2 and Σ_3 meet the constraint; and so on.

In 5.4.3 we described simple topic-chains, in which each sentence comments on the topic that is stated, in nominative case, in the first sentence, and optionally repeated in any later sentence. In the case of an iterated sentence, such as (472), we explained in 5.3.3 that the primary topic, *bayi yaṛa*, can be taken as implicating a secondary topic, *balan ḍugumbil*; this then implicates a further secondary topic, *ŋinda*; and so on. The implication of a secondary topic can be regarded as a 'subroutine' within the topic-chain. The subroutine can at any time be terminated; the chain will then naturally revert to comment on the original topic. For instance, (472) could be extended by *miyandaṇu* 'laughed', which must be taken to refer to the topic, *bayi yaṛa*. Thus:

(473) *ŋaḍa bayi yaṛa gigan bagun ḍugumbilgu wawulṇaygu ŋinungu mundalṇaygu bagu miḍagu wambalṇaygu (bayi) (yaṛa) miyandaṇu* man was told by me to fetch the woman to bring you to build the house; (and the man) laughed

with tree representation:
(lxi)

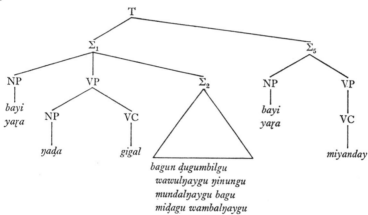

where Δ abbreviates structural detail identical to that dominated by Σ_2 in (lx).

It was mentioned in 4.5.4 that a simple sentence can be extended by more than one implicated NP, and that we can have a (non-iterative) 'double favourite construction' built upon a single topic. Thus (cf. (138)):

(474) *balan ḍugumbil baŋgul yaṛaŋgu gigan bagun bunigu mabalṇaygu bagun nayinbagu ḍaymbalṇaygu* man told woman to light fire and find girls

which has underlying representation:
(lxii)

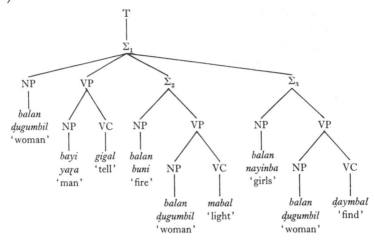

The -*ŋay* transformation is applied to Σ_2 and Σ_3. Constraint II, and rule (δ-i), are now applied to the pairs (Σ_1, Σ_2) and (Σ_1, Σ_3), in either order. Appropriate case and verb marking then produces (474).

It will now be seen that (472) is actually five-ways ambiguous; however, the 'unmarked' interpretation is that represented in (lvi).

5.4.6   Further cases of implication. We saw in 4.5.1 that there exist in Dyirbal perfectly grammatical 'minimal sentences' that involve no VP. In such cases the NP must involve a demonstrative, or an adjective, or something similar. Sentences of this type are discussed in 5.9 below; essentially, we have to allow underlying representations:
(lxiii)

T
|
Σ
|
NP

Thus, parentheses should be inserted round VP in rule (li).

We also noted, in 4.4.3 and also in 5.3.4, that the FIRST sentence of a topic-chain can involve an implicated VC, as in (cf. (89), (451)):

(475) *bayi yaṛa yanuli*   man has to go
(476) *balan ḍugumbil baŋgul yaṛaŋgu balgali*   woman has to be hit by man

Sentence (475) can be represented by:
(lxiv)

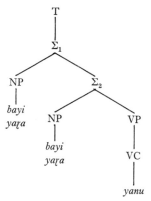

This satisfies constraint II, the lower *bayi yaṛa* is deleted by rule (δ-i), and (475) results.

Similarly, for (476):
(lxv)

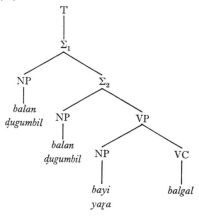

This satisfies constraint II; rule (δ-i) deletes the leftmost NP in Σ_2, giving:
(lxvi)

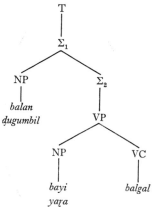

which, with case and verb markings according to (β') and (ϵ), gives (476).

We thus have two kinds of evidence suggesting that VP is an optional constituent in a Σ not dominated by any higher Σ.

There are also sentences that involve a dative NP but no verb in -*ŋay* or in purposive inflection – 4.4.1. Thus (cf. (62), (448)):

(477) *balan ḏugumbil baŋgul yaṛaŋgu mundan bagum miraŋgu*   man took woman to (concern herself with) beans

In this case we set up, as underlying tree representation of (477): (lxvii)

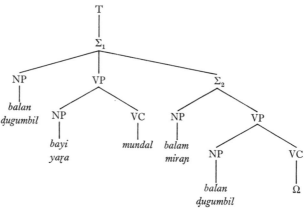

where Ω is a dummy verb. The -*ŋay* transformation then applies to Σ_2, putting it in a form in which constraint II will be satisfied; rule (δ-i) deletes the leftmost NP in the lower sentence and a special rule has to be set up to excise the dummy verb. This produces: (lxviii)

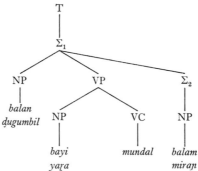

which is, by the case marking convention (β'), realised as (477).

An alternative treatment would be to suggest that the underlying tree representation of (477) was simply (lxviii), without invoking any 'dummy verb'.
However, constraint II could not be satisfied in the case of a deep representation
(lxviii), and the tree would have to be rejected as illicit. Thus, if we wished
to persist with this alternative, constraint II would have to be modified.

We gave evidence above suggesting that VP was optional in a top Σ. It might
appear quite natural to extend this, and say that VP is optional in any Σ, so
that it would be in order to have Σ_2 consisting just of NP, in a deep representation like (lxviii). However, this would then allow trees of the form:
(lxix)

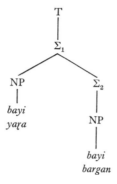

giving:

*(478) *bayi yaṛa bagul bargangu*   man [is going] to [concern himself with]
wallaby

We noted in 4.5.1 that sentences such as (478), containing just a nominative
NP and a dative NP, do occur in texts and conversation, but are firmly rejected
by informants as ungrammatical. (It seems that, if Σ_1 dominates Σ_2, then Σ_2
must contain a lexical verb if Σ_1 does not contain one.)

The fact that the alternative treatment of (477) – setting up (lxviii) as deep
representation – (1) goes against constraint II; and (2) results in the generation
of ungrammatical sentences such as (478), suggests that our original treatment
– giving (lxvii) as deep representation of (477) – is to be preferred.

Our treatment of (477) thus effectively specifies it as an 'elliptical'
version of the favourite construction. In 4.4.1 we mentioned, when
discussing (62 = 477) that 'in contrast to allative, which indicates just
"motion towards", a dative NP indicates the expectation of implication
of the beans (as goal) in some imminent action involving the woman
(as actor)'. It thus seems appropriate to include Ω in the deep, but not
in the surface, representation, as a token of the 'imminent action'.

The rule deleting the dummy verb in (lxvii) can be stated:

(ζ) DUMMY VERB DELETION

X	$_\Sigma$[X	VP	$_\Sigma$[X	VC]$_\Sigma$	X]$_\Sigma$	X
1	2	3	4	5	6	7
⇒ 1	2	3	4	∅	6	7

IF $5 = \Omega$

and 3 is non-null

The condition is required to limit the deletion of Ω to sentences in which there is a VP in Σ_1, thus preventing the generation of sentences such as (478).

5.4.7 Types of -ŋay construction. In 4.4.3 we mentioned that:

(479) *balan ḍugumbil baŋgul yaɽaŋgu balgan*   man hit woman
(480) *balan ḍugumbil baŋgul yaɽaŋgu balgali*
(481) *bayi yaɽa bagun ḍugumbilgu balgalŋaɲu*
(482) *bayi yaɽa bagun ḍugumbilgu balgalŋaygu*
(483) *bayi yaɽa baŋgun ḍugumbiɽu balgalŋaɲu*

are grammatical, but that:

*(484) *bayi yaɽa baŋgun ḍugumbiɽu balgalŋaygu*

is unacceptable – see examples (65), (67), (69), (90–2), above.

Clearly, it will be a crucial test of the syntactic representation we have adopted to see whether it can explain the acceptability of (479–83) and the unacceptability of *(484).

(479) and (480) have been dealt with above, in terms of trees (xxxix) and (lxv) respectively. (483) has the same underlying representation as (479), but involves the -ŋay transformation, producing (xl).

(482) has underlying representation:

(lxx)

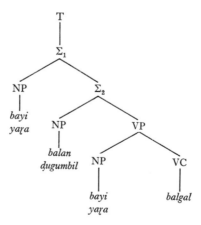

Applying the *-ŋay* transformation to Σ_2 we get:
(lxxi)

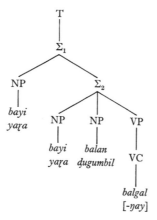

This satisfies constraint II, and rule (δ-i) then applies, producing:
(lxxii)

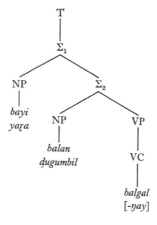

which is, by conventions (β') and (ϵ), realised as (482).

(481) is more difficult. We mentioned in 4.4.2 that the difference between (483) and (481) lies in the fact that in (483) the actor, goal and action simply make up an event; (481) implies something more – that the actor positively implicates the goal in the event. In terms of the underlying syntactic relations discussed in 5.3, we would say that underlying (479) is:

(lxxiii)   *[balan ḍugumbil, [balgal, bayi yaṛa]]*

And that in the case of (483) *bayi yaṛa* is lifted out of the inner brackets, giving:

(lxxiv)   [*bayi yaṛa, balan ḍugumbil, balgal*]

With case conventions similar to (β′), (lxxiv) would be realised as (483). We could then say that underlying (481) are (lxxiv) and:

(lxxv)   [*bayi yaṛa* →– *balan ḍugumbil*]

The case conventions would specify that any NP to the right of →–, in a relation such as (lxxv), is to be marked as dative. Thus, on the basis of (lxxiv) *balan ḍugumbil* should be in ergative case, and on the basis of (lxxv) it should be in dative. We can then introduce a further, quite natural, convention that a dative specification prevails over an ergative specification; this explains how *balan ḍugumbil* in (481) is, in fact, in dative case. (The 'naturalness' of this convention is in terms of the positive nature of dative specification, as against the negative nature of ergative marking – 'all other NP's' – in (β′).)

We can now provide a tree representation for (481). The verb, which inflects for tense, must be in Σ_1; NP *bagun ḍugumbilgu*, which is in dative inflection, must be in Σ_2. Thus:

(lxxvi)

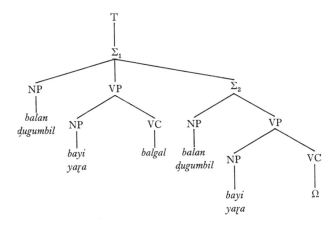

In trees such as (lxvii) the dummy verb symbol, Ω, indicates an 'anticipated' action involving the referents of the lower sentence NP's. It seems syntactically most straightforward to use the same symbol, Ω, in the syntactically analogous tree (lxxvi). However, if a more sematically orientated deep structure is required, the verb *balgal* could be repeated in the lower sentence of (lxxvi) in place of Ω; in this case rule (ζ) would have to be extended to delete a lower sentence VC when it is identical to the VC of the next higher sentence.

Now the *-ŋay* transformation is applied in the cycle on Σ_2 and also in the cycle on Σ_1, producing:

(lxxvii)

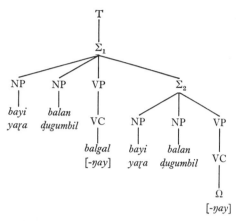

This satisfies constraint II, and rule (δ-i) applies, deleting the leftmost NP in Σ_2 under identity with the leftmost NP in Σ_1. Rule (ζ) applies, deleting Ω and its accompanying feature *[-ŋay]*:

(lxxviii)

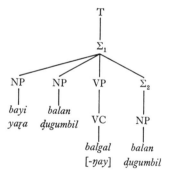

In order to derive (481) we need a rule which deletes the non-topic NP in Σ_1 under identity with the leftmost NP in Σ_2. This can be stated:

(η) IDENTICAL NP DELETION

	X	$_\Sigma$[NP	NP	X	$_\Sigma$[NP	X]$_\Sigma$]$_\Sigma$	X
	I	2	3	4	5	6	7
$\Rightarrow$	I	2	$\emptyset$	4	5	6	7

IF 3 and 5 have identical reference and 2 and 3 are directly dominated by the same Σ node

Applying rule (η) to (lxxviii) we get:

(lxxix)

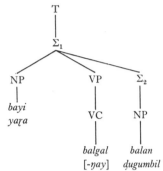

which, applying case convention (β'), is realised as (481).

Rules (δ-i) and (η) could be regarded as particular cases of a general 'identical NP deletion' rule (cf. Rosenbaum [1967] for identical NP deletion in English). It appears that NPs directly dominated by a Σ have an 'order of seniority':

[1] leftmost NP in top Σ

[2] leftmost NP in lower Σ

[3] non-leftmost NP in any Σ

If two NPs are identical, the more junior one is deleted. Thus, rule (δ-i) deletes an NP of type [2] under identity with an NP of type [1]; rule (η) deletes an NP of type [3] under identity with an NP of type [2].

A general 'identical NP deletion' rule of this type perfectly brings out the 'topic orientation' of Dyirbal syntax: a topic NP has the highest level of seniority, a secondary topic NP the next level, and any other NP the lowest level.

We have now accounted for (479–83). We find, in addition, that it is impossible to generate *(484) through the type of tree representation we have adopted. To obtain the form *balgalŋaygu*, *balgal* would have to be in a lower Σ; the possible underlying representations are (lxxi), or some variant of (lxxvii), with *balgal* in place of Ω. In each case *balan ḏugumbil* would finish in dative inflection, and not in ergative case as required for *(484). Thus *(484) is ungrammatical, according to our grammar of Dyirbal. The grammar passes the test imposed by (479–84).

Finally, we can review tree representations for the two kinds of favourite construction, from 4.5.3. The first type involves the second verb in purposive inflection; in the second type, both verbs take a tense inflection:

(485) *balan ḍugumbil baŋgul yaṛaŋgu mundan bagum miraŋgu babilŋaygu*
(486) *balan ḍugumbil baŋgul yaṛaŋgu mundan bagum miraŋgu babilŋaɲu*
man brought woman to peel beans

The tree representation for a *-ŋay* construction of the first type has already been described in (l), (liv), (lv).

The tree representation for (486), a tree representation of the second type, would be:
(lxxx)

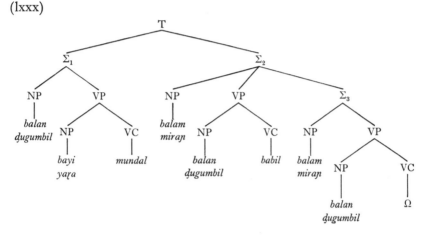

That is, we have Σ_1 and Σ_2 joined together as a 'simple topic-chain' (5.4.3) and then Σ_3 as a complement within Σ_2.

The *-ŋay* transformation applies in the cycles on Σ_3 and Σ_2, producing:
(lxxxi)

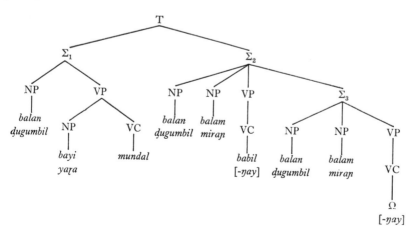

Now Σ_1 and Σ_2 satisfy constraint I, and Σ_2 and Σ_3 satisfy constraint II.
Applying rules (δ-i), (η) and (ζ) we obtain:
(lxxxii)

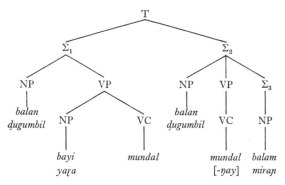

which, after the application of conventions (β') and (ϵ), yields (486).

An alternative to having Σ_2 dominated by Σ_1, as in (l), would be to have Σ_2 directly dominated by the VP that is directly dominated by Σ_1 (thus bringing this description of Dyirbal into closer alignment with recent grammars of English complementation – e.g. Rosenbaum [1967]). The arguments against doing this include: [1] we can have a lower sentence Σ_2 without there being a VP in Σ_1, as in (lxiii–lxv) etc.; [2] to attach Σ_2 to Σ_1 ties in better semantically with our conclusion in 5.3, that it is the topic NP (the only obligatory constituent of Σ_1) that 'implicates' the leftmost NP, and the VC, of Σ_2. In 5.6 we suggest that a *-ŋura* construction involves a node T immediately dominated by VP.
    It will be noted that the representations given above differ in some respects from the ad hoc analyses provided in chapter 4. For instance, in 4.5.3 we suggested that underlying (486 = 125) were *balan ḍugumbil baŋgul yaṛaŋgu mundan bagum miraŋgu* and *balam miraɲ baŋgun ḍugumbiṛu babili*. Here, we are effectively claiming that the first underlying sentence is simply *balan ḍugumbil baŋgul yaṛaŋgu mundan*. It should be stressed that the remarks in chapter 4 were entirely ad hoc suggestions, and were independent of any rigorous theoretical interpretation.

We have, in 5.4.2–7, dealt with points [6], [8–10], [12] and [17c] from 5.1.

5.5 Relative clauses and possessive phrases

5.5.1   Relative clauses. In 4.10 we mentioned that if the topic NP of any sentence has the same referent as any NP of a second sentence, then the (rest of the) first sentence can be embedded as relative clause on to the NP of the second sentence. We will, in tree representation, attach the Σ node of a relative clause to the appropriate NP node of the matrix sentence.

Thus, underlying (cf. (286)):

(487) *bayi yaṛa baŋgul yuṛiŋgu bagalŋaɲu banagaɲu*   man who had speared kangaroos is returning home

is:

(lxxxiii)

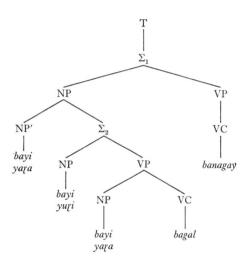

To produce such a tree, we need a PS rule:

(lxxxiv)   NP → NP′ (+Σ)

This does not necessitate the revision of any rules described above. The *-ŋay* transformation, for instance, moves a complete NP, including its relative clause.

Now, as stressed in 4.10, the leftmost NP in Σ$_2$, and NP′, must have identical reference. This can be expressed through a further constraint (that is remarkably similar in form to constraints I and II):

CONSTRAINT III

In: X $_{NP}$[NP′ $_Σ$[NP   X]$_Σ$]$_{NP}$ X
     I   2   3   4   5

the head nouns of 2 and 3 must have identical reference.

As it stands, (lxxxiii) does not satisfy constraint III. We have first to apply the *-ŋay* transformation in the cycle on Σ_2, deriving:
(lxxxv)

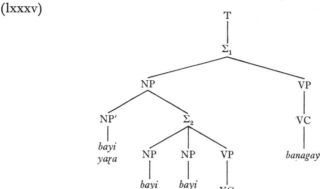

This satisfies constraint III. The topic NP in Σ_2 must now be deleted; this suggests an extension of rule (δ-i):

(δ-ii) LOWER TOPIC DELETION. Obligatorily applied if constraint III is satisfied.

	X	NP[NP'	Σ[NP	X]Σ]NP	X
	I	2	3	4	5
⇒	I	2	∅	4	5

From (lxxxv), rule (δ-ii) derives:
(lxxxvi)

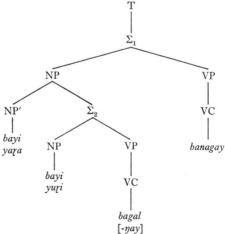

which is the surface structure of (487).

We must now add to the case and verb marking conventions:

(β'-iv) If NP immediately dominates NP', then NP' has the same case marking as NP.

(ϵ-iii) A VC, whose lowest dominating Σ is dominated by NP, is given the inflection REL (i.e.-*ŋu*(*ɲɖin*)-) plus the case inflection of the NP.

Revised conventions (β') and (ϵ) now give (487) as the realisation of (lxxxvi).

The rules and conventions allow the generation of all types of relative clauses. (We have not thus far given rules for generating locative nouns; once this is done, it is a simple matter to allow for modifying relative clauses – see 4.10, and also the discussion at the end of 5.6.)

In M only there are two kinds of relative clause. A clause marked by a -*mi* inflection will refer to an action that is completed, while a -*ŋu* clause refers to something that is still going on. Relative clauses in M have thus to be marked for aspect, in much the same way that topic-chains, in all dialects, are marked for tense. One of several ways of achieving this is through features attached to T and Σ nodes:

(lxxxvii) $T \rightarrow T [\pm$ future tense]
(lxxxviii) $\Sigma \rightarrow \Sigma [\pm$ perfect aspect]/NP'-

We must now revise part of the verb marking convention for M:

(ϵ-iii') If a Σ is dominated by NP, the aspect feature of the Σ is transferred to the nearest VC that is dominated by the Σ; this VC also receives the inflection REL, and the case inflection of the NP.

Participles can be accounted for in terms of the relative clause construction – see 5.9.

5.5.2 Possessive phrases. We have not so far discussed the syntactic status of possessive phrases. At first sight it might seem that the relation between a possessive phrase and the NP it qualifies should be treated as an additional type of syntactic relation. We shall show that it can more revealingly be treated as a special instance of the relative clause construction.

There are a number of striking similarities between relative clauses and possessive phrases:

[1] PHONOLOGICAL IDENTITY OF INFLECTIONS. Simple genitive inflection, *-ŋu*, is identical with the inflection verbs bear in relative clauses. General genitive inflection, *-mi*, is identical with the inflection in a second type of relative clause that occurs only in M.

[2] DISTRIBUTIONAL SIMILARITY. Genitive *-mi* is far less common than the simple genitive *-ŋu*; in addition, *-mi* inflections occur only on nouns and adjectives, whereas *-ŋu* also occurs on noun markers and pronouns. As we have mentioned, *-mi* relative clauses are only attested in the M dialect.

[3] SEMANTIC SIMILARITY. In M, *-ŋu* relative clauses involve 'imperfective' and *-mi* clauses 'perfective' aspect. In all dialects, genitive *-ŋu* indicates a relation of present possession, whereas *-mi* indicates a past owner.

[4] SYNTACTIC SIMILARITY – 1. A sentence can consist of just a noun-plus-marker and a possessive form – see (102), (322); similarly, a sentence can consist of just a noun-plus-marker and a relative clause – see (304), (306).

[5] SYNTACTIC SIMILARITY – 2. Both relative clauses and possessive phrases can qualify nouns in nominative, ergative, dative, instrumental, and locative cases. There is a difference in that possessive phrases – but not relative clauses – can qualify nouns in allative or ablative case.

[6] SYNTACTIC SIMILARITY – 3. An NP in a relative clause can be qualified by a further relative clause; similarly, a possessive phrase can be qualified by a relative clause.

[7] MORPHOLOGICAL SIMILARITY. Both a genitive noun, and the verb of a relative clause, agree in case with the noun they qualify.

This suggests that the underlying representation of a possessive phrase be a relative clause whose VC is the dummy verb POSS[esses]. Thus, corresponding to (cf. (307)):

(488) *bayi waŋal baŋul yaɽaŋu baŋgun ḏugumbiɽu buɽan*   woman saw man's boomerang

we have:
(lxxxix)

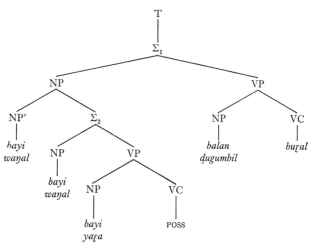

NOTE: Trees are simplified by the omission of NP′ nodes, unless there is a sister relative clause.

(lxxxix) satisfies constraint III, and rule (δ-ii) then applies, deleting the leftmost NP of Σ_2. Case and verb marking conventions yield:
(xc)

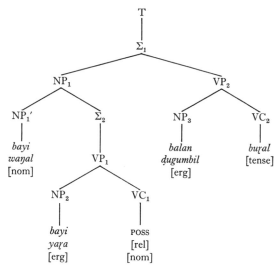

We can now suggest a rule that replaces the case feature of NP_2 by the features attached to POSS, and deletes POSS.

Generally, where [case] stands for whatever case has been assigned to the NP by (β'), the rule can be stated:

(θ) POSSESSIVE FORMATION RULE

$$\text{X} \quad {}_{\text{NP}}[\text{NP}'_{[\text{case}]} \quad {}_{\Sigma}[\text{NP}_{[\text{erg}]} \quad \text{VC}_{[\text{rel}]\,[\text{case}]} \quad]_{\Sigma}]_{\text{NP}} \quad \text{X}$$

I	2	3	4 5	6 7 8	9
I	2	3	4 7 8	Ø Ø Ø	9

IF 6 = POSS

and 6 does not involve the feature [-*ŋay*]

In M, the feature [± perfect aspect] will occur with [rel] and will be transferred to NP_2 by rule (θ).

We have suggested that alienable possession involves an underlying relative clause with verb POSS; but that, by rule (θ), the inflections on POSS are transferred to the 'possessor' NP, POSS itself being deleted.

Applying rule (θ) to (xc) we get:

(xci)

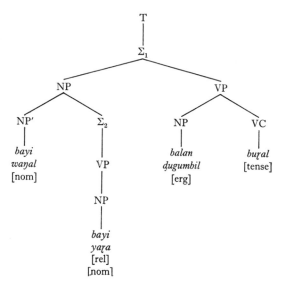

which is precisely (488).

It should be noted that as rule (θ) is stated it must apply after case and verb marking conventions (β') and (ϵ). It would be possible to formulate the possessive formation rule in such a way that it applied after constraint III but before (β') and (ϵ). We could have a rule that simply deleted POSS:

(θ') POSS DELETION

X	$_\Sigma$[X	VC]$_\Sigma$	X
I	2	3	4
I	2	$\emptyset$	4

IF 3 = POSS

and 3 does not have the feature [-ŋay]

Now, convention (ϵ-iii) would have to be modified. In the case of a normal relative clause (illustrating by reference to nodes in (xc)) we can think of Σ_2 as 'handing down' a feature [rel] to VP_1 and then to VC_1; similarly, NP_1 hands down its [case] feature to Σ_2 to VP_1 to VC_1. In the event that VC_1 has been deleted before (ϵ-iii) is applied, we can adopt the convention that the features [rel] and [case] are handed down by VP_1 to the only node it now dominates, that is NP_2, and replace the case marking that NP_2 has from (β'-iii).

These two treatments are entirely equivalent, and there appears to be no syntactic reason to prefer one over the other.

Dyirbal has no sentences in which the SUBJECT of an underlying possessive relative clause is identical with some noun in the matrix sentence (sentences like 'The man who owns the dog is coming'). That is, we cannot allow a possessive clause similar to the relative clause in (lxxxiii), with the -ŋay transformation having to be applied to obtain a tree that satisfies constraint III. Rules (θ) and (θ') have been phrased to exclude illicit possessive clauses – if POSS is marked as [-ŋay], the structural description for (θ) and (θ') is not satisfied, and POSS will not be deleted. The dummy POSS should not appear in surface structure, and so an illicit surface string results.

Sentiments like 'The man who owns the dog is coming' are dealt with through a quite different construction, involving -*bila* – see 4.11.1 and 6.1.1.

Dyirbal has no purely grammatical verbs (that is, verbs without concrete reference) such as 'to be', 'to become', 'to have', 'to make (cause to do)'. It is thus entirely natural that POSS should not be realised as a phonological word, but should trigger rule (θ), and be deleted by that rule.

The argument supporting this 'naturalness' can be formulated as follows. It appears that all grammars involve certain deep grammatical relations such as 'possession', 'adjectival predication', 'causation', and so on. In some languages these relations are realised through separate words ('surface verbs') such as English 'have', 'be', 'make (do)', etc. In other languages they are realised not as separate words, but either overtly as affixes, or covertly through the triggering of transformational rules that affect other constituents. Now it is an empirical fact (although admittedly of a type that linguists have paid little attention to in recent years) that languages tend EITHER to have 'surface verbs' realising most or all of these deep relations, OR ELSE to have 'surface verbs' realising none of them. Dyirbal is of the latter type, and it is in view of this that it is said to be 'natural' for POSS not to be realised overtly as a surface verb, but only covertly through its triggering of rule (θ).

Dixon [1969] compares the syntax of relative clauses and possessive phrases in Dyirbal and Gumbaiŋgar, and concludes that the two languages demand a common set of rules, but with different conditions and slightly different ordering. The *-mi* affix on nouns and verbs was not clearly understood when this paper was written, and discussion was confined to *-ŋu* forms. The additional data given above provides further strong support for the solution given in 1969.

Further discussion of *-mi* in M is in 10.3.2.

In this section we have dealt with points [17a–b] from 5.1.

5.6   *-ŋura* constructions

The *-ŋura* construction can be represented by a tree in which VP dominates a second T node. Thus, underlying (cf. (147)):

(489) *bala yugu baŋgul yaɽaŋgu madan (bayi yaɽa) wayṇḍiŋura*   man threw stick and then he immediately went uphill

is:

(xcii)

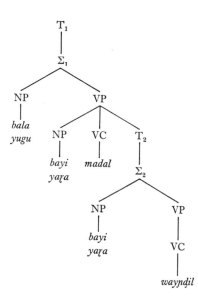

In such a tree, the leftmost NP dominated by VP, and the topic of T_2, must have identical reference. This requires a further constraint:

CONSTRAINT IV

In: X $_{VP}$[NP X $_T$[$_\Sigma$[NP X]$_\Sigma$ $_\Sigma$[NP X]$_\Sigma$...$_\Sigma$[NP   X]$_\Sigma$]$_T$]$_{VP}$ X
   1   2 3   4 5   6 7   2n 2n+1   2n+2
     where n $\geqslant$ 2
     the head nouns of 2, 4, ..., 2n must have identical reference

Then, all or part of the portion of each 2i (i $\geqslant$ 2) that is also included in 2i-2 can optionally be deleted.

Tree (xcii) meets this condition. Convention (β') assigns cases to the NPs in (xcii) that correspond to those in (489). To deal with the inflection on *wayɲḍil* a further clause must be added to convention (ϵ):

(ϵ-iv) a VC whose lowest dominating Σ is dominated by T, that T being itself dominated by VP, is given inflection *-ɲura*.

As a further example, consider (cf. (153)):

(490) *bala yugu baŋgul yaṛaŋgu nudin/ (bayi yaṛa) bagul ɲalŋgagu bunḍulɲaɲura*   man cut tree [until he stopped to] spank boy

This has tree representation:
(xciii)

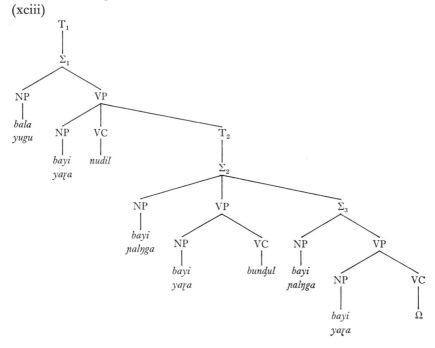

(xciii) does not satisfy constraint IV. We can, however, apply the *-ɲay* transformation in the cycles on Σ_3 and Σ_2; and then, constraint II being satisfied for Σ_2 and Σ_3, transformations (δ-i), (ζ) and (η) apply, producing:

(xciv)

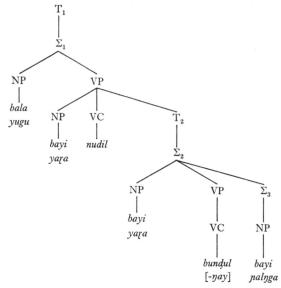

which does satisfy constraint IV. Conventions (β') and (ϵ) now give (490) as the realisation of (xciv).

A *-ɲura* construction, which involves a VP dominating T, is rather different from a purposive construction, in which Σ dominates Σ. A purposive construction establishes a 'subroutine' WITHIN a topic-chain; this may terminate at any point, and the chain will then continue with comment on the original topic – 5.4.5. *-ɲura* marks the termination of one topic-chain and the establishment of a new one; it is impossible in this case simply to 'revert' to the original topic.

There is no strong syntactic evidence pointing to the 'correctness' of our tree representation of *-ɲura* constructions – as there was, for instance, supporting the analysis of possessive phrases in 5.5.2. The most we can say is that the analysis given above agrees well – in terms of constraint IV – with conditions in other parts of the grammar, and explains the case inflections in the *-ɲura* construction.

Empirical evidence in favour of this analysis lies in the occurrence of sentences with more than one verb in *-ɲura* inflection, e.g. *balan baŋgul balgan (bayi) ɲinaɲura miyandaɲura* 'he hit her, sat down, and laughed'. Here we appear to have a genuine topic-chain, dominated by VP.

Point [20] in 5.1 drew attention to the fact that the -ɲura inflection on verbs is identical to the inflection a verb receives in a relative clause to a locative noun – -ɲu + -ra, as in (298–9). The fact that certain verbs select only locative qualifiers, whereas others occur only with allative or ablative forms (3.4.6) suggests that locational qualifiers be regarded as constituents of VP. Thus, underlying (cf. (298)):

(491) *bayi yaṛa ɲinaɲu buniŋga ɲaduɲura baŋgun ḍugumbiṛu*   man is sitting by fire woman made

is (using LocP for the constituent involving verb marker and/or locational noun):
(xcv)

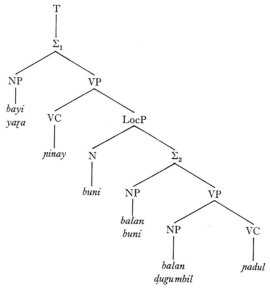

It is interesting to note the syntactic similarity between the -ɲura verb in (489) and the verb in -ɲu + -ra inflection in (491). In each case the VC is dominated by VP which is dominated by Σ; this is in turn, at one step remove, dominated by VP. The difference is that in the first case the intermediate node is T and in the second case LocP. This syntactic similarity – coupled with phonological identity – may be entirely coincidental; it may, on the other hand, provide a clue to the historical origin of -ɲura constructions (see also 5.7.6). Further work is required on this issue.

We have, in this section, dealt with point [11] from 5.1.

5.7   Instrumental and comitative constructions

5.7.1   The data. In 4.9 two types of construction were given, one involving an instrumental NP, the other an instrumentive VC. Thus (cf. (242), (253)):

(492) *balan ḍugumbil baŋgul yaɼaŋgu baŋgu yuguŋgu balgan*   man is hitting woman with stick

(493) *bala yugu baŋgul yaɼaŋgu balgalman bagun ḍugumbilgu* ⟨as (492)⟩

These two sentences have a high degree of synonymy – their main difference lies in the fact that a different NP is identified as topic in each case. A bilingual informant explained that (493) meant 'that stick that killed that woman...' whereas (492) was 'that woman that was killed...'.

In 4.9.2 we informally suggested that (493) might be regarded as transformationally derived from (492). However, the changes that were listed are quite ad hoc, and do not interrelate with any other processes in the grammar. Constructions like (492), and those like (493) can in fact be related together rather more revealingly, in terms of the types of tree representation already described.

5.7.2 Instrumental NPs. We posit that underlying both (492) and (493) are two ternary deep relations:

(xcvi) [*bala yugu*, [INST, *bayi yaɼa*]]   man INST stick

(xcvii) [*balan ḍugumbil*, [*balgal*, *bayi yaɼa*]]   man hits woman

INST is a dummy verb that can be glossed 'uses (as instrument)'.

In the case of (492), (xcvi) functions as a relative clause qualifying the NP *bayi yaɼa* in (xcvii). The deep representation of (492) is thus:

(xcviii)

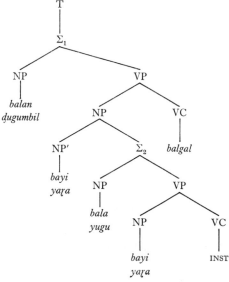

To satisfy constraint III, the *-ŋay* transformation must be applied in the cycle on Σ_2, producing:
(xcix)

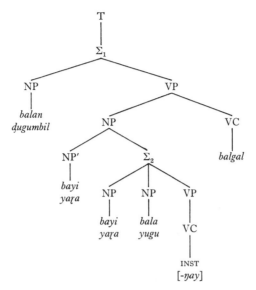

Rule (δ-ii) deletes the lower *bayi yaṛa*. Conventions (β') and (ϵ) give, as the realisation of (xcix):

(494) *balan ḍugumbil baŋgul yaṛaŋgu baŋgu yuguŋgu* INST[*-ŋay*] [rel] [erg] *balgan*

The three NPs in (494) are in the correct inflections, qua (492). If we include a rule deleting INST and all features attached to it, the surface structure of (492) will result. The rule has the form:

(ι) INST DELETION

X	VC	X
1	2	3
⇒ 1	∅	3

where 2 = INST

A revised statement of this rule, following the discussion in 5.8.1, is in 5.11.2

We have thus described a possessive phrase as a special type of relative clause in which the dummy verb INST is simply deleted; there is no transfer of features to an NP as there was in the case of POSS. This representation explains:

[1] the identity of ergative and instrumental inflections. In terms of the representation above, an instrumental NP receives ergative marking according to convention (β'), by virtue of being non-topic NP in a relative clause.

[2] the occurrence of instrumental NPs in both transitive and intransitive sentences. A relative clause involving INST can qualify either an A or an S NP (5.8.1). Thus, for instance:

(c)

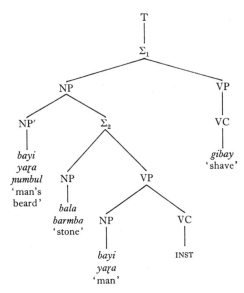

yields (cf (251)):

(495) *bayi yaṛa ɲumbul baŋgu barmbaŋgu gibaɲu*   man shaved his beard with stone

[3] the fact that an instrumental NP is, unlike an ergative NP, unaffected by the *-ŋay* transformation.

Suppose that the *-ŋay* transformation had applied in the cycle on Σ_1 in (xcix). In the absence of rule (ι), the realisation would have been

(496) *bayi yaṛa baŋgu yuguŋgu* INST[*-ŋay*] [rel] [nom] *baŋgun ḍugumbiṛu balgalŋaɲu*

INST in (496) has the case feature [nom], whereas in (494) it has [erg]. However, rule (ι) deletes INST and all its features. The final realisation is thus still (492). The vital point here is that the *-ŋay* transformation does not affect the inflection on an NP WITHIN a relative clause.

5.7.3   Instrumentive VCs. We suggest that (xcvi) and (xcvii) also
underlie (493), but that in this case (xcvi) is in *-ŋura* construction with
(xcvii). The tree representation is:
(ci)

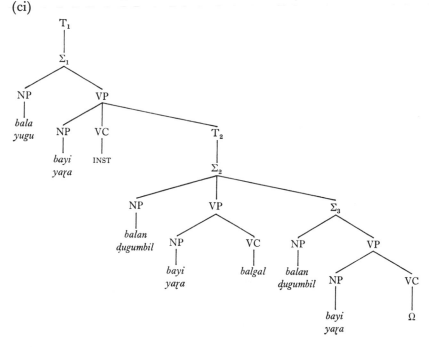

(xcvii) is 'repeated' with dummy verb Ω, as complement to itself, to
account for the fact that the *-ŋay* construction is of the 'O NP in
dative case' variety – cf. (481) in 5.4.7.

The *-ŋay* transformation is applied in the cycles on Σ_3 and Σ_2.
Constraint II is satisfied for the pair (Σ_2, Σ_3) and rules $(\delta\text{-i})$, (ζ) and
(η) apply, yielding:

(cii)

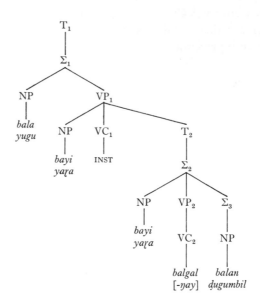

Constraint IV is now satisfied for the pair (Σ_1, Σ_2); the lower *bayi yaṛa* is optionally deleted. The realisation of (cii) would now be:

(497) *bala yugu baŋgul yaṛaŋgu* INST[$\pm$ future tense] *balgal[ŋay] [ŋura]
bagun ḍugumbilgu*

The three NPs in (497) are in their correct inflections, qua (493).

We can postulate a rule which raises *balgal* from VP$_2$ and attaches it to VP$_1$, INST from VC$_1$ becoming a feature on *balgal* in place of [-ŋay]. At the same time Σ_3 is raised, and attached to Σ_1. T$_2$ and Σ_2 are now excised. Thus from (cii) we derive:

(ciii)

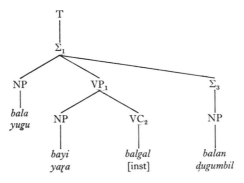

The realisation of (ciii) is now:

(498) *bala yugu baŋgul yaṛaŋgu balgal* [inst] [$\pm$ future tense] *bagun ḍugumbilgu*

which, under the convention that [inst] is realised as *-mal~-(m)bal* (4.9), is (493).

The VC raising rule can be stated:

(κ) INST INCORPORATION

$_T[_\Sigma[X$	VC	$_T[_\Sigma[NP$	$VC_{[-\eta ay]}$		$_\Sigma[NP]_\Sigma]_\Sigma]_T$		$X]_\Sigma$	$X]_T$
I	2	3	4	5	6	$\emptyset$	7	8
$\Rightarrow$ I	$4_{[2]}$	$\emptyset$	$\emptyset$	$\emptyset$	$\emptyset$	6	7	8

IF 2 = INST

We have thus suggested that the occurrence of INST, in *-ŋura* construction with a Σ containing a lexical verb, triggers the raising of the verb to the node occupied by INST, INST now becoming a feature on the verb. INST is thus similar to POSS in that it triggers a rule that, amongst other things, takes away its own status as a node label.

Justification for the analysis given above is in 5.7.5.

5.7.4 Comitative VCs. The comitative affix, *–mal~-(m)bal*, can be added to a stem which is surface intransitive, producing a stem that functions transitively. Thus, from intransitive *maril* 'follow' is derived comitative *marilmal* that can, for instance, occur in a VC with transitive *banḍal* (compare with (455)):

(499) *balan ḍugumbil baŋgul yaṛaŋgu marilman banḍan*   man followed woman

Comitative and instrumentive affixes have identical form and considerable semantic similarity. However, comitative has considerably wider semantic possibilities than instrumentive, and in chapter 4 it seemed wisest to distinguish two distinct processes, one applying to intransitive and one to transitive stems.

We can provide a deep representation for a comitative construction that is rather similar to that given above for instrumentives. Thus:

(civ)

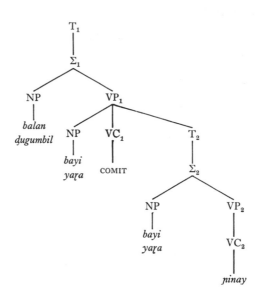

And a rule similar to (κ) raises *ɲinay* from VP_2 to VP_1, COMIT then becoming an affix to the lexical verb:

(λ) COMIT INCORPORATION

$_T[_\Sigma[X$	VC	$_T[_\Sigma[NP$	$VC]_\Sigma]_T$	$X]_\Sigma$	$X]_T$
1	2	3	4	5	6
$\Rightarrow$ 1	$4_{[2]}$	$\emptyset$	$\emptyset$	5	6
IF 2 = COMIT					

Applying (λ) to (civ) we get:
(cv)

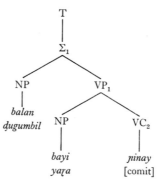

which, with the convention that [comit], like [inst], is realised by
-*mal* ~ -(*m*)*bal*, gives (cf. (258)):

(500) *balan ḍugumbil baŋgul yaɽaŋgu ɲinayman*   man is sitting down
with woman

Tree (cv) correctly assigns a surface structure to (500) that shows
ɲinaymal to be transitive – see 5.4.2.

Rule (λ) is similar to (κ). There is, however, one important difference.
Rule (κ), which applies if there is more than one NP dominated by
Σ_2, raises VC_2 but deletes the [-*ŋay*] feature. Rule (λ), which applies
if there is only one NP dominated by Σ_2, raises VC_2 and retains all
features attached to this node. Thus, comitative can be added to a root
that is already in -*ŋay* form, as in (265), and the -*ŋay* inflection is
in this case preserved.

It was noted in 4.9.3 that comitative can co-occur with reflexive.
There are several possibilities:

[1] reflexive plus comitative. In the case of (cf. (267)):

(501) *balan ḍugumbil baŋgul yaɽaŋgu buybayirimban*   man hides himself
with woman

the deep representation is:
(cvi)

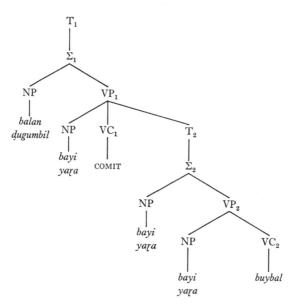

7-2

Reflexive transformation (γ), applied to Σ₂ in (cvi), deletes the NP dominated by VP₂ and marks VC₂ as [refl]. Applying rule (λ), and the case conventions, we obtain (501).

[2] comitative plus reflexive. In this case we have Σ₁ with VC COMIT and an intransitive Σ₂; (λ) applies, raising the lexical verb in Σ₂ into Σ₁. The reflexive rule (γ) applies in the cycle on Σ₁, yielding a sentence like (270–1). (λ) and (γ) can be applied in either order.

[3] comitative plus reflexive plus comitative. The deep representation involves three Σ's, with Σ₁ in *-ɲura* construction with Σ₂ and Σ₂ in *-ɲura* construction with Σ₃. Σ₁ and Σ₂ have COMIT as VC, whereas Σ₃ involves an intransitive lexical verb. Rule (λ) raises the lexical verb into Σ₂; reflexive rule (γ) applies in the cycle on Σ₂; and rule (λ) raises the lexical verb of Σ₂ – which is now marked as [comit] and [refl] into Σ₁. A sentence such as (272) will result.

See also 5.10.1, below.

5.7.5 Justification for analysis. There is a stem-forming verbal affix *-ɖay* which (roughly) indicates that an event is repeated, with different tokens of the same topic type, many times within a short interval of time. A full discussion is in 6.3.2. Thus:

(502) *bayi yaṟa ɲinanḏaɲu*   many men are sitting down

Now a verb form can include *-ɖay* either BEFORE or AFTER the comitative affix *-mal ∼ -mbal*. Thus:

(503) *bala dayibul baŋgul yaṟaŋgu ɲinanḏáymban*   many men are sitting at a table
(504) *bala dayibul baŋgul yaṟaŋgu ɲinaymálḏaɲu*   man is sitting at many tables (i.e. keeps moving from one to the other)

The deep tree for (503–4) is:
(cvii)

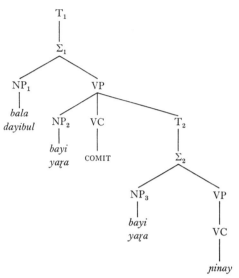

In (503) *-ḍay* applies in Σ_2 and thus refers to a number of different tokens of the topic NP$_3$, i.e. 'many men'. *-ḍay* is attached to *ɲinay* and then, after raising rule (λ) has applied, [comit] is attached to *ɲinanḍay*.

In (504) *-ḍay* applies in Σ_1, i.e. 'many tables', and *-ḍay* is attached to COMIT. Rule (λ) then raises *ɲinay* to Σ_1, and adds to it features [comit] plus *-ḍay*.

Thus, the difference between (503) and (504) can be explained by *-ḍay* applying to Σ_2 in one case, and to Σ_1 in the other. This provides justification for our analysis of comitative forms in terms of two underlying Σ's, joined in a *-ŋura* construction.

Analogous justification can be given for the analysis of instrumentive VCs in 5.7.3. Thus:

(505) *bala bari baŋgul yaɽaŋgu núdilḍáymban bagu yugugu*   man cut down many trees with axe

(506) *bala bari baŋgul yaɽaŋgu núdilmálḍaɲu bagu yugugu*   man cut down tree with many axes

In (505) *-ḍay* applies to Σ_2 with topic *bala yugu* 'tree', and in (506) to Σ_1 with topic *bala bari* 'axe'.

The M informant gave versions of (505) and (506) in which he used *gunbalḍariman* and *gunbalmalḍaɲu* respectively; *gunbal* 'cut' is the M correspondent of D *nudil*. The interesting feature is his inclusion of reflexive *-ri-* after *-ḍay* and before *-mal*; because of this the *-mal* in *gunbalḍarimal* has to be identified as the comitative, and not the instrumentive, affix. This is one of many examples of the similarity and partial interchangeability of comitative and instrumentive – note also the similarity between rules (κ) and (λ). Yet there are significant differences, sufficient to prevent our collapsing instrumentive and comitative into a single suffix, or deriving them from a single dummy verb.

5.7.6   Verbalisation. This section should be read after 5.9.

Comitative and instrumentive affixes are phonologically similar to the transitive verbalising affix *-mal ~ -(m)bal*, that can occur with adjective and noun stems, with locative and allative forms, and with some particles (4.7). In 5.9 it is suggested that:

(507) *bayi yaṛa gulgiṛi*   man is pretty (i.e. prettily painted)

has tree representation:

(cviii)

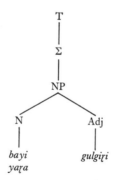

whereas

(508) *bayi yaṛa baŋgul gubiŋgu gulgiṛimban*   the gubi made man pretty

has representation:

(cix)

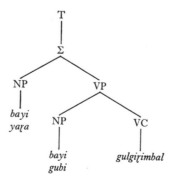

We could posit a further dummy verb CAUS[ative] – along the lines of INST and COMIT – and say that the DEEP representation of (508) is:
(cx)

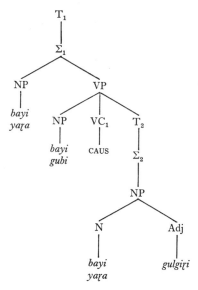

and say that a transformation, remarkably similar in form to (λ), lifts *gulgiṛi* and attaches it to VC$_1$, CAUS then becoming a feature to the adjective. With CAUS realised as *-mal ~ -mbal*, (cix) results.

Such a 'causative incorporation' rule (the formulation is straightforward) would go some way towards 'explaining' the phonological similarity between comitative and instrumentive affixes on verbs, and the transitive verbalising affix (at least as it occurs with adjectives). Similar treatment can be given for the intransitive verbaliser *-bil*.

The occurrence of the verbalisers with nouns, locative and allative forms, etc. would also need to be explained.

Note that [1] we are explaining verbalisation in terms of an underlying *-ŋura* construction; and [2] locative nouns can be verbalised. This may be found to provide further support for the idea – mentioned in 5.6 – that *-ŋura* constructions may in some way have evolved from sentences involving a relative clause to a locative noun.

We have, in 5.7.1–6, dealt with points [13], [17e] and [21–5] from 5.1.

5.8 Actor NPs

5.8.1 Instrumental relative clauses.
In 5.7.2 we explained instrumental NPs in terms of relative clauses involving the dummy verb INST. In fact, relative clauses of this type can only qualify S and

A NPs – as in (c) and (xcviii) respectively; an instrumental relative clause cannot occur with an NP in O function.

This suggests setting up a feature [+actor] that applies to S and A NPs; other NPs will be marked as [−actor]. An appropriate PS rule would be:

(cxi) (a) NP → NP [+actor]/−VC
       (b) NP → NP [−actor]

Now only [+actor] NPs can involve a relative clause in which the verb is INST.

5.8.2 Pronoun cases.

In 5.2 we showed that, despite the case marking on pronouns, the syntax of Dyirbal followed an entirely nominative-ergative pattern. However, we still have to explain pronominal inflections.

This can be done in terms of the feature [+actor]. The case marking convention (β') applies in the case of pronominal NPs just as it does for non-pronominal NPs. But whereas the inflections of nouns depend only on case marking, pronominal inflections take account not only of case but also of the polarity of the [actor] feature. Thus, in the case of the first person singular pronoun, for instance (compare with the paradigm in 3.3.1):

(cxii) REALISATION RULES

	its pronominal head has the form:	
if the NP has features:	in G	in D
[1] [nominative] and [+actor]	ŋayba	ŋaḍa
[2] [ergative] and [+actor]	ŋaḍa	ŋaḍa
[3] [nominative] and [−actor]	ŋaɲa	ŋayguna

It will be seen that for singular pronouns in G there is a different form corresponding to each combination of case and actor features. In D and M however (and for non-singular pronouns in G) there is a single form of each pronoun, used in [+actor] NPs, IRRESPECTIVE OF THE CASE MARKING.

Realisation rules (cxii) explain why there is only one type of -ŋay construction involving pronouns, although there are two varieties involving nouns (point [7] in 5.1).

In the case of nouns we have (cf. (481), (483) etc.):

(509) *bayi yaṟa bagun ḍugumbilgu balgalŋaɲu*   man hit woman
(510) *bayi yaṟa baŋgun ḍugumbiṟu balgalŋaɲu*   man hit woman

with surface trees (after case and verb marking conventions have applied):
(cxiii)

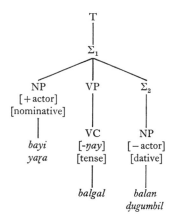

and
(cxiv)

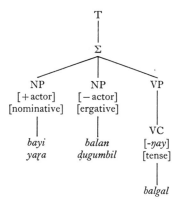

respectively.

Now suppose that the O NP is 'first person singular pronoun' in (cxiii) and (cxiv). Corresponding to (509) we get:

(511) *bayi yaṟa ŋaygungu balgalŋaɲu*   man hit me

However, the surface structure corresponding to (510) and (cxiv) would be:

(cxv)

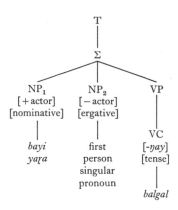

Note that the pronominal NP is marked as [ergative] and also as
[−actor]. But (cxii) gave a full list of pronominal forms corresponding
to NPs with case markings [nominative] and [ergative]; it will be seen
that there is NO pronominal form corresponding to the features [ergative]
and [−actor]. There is thus NO FORM that can be the realisation of
NP₂ in (cxv), and it is almost certainly because of this that there is
NO CONSTRUCTION, involving a pronominal O NP, corresponding to
(510).

A pronominal A or S NP prefers to occur sentence initial, before even a topic
NP – see 7.8; there must thus be a phonological rule moving any NP that
has the feature [+actor], and that involves a pronoun, to the front of any
other NP in the sentence.

5.8.3   Nominal affix -ɲa. In 3.2.1 we mentioned that the affix -ɲa
can occur on a noun in a nominative NP in O function, but not in
a nominative NP in A function. Nominal -ɲa is similar in form – and
may be genetically related to – the affix -na ~ -ɲa occurring in the
O forms of pronouns (1.5, 1.6, 3.3.1, 6.1.1, 6.2). There is also some
semantic similarity – -ɲa is commonly used with proper nouns, and
with common nouns referring to humans; all pronouns in Dyirbal
necessarily have human reference.

    The rule for the use of -ɲa can be stated (cf. (cxii-3)):

(cxvi) if an NP has features [nominative] and [−actor], its head noun
        can, optionally, take the affix -ɲa.

5.8.4   Cases on the interrogative pronoun. At first sight, the
inflectional paradigm of the interrogative pronoun appears rather
different from both pronoun and noun paradigms (3.3.3).

A closer examination reveals that the interrogative pronoun inflects exactly like a noun EXCEPT THAT the affix *-ɲa ~ -na* is obligatory in the case of a nominative NP marked as [−actor]. (The interrogative pronoun always has human reference.)

(cxvii) REALISATION RULES

if the NP has features:	its interrogative pronominal head has the form:
[1] [nominative] and [−actor]	*waɲuna*
[2] [nominative] and [+actor]	*waɲa*
[3] [ergative]	*waɲḍu*

The root has three slightly different forms – it is *waɲu-* in line [1], *waɲa-* in line [2], and *waɲ-* in line [3]; the ergative is thus formed from *waɲ-* by the usual rule – a homorganic stop plus *-u* (3.2.1).

In G, the form *waɲa* has evidently become an interrogative noun (corresponding to DM *miɲa* – 3.2.4) and the gap in the interrogative pronoun paradigm has been filled by *waɲuɲa*.

Note that none of the languages surrounding G has *waɲa* for 'what'. Wargamay, to the south, has *miɲa*, while Waruŋu, to the west, has *ŋani*.
    In terms of the above analysis of interrogative pronominal forms we should expect there to be two kinds of *-ŋay* construction involving this pronoun, corresponding to (509) and (510). However, while *bayi yaṛa waɲungu balgalŋaɲu* is perfectly acceptable, the other type of *-ŋay* construction – as in **bayi yaṛa waɲḍu balgalŋaɲu* – is judged ungrammatical by all informants.

5.8.5 Imperatives. The non-embedded sentences of a topic-chain must either [1] all be in non-future tense, or [2] all be in future tense, or [3] all be in imperative form. This suggests that features be assigned:

(cxviii) [1] T → [±imperative]
       [2] [−imperative] → [±future tense]

(cxviii) now replaces rule (lxxxvii). We must now rewrite (ε-ii) as:

(ε-ii') if a Σ is directly dominated by T, the [imperative] and [future tense] features of the T are transferred to the nearest VC that is dominated by the Σ.

It was stated in 4.12.1 that [1] in an imperative construction the head of the S or A NP can be a pronoun; or else [2] there need be no head stated, it then being understood that the addressee(s) are the actor(s). Note that the crucial NP, in an imperative construction, is that with the feature [+actor].

We can set up the underlying representation of an imperative of the second type to include a 'second person pronoun' (unspecified for number). This can be deleted by rule:

(μ) IMPERATIVE

X	$_\Sigma[$X	NP$_{[+actor]}$	VC$_{[imperative]}$	X$]_\Sigma$	X
1	2	3 4	5 6	7	8
$\Rightarrow$ 1	2	$\emptyset$ $\emptyset$	5 6	7	8

IF 3 = 'second person pronoun'

It might be thought that our recognition of the feature [actor], which is attached to intransitive and transitive deep subject, is an admission that Dyirbal does have SOME nominative-accusative character. Such a suggestion is easily refuted. Thus [+actor] is needed to explain the inflection of pronouns – yet in 5.2 we were able conclusively to demonstrate that the syntactic behaviour of pronouns is entirely nominative-ergative in character.

Similarly, although the imperative transformation (μ) refers to the feature [+actor] – which is attached to S and A NPs – imperatives take part in topic-chains exactly as do non-imperative sentences; these topic-chains are constructed according to a nominative-ergative principle. Note also the two kinds of transitive imperative:

(512) (*ŋinda*) *bayi yaṟa balga*   (you) hit the man!
(513) (*ŋinda*) (*bagul yaṟagu* OR *baŋgul yaṟaŋgu*) *balgalŋa*   (you) hit (the man)!

(In G the pronoun in (512) would be *ŋinda* and in (513) *ŋinba*.) Every Dyirbal sentence must contain a topic NP, unless deleted by rule (μ). Thus *bayi yaṟa* cannot be omitted from (512). In (513), however, the topic *ŋinda* can be deleted by rule (μ), and the O NP can be omitted (as described in 4.5.1).

Note Hale's comment [1970: 771/2]: 'in the majority of [ergative] languages in Australia, the rules and constraints in the grammar which make reference to the relation 'subject-of' show that the subject of a nontransitive sentence is the NOMINATIVE NP and that the subject of a transitive sentence is the ERGATIVE NP...(The rules and constraints relevant here include: (1) the imperative (the subject must be 2nd person); (2) obviative and proximate conjoining (obviate if subjects distinct, proximate if identical); (3) complementizer insertion (depending on identity of embedded subjects with NP object or subject in superordinate sentence); (4) subject agreement in AUX, for those languages which have it; (5) deep structure constraints associated with certain superordinate verbs. In fact, most rules and constraints which depend on the identity or distinctness of NP's require reference to the notion 'subject-of-S'.)'

Some of Hale's points indicate the need for a feature [+actor] as described above – subject agreement in AUX is closely related to pronominal inflection, and so on. As we have shown, the need for such a feature, to explain a number of rather superficial aspects of the grammar, does not imply that a language is basically, or even partially, nominative-accusative in syntax. Pace Hale's final point, it has been shown above that the rules of NP deletion in Dyirbal depend predominantly on topic identification (as does the whole syntax of complementizer insertion) – see rules (δ-i, ii), (η), and constraints I–IV.

In 5.8.1–5 we have dealt with points [3–4], [7] and [26] from 5.1.

5.9 Minimal sentences

Any Dyirbal utterance necessarily involves a 'topic' noun (which is in nominative case) and some 'comment' on it. The comment can be verbal as in all earlier discussion in this chapter, or it can be adjectival; the types are exemplified in:

(514) *bayi yaɽa yanu*   man is going
(515) *bayi yaɽa bulgan*   man is big

The difference between these types can be seen by comparing (515) with the verbal comment sentence:

(516) *bayi yaɽa bulganbin*   man has become big

The difference between (515) and (516) is exactly paralleled by that between (517) and (518):

(517) *bayi yaɽa bulgan wuḍiɲu*   big boy grew up
(518) *bayi yaɽa bulganbin wuḍiɲu*   boy grew up, becoming big

The entire difference between (517) and (518), and between (515) and (516), is that *bulgan* indicates a state of being (roughly, 'a nominal quality'), whereas *bulganbil* indicates an activity ('a verbal quality'). The semantic difference can be brought out in the case of (517) and (518) through tree representations:

(cxix)

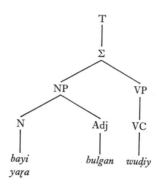

and
(cxx)

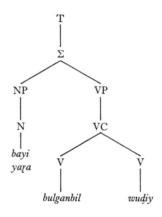

respectively.

This suggests deep structures for (515) and (516):
(cxxi)

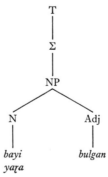

and

(cxxii)

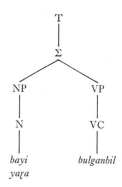

respectively.

We are thus viewing (515) as a sentence that consists of JUST AN NP; within the NP the noun is the topic and the adjective the comment. Thus, if an NP contains an adjective and there is also a VP or embedded Σ in the sentence, then the adjective is part of the 'topic', as in (517). However, if an NP contains an adjective and the NP is the sole constituent of a sentence, then the adjective is the 'comment', as in (515).

Support for the above analysis is provided by the occurrence of *gulu* 'not' in sentences that do not involve a verb (see 4.15.3). In M, (515) can be negated by placing *gulu* at the front of the sentence: *gulu bayi yaṛa bulgan* 'the man is not big'. If *bulgan* were dominated by the node VP in (515), we would expect **bayi yaṛa gulu bulgan* to be grammatical; it is not.

The three functions of *aɲḍa* (4.15.2) are [1] to introduce a new topic; [2] to introduce a new type of verbal comment; and [3] to introduce a new type of adjectival comment. A detailed examination of the behaviour of *aɲḍa*, and its semantic effect, thus provides support for the analysis given here.

Any attempt to formulate a universal syntactic policy on adjectival modification must set out with the recognition that the relation of 'big' to 'man' in 'the big man is going' is the same as that in 'the man is big' (in Dyirbal, that the relation of *bulgan* to *yaṛa* in *bayi yaṛa bulgan yanu* is the same as that in *bayi yaṛa bulgan*). There are then two main possibilities:

[1] since 'the man is big' appears in some languages to involve a predication, then adjectival predication is said to underlie 'the big man is going'. Thus 'adjectival comment' is regarded as a special type of 'verbal comment' [Lyons, 1966, after Chomsky, etc.].

[2] since 'big' is an intra-NP modifier in 'the big man is going' it is also syntactically this in 'the man is big'. This is the analysis adopted here.

Languages vary in whether or not sentences which involve only adjectival

comment are given tense qualification. For languages – such as Dyirbal – in
which they are not, analysis [2] is clearly preferable. The difference between
(515) and (516) is exactly expressed by the different syntactic statuses of the
comment in the two cases; and note that in addition to tense, *bulganbil* can
bear the full range of verbal affixes (6.3), whereas *bulgan* can bear only nominal
affixes. To adopt analysis [1] for Dyirbal would be needlessly to complicate
the description.

In the case of languages that do provide tense qualification for adjectival
sentences there is little to choose between analyses [1] and [2]. If tense is
regarded as a feature applying to a complete sentence, not just to the VC, then
the fact that adjectival sentences are marked for tense is no argument for
regarding adjectives as 'a kind of verb'. If analysis [2] were applied to English,
the copula could be thought of as a 'dummy' brought in to carry tense when
there is no verb available. (Russian provides support for this position –
adjectival comment sentences involve a copula only when referring to past or
future time; if the reference is to present time noun and adjective are sufficient.)

Minimal sentences involving a head noun, and a modifier noun with
some suitable affix, can be classed with noun-plus-adjective constructions; *-ŋaŋgay* 'without' in (106), *-bila* 'with' in (525), and *-ŋaru*
'like a' in (107) serve to derive an adjectival stem from a noun root.

Participles function exactly like adjectives. They can be regarded as
syntactically derived from relative clauses. Thus the surface representation of the relative clause construction:

(519) *bayi yaṟa ḍanaŋu*   man has been standing

is:

(cxxiii)

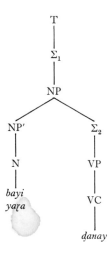

We can give the representation of the participial sentence:

(520) *bayi yaṛa ḍanay*   man habitually stands around

as:

(cxxiv)

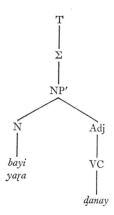

Thus, to form a participial structure from a relative clause, *ḍanay* (and the VC node that dominates it) are detached from VP in Σ_2 and attached to the node Adj[ective].

Similarly, in the case of an NP-incorporating participle (4.6); the representation for:

(521) *bayi yaṛa baŋgun ḍugumbiṛu bunḍulŋaŋu*   man has been spanking woman

is:

(cxxv)

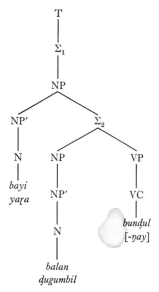

The representation of:

(522) *bayi yaṛa ḍugumbilbunḍul(ŋay)muŋa* man habitually spanks
      women

can be shown:
(cxxvi)

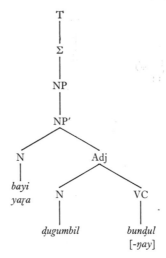

There are three important differences between (521) and (522): [1]
ḍugumbil is in ergative case in (521) but bears no inflection in (522);
[2] *ḍugumbil* can be accompanied by a noun marker in (521) but not
in (522); and [3] *-ŋay* must be affixed to *bunḍul* in (521) but can
optionally be omitted in (522). These differences are accounted for by
saying that *baŋgun ḍugumbiṛu bunḍulŋaṇu* is dominated by Σ in (cxxv),
whereas *ḍugumbilbunḍul(ŋay)muŋa* is dominated by Adj WITHIN the
topic NP in (cxxvi).

In 5.5.2 we described possessive phrases in terms of relative clauses; in surface
representation a possessive NP was shown as still dominated by the relative
clause Σ. An alternative would be to say that the possessive NP is transferred
to the Adj node, as in the case of a participle. There is in fact no syntactic
evidence favouring one of these alternatives over the other. (Note that a sentence
can involve just a noun plus relative clause, or just a noun plus adjective, or
just a noun plus possessive phrase – the latter could thus conceivably be
'identified' with either of the first two.)

There is a further type of intra-NP comment, the demonstrative
noun marker, *giṇa-*, as in (cf. (101):

(523) *giyi bayi yaṛa*   the man's here OR this is the man

for which a suitable tree representation would be:

(cxxvii)

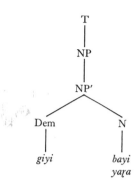

One final constituent of an NP which has not been dealt with above is a modifier noun, indicating inalienable possession – 4.2.1. Such a noun can be a comment (and can be qualified by an adjective, although not by a noun marker). Thus:

(524) *bayi yaṟa gagalumɲunu guwu bulayi*   the man, from the moon, has two noses

Compare with the construction involving alienable possession:

(525) *bayi yaṟa bayiɲambila waɲalbila*   the man has a boomerang

There are no nominal sentences (showing inalienable possession) of the type 'the nose belongs to the man', similar to *baɲul yaṟaɲu bayi waɲal* 'the boomerang belongs to the man', which involves alienable possession.

It thus seems appropriate to consider an inalienably possessed noun as a further constituent of NP'. The underlying representation of (cf. (39)):

(526) *giɲan balan ḍugumbil mambu baŋgul yaṟaŋgu balgan*   man is hitting this woman's back

would now be written:
(cxxviii)

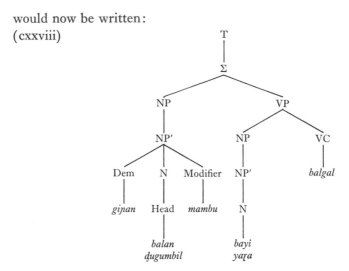

In this section we have taken account of points [14–16] from 5.1.

5.10   Set representation

5.10.1   Reciprocals. There are some syntactic processes in Dyirbal
that cannot be fully described in terms of the representations used so
far. Consider reciprocals, for instance. A simple reciprocal such as:

(527) *ŋali bayi yaṛa baṛalbaṛalnbariɲu*   we two (man and I) are fighting
each other

could be given deep representation:
(cxxix)

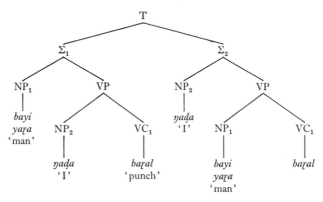

(The sequence in which Σ_1 and Σ_2 occur is, of course, immaterial.)

We could then formulate a transformational rule, similar to the reflexive rule (γ), which would derive:
(cxxx)

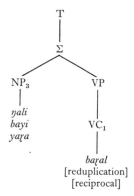

from (cxxix). Here the referent of NP_3 is the sum of the referents of NP_1 and NP_2. Tree (cxxx) correctly shows that a reciprocal verb is surface intransitive. Verbal reduplication normally indicates that an action is performed 'many times' or 'to excess' (6.3.4). The obligatory reduplication of a reciprocal is appropriately mirrored by a deep representation like (cxxix), which involves two occurrences of the verb root.

However, a deep representation of the type (cxxix) is less suitable for:

(528) *bayi yaɽarḍi baɽalbaɽalnbariɲu* (all) the men are fighting each other

If the plural noun *yaɽarḍi* refers to a group of n men, the deep representation for (528) would have to involve $(n-1)!$ coordinated Σ's (man_1 fought man_2, man_1 fought man_3, ..., man_{n-1} fought man_n). Such a representation would be unbearably long and clumsy. Another unsatisfactory feature is that it must refer to the number of men, n, in the group, although (528) could be understood perfectly well without any exact count having been taken.

Reciprocals of all types can be more revealingly explained in terms of set inclusion. We say that any surface structure of the form (cxxix), that is:

(cxxxi) $[NP_1, VC_{1[redupl]\ [recipl]}]$

has the following deep representational basis:

[1] NP$_1$ refers to a set, S

and [2] for every x and y such that x and y are members of S, then
[NP$_x$, [VC$_1$, NP$_y$]] and [NP$_y$, [VC$_1$, NP$_x$]] hold.

This type of explanation could be extended to deal with comitative-plus-reflexive type constructions – 5.7.4.

In this section we have taken further account of point [12] from 5.1.

5.10.2   -*gara* and -*maŋgan*. Consider (cf. (43) and 6.1.1):

(529) *bayi yaṛagara balan ḍugumbilgara baniɲu*   man, being one of a
        pair, and woman, being the other of the pair, are coming

It might be thought that the deep representation of (529) could be simply:

(cxxxii)

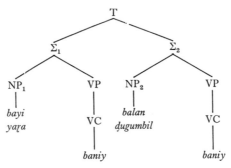

with -*gara* a marker of the coordination.

However, this approach would be less satisfactory for the perfectly grammatical:

(530) *bayi yaṛagara baniɲu*   man, being one of a pair, is coming

since the deep representation would have to involve a 'dummy' NP$_2$ that was then deleted. And it would be highly unsatisfactory in the case of:

(531) *bayi yaṛamaŋgan baniɲu*   man, being one of many people, is
        coming

and of:

(532) *bayi yaṛamaŋgan bayi gubimaŋgan baniɲu*   man, being one of
        many people, and the gubi, being another of many people, are
        coming

For these sentences we would need deep representations involving an indefinite number of conjoined Σ's, all but one or two of which have dummy NPs.

-*gara* and -*maŋgan* constructions can be explained quite straight-forwardly in terms of set inclusion. Consider a sentence:

(533) $NP_1 - \text{AFF} - NP_2 - \text{AFF} - \ldots - \text{AFF} - NP_n - \text{AFF} - VP_1$

where AFF is either -*gara* in each case, or -*maŋgan* in each case. We can say that underlying (533) is a deep relation:
(cxxxiii)

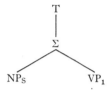

where the referent of NP_s is a set, S, consisting of m individuals $(m \geqslant n)$. Now the referents of NP_1, $NP_2 \ldots$, NP_n are each members of S. If $m = 2$, AFF in (533) must be -*gara*; if $m > 2$, AFF in (533) must be -*maŋgan*.

Sets are also needed to explain the grammar of -*mumbay* (6.1.1).

5.11   Summary of rules

5.11.1   Well-formedness conditions on trees. A number of PS rules have been mentioned above, but no comprehensive list has been given. The trees used in the chapter could be dealt with through PS rules, or through tree formation rules, or through well-formedness conditions on trees (i.e. node admissibility conditions) – McCawley [1968]. Well-formedness conditions seem most appropriate in this case. Thus, following the notation in McCawley:

STRUCTURAL CONDITIONS

Topmost node: # T #
1. $\langle T; \Sigma^n \rangle$
2. $\langle \Sigma; NP, VP, (\Sigma) \rangle / \underline{\Sigma}$
3. $\langle \Sigma; NP, (VP), (\Sigma) \rangle$
4. $\langle VP; \begin{Bmatrix} NP, VC_{tr} \\ VC_{intr} \end{Bmatrix}, (T) \rangle$

5. ⟨NP; NP′, (Σ)⟩
6. ⟨NP′; (Dem), N, (Modifier) (Adj)⟩
7. ⟨N; $\begin{cases} \text{Noun Marker, Noun} \\ \text{Pronoun} \end{cases}$⟩
8. ⟨Modifier; Noun⟩

FEATURE SPECIFICATIONS

9. T → [±imperative] /#−
10. [−imperative] → [±future tense]
11. Σ → [±perfect aspect]/$\overline{\text{NP}}$
12. NP → [+actor]/−VC
13. NP → [−actor]

The context specification $\underline{X}$ in a condition of the form $< Y; Z >/\underline{X}$ indicates that Y may dominate Z only when it is itself directly dominated by X. 11 applies for the Mamu dialect only.

These conditions only provide a partial specification of the trees needed to deal with all aspects of Dyirbal syntax. We leave the reader to formulate the straightforward augmentations needed to deal with locational phrases, time qualifiers, particles, and so on.

5.11.2 Transformational rules, constraints and marking conventions

(α) -*ŋay* TRANSFORMATION (optional)   [p. 152]

X	[		NP	$_{\text{VP}}$[NP	VC]$_{\text{VP}}$	X	]	X
1		∅	2	3	4	5		6
⇒ 1		3	2	∅	4$_{[\text{-ŋay}]}$	5		6

IF 4 is a lexical verb (i.e. not INST, COMIT, POSS, etc.)

The condition in (α) is to account for the fact that the -*ŋay* affix always occurs next to the verb root; unlike reflexive, -*ŋay* cannot follow an instrumentive/comitative affix.

(γ) REFLEXIVE (obligatory)   [p. 152]

X	$_Σ$[NP	$_{\text{VP}}$[NP	VC]$_{\text{VP}}$	X]$_Σ$	X
1	2	3	4	5	6
⇒ 1	2	∅	4$_{[\text{refl}]}$	5	6

IF the referent of 2 is identical to or included within the referent of 3

The false reflexive transformation is identical to (α), with feature [refl] in place of [-*ŋay*] and without the condition that 4 be a lexical verb.

(δ) LOWER TOPIC DELETION

(i)   X   ₂[NP   X   ₂[NP   X]₂]₂   X   [p. 157]

	I	2	3	4	5	6
	I	2	3	4	5	6
⇒	I	2	3	Ø	5	6

obligatorily applied after constraint II is satisfied

(ii) X   ₙₚ[NP'   ₂[NP   X]₂   ]ₙₚX   [p. 178]

	I	2	3	4	5
	I	2	3	4	5
⇒	I	2	Ø	4	5

obligatorily applied after constraint III is satisfied

(η) IDENTICAL NP DELETION (obligatory)   [p. 173]

   X   ₂[NP   NP   X   ₂[NP   X]₂]₂   X

	I	2	3	4	5	6	7
	I	2	3	4	5	6	7
⇒	I	2	Ø	4	5	6	7

IF 3 and 5 have identical reference
and 2 and 3 are directly dominated by the same Σ node

(ζ) DUMMY VERB DELETION (obligatory)   [p. 170]

   X   ₂[X   VP   ₂[X   VC]₂   X]₂   X

	I	2	3	4	5	6	7
	I	2	3	4	5	6	7
⇒	I	2	3	4	Ø	6	7

IF 5 = Ω
and 3 is non-null

(θ) POSSESSIVE FORMATION RULE (obligatory)   [p. 182]

   X   ₙₚ[NP'₍case₎   ₂[NP₍erg₎   VC₍rell [case]₎]₂]ₙₚ   X

	I	2	3	4	5	6	7	8	9
	I	2	3	4	5	6	7	8	9
⇒	I	2	3	4	7	8	Ø	Ø	Ø	9

IF 6 = POSS
and 6 does not involve the feature [-ŋay]

(The second condition on (θ) is not strictly necessary, in view of the condition on (α); the -ŋay transformation cannot be applied to a Σ whose VC is not a lexical verb, thus POSS could not involve the feature [-ŋay].)

(ι) INST DELETION (obligatory)   [p. 189]

   X   NP'₍₊actor₎   ₂[X   VC]₂   X

	I	2	3	4	5	6
	I	2	3	4	5	6
⇒	I	2	3	4	Ø	6

IF 5 = INST

As mentioned in 5.8.1, only an NP marked as [+actor] can take an instrumental relative clause. If the NP does not have this marking, rule (ι) does not apply and INST goes through to surface structure, an illicit string resulting.

(κ) INST INCORPORATION (obligatory)   [p. 193]

$$_T[_\Sigma[X \; VC \; _T[_\Sigma[NP \quad VC_{[-\eta ay]} \; _\Sigma[NP]_\Sigma]_\Sigma]_T \qquad X]_\Sigma \quad X]_T$$

	I	2	3	4	5	6	$\emptyset$	7	8
$\Rightarrow$	I	4[2]	$\emptyset$	$\emptyset$	$\emptyset$	$\emptyset$	6	7	8

IF 2 = INST

(λ) COMIT INCORPORATION (obligatory)   [p. 194]

$$_T[_\Sigma[X \qquad VC \; _T[_\Sigma[NP \qquad VC]_\Sigma]_T \; X]_\Sigma \qquad X]_T$$

	I	2	3	4	5	6
$\Rightarrow$	I	4[2]	$\emptyset$	$\emptyset$	5	6

IF 2 = COMIT

(μ) IMPERATIVE   [p. 204]

$$X \; _\Sigma[X \quad NP_{[+actor]} \quad VC_{[imperative]} \; X]_\Sigma \; X$$

	I	2	3	4	5	6	7	8
$\Rightarrow$	I	2	$\emptyset$	$\emptyset$	5	6	7	8

IF 3 = 'second person pronoun'

These are only a sample of the full set of rules required for Dyirbal. Other rules, which are quite straightforward, include [1] coordinating two VCs which agree in surface transitivity, and in tense or other final inflection; [2] specifying that Dem[onstrative] can only be included in an NP which is surface structure topic; [3] optionally deleting any non-topic NP (4.5.1); and so on.

CONSTRAINT I (when Σ is dominated by T)   [p. 155]

In: $_T[_\Sigma[NP \qquad X]_\Sigma \; _\Sigma[NP \qquad X]_\Sigma \; \ldots \; _\Sigma[NP \qquad X]_\Sigma]_T$

I	2	3	4	2n-I	2n	(n $\geqslant$ 2)

the head nouns of 1, 3, ..., 2n–1 must have identical reference.

CONSTRAINT II (when Σ is dominated by Σ)   [p. 157]

In: $X \quad _\Sigma[NP \quad X \quad _\Sigma[NP \quad X]_\Sigma \;]_\Sigma \; X$

I	2	3	4	5	6

the head nouns of 2 and 4 must have identical reference

CONSTRAINT III (when Σ is dominated by NP)   [p. 177]

In: X $_{NP}$[NP′ $_\Sigma$[NP   X]$_\Sigma$]$_{NP}$ X
    1   2   3   4   5

    the head nouns of 2 and 3 must have identical reference

CONSTRAINT IV (when T is dominated by VP)   [p. 185]

In: X $_{VP}$[NP   X $_T$[$_\Sigma$[NP   X]$_\Sigma$ $_\Sigma$[NP   X]$_\Sigma$…$_\Sigma$[NP   X]$_\Sigma$]$_T$]$_{VP}$ X
    1   2   3   4   5   6   7   2n 2n+1   2n+2

    $(n \geqslant 2)$ the head nouns of 2, 4, …, 2n must have identical reference

(β') CASE MARKING CONVENTION   [pp. 152, 158, 179]

    (i) the leftmost NP immediately dominated by a Σ, that is itself immediately dominated by T, is in nominative case;

    (ii) the leftmost NP immediately dominated by a Σ, that is itself immediately dominated by Σ, is in dative case;

    (iii) all other NPs are in ergative case;

    (iv) if NP immediately dominates NP′, then NP′ has the same case and actor marking as NP.

(ϵ) VERB MARKING CONVENTION   [pp. 158, 179, 185, 203]

    (i) a VC whose lowest dominating node is itself directly dominated by Σ is placed in purposive inflection (and does not receive any tense inflection);

    (ii′) if a Σ is directly dominated by T, the [imperative] and [future tense] features of the T are transferred to the nearest VC that is dominated by the Σ;

    (iii) a VC, whose lowest dominating Σ is dominated by NP, is given the inflection REL (i.e. *-ŋu(ɲḍin)-*) plus the case inflection of the NP (and see p. 179 for ϵ-iii′);

    (iv) a VC whose lowest dominating Σ is dominated by T, that T being itself dominated by VP, is given inflection *-ŋura*.

5.11.3   Ordering of rules. Only two rules are in the 'cycle' (which applies from the lowest Σ upwards, as in Chomsky [1965]) – (α) and (γ). Only one can apply in the case of any Σ, but obligatory rule (γ) could be said to be ordered before optional (α), since if a Σ meets the structural description of (γ), rule (γ) must apply and (α) cannot apply.

    Constraints I–IV apply immediately after the cycle; (δ–i) must apply if constraint II is met, and (δ–ii) if constraint III is met. (η) is ordered after (δ–i). (κ), (λ), (ι), (ζ) and (μ) apply post-cyclically, but with no relative ordering. (As they are stated, rule (κ) should apply before rule (ι), otherwise the latter may delete an occurrence of INST that should have been raised by the former; however, rule (ι) could easily be restated so that it could apply before (κ).) The ordering of (θ) was discussed in 5.5.2.

Marking conventions (β') and (ϵ) normally follow transformations. However, the optional rule that deletes some or all of a repeated topic (mentioned informally as the last sentence of constraints I and IV – pp. 155 and 185) must follow (β'), if incorrect case assignments are to be avoided.

As mentioned in 5.4.5, the constraints must apply from the topmost Σ downwards.

An argument could be made out for (λ) being in the cycle – see (272) and 5.7.4; there are, however, equally compelling reasons for regarding it to be post-cyclic.

6 *Morphology*

6.1 Morphology of nouns and adjectives

6.1.1 Stem-forming affixes.
There are about a score of affixes in Dyirbal that form nominal stems from nominal roots; some of them also function as affixes to members of other word classes. Some of the affixes are important syntactically – for instance *-bila* 'with' as a type of possessive, and *-gara* and *-maŋgan* as coordinators; others merely provide semantic qualification of the noun or adjective they occur with. NPs involving certain of the affixes can make up complete sentences; this is not so in the case of other affixes.

The full functional possibilities of each affix are described below. The section ends with a discussion of the use of bound forms *dayi*, *galu*, etc. (3.2.3) as nominal affixes.

[1] *-ɲa* This affix has already been discussed in 3.2.1 and 5.8.3. It is listed as a stem-forming affix, rather than as a case inflection, because [i] it is always optional with nouns; and [ii] it can be followed by other stem-forming affixes. *-ɲa* is generally added only to a nominal referring directly to a particular person or persons – a proper name, or else a noun used in a particular instance as a proper name.

In the case of a stem of three or more syllables ending in a vowel, ergative and dative inflections coincide; thus *burbulagu* is ambiguous – it could be either ergative or dative. Now a considerable proportion of proper names are of three or more syllables, and are thus open to this ambiguity. But it is with proper names that *-ɲa* is most used, and the inclusion of *-ɲa* can help to resolve the ambiguity – *burbulaɲangu* is unequivocally dative (an ergative form cannot involve *-ɲa*). *-ɲa* does not normally occur with common nouns; but the majority of the most frequent common nouns are disyllabic, with distinct ergative and dative forms (3.2.1).

-ɲa commonly occurs as a suffix to *balagara* and *balamaŋgan*: the *ɲ* drops with *balamaŋgan*, so that we have *balagaraɲa* and *balamaŋgana*. The dative inflection of *balagaraɲa* can thus be *bagugaraɲa*, *balagaraɲangu* or *bagugaraɲangu* (3.3.2). *-ɲa* can also occur with noun markers and interrogative noun markers, but only in the presence of a further affix – 6.5.6.

[2] -*bila* DG, -*ba* M 'with – '. -*bila* can be suffixed to a noun, the resulting form functioning as an adjective:

(534) *bayi yaṟa yugubila baniɲu*   man with stick is coming

It can also be suffixed to adjectives, and to noun markers that are already in -*ɲa* form, i.e. *bayiɲambila, balanambila, balamambila, bala-ɲambila*. We can thus have a complete 'comitative NP', modifying a head noun, e.g. *balaɲambila yugubila bulganbila* 'with big stick', from *bala yugu bulgan* 'big stick' in:

(535) *bayi yaṟa balaɲambila yugubila bulganbila baniɲu*   man with big
      stick is coming

or else just:

(536) *bayi yaṟa bulganbila baniɲu*   man with big thing is coming

However, a noun-plus-*bila* is only infrequently accompanied by a noun-marker-plus-*bila* (as against a head noun, which is usually accompanied by a noun marker).

With a nominal-plus-*ɲa* form we get simply -*ɲaymba* in M, but -*ɲalaymbila* in D and G:

(537) DG *ŋali ḍumbuluɲalaymbila baniɲu* ⎫
      M *ŋali ḍumbuluɲaymba baniɲu*   ⎬ we two came with Dyumbulu
                                           ⎭

As mentioned in 4.11.1, a sentence can consist of just a head noun and a noun-plus-*bila*:

(538) *ŋaḍa (balanambila) gudabila*   I have a dog [literally: I, with dog]

compare with:

(539) *ŋaygu balan guda*   the dog is mine

However, constructions like (538) are not simply the converses of constructions like (539), and should not be related to the dummy verb POSS (5.5.2). Consider:

(540) *ŋayguna baŋgun gudaŋgu yaṟaɲuṇḍindu baḍan*   man's dog bit me

This states that a dog bit me, and that the dog belongs to a certain man; it carries no inference that the man is involved in the action – he could have been encouraging the dog, or he could have been many miles away. Now consider:

(541) *ŋayguna baŋgul yaṟaŋgu gudabilagu balgan*   man with dog hit me

This implies that the man hit me; that the man has a dog; and also that the dog assisted the man in hitting me. It is thus NOT equivalent to the English 'man who has/owns a dog hit me'. Whereas possessive phrases appear to function like relative clauses (5.5.2) -*bila* forms appear quite unlike relative clauses.

A typical topic-chain involving a *-bila* form in ergative inflection is, in M:

(542) *baŋgul   gamabagu   balan   biḏaman |balan*
THERE-ERG-I gun-WITH-ERG THERE-NOM-II swive-PRES/PAST THERE-NOM-II
mugu   wugariɲu   diranayaɲu   minbali   gamaŋgu
PARTICLE give-REFL-PRES/PAST threaten-REL-NOM shoot-PURP gun-INST
he, with a gun, swived her; she had to give herself, having been
threatened that she would be shot with the gun

[3] *-baray* M 'with a lot of – '. Thus, *bayi yibiba baniɲu* refers to
a man accompanied by one woman, *bayi yibibaray baniɲu* refers to
a man amongst a crowd of women. *-baray* occurs most commonly with
nouns referring to humans; unlike *-bila ~ -ba* it cannot be affixed to
noun markers. A noun that involves *-baray* is frequently (but not
necessarily) reduplicated.

[4] *-ŋaŋgay* DM, *-biday* G 'without – '. *-ŋaŋgay* can be suffixed to
a noun, the resulting form functioning as an adjective. It can also, like
-bila, be suffixed to adjectives; but unlike *-bila*, it can NOT be suffixed
to noun markers. Thus:

(543) *bayi yaɽa yuguɲaŋgay baniɲu*   man without a stick is coming
(544) *bayi yaɽa baŋgayɲaŋgay bulganɲaŋgay baniɲu*   man with no big
        spears is coming
(545) *bala yugu baŋgul yaɽaŋgu ḏugumbilɲaŋgayḏu maŋgan*   man with
        no wives picked up stick

Sentences frequently consist of just an NP, that includes a *-ŋaŋgay*
form:

(546) *bala miḏa banaɲaŋgay*   there's no water at the camp (literally:
        the camp is without water)

See also (106) in 4.5.1. The form *waɲaɲaŋgay* is discussed in 6.6.

Most Australian languages have nominal affixes with similar meaning and
function to Dyirbal *-bila* and *-ŋaŋgay*; however, none of these affixes appear
to be cognate with the Dyirbal forms – see 1.6.

[5] *-ginay* 'covered with – , full of – '. This affix can be suffixed to
a noun, the resulting form functioning as an adjective. *-ginay* has very
restricted use: it is normally used only of 'something dirty or unpleasant',
and is apparently used less nowadays than previously. Thus we can
have *bala ḏina banaginay* 'foot covered with water' to refer to someone
who has been walking in puddles and tramples water into a house.
Other typical uses are *ḏuḏaɽginay* 'covered with urine', *gunaginay*
'covered with faeces' and *muraginay* 'covered with, or full of, semen'

(text reference xxx: 7, 10). Note also *balan warayi wurmburginay* 'a bream full of bones (making it a difficult fish to eat)'. *-ginay* cannot be suffixed to noun markers, and has not been observed occurring as an adjectival suffix.

[6] *-ɲunu* 'out of – , from – ' can be suffixed to nouns and adjectives, the resulting form functioning as an adjective; it cannot be suffixed to noun markers. With nouns, *-ɲunu* can refer to location or to time (it can also be affixed to time words, see 6.4):

(547) *bayi   ḍaban   baŋgun   mawaŋgu*
THERE-NOM-I eel-NOM THERE-ERG-II shrimp-ERG
ḍuɲaɲunugu   ḍaŋganaɲu
leaves in water-FROM-ERG eat-ɲay-PRES/PAST
eel eats shrimps from the leaves

(548) *ŋaḍa bayi yaṛa ɲalŋgaɲunu wuḍiman*   I brought the man up from a boy

See also *banaɲunugu* in text xv, line 71 (p. 380).

A *-ɲunu* form is not sufficient 'comment' to make up, with a topic noun, a complete sentence. Thus **bayi bulganɲunu* ['he used to be big'] is not an acceptable sentence; however:

(549) *bayi bulganɲunu margibin*   he has become skinny, from (being) fat

which also involves the derived verb *margibil*, is grammatical.

The nominal affix *-ɲunu* must not be confused with ablative inflection *-ɲunu* – see 6.1.5.

[7] *-bara* 'a person or animal who is concerned with – '; often 'who comes from – ' or 'who lives at or on – '. See also 9.1.2. *-bara* can be suffixed to nouns, most often to nouns referring to places. Thus from *gambil* 'tableland' is derived *gambilbara* 'person from the tableland' (i.e. a member of the more northerly of the two hordes of the Dyirbalŋan tribe). The writer was referred to as *bayi landanbara* 'a person who comes from London'; and see (105). Sometimes *-bara* can be suffixed to an adjective: *guyimbara* 'murderer' from *guyi* 'dead' (however, *-bara* cannot be suffixed to a noun and to an adjective qualifying the noun). There is also *yalamaynbara* 'thing or state which is like this one' from *yalamay* 'do it like that';

(550) *yalamaynbaragu ŋayguna yuguŋgu balgan*   a stick similar to that one hit me

(551) *yalamaynbara bani/balgun*   you can come like that, naked (i.e. it doesn't matter about clothes)

yalamaynbara is used as a noun in (550), and as an adjective in (551).

The form is *yalamaynbara* in both D and M, even though the M form corresponding to D *yalamay* is *yalabay*.
    A *-bara* form always functions as a noun. *-bara* is the only nominal affix that can form part of a noun root, e.g. *balan wabubara* M 'dingo' (cf. *bala wabu* 'scrub'), *balan ganibara* DG 'dingo' (cf. *gani* 'a long way'); *bala ḍawunbara* G 'English bee' (cf. *bala ḍawun* 'dilly bag') – see 9.1.2.

[8] *-ŋaru* 'is like a – '. *-ŋaru* can be suffixed to a noun, the resulting form functioning as an adjective, e.g. *yaṟaŋaru* '[looks] like a man', *gugulaŋaru* '[dives] like a platypus':

(552) *baŋgun ḍugumbiṟu ŋayguna yaṟaŋarugu balgan*   the woman that looks like a man hit me

(553) *bayi yaṟa gugulaŋaru mulmaɲu*   the man dives like a platypus

And see text xxxib, line 15 (p. 384).
    A *-ŋaru* form may be the complete 'comment' in a sentence – see (107).
    -ŋaru may modify a multi-word NP which then functions as an adjective phrase modifying a head noun, e.g. *bayi yaṟa ḍugumbilŋaru midiŋaru* 'the man is like a little woman'. In the case of a sentence like *bayi yaṟa ŋaygu damanŋaru* 'the man is like my son', *-ŋaru* is usually suffixed to the head of the modifying phrase, although it is possible but less acceptable to have, say, *bayi yaṟa ŋayguŋaru daman* 'the man is like my son', with *-ŋaru* suffixed to *ŋaygu*. We could also have *bayi yaṟa ŋayguŋaru* 'the man is like someone of mine'. However, it appears that *-ŋaru* cannot in this case occur with both words in the modifying phrase; thus **bayi yaṟa ŋayguŋaru damanŋaru* is not an acceptable Dyirbal sentence.

Kerr [1968: 21–2] mentions that Nyigina has a suffix *-ŋaru* 'resemble, be like'. Note that Nyigina has a number of other forms that resemble Dyirbal words and suffixes in both form and meaning, e.g. *giɲa* 'that one' (see 6.5.3).

[9] *-baḍun* 'really – ' or 'very – '. This suffix does not change the syntactic function of a word to which it is attached.
    -baḍun is most commonly suffixed to adjectives; here it can be glossed 'very' – *bulganbaḍun* 'very big'. It can also be suffixed to nouns, indicating that the noun is indeed a proper description of its referent,

8   D D L

e.g. *balan banabaḏun* 'proper water (i.e. with no impurities)', *bayi waŋalbaḏun* 'a proper boomerang (i.e. made from the correct sort of wood)'; *bayi yaṛabaḏun* 'a proper man (i.e. he is beyond doubt a man and not a woman)'. *-baḏun* can also be suffixed to noun markers, attracting attention to the referent of the noun, e.g. *bayimbaḏun* 'he's the one (e.g. that I was telling you about)'; *balanbaḏun ḏugumbil ḏanaɲu* 'a whole lot of women are standing there'. A topic noun plus *-baḏun* can make up a complete sentence – as in (104).

-baḏun can also be suffixed to time words – 6.4.

A form *baḏun* occurs in Wargamay, most typically following *ɲuɲa* 'he', with the meaning 'that's the one'. It is likely that the Dyirbal/Wargamay affix is cognate with Gugu-Yimidir *-buḏun* 'very, extremely' [Roth, 1901 a: 25; Haviland, forthcoming] and Gugu-Yalanji *-baḏagu* 'very' [H. Hershberger and Pike, 1970: 802].

[10] *-baṛa* comparative; occurs predominantly with adjectives, although it can qualify a noun, e.g. *yaṛabaṛa* 'more of a man'.

The function of *-baṛa* is best understood by studying its occurrence in texts. First (text XXXIX) a conversation between J (a speaker of G) and G (an M speaker):

(554) J: ...*gariḏin   budin*
            kerosene [tin]-NOM carry-PRES/PAST
            [I] carried the kerosene tin [with the honey in it]
    G: *ŋa/ gulu   gayuŋga   budin*
            YES PARTICLE bark bag-LOC carry-PRES/PAST
            Yes, [you] didn't carry [the honey] in a bark bag?
    J: *maya/ ḏigalbaṛa   balan   bigaybila*
            NO   good-COMP THERE-NOM-II handle-WITH
    No, it [kerosene tin] is better [than a bark bag] since it has
    a handle

Second (text VIII: 28–30) a conversation between P and M (both speakers of G) concerning a projected fishing expedition:

(555) P: ...*banuŋgulbalbulu/*
            THERE-NOM-II-THAT ONE-DOWN-WATER-LONG WAY
            gunbayḏa   buḏabuḏaygu
            Gunbay-LOC bathe-REDUP-PURP
            that's the one [pool in the river] a long way downstream;
            [we] should bathe at Gunbay

M: *ɲuɽindan   ban   gamu*
deep-EMPH THERE-NOM-II water-NOM
That water's too deep

P: *balidawulugu*
THERE-ALL-DIRTN-UP-WATER-LONG-WAY-?
wandin   buḏaygu/   ḏalabaɽagu
motion upriver-PRES/PAST bathe-PURP shallow-COMP-ALL
[we'll] go upriver to bathe, to a shallower place [than Gunbay]

Third (text XXIII: 31) a myth telling how the blue-tongue lizard was the original owner of water, and of the other animals' attempts to find where he has hidden it. Each tries to follow but is detected. Finally, the kangaroo turns to a small mouse and asks:

(556) *ɲinda/ɲinda midibaɽa/ baŋgul gulu buɽan*
[how about] you? You are smaller [than us], and will not be seen by him

In each example the object of comparison is not explicitly mentioned in the comparative sentence; it is, however, quite clear what the object of comparison is from the preceding sentences and/or from the situational context (we thus have a classic example of 'contextual correlations' – Dixon, 1965). If a comparative sentence is given to an informant in isolation there is likely to be ambiguity. Thus:

(557) *balan ḏugumbil baŋgul yaɽaŋgu midibaɽagu balgan*
could mean 'the smaller man hit the woman', *midibaɽagu* being taken as part of the ergative NP; or else as 'the man hit the woman with a smaller [stick]', where *midibaɽagu* is taken to be in instrumental case.

If an explicit comparison is needed (that is, if there has been no previous mention of the object of comparison) the following form is likely:

(558) *ŋaḏa bulganbaɽa bayi mididilu* I'm bigger [than him]; he's really small

or else:

(559) *ŋaḏa bulganbaɽa bayi midibaɽa* I'm bigger [than him]; he's smaller [than me]

However:

(560) *bayi bulgan ŋaḏa bulganbaɽa* he's big; [but] I'm bigger

may also be used.

A sentence may, in an appropriate textual context, consist of just a topic noun or pronoun and a *-baṟa* form (as *ɲinda midibaṟa* in (556)). Note the contrast between:

(561) *bayi bulganbaṟa*   he's bigger [than someone else]

and:

(562) *bayi bulgan aɲḍa*   he's bigger [than he used to be]

-baṟa also occurs as a comparative with time qualifiers (6.4) and bound forms *bayḍi* etc. (6.5.7).

[11] *-gabun* 'another –'. The addition of this suffix does not change the syntactic function of a word; *-gabun* can be suffixed to a noun or to an adjective. For example:

(563) *bayi yaṟa ɲinaɲu/bayi yaṟagabun wayɲḍin*   one man is sitting down, and another man is going uphill

-gabun thus marks reference to a further token of the same type. Not infrequently, *-gabun* is affixed to EACH token of a certain type:

(564) *bayi yaṟagabun ɲinaɲu/bayi yaṟagabun wayɲḍin*   ⟨=(563)⟩

From the adjective *wura* 'little, small' is derived the very common Dyirbal form *wurawuragabunda* 'quite a considerable amount (literally: at more than a little)':

(565) *balan ḍugumbil ɲalŋgirgan wurawuragabunda*   woman is certainly very good-looking

and (text XXXIa: 3):

(566) *walawalaygu bayi wurawuragabunda*   he certainly danced shake-a-leg style well

wurawuragabunda is always a sentence qualifier. (An alternative would be to consider it as submodifier to an adjective, in certain constructions; the fact that *wurawuragabunda* cannot take any further inflection shows this analysis to be incorrect.)

-gabun plus locative inflection can also be involved in time expressions – 6.4. *-gabun* occurs with particle *-ŋuri* – 4.15.3.

[12] *-ḍaran* 'two –' or 'each of two –'. This suffix can be attached to a noun or an adjective and involves no change in syntactic function. Thus:

(567) *bayi yaṛaḍaran baniɲu*   two men are coming
(568) *balan ḍugumbil baŋgul yaṛaḍarandu balgan*   two men are hitting woman

Compare with the adjective *bulay(i)* 'two' (6.1.7):

(569) *bayi yaṛa bulay baniɲu*   two men are coming
(570) *balan ḍugumbil baŋgul yaṛaŋgu bulaydu balgan*   two men are hitting woman

The words in (569) and (570) can occur in any order; in (567) and (568) -*ḍaran*, like all stem-forming affixes, is in fixed position following *yaṛa*, as part of the noun stem *yaṛaḍaran*. Note that -*ḍaran* can be affixed to either noun marker or noun but not both; thus we can have:

(571) *bayiḍaran baŋguy balay ɲinaɲu*   two frogs are sitting there

or:

(572) *bayi baŋguyḍaran balay ɲinaɲu*   ⟨=(571)⟩

but not:

*(573) *bayiḍaran baŋguyḍaran balay ɲinaɲu*

However, -*ḍaran* can be affixed to both noun and adjective:

(574) *bayi yaṛaḍaran midiḍaran baniɲu*   two small men are coming

In (567–70) the affix -*ḍaran* appears to be synonymous with number adjective *bulay(i)*. In fact, although there is some overlap in meaning, -*ḍaran* frequently has a 'distributive' sense, contrasting with the simple enumeration of *bulay(i)*. Thus, in M:

(575) *balan buṛba bulayi maṛuḍaranba*   two swamps, each with mud
(576) *bayi bulayi yaṛa ɲirmagabundaran wurbaɲu*   two men, each speaking two (different) languages [i.e. there are in all four languages known]

(The use of -*gabun* in (576) is similar to that in (564).) The contrast between *bulayi* and -*ḍaran* is highlighted by the use of -*ḍaran* as an affix to the number *yuŋgul* 'one', as in *baŋugaraɲu yuŋgulḍaran* 'the two [people] have one each' (literally 'belonging to the two people, one each'). See also text xv, line 62 (p. 379) *malaḍaranda bulay* 'two pieces, one in each hand'.

bula occurs as the number adjective 'two', and *(gu)Ḍara(n)* as a dual affix, in many Australian languages; in other languages the functions are reversed – see 1.6.

[13] *-mumbay* 'all (and only) the –'. This suffix can be attached to a noun or adjective and involves no change in syntactic function. Thus:

(577) *bayi yaṛamumbay baniɲu*   all [of a certain community of] men are coming

In spontaneous conversation one woman asked another whether she had told the writer the Dyirbal names of all the fishes (*bayi ḍabu* 'fish'; *wanḍay* 'call a name'; text reference IX: 6):

(578) *ɲindama ḍaɲḍa wanḍaɲu ḍabumumbay*   have you called the names of all the fishes?

-mumbay can be given a deep representation in terms of set inclusion (as in 5.10). Thus [Noun$_S$-*mumbay*, VC] implies that 'Noun$_S$' refers to some 'natural' set of objects S; and that for every member, x, of S [Noun$_x$, VC] holds, where Noun$_x$ has reference x.

[14] *-gara* 'one of a pair' (cf. *balagara*, 3.3.2). *-gara* can be added to certain nouns, and involves no change in function. It is most commonly used with proper nouns and indicates that the person referred to is one of two people involved in a general set of events. *-gara* can also be used with some kinship terms, indicating two of a type. Thus *balan yabundigara* refers to two mothers (say, the two mothers of two men mentioned earlier in the discourse). An example of *-gara* with a proper noun:

(579) *burbulagara baniɲu*   Burbula and another person are coming

Both of the pair may be specified, each with a *-gara* suffix:

(580) *burbulagara badibadigara baniɲu*   Burbula, being one of a pair, and Badibadi, being the other of the pair, are coming

-gara effectively functions as a coordinator within an NP – see also 4.2.1, 5.10.2. Thus, if one wanted to say that both a kangaroo and a wallaby were speared, one could either [i] use a *-gara* construction:

(581) *ɲaḍa bayi yuṛigara bayi bargangara ḍurgaɲu*   I speared kangaroo and wallaby

or [ii] repeat the verb:

(582) *ɲaḍa bayi yuṛi ḍurgaɲu/aṇḍa ɲaḍa bayi bargan ḍurgaɲu/bulayimban*
⟨=(581)⟩

Here *aɲḍa* marks a new topic, and the verbalised number adjective *bulayimban* 'do twice' emphasises that the action is repeated.

A -*gara* NP can function equally well as actor:

(583) *ŋayguna yaɽagaragu ḍugumbilgaragu ḍilwan*   man and woman kicked me

When confronted with the ungrammatical sentence

*(584) *ŋayguna yaɽaŋgu ḍugumbiɽu ḍilwan*

an informant said that the only way to attach any sense to it was to assume that the kicker was a person half-man and half-woman.

[15] -*maŋgan* 'one of many' (cf. *balamaŋgan*, 3.3.2). -*maŋgan* is exactly analogous to -*gara* except that it refers to one amongst many, not to one amongst two. Several of the people in a crowd can be specified, each with suffix -*maŋgan*:

(585) *burbulamaŋgan badibadimaŋgan baniɲu*   many people, including Burbula and Badibadi, are coming

An underlying set representation for -*gara* and -*maŋgan* sentences was discussed in 5.10.2.

[16] -*ḍilu* DG, -*ḍu* M. This is an intensifier that can be suffixed to nouns, adjectives and noun markers, without any change in syntactic function; it can be attached either to a head noun in an NP, or to its noun marker, but not to both. -*ḍilu* cannot be given any overall single English gloss; it can sometimes be taken to carry 'reflexive meaning' (cf. 4.8.1, 6.5.6), e.g. *bayinḍilu yaɽa* 'the man himself' and, in M (text xxv, line 58, p. 392):

(586) *balanḍu ŋambaɲambariɲu buɲali*   she kept thinking about going down [there] herself

In other instances a form like *yaɽaḍilu* can mean 'man on his own'.

-*ḍilu* occurs very frequently, and examination of some of its occurrences in the texts that are given at the end of the book will give some idea of its use as an intensifier.

-*ḍilu* also occurs with pronouns (carrying a reflexive meaning), with time words (6.4), verb markers (6.5.6), with particles such as *biri* and *ḍamu* (4.15.3), and with interjections: *yimba* 'no', *yimbaḍilu* 'certainly not, no indeed', and *ḍuru* 'I don't know', *ḍuruḍilu* 'I definitely do not know' (4.17).

O'Grady et al. [1966: 133] mention that in Wadjuk there is a suffix *-ḏil* with 'assertive reference'; there is a chance that this may be cognate with Dyirbal *-ḏilu*.

[17] *-gayul* 'the same –' has complex syntactic function which includes its functioning as a stem-forming nominal affix. *-gayul* is discussed in 6.1.4.

[18] bound forms *-bayḏi* etc. and *-gali* etc. (3.2.3). These fifteen bound forms function mainly as suffixes to noun and verb markers. Some of them can also, far less commonly, occur as stem-forming nominal affixes, e.g. *bala biguŋgalugalu* 'very long fingernails' from *bala biguɲ* 'fingernails' and *-galu* 'out in front' (text xxxib, line 15, p. 384). And:

(587) *bayi baniɲu diŋgaldayi*   he's coming with his head held very high
(588) *bayi baniɲu diŋgalbayḏi*   he's coming with his head held very low
(589) *bayi baniɲu diŋgalgalu*   he's coming with his head bent down (to charge)

See also *diradayi* 'point up' in text xv, line 53 (p. 377). A common Dyirbal expression for 'upside down' is *munudayi* from *bala munu* 'arse, bottom'.

Of the fifteen forms in 3.2.3 only *bayḏi, dayi, galu, gala* and *gali* have been elicited functioning as stem-forming affixes; only *dayi* and *galu* occur with this function in the corpus of texts. The bound forms are commonly reduplicated when occurring with nouns whereas they cannot be reduplicated when occurring with noun or verb markers.

The difference between, for example, *balagalu biguɲ* and *bala biguɲgalu* is very important: roughly, the form in which *galu* is suffixed to the noun marker, *bala*, indicates POSITION, i.e. that the fingernails are way out in front; the form in which *galu* is suffixed to the noun, *biguɲ*, indicates EXTENSION, i.e. that the fingernails stretch FROM here TO way out in front.

Participles function exactly like noun roots, taking the full range of nominal affixes. Thus *bayi yibiwadilwadilḏaran* 'two woman-swivers' and *bayi miḏaŋga ɲinayɲinaybaḏun* 'a man who really sits all the time in camp'.

6.1.2 Ordering of affixes. Some affixes appear to have fairly fixed ordering qua root and case inflections. Thus *-bara* is only attested immediately after a root; *-gara* and *-maŋgan* appear to belong in the next order, followed by *-ɲa*. At the other extreme, *-ḍilu* always immediately precedes case inflections. The other affixes occur between *-ɲa* and *-ḍilu*, but there is no fixed relative ordering; however, each difference in ordering carries a semantic difference. Thus we can have *yaɽagabunḍaran* 'two other men' and also *yaɽaḍarangabun* 'another two men'; and *bayi yaɽa waɲalḍaranbila* 'man with two boomerangs' as well as *bayi yaɽa waɲalbilaḍaran* 'two men each with boomerang'.

Investigation of ordering is hampered by the fact that Dyirbal words seldom involve more than one nominal affix; the only combinations of affixes that have been observed outside elicitation sessions are *-gara + -ɲa*, *-maŋgan + -ɲa*, *-ḍaran + -bila*, *-bila + -ḍaran + -ḍilu*, *-mumbay + -bila* and *-bara + ḍaran*. It seems that each affix has its own individual potential for combining with other affixes, so that no glib overall statement of relative ordering is possible. (It is probable that only a native speaker, who was trained as a linguist, would be able to give a full account of this topic.)

For instance, *-ŋunu* can occur with *-ḍaran* in:

(590) *giyi midinḍaran yugariḍaranŋunu*   those (are) two possums, out of two hollow logs (i.e. each out of its own hollow log)

but it cannot occur with *-bila* in:

*(591) *balan ḍugumbil gunabila midiɲunubila baniɲu*   [woman is coming with child's faeces]

instead, we must say simply:

(592) *balan ḍugumbil gunabila midiɲunu baniɲu*   woman is coming with child's faeces

Combinations of affixes that have been elicited include (together with the noun used): *miḍagabunɲunu* 'from another camp', *miḍagabungabunɲunu* 'from all the camps', *gugulabaḍunɲaru* 'like a real platypus', *gambilbaragara* 'a person from the tableland, being one of a pair', *bulganbaḍunbila* 'with a really big (thing)', *waɲalmumbaybila* 'with all the boomerangs', *midibaḍunɲaŋgay* 'without any really small (ones)', and in M *midibaḍunḍarangabunba* 'with another two really small (ones)'.

It appears that no other affix can occur with a bound form *bayḍi* etc. functioning as nominal affix. We can have, for instance, *bayi yaɽa ɲumbulgalugalu ɲumbulbila* 'man has a long beard' (*bala ɲumbul* 'beard') but not **bayi yaɽa ɲumbulgalugalubila*.

6.1.3 Kinship duals. Certain kinship terms can be described as 'reciprocal' – if A is in X-relation to B, then B is also in X-relation to A. Thus a child will call his or her mother's father *ŋagi*, and the grandfather will call this child *ŋagi*. Similarly a child will call its mother's older brother *mugu*, and this uncle will in return refer to the nephew or niece as *mugu*.

There is an affix *-ḍir* which occurs with reciprocal kinship terms and refers to two people who are in the reciprocal relation to each other. Thus *ŋagiḍir* 'maternal grandfather and grandchild', as in:

(593) *bayindayi ŋagiḍir baniɲu* two people, one of whom is maternal grandfather of the other, a short way uphill are coming

It appears that there are only six or seven reciprocal kin terms that can take the dual affix *-ḍir*. They are:

[1] *bulu* 'father's father'
[2] *babi* 'father's mother'
[3] *ŋagi* 'mother's father'
[4] *gumbu* 'mother's mother'
[5] *bimu* 'father's elder brother or sister'
[6] *mugu* 'mother's elder brother'; and *mugunan* 'mother's elder sister' – the dual form is said to be *muguḍir* in each case.

The terms for a parent's younger siblings are not reciprocal, and do not occur with *-ḍir*. The forms used are:

relation to ego	ego calls the relative	ego is called by the relative
father and father's younger brother	*ŋuma*	*galbin*
father's younger sister	*ŋalban*	*galbin*
mother and mother's younger sister	*yabu*	*daman*
mother's younger brother	*gaya*	*daman*

There are two further dual forms:

[1] *ŋumaygir* – two people who are in *ŋuma/galbin* relation, e.g. a father and child (son or daughter)
[2] *ginagir* – two people who are in *yabu/daman* relation

Note that while *ŋumaygir* is clearly related to *ŋuma*, the suppletive form *gina* is encountered – where *yabu* would be expected – in *ginagir*.

There appear to be no dual forms referring to two people who are in *ŋalban/galbin* or *gaya/daman* relation.

Reduplication of the root part of a *-ḍir* or *-gir* dual implies inclusion of more than one member of the younger generation in a pair. Thus *ŋagiŋagiḍir* is 'a man, together with two or more of his daughter's children', *ŋumaŋumaygir* is 'a man, together with two or more of his own, or of his elder brother's, children'.

The noun class of a *-ḍir* or *-gir* form depends on the sex of the member of the OLDER generation; thus *ginaginagir* might refer to a woman accompanied by her six sons, but would always take noun marker *balan*.

-ḍir/-gir can be followed by some, but not all, nominal affixes, e.g. *ŋagiḍirbila*, *ŋagiḍirbaḍun* but not **ŋagiḍirḍaran*.

There is nothing unusual in an Australian language having kinship-determined affixes; as mentioned in 1.5, a number of languages have several sets of pronouns, depending on the relationship of the people referred to.

6.1.4 gayul. *-gayul* occurs in D as a stem–forming affix only in stems that receive a locational (allative, ablative or locative) case inflection: *miḍagayuṛa* 'at the same camp', *miḍagayulgu* 'to the same camp', *miḍagayulŋunu* 'from the same camp'. A nominal-plus-*gayul* stem cannot occur in a non-locational inflection in D; we cannot have, for example:

**(594) ŋayguna baŋgul yaṛagayuṛu balgan   the same man hit me

It appears that in M stems involving *-gayul* can receive ANY case inflection; thus (594) is an acceptable sentence in M (and appears to be synonymous with (595)).

gayul also occurs in both D and M as a particle, to indicate that an action is repeated with the same actor (if an intransitive action) or actor and goal (if a transitive action):

(595) *ŋayguna baŋgul yaṛaŋgu gayul balgan*   the same man hit me again
(596) *bayi gayul yaṛa baniŋu*   the same man is coming again

As a particle *gayul* can occur anywhere before the verb.

-gayul thus marks reference to the same token of the same type – it contrasts with *-gabun* 'another', 6.1.1.

The behaviour of *gayul* tends to support the view that Dyirbal is gradually getting more 'synthetic' (in terms of the general view that modern Australian

languages have evolved from an ancestor that was considerably less synthetic
– 1.12). *gayul* appears to be gradually acquiring the status of an affix, and
has moved further in this direction in M than in D.

6.1.5 Case inflections. Case inflections can be added to any nominal
stem – a full paradigm was given in 3.2.1. With a few exceptions
(*-bu*, *-ru*, *-bi* – 6.7; *-ḍan(a)* – 6.1.6) nothing can follow a case inflection
within the same word. Sentence clitics (*-ma*, *-riga*, *-gira* – 4.16) are
enclitic to the first word of a sentence, whatever it is or whatever its
inflection.

Dative and allative are both realised by *-gu* in the case of nouns.
There are, however, a number of syntactic differences between the
two case forms:

[1] a noun-plus-*gu* will be accompanied by a dative noun marker
(*bagul*, *bagun*, *bagum* or *bagu*) if it is in dative case; and by an allative
verb marker (*balu* or *bali*) if the *-gu* marks allative case.

[2] a dative, but not an allative, noun can be qualified by a relative
clause.

[3] a dative, but not an allative, noun can be the basis for a favourite
construction.

[4] an allative, but not a dative, noun can be verbalised.

[5] an allative, but not a dative, noun can be augmented by affix *-ru*
(3.4.6).

In most instances there is sufficient information WITHIN a sentence to tell
whether a *-gu* form is dative or allative; in case of doubt the ambiguity can be
resolved by asking the informant whether the form could be verbalised, or
qualified by a relative clause, and so on.

Semantically, dative *-gu* and allative *-gu* are fairly distinct (translation into
English, where they can both be rendered by 'to', tends to obscure this).
There is, however, an ELEMENT of common meaning between allative and
dative in Dyirbal, as in other languages. Further general discussion of this
point would be outside the scope of the present work.

The ablative case, and the stem-forming nominal affix 'out of – ,
from –' have the same realisation: *-ŋunu*. These are semantically similar
but differ functionally: the nominal affix can be followed by a case
inflection, whereas the ablative case inflection must be word-final; a
nominal plus stem-forming affix *-ŋunu* behaves like an adjective,
modifying the head noun in an NP, whereas a nominal in ablative case
provides locational qualification for the head noun in a VP, agreeing
with the verb marker in locational choice (i.e. co-occurring only with
verb markers *baŋum*, *yaŋum*). Informants gave sentences (547–8) and:

(597) *bayi   mulmaɲu |balugali |banagu |*
THERE-NOM-I dive-PRES/PAST THERE-TO-PLACE-DOWN water-ALL
ŋalgalaygu   ḍabangu maṛaluɲunugu
poke-*ɲay*-PURP eel-DAT hollow log-OUT OF-DAT
they dive down into the water to poke eels [with sticks] out of
hollow logs [under the water]

(598) *ŋaḍa ɲinaɲ yaṛaŋga yiŋariŋunuga* I'll sit by the man from the
hole [e.g. a man that had fallen into a hole and had to be pulled
out again]

It appears impossible to have a word involving two *-ɲunu's* – a stem-forming
affix followed by ablative inflection. Thus informants rejected:

*(599) *ŋaḍa baniɲu baŋum yaṛaɲunu yiŋariŋunuŋunu*

in favour of:

(600) *ŋaḍa baniɲu baŋum yaṛaɲunu yiŋaribaraŋunu* I'm coming from man
from hole

Although the simple genitive cases in Dyirbal have some semantic
similarities with genitive and dative cases set up for other languages
(for example, Latin) there are significant differences. For example,
wugal 'give' typically occurs in a proleptic construction; that is, the
giver will be in the ergative case, that which is given in the nominative
case, and the recipient in the simple genitive case, as a possessive
phrase qualifying that which is given:

(601) *balam miraɲ baɲun ḍugumbilɲu baŋgul yaṛaŋgu wugan* man gave
woman beans

literally 'man gave beans, which belong to woman [understood: beans
are given to person to whom they belong]'. This kind of construction
is consistent with the Dyirbalŋan's belief that something must belong
'by right'; there is very little spontaneous non-necessary giving, but
a great deal of necessary giving, according to the people's habits of
sharing most things with their relatives etc. – 2.4. A full account of the
considerable syntactic possibilities of *wugan* is in 8.2.3.

The locative case has, in addition to its central use as an indicator
of position, the following uses:

[1] when something is done because of X, X can receive locative
inflection. There is very frequently an element of fear involved here:
what is done may be done to avoid contact with X. For example
(text xv, lines 24 and 36, pp. 373–4):

(602) *giyiɲaŋgadayi ŋali buybarigu*   let us hide ourselves away from him
(603) *yuɽay ŋali ɲina/baɲulḍinda*   we must sit quietly, because of that
which belongs to him (i.e. so that we do not become involved
with it)

A locative inflection of this type can go on to:

either [a] a noun marker plus *-ɲa*, e.g. *bayiɲaŋga* 'for fear of him
there', *yayiɲaŋga* 'for fear of him here'
or [b] a noun marker in genitive inflection, e.g. *baɲulḍinda*,
yaɲulḍinda
or [c] a noun in genitive inflection, e.g. *ḍumbuluɲuɲḍinda*

However, it cannot go on to a simple noun root, or a noun root plus
-ɲa; thus (qua this sense) **ḍumbuluga*, **ḍumbuluɲaŋga*.

Forms of type [c] can co-occur with type [a] or with type [b]:

(604) *galga yanum bayiɲaŋga ḍumbuluɲuɲḍinda*   don't go for fear of
Dyumbulu
(605) *galga yanum baɲulḍinda ḍumbuluɲuɲḍinda*   ⟨=(604)⟩

A locative in sense [1] can involve a relative clause:

(606) *ŋaliḍi buybayiri bayiɲaŋga baniɲura*   hide for fear of him that
has [/may] come

Note that the verb inflection *-bila* (4.13.1) can occur with dative but
not with locative inflection.

Further examples are in text xxxib, lines 1 and 2 (p. 383).

[2] locative inflection is used in some cases when (on the basis of
English 'to') dative might be expected; that is, locative marks certain
'objects' of adjectives etc. Thus *ḍilbay* means 'know how to do something, e.g. used to the job'; it can also mean 'know a certain person,
i.e. familiar with their ways and habits', as in:

(607) *bayi ḍilbaybin ŋaygudinda*   he's used to me (say, he knows he
can treat my place like home, and help himself to my food, etc.)

[3] locative can also mean 'amongst –, of –':

(608) *bayi mididaran bulayi yaɽaŋga bulgangaydḍa*   they are the smallest
two of the men [literally. they are two small amongst big(ger)
men]

[4] when talking about language activity, the name of a language or

style of speech (e.g. *guwal, ḍalŋuy*) may be in locative case, e.g. *giramayḍa* 'in Giramay', *ḍirbaɽa* 'in Dyirbal':

(609) *ŋinda wurba giramayḍa*   you talk in Giramay!

or *wiyaman ḍalŋuyḍa* 'how is it done (i.e. said) in Dyalŋuy?'.
    Note that an alternative to (609) is:

(610) *ŋinda giramay wurba*   you talk Giramay!

where the noun referring to 'language' is in the topic NP (here *ŋinda giramay* should perhaps be regarded as an instance of inalienable possession).
    [5] locative is the only case inflection that can occur with DM *yimba*, G *maya* 'nothing'; thus *yimbaŋga* 'concerning nothing' – see (351) and 4.17.

6.1.6   -ḍana, -ban. Affixes *-ḍana* and *-ban* can be placed at the end of various types of words; they do not appear to have any clear cognitive meaning, nor any very fixed or strong syntactic function.
    -ḍana can be affixed to noun markers, demonstrative markers, pronouns and time qualifiers. It draws attention to a certain person or thing: 'this is the one'.

(611) *ŋindaḍana ŋayguna ŋundaɲu*   you're the one that blamed me
(612) *ŋaygunaḍana ŋinda ŋundaɲu*   I'm the one you blamed

One use of *-ḍana* is in replying to a question about some earlier sentence that was not clearly understood. Thus, if a speaker said:

(613) *gilu ŋaḍa yanuɲ*   I'll go later on today

but the addressee, not hearing clearly, asked:

(614) *miɲay*   when?

the speaker would be likely to say:

(615) *giluḍana ŋaḍa yanuɲ*

emphasising the *gilu* by means of *-ḍana*.
    -ḍana cannot normally be affixed to more than one word in an NP (or, for that matter, in a sentence). Thus we can say *bayinḍana yaɽa dungaraɲu* 'man cried' or *bayi yaɽaḍana dungaraɲu* but not **bayinḍana yaɽaḍana dungaraɲu*.

-*ḍana* is sometimes shortened to -*ḍan* in discourse – see (555). The common imperative particle form *gaḍiḍan* (4.15.1) probably involves this affix.

-*ban* can be affixed to (at least) noun markers, predominantly in M, and provides a degree of emphasis. Thus DM *bayimban*, G *bayinban* is a more emphatic form than *bayi*. -*ban* also occurs with interjections, e.g. *yimbaban, mayaban, mayaḍiluban* – see 4.17.

6.1.7 Cardinal and ordinal numbers. The cardinal numbers are:

DG	M	
yuŋgul	*yuŋgul*	'one'
bulay(i)	*bulayi*	'two'
gaṛbu	*waraɲuŋgul*	'three'
mundi	*gaṛbu*	'a good few (from 4 to about 50 or more)'
muɲa	*ḍulun*	'a lot (about 100 or more)'

There is also a number term *gibaṛ*, meaning a certain order of magnitude (said by informants to be 'one hundred'). A message stick summoning a tribe to a fighting corroboree had a set of marks indicating how many *gibaṛ* of other tribes were going to take part (one mark would indicate one *gibaṛ*).

There are also 'marked' terms for higher numbers, e.g. *bulayirin-bulayirin* 'four'; *bulayigaṛbu* DG 'five' (in M *bulayibulayiyuŋgul* is used for 'five' in preference to **bulayiwaraɲuŋgul*); *gaṛburungaṛburun* DG 'six'. The NP *mala yuŋgul* 'one hand' is also commonly used for 'five'; and so on. Thus, four objects can be referred to by the general term *mundi*, or more specifically by *bulayirinbulayirin*, and similarly in other cases.

There is a set of ordinals based on *yuŋgul*:

> *yuŋgul* 'one'
> *yuŋgugan* 'a second one'
> *yuŋgularu* 'a third and succeeding one'

And another set based on *bulay(i)*:

> *bulay(i)* 'two'
> *bulayiru* 'a second or later pair'

There exist, analogously, *gaṛburu, waraɲuŋgularu, mundiru* etc. (The

M informant stated that *bulayiru* was pretty well synonymous with *bulayigabun*.) A general discussion of the affix *-ru* is in 6.7.1.

muɲa is used for 'a lot' and *muɲagabun* for 'another lot (of the same thing)'; *muɲarnbara* is commonly used to refer to 'a big crowd', there being also *muɲarnbararu* 'another big crowd'.

In M at least there is a common phrase *yuŋgul yuŋgulba* 'one by one' (literally: 'one with one').

See 6.1.1 for discussion of the contrast between *bulay(i)* and dual affix *-ḍaran*.

6.1.8   Vestigial plurals. As a rule, plural forms of nominal roots are obtained by reduplication. However, there are separate plural forms for one adjective and a handful of nouns:

root	plural form	
DM *bulgan*	*bulgangay* ⎱	'big'
G *ḍagiɲ*	*ḍagiŋgay* ⎰	
yaṟa	*yaṟarḍi*	'man'
barŋan	*barŋanmi* (M only)	'young boy (just before initiation)'
ṟugun	*ṟugunmi*	'youth (initiated)'
gaḍiya	*gaḍiyami*	'young girl (just before puberty)'
nayi	*nayinba*	'girl (past puberty)'
ɲalŋga	*ɲalŋgaymbaṟu* (M only)	'child (any age up to puberty)'

It is interesting to note that there is a separate plural form for 'man' but not for 'woman'; in fact *yaṟa* occurs in all three dialects, whereas the term for 'woman' is *yibi* in M, *ḍugumbil* in D and *gumbul* in G. Other 'age-group terms' do not have a special plural – thus *ḍaḍa* 'baby' and *ḍaḍaḍaḍa* 'many babies'.

It is also interesting to note that the different words for 'big' in DM and G form plurals in the same way. In contrast, the Dyalŋuy correspondent *gagiṟ* can only form a plural by reduplication; similarly the Dyalŋuy correspondents of the six nouns listed above all lack plural forms (beyond the usual reduplication).

Plural forms are used to denote more than two things; *-ḍaran* (6.1.1) or *bulay(i)* (6.1.7) are used for explicit reference to two things. For all other nominals number is an optional category – the root is the unmarked form which can be taken to refer to one, two or many things (or, in marked context, it can mean 'one' in contrast to a dual (*-ḍaran*) or a plural (reduplicated) form). However, number is an obligatory category for the seven words listed above: the simple root always has reference to just 'one' thing.

6.1.9   Reduplication. Any nominal root can be reduplicated (the whole root is repeated) – indicating plurality (generally 'three or more'); the exceptions are the seven forms listed in the last section which have idiosyncratic plural forms. A reduplicated adjective indicates reference to more than two things with that property, e.g. *midimidi* 'lots of little ones', *gulgiɹigulgiɹi* 'lots of prettily painted men'. An unreduplicated root can refer to any number of objects; the 'marked' reduplicated form refers to more than two:

(616)   *balan ḍugumbil baŋgun ɲalŋgaŋgu buɹan*   girl(s) saw woman/women

(617)   *balan ḍugumbil baŋgun ɲalŋgaɲalŋgagu buran*   girls saw woman/women

Note that *ɲalŋga*, a two-syllable stem, has ergative inflection *-ŋgu*; *ɲalŋgaɲalŋga*, a stem of more than two syllables, has ergative inflection *-gu* (cf. the paradigm in 3.2.1). With *balan gabul* 'carpet snake':

(618)   *balan maga baŋgun gabuɹu ḍaŋgaɲu*   carpet snake(s) ate rat(s)

(619)   *balan maga baŋgun gabulgabuɹu ḍaŋgaɲu*   carpet snakes ate rat(s)

Here root-final *-l* occurs in the reduplicated root, even though it has been lost stem-finally before the ergative inflection.

Some stem-forming nominal affixes can be reduplicated: with *-gabun* and *-baḍun* this has the same effect as reduplicating the root to which they are suffixed, i.e. it indicates plurality. Thus *bayi yaɹagabungabun* 'lots of other men, OR lots of strangers', *midibaḍunbaḍun* 'lots of very small ones'; these are semantically equivalent to *bayi yaɹayaɹagabun* and *midimidibaḍun* respectively. A root and an affix may not both be reduplicated: we cannot have **midimidibaḍunbaḍun*, and so on. *-mumbay* can be reduplicated, emphasising that a VERY large number is involved; *-ginay*, indicating excessive contamination – *gunaginayginay* 'totally covered with faeces'; and *-ŋaŋgay*, emphasising that there is nothing at all – *banaŋaŋgay* 'without water', *banaŋaŋgayŋaŋgay* 'with absolutely no water at all'. *-bila*, *-ḍaran*, *-ŋaru*, *-baɹa* and probably most of the other affixes listed in 6.1.1 can never be reduplicated (the common reduplication of *galu*, *dayi* etc. functioning as nominal affixes was mentioned in 6.1.1 – this carries no implications of plurality).

Some four-syllable noun roots appear to be in reduplicated form (but in almost every case the unreduplicated form does not exist): *bala ḍibanḍiban* 'a wart', *bayi naŋgalnaŋgal* 'small black ants', *bala ḍuluḍulu* 'Johnson hard wood', *bayi gurilnguril* 'a storm bird' – see 9.4.

Reduplication of noun markers and demonstrative noun markers is dealt with in 6.5.5.

6.2 Pronominal morphology

Pronominal forms (listed in the paradigm of 3.3.1) can be analysed in terms of categories of first and second person, and of singular, dual and plural number. For each person and number we can recognise a 'general root':

	first person	second person
singular	*ŋaygu*	*ɲinu*
dual	*ŋali ~ ŋaliḍi*	*ɲubala ~ ɲubalaḍi*
plural	*ŋana ~ ŋanaḍi*	*ɲura(y) ~ ɲuraḍi*

The case forms in D and M can now be analysed (cf. 5.8.2):

	singular	non-singular
[+actor] form	[see below]	general root
[−actor] plus nominative form	general root + *-na*	general root + *-na*
genitive	general root	general root + *-nu ~ -ŋu*
dative	general root + *-ngu*	general root + *-na + ngu*

and in G:

	singular	non-singular
[+actor] form	[see below]	general root
[−actor] plus nominative form	[see below]	general root + *-ɲa*
genitive	general root	general root + *-nu ~ -ŋu*
dative	general root + *-ngu*	general root + *-ɲa + -ngu*

In the table of 3.3.1 G appears to have borrowed the D form for the second person dual pronoun, except that the distinctive G second vowel *i* is retained; it seems that the forms given in 3.3.1 are in free variation with forms that would be expected from the rule above.

The genitive inflection is in all dialects *-ŋu* on to a disyllabic stem and *-nu* on to a stem of three or more syllables.

Note that the pseudo-pronoun *balagara* (3.3.2) forms a genitive by adding
-*ŋu*, showing that it inflects as a noun and not as a pronoun.

Note also that -*ɲa* is optional on [−actor] nouns and – since other stem-
forming affixes can follow it – is best regarded as a stem-forming affix and not
as a case inflection with nouns. With [−actor] plus nominative pronouns,
-*na* (DM) ~ -*ɲa* (G) is obligatory and must be regarded as a case inflection.
balagara and *balamaŋgan* behave like nouns in this respect.

-*ḍin* can be added to a genitive form (4.11) and the resulting form
given any case inflection; in the case of dual and plural pronouns the
genitive -*ŋu* ~ -*nu* affix can optionally be omitted in -*ḍin* forms. We can
thus have either *ŋaliɲuɳḍinda* or *ŋaliḍinda* 'at that which belongs to us
two'. A form *ŋaliḍinda* is structurally analogous to the -*ḍin* plus locative
form of a singular pronoun, where the genitive form is just the general root.

Similarly, in the case of the interrogative pronoun, *waɲuḍin* alternates with
waɲuɲuɳḍin.

Non-singular dative forms can be regarded as derived from [−actor]
plus nominative forms by the addition of -*gu*; the -*n*- is a predictable
phonological intrusion (7.5.1). In D and M the -*na*- is usually dropped
from dative forms. However, this is not absolutely obligatory – D
speakers have been heard to use *ɲubalaḍinangu* rather than *ɲubalaḍingu*,
and informants accepted the first form as possible although preferring
the second (on the grounds that it was 'shorter').

We must assume the -*na*- is present in the underlying forms (of both singular
and non-singular pronouns) in order to explain the presence of -*n*- in non-*ḍi*
forms – by a rule of 7.5.1, *n* is inserted before dative -*gu* only when immediately
following a stressed vowel.

The seventh pronoun in M, a special type of first person dual, has
general root *ŋanaymba*, and inflects like the regular duals and plurals.

The singular pronouns show additional complexities that suggest
the postulation, in addition to the general root, of what we can call
a 'basic root'. Thus:

	basic root	general root
First person singular	*ŋay*	*ŋaygu*
Second person singular	*ɲin*	*ɲinu*

We could say that the pronoun forms not dealt with above are
derived from the basic root:

[+actor] form in D and M ⎫ [+actor] plus ergative form in G ⎭	basic root + -*da*
[+actor] plus nominative form in G	basic root + -*ba*
[−actor] plus nominative form in G	basic root + -*ɲa*

In all other cases G pronouns involve *-ɲa* where D and M have *-na*. The justification for recognising *-ɲa* rather than *-na* in the singular [−actor] plus nominative forms is [1] the common Australian affix is *-N̪a*, realised as *-n̪a* in languages having a laminal contrast, and as *-ɲa* in languages with a single laminal series (1.2, 1.5). Gugu-Baḍun has a pronoun paradigm very similar to that of G; it differs from G in that it has two laminal series instead of one. The first person singular object pronoun in Gugu-Baḍun is *ŋan̪a* against G's *ŋaɲa*. [2] if the affix is recognised as *-ɲa*, we have *ŋin+ɲa → ŋina* in G. This agrees with the rule needed for genitives and for *balamaŋgan, balan* plus *-ɲa* – in certain circumstances, the first of two consecutive nasals is dropped – 3.2.1, 6.1.1.

Against this is the consideration that *-yn-* is an impossible sequence intra-morphemically, being replaced by *-ɲ-* (7.5.2). Thus if the affix were *-na*, *ŋaɲa* would be simply explainable; if the affix is *-ɲa* we have an apparently un-motivated dropping of *-y-* from *ŋayɲa*.

There are synchronic grounds for considering *-ba* a case affix in G. However, the likely historical explanation is that [−actor] plus nominative forms were originally just the basic root – as is the case nowadays with east coast languages such as Gabi (1.5). *-ba* has been added to roots in a number of languages for PURELY PHONOLOGICAL REASONS, e.g. so that every word should be at least disyllabic (probably the reason here), or so that every word should end in a vowel [Hale, mimeo-c: 93ff].

The affix *-da* provides a tidy analysis – *-yd-* is not a possible intramorphemic cluster, and would be replaced by *-ḍ-* (7.5.2). However, once it is realised that *-ba* is not properly a case affix, the recognition of *-da* as an affix becomes less plausible. Historical investigation may eventually relate *-da* (∼ *-du* in other languages) to ergative *-lu*; but it is equally likely that further study will show that there is insufficient evidence to justify any kind of analysis of *ŋaḍa* and *ŋinda*.

The general root appears to be derived from the basic root, by the addition of *-gu* in the first person and *-u* in the second.

The [−actor] plus nominative form – which is the nearest pro-nominal equivalent of the 'topic' form of nouns – appears to be syntactically central. Thus the affix *-bila* 'with' occurs with what appears to be this form:

(620) ŋaḍa ɲinaɲu   dibanda/ diban   balbaliɲu
I-SA sit-PRES/PAST stone-LOC stone-NOM roll-PRES/PAST
ŋaygunalaymbila
I-WITH
I sat on the stone; the stone rolled [downhill] with me

Compare the occurrence of *-bila* with proper nouns, e.g. *ḍumbuluɲalay-mbila* in (537), 6.1.1.

There are no allative, ablative or locative inflections of pronouns.

In D, the plural pronouns can be reduplicated, in a kind of joking exaggeration: *ŋanaŋanaḍi* 'all of us' (text reference IX. 41) and *ɲuraɲuraḍi*.

Affixes *-baḍun, -ḍilu, ḍan(a), -ru, -bu* and *-bi* can be added to pronouns, the affix always following the case inflections. The only noted instance of two affixes to the same pronoun involves *-ḍilu* and *-bu*; then the order is *-buḍilu* (the same order as with noun markers, but the opposite of that with nouns).

6.3 Verbal morphology

6.3.1 Verbal word structure.

Each verbal word (whether verb or adverbal) must involve [i] a root, and [ii] a final inflectional ending. Between these constituents can occur:

[1] *-ŋay*, 4.4.2
[2] reciprocal *-nbariy*, 4.8.2
[3] aspectual affixes *-galiy ~ -nbal*; or *-yaray*; or *-ganiy*, 6.3.2
[4] aspectual affix *-ḍay*, 6.3.2
[5] reflexive *-riy ~ -yiriy ~ -mariy*, 4.8.1
[6] comitative/instrumentive *-mal ~ -mbal*, 4.9

At first sight there appears to be no strict ordering between these affixes. Thus we get [4] both before and after [6] – *nudilḍayman* and *nudilmalḍaɲu* – and [5] both before and after [6] – *buybayirimban* and *ɲinaymariɲu*. Further, we can get a verbal word with two occurrences of [6] – *ɲinaymariman*. If a table of 'affix orders' were constructed we would have to allow the 'threading' of the table to loop back and pass through parts of it at least twice.

All the complexities just mentioned involve the comitative/instrumentive affix *-mal ~ -mbal*. Now we showed in 5.7 that any surface structure which involves this affix can be provided with a deep structure involving two Σ's. This suggests rules for deriving verbal word structure:

1. $\text{V} \rightarrow \text{Root} + \left(\left\{ \begin{matrix} \text{-}\eta ay \\ \text{RECIP} \end{matrix} \right\} \right) + \left(\left\{ \begin{matrix} \text{-}gali \sim \text{-}nbal \\ \text{-}yaray \\ \text{-}ganiy \end{matrix} \right\} \right) + (\text{-}ḍay) + (\text{REFL}) + (\text{V}') + \text{I}$

(here I indicates the final inflectional ending)

2. $\text{V}' \rightarrow \text{-}mal \sim \text{-}mbal + \left(\left\{ \begin{matrix} \text{-}gali \sim \text{-}nbal \\ \text{-}yaray \\ \text{-}ganiy \end{matrix} \right\} \right) + (\text{-}ḍay) + (\text{REFL}) + (\text{V}')$

With the proviso that only a transitive root can accept -*ŋay*, reciprocal
or reflexive affixes, and then becomes intransitive. Thus only one of
these three affixes can be chosen in rule 1.

These rules explain FIRSTLY the fact that -*ŋay* and reciprocal affixes
occur immediately after a verb root; SECONDLY the fact that -*ŋay* and
reciprocal can be followed by aspectual affixes, e.g. *dumbalnbarigalin-
ḍaygu, nudilŋanḍayman, duyginayaraygu* (text xxv, line 58, p. 392);
THIRDLY, the fact that reflexive can be preceded by aspectual affixes,
e.g. *gunbalganiḍariman*.

Thus, following 5.7, we regard -*mal* ~ -*mbal* as a type of verb root,
that can 'take' any verbal affixes with the exception of -*ŋay* and
reciprocal. In practice, no form involving more than two comitative
affixes has been encountered (this implies two applications of rule 2
above); the instrumentive affix has been encountered followed by an
aspectual affix, but not by reflexive.

Each verb must take a final inflectional ending. The possibilities are:

[1] tense (3.4.3)
    [a] future – DM -*ɲ* with deletion of stem-final consonant; G -*ḍay*
    to an -*l* stem, and -*nḍay* with deletion of stem-final -*y* in the
    case of a -*y* stem
    [b] non-future – -*n* to an -*l* stem and -*ɲu* to a -*y* stem, with
    deletion of stem-final consonant in each case

[2] imperative (4.12)
    [a] positive – deletion of stem-final consonant
    [b] negative – DM -*m* replacing stem-final consonant; G -*mu*
    with loss of stem-final -*y* but retention of -*l*

[3] -*ŋura* (4.5.5)

[4] purposive – -*gu* to a -*y* stem and -*i* to an -*l* stem (4.4.3)

[5] -*bila* ~ -*ba* (details in 4.13.1); can in some circumstances be
    followed by -*gu*

[6] in M only: -*ga* (4.13.2)

[7] relative clause
    [a] -*ɲu*
    [b] in M only: -*mi*   } followed by case inflection (4.10)

[8] participial
    [a] simple stem
    [b] stem + -*muɲa*   } followed by nominal affixes and case
    [c] stem + -*ginay*   inflection (4.6)

6.3.2 Aspectual affixes. In addition to the affixes that mark types of construction, there are also four stem-forming 'aspectual' affixes:

> [1] *-nbal* ~ *-galiy* 'do it quickly'. The alternants occur as follows:
> > [a] *-nbal* with transitive *-l* stems;
> > [b] *-galiy*, plus elision of stem-final *-y* or *-l*, with all other stems (i.e. with intransitive *-l* stems, and with all *-y* stems).

Thus, with transitive roots *ḍurgay* and *buybal*, and intransitive *baniy* and *wayṇḍil*:

(621) *ŋaḍa bayi bargan ḍurgagaliṇu*   I quickly speared the wallaby
(622) *ŋaḍa giṇa buybalnban*   I hid that thing quickly
(623) *bayi yaṛa banigaliṇu*   man came quickly
(624) *ŋaḍa wayṇḍigaliṇu*   I went uphill quickly

It appears that in M *-galiy* can be used with all stems, although *-nbal* is PREFERRED with transitive *-l* stems; in D, ONLY *-nbal* occurs with transitive *-l* stems.

The basic form of alternant *-nbal* can be regarded as *-bal*, the *-n-* being brought in by a phonological rule (7.5.1).

A case could be made for considering the reciprocal affix *-(n)bariy* as morphologically analysable into *-(n)bal* and reflexive *-(yi)riy*. Arguments against this are [1] such an analysis would be semantically unrevealing – there being no implication of 'quickness' in *-(n)bariy*; [2] the *-(n)bal* alternant is only used with *-l* stems, whereas *-(n)bariy* can be used with any transitive root (obligatorily reduplicated) – we thus have *ḍurgagaliṇu* 'spear quickly' and *ḍurgayḍurgaybariṇu* 'spear each other' but not **ḍurga(y)ban*.

There are also forms that appear to be false reciprocals, exactly like false reflexives: thus *maŋgalmbarigu* (text XXXIb, line 9, p. 383) and *yubalnbarimali* (text XV, line 76, p. 381). These forms involve a transitive root with the reciprocal affix, but show no reduplication; they function intransitively. We can either regard them as 'false reciprocals', or else as 'false reflexives' with the reflexive affix preceded by *-nbal*; there is no evidence preferring either solution. It should be noted that, even though we chose not to relate reciprocals to reflexives (in the past paragraph) we are still free to relate 'false reciprocals' to 'false reflexives'.

> [2] *-ganiy* 'do it repeatedly'. When used with a *-y* stem, stem-final *-y* is replaced by *-n-*; stem-final *-l* is retained in G and M but lost in D.

(625) *balan ḍugumbil baŋgul yaṛaŋgu balgaganiṇu*   man has hit woman many times
(626) *bayi yaṛa baninganiṇu*   man has come here many times

[3] -*yaray*, with deletion of the final -*l* or -*y* of a stem to which it is attached. This affix is not so easily translatable into English as -*nbal*~ -*galiy* or -*ganiy*. It appears to mean either 'do it a bit more' or 'start to do it' or 'start to do it a bit more':

(627) *bayi yaɽa yanuyaraɲu*   man went a bit further away
(628) *balan ḍugumbil baŋgul yaɽaŋgu balgayaraɲu*   man started to hit woman (i.e. he raised his stick, and started to bring it down to hit her) OR man hit woman a bit harder
(629) *bayi yaɽa banagayaraɲu*   EITHER man carried on returning (i.e. he is now on the last half of his journey back) OR man returned again (having already returned once and gone away again)

[4] -*ḍay* (when used with a -*y* stem, stem-final -*y* is replaced by -*n*-). This affix appears on the surface to have two quite different semantic effects, implying:

EITHER [a] that an action is repeated (the action often being performed not with respect to some known goal, but blindly, everywhere, in the hope of encountering a goal):

(630) *bayi yaɽa ŋandandaɲu*   he called out in all directions (i.e. not knowing if there was anyone there to hear him)
(631) *bayi yaɽa bilindaɲu*   he climbed many trees (e.g. looking for possum, not knowing where any might be)
(632) *ŋaḍa buɽaldaɲu*   I looked everywhere

OR [b] that an action involves many objects (realising deep function S or O):

(633) *bayi yaɽa ɲinandaɲu*   many men are sitting down
(634) *balam miraɲ baŋgul yaɽaŋgu gundaldaɲu*   he put lots of beans in [the dilly bag]

The first type of meaning of -*ḍay* appears to have some similarities with the meaning of -*ganiy*.

-*ḍay* can best be explained, and contrasted with *ganiy*, as follows: -*ganiy* indicates that an event is repeated many times OVER A LONGISH TIME SPAN, each event being an exact repetition (same action, objects, etc.) of the original event. -*ḍay* indicates that an event is repeated many times WITHIN A SHORT TIME SPAN, the events being taken to be exact repetitions if this would be situationally plausible; if it is situationally implausible for an event to be exactly repeated many times within a short time span then the repetition is understood to involve some difference of token (but not of type) of one aspect of the event.

Thus *bilinganiy* might refer to a person climbing the same tree every morning for a week, while *bilinḍay* would normally be taken to refer to a person climbing many different trees within the space of an hour, say. *ŋabal* is a transitive root 'duck [a person under the water]'; the form *ŋabalganiy* means 'repeatedly duck', while *ŋabalḍay* is 'drown'. *ɲinay* is a 'durative' verb indicating an act of sitting down or staying put for some time (and not just the action of getting into a sitting position, which would be *ɲinayaray*) and so *ɲinanḍay* is normally taken to refer to a number of people all sitting down. In the case of *gundalḍay* it is implausible to suppose that one thing should be put many times into a single container, or put into many different containers – the unmarked interpretation of *gundalḍay* is of many things being put into a single container.

The difference of token between successive events referred to by a -*ḍay* form are EITHER [1] differences of location or direction – as in *bilinḍay, ŋandanḍay, buṛalḍay*; OR [2] different tokens of a (deep) topic NP. -*ḍay* can never refer to different tokens of an A NP.

wugal 'give' has wide syntactic properties (see 8.2.3). That which is given can be in instrumental case, with the recipient as O NP; or that which is given can be head of the O NP. -*ḍay* will refer to whatever is in the nominative case:

(635) *bayi yaṛa baŋgul wuḍuŋgu wugalḍaɲu*   he gave the food to lots of
      men
(636) *baŋgul balam wuḍu wugalḍaɲu*   he gave all the food away

See also (503–6) in 5.7.5.

Only one of the three affixes -*nbal* ~ -*galiy, yaray* and *ganiy* can be chosen in each of rules 1 and 2; however, any of these affixes may be followed by -*ḍay*. When -*yaray* and -*ḍay* occur together the meaning of -*yaranḍay* is 'has been doing it habitually':

(637) *balan ḍugumbil baŋgul yaṛaŋgu ŋanbayaranḍaɲu*   the man would
      always ask the woman (i.e. ask the same thing)
(638) *balan ḍugumbil yanuyaranḍaɲu*   woman would go over regularly
      (e.g. to see a sick relative)

6.3.3 The irregular verb *yanu*. The verb 'go' effectively has two roots – *yana(l)* in positive imperative forms, and *yanu(l)* in all other (including negative imperative) forms. The unmarked tense form is *yanu* and not **yanun*. Otherwise, *yanu(l)* and *yana(l)* behave like *-l* roots, except that root-final *-l* can optionally be dropped when not followed by a plosive (*-l-* is more likely in G than in D to be retained before nasals). We thus have *yanuman ~ yanulman*, but *yanulḍaɲu* rather than **yanuḍaɲu*; and positive imperative forms *yana*, *yanamalḍa*, *yanagali*, etc.

In addition to *yanu(l)mali*, the form *yanamali* has been heard – see (668) – and is confirmed by informants as a bona fide Dyirbal form, contrasting with *yanumali*. This can only mean that the lower sentence in a *-ɲura* construction (in which the higher sentence is COMIT) can be EITHER imperative OR non-imperative. This distinction is shown in the final form of the verb ONLY IN THE CASE OF *yanu*! Probably only a linguist who was a native speaker of Dyirbal could gain any real understanding of this point.

6.3.4 Reduplication. Any verbal root can be reduplicated – this involves the repetition of the first two syllables of the root only, in front of the main occurrence of the root (compare with nominal reduplication where the whole root is repeated, irrespective of how many syllables long it is): thus *baniɲu* 'come', *banibaniɲu*; *balgan* 'hit' *balgabalgan*; but *miyandaɲu* 'laugh', *miyamiyandaɲu*; *banagaɲu* 'return', *banabanagaɲu*.

It seems that the final consonant of a two-syllable root can appear in the reduplicated prefix only if it is preserved AS IS in the final form of the verb; and even then its reduplication is optional. In fact the reciprocal of *baṛan*, M, 'punch' has been noted as either *baṛabaṛalnbariɲu*, *baṛalbaṛalnbariɲu*, *baṛanbaṛalnbariɲu* or *baṛalnbaṛalnbariɲu* (the two intrusive n's being explained by a phonological rule – see 7.5.1).

Semantically, reduplication indicates that an action was or is being performed to excess: thus *miyamiyandaɲu* 'laugh more than is appropriate', *miḍumiḍun* 'having to wait [for someone] longer than one should have to'; *baŋgabaŋgan* 'put too much paint on', *balgabalgan* 'hit too much'.

Reduplication of the root of a verbal form is optional, except in the case of reciprocal forms when it is obligatory; verbal affixes cannot be reduplicated.

If a nominal form acting with nominal function is reduplicated, the whole root is repeated; but if a verbalised nominal (i.e. a form with verbal function) is reduplicated only the first two syllables are repeated. Thus we have nominal *gulgiṛi* 'prettily painted [of a man]' and *gulgiṛigulgiṛi* 'lots of prettily painted [men]'; and verbalised *gulgiṛibin* 'become prettily painted' and *gulgigulgiṛibin* 'become painted with too much paint'.

6.4 Morphology of time qualifiers

Time qualifiers (3.5, 4.14) can take the following affixes:

[1] *-baḍun*. As with nouns (6.1.1), this affix indicates 'certainty' (that a particular event has happened or will happen at a particular time):

(639) *gilu bayi yaṛa baniɲ*   man will come later on today
(640) *gilubaḍun bayi yaṛa baniɲ*   man is certain to come later on today

It appears that *-baḍun* can occur with all time words.

[2] *-baṛa* (see 6.1.1). As with nouns, *-baṛa* has a comparative meaning; thus *ḍaɳḍarubaṛa* refers to a time earlier than *ḍaɳḍaru* (but still 'earlier on today'); and *gilubaṛa* to a time later than *gilu* (but still 'later on today'). *-baṛa* can occur as an affix to words referring to past or to future time but not to *ḍaɳḍa* 'now'.

[3] *-ḍilu* DG, *-ḍu* M (see 6.1.1). This 'emphatic' affix is attested with all time words. It appears to have much the same effect as *-baṛa*; the emphasis that *ḍaɳḍarudilu* carries implies that it refers to a time earlier than *ḍaɳḍaru*, etc.

[4] durational inflections: [a] *-(ŋ)gu* 'until'. This cannot occur with past time words. The affix is *-gu* in some cases and *-ŋgu* in others; thus *ɲulgagu* 'until tomorrow', *ḍadagu* 'for a few days' but *giluŋgu* M, *gilugu* D 'until later on today'. *-gu* can also occur with *ḍaɳḍa* 'now' (in M at least) and adds some kind of emphasis; thus *ḍaɳḍa bani* 'come now' and *ḍaɳḍagu bani* 'you MUST come now'.

-(ŋ)gu, but not *-mu*, forms can be verbalised.

In 4.14 we gave examples of locational and nominal expressions that can have a time meaning: *yaŋgu(n)bayḍigu* 'next week', and *yaŋgungagaṛagabunda* 'next month'. These plainly involve the ergative/instrumental inflection and suggest that 'time until' *-(ŋ)gu* might be historically related to the ergative/instrumental rather than to the dative nominal inflection.

[b] *-mu* 'since'; this occurs only with past time words – *bandagaymu* 'since many years ago', *ɲumbuŋgamu* 'since yesterday'. (*-mu* is commoner in D than in M; strictly speaking, it may be confined to the D dialect.) *-mu* has semantic affinity with *-ɲunu*, used in a time sense (cf. (548) in 6.1.1):

(641) *ban ḍugumbil yaṛinbin/ ḍamiɲunu gubilamu* woman is slim, but was fat some years ago (literally: woman has become slim, from being fat some years ago)

-mu only occurs next to the root of a time qualifier. If any other affix intervenes, the 'from' form is *-ɲunu* – thus *bandagaymu* but *bandagay-baṛaɲunu*. This suggests that *-mu* should be considered an allomorphic variant of *-ɲunu*. In some cases an affix has been observed FOLLOWING *-mu* – thus *ɲudaŋgamubaṛa balay bayi ɲinaɲu* 'he's been sitting there quite a while!'

-mu or *-ɲunu* can often be omitted, the durational meaning still being evident from the rest of the sentence. There are, however, considerable complexities. Consider, in M (*gala* is 'earlier on today':)

(642) *ɲaḍa yalay galabaṛa ɲinaɲu* I've been sitting here for hours

(643) *ɲaḍa yalay ɲinaɲu galabaṛaɲunu* I'm sitting here [for a rest because, say, I've been walking] for hours

A possible explanation of the difference between (642) and (643) is that the underlying representation of (642) involves inflection *-mu*, which is deleted by a 'performance-rule'; and that *-ɲunu* in (643) is not a 'since' inflection but the stem-forming affix *-ɲunu*, as in (548).

[5] affixes *-ban* and *-ḍana* (6.1.6) can occur with time words – *ḍaṇḍaban, giluban, giluḍana*.

Non-time words, often with nominal inflection *-gabun* 'another', can be used in a locative inflection, with time reference. Thus *bala ḍagun* 'a sleep', and *ḍagungabunda* 'next night', as in (text xxxIb, line 19, p. 385):

(644) *baɲum balan yuŋgugan ḍagungabunda ɲaḍa ɲamban* then I heard another [Dambun spirit] the next night

And *garimaṛa* 'in the summer', *garimalgabunda* 'in the next summer'; *birgiṛa* 'in the wintertime', *birgilgabunda*; *gagalumgabunda* 'next month' etc.

There is also D *yalamayɲḍa*, M *yalamayɲḍay* 'at the same time' (cf. *yalamay* in 3.4.4, and note that the M time form involves *yalamay* even though the M verb is *yalabay*). Thus:

(645) *yalamayɲḍa ɲaliḍi yuban* we both put it down at the same time

and also (for *-bu* 'only' see 6.7.2):

(646) *yalamayɲḍabu ɲaliḍi ɲinaɲu yalay* it's the first time we've both sat here together (literally: 'the only same time')

Time words also take affix *-bi* – 6.7.3.

6.5   Morphology of noun and verb markers

Morphologically there are three types of marker: [1] noun and verb markers formed from root *bala-* (unmarked, and 'there'), *yala-* ('here'), *ŋala-* ('unseen'), or from the interrogative root *wuɲḍa-* ('where'); [2] quasi noun and verb markers based on root *gila-* 'somewhere'; [3] demonstrative noun markers based on root *giɲa-* DM, *ɲiɲa* G.

6.5.1   *bala-*, *yala-*, *ŋala-* and *wuɲḍa-* markers. At first sight there appears to be a lack of congruence between the *bala-/yala-/ŋala-* paradigm, and the *wuɲḍa-* paradigm (3.2.2, 3.4.5):

	bala-forms (class II)	*wuɲḍa*-forms (class II)	
nominative	*balan*	*wuɲḍan*	⎫
ergative/instrumental	*baŋgun*	*wuɲḍaŋgun*	⎬ noun markers
dative	*bagun*	*wuɲḍagun*	
genitive	*baɲun*	*wuɲḍaɲun*	⎭
allative (place)	*balu*	*wuɲḍaru*	⎫
allative (direction)	*bali*	*wuɲḍari*	⎬ verb markers
ablative	*baɲum*	*wuɲḍaɲum*	
locative	*balay*	*wuɲḍay*	⎭

At a glance the roots are *ba-* and *wuɲḍa-*. Ergative/instrumental, dative, genitive and ablative forms appear to involve the same inflections. But nominative is *-la-* in the case of *ba-* and zero for *wuɲḍa-*; the allatives are *-lu* and *-li* with *ba-* and *-ru* and *-ri* with *wuɲḍa-*; and locative is *-lay* with *ba-* but *-y* with *wuɲḍa-*.

The forms listed above are those that occur most frequently. But there are variant *bala-* etc. forms that are heard only occasionally; these are generally longer than the forms given above:

normal forms	variants	
balan	..	nominative
baŋgun	*balaŋgun*	ergative/instrumental
bagun	*balagun*	dative
baɲun	*balaɲun*	genitive
balu	*balaru*	allative (place)
bali	*balari*	allative (direction)
baɲum	*balaɲum*	ablative
balay	..	locative

(There are no variant *wuɲḍa-* forms.)

There is a semantic difference between the two columns: the longer forms imply an indefiniteness of locational specification. Thus *balu* 'to there', implying some specific place, but *balaru* 'to some place or other over there' (possibly also implying a circuitous route); and so on. *balaŋum* is used in the first line of text xv and also of text xxv, to indicate the indefinacy of origin of the main character in each story; elsewhere in these two texts the form *baŋum* is employed.

This suggests that we recognise roots:

bala-, yala-, ŋala- and *wuɲɖa-*

and case inflections:

noun markers	verb markers
nominative – zero	allative (place) – *-ru*
ergative/instrumental – *-ŋgu*	allative (direction) – *-ri*
dative – *-gu*	ablative – *-ŋum*
genitive – *-ŋu*	locative – *-y*

together with noun class endings (in the case of noun markers only):

class I *-l*; class II *-n*; class III *-m*; class IV zero

In the case of *bala-, yala-* and *ŋala-* markers there is elision and consonant change:

[1] *-la-* of the root drops before ergative/instrumental, dative, genitive, allative and ablative inflections;

[2] then, allative *-ru* and *-ri* become *-lu* and *-li* respectively.

The normal situation is for rules [1] and [2] to apply. If they do NOT apply 'indefinite' forms (that are many times less frequent than the shorter, normal forms) result.

If *-la-* were omitted from nominative and locative forms a word of only one syllable would result; as we have already noted, all Dyirbal words (except interjections *ŋa* and *ŋu*) have at least two syllables. However, *ban* and *bam* do occur as variants of class II and III nominative markers *balan* and *balam* (*balan* and *ban*, *balam* and *bam* are in free variation; there is in this case no 'indefiniteness' attached to the longer forms); *bala* and *balay* can not be shortened.

Allative *-ru* is probably related to the *-ru* that can be added to allative and locative forms of nouns (3.4.6). It is significant that although we can have *balu miɖagu* ('in the direction of the camp') and also *balu miɖaguru*, *-ru* cannot be affixed to *balu*: **baluru miɖagu(ru)*. This is explainable under our hypothesis that *-ru* is already included in *balu*. Rule [2] is similar to rules that are needed to explain other phenomena in Dyirbal: intransitive roots *barmiliy* and *balbaliy* are certainly historically related to the reflexive (*-riy*) forms of *barmil* 'look back' and *balbal* 'roll' (9.1.1).

There is nowadays no affix *-ri* similar to *-ru* (but see *ḍina* 'foot' and *ḍinari* 'root under water' – 9.1.2).

Verb marker inflection *-ŋum*, noun inflection *-ŋunu*, and time qualifier inflection *-mu* are quite possibly cognate, being derived from a single affix in an earlier stage of Dyirbal.

Our analysis of the noun and verb marker paradigms is also supported on historical grounds. *bala* recurs in a number of other Australian languages with a similar meaning and function to that which it has in Dyirbal, but without such complex morphology.

For instance, Pitjantjatjara [Trudinger 1943: 212] has a form *bala* 'that (definite, specified)'. In the Western Desert language [Douglas 1964: 72] there are demonstratives referring to 'near', 'mid-distance' and 'far'; the mid-distance form is given as *balaŋa*. O'Grady et al. [1966: 136–7] report that Wanman shows none of the normal Australian pronouns, but has a pronoun paradigm based on the root *bara*; this may possibly be cognate with Dyirbal *bala-*. See also 6.5.3.

6.5.2 *gila*- markers. In D and M (but not in G) there is a defective marker paradigm based on the root *gila-* 'somewhere'. Thus there are noun markers:

	nominative	ergative/instrumental	dative	genitive
class I	*gila*	*gilaŋgul*	*gilagul*	*gilaŋul*
class II	*gila*	*gilaŋgun*	*gilagun*	*gilaŋun*
class III	*gila*	*gilaŋgum*	*gilagum*	..
class IV	*gila*	*gilaŋgu*	*gilagu*	*gilaŋu*

There are also verb markers:

allative of place	*gilaru*
allative of direction	*gilari*
ablative	*gilaŋum*
locative	*gila*

Thus, *gila*- markers are morphologically exactly like *bala*- markers EXCEPT THAT: [1] there is no *-la*- deletion; [2] all nominative forms are simply *gila*, i.e. there is no class indication in this case; and [3] the locative verb marker is also *gila*.

An NP that includes a *gila*- marker may also include a *bala*- type marker (or a *giña*- type marker). *gila*- markers, like *bala*- markers, can occur in NPs with interrogative *wuɲḍa-* markers. Thus we can have (text reference XXIV: 89):

(647) [*bayi yaɽa*] *gilaguya buɽbaŋga galgan*   man was left somewhere over on the other side of the river, by the swamp

and (text reference XI: 74):

(648) [*bayi yaɽa*] *gilagunbawal wuɲḍagun warḍangu galgaɲugu bana-gayarayman*   [man] was taken back to the boat, which has been left somewhere – where exactly? – out there

also (text XXXIa: 5):

(649) *yugubaragira gila giyi ɲandaygu*   this yugubara spirit is bound to call out somewhere [around here, soon]

In (647) *gila* is a locative verb marker, agreeing with *buɽbaŋga* 'at the swamp'; in (648) *gilagun* is a dative class II noun marker, agreeing with *wuɲḍagun* 'to the class II object, which is where?', *warḍangu* 'to the boat', and *galgaɲugu* 'to that which had been left' (a relative clause qualifying *warḍangu*); in (649) *gila* is a nominative class I noun marker, agreeing with *yugubara* and *giyi* 'this class I object'.

In G, locative forms of noun markers and (especially) demonstrative markers are used where D and M would employ *gila* markers (see next section).

6.5.3 Demonstrative noun markers. In D and M there is a demonstrative root *giɲa*, that occurs only in nominative case, taking the usual noun class endings. *giɲa-* forms occur in place of nominative *yala-* forms (however, in some dialects *giɲa-* – unlike *yala-* – cannot take affix *-ɲa*, and nominative *yala-* forms do occur before this affix – 3.2.2).

Leaving aside *gila-* (which does not show noun class in nominative case), all nominative plus class I forms are exceptions to the rules we have given. Thus:

	actual form	form predicted by rules
	bayi	**balal*
	(similarly for *yayi*, *ŋayi*)	
	wuɲḍiɲ	**wuɲḍal*
	giyi	**giɲal*

In each case the last two or three segments of the 'expected' form are replaced by two laminal segments.

Roots *giɲa-* and *bala-* both occur (roughly, as third person singular pronouns) in Garadjari, in north-west Western Australia [Capell, 1962 a: 69]. *giɲa-* also occurs in Nyigina, to the north of Garadjari [Kerr, 1968: 30]; note that Nyigina also has affix *-ŋaru* 'like a –' that may be cognate with Dyirbal *ŋaru* – 6.1.1. Lardil also has demonstrative *giːn* 'that' (in Lardil, underlying forms cannot end in *-ɲ*); and Mbabaṟam *ŋgiɲ* 'there'.

Hercus [1969: 58] lists nine demonstrative pronouns for Wembawemba. She does not provide any morphological analysis of the nine forms, but six of these pronouns can be arranged in a suggestive paradigm:

giɲa 'this one right here', expressing close proximity to the speaker	*gila* 'this one now', tending to have a temporal meaning
ɲuɲa 'this one in the vicinity'	*ɲula* 'this one then', usually, not always, having a temporal nuance implying the immediate past
maɲa 'that one', 'that one some distance away and out of sight'	*mala* 'that one quite a long way off, in space or in time'

We can analyse these forms into two elements. The first element is either *gi-* 'near', *ɲu-* 'mid-distance' or *ma-* 'far'. The second element is *-ɲa*, referring to location, or *-la* which appears to have primary reference to time.

Of the Wembawemba forms *giɲa* and *gila* are clearly cognate with two of the noun marker roots in Dyirbal. However, since the rest of the paradigm is lacking in Dyirbal, it is not possible in Dyirbal to support an analysis of *giɲa* and *gila*, as it is in Wembawemba.

G has a set of demonstrative markers based on the root *ɲiɲa* that occur in nominative and locative inflections:

	class I	class II	class III	class IV
nominative	*ɲiyi*	*ɲiɲan*	*ɲiɲam*	*ɲiɲa*
locative	*ɲiyiŋga*	*ɲiɲaŋga*	*ɲiɲamga*	*ɲiɲaga*

Note that the locative inflection *-(ŋ)ga* is added AFTER class inflections.

We can thus have, for instance, *ɲiɲaga waɲaŋga* 'what is it that [the topic of the sentence] is at?'; and so on.

In addition, locative inflection can be added to (at least nominative and dative) noun markers, in G (but not in D or M): *bayiŋga, yagulga*, etc.

G demonstrative markers and noun markers in locative inflection are translation equivalents of *gila* forms in D and M. Specific instances of translation equivalences given by informants are:

G	D
yagulga	*gilagul* OR *balagul*
ɲiɲaga	*gila giɲa*
nayinba ɲiɲanga	*gilabi nayinba*
ɲiyiɲiyiŋgabawal	*gilagilabawal*

In the fourth example, the D word is not specified for class whereas the G equivalent is. The absence of class indication in nominative *gila* forms makes it sometimes necessary for two words to be used in D where one will do in G – as in the second example above.

Locative inflection, *-ga*, can also be added to verb markers in G: there are forms *yaluga*, *balayga*, and so on. The D translation equivalent of *baluga* is just *balaru*, that of *balayga* is *balaɲunda* (for *-ŋunda* see 6.5.6). The *-ga* appears to indicate that the state of motion or position took place 'at' some place; in many cases *-ga* appears to add a degree of indefiniteness (of location) to a verb marker.

6.5.4 *baŋuniɲ/baŋunday*. There are forms:

DG	M	
baŋuniɲ	*baŋunday*	'person/thing from there'
yaŋuniɲ	*yaŋunday*	'person/thing from here'
ŋaŋuniɲ	..	'person/thing remembered from past'
wuɳḍaŋuniɲ	*wuɳḍaŋunday*	'person/thing from where?'

that inflect like nominals:

(650) *yaŋuniɲḍu wuɳḍaŋgul baŋgul yanuŋuru bala budin* where is the person from here who took the thing [from here] and went away [with it]?

(651) *yaŋuniŋgu wuɳḍagul/ gaḍi mari gilagulgalu guninaygu* where is that person from here? – you'd better follow him to find him, he's somewhere out in front

(652) *baŋgul yaɻaŋgu wuɳḍaŋundayḍu ŋaygu galbin balgan* where does the man come from who killed my son?

In text xxv, line 2 (p. 388), *baŋunday* agrees in (dative) case inflection with *milbirŋunu* (involving stem-forming affix *-ŋunu*) *baŋundaygudayi milbirŋunugu* 'for that which is from up there in the slippery blue fig tree'. However, syntactically and semantically there are similarities between *baŋunday* forms and *-ḍin* possessive forms; for instance *yaŋuniɲḍa* 'for fear of [the man] from here' is common – cf. 6.1.5.

6.5.5 Reduplication. Any noun or verb marker, whether based on root *bala-*, *yala-*, *giɲa-/ɲiɲa-*, *ɲala-* or *gila-* (and whether or not bearing any bound affix *bayḍi* etc.) can be reduplicated; in this case the re-duplication involves repetition of the first two syllables of the form and appears to have the semantic effect of intensification: *yalay* 'here', *yalayalay* 'right here'; *bayinbayi* G, *bayimbayi* DM 'he himself'; and also *gilagilaru*, *balaymbalay*, *yaŋguyaŋgumaŋgandu*, *balubalubayḍu*, and so on.

Affixes to noun and verb markers, including the bound forms *bayḍi*, *gali* etc., cannot be reduplicated.

Two, slightly different, verb markers can occur together, for stylistic emphasis; thus *baliyalugalumban* in text xxv, line 54, p. 392. Markers can only occur to-gether if they show the same case – both *bali* and *yalu* are allatives, the difference being that *bali* is a 'direction' allative and *yalu* a 'place' form, and that *bali* is the 'there (or unmarked)' marker whereas *yalu* refers to 'here'.

6.5.6 Affixes. Noun markers can take affixes *-baḍun*, *-ḍaran* and *-ḍilu* (see 6.1.1), as well as the universal affix *-bu* (6.7.2). *-bu* precedes *-ḍilu* when both occur with a marker (the same happens with pronouns; with nouns, *-ḍilu* precedes *-bu*).

There are no allative, ablative or locative inflections of noun markers. However, a nominative noun marker may have *-ɲa* added to it, and then the locative inflection. In such cases the locative inflection is normally to be interpreted in the 'fear' sense (6.1.5), rather than as having any locational reference. Thus (text reference xxxic: 11):

(653) *bayiɲaŋga ḍigubinaga yuɽay muḍan buni ɲina* [we] must sit quietly, with the fire extinguished, for fear of Dyigubina (i.e. lest he sees the fire and come to torture us)

See also *ɲanaŋga* (from *ɲan ~ ɲalan* 'class II, not visible' + *-ɲa* + *ŋga*) and *wuɳḍanaŋga* in text xxxib, lines 1 and 2, p. 383.

We saw in 3.2.1, 6.1.1 that a noun such as *ḍumbulu* can have the forms *ḍumbuluɲa* (nominative), *ḍumbuluɲangu* (dative), *ḍumbuluɲaŋga* (locative) and *ḍumbuluɲalaymbila* (*-bila* form). We have mentioned that a noun marker, *bayi*, has the forms *bayiɲaŋga* and *bayiɲambila*. How ever, forms *bayiɲa and *bayiɲangu do not occur. That is, *-ɲa* can only occur with a noun marker in the presence of *-bila* or the locative inflection.

-gara and *-maŋgan* (6.1.1) can occur with *bala-* and with *giɲa- ~ yala-*

within quasi-pronominal forms *balagara, balamaŋgan* etc. (3.3.2); these forms can occur with *-ɲa* in the same way that a proper noun can.

gilamaŋgan is also attested, e.g. *gilamaŋgan yalay miyandaɲu* 'some people here laughed' (said when the speaker is not sure who did it). *gilagara* is impossible in normal circumstances – the specificity of *-gara* 'two' cannot be combined with the vagueness of *gila* 'someone'. However, *gilagara* can be used in avoidance talk between children – if a child wishes to refer to two people whose names he should not mention (because of kinship taboo) he may use *gilagara*, making it explicit how many people he is referring to but preserving a proper 'distance' by the vague use of *gila*.

There is another suffix, that occurs ONLY with noun and verb markers: *-(y)uŋgul* 'that's the one' (cf. number adjective *yuŋgul* 'one'); it occurs with all markers but most frequently with *giɲa- ~ yala-* forms. From demonstrative markers *giyi, giɲan, giɲam* and *giɲa* are derived *giyiɲuŋgul, giɲanuŋgul, giɲamuŋgul* and *giɲayuŋgul*; from ergative noun marker *yaŋgul* 'this one [did it]' we get *yaŋguluŋgul* 'this is the one [that did it]'; from *yalu* 'to this place', *yaluyuŋgul* 'this is the place [we're going] to'. The difference between *yuŋgul* 'one' as an adjectival modifier, and *-(y)uŋgul* as an affix is important:

(654) *giɲan yuŋgul baniɲu*   this one [woman] is coming
(655) *giɲanuŋgul baniɲu*   this is the [woman] coming

See also (555).

For a discussion of the phonological changes involved with *-(y)uŋgul*, and of the problems of disambiguation cast up, see 7.5.2.

Another affix *-ɲunda* 'somewhere' occurs in D (it does not occur in G and is not so far attested for M). It comes immediately after a noun marker, and before *-ḍilu* or a *bayḍi* etc. form. *-ɲunda* occurs frequently with *bala, yala* and *gila* class IV nominative markers (and once with *yaɲum* in the corpus of texts). *balaɲunda* 'somewhere there', *yalaɲunda* 'somewhere here', *gilaɲunda* 'somewhere – anywhere at all' appear to function as verb markers, and not as noun markers. It may be that *bala* in *balaɲunda* should be regarded simply as the root *bala-*, and not as an inflected form (but it still remains to account for *yaɲum*). The G translation equivalent of *balaɲunda* is *balayga*.

Verb markers are more limited in their morphology. Besides *bayḍi, gali* etc. bound forms, verb markers can take emphatic affix *-ḍilu* (6.1.1), e.g. *yaliḍilu*. Some allative forms can occur with *-ɲunu* (and can then, unlike ablative markers, be verbalised); examples are in 4.7.2.

In M at least, *balaru* can be followed by an affix *-ba*, with the implication that something is done over a large area – see text xv, line 39, p. 375.

A noun or verb marker can take, in order:

[1] any of the affixes mentioned above;

[2] one of the twelve (thirteen in M) bound affixes *bayḍi*, etc.;

[3] one of *gali, galu, gala*.

6.5.7   Bound forms *bayḍi, gali* etc. Ten forms of the *bayḍi* set (see table in 3.2.3) can be analysed as follows (in terms of the phonological description of chapter 7):

[1] Each form involves either component 'up', realised by *da*[S-V], or component 'down', realised by *ba*L[Stop]. Here [S-V] is a segment specified only as to the manner feature 'semi-vowel', and [Stop] a segment specified only by the feature 'stop' – 7.1. L covers the set of four segments that must occur initially in a medial cluster – *l, r, ṛ* and *y* (7.2.1).

[2] Each form also involves either component 'non-water', realised by localisation feature [Lfr] (roughly 'front-lingual' or 'lamino-alveopalatal'), or component 'water', realised by feature [Lab] (labial).

The up/down and non-water choices then generate:

$$da \begin{bmatrix} \text{S-V} \\ \text{Lfr} \end{bmatrix}, \; da \begin{bmatrix} \text{S-V} \\ \text{Lab} \end{bmatrix}, \; ba \; \text{L} \begin{bmatrix} \text{Stop} \\ \text{Lfr} \end{bmatrix}, \; ba \; \text{L} \begin{bmatrix} \text{Stop} \\ \text{Lab} \end{bmatrix}$$

L + [Lfr] is realised as *y*, and L + [Lab] as *l* (which involves the unmarked localisation feature [Lin]; none of *y, l, r* or *ṛ* include the feature [Lab]). From the table of 7.2.1 [S-V; Lfr] is *y*, [S-V, Lab] is *w*, [Stop, Lfr] is *ḍ*, and [Stop, Lab] is *b*. The forms are then:

day-, daw-, bayḍ-, balb-

Any explanation of why L + [Lfr] is realised as *y* (= [S-V, Lfr]), rather than as *r* (+ [Liq, Lfr]), must involve the feature [S-V] being considered 'unmarked', within the manner system, with respect to marked [Liq].

[3] Each form also involves: with a 'non-water' choice, either component 'long distance', realised by *-u*, 'medium distance', realised by *-a*, or 'short distance', realised by *-i*; with a 'water' choice a form will involve either 'long distance' or 'medium distance'. The 'long distance' choice is the unmarked one, and of the remaining two choices 'short distance' is unmarked with respect to marked 'medium distance' (see 9.2.1).

With the distance choices the full forms are now:

dayu, daya, dayi; dawu, dawa; bayḍu, bayḍa, bayḍi; balbu, balba

The other forms of the *bayḍi* set: *guya* 'across the river', *bawal* 'long way (in any direction)' and (M only) *ŋaru* 'behind' are not further analysable.

At first sight the *-u*, *-a* and *-i* of *galu*, *gala* and *gali* appear to be semantically rather different from the *-u*, *-a* and *-i* of distance choices. Thus *gali* is 'vertically down', *gala* 'vertically up' and *galu* 'straight in front'. However, it could be argued that we can only see a short distance down (to the ground); a fair distance up; and a longer distance straight ahead.

In support of this, there are in Awabakal three demonstrative forms *ŋali* 'here', *ŋala* 'there' and *ŋaloa* 'yonder' [Threlkeld, 1892: 19]; there is a chance that these forms are cognate with Dyirbal *gali*, *gala* and *galu*.

The 'up river' and 'down river' forms vary in the three dialects:

	G	D	M
long way up river	*dawulu*	*dawulu*	*dawu* or *dawulu*
medium way up river	*dawaṛa*	*dawala*	*dawa* or *dawala*
long way down river	*balbulu*	*balbulu*	*balbu* or *balbulu*
medium way down river	*balbaṛa*	*balbala*	*balba* or *balbala*

The difference between *dawulu* and *dawu*, and *balbulu* and *balbu*, can be explained in terms of the longer forms involving the universal affix *-ru* (6.7.1). Thus *dawu* is 'long way up river', whereas *dawulu* is 'further up river'. In M at least, forms **dawuluru* and **balbuluru* are not possible (whereas *bayḍiru*, *guyaru*, *bawalaru* etc. ARE possible). We would thus suppose that *dawuru* had given rise to *dawulu* by a regular phonological change – see 7.7. There is nowadays no parallel suffix *-ṛa* (or *-la*) and there is no evidence to support a similar origin for *dawaṛa* and *balbaṛa*.

Noun or verb markers plus bound forms *bayḍi*, *gali* etc. can take the comparative affix *-baṛa* – thus *balubalbulubaṛa* '(to) further down-river', *bayingalabaṛa* '(he) further up'.

We stated in 3.2.3, 3.4.5 that *bayḍi*, *gali* etc. are bound forms, and can only occur following a noun or verb marker (or as affix to a noun or adjective – 6.1.1). This was an oversimplification. The forms cannot occur alone – that is **bayḍi*, **galu*, and so on, are not acceptable Dyirbal words; however, they can occur WITHOUT a noun or verb marker IF they have one of a certain set of suffixes:

[1] There are 'comparative adjectives' formed from bound forms *baydi* etc. and affix *-baṟa* – the commonest are *dayibaṟa* 'higher' and *baydibaṟa* 'lower'.

[2] Allative and locative verb markers, with or without bound forms, can be verbalised: *balumban, baluguyamban, balaydayimban*. The bound forms can be verbalised WITHOUT a verb marker, e.g. *guyamban* (text xv, line 22, p. 372), and *dayimban* (text xxv, line 7, p. 388). However, verbalisations that do not involve a verb marker are comparatively rare in Guwal (although they are common, and are in some cases institutionalised verbs, in Dyalŋuy – see 9.2.1 and Dixon, 1971).

[3] The universal affix *-ru* (6.7.1) can be added to some bound forms, and sometimes involves a non-predictable change in meaning. Thus *baligaluru* '(to) further in front', *baligalaru* '(to) inside', *baligaliru* '(to) underneath', '(to) outside'. Bound forms plus *-ru* are also encountered, with no verb marker – thus *galaru* 'inside', *galuru* 'in front' (*galuru* can also mean 'the first one (to do something, or to have something done to him)'; and cf. *galurumi* 'eldest child in family').

guŋgari 'north', *guyŋguru* 'south' and *ṟuwa* 'west' (there is no comparable term for 'east', which would be in the direction of the Coral Sea) function as free forms and also as affixes to verb markers, just like *baydi, gali* etc.; in the latter function they come after *-ŋunda* and before *baydi* forms. It is likely (although there is no really strong evidence) that these three words are gradually acquiring the status of affixes.

6.6 Morphology of interrogative forms

There are four interrogative (sub-) roots in *Dyirbal*: [1] *miɲa*; [2] *wiyama ~ wiyaba*; [3] *wuɲḍa*; and [4] *waɲ(u/a)*. Words based on the first two roots are interrogative members of open (i.e. lexical) word classes; words based on the third and fourth roots are members of closed (i.e. grammatical) classes – see chapter 9.

[1] *miɲa* forms:

    [a] DM *miɲa* 'what' ranging over those members of the class of nouns with non-human referent (3.2.4); the corresponding G form is *waɲa* (5.8.4).

    [b] *miɲaɲ* 'how many', ranging over the subclass of number adjectives (6.1.7).

    [c] DM *miɲay*, G *miɲi* 'when' ranging over the class of time words (3.5, 4.14).

miɲa and *miɲaɲ* inflect like nominals (3.2.1). Some nominal affixes –
e.g. *-bila*, *-ŋaŋgay*, *-ginay*, *-ŋunu*, *-ŋaru*, *-ḍaran* – can occur with *miɲa*;
others – e.g. *-baṛa*, *-gara*, *-ɲa* – cannot. *miɲaɲ* can occur with, for
example, *-bila*.

*miɲabara is not possible, *wuɲḍaɲumbara* 'man belonging to where'
being preferred.

[2] *wiyama ~ wiyaba* forms:

[a] DG *wiyamay*, M *wiyabay* 'do what/do how' (intransitive).
[b] DG *wiyamal*, M *wiyabal* 'do what/do how' (transitive).

Occurring in a VC without any other verb, one of these forms acts
as an interrogative verb; occurring in a VC with a verb it acts as an
interrogative adverbal (3.4.4).

[3] *wuɲḍa*. From this root are formed a full array of noun and verb
markers (3.2.4, 3.4.7, 6.5). *-ɲa* can occur with nominative interrogative
markers only when a locative inflection follows. It appears that interrogative markers can take no other affixes (in particular, bound forms
bayḍi, *gali*, etc. cannot be affixed to interrogative markers).

[4] *waɲa ~ waɲu- ~ waɲ-* 'who'. The paradigm of the interrogative
pronoun was given in 3.3.3. Inflection basically follows the nominal
pattern except that *-ɲa* is obligatory with [−actor] plus nominative
forms – 5.8.4. (There is one other respect in which *waɲ-* resembles
pronouns – the dative inflection is preceded by *-n-*; thus, *waɲungu*.)

Semantically, *miɲa* 'what' refers to anything non-human (including
animals); *waɲa* refers to anything human. Thus a reply to *miɲa* would
normally involve a noun and not a pronoun; a reply to DM *waɲa*
could involve either a noun or a pronoun.

In many instances Dyirbal *waɲa* or *miɲa* would be better translated by English
'someone' or 'something' than by 'who' or 'what'. As mentioned in 2.4,
vagueness is held to be a severe fault amongst the Dyirbalŋan; thus it is quite
natural that a non-specific description should at the same time ask for
specification.

waɲa 'who, someone' can occur with affix *-ŋaŋgay* 'without' –
waɲaŋaŋgay is then, literally, 'with no one'. Thus:

(656) *miḍa ŋaḍa bala ḍaymban waɲaŋaŋgay*   I found no one in the
camp [literally: I found the camp with no one]

waɲaŋaŋgay can inflect like a noun or adjective:

(657) *ŋayguna baŋgul waɲaŋaŋgayḍu buṛan*   he saw me by himself
[literally: he, with no one, saw me]

Interrogative forms cognate with *miɲa* are found in a number of languages in the eastern half of the continent. Thus Wargamay *miɲa*, Gumbaiŋgar *mi꞉ɲa* [Smythe, 1948/9: 40], Gabi *miɲaŋgay* [Mathew, 1910: 210], Awabakal *min* [Threlkeld, 1892: 20], Narrinyeri *minye* [Taplin, 1880: 13], Thangatti and Kattang *miɲa(ŋ)* [Holmer, 1966: 71], and Pittapitta *mina* [Roth, 1897: 28].

Interrogatives of the type *waɲ-* occur in Yidin and Waruŋu but have not been reported for languages outside the North Queensland region.

6.7   Universal affixes

There are three affixes that can occur with almost any type of word.

6.7.1   *-ru*. Affix *-ru*, following a vowel; *-aru*, following a consonant. This cannot be given any effective English gloss; however 'another' and 'again' covers part of some of its meanings. *-ru*, which follows all other affixes, occurs with at least the following:

[1] number adjectives; thus *bulayi* 'two', *bulayiru* 'another two' – 6.1.7.

[2] pronouns, e.g. *ŋindaru bani* 'you (can) come too!'; and quasi-pronouns, e.g. *balagararu*.

[3] noun markers; in D *-ɲa* must precede *-ru*. Thus D *bayiɲaru bani*, M *bayiru bani* or *bayiɲaru bani* 'he (can/must) come too!'.

[4] some particles, e.g. *aɲḍa* – see (668); D *ḍamu*, M *yurmu* 'just' – see 4.15.3, and:

(658) *yurmu ŋaḍa bayi baniɲu*   I just came here (i.e. did nothing else)
(659) *yurmuru ŋaḍa bayi baniɲu*   I just [want to] keep on coming here

and *ŋuri* 'in turn' (this is a D example):

(660) *ɲuraḍi ŋuriru ŋuriru budi*   You(all) carry [the children], turn and
     turn about

[5] verbs in unmarked tense inflection (indicating that an action happens twice):

(661) *bayi baḍiɲu balay/ ŋaḍaru balaygayul baḍiɲuru*   he fell down
     there; I too fell down at the same place

Versions of (661) in which *-ru* is attached to *ŋaḍa* but not to *baḍiɲu*, to *baḍiɲu* but not to *ŋaḍa*, or to neither, are all quite acceptable.

Note also *yalamanaru* 'do the same thing again'.

[6] adjectives – thus *midi* 'small', *midiru* 'smaller'.

[7] nouns – as in *bayi yaɽa baniɲu/ ḍugumbilaru baniɲu* 'the men are coming and the women are coming too'.

[8] most of the bound forms *bayḍi*, *gali* etc. The affix has the form

-ru ~ -aru in D, *-ndu ~ -andu* in certain varieties of M (probably Waṟibara) and *-gu ~ -agu* in other types of M (probably Dulgubara). Thus, *bawalaru* refers to a distance further than *bawal*; and:

(662) *ŋaḏa yanu baluguya*   I'm going (to) there across the creek

(663) *ŋaḏa yanu baluguyagu*   I'm going (to) there across another creek

It appears that *bayḏiru* refers to something NEARER than *bayḏi* 'short distance downhill'; thus *bayḏiru* is used for 'underneath', etc. *bayḏa* 'medium distance downhill' cannot occur with *-ru*. *bayḏuru* refers to a distance FURTHER than *bayḏu* 'long way downhill'. Similarly with the other sets of bound forms. Here *-ru* appears to be an intensifier: a shortER or a longER distance. (See also 6.5.7.)

[9] interrogatives – *-ru* often serves to derive a negative from an interrogative/indefinite root. Thus the interrogative pronoun plus *-ru* has the meaning 'no one' (text reference VII: 3):

(664) *waɲḏu bayi ŋaṟin*   who answered him?

(665) *waɲḏuru bayi ŋaṟin*   no one answered him

Similarly, a *wiyama* form plus *-ru* will mean 'can't do it'; in fact the form *wiyamaliru* often has the sense 'don't like to do it':

(666) *giɲabawal*   *ŋaḏa ŋaḏilman*   /   *ṟala*
      THIS-NOM-IV-LONG WAY I-SA lose-INSTR-PRES/PAST ṟala-stick-NOM
      wiyamaliru   *ŋaḏa bayali*   *ŋinu*/
      do what-PURP-*ru* I-SA sing-PURP you-GEN
      ḏaŋala
      ḏaŋala-style songs-NOM
      I've lost this *ṟala*-stick; now I can't sing *ḏaŋala* songs for you

(667) *ŋaḏa giɲan wuygi*/ *wiyamaliru balabala*/ *ṟubimali*   [now] I'm old
      I can't/don't like to eat meat [any more]

(668) *yanama wuygi balam*/ *wiyamaliru aɲḏaru ŋuṟbili*/ *yanama budi* take
      away this useless food; I no longer like to taste it; carry it away!

Care must be taken not to confuse the universal affix *-ru* with [1] the ergative inflection, *-ru*, on the verb in a relative clause; and [2] the 'motion' affix *-ru*, that occurs with allative and locative nouns (3.4.6) and is incorporated into verb markers *balu* and *yalu* (6.5.1).

-ru appears to have some semantic similarity to the comparative affix *-baṟa*. It is likely that native speakers recognise *-ru* and *-baṟa* to provide different kinds of qualification of an adjective. But bilingual informants did translate both *midiru* and *midibaṟa* as 'smaller', and then said that *midiru* referred to something smaller than did *midibaṟa*; *midibaṟaru* 'very much smaller' is also

quite acceptable. Note that *-baɽa* occurs only with adjectives, nouns, and bound forms *bayḍi* etc.

6.7.2   -bu. The affix *-bu* 'only' (in D and G, not in M) can be added to (at least) a nominal form, a noun marker, a pronoun, a verbal form, or a time qualifier. It is always added AFTER any case, tense or other inflectional ending. Thus:

(669) *yaɽaŋgubu bala budin*   only men brought it (i.e. women had no hand in it)

(670) *bayi waŋalbilabu baniɲu/ biginɲaŋgay*   the man is coming with boomerangs only, not with shields

(671) *giɲa ŋumaɲubu bala baya*   that belongs only to father

(672) *bandagay bayi ɲinaɲu balay/ ŋudaŋgabu bayi yanu*   he'd been living there for years, he left only the other day

(673) *giramaybu bayi wurbaɲu*   he only speaks Giramay

(674) *ŋaḍa maymiɲubu*   I was only visiting (to be given) food

-bu occurs with verbs predominantly in G (to a far lesser extent in D). A further example of *-bu* is in text xxxib, line 28, p. 386. See also (646).

With noun markers and pronouns (but not with nominals) *-ḍilu* must come after *-bu*.

-bu does not occur in M; an informant variously used *-mumbay*, *-ḍu* (~ *-ḍilu*), particle *yurmu*, and *ɲamuy* 'do on one's own' (which is probably another particle), when translating into M sentences from D involving *-bu*. Thus (673) was translated as:

(675) *bayi giramayḍu wurbaɲu*   he speaks only Giramay

and (669) was translated as:

(676) *yaɽaŋgu ɲamuy bala budin*   only the man brought it

6.7.3   -bi. *-bi* can be affixed to nouns, noun markers, demonstrative markers, pronouns, verbs and time qualifiers. Informants sometimes used 'too' in the translation of sentences including *-bi*; *-bi* often occurs in questions:

(677) *bayinbi banigu*   is he coming as well?

but can also occur in many other types of sentence. *-bi* occurs in all three dialects but is particularly common in G.

In some instances *-bi* appears to have a similar meaning to *-ru*. Thus *ŋindaru* and *ŋindabi* might both be glossed 'you, too...'. Roughly, *-ru* appears to mean 'a second participant' as against *-bi* 'this one as well'. *ŋindarubi bani* is attested, with a meaning something like 'do you want to come too, in addition to the others?'.

7 *Phonology*

Each Dyirbal sentence has both a grammatical and a phonological description. The phonological description consists of a number of 'phonological words': each of these is based on a single 'word class' root, the phonological form of the root undergoing phonological addition or alteration corresponding to (optional) stem-forming or derivational processes and (obligatory) inflectional processes.

The word as a phonological unit is marked by an initial stressed syllable, final inflectional ending, and a fixed form: that is, the 'constituents' of a word cannot be permuted within the word. There is, however, considerable freedom of the order in which words can appear in a sentence (7.8).

Each word is a sequence of phonological segments, a segment being a set (or 'bundle') of phonological features; each feature belongs to a phonological system. A single statement of possible word structures can be given (covering words of all grammatical types). The possible phonic realisations of each phonological feature are described (RELATIVE TO the realisations of the other features in the system).

Dyirbal words tend to be phonologically rather compact: that is, certain phonological processes of insertion, assimilation, elision and conflation act to ensure that, say, a consonant cluster is not only one of the 'possible' clusters for the language, but is also one of the more frequent or 'popular' clusters (7.5). There is no phonological cohesion (sandhi and so on) BETWEEN words.

Within a word the phonological possibilities at morpheme boundaries (say, between a root and a stem-forming affix, or at a reduplication boundary) are wider than the intramorphemic possibilities.

7.1 Systems of phonological features

A purely phonemic analysis would recognise a sixteen-term system for Dyirbal:

[1] four stop-nasal series, distinguished in terms of active articulator;

this can be the lower lip, or the tip, blade or back of the tongue:

	stop	nasal
labial	*b*	*m*
apical	*d*	*n*
laminal	*ḍ*	*ɲ*
dorsal	*g*	*ŋ*

The labial series involves the lower and upper lips. In the case of apicals the tip of the tongue touches the alveolar ridge. Laminals involve the blade of the tongue in contact with the hard palate, the alveolar ridge, and often the top teeth, with the tongue tip in the region of the lower teeth (the teeth being slightly apart) – cf. 1.2. For dorsals the primary contact is of the anterior part of the tongue with the soft palate; there is often a secondary contact, of the tongue tip with the alveolar ridge.

[2] three liquids: an alveolar lateral, *l*; and two grooved-tongue sounds – *r*, which is generally either an alveolar tap (intervocalically and word-finally) or a trill (preconsonantally); and *ɽ*, which is generally a semi-retroflex continuant with the tongue tip turned back to touch the anterior part of the hard palate.

[3] two semi-vowels – lamino-alveopalatal *y*; and *w*, which involves lip rounding and raising of the dorsal part of the tongue towards the soft palate.

[4] three vowels – open *a*, close back rounded *u*, and close front unrounded *i*. Each vowel covers a considerable phonetic range – thus /u/ is realised as [o] or even [ɔ] word-finally and before /y/, and as [u] after /g/. /a/ can be realised as [ɛ], following a laminal consonant, or as [ɔ], after a dorsal. And so on.

However, a more revealing description of Dyirbal phonology is in terms of two systems of phonological features:

[1] a four-feature 'localisation' system:

[Lin]	(unmarked) lingual
[Lfr]	front (marked) lingual
[Lba]	back (marked) lingual
[Lab]	labial

[2] a five-feature 'manner' system:

[Stop]
[Nas]   nasal
[Liq]   liquid
[S-V]   semi-vowel
[Vow]   vowel

Each feature has a 'range' of possible phonetic realisations, relative to the realisations of the other features in its system (7.3).

A 'bundle' consisting of one feature from the localisation system, and one feature from the manner system, constitutes a phonological segment; except that [Liq, Lab] is not a possible segment. Correspondences between these segments and letters used in the orthography (= phonemes) are:

	[Lin]	[Lfr]	[Lba]	[Lab]
[Stop]	*d*	*ḍ*	*g*	*b*
[Nas]	*n*	*ɲ*	*ŋ*	*m*
[Liq]	*l*	*r*	*ɽ*	
[S-V]	*w*	*y*	*w*	*w*
[Vow]	*a*	*i*	*u*	*u*

It will be seen that there is no one-to-one correspondence between the phonemic orthography and the segments of the phonological description (cf. Henderson, 1966). Where the 'same letter' occurs more than once (in the cases of *w* and *u*) the segments concerned are in fact phonetically identical, but have different underlying phonological descriptions.

The setting up of the two phonological systems can be justified on three counts: [1] it is phonetically plausible – that is, straightforward, non-disjunctive statements of phonic realisation can be given for the features in the systems (7.3); [2] it makes the statement and explanation of the main morphophonological rule optimally simple (7.6); [3] it is supported statistically (7.4).

For reference to other languages in which liquids and semi-vowels can be placed in 'localisation series', see Trubetzkoy, 1969: 138–9.

[Lin] can be regarded as the 'unmarked' member of the localisation system on the following grounds:

[1] it is phonetically unmarked, involving minimum movement of the tongue from rest position – 7.3.

[2] it is statistically unmarked – see the tables in 7.4.2.

[3] -*n*-, involving [Lin], is 'inserted' into Dyirbal words by a special process (7.5.1); no other segment is introduced in this way.

[4] non-homorganic nasal-stop or nasal-nasal clusters must have [Lin] in the first segment – 7.2.1.

[5] the overall probabilities of occurrence of segments involving [Lin] are significantly different from those of segments involving [Lfr], [Lba] and [Lab] – words rarely begin with *d* or *n*, never with *l*; on the other hand, *n* and *l* are the most common root-final consonants (7.4.1).

See also Trubetzkoy [1969: 167].

7.2   Word structures

7.2.1   Segments. A Dyirbal root has phonological structure:

$$C_1VC_2V(C_2V)^n(C_3), \quad \text{where } n \geqslant O$$

That is, it consists of two or more syllables, each of which involves a single vowel segment. It can end in a vowel or one of a set, C_3, of consonants.

The possibilities at the structural positions are:

V   is any segment involving [Vow], i.e. *a*, *i* or *u*

C_1 is any segment involving [Stop], [Nas], or [S-V]; or the segment [Liq, Lba], i.e. *b*, *d*, *ḍ*, *g*, *m*, *n*, *ɲ*, *ŋ*, *w*, *y* or *ɼ*

C_3 is any segment involving [Nas] and NOT [Lba]; any segment involving [Liq]; or the segment [S-V, Lfr], i.e. *m*, *n*, *ɲ*, *l*, *r*, *ɼ* or *y*

C_2 can be any sequence of one, two or three consonants, subject to the following constraints:

    [1] only one of *l*, *r*, *ɼ* and *y* can occur in a sequence; it must always be the initial consonant in the sequence;

    [2] only one of *b*, *d*, *ḍ*, *g* and *w* can occur in a sequence; it must always be the final consonant in the sequence;

    [3] *w* cannot be preceded by a nasal;

    [4] *n* can [a] be followed by any nasal or stop; [b] be preceded by *l* or *y* only, and then only when followed by a non-homorganic nasal or stop; *d* can only be preceded by *n*;

    [5] otherwise, all nasals and stops in a sequence must be homorganic;

    [6] a sequence cannot involve two identical segments.

An alternative statement is:

C_2 can be either [1] *b, d, ḍ, g, m, n, ɲ,* or *ŋ*;

or [2] *mb, nd, ɲḍ,* or *ŋg*;

or [3] *w*;

or [4] *y, l, r* or *ɽ*;

or [5] *n* followed by *b, ḍ, g, m, ɲ* or *ŋ*; i.e. *n* followed by [1] excluding [Lin] segments;

or [6] *y, l, r* or *ɽ* followed by *b, ḍ, g, m, ɲ, ŋ, mb, ɲḍ, ŋg* or *w*; i.e. [4], followed by [1], [2] or [3], excluding [Lin] segments;

or [7] *l* or *y* followed by *nb, nḍ, ng, nm, nɲ,* or *nŋ*; i.e. *l* or *y* plus [5].

Two words have been encountered that involve C_2 clusters not covered by the above rules: Guwal *bala guyaŋgu,* 'water-gum tree', and Dyalŋuy *bala mulumdayman* 'message'. The rules could be extended, to cover these two words, by saying that ANY nasal can be followed by ANY stop. However, over a hundred non-homorganic sequences have been encountered with initial segment *n*, as against a single example with *ɲ*, a single example with *m*, and no example at all with *ŋ*. We thus prefer to state the rule as above, and to consider *guyaŋgu* and *mulumdayman* to be 'exceptions' to it.

Note that the further after a stressed vowel a C_2 sequence occurs, the less complex it is likely to be.

There are also two general constraints on word structure:

[1] *-iy-* can occur only when immediately followed by *-i*; that is, we have *-iyi-* but not **-iya-, *-iyu, *-iyɲ-, *-iyḍ-, *-iyb-* etc.

[2] *-wi-* can occur in a stressed syllable only (for stress see 7.2.2).

Noun and adjective roots have phonological forms corresponding to all possibilities of word structure; verbal roots end in *-al, -il, -ul, -ay* or *-iy* (but not in *-uy*) but otherwise cover all possibilities.

There is one exception to the general statement that all words begin with a consonant – the particle *aɳḍa,* 4.15.2. Six monosyllabic words are known – interjections *ŋa* 'yes' and *ŋu* 'alright' (4.17), and variant forms *ban, bam, ŋan* and *ŋam* of class II and III nominative noun markers (3.2.2, 6.5.1). A high proportion of Dyirbal words (especially the most frequent) have EXACTLY two syllables.

It appears that affixes have the same phonological possibilities as roots, except that they can be monosyllabic. Thus, all affixes begin with a single consonant. (The appearance of clusters such as *-lnb-* at root-affix boundaries is due to the insertion of *-n-* by a special phonological process – 7.5.1.)

At certain morpheme boundaries within a word, consonant clusters can have wider possibilities than those listed for C_2 – effectively, we can have any C_3 followed by any C_1 consonant. For instance, *-ɲŋ-* in *guliɲŋunu* (text xv, line 1, p. 368). Clusters of this type probably only occur at root-affix and reduplication boundaries within noun and adjective stems; within verb, and noun and verb marker, stems phonological rules normally act to produce clusters of type C_2.

It is not easy to formulate a criterion for dividing up Dyirbal words into syllables. A syllable is always centred on a vowel; plainly a C_1 consonant goes with the following vowel, and a C_3 segment with the preceding vowel. However, a three-segment C_2 cluster can be divided between syllables in several ways. Consider *ḍalnbil* 'dance'; the first syllable involves *ḍal* and the second *bil*, *n* could be assigned in either direction. There is a selectional dependency between the *l* and *n* of the cluster (we could not have **ṛn*, for instance) and also between *n* and *b* (**ɲb* is impossible). (And see the discussion in 7.5.1.)

7.2.2 Stress. Dyirbal words have a 'preferred' stress pattern – that the first syllable should be stressed, and that there should be exactly one unstressed syllable between each two successive stressed syllables. The ideal situation is for the first and all odd-numbered syllables to be stressed, and for the second and all even-numbered syllables to lack stress. Final syllables are never stressed (cf. Trubetzkoy, 1969: 286).

The first syllable of every root (and thus of every word) is stressed. Reduplicated roots have reduplicated stress. Some compound roots have stress on the third syllable: thus *múnumádal* 'chuck it in', *bándubánal* 'bend it over' – 9.1.1.

The lack of stress on the final syllable of a word can be explained in terms of the obligatory stress on the first syllable: to have two consecutive syllables stressed would be counter to the stress preferences of Dyirbal.

All affixes, with the exception of the reflexive alternant *-yiríy* in D, have the first syllable stressed. However, the first syllable of an affix loses its stress:

[1] when immediately following a stressed syllable. Thus, with roots *ɲínay* 'sit', and *búybal* 'hide' and affixes *-mál* ~ *-mbál* 'comitative/instrumentive', and *-ríy* 'reflexive' (in M), we get (in unmarked tense inflection):

búybaríɲu	*ɲínayman*
búybarímban	*ɲínaymáriɲu*

[2] when word-final. Thus:

ɲínaɲúmi but *ɲínaɲu*   (unmarked tense plus 'perfective' relative clause inflection, in M)

wáyɲḍiɲúgu but *wáyɲḍiɲu* (relative clause inflection plus dative case)

A number of Dyirbal affixes have alternant forms that are used whenever a word does not exhibit the 'preferred' stress pattern. For instance, the comitative/instrumentive affix is *-mál* next but one after a stressed syllable (that is, when the preferred stress pattern prevails) but *-mbál* in all other cases. We thus have (all forms are in unmarked tense inflection):

núdin	*núdilḍáɲu*	*núdilman*
núdilḍáymban	*núdilmálḍaɲu*	*núdilḍáriman*

(cf. 5.7.5)

Also: *bánagaɲu* 'return', *bánagaymban*, *bánagaymbáriɲu*.

In the case of *ɲínay* 'sit' the comitative form is *ɲínaymál*; with unmarked tense inflection this becomes *ɲínayman*, the final syllable losing its stress by rule [2]. The reflexive affix can be added to *ɲínaymál*; this is, in D, *-yiríy* next but one after a stressed syllable, and *-ríy* in all other cases. The form *ɲínaymáriy* results; by rule [1] *-ríy* loses its stress immediately after a stressed syllable, producing *ɲínaymáriy*. The comitative affix can again be added – the alternant used is *-mál*, since the affix comes next but one after a stressed syllable – and *ɲínaymárimál* results. With unmarked tense inflection we get *ɲínaymáriman*, as in (272) of 4.9.3.

It might be suggested that two degrees of stress should be recognised for Dyirbal: primary stress, occurring on the first syllable of a word, and secondary stress, occurring elsewhere. We would then be able to account for two kinds of alternation in the form of affixes:

FIRSTLY [a] instrumentive/comitative in all dialects, and [b] reflexive on to *-l* stems in D (4.8.1) have one form next syllable but one after ANY DEGREE OF STRESS, and another form elsewhere.

SECONDLY [a] transitive verbaliser (4.7), and [b] reflexive on to *-y* stems in all dialects (4.8.1) have one form next syllable but one after PRIMARY stress, and another form elsewhere.

We would be able to disambiguate (170) and (172) if two degrees of stress were recognised. Writing ′ for primary and ` for secondary stress, (170) would be *ḍúgumbilbùnḍulmùŋa bániɲu* against (172) *ḍúgumbil bùnḍulmùŋa bániɲu*. A further pair of sentences that would be disambiguated is (cf. 654–5):

(678) *gíɲa yúngul báḍiɲu* that one [class IV object] is falling
(679) *gíɲayùngul báḍiɲu* that's the [class IV object] falling

(This problem only arises in the case of class IV markers.)

However, there is no evidence that speakers of Dyirbal do phonetically distinguish two degrees of stress. It may be thought convenient to define 'secondary stress' as 'stress on any syllable that is not word-initial' but this would be a mere analytic ploy – distinguishing two degrees of stress IN TERMS

OF word boundaries, etc. There is no evidence that speakers identify word boundaries IN TERMS OF prior perception of primary and secondary stress.

We shall, below, recognise only one degree of stress (contrasting with the absence of stress).

7.3 Phonic realisations of phonological systems

Relative phonic realisations of the features in the two phonological systems are (cf. Abercrombie, 1967):

LOCALISATION SYSTEM

[Lin] articulation with minimal movement of the tongue from rest position

[Lfr] articulation with significant movement of the tongue from rest position with respect to a relatively front part of the mouth

[Lba] articulation with significant movement of the tongue from rest position with respect to a relatively back part of the mouth

[Lab] articulation involving the lips

MANNER SYSTEM. Phonic realisations of the features of this system involve three variables:

[1] whether the articulation has either [a] a stricture of complete closure across the whole width of some part of the tongue; or [b] a stricture of complete closure involving only part of the width of some part of the tongue; or [c] no stricture of complete closure.

[2] whether there is also velic closure or not.

[3] whether the articulation is on the peak of a chest-pulse or not.

Relative phonic realisations are now:

	[1]	[2]	[3]
[Stop]	complete closure	closure	not peak
[Nas]	complete closure	no closure	not peak
[Liq]	partial closure	closure	not peak
[S-V]	no closure	closure	not peak
[Vow]	no closure	closure	peak

STRESS SYSTEM. Each syllable chooses one of the two features:

[Stress]   relatively more forceful chest pulse

[Lack of Stress]   relatively less forceful chest pulse

These realisational statements give the significant phonic differences corresponding to features in the systems. The phonic realisation of each bundle of features (or segment) may involve other, non-defining phonic components:

STOPS, i.e. segments involving feature [Stop]. *d* (feature [Lin]) involves minimal movement of the tongue from rest position – the tip moves up to touch the alveolar ridge. *ḍ* – feature [Lfr] – requires a considerable portion of the blade of the tongue to be raised into contact with the hard palate, alveolar ridge and teeth. In the case of *g* (feature [Lba]) the dorsal section of the tongue is raised to the velum, and the tip often also raised to the alveolar ridge. *b* (feature [Lab]) is a simple bilabial stop.

NASALS, i.e. segments involving feature [Nas], are exactly analogous to the corresponding stops.

LIQUIDS, i.e. segments involving feature [Liq]. The least movement of the tongue from rest position that will form a stricture across part of its width is the raising of the central part – producing lateral *l* (= [Liq, Lin]). Non-minimal movement from rest position is involved in raising the sides of the tongue, to form a grooved-tongue sound. [Lfr] produces *r*, articulated further forward in the mouth than *ɽ*, which involves [Lba]. In each case the articulation can be continuous or discontinuous – statistically, *r* is more frequently tapped or trilled, and *ɽ* more frequently a continuant.

Considered merely qua 'absolute place of articulation' *l* and *r* are both closest to the apico-alveolar series *d* and *n*, with *ɽ* being nearest to the lamino-alveopalatals *ḍ* and *ɲ*. However, the phonological statement attempted here refers to RELATIVE MOVEMENT rather than ABSOLUTE POSITION for grouping *l* with *d* and *n*, *r* with *ḍ* and *ɲ*, and *ɽ* with *g* and *ŋ*.

VOWELS. The realisation of [Lab] is defined in terms of lip articulation; [Vow, Lab] also involves significant movement of the tongue qua an anterior part of the mouth, i.e. raising of the tongue towards the velum. The realisation of [Lba] is defined as movement of the tongue at the rear of the mouth; [Vow, Lba] also involves lip rounding. Thus both [Vow, Lab] and [Vow, Lba] are realised as the rounded back vowel *u*. *a* is [Vow, Lin], involving no movement at all of the tongue from rest position. [Vow, Lfr] – that is, *i* – involves significant movement of the tongue in the front portion of the mouth, towards the hard palate.

SEMI-VOWELS. The bundles involving [Lab], [Lba] and [Lfr] are realised as *w*, *w* and *y* respectively, following the arguments for vowels. [S-V, Lin] is also related to *w*, largely on the basis of the realisation of /-*awa*-/ as [-*a:*-], in [1] below, and the statistical association between *a* and *w* – 7.4.2. However, there does seem to be some phonetic basis for the assignment – *w* certainly appears to involve less tongue movement from rest position than does *y*, for instance, and can on this basis be described as the 'unmarked semi-vowel'.

Further evidence supporting the phonological description of vowels and semi-vowels is:

[1] /-*awa*-/ can be alternately realised as [-*awa*-] or [-*a:*-], /-*uwu*-/ as [-*uwu*-] or [-*u:*-], and /-*iyi*-/ as [-*iyi*-] or [-*i:*-]. Thus *máwa* 'shrimp' is heard as either [*máwa*] or [*má:*]; *gíyi*, class I demonstrative noun marker, as [*gíyi*] or [*gí:*] *gúwu* DM 'nose' as [*gúwu*] or [*gú:*]; and similarly in other cases. Informants use different phonetic forms quite interchangeably and insist that they are equivalent.

However, some factors (including the factor of habit) may determine which is used, e.g. *gíyi* is usually [*gí:*] in isolation but [*gíyi*] with a bound form, e.g. [*gíyimbáyḍi*]; [*máwa*] in monologue but [*má:*] as a shout ('there are shrimps here!'); [*bá:l*] normally but [*báwal*] with an indefinite verb marker (6.5.1), i.e. [*bálubá:l*] but [*bálarubáwal*]. But note that informants did not correct the writer when, purposely, he repeated something they had just said using the alternative realisation – a sure identification that a difference is 'etic' rather than 'emic'.

[2] most words beginning with /*wú*.../ can be realised as [*wú*...] or as [*ú*...]; similarly, most words with initial /*yí*.../ as [*yí*...] or [*í*...]. However, words beginning with /*wá*.../ can NOT be realised as [*á*...]. Different forms are used quite interchangeably and informants again insist that they are equivalent (and furthermore insist that [*wú*...] and [*yí*...] are really the 'correct' pronunciations).

It appears that words beginning with /*wú*.../ can be realised as [*ú*...] UNLESS the first C$_2$ is simply -*l*- or -*y*-; similarly, words beginning in /*yí*.../ can be realised as [*í*...] UNLESS the first C$_2$ is simply -*l*-, -*y*- or -*r*- (no words beginning /*yíwV*.../ or /*yíṛV*.../, where V is any vowel, are known).

In some roots, which appear to be in reduplicated form and which begin with *yi*- or *wu*-, the medial *y* or *w* is elided to avoid an impossible consonant sequence. For instance, *balan yímalímal* 'welcome swallow', *bala wúrbunúrbun* G 'tassel fern' (*-*ly*- and *-*nw*- being impossible clusters). There is no elision in, for instance, *bayi wúṇḍirwúṇḍir* 'midge', -*rw*- being a quite normal cluster.

Thus all words in Dyirbal can be regarded as beginning with a consonant. The single exception is the particle *áṇḍa* (4.15.2); note that this DOES NOT have a variant form [*wáṇḍa*]. It is possible – as one informant once suggested – that *aṇḍa* is an introduction within the last fifty years, based on English 'and'; but this can not be regarded as more than an unsubstantiated possibility.

7.4 Statistical support for phonological description

7.4.1 Probabilities of occurrence. The features in a phonological system have different relative probabilities of occurrence with respect to different functional possibilities. In the first (stressed) syllable of a word relative probabilities of vowel occurrence are:

á 0·4 í 0·2 ú 0·4

whereas in the second (unstressed) syllable the probabilities are:

a 0·5 i 0·25 u 0·25

These figures, and others given below, are based on a 2,200-word vocabulary sample.

An examination of running text would be likely to give slightly different figures. For instance, the high frequency of pronominal forms beginning with *ŋ-* and *ɲ-*, and of noun and verb markers beginning with *ba-*, might increase the scores of these segments.

Relative probabilities of occurrence of consonants in root-initial (C_1) and of consonants and vowels in root-final (C_3 or V#) positions are (with the root-initial figures referring to all classes, but the root-final ones referring to nouns and adjectives only, since verbal roots all end in *-y* or *-l*):

	root initial		root final	
b	0·15			
d	0·04	0·55		
ḍ	0·15			
g	0·21			
m	0·12		0·02	
n	0·02	0·25	0·16	0·21
ɲ	0·04		0·03	
ŋ	0·07			
l			0·12	
r			0·05	0·22
ṛ	0·03		0·05	
w	0·10	0·17		
y	0·07		0·07	
a			0·23	
i			0·09	0·50
u			0·18	

Root-final probabilities were computed for noun and adjective separately – but did not differ significantly.

There are a large number of possibilities at medial (C_2) positions. Considering those words with just a stop at first C_2, relative probabilities are:

$$b \ \ 0.29 \qquad d \ \ 0.16 \qquad ḍ \ \ 0.26 \qquad g \ \ 0.29$$

And for those words with just a nasal at first C_2:

$$m \ \ 0.40 \qquad n \ \ 0.21 \qquad ɲ \ \ 0.15 \qquad ŋ \ \ 0.24$$

It will be seen that apico-alveolar stop and nasal (*d* and *n*) are seldom found root-initial, *n* is often found root-final, and *n* and *d* have fairly average probabilities of occurrence in word-medial position.

Homorganic nasal-plus-stop clusters are several times more common than non-homorganic clusters; the three types of non-homorganic cluster (*nb*, *nḍ*, and *ng*) are about equally common – each occurred about thirty times in the 2,200-word vocabulary sample. Nasal-plus-nasal clusters are very rare: ten words involving an *-nm-* cluster occurred in the sample; *-nɲ-* and *-nŋ-* clusters were each represented by a single root.

Quantitative considerations are relevant to a discussion of certain cases of possible ambiguity. For instance, the ergative/instrumental inflection on to a nominal ending in a nasal is a homorganic stop plus *-u*. Thus it is *-bu* on to a nominal ending in *-m*. But there is also the universal affix *-bu* 'only' (6.7.2). Encountering a form *búrguɽumbu* (*bayi búrguɽum* 'jumping ant') we might thus not be able to tell whether it was in nominative inflection plus affix *-bu* 'only', or in ergative/instrumental inflection. There would in fact be the possibility of ambiguity in such cases. But it will be seen from the figures given above that *-m* is the least common root-ending segment – only about 2% of nominals (none of these being very frequent ones) end in *-m*. We could say that the chances of this ambiguity coming up are so small that the language 'tolerates' it.

However, the ergative/instrumental inflection of a nominal ending in *-ŋ* would presumably be *-gu*, identical with the dative inflection. This would be a serious syntactic ambiguity, and would be less likely to be resolvable by 'common sense' considerations than the *-bu* one. In fact no Dyirbal root ends in *-ŋ*. We could say that the possibility of so serious an ambiguity is NOT tolerated by the language; and that to avoid it Dyirbal does not allow any nominal to end in *-ŋ*.

Nyawigi, the language to the south of Wargamay, does have nominal roots ending in *-ŋ*: thus Nyawigi *búndiŋ* as against Wargamay and Dyirbal *búndiɲ* 'grasshopper' (the form is *búndim* in Yidin, and *búndi* in Mbabaram).

See also the discussion of *-ɲá* occurring with proper names – 6.1.1.

If two words differed only in their final segments, each being chosen from the set *l, r, ɾ*, then their ergative/instrumental forms would be identical. However, this only leads to homonymy in a certain syntactic function (and Dyirbal, like most languages, tolerates a good deal of root homonymy) and not to syntactic ambiguity as in the examples above.

7.4.2 Statistical association. It is a fact of Dyirbal phonology that there is a greater than chance expectation that two successive segments in a word will contain the same features from the localisation system.

For example, a 2,200-word sample includes 594 words beginning with *b* or *m*. There is thus a 0·27 probability that any word begins with *b* or *m*. 880 words in the sample have *u* as their first vowel – a probability of 0·40. If there were no 'association' between C_1 and following V segments, the probability that a word has initial *bú-* or *mú-* should be 0·27 × 0·40 = 0·108. That is, we would expect 238 words of the sample to begin with *bú-* or *mú-*; in fact 262 do. The actual to expected ratio – 262 ÷ 238 = 1·10 – shows that there is positive association between choice of the feature [Lab] at C_1, and of [Lab]/[Lba] at the following V.

C_1	V			greatest association with	medium association with	least association with
	ú	*i*	*á*			
b or *m*	1·10	0·85	0·97	*ú*	*á*	*i*
g or *ŋ*	1·15	0·70	0·95	*ú*	*á*	*i*
ḍ or *ɲ*	0·77	1·35	1·07	*i*	*á*	*ú*
d or *n*	0·63	1·30	1·25	*á, i*		*ú*
w	0·68	0·50	1·36	*á*	*ú*	*i*
y	0·68	1·77	0·98	*i*	*á*	*ú*
ɾ	1·30	0·60	0·83	*ú*	*á*	*i*

The values of the actual to expected ratio for all possible C_1 and following V choices are shown in the left half of the table above. The right half of the table orders the vowels, for each type of initial segment, as they have greater or lesser association with the initial segment. Comparing this table with that in 7.1 it will be seen that an initial consonant always has POSITIVE association with the vowel involving the SAME choice from the localisation system, and NEGATIVE association with the vowel involving a DIFFERENT, MARKED choice. It has fairly NEUTRAL association with $\acute{a}$, involving the UNMARKED localisation feature. It should be noted that w, placed in the same column as both $\acute{u}$ and $\acute{a}$ in the table of 7.1, has greatest association with $\acute{a}$, and considerably less with $\acute{u}$ (although not so little as with $\acute{\imath}$); this contrasts with the phonetic possibility of dropping $[w]$ from $/w\acute{u}.../$ but not from $/w\acute{a}.../$. (Relatively few words begin with d and n – the initial consonants that involve the unmarked feature from the localisation system – so that here we are dealing with a 'small sample', that may not be sufficient as basis for working out associations.)

In fact there is always positive association of localisation features between successive segments at certain positions in word structure, but not at certain other positions.

There is positive association between:

[1] C_1 and a following V;

[2] V and a following l, r, $ʅ$ or y beginning or constituting a C_2 cluster;

[3] the final segment of a C_2 cluster and the following V;

[4] a nasal and a following stop within a C_2 cluster.

There is no appreciable association between:

[1] a vowel, and the nasal and/or plosive part of a following C_2 cluster;

[2] a vowel, and a following C_3.

For instance, the average actual-to-expected ratios between C_2 and a following vowel, for just those words whose C_2's are a nasal, a stop or a homorganic nasal-plus-stop sequence are:

for the same choice from the localisation system (not [Lin]) at C_2 and the following vowel – 1·18

for different choices (one being [Lin]) – 0·95

for different choices (neither being [Lin]) – 0·81

For cases of positive association the 'actual' numbers are 10 to 30 per cent higher than the 'expected' figures. This is not a very large percentage, but it is significant, and is consistently noticed to hold between segments in the syntagmatic sequences noted above. This consistency provides support for the setting up of these particular phonological systems, and of relating vowels and consonants to the same localisation system.

The figures are significant on the chi-squared test. In the case of the C_1-V table, for instance, chi-squared is approximately 90, in a system with twelve degrees of freedom. This implies a chance of much less than one in a million that the figures imply no association. In other words, the table is statistically quite conclusive.

The identification of *l*, *r* and *ɽ* with [Lin], [Lfr] and [Lba] is given some support by tables such as the one below, which shows actual-to-expected ratios between a vowel, and the initial liquid of a following C_2 cluster.

V	initial part of C_2		
	ɽ	*r*	*l*
ú	1·2	1·0	0·95
í	0·6	1·3	0·9
á	1·1	0·9	1·05

Note also that when *y* makes up all of C_2 it prefers to select *í* as the preceding vowel, *w* prefers *ú* or *á*, *r* prefers *í*, *ɽ* prefers *ú* or *á*, and *l* appears to be selectionally neutral. The identification of *l*, *r* and *ɽ* with [Lin], [Lfr] and [Lba] can thus be supported phonetically, statistically and morphophonologically; but it remains the part of the phonological description about which the writer has most reservations.

No segment has been recognised that involves the bundle [Liq, Lab]. In fact, there is no convincing statistical, phonetic or other support for identifying *l*, say, with [Liq, Lab] as well as with [Liq, Lin] (in the way that *w* was identified with [S-V, Lab], [S-V, Lba] and also with [S-V, Lin]); or for any other identification here.

7.5 Special phonological processes

7.5.1 Insertion and assimilation.
A number of special phonological processes (or tendencies) can be noted that affect the generation of phonological words from the phonological forms of roots:

[1] INSERTION OF -*n*-. The sooner a medial consonant cluster, C_2, comes after a stressed vowel the more tendency there is for it to include a nasal. Process [1], which is extremely widespread and important in Dyirbal, involves the insertion of -*n*- at certain grammatical boundaries within a word.

[2] ASSIMILATION. As described in the last section, there is a tendency for consecutive segments – at certain positions in word structure – to choose the same feature from the localisation system. Correlating with this, an inserted -*n*- is in many (but not all) cases assimilated in localisation feature to a following stop. (See also 7.6.)

A full list of the applications of processes [1] and [2] follows:

[i] dative inflection is -ngú when immediately after a stressed syllable (with nominal affix -ɲá, and pronominal -ná/-ɲá), but -gú when at least one stressed syllable intervenes. We can take -gú as the dative inflection, the -n- being inserted by process [1].

[ii] between simple genitive -ɲú and catalytic affix -ḍín, -n- is inserted by process [1] and assimilated to ɲ by process [2]. Thus we have báɲul and báɲulḍin, but ɲáliɲu, ɲáliɲúɲḍin; yáɽaɲu, yáɽaɲúɲḍin (4.11.1).

[iii] the transitive verbalising affix to nominals etc. has form -mál, with a stem of two syllables, and -bál with a longer stem. -n- is often inserted before -bál, and usually assimilated to -m- (4.7).

[iv] verbal stem-forming affix -bál 'do it quickly' always has -n- inserted before it (the affix can only occur with -l stems); affixes -gániy and -ḍáy have -n- inserted before them with a -y stem, the -y then being deleted (6.3.2).

[v] the reciprocal affix -báriy often has -n- inserted before it when following an -l stem, but never after a -y stem (4.8.2).

[vi] when nominal affix -bíla DG, -bá M occurs with -ɲá, an -n- is inserted and then assimilated to -m-: -ɲámbila (6.1.1). (See also M yúŋgul yúŋgulnba 'one by one' – 6.1.7.)

[vii] -n- is frequently inserted before a noun or verb marker ending in a vowel or -y, and a following bound form; thus báyingúya, báyimbáwal. And in reduplicated forms of markers: báyimbáyi, bálaymbálay. In gíyiɲúŋgul, báyiɲúŋgul there is insertion of -n-, and then replacement of -yn- by -ɲ- (see 7.5.2). In such forms n is always assimilated before b.

[viii] with verbal affix -bíla and a -y stem, -n- is inserted, assimilated to -m-, and the -y- dropped (4.13.1).

The justification for saying that -n- is inserted and then assimilated to -m- in cases [iii], [vi], [vii] and [viii], and to -ɲ- in [ii], rather than just saying that m or ɲ is inserted in such cases, lies in the fact that this assimilation does not take place in the G dialect. So that we get báyimbáyi in D and M but báyinbáyi in G; and with the verbal ending -bíla and exact translation equivalents ḍáŋgay D and búɽṇḍal G 'eat' we get -ŋay forms ḍáŋganámbila and búɽṇḍalɲánbila.

The examples listed above involved the insertion of -n- at a morpheme boundary. There is also evidence that certain nasals within roots could be regarded as inserted by process [1] (and, in some cases, assimilated by process [2]):

FIRSTLY note that when the writer first encountered the unanalysable root *ŋáɽḍambay* 'plan some rather difficult action', in the form *ŋáɽḍambaɲu*, the informant repeated the word very slowly as *ŋárḍa – báɲu*; that is, when a single-stressed word was said at 'dictation speed', with two stresses, the -*m*- was omitted. The same thing was noticed in a number of other instances.

SECONDLY, there are a number of trisyllabic verb roots that 'lose the nasal' from the final intervocalic cluster when reduplicated. Non-future tense forms are quoted:

simple root	reduplicated	
gíndimban	*gíndigíndiban*	'warn'
gúwurmban	*gúwurgúwurban*	'gather up'
gúdaymban	*gúdaygúdayban*	'pass by'
gáḍilmbáɲu	*gáḍilgáḍilbáɲu*	'prevaricate'

The transitive verbs *gíndimbal*, *gúwurmbal* and *gúdaymbal* COULD be regarded as verbalised adjectives – there is, in fact, the cognate intransitive verb *gíndibil* (but adjectives *gíndi*, *gúwur* and *gúday* have NOT been encountered; and note that, by the rules given in 4.7, the unreduplicated transitive stems should be *gíndimal*, *gúwurmal* and *gúdaymal*). However, the intransive verbs *ŋáɽḍambay* and *gáḍilmbay* could NOT be explained in this way – there is no verbalising affix -(*m*)*bay* (but see 9·4).

All these forms, and their alternations, may be a relic of rules in an earlier stage of the language.

The facts given above might be taken to suggest that a Dyirbal word could be described as a succession of syllables, each of structure $C_1V(C_3)$, with insertion and assimilation of -*n*- in some instances. That is, the cluster in a disyllabic root such as *ḍálnbil* 'dance' could be analysed as $C_3 + n + C_1$. Against this, we can note that the possibilities at C_2 are generally much narrower than those allowed by $(C_3) + (\text{nasal}) + C_1$ – for instance *ɲb*, *mŋ*, *ly* and *rɽ* are NOT possible at C_2; and C_2 does cover some segments (-*l*-, -*r*-) that are NOT generated by $(C_3) + (\text{nasal}) + C_1$. Overall, it seems most appropriate to set up a separate functional position C_2 (as was done in 7.2.1).

Whether or not an -*n*- is inserted – and once inserted whether it is assimilated – at the boundary of two phonological forms depends on [1] the grammatical nature of that boundary; [2] the final segment of the first form; and [3] the first segment of the second form.

An -*n*- will only normally be inserted if the second form begins with a stop; it is more likely to be inserted if the first form ends with a -*y* than if it ends with an *-l*: we have *bálaymbálay* but just *báŋgulbáŋgul*, for instance, and the insertion of *-n-* after *-y* verbal stems but not after *-l* stems with *-gániy*, *-ḍáy* and *-bíla* (although we do have *-n-* inserted between an *-l* stem and *-báriy* or *-bál*). An inserted *-n-* is more likely to be assimilated to a following *b* than to a following *g*: we have *bálaymbálay* and *báyimbáyḍi* but *báyingúya*.

Some words exist only in reduplicated form (and there is generally no corresponding unreduplicated form) – see 9.1.2, 6.1.9. At the boundary in the middle of a reduplicated form – just before the second stress – clusters can occur that would not be allowed at C$_2$ position: *-ɲb-*, *-ɲg-* and *-ln-*, for instance, as in *báyi báriɲbáriɲ* 'chicken hawk', *bála gíriɲgíriɲ* 'sharp scream' and *báyi náŋgalnáŋgal* 'small black ant'. In some cases, however, an *-n-* appears to have been inserted.

[1] between *y* and *b* or *g*, an *n* is inserted and assimilated:

bála báraymbáray 'dawn', báyi gúgayŋgúgay 'host of teenage boys'

[2] between *l* and *g*, an *n* is inserted but not assimilated:

bála gábalngábal 'sandy ridge', báyi gúrilngúril 'a storm bird'

[3] however, between *l* and *b*, no *n* is inserted:

bálan bíyilbíyil 'peewee bird', báyi or bálan búrgulbúrgul 'a child that never matures'

Similarly, no *n* is inserted between *ṛ* and *g*. (There are about fifty roots in apparently reduplicated form – none of them involves *-yḍ-*, *-lḍ*, or similar boundaries.)

(The examples above are all roots that appear to be in reduplicated form; productive reduplication of a simple root never involves any insertion.)

It thus appears that [1] final *-y* is a stronger 'demander' of a following *-n-* than final *-l*; and [2] an intra-root reduplication boundary is a stronger 'demander' than a noun or verb marker plus affix boundary. We have the following insertions/assimilations:

marker-affix boundary: final			reduplication boundary: final		
initial	*y*	*l*	initial	*y*	*l*
b	*m*	. .	*b*	*m*	. .
g	*n*	. .	*g*	*ŋ*	*n*

Whereas normal reduplication involves repetition of the whole root, verbal reduplication only involves the first two syllables. Generally, only the initial C$_1$VC$_2$V is repeated; however, a following liquid or *y* may appear in the reduplicated root ONLY IF it is preserved 'as is' in the final inflected form. An *-n-*, inserted before reciprocal affix *-báriy*, may optionally be reduplicated – 6.3.4.

7.5.2 Elision and conflation. In the generation of a phonological word from the phonological form of a root, segments may be conflated or elided in order to produce clusters that are 'possible' (according to the rules of 7.2.1) or else in order to produce 'popular' or frequent clusters rather than possible but less frequent ones.

[1] to avoid impossible sequences. When the affix *-yúŋgul* 'that's the one' is added to class I demonstrative noun marker *gíyi*, an *n* is inserted: *gíyinyúŋgul* (this is one of the few instances of *n* being inserted when the following consonant is not a stop – without the *n* there would be an unacceptably long stretch involving just vowels and semi-vowels). **-ny-* is not a possible cluster, and is replaced by *-ɲ-*, giving *gíyiɲúŋgul*. Notice that in the case of class II demonstrative form *gíɲan*, the *-yúŋgul* derivative is *gíɲanúŋgul*. That is, the initial *-y* of the affix drops before root-final *-n-* but is fused with an *-n-* introduced by process [1].

In M the form *gíyiɲáligu* 'this fellow here' has been encountered. This involves *gíyi* plus *yáli* with an inserted *n*, that is then fused with the following *y*.

Sequences *yn and *yd are impossible, and would naturally be replaced by *ɲ* and *ḍ* respectively. Thus (6.2) pronominal form *ŋáḍa* can be analysed into *ŋáy + da*; and the non-future tense inflection on a *-y* stem, *-ɲu*, can be analysed into *-y + nu* (10.3.2).

Note that *i* is inserted between *y* and *n* in loan words, as in *balam ḍugagayin* 'sugar cane' – 9.3.1.

In many cases *y* is simply deleted where an impossible sequence would otherwise result. Consider verbal stems *bániy*, *wáymbay*, together with purposive inflection *-gú*: resulting forms are *wáymbaygu* but *bánigu*, the *-y-* being elided in the second form in view of the fact that *-iy-* can only occur as part of the sequence *-iyi-* (7.2.1). Similarly, when *-yúŋgul* is affixed to *báŋgul* or *gíɲan*, for instance, the resulting forms are *báŋgulúŋgul*, *gíɲanúŋgul*, *y* being elided to avoid impossible sequences **-ly-* and **-ny-*.

In other cases the second of two nasals is dropped, to avoid an impossible sequence. Thus, when *-ɲá* is added to class III noun marker *bálam*, and class I and III interrogative markers *wúɳḍiɲ* and *wúɳḍam*, the resulting forms are *bálama*, *wúɳḍiɲa* and *wúɳḍama* respectively (note that with *báyi*, *bála* and *wúɳḍa* we get *báyiɲa*, *bálaɲa* and *wúɳḍaɲa* respectively). (These forms only occur with *-bíla* or the locative inflection – 6.5.6.)

[2] to avoid infrequent clusters. Sequences of *n* with another nasal do occur in all medial clusters in Dyirbal, but are rare. When adding -*ɲá* to -*máŋgan*, *bálan* or *wúɳḍan* (6.1.1, 6.5.6) the second nasal is dropped, producing -*máŋgana*, *bálana* and *wúɳḍana*.

Similarly, the simple genitive inflection on a noun has canonical form -*ŋú*, but after a nasal the -*ŋ* drops: *yáɽa*, *yáɽaŋu* but *mídin*, *mídinu; wádam*, *wádamu* (3.2.1).

However, the second nasal is retained when the genitive affix is non-word-final and retains its stress – *bálamáŋgannyúɳḍinda* and *mábimáŋgannyúɳḍinda* are attested; this indicates that the 'nasal elision rule' must follow the 'stress reduction rule' [2] of 7.2.2.

In the formation of the [− actor] plus nominative form of the second person singular pronoun in G, -*ɲá* is added to *ɲín*, *ɲína* resulting after elision of the second nasal.

In some cases a word can be formed from a root ending in -*m* and an affix beginning with *m*, e.g. (in Dyalŋuy) *yígam* 'frightened' plus transitiviser -*mál*. In normal speech one -*m*- will simply be omitted: [*yígaman*] 'make someone frightened'; but in pronouncing the word very slowly for the writer an informant would say [*yígam*] – [*mán*]. We could either say [1] that there is phonological elision here – the phonological word being /*yígaman*/; or [2] that it is phonologically /*yígamman*/ but phonetically [*yígaman*]. (A third alternative might be to preserve the second -*m*- when the -*mál* retained its stress, as in the case of genitives.) Similar comments apply to the sequence -*ɲn*- in *wuɳḍiɲ*+*ɲa* (note that there are no putative -*nn*- or -*ŋŋ*- sequences – stems cannot end in -*ŋ*, and no nominal affix begins with *n*-).

There is no evidence favouring either alternative over the other. If we took /*yígamman*/ as the underlying form, constraint [6] should be omitted from the specification of phonological word structure in 7.2.1. If /*yígaman*/ is taken as the form, then we would say that one *m* is elided, as in the examples above.

7.6   A morphophonological rule

As described in 3.2.1, there are a number of alternate realisations of the ergative inflection, depending on the final segment of the nominal stem:

[1] -*gú* with a stem of three or more syllables, ending in a vowel;

[2] -*ŋgú* with a disyllabic stem, ending in a vowel;

[3] a homorganic stop plus -*ú* after a nasal or -*y*;

[4] -*ɽú*, with deletion of the stem-final consonant, in the case of a stem ending in -*l*, -*r*, or -*ɽ*.

We take the canonical form of the ergative affix to be -*gú*; it is simply this that is involved in case [1]. In case [2] a nasal is inserted by process [1] and assimilated to the following consonant by process [2] of 7.5.1. For case [3] the first segment of the case affix is regressively assimilated to the preceding consonant segment:

$$
\begin{bmatrix} \text{Stop} \\ \text{Lba} \end{bmatrix} \longrightarrow \begin{bmatrix} \text{Stop} \\ x \end{bmatrix} \Big/ \left\{ \begin{bmatrix} \text{Nas} \\ x \end{bmatrix} \\ \begin{bmatrix} \text{S-V} \\ x \end{bmatrix} \right\} \underline{\quad\quad}
$$

where x ranges over the features of the localisation system.

In case [4] we can suggest that a bundle is formed consisting of the manner feature of the stem-final consonant, and the localisation feature of the affix-initial segment:

$$
\underline{\quad\quad} \underbrace{\begin{bmatrix} \text{Liq} \\ x \end{bmatrix}}_{\text{stem}} \underbrace{\begin{bmatrix} \text{Stop} \\ \text{Lba} \end{bmatrix}}_{\substack{\text{ergative} \\ \text{affix}}} \underline{\quad\quad} \rightarrow \underline{\quad\quad} \begin{bmatrix} \text{Liq} \\ \text{Lba} \end{bmatrix} \underline{\quad\quad}
$$

The complex alternations involved in the ergative inflections are thus explained entirely naturally in terms of the phonological feature analysis of 7.1. Note that this explanation depends upon recognition of a feature common to y, *ɲ* and *ḍ*; and (more controversially) one common to *ɽ* and *g*.

The canonical form of the ergative inflection is thus identical with that of the dative affix, -*gú*. But whereas dative -*gú* is relatively immutable (allowing the insertion of -*n*- only in limited circumstances and then no assimilation – 7.5.1), ergative -*gú* readily accepts an inserted nasal and assimilates it, or is itself assimilated to a preceding segment.

Other phonological phenomena, that are not dealt with here, include: the retention of stem-final -*y* or -*l* before some verbal affixes and loss before others; the apparent replacement of stem-final -*y* by -*n* in some cases (this could of course be said to involve insertion of -*n*-, by process [1], and then elision of -*y*- to avoid an impossible sequence *-*yn*-); the fact that the -*ŋáy* inflection is -*náy* on to a -*y* stem, with loss of stem-final -*y*, as against -*ŋáy* with retention of -*l* in the case of an -*l* stem; the fact that the genitive inflection on pronouns is -*ɲú* to a disyllabic and -*nú* to a longer root.

7.7 *r* and *l*

There is some evidence that when, by linguistic change, a root plus affix takes on the status of an unanalysable root, then an *l* in the new root may correspond to *r* in the original affix. The evidence is:

[1] there are forms *bálbaliy* 'roll' and *bármiliy* 'look back' which are exact intransitive analogues of transitive *bálbal* and *bármil* (9.1.1). *bálbal* and *bármil* do not have reflexive forms: if these did exist they would be expected to be *bálbayiríy*, *bármiyiríy* in D, *bálbaríy*, *bármiríy* in M and G. We can posit that roots *bálbaliy*, *bármiliy* have been formed from stems *bálbaríy*, *bármiríy* by the substitution of *li* for * rí* in each case.

[2] we posited underlying roots *bála* and *yála* for verb markers, and suggested that *bálu*, *yálu* are derived from *bálaru*, *yálaru* by the deletion of *-la-* and substitution of *-l-* for *-r-* (6.5.1).

[3] we also mentioned the possibility that bound forms *dáwulu*, *bálbulu* are formed from *dáwu+rú*, *bálbu+rú*, with *-l-* substituting for *-r-* (6.5.7).

[4] *bala máɽalu* 'hollow log, shirt' is probably etymologically related to *bala máɽa* 'hole' (see 9.1.2), and possibly through the ubiquitous locational affix *-rú* 'along, through', with substitution of *-l-* for *-r-*.

Note that the *-rú* involved in [2] and [4] is the 'motion' affix mentioned in 3.4.6; the *-rú* in [3] is the universal affix of 6.7.1.

The change from *-r-* to *-l-* would be an entirely natural one; both involve feature [Liq] – the change involves the substitution of unmarked localisation feature [Lin] for marked feature [Lfr].

There is one instance of an alternation between *r* and *d* in the present-day language. When occurring with bound forms *báyḍi* etc. the universal affix has the form *-rú* in D, *-gú* in some dialects of M, and *-ndú* in other M dialects and probably in Ngadyan (3.2.3, 6.7.1). Thus *yáludáyiru ~ yáludáyigu ~ yáludáyindu*. In normal speech *bálarubáwal* was said by the main D informant as [*bálarubá:l*], but when said very slowly, in teaching Dyirbal to the writer, it was [*bá-lá-dú-bá-wál*]. Commenting on the difference, the informant said that *dú* became *rú* when 'said quickly' (i.e. in a normal stream of speech). The underlying affix can be taken as *-dú*, this appearing as *-rú* in ordinary D speech through some as yet insufficiently understood alternation between *d* and *r*, and as *-ndú* in the more northerly dialects, the *n* being inserted before the stop by process [1] of 7.5.1 (this process normally inserts *n* only before stops, not before liquids).

That the underlying representation of at least some occurrences of *r* is *d*, is not inconsistent with the phonological description given in this chapter. Note that *d* and *l* share the same localisation feature, [Lin]. Thus, there could conceivably have been a synchronic rule *d → r*, and then a diachronic change *d > l*, explaining the *r ~ l* alternations described above.

7.8   Word order

Word order is exceptionally free in Dyirbal. There are two types of restriction on order:

[A] certain particles must precede the verb – 4.15.3.

[B] in sentences involving iteration of the favourite construction, the verbs of the succeeding embedded Σ's serve as foci for order restrictions: a word dominated by a lower-sentence node Σ_n must generally occur before the verb of Σ_{n+1} where Σ_{n+1} is dominated by Σ_n

However, there is a most frequent order; the preferences include:

[1] time qualifiers tend to precede all other words;

[2] some particles precede all but time qualifiers; other particles prefer to occur immediately before the verb (see the list in 4.15.3);

[3] a [+actor] pronominal NP will precede any other NP;

[4] nominative NPs precede ergative and dative NPs;

[5] ergative NPs precede the verb;

[6] dative NPs follow the verb;

[7] verb markers and locational nominals follow the verb;

[8] a noun marker precedes its noun;

[9] adjectives follow nouns;

[10] adverbals precede verbs;

[11] a relative clause follows the noun it qualifies;

[12] a possessive phrase precedes the noun it qualifies;

[13] a demonstrative noun marker comes first in an NP.

However, any or all of these 'preferences' can be ignored in a particular sentence. Words are not only free within phrases, they can occur in any order in a sentence (subject only to restrictions [A] and [B] above – see (321)). It is even quite common for an implicated VC to precede the VC (with tense-inflected verb) of a higher verb; thus (cf. (78)):

(680) *bayi   yaṛa   biligu   ḏiŋgaliɲu*
THERE-NOM-I man-NOM climb-PURP run-PRES/PAST
man runs [to tree] to climb [it]

The relative ordering 'preferences' listed above are more likely to be adhered to if ambiguity would otherwise result.

Note that within a participle the order is fixed – 'object noun' must precede the verb root – cf. [4–5] above.

8 Semantics

A full account of the semantics of Dyirbal would be considerably more lengthy than the description of the grammar and phonology, in chapters 3–7. In this chapter we refer briefly to some of the main points of Dyirbal semantics, paying attention to aspects that reinforce and help to explain parts of the syntax. A complete account of the semantics, in the form of a comprehensive dictionary-thesaurus of the language, is in active preparation. A provisional statement of verb semantics, going into considerably more detail than is attempted here, will be found in Dixon [1971].

8.1 Guwal-Dyalŋuy correspondences

We mentioned in 2.5 that when a speaker was within earshot of a 'taboo' relative he had to use Dyalŋuy, the so-called 'mother-in-law' style. In all other circumstances he had to use Guwal, the 'everyday' style. Every dialect has its own Guwal and Dyalŋuy. Each Dyalŋuy has identical phonology, and almost exactly the same grammar, as its Guwal. However, it has an entirely different vocabulary, there being not a single lexical item common to the Dyalŋuy and Guwal of a tribe.

Confronted with a Guwal word a speaker will give a unique Dyalŋuy 'equivalent'. And for any Dyalŋuy word he will give one or more corresponding Guwal words. It thus appears that the two vocabularies are in a one-to-many correspondence: each Dyalŋuy word corresponds to one or more Guwal words (and the words so related are in almost all cases not cognate with each other). For instance, M Guwal has terms *bala magur* 'haze', *bala gumburu* 'mountain mist', *bala garan* 'smoke' and *bala ḍawuy* 'steam' – in M Dyalŋuy there is a single noun, *bala garmban*, covering the meanings of the four Guwal terms (and note that there is no generic term in Guwal relating together the four phenomena).

Dyalŋuy thus operates on a considerably more general level than does Guwal. Whereas vagueness is held to be a severe fault in normal conversation (2.4), it is appropriate to the 'social distance' that must be observed in the presence of a taboo relative (and see the example in 6.5.6). However, specificity CAN be achieved in Dyalŋuy by adding a qualifying phrase or clause to a term such as *bala garmban*, describing some critical property of the specific phenomenon referred to.

Dyalŋuy has not been actively spoken since about 1930. However, the writer persuaded several old people to talk to each other in Dyalŋuy, and recorded four sizeable texts. In addition, the Dyalŋuy equivalents of about two thousand Guwal words were asked, from each of two informants; many words were asked again two or three years later, in order to check the consistency of the data obtained. There was, in fact, a high level of agreement, indicating that Dyalŋuy was being accurately remembered.

Dyalŋuy contains far fewer words than Guwal – something of the order of a quarter as many. Whereas Guwal has considerable hypertrophy, Dyalŋuy is characterised by an extreme parsimony. Every possible syntactic and semantic device is exploited in Dyalŋuy in order to keep its vocabulary to a minimum, it still being possible to say in Dyalŋuy everything that can be said in Guwal. The resulting often rather complex correspondences between Guwal and Dyalŋuy vocabularies are suggestive of the underlying semantic relations and dependencies for the language.

8.2   Verb semantics

8.2.1   Nuclear and non-nuclear verbs. The data on Guwal–Dyalŋuy correspondences in the case of verbs suggests a classification of verbs into two sets, 'nuclear' and 'non-nuclear':

[1] There are a fairly small number of NUCLEAR verbs, these are the most important verbs of the language with encompassing, generic meanings. Nuclear verbs cannot be semantically defined in terms of other verbs (they may, however, be related together through componential description – Dixon [1971]).

[2] The set of NON-NUCLEAR verbs is considerably larger. Each non-nuclear item effectively provides a rather detailed specification of some aspect of the meaning of a nuclear verb. Semantically, a non-nuclear verb can be 'defined' in terms of a nuclear verb, and certain grammatical processes and relations (sometimes also involving other lexical items).

The set of nuclear verbs includes [1] *madal* 'throw'; and [2] *biḍil* 'hit with a rounded object'. Amongst non-nuclear verbs are [1] *dabil*

'throw a handful of solid bits (e.g. sand or nuts) at someone', *nalŋil*
'sieve', *bulwal* 'expel breath in big gasps', all of which are semantically
definable in terms of nuclear *madal*; and [2] *ḏilwal* 'kick, or shove with
knee'; *dudal* 'mash [food] with stone', *daliy* 'deliver blow to someone
lying down, e.g. fall on them, drop stone on them', all of which are
semantically definable in terms of nuclear *biḏil*.

An account of the procedure followed in eliciting Guwal-Dyalŋuy
correspondences will give some idea of the justification for a nuclear/
non-nuclear division of Dyirbal verbs.

The field technique fell into two parts. First, about seven hundred
Guwal verbs were gone through separately with each of two informants,
and their Dyalŋuy correspondents were elicited. About a hundred and
fifty Dyalŋuy verbs were involved, most occurring several times, as
correspondents of different Guwal items. Thus Dyalŋuy verb *ɲuɽimal*
was given as correspondent of, amongst others:

> *buɽal* 'look at, see'
> *wabal* 'look up at'
> *ɽugal* 'watch [someone] going'
> *ɲaɽɲḏay* 'stare'
> *gindal* 'look with the aid of a light (at night)'
> *wamil* 'watch someone without their being aware they are being
> watched; take a sneaky look'

At the end of the first stage of the elicitation the writer made out
a card for each Dyalŋuy verb, listing on it all Guwal verbs for which
it had been given as correspondent. Thus the card for *ɲuɽimal* included
buɽal, wabal, ɽugal, ɲaɽɲḏay, gindal and *wamil*. Now, at the second
stage, each of these cards was gone through with the informant. He
was asked to verify that *ɲuɽimal* was a bona fide Dyalŋuy item and
was then asked how he would render *ɲuɽimal* in Guwal. There were
at this stage a number of possibilities open to the informant. He could
have said *buɽal, wabal, ɽugal, . . .*, listing all the items for which he
had said *ɲuɽimal* in stage 1; or he could have just mentioned ONE of
these Guwal verbs. In fact his response was of the second type: he
simply gave *buɽal* as the equivalent of *ɲuɽimal*; and he had to be
prompted – in the second stage – to say that *wabal, ɽugal, ɲaɽɲḏay*,
and so on, were also Guwal equivalents of Dyalŋuy *ɲuɽimal*.

The writer then went into the second stage of elicitation with his
other main informant. Exactly the same results were obtained – again

just *buṟal* was given as Guwal correspondent of *ɲuṟimal*. And the same
thing happened for every one of the Dyalŋuy verbs. Although from
two to twenty verbs were listed on each card – those Guwal words
for which the Dyalŋuy item had been given as correspondent in stage 1
– each informant gave just one of these as Guwal equivalent in stage 2;
and in each case the two informants picked THE SAME ITEM.

It is fairly obvious what is happening here. Each card contained
one nuclear Guwal verb and a number of non-nuclear verbs. When the
nuclear Dyalŋuy verb was put to an informant, he ALWAYS chose the
nuclear Guwal verb as its correspondent, NEVER one of the non-nuclear
verbs. These results provide not only justification for the nuclear/non-
nuclear distinction, but also a procedure for checking which of the
everyday language verbs are nuclear.

The writer next checked with informants that Guwal verbs *buṟan*
and *waban* did differ in meaning, despite the fact that they had both
been rendered by the same Dyalŋuy verb, *ɲuṟiman*, in stage 1. (Unmarked tense forms were quoted.) The informant was asked how this
difference in meaning could be expressed in Dyalŋuy, if it were necessary
to do so. He replied that *buṟan* would just be rendered by *ɲuṟiman* but
that *waban* would be expressed by *yalugalamban ɲuṟiman*, with the
verb preceded by a verbalised verb marker involving the bound form
gala 'vertically up'. Similarly, when confronted by the pair *buṟan* and
ṟugan, he said that for *buṟan* the Dyalŋuy translation would be just
ɲuṟiman but that *ṟugan* would be *ɲuṟiman yalugalumban bawalbiɲu*
'look out in front at [someone] who is going'; *bawalbiɲu* is a relative
clause involving Dyalŋuy verb *bawalbil* 'go', the correspondent of
Guwal *yanu* (9.2.1). The same procedure was followed for all verbs
on the card; when the *ɲuṟiman* card had been dealt with the field note-
book read, in part:

ɲuṟiman

buṟan	
waban	*yalugalamban ɲuṟiman*
ṟugan	*ɲuṟiman yalugalumban bawalbiɲu*
ŋaṟɳḍaɲu	*ḍungurugu ɲuṟiman*
gindan	*ŋarganagu ɲuṟiman*
wamin	*gilari ḍubuɳḍu ɲuṟiman*

In the case of *ŋaṟɳḍaɲu* the adjective *ḍunguru* '(action done) hard', in
ergative inflection, is added to *ɲuṟiman*; thus *ŋaṟɳḍaɲu* is effectively

defined as 'look hard'. For *gindan, ŋargana* 'light', in instrumental inflection, is placed in syntactic relation with *ɲuṟiman*. The Dyalŋuy equivalent of *wamin* involves, besides *ɲuṟiman*, verb marker *gilari* and the adjective *ḍubuɲ* 'quiet, with stealth' in ergative inflection.

Similar results were obtained for all the cards, for both informants. The Guwal nuclear verb was always left with just the Dyalŋuy verb as correspondent, and 'definitions' were given for the nuclear verbs. Informants sometimes gave identical definitions for a non-nuclear verb – both gave *yalugalamban ɲuṟiman* for *waban*, and *yalugalumban ɲuṟiman bawalbiɲu* for *ṟugan*, for instance – and sometimes rather different ones; but they agreed in ALWAYS giving SOME definition for a non-nuclear verb, and NEVER attempting one for a nuclear verb.

The 'definitions' of non-nuclear in terms of nuclear verbs will be seen to be of a number of different kinds. They can involve the addition of some grammatical process to a nuclear verb (for instance, an aspectual affix, or reduplication), or the specification of some other word which is in a certain syntactic relation to the nuclear verb. Thus, the definitions of *waban* and *ṟugan* involve a verbalised verb marker within the same VC, and *wamin* involves verb marker *gilari*; *gindan* involves specification of the head of an instrumental NP, and *ŋaṟɲḍaɲu* and *wamin* each involve an adjective modifying the head of the A NP; *ṟugan* involves a relative clause to the head of the O NP. Definitions utilise the full syntactic possibilities of the language – including reflexive, comitative, -*ŋay* constructions, and so on; a fullish list is in Dixon [1971].

During the elicitation, verbs were put to informants within a simple sentence – with pronominal subject/object etc. In the account above this minimal NP specification – which was common to Guwal question and Dyalŋuy response in stage 1, and to Dyalŋuy question and Guwal reply, in stage 2 – has been silently omitted.

8.2.2 Syntactic possibilities. There are in Guwal pairs of verbs that appear to have the same semantic content but to differ in transitivity: thus intransitive *maril* and transitive *banḍal* 'follow', intransitive *ḍanay* and transitive *ḍaral* 'stand', intransitive *maɲḍay* and transitive *ḍaŋgay* 'eat' etc. Such pairs are of two distinct types according as the realisation of the subject of the intransitive verb corresponds to:

[1] the realisation of the object of the transitive verb (the case $S \equiv O$); or

[2] the realisation of the subject of the transitive verb (the case $S \equiv A$).

Dyalŋuy, with its lexical frugality, makes do with a single transitive verb in cases when Guwal has a transitive and intransitive pair. The Dyalŋuy verb corresponds to the transitive member of the Guwal pair, and the false reflexive form of the Dyalŋuy verb is used in cases when Guwal would employ the intransitive member.

Examples are (M Dyalŋuy):

[1] S ≡ O

	Guwal	Dyalŋuy
[a]	*ḍaran*, tr, *ḍanaɲu*, intr 'stand'	*dindan*, tr
	balan bangul ḍaran, 'he stands her up'	*balan bangul dindan*
	balan ḍanaɲu, 'she is standing up'	*balan dindariɲu*
[b]	*bundin*, tr 'take out'; *mayin* intr 'come out'	*yilwun*, tr
	balan bangul bundin 'he takes her out'	*balan bangul yilwun*
	balan mayin, 'she comes out'	*balan yilwuriɲu*
[c]	*walmbin*, tr, *walmaɲu*, intr 'get up, waken'	*ḍulwan*, tr
	balan bangul walmbin, 'he wakens her'	*balan bangul ḍulwan*
	balan walmaɲu, 'she wakens'	*balan ḍulwariɲu*

[2] S ≡ A

	Guwal	Dyalŋuy
[a]	*banḍan*, tr, *marin*, intr 'follow'	*gaɲḍaman*, tr
	balan bangul banḍan 'he follows her'	*balan bangul gaɲḍaman*
	bayi marin, 'he follows'	*bayi gaɲḍamariɲu*
[b]	*buwaɲu*, tr 'tell', *wurbaɲu*, intr 'talk, speak'	*wuyuban*, tr
	balan bangul buwaɲu 'he tells her'	*balan bangul wuyuban*
	bayi wurbaɲu 'he talks'	*bayi wuyubariɲu*
[c]	*ḍaŋgaɲu*, tr, *maɲḍaɲu*, intr 'eat'	*yulmiɲu*, tr
	balam bangul ḍaŋgaɲu 'he eats food'	*balam bangul yulmiɲu*
	bayi maɲḍaɲu 'he eats'	*bayi yulmimariɲu*

We are oversimplifying here since there is in fact a slight difference in semantic content for the 'eat' pair. *maɲḍaɲu* is 'eat fruit or vegetables to appease hunger' while *ḍaŋgaɲu* is 'eat fruit or vegetables (whether or not particularly hungry)'; there is a different verb, intransitive *ɾubiɲu*, for the eating of fish or meat. However, for all the other pairs mentioned here transitive and intransitive members have exactly the same semantic content.

It appears that all Guwal transitive verbs can occur in 'false reflexive' form – 4.8.1 (in addition, all verbs may – if it would be semantically plausible – form true reflexives). A false reflexive involves the original A NP taking on S function – see (219–28), and:

(681) *balan ḍugumbil baŋgul yaɽaŋgu walmbin*   man woke woman
(682) *bayi yaɽa walmbiyiriɲu bagun ḍugumbilgu*   ⟨as (681)⟩

Thus pairs of stems *ḍaŋgay, ḍaŋgaymariy* and *walmbil, walmbiyiriy* are of the type S≡A.

Now in the case of pairs of roots of type S≡A, false reflexives are formed in Dyalŋuy on the same syntactic pattern as in Guwal. Thus *ḍaŋgaymariy* is effectively synonymous with *maɲḍay*, and so it is entirely appropriate to have *yulmiy* corresponding to *ḍaŋgay*, and *yulmimariy* to *maɲḍay*. However, in the case of root-pairs of type S≡O, Dyalŋuy false reflexives are formed on an entirely different pattern from that employed in Guwal. Thus *walmbiyiriy* in (682) is NOT synonymous with *walmay* in [1c] above, but Dyalnuy DOES have *ḍulwal* corresponding to *walmbil* and *ḍulwayiriy* for *walmay*.

We have seen that in Guwal transitive verbs of type S≡O and of type S≡A form false reflexives on the same pattern; but that in Dyalŋuy the Guwal pattern is followed for S≡A verbs, and a quite different pattern in S≡O instances.

The comitative construction has two quite different semantic interpretations, correlating with the S≡O/S≡A distinction and, in this case, the correlation applies in both Guwal and Dyalŋuy. Thus *marilman* is syntactically and semantically equivalent to *banḍan*, as is *wurbayman* to *buwaɲu* and *maɲḍayman* to *ḍaŋgaɲu*. Comitative *balan baŋgul marilman* 'he is following her' could be realised by the same event as *balan baŋgul banḍan*; *marilman* and *banḍan* appear to be exact synonyms. However, *ḍanayman* and *ḍaran, mayilman* and *bundin, walmayman* and *walmbin* are not syntactically and semantically equivalent. Comitative *bala baŋgun ḍanayman* 'she is standing with it (e.g. a stick in her hand)' corresponds to *balan ḍanaɲu* 'she is standing', which could be realised by the same event as *balan baŋgul ḍaran* 'he is standing her up (e.g. if she is a child that cannot stand well, say, or a sick woman)'.

Syntactically, the relation between a transitive verb of type S≡O and its intransitive equivalent is that of transitive verbaliser *-mal* or *-mbal* to intransitive verbaliser *-bil* (this is borne out by Dyalŋuy correspondent *bawalbin* for *yanu* 'go' and *bawalban* for *mundan* 'lead'

– 9.2.1.) The relation between a type S ≡ A transitive verb and its intransitive equivalent is that of *-bilmban* (*-bil* plus comitative *-mal*) to *-bil*, or of an intransitive verb in comitative form to one not in comitative form.

8.2.3 Verb types and their syntactic properties.

Dyirbal verbs fall, on syntactic and semantic grounds, into seven sets or types (the sixth of which is a residue set). Each set (except the sixth) is semantically homogeneous; that is, a collection of semantic systems, arranged in a single dependency tree, serve to generate the componential descriptions for nuclear members of the set (for details see Dixon [1968*a*] and [1971]). Each type involves one or more nuclear verbs and a considerable number of related non-nuclear items.

In this section we list the types and mention some of their more important syntactic characteristics:

[1] POSITION. Verbs in this type clearly fall into two selectional sets – verbs of motion that can occur with allative or ablative qualifiers, and verbs of rest that are restricted to locative qualification (3.4.6). We can distinguish 'simple motion' ('come', 'motion uphill', 'swim' etc.), simple rest ('sit/stay', 'lie down' etc.) and also 'induced motion' ('carry', 'shake' etc.) and 'induced rest' ('hold').

The position type includes both transitive and intransitive verbs. Of the ten or more transitive-intransitive pairs all but one are of type S ≡ O; the exception is *baṇḍal-maril* 'follow' which is S ≡ A (see [2a] above). This pair is best regarded as the CONVERSE [Lyons, 1963: 72] of the S ≡ O pair *mundal-yanu* 'lead/go' (9.2.1) – thus we have SHE GOES / HE LEADS HER / SHE FOLLOWS HIM / SHE FOLLOWS. The relation 'converse' involves interchange of subject and object functions (for a fuller discussion see Dixon, forthcoming-a). We can thus say that all position verbs are basically of type S ≡ O, and that 'follow' is DEFINED in terms of the more basic 'lead'.

Informants agreed that *bayi baŋgun baṇḍan* 'she followed him' and *balan baŋgul mundan* 'he led (or took) her' are synonymous, the only difference being that a different NP is 'topic' in the two cases.

[2] AFFECT. All verbs in this type are transitive (the single exception – *bundalay* 'fight' – is probably a fossilised reciprocal form and requires plural subject). Affect verbs cannot normally occur with allative or ablative qualifiers (although, like all verbs, they can accept 'unmarked' locative qualification). Affect verbs ('hit', 'cut', 'tie' etc.) commonly

take an instrumental NP, and occur with instrumentive VCs. The actions realising verbs from this type induce a 'state' in the object, that can be described by a (normally non-cognate) adjective – see 8.5.

[3] GIVING. This type includes nuclear *wugal* 'give' and at least seven other non-nuclear verbs, all transitive. (There is one verb that is surface intransitive – *muṇḍal* 'divide'; however, it must have plural subject, and can be described as a 'deep transitive' verb, with lexical insertion following the reciprocal transformation.)

Semantically, these verbs can be related to the dummy verb POSS that in the syntax underlies possessive constructions (although, as described in 5.5.2, POSS itself is not realised as a 'surface verb' in Dyirbal; instead it triggers rule (θ) and is itself deleted by that rule).

Verbs of giving are marked by their very wide syntactic possibilities. 'Giver', 'what is given' and 'who given to' can be assigned syntactic function in several different ways:

	giver	what is given	who given to
[i]	A	instrumental NP	O
[ii]	A	O	implicated NP
[iii]	A	O	possessive NP to O

Thus *bayi baŋgun baŋgum wugan* (and, elliptical variants: *bayi baŋgun wugan, bayi baŋgum wugan*), *balam baŋgun wugan bagul* and *balam baɲul baŋgun wugan* 'she gave food to him'. The proleptic construction – type [iii] – occurs most frequently – see 6.1.5 and also 4.9.1, 6.3.2. Line 20 of text XV (p. 372) involves two occurrences of *wugal*, the first in a construction of type [iii] and the second in one of type [i]; the topic NP 'the child' (which is not actually stated in the sentence) is 'what is given' for the first occurrence of *wugal*, and 'who given to' for the second occurrence.

bilal 'send' and *yuṟal* 'give through something, e.g. through a window' normally select motion (allative or ablative) qualification; the remainder select unmarked locative.

[4] ATTENTION. Positive verbs in this type ('see', 'hear' and their hyponyms) can select ablative/allative or locative qualification with equal facility; negative verbs ('take no notice'; 'ignore') are usually confined to unmarked locative qualification. All verbs in the type are transitive with the exception of *barmiliy* 'look back' which can be regarded as the fossilised reflexive form of transitive *barmil* (7.7).

[5] SPEAKING. Verbs of this type (which include 'tell', 'ask', 'call', 'sing' and 'tell to do', 'stop doing') typically have the 'person who is told/asked/sung to/etc.' as O NP, with the name of the speech or song-style, in locative inflection, as a verbal qualifier. The type contains both transitive and intransitive verbs – all pairs are of type S $\equiv$ A.

[6] CORPOREAL. Verbs which do not fall into any of the other sets are grouped together in this type. These verbs have no common semantic feature, but they do appear to have a vague overall resemblance – they are all concerned with 'bodily activity' (other than seeing, hearing and speaking): 'eat', 'kiss', 'laugh', 'cough', 'smell', 'swive' etc. All transitive-intransitive pairs are of type S $\equiv$ A.

[7] BREAKING OFF. Verbs in the final type refer to the 'breaking off' of some state or action; they are thus in a sense 'meta' with respect to verbs of other types. If intransitive *gayṇḍal* occurs in a VC with a verb X it means 'the action referred to by X was broken off, i.e. stopped'; in a VC by itself the unmarked realisation of *gayṇḍal* is 'something – e.g. a branch – breaks'. The type also includes *baḍiy* 'fall down' (i.e. the breaking off of a state of motion). There is a single Dyalŋuy verb, *dagaray*, corresponding to Guwal *gayṇḍal*, *baḍiy* and other verbs of this type (and see 9.2.1).

8.3   Adverbal semantics

The Dyirbal corpus yields about two dozen adverbals, that qualify verbs in much the same way as that in which adjectives qualify nouns. Most of the adverbals fall into pairs, where the members of each pair have a common semantic content but differ in syntactic orientation. For instance:

[1] the basic content 'do badly' occurs in two transitive verbs, *daral* – involving   object   orientation – and   *ganbil* – involving   subject orientation. *daral* implies that the event was unsatisfactory because of some property of the object, *ganbil* that the subject was at fault. For example, *daral ḍaŋgay* is 'eat something that is, say, stale (but there was nothing else to eat)' as against *ganbil ḍaŋgay* 'eat sloppily'.

[2] The concept 'start doing/do first' appears in *ŋayṇil*, together with subject orientation, and in *ŋunbiɣal*, together with object orientation. *ŋayṇil* indicates that the agent starts doing a certain action first, i.e. before anyone else starts doing it OR that he starts it next, i.e. before he starts doing anything else; thus *ŋayṇil nudil* can mean 'be first to

start cutting trees down'. *ŋunbiɽal* indicates that an action is BEGUN with respect to an object – to test or try the object; e.g. *ŋunbiɽal nudil* 'cut a tree a little, say, to see whether it is hard or soft'.

Guwal-Dyalŋuy correspondences provide support for our grouping adverbals into pairs. In most cases there is a single Dyalŋuy verb corresponding to both members of the Guwal pair; for instance, both *ŋaypil* and *ŋunbiɽal* are translated by Dyalŋuy *ŋunil*.

There are some pairs of verbs in English that exhibit the same kind of syntactic orientation. Thus 'finish' involves object orientation, while 'cease' and 'stop' refer to the subject; similarly in the case of 'begin' and 'start'. However, the phenomenon is much more limited in English than it is in Dyirbal – a fullish discussion is in Dixon [1970c].

In some cases the 'basic semantic content' of adverbal pairs in Dyirbal has strong resemblances to the semantic components of stem-forming verbal affixes, of verbal reduplication, of certain particles, and of value adjectives.

 [i] related to verbal affixes (6.3.2):

  [a] 'start doing/do first' which appears to be a simple non-disjunctive concept in Dyirbal but is difficult to explain in English – it is related to aspectual affix *-yaray*; [b] 'do quickly' – cf. aspectual affix *-galiy* ~ *-nbal*; [c] 'do over and over, within a short time span' cf. aspectual affix *-ḍay*; [d] 'do again, at intervals' cf. aspectual affix *-ganiy*.

 [ii] related to verbal reduplication (6.3.4) 'do to excess'.

 [iii] related to particles (4.15.3):

  [a] 'do something that shouldn't be done' – cf. *wara*; [b] 'can't do, despite tries' cf. *ŋaɽa*.

 [iv] related to value adjectives:

  [a] 'do well'; [b] 'do badly'.

8.4 Noun semantics

The class of nouns is semantically less tightly structured than the class of verbs: the nuclear/non-nuclear distinction is not generally appropriate, and revealing 'definitions' can only be provided in a minority of cases. Nouns can instead be represented as a semantic taxonomy with a number of cross-links, and so on.

Three main criteria are involved in establishing this taxonomy:

[1] generic terms in Guwal; [2] Guwal-Dyalŋuy correspondences; and [3] noun class membership. The criteria frequently interrelate – thus a set of birds (comprising three willy wagtails) [1] are not included under the generic term *dundu* 'bird'; [2] have a single Dyalŋuy correspondent; [3] belong to noun class I whereas most birds are class II.

It will be seen below that the semantic organisation of the class of nouns is related on many points to the mythological beliefs of the Dyirbalŋan.

8.4.1 Generic terms in Guwal. There are a number of important generic terms in Guwal; although they are translated by bilingual informants as 'snake', 'bird', 'fish', 'tree' etc., they do not have exactly the same scopes as the English terms:

[1] Of the twenty or so snakes known to the writer, all but three are covered by the general term *bayi wadam*; the exceptions comprise three carpet snakes. Significantly, these carpet snakes are the only snakes normally eaten by the Dyirbalŋan.

[2] The generic term *balan dundu* covers about three-quarters of the birds. It does not cover (1) the giant flightless birds – emu and cassowary; (2) the scrub hen and scrub turkey, the only birds whose eggs are regularly eaten by the Dyirbalŋan; (3) certain birds that appear in myths. Thus *balan baḍinḍila*, 'satin bird', the bird who snatched the fire from the clutches of the rainbow-snake, *balan guŋgaga* 'kookaburra', the bird who warned of the return of *giḍiya* from the land of spirits, and eight or nine other birds who have mythological status, are not included under *balan dundu*.

[3] Generic term *bayi ḍabu* covers all fishes (but not crustaceans or molluscs) except gar fish, stone fish and stingaree, the three fishes that are harmful to men.

[4] *bala yugu* covers a great number of trees; it does not, however, include ALL plants that are 'trees' in English. A main criterion appears to be height. Plants that are not covered by the generic term include *balam gubungaṟa* 'palm (Archontophoenix Alexandrae)', *balam ḍaguru* 'umbrella palm (Licuala Muelleri)', *bala yagal* 'pandamis tree'. It is interesting to note that of the two trees injurious to man, one – *balan giyara* 'big softwood stinging tree' – is included under *yugu* whereas the other – *balan ḍaŋali* 'small stinging tree' – is not.

Note that (despite its tendency to generic terms) Dyalŋuy has no correspondent of Guwal *balam wuḍu* 'wild fruit and vegetable food';

in fact the scope of *wuḍu* is coextensive with that of noun class III –
everything that is in class III is *wuḍu*, and vice versa – and Dyalŋuy
just uses noun marker *balam* where Guwal would have *balam wuḍu*.

However, this would appear to lead to some difficulties, since the syntactic
possibilities of *balam* are more limited than those of *wuḍu*. Thus, although
wuḍubila 'with food' can be rendered easily enough in Dyalŋuy by *balamabila*,
wuḍuŋaŋgay 'without food' (e.g. in the sentence *ŋaḍa wuḍuŋaŋgay* 'I've no food')
cannot be rendered in Dyalŋuy: noun markers can occur with affix *-bila* but
not with *-ŋaŋgay* (6.1.1). The writer discussed this point with an intelligent
informant who was unable to resolve the problem. Other informants translated
'I've no food' into Dyalŋuy by 'I've no black beans, and no fruit that can be
eaten raw,...' (i.e. merely giving a list of specific Dyalŋuy names for types
of *wuḍu*, each with affix *-ŋaŋgay*).

8.4.2 Guwal-Dyalŋuy correspondences: taxonomic grouping. It
has often erroneously been stated that Australian languages have a
relative lack of generic terms; this has sometimes been taken to imply
that aborigines have not developed the power of abstract thinking.

The facts are: (1) It is a cultural fault to be vague – if an aborigine
sees a snake, he should if possible refer to it by as specific a name as
possible; thus generic terms may not be as widely used as in other
languages. (2) There ARE a FAIR number of generic terms in Guwal.
Roughly, just those generic terms that ARE needed, exist in Guwal;
thus someone might see the tail of a snake and not be able to identify
the species – he would then use the generic term *bayi wadam*. However,
it would be impossible (because of size) to confuse a kangaroo with
a wallaby – a generic term covering kangaroo and wallaby is not
needed; such a term does not exist in Guwal. (3) There ARE a LARGE
number of generic terms in Dyalŋuy; for instance, *bayi yuŋga* is the
Dyalŋuy equivalent of Guwal *bayi yuṛi* 'kangaroo' and also of *bayi
bargan* 'wallaby'.

In the case of animals, the taxonomic groupings revealed by Dyalŋuy
correspond reasonably closely to the scientific taxa of zoologists. Thus
there is a single Dyalŋuy term for all lizards and guanas; there is one
term for all possums, gliders, flying squirrels and also some rats; there
is another term for flying foxes and bats; and a term for lice and tics.
Other generic terms in Dyalŋuy (in cases where Guwal has only
specific names) are 'grub', 'frog and tadpole', 'worm', 'snail', 'ground
ant', 'leech', 'grasshopper', 'locust', 'eel'.

The criteria for taxonomic grouping are in some cases rather interesting. Thus, the writer was told that three types of parrot (each with its own name in Guwal) were grouped together as *balan guliliɲ* in M Dyalŋuy because they have the same sort of beak and food. The brown pigeon, the grass quail, the curlew and two other birds are covered by *balan ḍinbaybara* in M Dyalŋuy, because they all lay eggs on or near the ground (*ḍinbaybara* is literally 'belonging to the ground – see 9.2.2). *bala miyabuṟ* 'black oak', *bala ḍungan* 'bull oak', *bala guray* 'red oak' and *bala ḍuɲḍurḍuɲḍur* 'pink oak' are all rendered by *bala guruɲun* in M Dyalŋuy since they all have the same sort of grain, although they differ in colour. Four other trees have a common name in Dyalŋuy on the grounds that they have the same sort of milky sap; two others because their wood is extraordinarily hard; two others because their bark is particularly suitable for making waterbags.

8.4.3 Metaphoric naming. There appears in Guwal to be a fair amount of homonymy. Thus, for instance:

balan gaḍin	'girl'	*bala gaḍin*	'yamstick'
balan gabal	'crane'	*bala gabal*	'sand'
balan gari	'hairy mary grub'	*balan gari*	'sun'

There is, however, a connection between the members of each pair – yamsticks are used a great deal by girls, cranes are frequently seen walking on the sand, and the sting of the hairy mary grub feels like sunburn. Furthermore, the apparent homonymy carries over into Dyalŋuy – *balan gabay* 'girl', *bala gabay* 'yamstick', and so on. This suggests that there is at work in Guwal a general principle of 'metaphoric naming': object X may be given the same name as object Y because X looks like, feels like, or is behaviourally associated with Y.

This principle is applied far more extensively in Dyalŋuy. Thus Dyalŋuy groups together (by having a single term for both) 'milky way' with 'road', 'shell-fish' with 'shell', 'pee-wee' with 'shield' (since the bird is coloured like a shield), 'white man' with 'spirit of a man', and 'white woman' with 'spirit of a woman' (since European settlers looked the colour of treated dead bodies).

In addition to metamorphic naming based on 'real world' similarity or association between objects, Dyalŋuy also groups together objects that are associated together through myth or belief. Thus birds are believed to be the spirits of dead women – both Guwal *balan dundu* 'bird' and *balan guyŋgan* 'spirit of a dead woman' are rendered by

Dyalŋuy *balan muguyŋgun* (as noted in the last paragraph *balan miḍiḍi*
'white woman' is also translated by Dyalŋuy *balan muguyŋgun*). In
some cases there is both mythological and visual similarity – 'kingfisher'
and 'storm bird' are both identified with 'eel' in Dyalŋuy (each has
a long tail like an eel, and the eel is believed to be able to turn into
either of these birds).

Thus, in keeping with its general tendency towards lexical economy,
Dyalŋuy frequently has a single lexical item corresponding to three or
four items of quite different taxonomic kinds in Guwal. For instance
bayi yamani 'rainbow' is *bayi gagilbara* in Dyalŋuy; *balan ŋiriwuŋal*
'green pigeon' is *balan gagilbara*, on the grounds that its colour is like
the green in the rainbow; and *bala giwan* 'bloodwood tree', a plant that
is held to be sacred to the rainbow-snake (most powerful spirit of the
region), is in Dyalŋuy *bala gagilbara*. Note that there is unlikely to be
any confusion in Dyalŋuy as a result of this multiple-naming: the
tree, the bird and the rainbow all belong to different noun classes.
And *bala gagilbara* is included under the generic term *bala dandu*
'tree' in Dyalŋuy, just as *bala giwan* is included under *bala yugu* in
Guwal; similarly, *balan gagilbara* is included under Dyalŋuy *balan
muguyŋgun* 'bird' just as *balan ŋiriwuŋal* is under Guwal *balan dundu*.

Consider another example: Guwal nouns *balan ŋamun* 'breast, breast
milk', *bala mura* 'semen', *bala dambul* 'the bump at the reverse of the
handle on a shield', and loan words *bala milgi* '(cow's or goat's) milk'
and *balan bulugi* 'cattle' are all rendered by *ŋunŋun* in Dyalŋuy (with
the noun class preserved in each case). 'Semen' is grouped with
'breast milk' since it is a fluid, connected in some way with reproduction,
that comes out of a human's body; 'bump on a shield' is grouped with
'breast' since they look alike; 'milk' is grouped with 'breast milk'
since it looks and tastes like it, and has a similar origin; finally, 'cattle'
is named in Dyalŋuy according to its main functional characteristic –
the milk-giving udders.

Other Guwal nouns are given Dyalŋuy names that are grammatically
complex – involving a nominalised verb, or other verb form, or a noun
plus -*bara* or other nominal affix (6.1.1); see 9.2.2.

8.4.4 Semantic basis of noun class membership.
Each noun
belongs to one of the four noun classes, and is accompanied in an NP
by a marker of this class, agreeing with the noun in case (and also
indicating whether the referent of the noun is 'here', 'there' or

'unseen') – 3.2.2. A small group of nouns can occur with either class I or class II markers; these are all either kinship terms, e.g. *daman* 'female ego's child', *ŋagi* 'male ego's daughter's child', or age-group terms, e.g. *ḍaḍa* 'baby', *palŋga* 'child'; the class marker occurring with such a noun indicates the sex of its referent (masculine for class I and feminine for class II).

Noun classes are recognised, in any language, on syntactic/morphological grounds; however, it is an empirical fact that noun classes seem always to have some degree of semantic correspondence. The degree varies – it is seldom sufficient to be the basis for straightforward, categorical statements of semantic content, and seldom so slight that it can be ignored.

A first glance at the membership of noun classes in Dyirbal suggests that the semantic basis is vague and almost random.

I (bayi)	II (balan)	III (balam)	IV (bala)
men	women		parts of the body
kangaroos	bandicoots		meat
possums	dog		
bats	platypus, echidna		
most snakes	some snakes		
most fishes	some fishes		
some birds	most birds		
most insects	firefly, scorpion, crickets		bees and honey
	hairy mary grub		
	anything connected with fire or water		
moon	sun and stars		
storms, rainbow			wind
boomerangs	shields		yamsticks
some spears	some spears		some spears
etc.	some trees	all trees	most trees
	etc.	with edible fruit	
			grass, mud, stones, noises and language etc.

Lists as heterogeneous as the above might be taken to imply that allocation of nouns to the four classes lacks any principled basis – that there are so many exceptions to any general statements (such as 'snakes and fishes are class I, birds class II') for the latter to be of little use. However, speakers do not appear to have to learn the class of each noun individually, but rather to operate with certain general principles. As a further clue, loan words are immediately assigned by different speakers to the same class.

It will be seen that if we approach the question of the semantic basis of the classes in a rather more subtle way than by just asking 'what types of object belong to each class?', then we can reveal a quite principled basis of allocation.

Class membership can largely be explained in terms of (i) certain basic concepts associated with the various classes, and (ii) certain rules (for transferring class membership).

The basic concepts associated with the classes are:

class I (*bayi*): animateness; (human) masculinity

class II (*balan*): (human) femininity; water; fire; fighting

class III (*balam*): edible vegetables and fruit

class IV (*bala*) is a residue class, dealing with everything else

The rules are:

(1) If some noun has characteristic X (on the basis of which its class membership would be expected to be decided) but is, through belief or myth, connected with characteristic Y, then generally it will belong to the class corresponding to Y and not that corresponding to X.

(2) If a subset of nouns has some particular important property that the rest of the set do not have, then the members of the subset may be assigned to a different class from the rest of the set, to 'mark' this property; the important property is most often 'harmfulness'.

Humans are always specified for sex; other animate beings are not. Thus all (nouns referring to) human males are class I; all human females are class II. Animals, snakes and lizards, insects, fishes are class I by virtue of their 'animateness'. But birds are believed to be the spirits of dead human females; by rule (1), on the basis of this believed (human) femininity rather than on the basis of their actual (non-human) animateness, birds are class II. However, certain birds are excepted from this (and are not included under the generic term *balan dundu* 'bird'): these birds have, as individuals rather than as a class, mythical associations. Thus three willy wagtails are believed to be mythical men, and are class I. The satin bird is in a myth the bringer of fire (from the clutches of the rainbow-snake): fire is in class II, and so is the satin bird. And similarly in half-a-dozen other cases.

Fishes are mostly class I; but two particularly harmful fishes, the stone fish and the gar fish are, by rule (2), class II. In this as in other cases there is interrelation with other criteria for semantic grouping: stone fish and gar fish are not included in the scope of the generic *bayi ḍabu* 'fish' (the other fish that is not covered by the generic term is in class I – *bayi yaḍaɼ* 'stingaree'). Trees, bushes, vines, and grasses with no edible parts are class IV; but the two stinging trees and a stinging nettle vine are, by rule (2), class II. Hawks, the only birds that eat other birds, are in class I by rule (2), whereas the majority of birds are in class II.

Anything connected with water and fire (including light) is in class II. But the moon and sun are, in mythology, believed to be husband and wife: by rule (1) the moon is class I and the sun class II (the stars are, by their connection with fire, class II). Wind, having none of the positive characteristics 'animateness', 'fire', 'water', 'fighting', 'edible', is class IV. But storms and the rainbow are believed to be mythical men, and are class I, by rule (1).

Anything connected with fighting is, as a rule, class II: most fighting implements and the fighting ground itself. Thus fighting spears (which are also used for hunting kangaroos, etc.) are class II. But multi-pronged spears, used solely for spearing fish, are (like fishing line) class I, the same class as fish. And big short spears are, like yamsticks, class IV. (Note that Dyalŋuy has a single term for 'yamstick', 'big, short spear', 'woman's fighting stick', and 'echidna spikes'.)

It should be noted that rule (1) assigns the class of an item. Rule (2), as stated here, indicates that an item should belong to a different class from that expected, but does not specify which class. In examples of the application of rule (2): if a set of nouns is not class II, then a 'harmful' subset of the set is class II; if the set is class II, then the harmful subset is class I. There are insufficient examples, however, to justify incorporating this in rule (2).

Rule (2) might be stretched to explain the inclusion of 'bees' and 'honey' in class IV; everything else animate is in classes I or II. Honey provided the only real sweetness the Dyirbalŋan knew, and was the basis of the only drink they had besides water (a weak honey solution – Roth, 1901 *b*). Honey, and bees, thus had a unique and important status for the Dyirbalŋan. Note also the special semantic status of 'honey' in the Worora language of the North Kimberleys. Here noun class I refers to 'males, articles made by or associated especially with males', and class II to 'females, articles especially connected with females, and also sweet things such as honey' [Capell and Elkin, 1937].

The class-concept associations and the two rules do provide a simple and efficient explanation for the general organisation of the nouns into classes. They do not, however, explain all particular instances. For example, crickets are class II by rule (1): in myth crickets are 'old ladies'; the scorpion *balan malayigara* may be class II because of its recognised similarity to *balan yigara* 'crayfish' (an informant explained that a scorpion is like a crayfish with a large hand attached, cf. *bala mala* 'hand' – 9.1.2); the firefly is class II by its association with fire, and the hairy mary grub by its association with the sun (the grub's sting is said to feel like sunburn); but it is not known why dog, bandicoots, platypus and echidna are class II, rather than the expected class I. Again, *balan bima* 'death adder' is probably class II, rather than class I, by its mythical connection with *balan gurbuɽu* 'seven sisters' (believed to be a 'death adder in the sky') – rule (1); but it is not known on what grounds *balan munilan, balan marigal* 'chicken snakes' and *balan yunba* 'water python' are class II when all other snakes are class I. (Note that other water snakes are class I.)

Some unexplained individual class memberships may be due to the writer's lack of familiarity with some relevant myths or beliefs. But it seems likely that some are WITHOUT EXPLANATION (as would be the case in any natural language: some may have had an explanation in terms of an earlier stage of the language, but the class assignment has been retained and the explanation lost as the language has altered). However, the class-concept associations and the two rules do explain the vast majority of noun class memberships – a great deal of which appeared at first sight to be heterogeneous and without explanation.

The class I/class II correlation with male/female is obligatory for reference to humans; it can, exceptionally, be used to refer to the sex of an animal. Each name of an animal normally has fixed class membership (class I or II, except for bees, class IV). Thus *balan guda* (class II) 'dog', *bayi yuɽi* (class I) 'kangaroo'. But in order, exceptionally, to point out that a certain dog is male *bayi guda* can be used; similarly *balan yuɽi* to indicate that a certain kangaroo is female. Thus for dogs 'male' is the marked sex and 'female' unmarked; for kangaroos 'female' is marked.

Speakers of Dyirbal can also refer to the sex of animals by using nouns that normally refer to human relations, etc. Thus a female bird will be called *yabu* 'mother' and a male *wiru* 'husband'; a female snake can be called *bulgu* 'wife' or *yabu*, and a male *wiru*; female dog, kangaroo, horse and cattle can be called *gaḍin* 'young girl' and the male of these species *yaɽa* 'man'. Note that in referring to humans *ḍugumbil* is the opposite of *yaɽa*, *bulgu* the opposite of *wiru* and *baryan* 'young boy' probably the opposite of *gaḍin*.

Speakers of Dyirbal are able to 'manipulate' noun class to draw
attention to unusual phenomena. Thus, in all normal circumstances
yaṛa 'man' can occur only with the class I marker, *bayi*. However, the
writer heard *balan yaṛa* used jokingly to refer to an aboriginal hermaphrodite, the user of the class II marker pointing out the female
characteristics of this 'man' (and compare 4.7.1).

It will be seen that the explanation of the semantic basis of noun
classes in Dyirbal is not simply taxonomic, but involves rules for
transferring class membership; and that it depends on an intimate
knowledge of the beliefs and myths of the people. Three of the classes
are positively specified, in terms of definite concepts, whereas the
fourth class is only negatively specified, as 'everything else'. (It may
be that in any system of noun classes, there will always be one 'residue'
class, similar to class IV in Dyirbal.)

A fair number of other Australian languages have noun classes, with some
semantic and syntactic similarities to the classes in Dyirbal – see Dixon [1968c]
(from which the above discussion is largely repeated). Kirton [1971: 57–8]
has investigated noun classes in Yanyula along the lines similar to those
explained above and has gained similar results.

8.4.5 Loan concepts. When the Dyirbalŋan came into contact with
European civilisation they extended the meanings of some Guwal
words to cover the new concepts that were encountered. Thus *bala
maṛalu* 'hollow log' was extended to cover 'shirt'. In most cases,
however, they took over an English word, suitably cast into the mould
of Dyirbal phonology (9.3.1): thus *balan bigi* 'pig', *bala ḍuga* 'sugar',
balam ḍubayga 'tobacco', *bayi mani* 'money'.

Now we have seen that everything must have a different name in
Dyalŋuy from that which it has in Guwal; and we have also noted that
Dyalŋuy is extremely parsimonious, keeping its vocabulary as small as
possible. Consistent with this, Dyalŋuy most often dealt with loans
by extending the range of meaning of an existing Dyalŋuy term. Thus
balan bigi 'pig' is translated into Dyalŋuy by *balan ginga*, which was
already the Dyalŋuy correspondent of Guwal *balan gumbiyan* 'echidna';
pig is assigned the same taxonomic group as echidna (probably because
its tough bristles resemble the echidna's spines). *bala ḍuga* is, by its
texture, called in Dyalŋuy *bala waruɲ*, which was already the correspondent of Guwal *bala waguy* 'sand'. However, no existing Dyalŋuy
item could be extended to cover 'money' and in this case a new word
was introduced into Dyalŋuy: *bayi walba*. (Of the hundred or so

noun loans in Guwal, all but three or four are covered by an already existing Dyalŋuy term – the exceptions are 'money', 'policeman' and 'pipe'.)

The allocation of loan words to noun classes is largely predictable from the concepts and rules given in the last section. Fruit, flour, cake (made from flour), wine (made from fruit) are in class III; white man is in class I, white woman in class II; matches and pipe (concerned with fire) in class II but cigarettes (leaves that are 'consumed') in class III; sugar is, like honey, in class IV. Most else is in class IV; an exception is *bayi mani* 'money' whose referent was unlike anything already existing in Dyirbal culture, and is (unpredictably) placed in class I.

Again, noun class helps to disambiguate multi-sensed Dyalŋuy terms that involve loan concepts. Thus *balam ḍubayga* 'tobacco' is rendered by Dyalŋuy *balam garmban. bala garmban* was already the Dyalŋuy correspondent for Guwal terms for 'haze', 'mountain mist', 'smoke' and 'steam'; however 'tobacco' is class III whereas the other concepts are grouped into class IV. Thus *ḍubayga* is assigned a Dyalŋuy correspondent on the basis of the smoke it produces, but is placed in a noun class according to the fact that it is 'consumed'.

8.5   Adjective semantics

Dyirbal Guwal is particularly rich in adjectives. Not only are there adjectives covering all the semantic areas described by adjectives in English, but Dyirbal has an adjectival opposite for many adjectives, where English would use a verb form. Thus, the opposite of *gunga* 'raw' is *ɲamu* 'cooked' (which cannot be shown to be cognate with the verb *ɲaḍul* 'cook'), and the opposite of *mugulnba* 'whole' is *yagi* 'broken, split' (which is not cognate with verbs *ɽulbal* 'split' or *gayɲḍal* 'break' etc.).

A particular feature of Guwal is the wide range of meaning of *wuygi* 'no good'; this can be seen by listing its contraries, *wuygi* can mean 'not good for its purpose' as against *ḍigil* 'good for its purpose'; or 'old (material object)' as against *guɲu* 'new'; or 'not strong or sweet (e.g. tea)' as against *guli* 'strong and/or sweet'; or 'old (person)' as against a variety of terms for 'young woman', 'middle-aged man' etc.; or 'ill' as against *bambun* 'getting better (i.e. fatter)'; etc.

There are Dyalŋuy correspondents for most of the important Guwal adjectives, with some grouping together of concepts – thus there is a single Dyalŋuy adjective corresponding to Guwal 'sour' and 'bitter', one for 'hot' and 'dry', one for 'straight' and 'good', and so on. Just as *wuygi* has a wider range of meaning than any other Guwal adjective, so its Dyalŋuy correspondent *maŋgay* has a phenomenal range – at least fifty adjectives and verbs in Guwal have *maŋgay*, *maŋgaybil* or *maŋgaymal* as their Dyalŋuy correspondents. They cover 'stale, deaf or forgetful, lazy, tired, shaky, coarse (not finely ground), cunning, cheeky, frightened, broken-hearted or offended, ashamed, stupid, grumble at, feel ill, etc. etc.'

In some cases Guwal has an 'affect' verb referring to a certain action, and an adjective for the state resulting from that action. Dyalŋuy, in keeping with its general parsimony, will have a single item. Thus (in M):

	Guwal	Dyalŋuy	
transitive verb	*ɽulbal*	*yilgilmal*	'(to) split'
adjective	*yagi*	*yilgil*	'broken, split'
transitive verb	*ɲaḍul*	*durmal*	'(to) cook'
adjective	*ɲamu*	*durmanmi*	'cooked'

In the first case Dyalŋuy has an adjective, the Guwal verb being rendered by a verbalised form of this adjective; in the second case there is a verb in Dyalŋuy, the Guwal adjective being translated by the perfective form of this verb.

There is another class of adjectives that are analogous to adverbals – they provide the same semantic qualification of nouns as certain adverbals do of verbs. Again, Dyalŋuy has a single item:

	Guwal	Dyalŋuy	
intransitive adverbal	*wundiy*	*wurgalbil*	'do slowly'
adjective	*wunay*	*wurgal*	'slow'

8.6 Semantics of time qualifiers

Dyalŋuy classes together Guwal words referring to 'a certain time away in the past' and 'the same time away in the future'. That is, it has *ganba* for both 'earlier on today' and 'later on today' and *ganbagabun* (literally 'another *ganba*') for 'yesterday (or any further time in the past)' and 'tomorrow (or any further time in the future)'. (There are also one or two other, more specific Dyalŋuy time words.)

9 Lexicon

In this chapter we survey the structure of lexical roots, in both Guwal and Dyalŋuy.

Dyalŋuy data supports the recognition of a division between grammar and lexicon: all members of open word classes – that is, all nouns, adjectives, verbs, adverbals and time qualifiers – have a different form in Dyalŋuy from that which they have in Guwal. However, all grammatical forms – words such as pronouns, noun and verb markers and particles, and all affixes – have identical form in Guwal and Dyalŋuy. Consider the following sentence in Dyalŋuy (text reference XVIII: 35):

(683) *bawalbi ɲuɽimarigu wuɲḍagun bagumaŋganangu ɲalmarugu maḍirabiɲugu*

and its translation into Guwal:

(684) *yana buɽalaygu wuɲḍagun bagumaŋganangu ɲalŋgagu ɲinaɲugu*
  go and look [to see] where all the children are camping!

These sentences involve the following correspondences of lexical roots:

Guwal	Dyalŋuy	
yanu(l)	*bawalbil*	'go' (see 9.2.1)
buɽal	*ɲuɽimal*	'see, look at'
ɲalŋga	*ɲalmaru*	'child'
ɲinay	*maḍirabil*	'sit, stay, camp'

The interrogative noun marker *wuɲḍagun*, and the quasi-pronoun *balamaŋgan* (here in *-ɲa* plus dative form) are common to (683) and (684). Note that the informant providing the translation put *buɽal* into *-ŋay* form, to correspond to a false reflexive form of *ɲuɽimal* (on this see 9.2.1).

Dyalŋuy interrogatives also support the grammar/lexicon distinction. The interrogative pronoun *waɲ(u/a)* and noun/verb marker *wuɲḍa-* have identical form in Guwal and Dyalŋuy – these roots range over

[314]

grammatical classes. However, the interrogatives which belong to lexical classes – based on *miɲa* and *wiyama* roots – have different form in Dyalŋuy.

D Guwal has *wiyamay/l* and M Guwal *wiyabay/l*; the forms are reversed in Dyalŋuy – thus D Dyalŋuy has *wiyabay/l*, and M Dyalŋuy *wiyamay/l*. Dyalŋuy *mindir* corresponds to Guwal *miɲa* 'what' in both dialects; both *miɲay* 'when' and *miɲaɲ* 'how many' are rendered by *minay* in Dyalŋuy (cf. 6.6).

There are two exceptions to the statement that particles are unchanged in Dyalŋuy. Dyalŋuy *ŋurɲḍi* corresponds to Guwal *ŋuri* in both D and M; Dyalŋuy *mumba* corresponds to Guwal *mugu* in M (4.15.3).

In M Dyalŋuy only, the form *ɲulaɲ* is brought in between a noun or verb marker and a bound form (only) – thus *yaluɲulaɲdayi, bayiɲulaɲgalu,* etc.; *ɲulaɲ* carries no meaning – the M informant said it was needed 'to complete the language'.

Interjections have the same form in Guwal and in Dyalŋuy with one exception: *maya* G, *yimba* DM 'no, no more' is in Dyalŋuy *ḍagin* G, *ḍilbu* DM (4.17).

9.1 Structure of Guwal roots

9.1.1 Verb roots. Three kinds of resemblance can be noted between verb roots:

[1] There are a limited number of pairs of verb roots with the same form – save that one ends in *-y* and the other in *-l* – and the same meaning – save that the *-y* root is intransitive and the *-l* form transitive. The interrogative and deictic pair:

intransitive	transitive
yalamay D, *yalabay* M	*yalamal* D, *yalabal* M 'do like this'
wiyamay D, *wiyabay* M	*wiyamal* D, *wiyabal* M 'do what/do how'

have already been discussed (3.4.4). Other pairs include:

intransitive	transitive
ŋabay 'bathe'	*ŋabal* 'immerse in water'
gibay 'scratch oneself'	*gibal* 'scratch, scrape'
ginday 'look with a light'	*gindal* 'look with a light'

Intransitive *ginday* refers to someone using a light to find their way after dark; transitive *gindal* implies the use of a light to assist in hunting some animal, etc. Note that the reflexive form of *gibal* is used – for instance, to describe a man shaving himself.

In some Western Australian languages there are a considerable number of transitive/intransitive cognate pairs – considerably more than there appear to be in Dyirbal.

[2] There are a number of verb roots which appear to involve a disyllabic prefix to a popular disyllabic root:

bandubanal 'bend over'	*banal* 'break off'
galbabagal 'wash clothes'	*bagal* 'pierce with pointed implement'
garugaḍal 'go past'	*gaḍal* 'go past without seeing'
dabaḍanay 'duck down'	*ḍanay* 'stand'

The first three pairs are transitive and the last one intransitive. Note that there appears to be some semantic similarity between longer and shorter forms in each line. However, there are NO forms *bandu, galba, garu,* or *daba.*

There is also:

munumadal DM, *muyumadal* G   *madal* 'throw'
'chuck in (a task), give it up'

In this case the first element is an established noun: *bala munu* DM, *bala muyu* G 'bottom, arse'.

[3] There is another set of verb roots the FIRST part of which is identical with a common disyllabic root:

bundalay 'fight'	*bunday* 'break'
waymbaray 'go round something'	*waymbay* 'go walkabout'
mayilŋgay 'come out forcibly'	*mayil* 'come out'
baḍigay 'duck away'	*baḍiy* 'fall down'

All these roots are intransitive. *mayilŋgay* implies an exit through an obstruction – thus *mayil* would be used for going out through the door of a house, but *mayilŋgay* for breaking a hole in the back to get out (if, say, the front were on fire); *mayilŋgay* would be used for emerging from thick undergrowth into open forest, but *mayil* for coming out of the forest into a plain. *baḍigay* can refer to someone ducking down so that they are not seen, say, or to a fire going out.

Again, there is some similarity between longer and shorter forms in each line. It is possible (although there is no real evidence for this) that *mayilŋgay* is etymologically related to *mayil* through the aspectual affix *-galiy* 'quickly', and that *waymbaray* is historically derived from *waymbay* through *-yaray* 'start to do/do a bit more'.

The M informant recognised a number of other forms similar to *mayilŋgay* (which he glossed 'come out quickly'): *wayṇḍilŋgay* 'go uphill quickly' related to *wayṇḍil* 'go uphill'; *mabilŋgay* 'cross the river quickly' related to *mabil* 'cross the river'. These glosses support the derivation of *-ŋgay* forms from the affix *-galiy*. The process is not productive – thus there is no *buŋalŋgay* corresponding to *buŋal* 'go downhill'. (The D informant judged *wayṇḍilŋgay* and *mabilŋgay* to be ungrammatical in D.)

There are also intransitive roots *balbaliy, barmiliy* that can be regarded as 'fossilised reflexive' forms of *balbal* 'roll over' and *barmil* 'look back' (7.7). Note that *barmil/barmiliy* is a pair of type $S \equiv A$, whereas *balbal/balbalay*, which belongs to verb type 'position' (8.2.3), is of type $S \equiv O$ (although reflexive as a productive process in Guwal always produces pairs of type $S \equiv A$ – 8.2.2).

There are a number of verb roots that have the form of verbalised adjectives – *guwurmbal, gindimbal*, etc.; however, there are no adjective roots *guwur, gindi* etc. (see 7.5.1).

Some Australian languages have considerable numbers of compound verbs, generated by productive sets of prefixes, etc. – see 1.7.

9.1.2 Noun roots. Three kinds of 'structure' can be recognised for noun roots:

[1] There are a few compounds, made up of two simple roots:

balan malayigara 'scorpion'	*balan yigara* 'crayfish'
	bala mala 'hand'
bala ḍinaguda 'a softwood tree'	*balan guda* 'dog'
	bala ḍina 'foot'

Informants explained that a scorpion looks like a crayfish with a big hand, and that the *ḍinaguda* tree has a leaf that looks like the foot of a dog.

[2] There are a fair number of nouns the first part of which is identical with a disyllabic root:

bayi gubimbulu 'very clever man'	*bayi gubi* 'clever man' (see 2.4)
bala garimal 'summer-time'	*balan gari* 'sun'

bayi/balan ḍulbuṟuy 'married person'	*bayi/balan ḍulbun* 'recently married person'
balan guwugiṇḍu 'ibis'	*bala guwu* 'nose'
bala maṟalu 'hollow log' D	*bala maṟa* 'snake or rat hole'
bala yugari 'hollow log' G	[cf. *bala yugu* 'tree, wood']
bala ḍinari 'root under water'	*bala ḍina* 'foot'

The second parts of these roots cannot be positively identified with anything else in the language. Thus, there are no forms *-bulu, -ṟuy* or *-giṇḍu*; it is possible that the *-mal* in *garimal* is related to the transitive verbalising affix (and see the discussion of *gaygamali* in 9.3.3). We suggested in 7.7 that the *-lu* in *maṟalu* may be historically related to the affix *-ru* 'along, through'. It may be that the *-ri* in *yugari* and in *ḍinari* goes back to a productive affix from some earlier stage of the language (that may also have combined with roots *bala, yala* to give the allative of direction forms *bali* (~ *balari*), *yali* (~ *yalari*) – 6.5.1).

Tribal names are of a similar construction:

tribal name	language name
ḍirbalŋan	*ḍirbal*
giramaygan	*giramay*
ŋaḍanḍi	*ŋaḍan*

Further examples are in 2.2, 2.3; *-ŋan, -gan* (which appears unrelated to the feminine ending discussed below) and *-ḍi* do not recur in other types of compound in the language.

A number of kinship terms occur in two forms – a short form, and a longer form obtained by adding *-ndi* or *-(ɲ)ḍa* to the short form. *-ndi* is added in the case of 'mother' and 'father' and *-(ɲ)ḍa* in the case of terms for grandparents, parents' siblings, and parents-in-law (*-ɲḍa* is added after a vowel, and *-ḍa* after *-n*). Thus:

ŋuma	*ŋumandi*	'father'
ŋagi	*ŋagiɲḍa*	'mother's father'
waymin	*wayminḍa*	'mother-in-law'

The difference between the two sets of terms is obscure.

[3] Some nouns involve the affix *-bara* 'someone who is concerned with...' (6.1.1). Thus there are institutionalised names for two spirits:
bayi yugubara 'a bad spirit' (literally 'man of the woods'; from *bala yugu* 'tree')
bayi gububara 'a friendly spirit, about a foot high; he is put in a dilly

bag by a traveller and whispers or whistles to him, warning of any unseen danger ahead' (literally 'man of the leaves', from *bala gubu* 'leaf')

The names for the five hordes of the Mamu tribe, and the name for the tribe speaking Gulŋay, involve *-bara* – see 2.2.

A few nouns appear to involve the feminine affix *-gan* (1.6). These comprise the section names (2.4) and:

balan yalŋgayngan 'single woman (when beyond usual marrying age)';
cf. *bayi yalŋgay* 'single man (when beyond usual marrying age)'

balan ḍulbungan 'a woman who follows her promised man – the man and woman have been promised to each other in marriage, but the man is too shy or frightened to claim his bride, and she is forced to go to him'; cf. *bayi/balan ḍulbun* 'recently married person'

See also *bayi mugu* 'mother's elder brother'; and *balan mugunan* 'mother's elder sister'.

A considerable number of nouns appear to be in reduplicated form; however, the unreduplicated roots do not exist in the present-day language – examples were mentioned in 7.3, 7.5.1 (see also 9.4).

ŋambiya, DG 'what's it called' (there is no corresponding form in M) may be historically related to *ŋambal* 'hear'.

9.1.3 Adjective roots. A few adjective roots appear to be cognate with verbal forms:

adjective root	verb root
wugiḍa 'generous'	*wugal* 'give'
gunda 'inside'	*gundal* 'put inside'
garḍa 'alright'	*garḍul* 'do properly'
maɲḍay 'hunger satisfied'	*maɲḍay* 'eat vegetables when hungry'
miyay 'smile'	*miyanday* 'laugh'

The first three verbs are transitive and the last two intransitive. The adjective *maɲḍay* is identical with the participial form of the verb (4.6); however, it is nowadays felt to be a full adjective root, with a meaning rather different from that which the participle would have – *maɲḍaybil* 'to be satisfied' is a common verbalisation. There is no intransitive verb 'go in' and verbalisation *gundabil* is very common, as the opposite of *mayil* 'come out'. (See 10.3.4 for a discussion of the prehistory of verb root *wugal*.)

There is also an adjective *wudubalu* 'going straight on, blindly, without looking back', which can plausibly be derived from *bala wudu*, G, 'nose' and *balu* 'to a place in that direction' (literally 'nose going to a place in that direction'); *wudubalu* occurs in G, D and M although the word for 'nose' in D and M is *bala guwu*.

The number adjective 'three' in M is *waraɲuŋgul* (6.1.7) – this could be analysed as the particle *wara* 'the wrong thing, a strange thing' (4.15.3) plus *yuŋgul* 'one', with an *n* inserted and the impossible sequence *-ny-* replaced by *ɲ* – 7.5. (By this analysis *waraɲuŋgul* would be, literally, 'strange one'.)

From *yalamay* 'do it like this' are derived adjective *yalamay* 'like this' (e.g. *ŋaḍa yalamay bayi*, 'he's the same sort of man as me') and *yalamaynbara* 'thing or state which is like this one', which can function as noun or adjective – 6.1.1. There is also *yalamayṇḍa(y)* 'at the same time' – 6.4.

There were very few non-simple roots in the two to three thousand word vocabulary of Guwal that the writer collected during his first field trip. Further work since then has revealed an increasing number of compound words; it is likely that a full investigation of the ten thousand or so words that are likely to comprise the everyday working vocabulary of Dyirbal would uncover a considerable range of complex roots.

9.2 Structure of Dyalŋuy roots

Dyalŋuy vocabulary has plainly been assembled from a number of different directions. Although there is no lexical item common to the Guwal and Dyalŋuy of a particular tribe, what is a Guwal form for one tribe may turn up in the Dyalŋuy of a neighbouring people. Thus the Dyalŋuy time qualifier *ganba* 'earlier or later on today' (8.6) occurs in Wagaman with the meaning 'long time'. The M and D dialects have a number of 'double cross correspondences' – thus *bayi baḍiri* is the name for 'water guana' in M Guwal and D Dyalŋuy, while *bayi ḍiḍan* is the name in D Guwal and M Dyalŋuy. Interrogative and deictic verbs *wiyam/ba-* and *yalam/ba-* behave in the same way – the *-b-* forms occur in M Guwal and D Dyalŋuy, with the *-m-* forms being used in D Guwal and M Dyalŋuy (3.4.4).

Some Dyalŋuy forms look as if they are in some way 'derived' from the corresponding Guwal words – thus Guwal *guyŋgan*, Dyalŋuy *muguyŋgun* 'spirit of a dead woman'; Guwal *muray*, D Dyalŋuy

gumuray, M Dyalṇuy *ḏilmuray* 'head hair'; Guwal *buyal*, D Dyalṇuy
wuṇḏurmbuyal, M Dyalṇuy *buḏubuyal* 'blow, puff'. However, it may
be that in each case the two terms have evolved, by quite different
routes, from a single form in some ancestor language.

In other cases a Dyalṇuy form looks suspiciously like a 'deformation'
of the Guwal word – compare Guwal *banagay* with Dyalṇuy *walagay*
'return' – there appears to be substitution of the apical liquid *l* for the
apical nasal *n*, and of the bilabiovelar semivowel *w* for the bilabial
stop *b* (there is, of course no bilabial liquid). Another example is Guwal
ṇamiṟ, Dyalṇuy *gabiṟ* 'hungry', where nasals in the Guwal form are
replaced by corresponding stops in Dyalṇuy.

There are a number of other examples of similar forms, including Guwal
ḏilŋgal, Dyalṇuy *ḏilŋguwal* 'throw or pour water', and Guwal *ḏaywal*, Dyalṇuy
ḏaywil 'catch fish by dragging a net-like roll of grass through the water'. It
must be noted, though, that the vast majority of Dyalṇuy forms are lacking
any similarity with the corresponding Guwal words.

9.2.1 Verb roots. Dyalṇuy has a pair of verb roots corresponding to
each Guwal pair (where the forms differ only in the final consonant,
and the meanings only as regards transitivity). Thus:

Guwal	Dyalnuy	
ʃ*ŋabay*	*darubay*	'bathe'
ˋ*ŋabal*	*darubal*	'immerse in water'
ʃ*gibay*	*wirŋgay*	'scratch' (intransitive)
ˋ*gibal*	*wirŋgal*	'scratch' (transitive)

There is, in addition, at least one pair in Dyalṇuy that does not correspond to a 'cognate pair' in Guwal:

Guwal	D Dyalṇuy	
baḏiy	*dagaray*	'fall down' (intransitive)
gayṇḏal	*dagaray*	'break' (intransitive)
guṇḏil	*dagaral*	'take skin off, take clothes off' (transitive)

All three Guwal verbs belong to the semantic type 'breaking off'
(8.2.3), and it is thus quite natural for them to be dealt with in this way
in Dyalṇuy. Note that although M Dyalṇuy has *dagaray* corresponding
to *baḏiy* and *gayṇḏal*, it has *ḏuyal* as translation equivalent of *guṇḏil*.

There are a fair number of instances of Dyalṇuy having a single
verb where Guwal has a (non-cognate) transitive/intransitive pair with
the same semantic content (see 8.2.2).

Guwal verbs which appear to involve either a prefix or a suffix to a common root ([2] and [3] of 9.1.1) sometimes have the same Dyalŋuy correspondent as the common root. Thus:

Guwal	Dyalŋuy	
bundil	*yilwul*	'take out' (transitive)
mayil ⎫ *mayilŋgay* ⎭	*yilwuyiriy*	'come out' 'come out forcibly' ⎫ (intransitive) ⎭

However, the structure of a compound verb in Guwal is carried over into Dyalŋuy in at least one instance:

Guwal	Dyalŋuy
munumadal 'chuck it in'	*gumbunayŋul*
madal 'throw'	*nayŋul*
bala munu 'arse'	*bala gumbu*

In addition to the complex apparatus of bound forms referring to up hill, up river, down hill, down river and across river, Guwal has a set of verbs specifying the same parameters. In keeping with its general policy of parsimony, Dyalŋuy eliminates this redundancy by employing verbalised bound markers as institutionalised verbs of motion (cf. the table of bound forms in 3.2.3)

Guwal	Dyalŋuy	
yanu	*bawalbil*	'go'
wayɲḍil	*dayubil*	'motion uphill'
buŋal	*bayḍubil*	'motion downhill'
wandil	*dawulubil*	'motion upriver'
daday	*balbulubil*	'motion downriver'
mabil	*guyabil*	'motion across river'

These bound forms CAN occur verbalised without a verb marker in Guwal; however, a verb marker is included in the vast majority of cases in Guwal – see 6.5.7.

Note that the bound forms also involve specification of 'long', 'medium' or 'short' distance; the verbs lack this additional information. The 'long distance' form is used in the Dyalŋuy verb, indicating that 'long distance' is the unmarked choice in the 'distance system'. In the case of the 'hill' verbs informants sometimes gave *dayibil* and *bayḍibil*, involving the 'short distance' form; 'short distance' is unmarked relative to 'medium distance' – the latter type of bound form can never make up a Dyalŋuy verb.

There are also some transitive Guwal verbs of motion that involve
a bound form in Dyalŋuy:

Guwal	Dyalŋuy	
⎰ *yanu*	*bawalbil*	'go' (intransitive)
⎱ *mundal*	*bawalmban*	'lead' (transitive)
⎰ *daday*	*balbulubil*	'motion down river' (intransitive)
⎱ *dangal*	*balbulumbal*	'[river or flood] washes [something] away' (transitive)

The Guwal verb *baniy* 'come' is rendered in Dyalŋuy by *yalibil* –
that is, the verbalised form of the allative-of-place verb marker 'to
here'.

We stated in 4.7.2. that all allative and locative nominals and verb markers
can be verbalised. However, the writer once used *yalibil* within a Guwal
sentence, and was told that it was not acceptable, since it was a Dyalŋuy verb.
It appears that forms, generated by the grammatical rules, which have an
institutionalised status in Dyalŋuy may not be used in Guwal.

There are a few isolated instances of Dyalŋuy dealing with a Guwal
verb metaphorically. Thus M Dyalŋuy has *digir ḍulbambal* for Guwal
ŋambal 'hear, listen to'; *ḍulbambal* is 'put down' (Guwal *yubal*) and
bala digir is 'the side of the head between eye and ear – believed to be
the location of the "brain"' (Guwal *bala yagin*). *digir ḍulbambal* is thus
literally 'the brain is put down'. (Note that D Dyalŋuy does have
ŋarmil, as direct correspondent of *ŋambal*.)

A fair number of Guwal verbs are dealt with through adjectives in
Dyalŋuy – thus a number of verbs dealing with grumbling and illness
are verbalised forms of *maŋgay* 'no good, etc.' – 8.5.

A considerable proportion of Dyalŋuy verbs appear to have the form
of verbalised adjectives – that is, they end in *-bil* or *-mal~ -mbal~ -bal*
(the proportion is much higher than in Guwal). For instance *wuyubal*
'tell', *baŋarmbal* 'ask', *ḍubumbal* 'hit with a rounded object', *ɲuɽimal*
'see, look at', *maḍirabil* 'stay, sit'. In every case the forms are in fact
non-analysable – that is, there are no adjectives *wuyu, baŋar, maḍira*,
etc., nor verbs *wuyubil, baŋarbil, maḍirambal*, etc.

However, it is extremely likely that these forms are diachronically derived
from non-verbal roots by a verbalisation process. A residual indication of this
may be the 'preference' of such forms for false reflexive rather than *-ŋay*
constructions – see (683–4) above and the comments on reflexive alternant
-mariy in 4.9.3. Note that forms like *wuyubal, maḍirabil* etc. have all the
characteristics of loan words (9.3).

9.2.2   Noun roots. Compound roots in Guwal are frequently rendered by a simple form in Dyalŋuy:

Guwal	Dyalŋuy	
balan malayigara	*balan wurmbu*	'scorpion'
balan yigara	*balan wurmbu*	'crayfish'
bala ḍinaguda	*bala ɲimbaɽ*, M	'softwood tree'
balan guda	*balan ɲimbaɽ*, M	'dog'

The Dyalŋuy term is the correspondent of the second (head) element in the Guwal compound, in each case.

Dyalŋuy correspondents of Guwal nouns can have a variety of forms:

[1] We can have a simple Dyalŋuy noun, either in its 'central' meaning, or in a metaphorical extension (8.4.3).

[2] There are a number of nouns plus affix *-bara* – thus *balan ḍinbaybara* 'something concerned with the ground' is the Dyalŋuy name for five types of bird, all of whom lay their eggs on or near the ground; *bayi buɽulabara* 'something concerned with the fighting ground' is the name for three species of willy wagtail.

Other nominal affixes are sometimes involved in Dyalŋuy correspondents for simple roots from Guwal. Thus *bayi yalŋgay* 'single man (beyond usual marrying age)' is in Dyalŋuy *bayi muɲḍuɲaŋgay*, literally 'without woman'; similarly *balan yalŋgayngan* 'single woman (beyond usual marrying age)' is *balan bayabayɲaŋgay* 'without man'.

[3] Some Dyalŋuy nouns take the form of participles – thus *guyḍulmuɲa* 'he who bites a lot' for snakes, ants, mosquitos, march fly, shark; *ɲanbalmuɲa* 'he who pierces a lot' for borer, wasp, hawks, stone fish; *gilgarimuɲa* 'he who jumps a lot' for grasshoppers; *yirguɲḍimuɲa* 'he who laughs a lot' for laughing jackass; *maybarimuɲa* 'he who calls out a lot' for crickets; *bayŋguraybarimuɲa* 'he who sings a lot' for locusts, a beetle and a bird; *wirŋgarimuɲa* 'he who scratches a lot' for scrub-itch (a parasite similar to scabies); *yulɲimuɲa* 'he who dances a lot' for a bird; *bala nayɲuriyaray* 'that which has started to be thrown out' for *bala yabala* 'the flat [ground]'.

[4] A few Guwal nouns are rendered by Dyalŋuy adjectives (with appropriate noun classification) – for instance: *bala ɲingal* 'short' for *bala buɽumba* 'stump'; *bala ɲilu* 'cold' for *bala birgil* 'wintertime', *bayi ɲilu* for *bayi gubaguba* 'a type of pearl shell', *bayi/balan ɲilu*, M for *bayi/balan bilmbu* 'widower/widow'.

[5] Some common nouns in Dyalŋuy are descriptive in a way that

only place names can be in Guwal (cf. text xxv, line 29, p. 390): *bayi mayaḍayulmiyulmi* (literally 'grubeater') corresponding to *bayi yugaba* 'small brown rat'. And in the case of *balan yibaymalŋimalŋi* ('fire-bringer') corresponding to *balan baḍinḍila* 'satin bird', the mythological role of this bird in snatching the first fire away from the rainbow snake is described. Note that in both these 'fossilised clause' names the verb is reduplicated and the final consonant omitted from the root (as in positive imperatives): this almost certainly has no grammatical significance.

9.2.3 Adjective roots. Guwal adjectives are generally rendered by adjectives in Dyalŋuy. There are a very small number of compounds – for instance *yibayŋaŋgay* (literally 'without fire') was given as correspondent of Guwal adjective *muḍan*, '[fire] extinguished'.

Two position adjectives have M Dyalŋuy correspondents that are identical in form but for the final segment:

Guwal	M Dyalŋuy	
bilŋgi	*ŋalŋunday*	'on lap, across legs'
baɽay	*ŋalŋunda*	'[held] between legs'

Dyalŋuy has fewer number adjectives than Guwal, grouping together 'three', 'a good few' and 'a lot':

	Guwal	Dyalŋuy
'one'	*yuŋgul*	*ɲungul*
'two'	*bulay(i)*	*ginaynḍaran*
'three'	*gaɽbu* D, *waraɲuŋgul* M	
'a good few'	*mundi* D, *gaɽbu* M	*guwara* D, *waraɲ* M
'many'	*muɲa* D, *ḍulun* M	

The Dyalŋuy adjective 'two' is particularly interesting from a grammatical point of view; *-ginay* 'full of' and dual *-ḍaran* are normally nominal affixes (6.1.1). (The insertion of *n* here is predictable – 7.5.1.) Note that Waruŋu, the language to the west of Dyirbal, has *ɲungul* 'one' in its Guwal.

9.3 Loan words

9.3.1 Phonology of loans in Guwal. As mentioned in 8.4.4 many English words have been borrowed into Guwal, suitably cast into a phonological structure appropriate to a Dyirbal word. Loan words

differ phonologically in a single particular from indigenous words –
loans may begin with *l*, other words may not: *laymun* 'lemon', *lada*
'ladder', *landan* 'London', etc.

Consonants in initial, final and non-corresponding medial clusters
in English will be separated by vowels: *bala bilayŋgir* 'blanket', *bala
ḍaruḍa* 'trousers', *balam ḍugagayin* 'sugar cane', *bala gurugu* 'grog',
bala babuligan 'pub (publican)'. A consonant – usually *ŋ* – will be added
before an initial English vowel: *bala ŋayan* 'iron', *balam ŋariṇḍi*
'orange', *bala ŋaŋgiḍa* or *bala gaŋgiḍa* 'handkerchief'.

A vowel will be added after a final stop. The rule for choosing this
vowel appears to be:

(a) If the final syllable includes a postvocal glide *y*, then the word-
final vowel will be *i*;

(b) Otherwise the vowel in the final syllable is repeated word-finally.

Thus *balan miḍiḍi* 'white woman (missus)', *balan gawa* 'cow', *bala
buwu* 'fork', *balam gaygi* 'cake', *bala ṟaygi* 'rag'; and *bala gurugu,
balam ŋariṇḍi*.

Generally, Dyirbal *b* corresponds to English, *b, p, v, f*; Dyirbal *ḍ* to
English *s, ᴢ, ʃ, ᴣ*; Dyirbal *g* to English *g, k*; Dyirbal *d* to English *d* and
(in initial position) *t*; Dyirbal *r* to English *t* (when non-initial), and
some instances of *r* (when non-initial); Dyirbal *ṟ* to all initial and some
non-initial instances of English *r*; etc. Examples, besides those given
above, are *dina* 'dinner time', *bala diyi* 'tea', *balam burira* 'potato',
balam binara 'peanut', *bala ḍalgi* 'dray, sulky', *bala ḍuwa* 'shop, store',
girḍibi 'Christmas (time)'. Note also the adjective *maḍirim* 'mustering',
where final -*m* corresponds to -*ŋ* in English (Dyirbal stems cannot end
in -*ŋ*).

9.3.2 Syntax of Guwal loans. Loans are taken into Guwal as nouns,
adjectives or time qualifiers, never as verbs. Thus there is an adjective
waga M, *wagi* DG 'work[ing]' that typically occurs with the intransitive
verbaliser – *wagabil, wagibil* '(to) work'. The adjective *maḍirim*
'mustering' commonly occurs with the transitive verbaliser – *maḍirimbal*
'(to) muster'. There are, however, relatively few loans from English
verbs; most often the range of meaning of an established Guwal verb
is extended to cover a new type of action.

In not accepting loan words as verbs Dyirbal is typical of Australian languages;
see, for instance, R. Hershberger [1964*b*] on Gugu-Yalanji.

9.3.3 Dyalŋuy correspondents of Guwal loans. We mentioned in 8.4.4 that in most cases an already established Dyalŋuy word is used to render a loan item in Guwal. There are a few instances of compound Dyalŋuy correspondents – thus Guwal *bala ŋaŋgiḍa* or *bala gaŋgiḍa* 'handkerchief' becomes in Dyalŋuy *bala ḍurmbaybarimuŋa*, literally 'that which rubs [itself] a lot' (*ḍurmbaybal* is the Dyalŋuy correspondent of Guwal verb *ḍural* 'rub').

Examination of Dyalŋuy correspondences continually throws new light on problems in the analysis of Dyirbal. The word for flour (being introduced into the language with the advent of flour, in the late nineteenth century) is *balan gaygamali*. Now *bala gayga* is 'eye', and *gaygamali* could be a purposive form of transitively-verbalised *gayga*: literally 'in order to make an eye'. However, this seemed semantically implausible and informants were unable to shed any light on the matter; the writer at first assumed that the similarity was merely coincidental. But then the following Guwal-Dyalŋuy correspondences were uncovered:

Guwal	Dyalŋuy
bala gayga 'eye'	*bala diŋal*
balam gaygamali 'flour'	*balam diŋalmali*
balam damba 'damper'	*balam diŋal*
balam gaygi 'cake'	*balam diŋal*

Damper may possibly have been termed *diŋal* in Dyalŋuy since at a certain stage of its preparation it must look something like an eye: a hole is made in the middle of a mound of flour, and water poured in; it is then kneaded for some time from the centre. In any case the name for flour in terms of an analysis into *diŋal* plus -*mali* (=*gayga* plus -*mali*) now seems entirely reasonable. The identification of 'damper' with 'eye' could not otherwise have been guessed at (damper was very common in the early days of settlement but is hardly known nowadays, although of course flour is much used for other purposes) but is quite explicit in Dyalŋuy.

This analysis is supported by an analogous example from the present day. In the last few years the Dyirbalŋan have been able to buy dried apricots from the local store: the children refer to these as *maŋa* 'ear'.

Note also the Guwal noun *bala ḍinaman* 'boot, shoe' – cf. *bala ḍina* 'foot'.

9.4   Onomatopoeia

Speakers of Dyirbal are excellent mimics – by comparing their imitations of the calls of various birds etc. with the names of the birds, it was possible to establish that just over half the Guwal names for species of bird, locust and cricket are onomatopoeic.

A sample of sixty-two birds etc. yielded twenty-eight names that are completely onomatopoeic – that is, the full phonological form of the name occurred in the imitation. These included:

balan ḍiḍuluruy 'forest kingfisher'	*balan guṛur* 'brolga'
bayi ḍigirḍigir 'a willy wagtail'	*bayi dagu* 'hammer bird'

In some cases the name formed only a part of the imitation; thus the call of *balan baḍinḍila* D, *balan baḍinḍiladila* M 'satin bird' was given as [*báḍinḍiladíladíladíla*].

Four names involved partial onomatopoeia – that is, part of the name was recognised in the call:

name	call
balan ḍiwuɲu 'pink-chested kingfisher'	*ḍíwu-ḍíwu-ḍíwu*
balan bubunba 'pheasant'	*bú-bú-bú-bú*
balan guŋgaga 'kookaburra'	*gúgu-gúgu-gúgu*
bayi waḍa 'crow'	*wá-wá-wá*

The name for crow is *waga* or *waŋga* or something similar in many Australian languages; kookaburra is called by a variety of names, almost all of which begin with *gu-*.

Four of the birds etc. in the sample were said to have no call; two only whistle. Nine make a rasping gutteral sound that would not readily yield a form within the terms of Dyirbal phonology. The remaining fifteen have a call on which a name could be based, but in fact have a non-onomatopoeic name; for instance:

name	call
balan windan 'a yellow mountain bird'	*ḍáruḍánḍán*
bayi guṛuŋgul 'meat hawk'	*gí-gí-gí-gí*
bayi gayambula 'white cockatoo'	*gúruŋgára-gúruŋgára*

Thus, of sixty-two birds, locusts and crickets, forty-seven could be onomatopoeically named; thirty-two are.

Ten of the sixty-two names appear to be in reduplicated form; six of the ten refer to birds that are onomatopoeically named, two to birds that have a suitable call but are not onomatopoeically named, one to a bird with a gutteral cry on which a name could not easily be based, and one to a bird with no call at all. It will be seen that there is no particular correlation between reduplication and onomatopoeia.

No attempt has been made to give an accurate transcription of the imitations provided – these involve special voice qualities, lip positions, tonal fluctuations and other para-linguistic characteristics. Each call did appear to be clearly based on a form that obeyed the normal rules of Dyirbal phonology, and it is this form that is transcribed here. A call can be verbalised by adding -*bay*, thus the call of *balan ḍiwuɲu* 'kingfisher' was said as *ḍiwu*, pronounced as one lengthened syllable [*ḍiu*] with shrill, breathy voice; the intransitive verb *ḍiwunbay* '(to) call *ḍiwu*' shows no paralinguistic abnormalities and is pronounced like any normal verb.

One informant gave the call of the brown pigeon as *guguwuḍ* – a Dyirbal root cannot end in a stop, and the name of this bird is in fact *balan guguwuɲ* (another informant actually gave the call as *guguwuɲ*).

In some cases the M and D dialects have different names for the same bird; only one of these is onomatopoeic. Thus the M informant gave the call of the brown pigeon as *guguwuɲ*, although its name is *balan ḍuḍulu* in M. In other cases the two dialects have variants of the same, onomatopoeic name; for instance, a blue scrub pigeon is called *balan wangawa* in D but *balan wagawa* in M – the D informant imitated the call by [*wángawá*] and the M informant by [*wágawá*], the two imitations being identical in all paralinguistic aspects.

There is an account of onomatopoeia in some Kimberley languages in Worms [1938]; however, this should, like all Worms' work, be treated with caution.

Only one of the Dyalŋuy names for the sixty-two birds etc. could possibly be onomatopoeic. A black bird, *balan ḍawuḍala* in Guwal, *balan buḍaḍa* in M Dyalŋuy, has a long and complex call, said by an informant to be *ḍawuḍala wuɽaybuḍala ŋaygu waɲḍu yaŋum guguɽ buɲḍan ḍawuḍala wuɽaybuḍala.*

ŋaygu waɲḍu yaŋum guguɽ buɲḍan is 'who's been pulling up my young loya cane from here'; *wuɽaybuḍala* has no known meaning.

IO *Prehistory*

This chapter attempts to do two things. Firstly, to examine lexical and grammatical relationships between the dialects of Dyirbal and surrounding dialects in an attempt to assess the genetic relationships of the dialects and to reconstruct past tribal movement. Secondly, to assess ways in which individual dialects of Dyirbal differ from the general pattern of the language, with a view to internal reconstruction of some aspects of past stages of Dyirbal.

As mentioned in 1.1, it seems likely that most Australian languages (certainly, all those outside Arnhem Land and the Barkly Tableland) are genetically related; we can call this a 'weak genetic relation'. In this chapter we are interested in whether a pair of languages are 'strongly genetically related' – that is, whether they can be related to a common ancestor that is considerably less ancient than proto-Australian. If two languages belong to the same 'branch' or 'subgroup' of a family then they are said to be 'strongly related'; if they are members of different branches then they are 'weakly related'. Consider an Indo-European analogy: Welsh is strongly related to Breton and Cornish, and (slightly less strongly) to Irish, within the Celtic branch of Indo-European; it is only weakly related to languages such as Lithuanian, English and Greek.

In the discussion below we will use 'genetic relationship' to mean 'strong genetic relationship'. Thus we conclude that Dyirbal and Yidin, the language next to the north, are probably not genetically related; that is, to connect them on the 'family tree' of Australian languages one would probably have to pass through proto-Australian, at the apex. On the other hand, Dyirbal may well be genetically related to Wargamay, its southerly neighbour – that is, the common ancestor of these two languages may be a latter-day descendant of proto-Australian. It must always be borne in mind that over and above the (strong) genetic relationships that are discussed below, all Australian languages will probably in time be shown to be weakly genetically related.

10.1 Lexical diffusion in Australia

Recent archaeological work suggests that aborigines have been in Australia for something of the order of 25,000 to 30,000 years. The people are essentially nomadic, and it is likely that there has been considerable movement of tribes during this period. A tribe may have split into two and the parts moved in different directions; one of them might have merged with a further tribe (when numbers were reduced due to famine, say), and this new tribe could have then split, and so on (see Birdsell, 1958, and 10.2.2 below). This pattern of split, movement and merger has almost certainly been responsible for a great deal of lexical and grammatical diffusion throughout the continent.

A rather striking feature of Australian languages is their apparently high rate of vocabulary replacement. An account of the vocabulary of the tribe at the junction of the Murray and Darling Rivers, ninety years ago, mentioned 'when anyone dies, named after anything, the name of that thing is at once changed. For instance, the name for water was changed nine times in about five years on account of the death of eight men who bore the name of water. The reason is, the name of the departed is never mentioned from a superstitious notion that the spirit of the departed could immediately appear if mentioned in any way' [Taplin, 1879, p. 23]. For something to be changed nine times in five years is quite unusual, but there undoubtedly always has been considerable vocabulary replacement, due to this taboo on any common noun similar to a dead person's name, throughout Australia. The new noun, to replace the proscribed one, is likely to be borrowed from the dialect of a neighbouring tribe. (Some tribes, such as the Walbiri in Central Australia and the Tiwi on Bathurst and Melville Islands, have several alternative names for some common objects; one name will be the most frequently used, but if this should be proscribed then one of the other 'reserve' terms will at once replace it; however, this type of synonymy is quite absent from other regions – from the Cape York peninsula, for example.) Thus, if a tribe splits into two and the newly-formed tribes move so that they are separated by four or five other tribes, their vocabularies will quickly diverge; as words become taboo in each of the sister dialects they will be replaced with items from neighbouring dialects.

If the two dialects have been contiguous for a long enough time, they will have about 50% vocabulary in common. That is, if two dialects move into contiguity and, at the beginning have no (or very little) vocabulary in common, then – through borrowing from each other to replace proscribed items – the percentage of common vocabulary will build up until it levels off at about 50%. On the other hand, if a tribe splits into two and the two new tribes remain in contiguity, then they will at first have almost identical vocabularies; as different words become taboo at different times in the two sister dialects, and are replaced from neighbouring dialects, the percentage of common vocabulary will gradually decrease until it levels off at about 50%.

The way in which vocabulary is lost and gained can be illustrated from a hypothetical (and somewhat oversimplified) example. Suppose that in a narrow coastal strip, bounded by the sea to one side and a mountain range to the other, there are five dialects: from north to south, A, B, C, D and E. Suppose that each dialect has 50% vocabulary in common with the dialect to its north, and also with the dialect to its south; except that C has only 20% vocabulary in common with B. Suppose that in T years each dialect replaces 1% of its total vocabulary, by borrowing from its neighbours; suppose also that each dialect borrows equally (or almost equally) frequently from north and south. Now of the 1% lost by C one-fifth will be vocabulary that was in common with B; similarly for the 1% lost by B. But of the 1% gained by C, about half is likely to be borrowed from B; and, similarly, for the 1% gained by B. Thus, after T years the vocabulary in common to B and C will be $20 - 0.2 - 0.2 + 0.5 + 0.5 = 20.6\%$. But for C and D half the proscribed vocabulary will be material that was common to C and D; and half the gain will be new common vocabulary; after T years C and D's common material will be $50 - 0.5 - 0.5 + 0.5 + 0.5 = 50\%$. The percentage of vocabulary shared by B and C has increased, and will continue to increase until it reaches about 50%; the percentage shared by C and D, being already at the stable 50% level, does not alter.

Consider now the other case: suppose that each dialect shares 50% with its neighbours save for B and C, which this time share 70%. After T years B and C will now share $70 - 0.7 - 0.7 + 0.5 + 0.5 = 69.6\%$; and the vocabulary shared by these two dialects will continue to drop until it is about fifty percent.

We have thus suggested that the equilibrium figure for vocabulary shared by neighbouring dialects is 50%, and that after any two tribes have been in contiguity, as distinct tribal groups, for a sufficient period they will stabilise at about this figure.

It could be argued that a language is not likely to borrow equally frequently from each direction. For instance, if C shares a certain word with D, and the item is proscribed in C, then C presumably MUST borrow from B. Thus it would seem that if C has a higher percentage of vocabulary in common with D than with B, then it is likely to borrow rather more often from B than from D. It will be worthwhile to look at the mathematics of this borrowing situation in some detail (continuing with the coastal strip example):

Let p_{ij} be the fraction of vocabulary shared by languages I and J – that is, $p_{ij} = 0.4$ indicates that I and J have 40% vocabulary in common, and so on. Now C will have $1 - p_{bc}$ of its vocabulary DIFFERENT from B, and $1 - p_{cd}$ DIFFERENT from D. There is thus the expectation of $(1 - p_{bc})/(1 - p_{bc} + 1 - p_{cd})$ and that any new item borrowed by C will come from B, and the expectation of $(1 - p_{cd})/(1 - p_{bc} + 1 - p_{cd})$ that it will come from D.

Consider the case in which B and C each replace r% of their vocabulary, over a certain period of time. B will lose $r \times p_{bc}$ of the vocabulary it has in common with C, and C will lose an identical amount (note that $p_{bc} = p_{cb}$). Thus the total loss of common vocabulary will be $2r \times p_{bc}$.

Of the r% of vocabulary gain by B, $r \times (1 - p_{bc})/(2 - p_{bc} - p_{ab})$ will be borrowed from C; and of the gain by C $r \times (1 - p_{bc})/(2 - p_{bc} - p_{cd})$ will be borrowed from B. The total gain in common vocabulary will be the sum of these two figures.

Thus the 'net gain' in the fraction of the vocabulary of B and C which is common to the two languages can be formulated as total gain minus total loss, i.e.:

$$\text{Net Gain} = \frac{r}{100}\left(\frac{1}{1 + \dfrac{1 - p_{ab}}{1 - p_{bc}}} + \frac{1}{1 + \dfrac{1 - p_{cd}}{1 - p_{bc}}} - 2p_{bc} \right)$$

And the fraction of vocabulary common to B and C after the replacement of r% of the words in each language will be $p_{bc} + \text{Net Gain}$.

Now if each dialect has 50% vocabulary in common with its neighbours, except for B and C, which have 20%, the formula predicts that after 1% of the vocabulary has been replaced in each language, B and C will have 20.82% in common. And if each pair have 50% common vocabulary except for B and C who have 70%, the B–C figure after a 1% replacement will be 69.35%. Comparing these figures with those given above, we see that the percentages will move towards the equilibrium level of 50% rather more quickly if borrowing is 'weighted' than if each dialect borrows equally from all its neighbours.

Let us suppose that $p_{ab} = p_{cd} = m$. For each particular value of m there is a value of p_{bc} such that the Net Gain is zero. The figures are, approximately:

m	0.0	0.2	0.4	0.5	0.6	0.8	0.9
p_{bc} for zero gain	0.37	0.42	0.48	0.5	0.55	0.65	0.70

That is, if all other dialects have 20% vocabulary in common, and if B and C have 42% in common, then a small degree of lexical replacement (say 1%) would be likely to leave the B–C figure unchanged. This would not, however, be a stable situation, since the A–B and C–D figures would increase rapidly from a 20 % level, and as they rose so the 'equilibrium figure' for p_{bc} would (as can be seen from the table) approach the equilibrium figure of 50 % more and more closely. If the system of dialects were unaltered for a sufficient period (that is, if there were no further tribal split or merger, and no external cultural contact), the figures for all contiguous dialect pairs would eventually even out at around 50 %.

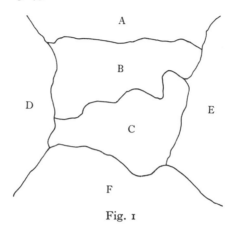

Fig. 1

The model we have discussed has been essentially a two-dimensional one. Some language contact situations in Australia do appear to follow this model, with a given tribe having extensive social contact with, and borrowing from, just two other tribes. However, some groups undoubtedly borrow from more than two directions. We can consider a three-dimensional model, in which each tribe shares boundaries with four other tribes. For instance, in fig. 1 B is contiguous with A, E, C and D, and C with B, E, F and D. Again, suppose that r % of each dialect's vocabulary is replaced over a certain period of time. The loss in the lexical items common to B and C will, as before, be $2 \times p_{bc}$.

Calculation of the gain is more complex than in the two-dimensional model. Through direct borrowing from C, B will increase the B–C common vocabulary by:

$$r \times (1 - p_{bc})/(1 - p_{ab} + 1 - p_{be} + 1 - p_{bc} + 1 - p_{bd}).$$

However, B will also borrow from D, and p_{cd} of D's vocabulary is held in common with C. Thus borrowing by B from D will increase the vocabulary common to B and C by:

$$r \times p_{cd} \times (1 - p_{bd})/(4 - p_{ab} - p_{be} - p_{bc} - p_{bd}).$$

Similarly in the case of borrowing by B from E; and by borrowing by C from D and E. The total increase in B–C common vocabulary after an r % replacement is now:

$$\text{Net Gain} = \frac{r}{100} \times \left(\frac{1 - p_{bc} + p_{cd}(1 - p_{bd}) + p_{ce}(1 - p_{be})}{4 - p_{ab} - p_{be} - p_{bc} - p_{bd}} \right.$$

$$\left. + \frac{1 - p_{bc} + p_{bd}(1 - p_{cd}) + p_{be}(1 - p_{ce})}{4 - p_{bc} - p_{ce} - p_{cf} - p_{cd}} - 2p_{bc} \right)$$

The Net Gain is zero if all p_{ij}'s in the formula are 0·5; this is the equilibrium situation.

Let us suppose that $p_{ab} = p_{be} = p_{bd} = p_{ce} = p_{cf} = p_{cd} = m$. The table giving the values of p_{bc} that will yield zero Net Gain for different values of m is:

m	0·2	0·4	0·5	0·6	0·8
p_{bc} for zero gain	0·31	0·44	0·5	0·56	0·69

That is, if m = 0·4 then any value of p_{bc} that is less than 0·44 will be raised in the direction of 0·44 after a period of lexical replacement; any value of p_{bc} that is more than 0·44 will be lowered by lexical replacement; if p_{bc} is exactly 0·44 then it will be unchanged under a small amount of lexical replacement. However, if each of p_{ab}, p_{be}, etc. are as low as 0·4, they will themselves be raised by the process of replacement, and the value of p_{bc} for zero gain will be altered accordingly, moving further in the direction of the 'stability figure' of 0·5.

The three-dimensional model thus yields similar results to the two-dimensional example: all percentages between contiguous dialects will in time tend toward 50%.

The question of whether the proportion of new vocabulary which B borrows from C depends upon the percentage which they at present have in common, or whether each language borrows fairly evenly from its neighbours, irrespective of how much vocabulary it has in common with each, cannot be settled on a priori grounds. Note that some support for the second alternative is provided by the figures for Ngadyan's borrowing from Yidin and Mamu since the operation of its 'long vowel rule' – 10.2.2. Note also that, if a certain form in B cannot be borrowed into C (because it is identical with the form that has just been tabooed in C, or because it already exists – with a different meaning – in C), then C may borrow a form that has a related meaning in B. For instance, *buŋgu* is 'knee' and *mugu* 'shin' in Waruŋu; however, in the contiguous Nyawigi *buŋgu* is 'shoulder' and *mugu* 'knee'.

Fifty per cent is an 'ideal' equilibrium figure. We would expect in practice two contiguous dialects, that had been borrowing back and forth for sufficient time, to have between 40% and 60% common vocabulary. Dialects not contiguous but separated by a single dialect (as A and C, for instance, in our coastal strip model) should eventually have 20–30% common vocabulary. Considering the amount of time that aboriginal languages have been occupying Australia we should expect most dialects to show common vocabulary percentages within these ranges; it seems that very many do so. Figures that fall outside the ranges can be significant:

(a) If two contiguous dialects have more than about 60% common vocabulary, then it is rather likely that they are (strongly) genetically related. That is, tribes speaking these dialects were formed, not too long ago, by the split of a single large tribe. The percentage of common vocabulary between the dialects has been dropping, but has not yet had time to reach the equilibrium figure.

(b) If two contiguous dialects have less than about 40% common vocabulary, then they are probably not (strongly) genetically related and have only been in contiguity for a relatively short time (that is, not long enough to achieve the equilibrium figure).

(c) If two non-contiguous dialects have more than, say, around 40% common vocabulary, then they may well be genetically related, as in case (a). Once sister dialects have moved apart, their common vocabulary is likely to drop to a very low figure (depending on how far apart they are); a figure of 40% indicates that the dialects have not had time totally to obscure their genetic relationship through lexical replacement.

In most instances grammatical similarity is a surer basis for judgements of genetic relationship than simple vocabulary counts. It is true that in many areas of the world the most basic vocabulary items are unlikely to be borrowed; however, this does not appear to be the case in Australia (or at least, not to the same degree as elsewhere) where any type of word seems liable to be replaced. Grammatical forms and constructions appear in all languages to be more stable, and less susceptible to large-scale borrowing, than dictionary items.

Percentages of common vocabulary are at best indicators: they can evoke suspicion of genetic relationship, which should then be checked by comparing the grammars of the languages. Grammatical change is normally rather slower than lexical replacement, and dialect pairs of types (a) and (c) should show significant grammatical similarity, if they are in fact genetically related.

For contiguous dialects with 40–60% common vocabulary it is impossible, on lexical grounds, to even hazard a guess as to whether (1) they are sister dialects, whose percentage of common vocabulary has in time dropped to the equilibrium level, or (2) the dialects are not recently related but have, through borrowing, achieved an equilibrium figure. In such cases detailed grammatical comparison is required before even tentative judgement of genetic relationship can be made.

A tentative classification of Australian languages has recently been produced by O'Grady, Wurm and Hale [see O'Grady, Voegelin and Voegelin, 1966].

This is based entirely on lexical similarity; the criteria include 'cognate density of…51–70 % for different languages or family-like languages of the same subgroup; and over 71 % for different dialects of the same language'. It appears that no account at all was taken of contiguity – we have mentioned that if two contiguous languages have about 50 % vocabulary in common this is not indicative of any strong genetic relationship, whereas a figure of 50 % for non-contiguous languages is highly significant. The O'Grady–Wurm–Hale classification clearly lacks any genetic implications but is rather a limited indication of whether languages have been in contiguity for a sufficient period to reach the 'equilibrium level' of 50 % common vocabulary.

In addition, it is clear that for the Cairns rain forest region, O'Grady, Wurm and Hale must have used old vocabularies that they attributed to the wrong dialect, for Nyawigi is grouped as a dialect of Dyirbal (there is in fact only around 20 % common vocabulary). It should also be noted that the 100-item list used by O'Grady, Wurm and Hale includes some grammatical items (such as pronouns) and would be expected to yield slightly higher cognate density counts than the list used in the present study. The map produced to accompany this classification bears a cartographer's error – the coast line between Cairns and Townsville is drawn entirely wrongly, showing a promontory and an inlet that do not exist; some of the languages are misplaced and others omitted.

10.2   Origin and movement of the Dyirbal tribes

10.2.1   Language grouping in the Cairns rain forest region. We can apply the comments of the last section to a classification of the tribal dialects in the rain forest region to the south of Cairns (see map 2, p. 25). The percentages of vocabulary shared by eight of these dialects are shown in table 10.1.

TABLE 10.1   *Percentages of vocabulary shared by eight dialects*

Yidin							
27	Ngadyan						
23	70	Mamu					
22	62	87	Dyirbal				
18	50	70	81	Giramay			
12	30	47	53	60	Wargamay		
14	27	43	46	47	46	Waruɲu	
16	15	17	18	15	9	13	Mbabaṟam

The table is based on a list of 221 lexical items – 138 nouns, 33 adjectives, 46 verbs, 'yesterday', 'tomorrow', 'yes' and 'no'. The 'common vocabulary' includes both identical, and non-identical but obviously cognate items. With the exception of Mbabaṟam and Ngadyan, which have undergone phonological changes described below, almost all common vocabulary is identical. Thus, the Wargamay–Giramay count includes 107 identical and 8 non-identical items. Even the non-identical items as a rule differ only slightly; thus we have for 'navel' *ḍúḍuṛ* in Dyirbal but *ḍúḍur* in Giramay; for 'grasshopper' *búndim* in Yidin, *búndiɲ* in Mamu, Dyirbal, Giramay, Wargamay and Waruŋu, *búndiŋ* in Nyawigi and *búndi* in Mbabaṛam (and see 10.3).

From the table, Ngadyan, Mamu, Dyirbal and Giramay are seen to have significantly high percentages of common vocabulary, indicating a probable genetic relationship; in fact these four dialects have almost identical grammars and are definitely related (for instance, unlike all other languages of the region each has a system of four noun classes).

The Yidin–Ngadyan figure is well below the equilibrium range of 40–60%: on lexical evidence this pair is unlikely to be genetically related. In fact these two dialects are very different grammatically; it appears that Yidin and Ngadyan came into contiguity relatively recently, and that the vocabulary they do share is largely the result of recent borrowing.

Mbabaṛam does not have much vocabulary in common with any of the other dialects; it is grammatically – and also phonologically – quite different from them. There is no evidence of genetic relationship. (Mbabaṛam is discussed in more detail in 10.2.4)

Waruŋu was spoken over a long tract on top of the range, in contiguity with Wargamay, Giramay and Dyirbal and also, to a lesser extent, with Mbabaṛam (and probably also with Nyawigi, to the south, and perhaps Wagaman, to the west of Mbabaṛam). In the table Waruŋu has lexical scores within the equilibrium range with Mamu, Dyirbal, Giramay and Wargamay – judgements of genetic affiliation or the lack of it thus depend on grammatical comparison. The writer has only a little grammatical data on Waruŋu, but it is sufficient to indicate that Waruŋu is grammatically quite different from Dyirbal and Wargamay; in addition, speakers of Dyirbal always refer to Waruŋu as a very 'difficult' language, far harder for them to speak and understand than Wargamay, for example. Waruŋu is pretty certainly not related to any of the other dialects in the rain forest region.

Waruŋu may be genetically related to languages to the west and south-west: it has about 45 % common vocabulary with Ilba – with which it is not contiguous, being separated by Kutjale according to Tindale's map – on the basis of Tompson and Chatfield's 1886 vocabulary of Ilba. Peter Sutton has recently done field work on Waruŋu, Gugu-Baḍun (immediately to the west of Waruŋu, and very similar to it), Biria, and other languages of what he calls the 'Burdekin' group; his (unpublished) results suggest that there is a family of languages covering a great deal of central Queensland, of which Waruŋu is the most north-easterly member.

Wargamay has 60% vocabulary in common with Giramay, at the upper extreme of the 'equilibrium range'. We must refer to grammatical comparison for evidence as to whether or not there is (strong) genetic relationship between the dialects – and the grammatical evidence is inconclusive. Wargamay has some important syntactic and morphological similarities with dialects of Dyirbal, but it also has considerable differences.

Similarities between the Dyirbal language and Wargamay include: [1] they both have -*ŋay* constructions – 4.4.2; [2] pronoun paradigms are identical (but for the idiosyncratic -*i*- in second person dual forms for G) – note that Wargamay has the *ŋayba/naḍa* and *ŋinba/ŋinda* distinction, in common with G (but not with any other dialects of the Dyirbal language); [3] intransitive and transitive verbalisers are -*bi* and -*ma* in Wargamay, as against -*bil* and -*mal* in Dyirbal (the transitive -*mal* form is common to many Australian languages; however, intransitive -*bi* does not appear to have a wide distribution); [4] Wargamay has *miɲa* 'what' in common with all dialects of Dyirbal but G. Other similarities encompass points that are common to a great many Australian languages – case inflections, verb conjugations, etc.

Differences include: [1] Wargamay has no noun classes, nor any noun markers (however, it has interrogative 'where' forms based on root *waṇḍa-*, that may be cognate with Dyirbal *wuɳḍa-*; and note that the third person pronoun, *ɲuŋa*, in Wargamay inflects – like nouns but unlike the other pronouns – on a nominative-ergative pattern); [2] Wargamay has a two-term tense system, but with a contrast between 'past' and 'non-past' as against Dyirbal's 'future' versus 'non-future'; [3] the interrogative pronoun 'who' is based on root *ŋan-* in Wargamay, as against *waɲ(a/u)* in Dyirbal; [4] many non-inflectional affixes are different – thus of the four aspectual affixes in Dyirbal only -*gani*- can be recognised in Wargamay; the affixes corresponding to Dyirbal -*bila* 'with' and -*ŋaŋgay* ~ -*biday* 'without' are -*giri* and -*biṛay* respectively.

A fuller comparison of the grammars of Dyirbal and Wargamay is planned for a later date, if it proves possible to collect more detailed syntactic data on Wargamay than the writer has so far obtained.

The data at present available does not allow us to make any definite judgement as to whether Dyirbal and Wargamay are or are not strongly genetically related. But we can conclude EITHER that there is a genetic relation, but the two languages have been separated for a very considerable time, allowing the vocabulary in common to contiguous dialects to drop to 60% and allowing the grammars to diverge in significant respects (noun classes in Dyirbal are likely to have evolved after the split-off from Wargamay), OR that the languages, although not strongly genetically related, have been in contiguity for a considerable period, allowing the common vocabulary to build up to the remarkably high level of 60%, and for there to have been a good deal of morphological and also syntactic diffusion. Note that these alternatives have in common the assumption that the two languages have been in contact for a longish time.

We have above talked of lexical similarity scores, which involve counting the proportion of nouns, verbs and adjectives (the items available from a maximal 221-word check list) that are held in common by two languages. However, borrowing is likely to involve a higher proportion of nouns than of verbs and adjectives. If we have two pairs of dialects, one pair genetically related and the other not, with the same lexical score, then we would expect the genetically related pair to have a larger number of verb and adjective correspondences – items that have NOT been replaced in the two sister dialects – and the other pair to have more noun correspondences – items that have been borrowed between the two dialects. This is confirmed by dialects from the rain forest region. For instance, Yidin has only 40% vocabulary in common with its northern neighbour, Dyabugay, but has significant grammatical similarities – Yidin and Dyabugay are almost certainly (strongly) genetically related. Note that the Dyabugay–Yidin lexical score is only half as much again as the Yidin–Ngadyan figure, but there are three times as many verbs common to Dyabugay and Yidin (and not to Ngadyan) as to Yidin and Ngadyan (and not to Dyabugay). And whereas Yidin and Ngadyan have no check-list adjectives in common, Dyabugay and Yidin share four. The 50% lexical score for genetically related dialects Ngadyan and Giramay includes thirty verbs (out of forty-six verbs in the check list) whereas the 60% score for Giramay and Wargamay includes only seven verbs; this could be taken as favouring the second alternative mentioned above – that there is NO strong genetic relationship between Dyirbal and Wargamay.

We conclude that there are, in the Cairns rain forest region, dialects belonging to at least five distinct 'languages':

1. Yidin (with dialects Yidin, Guŋgay and Madyay)
2. Mbabaṛam
3. Dyirbal (with dialects Dyirbal, Mamu, Giramay and Ngadyan, in addition to the extinct Gulŋay and Dyiru)
4. Waruŋu (with genetic affiliations to the west and south-west)
5. Wargamay (and possibly the extinct Bandyin)

The term 'language' is employed in many ways; we are here using it to describe a group of dialects that have almost identical grammars, so that it is most reasonable to write a single overall grammar for the language, with notes on dialectal variations. 'Languages' which are strongly genetically related to each other are said to form a 'language family'.

The three dialects of what we have chosen to call the 'Yidin language' appear to be as closely related to each other as do the dialects of Dyirbal. Yidin probably belongs to the same 'language family' as its northern neighbour, the Dyabugay language (with dialects Dyabugay, Bulway and (possibly) Yirgay).

From Armstrong and Murray's vocabulary [1886] it appears that Bandyin, spoken on Hinchinbrook Island, had 60 % vocabulary in common with Wargamay and 45 % with Giramay; no grammatical data is available on Bandyin. However, speakers of Giramay declare that Bandyin was more similar to Wargamay than to Giramay. Where such judgements – from the same informants – were checked out in other instances they were found to imply mainly grammatical similarity. Wargamay appears not to have any (strong) genetic connection with Nyawigi, its neighbour to the south.

10.2.2 Evolution of the Dyirbal dialects. Birdsell [1958] has argued that about 500 is the optimum size for a tribal group of hunting and gathering people. If a tribe gets very much larger it is likely to split into two groups, each of which becomes a tribe in its own right. If two nearby tribes have their numbers greatly reduced, for any reason, they are likely to amalgamate, creating a tribe of viable size. Now each tribe has its own 'language'; with tribal split there will also be language split. For a while the speech of sister tribes may be similar enough to be regarded, on the criterion used in this paper, as dialects of a single language; but after a long enough time (even if they do not geographically move apart) they are likely to diverge to such an extent that they must be regarded as distinct languages, although members of the same language family.

From their lexical and grammatical similarity it appears that the dialects of the Dyirbal language are descended from a single ancestor dialect. Ngadyan has been separated from the other dialects for the longest time. The second split involved the breakaway of Giramay; and then finally there was the split into Dyirbal and Mamu. This is illustrated in tree 1.

TREE I

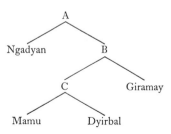

That the Dyirbal–Mamu split was relatively recent is emphasised by the fact that although there are names for the groups speaking Dyirbal, Ngadyan and Giramay (called Dyirbalŋan, Ngadyandyi and Giramaygan respectively) there is no single name for the tribe which speaks Mamu, only names for the five 'hordes' within the tribe (called Waṛibara, Dulgubara, Bagiṛgabara, Dyiṛibara and Mandubara). Proto-Mamu-Dyirbal was probably called Dyirbal (and the tribe speaking it, Dyirbalŋan). Insufficient data is available on the extinct Gulŋay and Dyiru dialects to suggest the stages at which they split off.

Although there is insufficient data to 'place' Gulŋay and Dyiru on the tree, they do appear to be part-way between Dyirbal and Mamu, both as regards grammar and in their lexicons. The last speaker of Gulŋay mixes his language with Dyirbal, and is a very poor informant. It was, however, possible to quiz him on a number of points on which M and D differ. It seems that Gulŋay is like M in having the emphatic affix -*ḏu* (D -*ḏilu*) and verbal affix -*ba* (D -*bila*), and in having the 'self and spouse' pronoun *ŋanaymba*; it is like D in not having perfective relative clauses, with affix -*mi*. Lexically, Gulŋay resembles M in having *balan yibi* 'woman' (D *balan ḏugumbil*) and *bayi maybaḏa* 'alligator' (D *bayi guḏagay*); it resembles D in having *gaṛbu* 'three' and *mundi* 'a good few' (M *waraŋuŋgul* and *gaṛbu* respectively).

Some lexical items are held in common by the non-contiguous dialects Ngadyan and Giramay, but are not found in Dyirbal and Mamu; such a word would have been present in languages A and B in the tree but replaced in C. In other instances Mamu and Giramay share a word that is not present in Dyirbal: the word would have been in languages B and C but replaced in Dyirbal, after the split with Mamu. This is additional evidence supporting the genetic affiliation of the dialects; in contrast, there are no words common to Ngadyan and Wargamay that are not also shared by Mamu and/or Dyirbal and/or Giramay.

There are also grammatical points on which Mamu and Giramay agree, and differ from the Dyirbal dialect. For instance, the negative imperative particle is *ŋaru* in M and G, but *galga* in D; reflexive allomorph -*riy* in M and G corresponds to -*yiriy* in D.

Assuming that each tribe replaces vocabulary at an approximately constant rate, we can calculate, by the technique mentioned in 10.1, that the times which elapsed between the Ngadyan split-off, the Giramay split-off, the Mamu-Dyirbal split, and the present day, must be approximately equal.

Ngadyan is the most divergent dialect of the Dyirbal language. It has basically the same syntax as the other dialects (including noun classes, -*ŋay* constructions, and so on) but differs in the form of some affixes. However, the most striking and interesting way in which Ngadyan diverges is in a detail of phonology. Unlike most languages of the region, the Dyirbal, Mamu and Giramay dialects have no significant vowel length. Most probably, there was length at one time (in language A) but this was simply dropped. Thus we have Dyirbal *waɲal* but Nyawigi *wa:ɲal* 'boomerang'. However, Ngadyan has undergone a simple phonological change that has reintroduced significant vowel length into the dialect. Before a consonant or a word boundary, a sequence of vowel plus *l*, *ɽ* or *y* is replaced by a long vowel, thus:

LONG VOWEL RULE
$$\begin{bmatrix} V \begin{Bmatrix} l \\ \mathstrut ɽ \end{Bmatrix} \\ ay \\ uy \end{bmatrix} \longrightarrow \begin{bmatrix} V: \\ a: \\ i: \end{bmatrix} \bigg/ \begin{Bmatrix} -C \\ -\# \end{Bmatrix}$$

where V indicates any vowel and C any consonant. The sequence *-iy-* does not occur except before a vowel. Examples of the change are:

D/M/G	Ngadyan	
waguy	*wagi:*	'sand'
ḍagal	*ḍaga:*	'cheek'
yalgay	*ya:ga:*	'road, track'
gibaɽ	*giba:*	'fig tree'
bilmban	*bi:mban*	'push'
gaɽbu	*ga:bu*	'a good few'
ɲumbul	*ɲumbu:*	'beard'

Note that the rule does not apply to sequence of vowel plus *r*.

The most remarkable thing about words that have undergone the long vowel rule in Ngadyan is that certain inflectional rules operate on the ORIGINAL phonological form of the word. For instance, the instrumental inflection of *baŋgay* 'spear' in D, M and G is *baŋgayḍu* (by the rules of 3.2.1); the instrumental inflection of *baŋga:* 'spear' in Ngadyan is *baŋga:ḍu*. It appears that in a grammar of Ngadyan we would have to give *baŋgay* as the underlying phonological representation of *baŋga:*; inflectional rules and so on would operate on this form, and the long vowel rule would apply as a late phonological rule.

The long vowel rule applied at a certain stage in the history of Ngadyan. Words that have been borrowed since this time have not undergone the rule (so that no recent loan words involve long vowels). Thus, *gugaɽ* 'black guana', *duguy* 'kauri pine', and so on. Now, D, G, and M have *guwuy* 'spirit of a dead man'; as would be expected the

form in Ngadyan is *guwi:*. When they first encountered white men
Mamu speakers imagined them to be reincarnations of their own
ancestors, and called them accordingly *guwuy*; Ngadyan borrowed this
form. Thus Ngadyan includes both *guwi:* 'spirit of a dead man' and
guwuy 'white man', both forms corresponding to M *guwuy*, but the
second being borrowed after the time of operation of the long vowel
rule.

The writer's corpus of Ngadyan Guwal includes 61 words with an
underlying sequence vowel plus *y*, *l* or *ɼ*, before a consonant or word
boundary. Of these, 44 have undergone the long vowel rule and 17 –
later borrowings – have not. Of the 44, 5 also occur in both Dyirbal–
Mamu and Yidin, 30 in Dyirbal–Mamu only, 4 in Yidin only and 5
cannot be traced in either Dyirbal–Mamu or Yidin. Of the 17 post-rule
borrowings, 4 occur in both Dyirbal–Mamu and Yidin, 5 in Dyirbal–
Mamu only, 5 in Yidin only, and 3 cannot be traced in either. Thus, it
appears that since the application of the long-vowel rule, Ngadyan
has borrowed about equally from Yidin and from the other Dyirbal
dialects. The 4 pre-rule words that occur in Yidin and Ngadyan but
not in Dyirbal–Mamu must have been borrowed between Ngadyan
and Yidin before the application of the long-vowel rule. Most of the
30 pre-rule words found only in Dyirbal–Mamu will be genetic
inheritance. The pre-rule items found in Ngadyan, Yidin and Dyirbal–
Mamu may have been borrowed by Yidin or Dyirbal–Mamu after the
time of the long vowel rule (we have seen that the original form of a
word is preserved as its underlying phonological representation in
Ngadyan; Yidin and Mamu could thus easily borrow from Ngadyan
the original form of the word). From these figures we can, using the
technique of 10.1, calculate that the long vowel rule must have operated
in Ngadyan soon after its split-off from Dyirbal–Mamu–Giramay;
earlier than or about the same time as the Giramay split-off. If this is
correct it should follow that there are no (or extremely few) words
common to Ngadyan and Giramay, but absent from Mamu and Dyirbal,
that have not undergone the long vowel rule in Ngadyan. Pre-rule
words occurring in only Ngadyan and Giramay would be genetic
inheritance from language A in tree 1 (or else borrowings from language
B into Ngadyan) that were replaced in language C. A post-rule word
occurring in only Ngadyan and Giramay would have to be an item
borrowed from C into Ngadyan, that was also in Giramay (the sister
language of B), and which was afterwards replaced in both Dyirbal

and Mamu – a rather unlikely thing to happen. In fact, all words common to Ngadyan and Giramay and absent from Dyirbal and Mamu HAVE undergone the long-vowel rule, providing some support for the hypothesis of tree 1 and for our attempt at relative dating.

The long vowel rule seems to have been applied in a rather limited manner in the type of Mamu spoken by the Waṛibara horde. Thus 'road' is *ya:ga:* in Ngadyan, *ya:gay* in Waṛibara Mamu, and *yalgay* in Dulgubara Mamu (the variety referred to throughout this book), and in D and G. Almost certainly, this is the beginning of the 'diffusion' of a phonological trait.

10.2.3   Dyalŋuy augmentation. Whereas Dyirbal and Mamu Guwals have 87% common vocabulary, their Dyalŋuys have only about 50% vocabulary in common. On the other hand, M and Ngadyan score 70% for Guwal vocabulary and about the same for Dyalŋuy.

The breakdown by parts of speech for D and M Dyalŋuys is – 67% of verbs in common, 41% of nouns, and 42% of adjectives; the Guwals have about 87% in common for each part of speech.

At first sight, the small percentage of vocabulary common to D and M Dyalŋuy seems puzzling. But it must be remembered that although an avoidance style of this type is very common in Australia, only SOME tribes have developed anything like so extensive an avoidance vocabulary; for instance, Kenneth Hale reports that for Walbiri there are probably less than fifty items that definitely belong to the mother-in-law style. The most likely hypothesis is that, although proto-Dyirbal would have had a limited Dyalŋuy vocabulary, this has only been expanded to its present size rather recently – in fact, SINCE the Dyirbal–Mamu split. The Dyalŋuy vocabulary extension has taken place independently for Dyirbal and Mamu (the Dyalŋuy augmentation in M being in fact more intimately connected with that in Ngadyan).

It is interesting to note that, although Dyirbal and Mamu dialects are closer to each other in grammar and vocabulary than either is to Giramay or Ngadyan, the Mamu tribe appears to have had its closest social associations with the Ngadyandyi, and the Dyirbalŋan with the Giramaygan. There may be a generalisation around here. If a large tribe B is to the south of A and to the north of C, then it may be that the circumstance leading to a split of B into tribes B_N (in the north) and B_S (in the south) is for the northern hordes of B to have developed close social associations with A and the southern hordes close connection with C – the new tribe B_N will now have rather more dealings with A than with B_S. If the northern hordes of B had closer connections with the southern hordes than with A, then tribe B would be unlikely to split into two. This would explain why Mamu should have more Dyalŋuy vocabulary in common with Ngadyan than with Dyirbal (Dyalŋuy vocabulary was greatly increased after the split-off from Dyirbal), although it has more Guwal vocabulary in common with Dyirbal – to which it is grammatically most similar – than with Ngadyan.

Although each dialect has no lexical items in common to its Guwal and Dyalŋuy it is frequently the case that a Dyalŋuy item for one dialect is identical with a Guwal item in a nearby dialect (2.5, 9.2). In a number of instances it appears that Dyirbal Dyalŋuy has borrowed a term from the Guwal of a tribe to the south, whilst Mamu has borrowed from the north. Thus, the word for 'body' is *yumal* in both Dyirbal and Mamu Guwals, but *buba* in Dyirbal Dyalŋuy and *gula* in Mamu Dyalŋuy; *buba* is the term in Nyawigi Guwal and *gula* that in Yidin Guwal. In connection with this example it is interesting to note that the Ngadyan Guwal word is also *yumal*, and not *yuma:*, indicating a post-long-vowel-rule borrowing from Mamu. Now in the process of expanding its Dyalŋuy vocabulary Mamu would be likely to take over a Guwal term from the contiguous dialect Ngadyan, if it differed from the Mamu Guwal term. It thus seems likely that before its recent borrowing of *yumal* the Ngadyan term for 'body' was *gula*, and that this was borrowed for Mamu Dyalŋuy. But since *yumal* occurs in Mamu, Dyirbal and Giramay, it was probably the term for body in proto-Dyirbal (language A in tree 1). We thus have the likelihood that immediately after its split from Dyirbal–Mamu–Giramay, Ngadyan Guwal had the form *yumal*; this was tabooed, and the form *gula* borrowed from Yidin to replace it; Mamu Dyalŋuy borrowed this form quite recently and even more recently *gula* itself was proscribed, *yumal* being borrowed from Mamu as a replacement.

It will be seen that the Dyalŋuy data provides general support for our hypotheses concerning dialect split, interaction, and so on. The Guwals of Australian languages appear all to taboo words and borrow replacements with some frequency. The augmentation of Dyalŋuy vocabulary follows the same principle – borrowing from neighbouring dialects, not to replace taboo terms, but to build up a full avoidance vocabulary, so that everything which can be expressed through Guwal lexical items can also be said using only Dyalŋuy words.

It is likely that many other cultural inferences will follow from a detailed study of Dyalŋuy vocabulary. For instance, Guwal *balan bigin* 'shield' and *balan biyilbiyil* 'peewee' are both rendered by *balan gigiba* in Dyalŋuy; the informant explained that this is because the bird looks like the painting on a shield. This could be taken to imply that shield painting was established before the bird was named in Dyalŋuy (unless, say, this name merely replaced an earlier Dyalŋuy name).

10.2.4 Mbabaṟam. Each rain forest tribe occupied an area that was considerably smaller than that of the average Australian tribe – the abundance of animal and plant food meant that a relatively small region could support a tribe of the standard size (of about 500 people). In contrast, Waruŋu – a typical 'inland' tribe – occupied a territory probably four or more times as big as that of Mamu or Yidin; but it was country that yielded perhaps only a quarter as much food per square mile.

The tribe speaking Mbabaṟam occupied a relatively small area on top of the range – no bigger than that of a tribe in the coastal belt, although Mbabaṟam country was as inhospitable as that of the Waruŋu. Mbabaṟam had most contact with Wagaman to the west, and Dyangun to the north (it has 23% vocabulary in common with Wagaman, and 16% with Dyangun). It also had some tribal boundaries in common with Ngadyan, Dyirbal, Waruŋu and Muluridyi (the latter intervening between Mbabaṟam and Bulway).

Fairly recently, Mbabaṟam has undergone a series of rather drastic phonological changes. Whereas words in surrounding languages must begin with a single consonant, must have at least two syllables, and cannot end in a stop, in Mbabaṟam they can begin with *a-*, with a single consonant, or with a homorganic nasal-plus-stop cluster, they can be monosyllabic and they can end in a stop. Surrounding languages all have a three-vowel system; Mbabaṟam has at least six vowels – *i, ε, a, ɔ, u* and the close unrounded back *ɯ*. Phonological developments which produced these forms include:

[1] STRESS SHIFT. Stress moves from first to second syllable within a word.

[2] VOWEL RAISING. An *a* in the second syllable of a word becomes *ɔ* if the word-initial consonant is *g-, ŋ* -or *w-*; it becomes *ε* if the word initial consonant is *ḍ-* or *y-* (or, presumably, *ɲ-*).

[3] INITIAL DROPPING. An initial CV-, with a short vowel, is dropped; initial CV:- is replaced by a-.

[4] FINAL DROPPING. In many words, final -C or -V is dropped.

[1–3] are definite rules, that applied at a certain point in time. Words borrowed since this time have not undergone the rules. [4], however, is more in the nature of a general tendency; unlike [1–3] it does not seem to be applied in any strict manner, and it is applied to some recent borrowings. Examples of the application of the rules are:

gúdaga	> dɔ́g 'dingo, dog'		gúwa	> wɔ́ 'west'
wúla-	> lɔ́- '(to) die'		ɖána-	> nɛ́ '(to) stand'
ɖáwa	> wɛ́ 'mouth'		ɖíba	> bɛ́ 'liver'
gúyu	> yú 'fish'		ŋáli	> lí 'we'
yí:bar	> abɛ́r 'south'		bámba	> mbá 'belly'

and examples of post-rule loans:

gúŋgaga	> gungág 'kookaburra'	bárŋan	> barŋán 'kangaroo rat'
búndiɲ	> búndi 'grasshopper'	búmba	> búmba 'ashes'

These are only SOME of the phonological changes that have taken place in Mbabaɽam (and the rules given here are extremely tentative and probably oversimplified) – a detailed account of Mbabaɽam, and the changes it has undergone, is in preparation. Note that these changes are similar to those that have taken place – apparently, quite independently – in Northern Paman [Hale, 1964] and in Arandic [Hale, personal communication].

Tindale and Birdsell [1941] hypothesised that twelve 'rain forest' tribes were 'Tasmanoid' in physical type, and possibly in other respects. In support of this position they maintained that the languages of these tribes were unAustralian. In fact eleven of the dialects cited (including the Dyirbal and Yidin languages) are typically Australian; the twelfth, Mbabaɽam (which is not in fact spoken in the rain forest region) appears aberrant on the surface, but – in terms of rules such as those given above – can be shown to have developed out of a language of the regular Australian pattern.

Cognates have been recognised in surrounding languages for 70 lexical items in Mbabaɽam (out of a total Mbabaɽam corpus of 210 lexical words, not counting proper and place names). Of these 51 have undergone rules [1–3] in Mbabaɽam, the remaining 19 being post-rule borrowings. The distribution of these cognates is shown in Table 10.2.

It can be seen that there are no post-rule forms that must have been borrowed from the Yidin-Dyabugay family; the three post-rule forms that occur in Yidin-Dyabugay are also in Dyirbal and Waruŋu. Mbabaɽam is not at present contiguous to Yidin-Dyabugay; the figures indicate that it has not been contiguous since the time of the stress shift, vowel raising and initial dropping rules. However, the fact that six pre-rule cognates are found only in Yidin-Dyabugay indicates that it probably was contiguous with them at one time.

Mbabaɽam appears to have replaced about 25–30% of its vocabulary since the operation of rules [1–3]. We saw in table 10.1 that it now has

TABLE 10.2. *Mbabaṟam cognates*

		Yidin-Dyabugay	Wagaman-Dyangun	Dyirbal language	Waruŋu
pre-rule forms in Mbabaṟam	cognates found in this language only	6	13	8	2
	cognates found in this and in one or more of the other three languages	24	29	21	12
post-rule forms in Mbabaṟam	cognates found in this language only	0	6	4	1
	cognates found in this and in one or more of the other three languages	3	9	12	8

about 16% vocabulary in common with Yidin: it would probably have had around 25% in common at the time of operation of the rules. Now Ngadyan has replaced 25–30% of its vocabulary since its long-vowel rule. Assuming that languages of this region replace vocabulary at about the same rate, this would indicate that these phonological changes in Mbabaṟam and Ngadyan took place at approximately the same time.

The discussion in 10.1 – concerning lexical diffusion and an 'equilibrium figure' of 40–60% for the vocabulary shared by contiguous dialects – only applies in the case of dialects that borrow quite freely from each other. Most of the words in Mbabaṟam (monosyllabic, often beginning with a vowel or consonant cluster, ending in a stop, sometimes stressed on a non-initial syllable) are so divergent, in terms of the phonologies of neighbouring languages, that they would be unlikely to be borrowed. Thus, although there is evidence that Mbabaṟam has in recent times borrowed from Wagaman, Dyangun, Waruŋu and Dyirbal, none of these languages appear to have borrowed from Mbabaṟam since the time of its phonological changes.

In a one-way situation such as this the language that borrows (but is not borrowed from) is likely to have more and more of its phonologically idiosyncratic words replaced by words from neighbouring languages, that conform to the standard Australian pattern. As it acquires more 'normal' words these will be borrowed by its neighbours to replace tabooed terms. Eventually, we are likely to get a language most of whose vocabulary is phonologically 'normal', but many of whose grammatical forms (being less liable to speedy replacement) will still display the deviant patterning.

10.2.5   Conclusion. We have drawn the following inferences:

[1] The six tribes speaking dialects of Dyirbal go back to a single tribe, speaking a single dialect. The original tribe grew and split into two separate tribal groups; then one or both of the new tribes grew and split again, and so on.

[2] The Dyirbal dialects have been in contiguity with Wargamay for a considerable period.

[3] The Dyirbal dialects have been in contiguity with Yidin for a relatively short period.

[4] The long-vowel rule in Ngadyan must have operated not too long after the Ngadyandyi split off from the main Dyirbal group, and emerged as a tribe in their own right.

[5] The long-vowel rule in Ngadyan must have operated fairly soon after the Dyirbal dialects came into contact with Yidin.

[6] Mbabaṛam was probably at one time contiguous to Yidin-Dyabugay; however, it has not been in contiguity with them since the time of operation of rules [1–3].

[7] Phonological changes in Mbabaṛam and in Ngadyan must have taken place at approximately the same time.

We have also:

[8] The recent discovery (2.4) that the rain forest in the lakes region of the Atherton Tableland (that is, in present-day Ngadyan territory) is only about 7,600 years old. No investigation has been made into the age of the rain forest nearer the coast, from Cairns down to Tully, but it is likely that it is considerably older than the higher, tableland forest. Let us take into consideration two more points:

[9] Each tribe of about 500 individuals needs a territory of a certain size, to provide it with sufficient animal and vegetable food. If one tribe increases in size and splits into two, it must be expanding its tribal territory. And it is likely to be doing this at the expense of some other tribe – that is, it would be pushing some other tribe out of its original territory into some probably less pleasant terrain.

[10] Sweeping linguistic changes frequently accompany cultural or social upheaval. Witness the great changes in Old Irish in the middle of the first millenium (with the coming of Christianity), and those in Algonquian accompanying the arrival of the Algonquians in buffalo

territory and the adoption of the Plains culture (which involved the buffalo as a main source of food). We may hypothesise that in each case the change was due to an estrangement between younger and older generations – without the conservative, dampening influence of older people's speech habits, the language of younger members of a community may change more rapidly and explosively than otherwise. The Mbabaṟam (but not the Ngadyan) changes would certainly be described as sweeping, and are likely to have been tied to some alteration in social circumstances. [The Old Irish and Algonquian examples are from Calvert Watkins – private communication.]

These points suggest the following hypothesis. Proto-Dyirbal was spoken in the southern part of the region at present occupied by the six tribes, contiguous with Wargamay; that is, its speakers lived in the coastal rain forest, to the south of Yidin (but perhaps not contiguous with it). Mbabaṟam was spoken inland from Yidin amongst the sclerophyll vegetation that ten thousand years ago grew on the Atherton Tableland. Gradually, the pattern of vegetation changed, sclerophyll scrub giving way to tropical rain forest. Meanwhile, the forest-dwelling Dyirbal tribe was expanding and splitting; needing more territory, it spread north along the coast (coming into contact with Yidin), and then north-west, into the emerging forest on the tableland. As it spread, it pushed the Mbabaṟam tribe before it, out of the pleasant tableland environment into a small, arid and rather undesirable territory on top of the dividing range. It was at the time of this forced change of habitat that Mbabaṟam words underwent three major phonological changes – stress shift, vowel raising and initial dropping.

Further work – by linguists, biogeographers, and perhaps archaeologists and others – would be needed before the hypothesis could be fully accepted. But note that it does provide explanation of why Mbabaṟam, although occupying country as inhospitable as that of the Waruŋu tribe, has a far smaller territory; and of why the tribes speaking Dyirbal extend further north in the tableland region than they do on the coastal fringe.

Mbabaṟam was probably a smallish tribe, which quickly perished with the invasion of European miners – there is today not a single full-blood Mbabaṟam living. Speakers of Dyirbal, on the other hand, have shown a definite will to survive. Their numbers were greatly reduced from the 1880s on through contraction of European diseases, and murder by settlers. But one group of thirty or so members of the Dyirbalŋan tribe was still living in the dense rain forest around the upper Tully River until twenty-five or thirty years ago, despite the presence of white settlers in the area for more than sixty years. Today, the Dyirbalŋan speak of increasing their numbers until they are strong enough to expel the white man, and can then resume occupation of their own rightful territory.

There is certainly a correlation – although it may well be irrelevant – between the recent aggressiveness and resistance of the Dyirbalŋan and the apparent meekness of the Mbabaṛam tribe, and the hypothesis we have suggested.

The discussion in 10.2.1–5 is largely repeated from Dixon [1970b].

10.3   Internal history of Dyirbal

Most words have either exactly the same form between dialects of Dyirbal, or else a totally different form. There are just a few examples of words similar but not identical; for instance:

[1] with *ṛ* in D and M corresponding to *r* in G:

    DM *bala ḍuḍaṛ*   G *bala ḍuḍar*   'urine'
    DM *bala ḍuḍuṛ*   G *bala ḍuḍur*   'navel'

[2] with *y* in D corresponding to *w* in M:

    D   *bayi yiriɲḍila*   M *bayi wiriɲḍila*   'dragon fly'
    D   *balan yugiyam*   M *balan wugiyam*   'firefly'

[3] with a vowel plus *-y* in one dialect corresponding to *-i* in another:

    DM   *miɲay*   G   *miɲi*   'when'
    M Dyalŋuy *bala ɲuɲaɲuy*   D Dyalŋuy *bala ɲuɲaɲi*   'teeth,
                                                seed, name'

It does not seem possible to draw any general conclusions about phonological change within Dyirbal from such limited examples of difference. It is, however, possible to attempt a measure of internal reconstruction from an examination of grammatical differences, and suchlike.

10.3.1   The origin of noun classes. With the exception of the universal affixes *-ru*, *-bu* and *-bi* (6.7) and emphatics *-ḍan(a)* and *-ban* (6.1.6), nothing can follow the case affix on a noun or adjective. It is significant, however, that in the case of noun markers the indicator of noun class FOLLOWS the case inflection. We can also note that some of the noun marker roots in Dyirbal – *bala, giɲa, gila* – occur in other Australian languages but do not as a rule inflect for case in the other languages, and never carry any information concerning noun classification

(6.5.1, 6.5.3). Wargamay, the language most similar to Dyirbal, has a demonstrative root *yala*, that occurs in locative, allative and ablative inflection but appears not to take ergative/instrumental, dative or genitive case endings. (None of the languages surrounding Dyirbal show noun classification.)

This suggests that Dyirbal may originally have had roots *bala*, *giɲa* etc. with a simple demonstrative-type meaning. That it then generalised the case inflections of nouns to these forms. And, finally, that indicators of noun class were added, at a rather late stage, to the root-plus-case forms. We mentioned in 6.5.1 that the *-la-* from a number of noun and verb marker forms has been dropped, to produce a form that better satisfies the stress preferences of the language (and see 10.3.4, below).

It remains to discover from what source noun class endings came. A full answer cannot at present be provided but we can make a suggestion concerning the ending *-m* for class III, which covers edible fruit and vegetables.

Firstly, note that there are a considerable number of languages in Arnhem Land and the Kimberleys that have noun classes, mostly involving a prefix to the noun and concordial prefixes throughout the sentence. Capell [1956: 41] has tabulated class prefixes for thirteen languages from these regions. Every one of the languages has a prefix referring entirely or almost entirely to vegetable foodstuffs. The prefixes have the following form:

ma-	in 6 languages
m-	in 4 languages
mi-	in 2 languages
mu-	in 1 language

Note the similarity to the class III suffix, *-m*, in Dyirbal.

Secondly, note that many Australian languages tend to include a generic term and a specific term together in an NP. For instance, in Dyabugay (eighty miles to the north of Dyirbal) a typical NP would be *miɲa wawun*, involving both *miɲa* 'animal' and *wawun* 'turkey'. It is significant that Dyirbal does NOT exhibit this behaviour. Now the generic noun for 'vegetable foodstuffs' over a large section of North Australia is *mayi*, or something similar (Dyabugay has *ma:* and Yidin *mayi*).

This suggests the following lines of development. In the Kimberleys and Arnhem Land, a specific name of a type of vegetable food was as a rule preceded by the generic noun *mayi* within an NP; then *mayi* gradually degenerated to become a prefix to the specific terms. The forms of the prefix in twelve of Capell's languages (*ma-*, *mi-* and *m-*) are entirely natural degenerate forms of *mayi*; *mu-* occurs in only one language, and suggests that there has been some sound change in this instance.

In the case of Dyirbal an NP may have typically involved: a form *bala, giɲa, ŋala* etc (in case inflection agreeing with the head noun), followed by a generic term (e.g. *mayi* 'vegetable foodstuff'), followed by the specific name of some particular edible plant. As in the Arnhem Land/Kimberleys area, the generic term gradually took on the status of an affix, but in Dyirbal it became a SUFFIX to the *bala, giɲa* etc. forms.

After *mayi* had been assimilated into the grammar in this way, Dyirbal must have borrowed (or otherwise acquired) its present generic term for non-flesh food, *wuḍu*. Note that the form *mayi* does occur in Dyirbal, as the name for 'English bee' – this must be a very recent borrowing, within the last two hundred years (that is, since the introduction of English bees into the continent). The discussion above is largely repeated from Dixon [1968c]; see also the discussion of the evolution of noun classes in Olgolo in Dixon [1970a].

10.3.2 Verbal and nominal inflections. The discussion in this section, which is largely concerned with inflectional variation between dialects, is restricted to D, G and M.

[1] General genitive inflection *-mi* on nouns and adjectives (3.2.1). The fact that this case affix has a rather limited distribution – it does not occur on noun markers or pronouns – suggests that it is a relatively late development. It was probably introduced into the language after noun markers had taken on their final, class indicator, segment (otherwise, we would expect to encounter noun markers in *-mi* inflection). Note that nominal *-mi* does occur in all dialects, suggesting that it was probably introduced into proto-Dyirbal (language A of tree 1, p. 341).

[2] Perfective relative clause inflection *-mi* (4.11.2). This affix occurs only in M; it is added AFTER the unmarked tense inflection (whereas relative clause *-ŋu* occurs INSTEAD of any tense inflection). This suggests that verbal *-mi* is a very late development, perhaps being introduced into Mamu after Mamu had split off from Dyirbal. (Note that verbal *-mi* does not occur in Gulŋay, for example; but it is in Ngadyan – its presence in both Mamu and Ngadyan could be explained in terms of diffusion, in either direction.) The introduction of verbal *-mi* appears

to involve generalisation from nominal *-mi*, on the analogy of nominal and verbal *-ŋu*.

[3] Verbal ending *-ga* (4.13.2). This occurs only in M. *-ga* is added after the unmarked tense inflection, but (unlike *-mi*) a vowel, *-u*, is added between an *-l* conjugation tense form ending in *-n*, and *-ga*. We thus have:

unmarked tense form	*-mi* form	*-ga* form
balgan	*balganmi*	*balganuga*
wayɲḍin	*wayɲḍinmi*	*wayɲḍinuga*
ɲinaɲu	*ɲinaɲumi*	*ɲinaɲuga*

It is important to enquire why the inserted vowel should be *-u-*. In many Australian languages a vowel that is inserted – for phonological felicity – is usually in some sort of 'harmony' with the previous vowel in the word [Hale, mimeo-c]. Exactly this happens in Dyirbal in the case of loan words, when the English item ends in a stop – the rule was stated in 9.3.1. The fact that *-u-* is included before *-ga*, whatever the last vowel in the verb stem is, suggests that the unmarked tense form, at the time that *-ga* was introduced, was *-nu* in the case of the *-l* conjugation. That is, we originally had *balganu* and *wayɲḍinu*, with the *-u* being dropped in a recent phonological change.

The only other instance of a vowel intruding between a consonant and a suffix involves the universal affix *-ru*, when following *bawal*; certainly in this case the inserted vowel is identical to the previous vowel – *bawalaru*.

We are led to the position that, at some time in its history, Dyirbal formed the unmarked, non-future tense by:

[a] in the case of an *-l* stem, replacing stem-final *-l* by *-nu*, and

[b] in the case of a *-y* stem, replacing stem-final *-y* by *-ɲu*.

This could be formulated as a single rule, in terms of the phonological features discussed in chapter 7. We can say that the unmarked tense inflection involves a consonantal segment, specified only for the feature [Nas], and vowel segment *-u*. And that a new segment is formed from the localisation choice of the stem-final segment, and the manner choice of the affix-initial segment. That is:

$$- \begin{bmatrix} y \\ x \end{bmatrix} \begin{bmatrix} \text{Nas} \end{bmatrix} u \rightarrow - \begin{bmatrix} \text{Nas} \\ x \end{bmatrix} u$$

$$\underbrace{}_{\text{stem}} \underbrace{}_{\substack{\text{tense} \\ \text{affix}}}$$

where y ranges over the manner system, and x over the localisation system.

The naturalness of this rule lends some plausibility to our suggestion. However, we still have to explain why the final *-u* should later be dropped from *-nu*, but not from *-ɲu* forms. There is a straightforward reason – the future tense inflection is *-ɲ* on all stems; thus if non-future *ɲinaɲu* were to lose its final segment, it would be indistinguishable from future *ɲinaɲ* (in contrast, *balganu* became *balgan*, which still contrasted with the future form *balgaɲ*).

[4] Future tense inflection in D and M involves the replacement of stem-final *-y* or *-l* by *-ɲ*. In G, on the other hand, future inflection involves:

    [a] the addition of *-ḍay* to an *-l* stem,

    [b] the addition of *-nḍay*, and loss of stem-final *-y*, in the case of a *-y* stem (3.4.3).

It is possible that the longer G form is more archaic, and that the DM form has developed out of this. Note that if the final *-ay* were elided from *ɲinanḍay*, *balgalḍay*, we would get forms ending in *ḍ*. Now words in Dyirbal cannot terminate in a stop, and it would be perfectly natural to change *-ḍ* to *-ɲ*. The *-l* or *-n* before this final *-ɲ* would have to drop, since no word can end in a consonant cluster.

This suggestion is highly speculative. However, slight support is provided by the name *guguwuɲ*, for a bird whose call was said to be *guguwuḍ* – here *ɲ* is substituted for word-final *ḍ* (9.4).

A similar hypothesis can be put forward for the negative imperative alternation (4.12.2). The inflection is *-m* in D and M, with loss of stem-final *-l* or *-y*. In G it is *-mu*, with loss of stem-final *-y* but retention of *-l*. We can suggest that the G form is nearer to the inflection in proto-Dyirbal, and that D and M have dropped the final *-u* (and then necessarily lost *-l* before *-m* to avoid a final consonant cluster).

We thus have the following likely changes:

    [a] roots such as *bala* and *giɲa* take case inflections (this applies to all Dyirbal dialects),

    [b] noun class indicators are added after these inflections (again, in all dialects),

    [c] the appearance of general genitive case inflection *-mi* (all dialects),

    [d] future tense inflection *-ḍay* reduced to *-ɲ* (D and M only)

    [e] appearance of verbal inflection *-ga* (M only),

[f] non-future tense inflection on -*l* stems loses its final vowel (this change has taken place in all dialects),

[g] the -*mi* inflection is generalised to verbs (M only).

The discussion above has indicated certain orderings between these changes: [b] must follow [a]; [c] must follow [b]; [f] must follow [e]; [f] must follow [d] (or there would be no bar to the loss of final vowel from the unmarked tense inflection on -*y* stems); [g] must follow [f]; and [g] must follow [c].

We can, rather speculatively, relate the changes to different 'stages' in tree 1, p. 341.

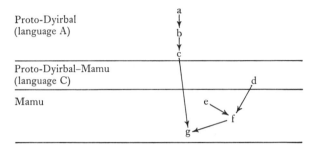

The fact that change [f] has applied in all dialects would have to be dealt with in terms of diffusion. We can date [f] after [e], and [e] appears to have taken place after the Dyirbal/Mamu split. However [f] could have originated in any of the dialects (not necessarily Mamu) and then spread to the others.

It appears from the above discussion that G is more conservative than either D or M. This would be expected in terms of the conclusion in 10.2.5 – G probably occupies the original tribal territory, and is in contact with Wargamay, the Dyirbal group's longest-known neighbour. It has thus been exposed to much less influence from other languages than the more northerly dialects.

G has not, however, remained static. Consider the addition of a locative inflection to a noun marker – *yagulga, giɲanga* – mentioned in 6.5.3; this is an innovation unique to Giramay (and it plainly post-dates change [b]).

We suggested change [a] on the evidence of other languages, which appear not to inflect *bala, giɲa* etc. forms. The change may have taken place in some ancestor language of Dyirbal, or it may have been as late as proto-Dyirbal (remembering that *yala* in Wargamay does not take the syntactic cases). Change [b] can confidently be assigned to proto-Dyirbal. Change [c] may belong in the same period, or it may have been somewhat later (after the original tribe had split) and then have diffused into all dialects.

All the remarks of this section are highly tentative, and subject to revision when more is known of dialectal differences within the Dyirbal language, and within neighbouring languages.

10.3.3 Pronominal cases. One of the most important grammatical differences between dialects concerns the singular pronouns. G has forms *ŋayba*, *ŋinba* for intransitive subject function, and *ŋaḍa*, *ŋinda* for transitive subject; D and M use *ŋaḍa* and *ŋinda* in both functions.

Gabi, in southern Queensland, and Gumbaiŋgar, in north New South Wales, both have different forms for the three functions S, A and O, for at least some pronouns – 1.5. (No grammatical information has been recorded for any other language between Wargamay and Gumbaiŋgar.) All languages to the north of Dyirbal appear to have a single pronominal form for both S and A function. It thus appears that the G dialect is the northernmost member of a considerable span of languages that distinguish pronominal S and A, and that D is the most southerly member of a northern chain that do not.

There are two possibilities: EITHER proto-Dyirbal had a pronominal system similar to that of G, and its northern dialects have lost the distinction between S and A forms of singular pronouns; OR proto-Dyirbal had pronouns along the lines of present-day D and M, and G has 'borrowed' the S/A distinction from Wargamay. (Note that G pronouns exactly follow those in Wargamay, even to the extent of having *ŋaɲa* where D and M have *ŋayguna* etc.)

It is difficult to find any evidence in favour of one or other of these alternatives. It might be that the fact of pronouns in Dyirbal behaving syntactically in so strictly a nominative-ergative manner (5.2.2) indicates that the first possibility is the more likely. But detailed descriptions of the underlying syntax of other languages, both with and without an S/A distinction in pronouns, would have to become available before this type of evidence could be satisfactorily evaluated.

Other grammatical points that can be interpreted to yield indications concerning the history of Dyirbal include [1] the reflexive alternant, *-mariy*, used with *-y* stems – see 4.9.3; and [2] the occurrence of *waɲa* in G corresponding to *miɲa* 'what' in D and M – 5.8.4. See also the discussion of *-ru ~ -ndu* in 7.7.

10.3.4 Syllable reduction. It was mentioned in 7.2.2 that Dyirbal 'prefers' just one (or at any rate, as few as possible) unstressed syllables between each two stressed syllables. It appears that the language tends, over a period of time, to reduce the number of syllables in a word more nearly to meet this requirement.

For instance, there are a number of forms in free variation in the modern languages:

> *máymiy ∼ máyimiy* '(to) visit in order to be given food or drink'
> *ḍúymal ∼ ḍúyimal* 'crawl under something'
> *ɲúbalḍína ∼ ɲúbalaḍína* second person dual accusative pronoun

It appears that in each case the shorter form is in the process of replacing the longer one. That is, an unstressed vowel is elided and a new consonant cluster formed, the new form of the word having one syllable less than the original form. (Note also the discussion of the elision of a complete syllable, *-la-*, from the forms of a number of noun and verb markers – 6.5.1.)

The long vowel rule in Ngadyan can provide evidence supporting doubtful cognates, besides demonstrating the process of syllable reduction. For instance, 'tongue' is *ḍalaɲ* in Wargamay, Nyawigi and Waruŋu, and in many other Australian languages. In Dyirbal, Mamu and Giramay 'tongue' is *ḍalŋgulay*. However, in Ngadyan it is *ḍalŋgula:*, with the long vowel rule having applied to the final *-y* but not to the first *-l-*. This suggests that *ḍalŋgulay* is the reduced form of a compound of *ḍalaɲ* with some form *gulay*. At the time of the long vowel rule the form was still *ḍalaɲgulay* in all four dialects (and became *ḍalaɲgula:* in Ngadyan), but since then the second vowel has been deleted and the *ɲ* assimilated to the following *g* (*ɲg* is an allowable cluster at a morpheme boundary but not within a morpheme).

This type of change may explain the fact that whereas clusters of three consonants are rare or non-existent in many Australian languages, they are rather common in Dyirbal (and in other languages of the region). Truncation could presumably only take place when an allowable consonant cluster would result (although there may have been processes of lenition at work – see the comments on *ḍ > ɲ* in 9.4, 10.3.2).

Almost all the most frequent roots in Dyirbal are disyllabic. A notable exception is *banagay* 'return home'. However this form only occurs in D and G, the M correspondent being disyllabic *ɲuṛbay*. There are two possibilities – either the form in proto-Dyirbal was *banagay*, and has been replaced in M; or else the original form was *ɳuɽbay*, and has been replaced in both D and G. Now the verb root 'return home' in Wargamay is disyllabic *bana*. At first sight it may be difficult to conceive how *bana* could be borrowed as *banagay*. But note that an imperative is formed from a verb stem in Dyirbal by deleting the final consonant of the stem. In Wargamay (at least for the *-y* conjugation, to which *bana* belongs) imperatives involve the addition of *-ga*. Thus, the imperative 'go home' is *banaga* in each language. And it does seem likely, on a priori grounds, that a verb should be borrowed in its imperative form.

All roots in Dyirbal must contain at least two syllables. It is unlikely that this requirement was applied quite as rigidly in proto-Australian. Thus, there is evidence suggesting that the original root '(to) give' was simply *wu-*; the form is *wuga-* in Dyirbal, and the *-ga-* may possibly relate to the imperative affix *-ga*, that occurs in perhaps the majority of Australian languages (though not in Dyirbal) – 1.7. Compare with the adjective *wugiḍa* 'generous' in Dyirbal (and the verb root *wugi-* 'give' in Wargamay).

Appendix A   Dyirbal logic

As part of what appears to be a continuing campaign to denigrate Australian languages (thereby demonstrating the supposed lack of intellect of their speakers) it has been pointed out that 'logical connectors' – 'or', 'because', 'if', and so on – are frequently lacking. Love [1938: 119] remarked of Worora, 'Alternative propositions do not occur. The Worora man does not say, Shall I do this or that? He says, Shall I do this? No. I shall do that. If asked in English, Will you have this or that? he will invariably reply, Yes, desiring both.'

Dyirbal does not have any particles exactly corresponding to English 'or', 'if' or 'because' (any more than English has words corresponding to Dyirbal *mugu*, *biri* or *wara*). The language is, however, quite as capable as English of expressing conditions, alternatives and implications. Amongst the syntactic means employed are:

[1] ENTAILMENT

The major construction here is that involving an implicated VC, in purposive construction – examples were given in 4.4.3, 5.3.3–4. An implicated VC refers to an action (action$_1$) that is the 'consequence' of the action (action$_2$) referred to by the preceding NP. There are two possibilities: (a) action$_1$ was done deliberately, just so that action$_2$ should be possible – e.g. run to a tree to climb it, hit someone to kill them; (b) action$_2$ is the unavoidable (but unplanned) consequence of action$_1$ – e.g. person$_1$ goes to a place and as a result encounters person$_2$ who (unknown to person$_1$) had settled at the place (see text xxv, line 40, p. 391). Type (a) appears, from an examination of Dyirbal texts, to be many times more common than type (b). It will be seen that implicated VCs in Dyirbal cover a wide spectrum of 'entailment'; there is no single connective or construction in English covering exactly the same ground.

Certain types of English construction, involving 'since' or 'because', would be translated by a Dyirbal sentence involving the particle *ŋuri* 'in turn'. Thus 'I punched him because he had kicked me' might be rendered:

(685) *ŋayguna baŋgul ḍilwan/ŋuri ŋaḍa bayi biḍin*

[2] 'IF'

An English sentence of the form 'if X, then Y' where X and Y have a common NP, would in most cases be rendered by a Dyirbal construction involving Y as main clause with FUTURE TENSE INFLECTION, with X being relative clause to the common NP in Y. Thus:

(686) *ŋama   bala   ŋinda ɲimaɲu*
     trigger-NOM THERE-NOM-IV you-SA squeeze-REL-NOM
     minbayiriɲ
     shoot-REFL-FUTURE
     If you squeeze the trigger [of a gun], [the gun] will go off
(687) *bayi yaṟa ṟudu balgaɲu/ guyibiɲ*   If a man is hit in the hollow in the back of his neck, he will die

The Dyirbal verbal inflection *-bila ~ -ba* (4.13.1) has some overlap of meaning with English 'if'. *-bila ~ -ba* typically occurs following a negative imperative:

(688) *galga bala ŋama ŋinda ɲimam/ minbayirimbila*   Don't you squeeze the trigger, lest [the gun] go off!

However, *-bila ~ -ba* can also be used in place of future tense in a sentence similar to (686–7). Note that *-bila ~ -ba* can only be employed if the 'consequence' is in some way unpleasant:

(689) *ŋinda   ŋaygu bulgugu   wadilɲaɲu   /ŋaḍa ŋinuna*
     you-SA I-GEN wife-DAT swive-ŋay-REL-NOM I-SA you-O
     maŋa   gunbalbila
     ear-NOM cut-*bila*
     If you swive my wife, I'll cut off your ears

Some English sentences involving 'if' are rendered by a purposive construction in Dyirbal – these involve a first clause describing an action deliberately undertaken by a human agent, in order that the action referred to by the second clause should come about:

(690) *ŋayguna ŋinda yanama/ dawungu/ ŋaḍa ŋinuna maniŋgu wugali*
     If you take me to town I'll give you some money

Something like (689) could be cast into the same type of construction:

(691) *ŋinda ŋaygu bulgu wadi(n)/ŋaḍa ŋinuna maŋa gunbali*

but would then have the nonsensical implication that 'you' deliberately intend to continue swiving 'my wife' so that you can get your ears cut off!

In a recording of everyday conversation, one speaker jokingly said to another (text reference XIX: 12):

(692) *wiyamaŋu   ɲinaymaŋu   yaŋun   daman*
     do what-REL-NOM marry-REL-NOM THIS-POSS-II child-NOM
     ŋaḍa yanumaɲ
     I-SA go-COMIT-FUTURE
     If I were married to her son, I'd take him away

The use of the interrogative verb (literally 'what would I do if I were...') is paralleled by the English construction 'were I married to her son, I'd take him away'. (692) does not appear to be typical of 'if' constructions in Dyirbal; certainly, none of the sentences the writer composed along the lines of (692) were liked by speakers – in every case a construction of type (686–7), or (689) or (690), was preferred.

[3] 'OR'

There are two kinds of statements of alternatives. Closed disjunction – X or Y or Z – insists that the listed alternatives exhaustively cover all possibilities. Open disjunction – X or Y or Z or... – can suggest that X, Y and Z are the most likely alternatives, but that there MIGHT be some unanticipated further alternatives. Some languages can show both kinds of disjunction (thus Chinese has different particles 'or' variously representing open and closed disjunction and also depending on the syntactic environment – I am grateful to M. A. K. Halliday for this information). English 'or' refers only to closed disjunction. Dyirbal, on the other hand, deals mainly with open disjunction, through the particle *yamba* 'perhaps, might be'. Thus the only way in which Dyirbal can translate 'I saw a fish, it was either a barramundi or a red bream' is through:

(693) *ŋaḍa guya buṛan/ gilabayḍi miɲa/ yuguṛ yamba/ yaŋgal yamba/*
     I saw a fish, what was it down there? – it might have been a barramundi, or it might have been a red bream

That is, the Dyirbal sentence leaves open the possibility that it was some other type of fish. (Although Dyirbal could add a rider stating that it could not have been anything else, i.e. closing the disjunction, just as English can create an open disjunction by including 'or something else'.)

It can be argued that 'closed disjunction' is a philosophical idealisation – in the real world it is seldom possible to exclude some further alternative, however much of a statistical longshot it might be. And that it is only in terms of this rather unrealistic idealisation that some logical paradoxes can be formulated (on this see Reichmann 1964: 120–1).

It is interesting to note the ways in which speakers of different dialects of English get around the limited possibilities of 'closed disjunction'. Thus in reply to a question 'when will he come?' a speaker of British English might reply 'probably at 10 or 11', with the 'probably' serving to leave open other alternatives. In American English a reply could be 'might be 10, might be 11'; this would be unacceptable in Standard British English, but is exactly paralleled by the construction in Dyirbal.

Other logical notions have straightforward expression in Dyirbal. Thus, 'all' is rendered by nominal affix *-mumbay* (6.1.1) or else by the adverbal *ḏayŋul* 'do all, finish' with object orientation (8.3):

(694) *giɲanḏana ḏugumbilmumbay*   all the people here are women
(695) *ŋaygu damandaman daligu mabin ḏayŋuyiriɲu*   all my sons have gone (crossed the river) to Tully

Appendix B   Previous work on Dyirbal

Previous work on the dialects of Dyirbal can be grouped into three categories. Firstly, work by amateurs who had no linguistic training and no understanding of or feel for the language. The earliest attempt was that of William Carron, botanist with the Kennedy expedition, on 26 May 1848. The three words given by Carron were probably taken from speakers of Giramay; they are [Carron, 1849: 9]:

'hammoo', fresh water (probably *gamu*)
'taa-taa' dog (probably G *guda*, possibly Wargamay *bada*)
'mocull' salt water (the original is unrecognisable)

The next publications were an eighty-word 'Vocabulary of the Kirrami tribe' by A. Douglas Douglas [1900] – mistakenly attributed to A. C. MacDougall in Craig [1967] – and a two-hundred-word 'Vocabulary of the Kiramai language' by the Rev. J. Mathew [1926]. Allowing maximum leeway for different possibilities of orthographic representation, only 20% of Douglas's words are correctly transcribed. John Mathew grew up as a speaker of Gabi and wrote a useful account of that language; he must, however, have had the most glancing of acquaintanceships with Giramay, and his transcription is less than successful, especially as regards vowels. More recently, Sydney May [1954] produced a list of 117 Mamu words; not only are these badly transcribed, but May attempts to hear a distinction in Mamu where there is none, to correspond to every contrast in English. He has *tipan* 'rock' but *tipun* 'stone' (both are *diban*), and *pookabin* 'dead' as against *porkarbin* 'to die (v)' (*bugabin* must have been meant, in each case).

Vocabularies such as the above could only have any value if they were the sole documentation of a language now dead. As it is, they have no claim to further consideration or listing. Much the same applies to the work of Aguas [1966] and Worms [Nekes and Worms, 1953]. Aguas was sponsored by the Australian Institute of Aboriginal Studies but her transcription of Dyiru words and sentences shows many inaccuracies. Father Worms had a considerable reputation in Australia as a linguist but his work on Dyirbal and surrounding dialects can only be described as wretched. He gives word lists in several dialects and a short 'Djirbal text'; this is actually in Mamu, with one Dyirbal word. Almost every word is mistranscribed: *gambil* is written *yambil*, *yumal* as *ŋumal* and both *baŋgul* and *baɲul* as *baɲul*. Verb form *bayiriɲu* (quoted as *baii riɲu*) 'turn oneself around' is split into two halves, *baii* (verbal root 'turn, twist, wring') being wrongly identified as the noun marker *bayi* 'he', and *riɲu* (reflexive affix plus unmarked tense inflection) is glossed 'turned'. Worms also mentions [1953: 67] 'analogies founded on the similarity of shape' and gives as example Dyirbal *bigun* which he says can mean 'shield' or 'fingernail', the language exploiting a similarity of convex form between the two objects. In fact *biguɲ* is 'fingernail' and *bigin* 'shield'; speakers of Dyirbal do not appear to observe any connection between the two objects. Worms' transcriptions are so bad, and his knowledge of the basic principles of descriptive and comparative linguistics so slight, that none of his inferences can be trusted. In particular, the cognate sets he recognises between languages in different parts of the continent are almost entirely spurious.

Banfield [1908, 1911, 1918, 1925] mentions a fair number of aboriginal habits and so on, sometimes attempting a transcription of a relevant word. Gladys Henry's [1967] collection of a score or so Dyirbal myths is the most ambitious amateur anthropological project from the area, and achieves a measure of success. The stories were taken down in English and are often only snatches of a longer tale, but a good deal of useful information has been recorded. The most interesting feature of her book is a map of the Tully and Murray Rivers, with aboriginal names for every bend and hillock. It is all the more disappointing that the transcription is so poor.

The second category includes the work of W. E. Roth. Employed first as a surgeon in the Gulf country Roth soon wrote a description of Pittapitta [1897] – this contained a good grammatical sketch but was phonetically poor. After his appointment as Northern Protector of Aborigines, based at Cooktown, Roth made several studies of sections of the six tribes speaking Dyirbal. In 1898 he wrote ethnological notes on three tribes encountered in the Atherton area – Chirpal-jĭ (Dyirbaldyi), Ngachan-jĭ (Ngadyandyi) and Ngikoongo-ĭ (this has not yet been identified). He recorded about two hundred words in each dialect – these were transcribed laboriously (with much use of diacritics) but on the whole accurately. He appears to have rewritten the three lists about 1900, simplifying and improving the transcription – thus diacritics are omitted, *-oo-* changed to *-u-*, and so on. Roth also secured a word list from a different group of Dyirbaldyi, at Herberton, in October 1900.

Roth's most important work in the Dyirbal area was the preparation, in September 1900, of a 104-page 'Scientific Report on the Natives of the Lower Tully River'; a 22-page appendix was added in December of that year, following a further visit to the Tully. Roth includes a great deal of important information on the Malanbara tribe's organisation, habits, songs, food, etc.; a considerable number of Gulŋay words and phrases are included, on the whole fairly accurately transcribed. This study, and the Atherton vocabularies and notes, remain unpublished [uncatalogued manuscript 216, Mitchell Library, Sydney], but some important extracts did appear in various of the *North Queensland Ethnography* bulletins [Roth, 1901–10].

All the indications are that Roth made a genuine attempt to assist the aborigines of North Queensland during his years as protector – for instance, he insisted that settlers who used aboriginal labour should pay regular wages. Roth took action against Lachlan (2.6) for 'associating with a native woman' and Lachlan was so incensed that, late in 1902, he filed a complaint against Roth with the Legislative Assembly in Brisbane. This appears to have been the beginning of a campaign to oust the protector. The month of Lachlan's complaint, Mr John Hamilton, the member for Cook, obtained by a subterfuge a photograph Roth had taken for 'ethnographic purposes' and circulated it in an attempt to discredit him. In 1905 a petition – whose signatories included Lachlan – was drawn up against Roth's reappointment; it was dismissed by parliament. But, with the controversy still continuing, Roth resigned on 10 June 1906, and went to British Guiana.

The attitude of the Queensland government towards aborigines gradually hardened in the years following Roth's departure. In 1914 aborigines from the Tully River area were taken, some in chains, to a settlement at Hull River; when that was destroyed by the 1918 cyclone they were removed to Palm Island. It is also worth noting that, in the fifty years after Roth, there was – in the whole of Queensland – just one piece of professional or semi-professional linguistic research undertaken: that of McConnel [1945 etc.].

Thirdly, a number of professional linguists – including Hale and West [Craig, 1967], and Wurm – have in the last decade or so done some work on dialects of Dyirbal. In each case only a few words have been gathered, all of which remain unpublished. N. B. Tindale has been working on the Cairns rain forest area on and off since the late thirties, and has gathered some incidental linguistic material (none of which has been published).

Texts

About forty texts in D, G and M have been obtained by the writer; four are in Dyalŋuy and the remainder in Guwal. They include myths, stories of recent events (the last cannibalism, an outrage by Lachlan – 2.6), and everyday conversations (semi-secretly recorded). The three texts given below have been chosen largely because they illustrate a wide range of grammatical features. Tapes of these texts, and both tapes and transcriptions of other texts mentioned above, have been deposited with the Australian Institute of Aboriginal Studies, P.O. Box 553, Canberra City, 2601, Australia.

Text XV

A myth told in Mamu; it concerns *ŋagaŋunu*, the 'first man', and explains where the first baby came from and how women gained their sexual organs.

1. *bayi*   *balaŋumguya*   *guliɲŋunu/ ŋagaŋunu*
   THERE-NOM-I THERE-ABL-ACROSS SEA east-ABL   'name'-NOM
   baniɲu   */banagu*   *bandalŋaɲu*   */*
   come-PRES/PAST water-DAT follow-ŋay-PRES/PAST
   gambilgubin   *wayɲdin*
   forest-ALL-INTR VBLSR-PRES/PAST motion uphill-PRES/PAST
   yalugalu   */balaydawu*
   HERE-ALL(PLACE)-UP THERE-LOC-UP-RIVER-LONG WAY
   duŋanbaraga   *ɲinayaraygu*   */*
   'place name'-LOC stay-START-PURP
   ŋagaŋunu ['the first man'] came from somewhere on the other side of the sea, from the east; and followed the fresh water [the Herbert River]; he went uphill right up here to the forest country; to settle there up river at [the place called] duŋanbara.

Each 'line' of each text is a complete topic chain; here the chain involves four sentences, whose VCs are [a] *baniɲu*, [b] *bandalŋaɲu*; [c] *gambilgubin wayɲdin*; and [d] *ɲinayaraygu*. Note that the fourth sentence – with VC in purposive inflection – is dominated by the Σ node of the third. The topic NP, *bayi ŋagaŋunu*, is stated once only, and its words are separated by *balaŋumguya guliɲɲunu*. *-guya*, which normally means 'across the river' here implies 'across the [Coral] sea' i.e. from the Barrier Reef or beyond. The long form of the ablative verb marker, *balaŋum*, indicates an indefinacy of origin.

2. *balay   baŋgul   miḍa   gadan*   /
   THERE-LOC THERE-ERG-I camp-NOM build-PRES/PAST
   He built a camp (i.e. a mia-mia) there.

3. *burubayḍu bayi   ŋaga   baganmi*   /
   boil-ERG   THERE-NOM-I leg-NOM pierce-PERF REL-NOM
   A boil had formed on his leg (literally: a boil had pierced his leg).

The topic NP shows inalienable possession, between *bayi* [*ŋagaŋunu*] and *bala ŋaga* – 'ŋagaŋunu's leg'.

4. *aɲḍa   baŋgul   burubay   ḍulman*   /*bayi*
   PARTICLE THERE-ERG-I boil-NOM squeeze-PRES/PAST THERE-NOM-I
   ɲalŋga   mayiyaraygu   /*bayi*   *ŋagaŋunu*   /
   child-NOM come out-BEGIN-PURP THERE-NOM-I 'name'-NOM
   baŋgul   ŋagaŋunugu/*yululumban   bayi   ɲalŋga*
   THERE-ERG-I 'name'-ERG rock-PRES/PAST THERE-NOM-I child-NOM
   baŋgul   /
   THERE-ERG-I
   The boil was squeezed by him, with the result that a male child came out; he [who came out] was [called] ŋagaŋunu; [and] he [who had squeezed it] was [called] ŋagaŋunu; [then] the child was rocked (i.e. nursed and sung to sleep) by him [i.e. the father].

The purposive inflection of the second VC suggests that *bayi burubay* 'the boil' and *bayi ɲalŋga* 'the child' should be regarded as different realisations of a single topic NP. Both father and son are called ŋagaŋunu (literally 'out of leg') and this is stated quite simply by having *bayi ŋagaŋunu*, agreeing in case with the topic NP, and then *baŋgul ŋagaŋunugu*, agreeing in case with the actor NP in the first, *ḍulman*, sentence. *aɲḍa* here 'introduces' a new topic.

5. *aɲḍa   bayi   yanu*   /*yuɽigu*   /*bargaŋgu*
   PARTICLE THERE-NOM-I go-PRES/PAST kangaroo-DAT wallaby-DAT
   ḍurganaygu   /*baŋum   bayi   ŋuɽbaɲu*   /
   spear-ɲay-PURP THERE-ABL THERE-NOM-I return-PRES/PAST
   yuɽiŋgu   ɽulguŋgu   wugalŋaygu   /*bagul   ɲalŋgagu* /
   kangaroo-INST heart-INST give-ɲay-PURP THERE-DAT-I child-DAT
   [Then] he [the father] went out to spear kangaroo and wallaby; then he returned home to give a kangaroo's heart to the child.

This topic chain consists of two favourite constructions; the topic NP is realised as *bayi* twice. However, *aɲḍa* before the first *bayi* indicates that there is change of topic (i.e. the topic is now 'the father'; in the previous line it had been 'the child'). *baŋum* 'from there' here has reference to time, rather than location. 'That which is given' – *yuɹi ɹulgu*, with a relation of inalienable possession – is in instrumental inflection (this is the first of the three kinds of 'giving' construction discussed in 8.2.3).

6. *ɹulgu   baŋgul   guɲḍan*   /
   heart-NOM THERE-ERG-I drink-PRES/PAST
   He [the baby] sucked [the blood from] the heart.

7. *maɲḍaybin   /yuban   gayuŋga/*
   full-INTR VBLSR-PRES/PAST put-PRES/PAST cradle-LOC
   [The child] became full; and was put in a cradle.

No topic NP is stated in this chain. However, *maɲḍay* is an adjective used only to describe satisfaction gained from drinking or eating, and it is clearly the child who becomes satiated, and is placed in a bark cradle his father has made for him.

8. *baraymbaray bayi   yanuga/ḍurganaygu   yuɹigu*   /
   next morning THERE-NOM-I go-*ga*   spear-*ŋay*-PURP kangaroo-DAT
   bargangu   /ɲuɹbaɲu   /
   wallaby-DAT return-PRES/PAST
   The next morning he [the man] went out to spear kangaroo and wallaby; [and] returned.

Verbal inflection -*ga* indicates that something is definitely done, and that there can be no going back (4.13.2). In the present instance it may imply that EVERY morning, the man went right away from the camp.

9. *ɹulguŋgu   bayi   wugayaranḍaɲu   ɲalŋga*   /
   heart-INST THERE-NOM-I give-HABITUALLY-PRES/PAST child-NOM
   guɲḍalɲaygu / garḍa   aɲḍa   /
   drink-*ŋay*-PURP alright-NOM PARTICLE
   He [the child] was always given a heart to drink; then he felt alright.

The inclusion of *aɲḍa* after the adjective *garḍa* indicates that the child felt alright after his daily drink of blood from the heart of a kangaroo, whereas he had not felt alright before (that is, he had been hungry).

10. *aɲḍa   ban   yibiḍaran   / baligayul*
    PARTICLE THERE-NOM-II woman-DUAL THERE-ALL(DIRN)-SAME
    banḍalɲaɲu   marin   /
    follow-*ŋay*-PRES/PAST follow-PRES/PAST
    Two women followed [the river] in the same direction.

Initial *aṇḍa* shows a change of topic. The VC involves transitive *baṇḍal* 'follow', in *-ŋay* form, and also intransitive *maril* 'follow'.

11. *bayi* *wabugayuṟa* *waymbaɲu* /
THERE-NOM-I scrub-SAME-LOC go walkabout-PRES/PAST
He [the man] went out into the same scrub [i.e. he went spearing kangaroos in the scrub he visited every day].

12. *balagara* *ḍurmangu buṟalŋaɲu* /
two people-NOM track-DAT see-ŋay-PRES/PAST
The two [women] saw the [man's] track [i.e. the path worn by his constant travel to and from the scrub].

13. *waɲuŋu giɲa* *miḍa* /
who-POSS DEM-NOM-IV camp-NOM
'Whose camp is this?' [one woman said].

14. *gaḍi* *ŋali* *wayɲḍi* *buṟalŋaygu* /
PARTICLE we two-SA motion uphill-IMP look-ŋay-PURP
'Come on, let's go up to have a look!' [the other replied].

15. *balagara* *wayɲḍin* / *miḍagu*
two people-NOM motion uphill-PRES/PAST camp-DAT
duyginaygu /
look inside-ŋay-PURP
The two of them went uphill, to look inside the mia-mia.

16. *yaludayimban*
HERE-ALL(PLACE)-UP-HILL-SHORT WAY-TR VBLSR-PRES/PAST
buṟan *gayuŋga* *bayi* *ɲalŋga*
look-PRES/PAST cradle-LOC THERE-NOM-I child-NOM
wandaɲu / *bubin* *baŋgugaragu* /
hang up-REL-NOM take off-PRES/PAST two people-ERG
Looking up, [they] saw a baby hanging there in a cradle; the two of them took [the baby and cradle] down.

bayi ɲalŋga is topic NP for this chain, which consists of two coordinated sentences, the first with VC *yaludayimban buṟan*, and the second with VC *bubin*. *wandaɲu* is the VC of a relative clause to the topic NP in the first sentence.

17. *ɲalŋga* / *gaḍi* *wuga* *ŋaḍa gulŋgan* /
child-NOM PARTICLE give-IMP I-SA breastfeed-PRES/PAST
'A baby! Go on, give [him to me]; I'll breastfeed [him]' [the smaller woman said].

Texts

18. *baŋgun*   *gulŋgan*   / *ŋamundu* /
   THERE-ERG-II breastfeed-PRES/PAST breast-INST
   She [the smaller woman] fed [the child] with her breast.

ŋamun can mean 'breast' or 'breastmilk'.

19. *bulgandu baŋgun*   /
   big-ERG   THERE-ERG-II
   [Then] the big[ger woman asked the smaller one]:

This sentence consists just of an NP in ergative inflection. Since it precedes direct speech, a transitive verb of saying ('tell' or 'ask') is to be understood.

20. *ŋaygu-nay ŋuri*   *wuga*   *ŋaḏa wugali*   *ŋamundu* /
   I-GEN-?   PARTICLE give-IMP I-SA give-PURP breast-INST
   'Give me [the child] for my turn, so that I can give [him] my breast!'

The two sentences involved in this topic-chain appear to be:

   [1] [*bayi ɲalŋga*] *ŋaygu* [*ŋinda*] *ŋuri wuga*
   [2] [*bayi ɲalŋga*] *ŋaḏa wugali ŋamundu*

That is, the first is a giving construction of type [iii] in 8.2.3 – where the 'thing given' is in nominative inflection and the 'recipient' in genitive case; the second sentence is of type [i], with the 'thing given' in instrumental inflection, and the 'recipient' in nominative. Thus the topic NP *bayi ɲalŋga* (which is not stated anywhere in the chain) is 'that which is given' for the first sentence, and 'recipient' for the second. The writer is unsure of the function or meaning of the affix *-nay*.

21. *ŋuri*   *baŋgun*   *bulgandu wugan*   /
   PARTICLE THERE-ERG-II big-ERG give-PRES/PAST
   The big[ger woman] gave [the child milk] for her turn.

22. *buṟan*   *guyamban*   *bayi*
   see-PRES/PAST across river-TR VBLSR-PRES/PAST THERE-NOM-I
   ŋuṟbaŋu   /
   return-REL-NOM
   He [the father] was seen [by the two women] across the river, returning home.

23. *ɲalŋga*   *ŋuṟbayarayman*   *balay*   *gayuŋga*
   child-NOM return-START-COMIT-PRES/PAST THERE-LOC cradle-LOC
   gundan   /
   put in-PRES/PAST
   [They] returned [to the mia-mia] with the baby; and put [him back] in the cradle there.

24. *giyiɲaŋgadayi*   *ŋali*   *buybarigu*   /
DEM-NOM-I-*ɲa*-LOC-UP-HILL-SHORT WAY we two-SA hide-REFL-PURP
'We must [do something to] hide ourselves from him.'

Here (as in lines 36 and 38, below) locative has a 'fear' meaning.

25. *balagara*   *ḏiŋgaliɲu*   / *yulgaraga*   *yuguŋga biligu*   /
two people-NOM run-PRES/PAST leaning-LOC tree-LOC climb-PURP
ban   *balagara*   *dira*   / *murgan*   / *ḏarga*   /
THERE-NOM-II two people-NOM name-NOM 'name'-NOM 'name'-NOM
balaragara   *dira*   /
two people-NOM name-NOM
The two of them ran, to climb a leaning tree; and the names of
the two of them were murgan [the bigger sister] and ḏarga [the
smaller one]; those were the names of the two of them.

26. *bayi*   *ɲuɽbaɲu*   *yuɽigu*   *madalŋayaraygu*   /
THERE-NOM-I return-PRES/PAST kangaroo-DAT throw-*ŋay*-START-PURP
He [the father] returned, and threw down a kangaroo.

27. *ɽulgu*   *baŋul*   *ɲalŋgaɲu* /*budin*   *baŋgul*   /
heart-NOM THERE-GEN-I child-GEN take-PRES/PAST THERE-ERG-I
He took the [kangaroo's] heart for the child.

Note that here *budil* 'take, carry in the hand' features in a proleptic construction
– 8.2.3.

28. *ɲalŋga*   *bubin*   *baŋumdayindu*   *gayuŋga* /
child-NOM take-off-PRES/PAST THERE-ABL-UP-HILL-*ru* cradle-LOC
yubali   *ŋamiŋga*/*gulŋgan*   *baŋgul*   *ɽulguŋgu* /
put down-PURP lap-LOC feed-PRES/PAST THERE-INST-I heart-INST
The baby was taken down from up there in its cradle, to be put
down in [the man's] lap; it was fed by him [the father] with
a kangaroo's heart.

29. *ɽulgu*   *baŋgul*   *ḏurɲaḏurɲaɲu*
heart-NOM THERE-ERG-I drink without stopping-REDUP-PRES/PAST
guɲḏan   /
drink-PRES/PAST
He [the child] drank from the heart without pausing for breath.

30. *munanḏaygu*   *bayi*   / *munanḏaɲu*
vomit-REPEAT-PURP THERE-NOM-I vomit-REPEAT-PRES/PAST
ŋamun   /
breastmilk-NOM
As a result he [the child] vomited a lot; he vomited up breastmilk.

Note that the NP topic is *bayi* [*ɲalŋga*] for the first sentence; it is 'elaborated' by the addition of [*balan*] *ŋamun* 'breastmilk' in the second sentence.

31. *bayi*   *ŋambaŋambariɲu*   /
    THERE-NOM-I listen-REDUP-REFL-PRES/PAST
    He [the man] thought a good deal:

32. *waɲḍu*   *ŋaygu ŋamundu*   *gulŋgan*   /
    who-ERG I-GEN breastmilk-INST breastfeed-PRES/PAST
    'Who's been feeding my [child] with breastmilk?'

The storyteller mentioned later that the man realised at this stage there must be women around, and that this aroused him.

33. *yubalnban*   / *ɲalŋga*   *gayuŋga*   *wandali*   /
    put down-QUICK-PRES/PAST child-NOM cradle-LOC hang up-PURP
    The baby was quickly put into the cradle, then it could be hung up [on a hook near the roof of the mia-mia].

34. *ḍaɲḍa bayi*   *guniguninaɲura*   / *ḍubulba*   /
    now   THERE-NOM-I search-REDUP-*ɲay-ɲura* erection-WITH-NOM
    ḍubul   *ḍanaɲu*   /
    erection-NOM stand-PRES/PAST
    Now he searched and searched [for the women], with an erection;
    [his] erection was standing up.

The A NP in line 33 is 'that man' (although this is not in fact stated in 33) – 'the man' becomes topic NP in 34, and the VC is accordingly placed in -*ɲura* inflection. Note that the topic NP in 34 is first stated as *bayi* [*ŋagaɲunu*] *ḍubulba*, and then restated as *bayi* [*ŋagaɲunu*] *ḍubul*, where *ḍubul* is shown as inalienably possessed by *ŋagaɲunu*.

35. *aɲḍa-* / *ban*   *midi*   *miyandaygu baŋun*
    PARTICLE THERE-NOM-II small-NOM laugh-PURP THERE-ERG-II
    bulgandu ḍabilganiɲu   /
    big-ERG   stop-KEEP ON-PRES/PAST
    The small[er woman] wanted to laugh [i.e. at the man's erection],
    [but] was stopped by the big[ger woman].

A VC in purposive inflection refers to something that can happen BY VIRTUE OF the action referred to by an earlier VC, or some extratextual event; unless anything is said to the contrary, it is assumed that the implicated event DID take place. Here, however, the sight of the man's erection made the younger woman want to laugh, but she WAS able to stifle the desire.

36. [*gayi*]/ *yuṟay*   *ŋali*   *ɲina*   *baɲulḍinda*   /
    sssh! quiet-NOM we two-SA sit-IMP THERE-GEN-I-*ḍin*-LOC
    'Sssh! We must sit quiet for [fear of] him!' [the elder sister said].

37. *bayimban*   *ḍubul*   *gunimariɲ*   /
THERE-NOM-I-EMPH erection-NOM search-REFL-FUTURE
'He will search us out with his erection' [she continued].

38. *ɲa/ bayiɲaŋga*   *yuɽay*   *ŋali*   *ɲina* /
yes THERE-NOM-I-*ɲa*-LOC quiet-NOM we two-SA sit-IMP
'Yes, we must sit quiet for [fear of] him!' [the other replied].

39. *balaruba*   *bayi*   *ŋandandaɲu*   /
THERE-ALL(PLACE)-EXTENT THERE-NOM-I call out-A LOT-PRES/PAST
ŋuɽbayaraɲu   / *bali*   *bayi*
return-START-PRES/PAST THERE-ALL(DIRN) THERE-NOM-I
garugaḍariɲu   /
pass by-REFL-REL-NOM
He was calling out everywhere there; he went back [to the camp again], passing [them up in a tree] on his way.

40. *balandayi*   *balagara*   *miyandaygul*
THERE-NOM-II-UP-HILL-SHORT WAY two people-NOM laugh-PURP
The two women up there [in the tree] wanted to laugh.

41. *baŋgun*   *bulgandu*   *ḍabilganiɲu*   / *[gayi]* /
THERE-ERG-II big-ERG stop-KEEP ON-PRES/PAST sssh!
The big[ger woman] stopped [the younger one from laughing, saying:] 'sssh'.

42. *baɲum*   *bayi*   *ŋuɽbaɲu*   / *walginagaligu*
THERE-ABL THERE-NOM-I return-PRES/PAST look in-*ɲay*-QUICK-PURP
ɲalŋgagu/ ŋuɽbayaraɲu   / *guninaygu*   /
child-DAT return-START-PRES/PAST search-*ɲay*-PURP
Then he returned [to the camp] to have a quick look in [the cradle] at the baby; [then he] started to go back, to search [for the women].

43. *midi*   *ban*   *aɲḍa*   *bandabandaɲu*
small-NOM THERE-NOM-II PARTICLE burst out-REDUP-PRES/PAST
miyandaɲu   / *mugu*   *aɲḍa*   *miyandaɲu*   /
laugh-PRES/PAST PARTICLE PARTICLE laugh-PRES/PAST
Then the small woman burst out laughing; she couldn't help laughing.

Particle *aɲḍa*, occurring after the topic NP but just before the VC, indicates a quite new kind of action involving an established topic, i.e. the smaller woman actually does laugh. Particle *mugu* indicates it was impossible to avoid laughing – that is, the desire to laugh overcame the strongest self-restraint.

44. *yalugalamban*   *baŋgul*
    HERE-ALL(PLACE)-UP-TR VBLSR-PRES/PAST THERE-ERG-I
    buɽan   /
    look-PRES/PAST
    He looked up [at the two women].

45. *aɲḍa*   *bayi*   *biliɲu*   /
    PARTICLE THERE-NOM-I climb-PRES/PAST
    [Then] he climbed up [the tree in which the women were hiding].

46. *midi*   *ban*   *bilŋgiŋa*
    small-NOM THERE-NOM-II across thighs-LOC
    buɲalman   / *ban*   *bundayman*
    descend-COMIT-PRES/PAST THERE-NOM-II break off-COMIT-PRES/PAST
    midi   /
    small-NOM
    [He] brought the smaller one down across his thigh; [he] pulled
    the smaller one [off the part of the tree she was clinging to].

47. *bulgan*   *ban*   *ŋaḍiŋa*
    big-NOM THERE-NOM-II on shoulder-LOC
    dimbaɲu   / *buɲalman*   /
    carry (other than in hand)-PRES/PAST descend-COMIT-PRES/PAST
    [He] carried the big woman over his shoulder, descending with her.

That is, the man brought down the two women together, one slung across his
shoulder, and the other against his hip.

48. *balaybayḍi*   *buḍuɽa*   *bayi*
    THERE-LOC-DOWN-HILL-SHORT WAY butt of tree-LOC THERE-NOM-I
    ḍinbiyaraɲu   /
    jump-BEGIN-PRES/PAST
    He jumped to the butt of the tree, down there.

49. *balayḍu*   *baŋgul*   *baɽabaɽan*
    THERE-LOC-EMPH THERE-ERG-I drive in-REDUP-PRES/PAST
    wadin   / *yimbaḍu*   /
    swive-PRES/PAST nothing-EMPH
    He [tried to] swive (i.e. have sexual intercourse with) [the smaller
    woman], driving in [with his thighs] right there [at the butt of the
    tree]; but there was nothing [i.e. he had no success].

50. *bulgan*   *ban*   *baŋgul*   *yubalnban*   /
    big-NOM THERE-NOM-II THERE-ERG-I put down-QUICK-PRES/PAST

wadili / *yimbaḍu* / *mundu* *buḍa* /
swive-PURP nothing-EMPH offended-NOM not sweet-NOM

[Then] he quickly [i.e. roughly] put down the bigger woman, to swive her; but there was nothing, [he had] no satisfaction.

mundu indicates that someone is 'offended' because he didn't get something that was his by right – for instance, wasn't given a share of some food, or (as here) wasn't brought to a sexual climax. *buḍa* is a general adjective 'not sweet enough'. *mundu buḍa* appears to be a stock phrase referring to lack of sexual satisfaction.

51. *baŋum* *bayi* *ŋambaŋambariŋu* /
THERE-ABL THERE-NOM-I listen-REDUP-REFL-PRES/PAST
ṛuwa bayi *yanu* /
west THERE-NOM-I go-PRES/PAST

Then he thought a lot; and he went out to the west.

52. *buṛan* *baŋgul* *barmba* *barmbiŋu* /
see-PRES/PAST THERE-ERG-I quartz-NOM glitter-REL-NOM
maŋgan / *bayguli* *dibanda* / *yagi*
pick up-PRES/PAST bash-PURP rock-LOC split-NOM
bulabili / *bala* *baŋgul*
two-INTR VBLSR-PURP THERE-NOM-IV THERE-ERG-I
ŋuṛbayman /
return-COMIT-PRES/PAST

He saw a piece of quartz glittering, picked it up, to bash it on a rock, so that it split into two pieces, which he took home.

53. *baŋgul* *buṛan* *balay* *balagara* /
THERE-ERG-I see-PRES/PAST THERE-LOC two people-NOM
ɲinayaranḍaɲu / *balay* *baŋgul* *guban* /
sit-HABITUAL-PRES/PAST THERE-LOC THERE-ERG-I cover-PRES/PAST
diradayi ḍanaygu /
point-UP stand-PURP

He saw the place where the two women habitually sat, [and put the two quartz pieces] there, covering them [with leaves, so that they were not visible], standing with their points uppermost.

54. *baŋum* / *balagara* *ŋuṛbaɲu* / *ɲinayaraɲu* /
THERE-ABL two people-NOM return-PRES/PAST sit-START-PRES/PAST
gunbali *baŋgu* /
cut-PURP THERE-ERG-IV

Then the two [women] returned home, and started to sit down [only] to be pierced by them [i.e. by the sharp quartz pieces].

It appears that the women originally had no sex organs at all (that is, no opening of any sort). ŋagaŋunu made them in three stages: [a] the vaginal openings were made through causing the women to sit on the slivers of quartz; [b] a kangaroo heart was joined on for the vulva, and kangaroo lungs for the vaginal lips; [c] cucumber halves were driven in (through the anus?) to make the inside firm, and capable of giving satisfaction (and, incidentally, producing the red colouration around that part of a woman).

55. *ganagala yuban   bulayimban*   /
    front-UP put down-PRES/PAST two-TR VBLSR-PRES/PAST
    aɲḍa   baŋgul   wadin | baɽabaɽan   /
    PARTICLE THERE-ERG-I swive-PRES/PAST drive in-REDUP-PRES/PAST
    yimba | mundu   buḍa   /
    nothing offended-NOM not sweet-NOM
    [He] put them both down belly up, and then he [tried to] swive [the smaller one], driving in, [but] there was nothing, no satisfaction.

56. *ban   bulgan   wadin | mundu*
    THERE-NOM-II big-NOM swive-PRES/PAST offended-NOM
    buḍa   /
    not sweet-NOM
    [He tried to] swive the bigger one; there was no satisfaction.

57. *baŋum   bayi   yanu | gunimariɲu*   /
    THERE-ABL THERE-NOM-I go-PRES/PAST search-REFL-PRES/PAST
    Then he went out, searching.

58. *ɽulgu   baŋgul   budin* | walŋgamu|
    heart-NOM THERE-ERG-I carry with hand-PRES/PAST lung-NOM
    ḍarban   baŋugaraŋundinda | wadin   /
    join on-PRES/PAST two people-GEN-ḍin-LOC swive-PRES/PAST
    yimba | mundu   buḍa   /
    nothing offended-NOM not sweet-NOM
    He carried heart and lungs [from a kangaroo] and stuck them on to the two women; [then he tried to] swive [them], but there was nothing, no satisfaction.

59. *baŋum   bayi   ḍanaɲu   buɽalɲaɲu*   /
    THERE-ABL THERE-NOM-I stand-PRES/PAST look-ŋay-PRES/PAST
    Then he stood and looked around.

60. *yaludayimban*
    HERE-ALL(PLACE)-UP-HILL-SHORT WAY-TR VBLSR-PRES/PAST
    buɾan | *bamgala* *bangula*
    look-PRES/PAST THERE-NOM-III wild cucumber-NOM
    wandalŋaŋu |
    hang-*ŋay*-REL-NOM
    Looking up, [he] saw a wild cucumber hanging [on a tree].

61. *bayi* *biliŋu* | *bagum* *bangulagu* |
    THERE-NOM-I climb-PRES/PAST THERE-DAT-III wild cucumber-DAT
    He climbed [the tree] for the cucumber.

62. *burbin* *baŋgul* | *madali* |
    pull-off-PRES/PAST THERE-ERG-I throw-PURP
    yagi *bulabili* | *maŋgan* *baŋgul* |
    split-NOM two-INTR VBLSR-PURP pick up-PRES/PAST THERE-ERG-I
    ŋuɾbayman | *maladaranda* *bulay* |
    return-COMIT-PRES/PAST hand-DUAL-LOC two-NOM
    He pulled [it] off, to throw [it] down, so that [it] would split into
    two pieces; he picked the two pieces up, and returned with them,
    one in each hand.

For discussion of the function of dual affix *-daran* and number adjective
bulay in constructions like *maladaranda bulay*, see 6.1.1.

63. *ban* *mambudaran* *ŋinaŋu* |
    THERE-NOM-II back-DUAL-NOM sit-PRES/PAST
    The [women] were sitting each with her back [towards him].

64. *yaliŋaru* *dulungaru* *baŋgul*
    HERE-ALL(DIRN)-BEHIND hip-LOC-MOTION THERE-ERG-I
    baɾan | *baŋgul* *baɾan* |
    drive in-PRES/PAST THERE-ERG-I drive in-PRES/PAST
    He pushed [the pieces of wild cucumber] in behind the [women's]
    hips; he pushed [them] in.

65. *miradaran* *balagaraŋa* | *daŋda wadin* |
    front-DUAL-NOM two-people-*ŋa*-NOM now swive-PRES/PAST
    garda | *dami* *aŋda* *wadin* |
    alright-NOM fat-NOM PARTICLE swive-PRES/PAST
    The two of them [were turned] front up; now he swived them; it
    was alright, it was satisfying swiving.

aɲɖa occurring after adjective *ɖami* – here used with a metaphorical meaning, to denote sexual satisfaction – indicates that the 'state' described by *ɖami* is a new one (previously there had been no satisfaction – *mundu buɖa*).

66. *balagara*   *aɲɖa*   *biŋgunbin* | *walŋga*
   two people-NOM PARTICLE tired-INTR VBLSR-PRES/PAST breath-NOM
   mayin   *baŋgul*   *wadinmi* |
   come out-PRES/PAST THERE-ERG-I swive-PERF REL-NOM
   muguymuguy |
   too much-REDUP-NOM
   [After awhile] the two of them became tired, fed up with being swived by him all the time.

aɲɖa here occurs after the topic NP and just before the VC – it indicates a new type of action concerning an established topic; they are, for the first time, tired of the swiving. Note that the topic NP is simply *balagara* for the first sentence; for the second sentence it is *balagara walŋga* – involving inalienable possession – and this NP has the perfective relative clause with VC *wadinmi*. *walŋga mayil*, literally 'breath come out, take a deep sigh' is a standard expression for 'fed up'.

67. *ban*   *midi*   *ŋanban* |
   THERE-NOM-II small-NOM ask-PRES/PAST
   The small[er woman] was asked [by her sister]:

68. *ŋinda/* *ŋali*   *wiyabaɲ* |
   you-SA we two-SA do what-FUTURE
   'You! What shall we do?'

69. *wiyabaɲ* | *ŋaɖa aɲɖa*   *biŋgunbin* |
   do what-FUTURE I-SA PARTICLE tired-INTR VBLSR-PRES/PAST
   'What indeed! I'm certainly tired [of him]' [the other replied].

70. *gaɖi*   *buɲɖangu*   *buŋa* |
   PARTICLE yellow walnut-DAT go downhill-IMP
   'Come on, let [us] go downhill for a yellow walnut!' [the first one said].

71. *buɲɖangu*   *balagara*   *buŋan*
   yellow walnut-DAT two people-NOM go downhill-PRES/PAST
   banaɲunugu |
   water-OUT OF-DAT
   The two of them went downhill [to pick] a yellow walnut out of the water.

72. budin   buṇḍan   / ŋuṛbayman   /
    carry-PRES/PAST yellow walnut-NOM return-COMIT-PRES/PAST
    gubali   *buniŋga/ maŋa*   *bagabagan*   /
    cover-PURP fire-LOC ear-NOM pierce-REDUP-PRES/PAST
    [They] carried the yellow walnut home, and covered it over in the
    fire [i.e. covered with ashes]; [they] whispered [to it]:

maŋa bagal, literally 'pierce ear' is the normal idiom for 'whisper'.

73. ŋaru   bandam   / waway / magul   miḍu
    PARTICLE burst-NEG IMP too soon meanwhile take no notice-IMP
    baŋgul   *ŋalina*   *garḍuli*   *gubali*   *yumaṛu* /
    THERE-ERG-I we two-O do properly-PURP cover-PURP body-ERG
    gilu   *bandaygu bagul*   *gandanaygu*   / ŋaru
    later on today burst-PURP THERE-DAT-I burn-ŋay-PURP PARTICLE
    ŋalina   *gandam*   /
    we two-O burn-NEG IMP
    'Don't explode too soon! Wait until he's covering us both properly
    with his body, then burst, so that [you] burn him. Don't burn us!'

The yellow walnut bursts when heated; the women were asking it to delay so
that it hurt the man but not them.

74. bayi   buṛan   ŋuṛbaŋu   /
    THERE-NOM-I see-PRES/PAST return-REL-NOM
    [They] saw him returning.

75. yuṛi   baŋgul   madalnban   /
    kangaroo-NOM THERE-ERG-I throw-QUICK-PRES/PAST
    He quickly threw down a kangaroo [he had speared].

76. bagugaraṇangu   ganagala yubalnbarimali   /
    two people-ṇa-DAT front-UP put down-RECIP-COMIT-PURP
    [Then he put something down] so that [he] could put the two of
    them on top of it.

yubalnbarimali appears to be a false reciprocal, or else aspectual affix 'quickly'
plus a false reflexive – there is, in fact, no syntactic difference; see 4.8.1, 6.3.2.
The comitative construction here is similar to that exemplified in (260) of
4.9.3.

77. ḍaṇḍawadin   / ḍaṇḍawadin   / ḍaṇḍawadin   /
    now swive-PRES/PAST now swive-PRES/PAST now swive-PRES/PAST
    Now [he] swived [them], and swived [them], and swived [them].

78. *wuḍu   ŋayi bam   buṇḍan   bandaɲu*
    fruit-NOM?   THERE-NOM-III yellow walnut-NOM burst-PRES/PAST
    [*bo:ŋ:*] /
    'noise'
    Then the fruit, the yellow walnut, exploded [making a noise]
    'bo:ŋ:'.

The informant said that the second word of this sentence was *ŋayi* 'then';
however, the writer has not been able to gather other instances of use of this
word.

79. *ḍaɲḍa bayi   walmawalmaɲu   ḍiŋgaligu/*
    now   THERE-NOM-I get up-REDUP-PRES/PAST run-PURP
    Then he jumped up, and ran off.

80. *balagara   yalabaɲu   /*
    two people-NOM do this way-PRES/PAST
    The two of them spoke:

The unmarked interpretation of a VC containing just a *yalab/may/l* form in
a context like this is that it refers to a speech act.

81. [*ʃo:*]/ *ŋaliḍinaru   wadili   /*
    phew we two-O-TOO swive-PURP
    'Phew! We'd been swived too much.'

82. *baŋum   bayi   aɲḍa   gulu   buɽan   /*
    THERE-ABL THERE-NOM-I PARTICLE PARTICLE(not) see-PRES/PAST
    baluɽuwa   bayi   ḍiŋgaliɲu   /
    THERE-ALL(PLACE)-west THERE-NOM-I run-PRES/PAST
    Then he was never seen again; he'd run away to a place out west.

Text XXXIb

Autobiographical story told in the Dyirbal dialect. The storyteller
recounts how, when as a girl she was sitting in the camp with the tribe
after dark, she heard a noise in the scrub and was told it was the Dambun
spirit. Despite warnings not to, she went looking for the source of the
noise, with a light, and found it was made by a curlew. The following
night she heard another noise, also said to be Dambun by the old
people, and found it was made by a mopoke owl.

It was said that the Dambun spirit – whose appearance is described
in the story – would put one in a lonely cave in the forest, and keep
one there for so long that the loneliness would drive the victim mad.

1. *dambunda   ŋanaŋga   muguru   ɲina /*
   dambun-LOC UNSEEN-NOM-II-*ɲa*-LOC quiet-NOM sit-IMP
   Sit quiet for fear of Dambun, who can be heard [now]!

ŋanaŋga is built on the root ŋala- 'audible but not visible'; in this sentence
and the next the locative inflection is used in the 'fear' sense.

2. *wuɲḍanaŋga   /*
   WHERE-NOM-II-*ɲa*-LOC
   Where is she that we fear?

3. *ŋan   bangaluɲunu*
   UNSEEN-NOM-II THERE-NOM-II-OUT IN FRONT-FROM
   yalgayḍaru   wandin   /
   road-LOC-MOTION motion upriver-PRES/PAST
   She can be heard going along the road up alongside the river there.

4. *ɲiralbila /*
   pin-*bila*
   [She] might pin [our chests, with her claw-like hands]!

5. *muymba   buni   / buṛalbila dambundu /*
   extinguish-IMP fire-NOM see-*bila* dambun-ERG
   Put out the fire lest Dambun see it!

6. *ŋanaḍina ḍindi   ɲiraɲ   /*
   we all-O chest-NOM pin-FUTURE
   [She] would pin our chests.

7. *wuɲḍan   /*
   WHERE-NOM-II
   Where is she?

8. *gilaɲunda   / ŋalan   / ŋalan*
   SOMEWHERE-LOC-SOMEWHERE UNSEEN-NOM-II UNSEEN-NOM-II
   ŋandaɲ   / mulgu   /
   call out-FUTURE noise-NOM
   She can be heard somewhere out there; she will call out her noise.

9. *ŋaḍa walmawalmagaliɲu   baŋum   maŋgalmbarigu*
   I-SA get up-REDUP-QUICK-PRES/PAST THERE-ABL pick up-RECIP-PURP
   duḍugu / gindalmali   /
   torch-DAT look with a light-INSTR-PURP
   I quickly got up from there [from where I was sitting in the camp]
   to pick up a torch, so that I could look by its light.

duḍu is an ad hoc English loan (it is not an established loan word). When the
text was played back the storyteller mentioned that she should have used
balan ɲaṛa 'flame, torch'.

10. *ḍaṇḍa ŋaḍa yanu*   /
    now   I-SA go-PRES/PAST
    Then I went out.

11. *baŋgumaŋgandu*   *gindimban*   /
    many people-ERG warn-PRES/PAST
    They all [all the old people of the camp] warned [me]:

12. [ε]/ *galga*   *ban*   *dambun*   *gindam*   /
    hey PARTICLE THERE-NOM-II dambun-NOM look with a light-NEG IMP
    banimbila |
    come-*bila*
    'Hey! Don't look for Dambun with the light, lest she come here!'

13. *ŋaḍa bala*   *gulu*   *ŋamban*
    I-SA THERE-NOM-IV PARTICLE(not) listen-PRES/PAST
    baŋumaŋganu   *guwal*   / *miḍuganiɲu*   /
    many people-GEN language-NOM take no notice-KEEP ON-PRES/PAST
    I didn't listen to what they were saying; I took no notice at all.

14. *baliḍilu*   *ŋaḍa yanu*   / *bagun*
    THERE-ALL(DIRN)-EMPH I-SA go-PRES/PAST THERE-DAT-II
    gindalŋaɲu   *dambungu*   /
    look with a light-*ŋay*-PRES/PAST dambun-DAT
    I went in that direction, looking for Dambun by [torch]light.

15. *ŋaḍa ban*   *buṛali*   *dambun*   /
    I-SA THERE-NOM-II see-PURP dambun-NOM
    miɲaŋarumban   *dambun*   /
    WHAT-LOOK LIKE-TR VBLSR-PRES/PAST dambun-NOM
    banḍana   *dambun*
    THERE-NOM-II-EMPH dambun-NOM
    gilagiɲan   *yaṛaŋarumban*
    SOMEWHERE-DEM-NOM-II man-LOOK LIKE-TR VBLSR-PRES/PAST
    balan | *muray*   *ḍuda* | *biguŋgalugalu* |
    THERE-NOM-II hair-NOM bushy-NOM nails-OUT IN FRONT-NOM
    margimargi | *wirmban* | *dayidayigala*   /
    very thin-NOM skin and bones-NOM UP-REDUP-UP-NOM
    I wanted to see Dambun; to see what Dambun looked like. That
    Dambun somewhere out there [is supposed to] look something

like a man, with bushy hair, long finger and toe nails, very skinny and emaciated, all bones and no flesh, very very tall.

16. *balubawal*   *ŋaḍa yanu* |
    THERE-ALL(PLACE)-OUT THERE I-SA go-PRES/PAST
    I went over there.

17. *yimba bangalu*   *buṟan*   *ŋaḍa guyibara*
    no   THERE-NOM-II-OUT IN FRONT see-PRES/PAST I-SA curlew-NOM
    yambiŋu |
    fly-REL-NOM
    Oh no! I saw the curlew flying.

18. *[giyu]/ [giyu]/ [giyu]/*   *ŋangalu*   *ban*
    'noise made by curlew' UNSEEN-NOM-II-OUT IN FRONT THERE-NOM-II
    yambin |
    fly-PRES/PAST
    '*Giyu, giyu, giyu,*' she could be heard flying.

19. *baŋum*   *balan*   *yuŋgugan* | *ḍagungabunda*
    THERE-ABL THERE-NOM-II another one-NOM night-ANOTHER-LOC
    ŋaḍa ŋamban | *bangalu*
    I-SA hear-PRES/PAST THERE-NOM-II-OUT IN FRONT
    mulgubiŋu | *balan*   *ŋamban*   *guɲu*
    noise-INTR VBLSR-REL-NOM THERE-NOM-II hear-PRES/PAST new-NOM
    dambun |
    dambun-NOM
    Then the next night I heard another [noise]; something was making an indistinct noise out there; it was another Dambun [I] heard.

20. *yanu*   *ŋaḍa*/
    go-PRES/PAST I-SA
    I went out.

21. *maŋgalmban*   *ŋaḍa duḍu* | *gindalmali* |
    pick up-INST-PRES/PAST I-SA torch-NOM look with a light-INST-PURP
    I picked up the torch, to look [for Dambun] with it.

22. *dambunda*   *yaŋgun* | *gindagindamalbila*
    dambun-LOC HERE-ERG-II look with a light-REDUP-INST-*bila*
    dambun |
    dambun-NOM
    [All the old people said:] 'This girl might shine a light on Dambun!'

23. *ŋanaḏi   ḍaṇḍa manmaygu   yaluguŋgari*   /
    we all-SA now   shift camp-PURP HERE-ALL(PLACE)-north
    'And we might all have to move camp to the north [to escape
    Dambun].'

24. *baliḏilu   ŋaḏa yanu   /*
    THERE-ALL(DIRN)-EMPH I-SA go-PRES/PAST
    gindalŋaɲu   /
    look with a light-*ŋay*-PRES/PAST
    I went out there looking with a light.

25. *buṟan   giɲanbayḏi   gugu*
    see-PRES/PAST DEM-NOM-II-DOWN-HILL-SHORT WAY owl-NOM
    ɲinaɲu   / mulgumbaɲu   /
    sit-REL-NOM noise-INTR VBLSR-REL-NOM
    I saw a mopoke owl sitting down there [in the grass] making a noise:

26. *[m̃m̃] /[m̃] /[m̃]/*
    'noise made by owl'.

27. *yalamaɲu   bangali   /*
    do like this-REL-NOM THERE-NOM-II-DOWN-HILL-SHORT WAY
    That's the way it [was making a noise], down on the ground.

28. *yidiṟa   ɲinaɲu   buybayiriɲu   gaygabu*
    grass-LOC sit-REL-NOM hide-REFL-REL-NOM eyes-NOM-ONLY
    bulgan   ŋaḏa ŋaṟban   /
    big-NOM I-SA frighten-PRES/PAST
    [Seeing] just [two] big eyes sitting hiding in the grass frightened
    me.

29. *banagayaraɲu   ŋaḏa buṟalaygu   ŋuymalaygu*
    return-AGAIN-PRES/PAST I-SA see-*ŋay*-PURP do properly-*ŋay*-PURP
    gaygagu bagun   /
    eyes-DAT THERE-DAT-II
    [But] I went back again to have a proper look at the eyes.

30. *balan   buṟan   gugu   ɲinaɲu   /*
    THERE-NOM-II see-PRES/PAST owl-NOM sit-REL-NOM
    [And] saw a mopoke owl sitting there.

31. *ḍaṇḍa ŋaḏa miyandaɲu   balayḍilu   /*
    now I-SA laugh-PRES/PAST THERE-LOC-EMPH
    I laughed, right there.

32. *baŋgumaŋgandu   ŋayguna ŋunḍaɲu   dambundu*
   many people-ERG I-O   blame-PRES/PAST dambun-ERG
   gidimbaɲu   /
   tickle-REL-NOM
   All the people [in the camp] put the blame [for the laughing] on
   me being tickled by Dambun.

33. *ban   -   ŋaḍa ban   miyandaɲu   bagun*
   THERE-NOM-II I-SA THERE-NOM-II laugh-PRES/PAST THERE-DAT-II
   dambu- ŋambiyagu   / gugugu /
           what's-it-called-DAT owl-DAT
   I was laughing at that Dambu – what's it called – that owl.

Text XXV

A myth told in Mamu. This concerns a legendary man, mubuɲinmi,
who has two sons and two daughters; in addition, each daughter has
a son. The women kill their brothers after they observe them cheating
– keeping for themselves all the large birds that they catch, and giving
the women the small ones. Mubuɲinmi leaves his home on Hinchinbrook
Island and follows the tracks of his children. He finds parts of his
sons' bodies and accuses the women of the murder; they confess.
Mubuɲinmi then turns himself into a snake [the rainbow-serpent] and
swallows his daughters. When the old man tells the two grandsons
what he has done, they plan their revenge. Pretending to be solicitous
for his comfort, they prepare a hollow tree for him to sleep in, taking
care to plaster over all the holes. When he is asleep, they stick lighted
torches into the trunk, to burn him. Half of the grandfather is burnt
away but the remainder, again in the form of a snake, breaks out, and
plunges into the river to try to put out the fire. He dives into one waterhole in the Tully River and emerges from another one, further up, and
so on, always keeping ahead of the pursuing grandsons. Eventually
he escapes, but leaves a large heel-mark in a rock just above Tully Falls
(that can be seen there to this day).

1. *balagara/ balamaŋgan/ balaŋumguya baniɲu/ yalu milbirmiguru/*
   Those two – that lot [two brothers and two sisters] came here to
   milbirmi [Cardwell] from somewhere over the other side [of the
   Hinchinbrook Channel] [i.e. from Hinchinbrook Island].

2. *baŋgun ḍurgayḍarandu gigan bayi/ ḍurgayḍaran biligu/ ḍiyilgu/*

*ḍiyilgu banalɲaygu baɲundaygudayi milbirɲunugu/ baŋgugaragu
ŋanbayaranḍaɲu/*
The two brothers were told by [their] two sisters to climb [the
slippery blue fig tree] for starlings, to pull off starlings from up
there in the slippery blue fig tree. They were continually asked
by the two [women]:

3. *giyigiyi midi madaɲ ḍiyil/ bulgangay wuɲḍan/*
   'These are all small starlings [you're] throwing down – where are
   the big ones?'

4. *baŋgugaragu/ balagaraɲa buwaɲu/*
   The two [brothers] told the two [sisters]:

5. *yimba/ midimidi yimba/ giɲan ɲali midimidi/ gundaɲ/*
   'No, there's nothing but small ones; its small ones we're putting
   into [our own dilly-bag].'

6. *ɲurɲuɲurɲu balagara maŋgalɲaɲu/*
   The two [sisters] were too busy picking up [starlings that had
   been thrown down to them] to notice [what exactly the brothers
   were doing].

7. *dayimban buṛan balagaraɲa bulgangaygu/ gundalɲaɲu ḍawunda/*
   [Then,] looking up [the sisters] saw the two [brothers] putting
   big ones into [their] dilly-bag.

8. *ɲubala bulgangay ban gundalḍaɲ/ giɲan ɲaliɲu midimidi madaɲ/*
   'You two keep putting big ones [into your dilly-bag], and throwing
   all these small ones down to us' [the sisters said].

9. *yimbaban ɲali midimidigu giyi gundalɲaɲ/*
   'Not at all, we're putting small ones into [our dilly-bag]' [the
   brothers said].

10. *balagara ban/ maɲa bagalbagalbariɲu/*
    The two women whispered to each other:

11. *ɲali/ gaḍindu baga balagaraɲa/ gulu wugalɲaɲu/*
    'We'll dig with a yamstick around our two brothers [in the tree],
    who wouldn't give [us any big starlings].'

12. *aɲḍa balagara gaḍindu bagalɲaɲu/ bagan bala miraŋgaru/*
    And so the two [women] dug with a yamstick; [they] dug along
    at the front [of the tree].

13. *baŋum waymbaraɲu/ mambuŋgaru bagalɲaygu/*
From there they worked round to dig at the back [of the tree].

14. *yugu aɲḍa gayɲḍan milbir/ banagu balgalɲaɲu/*
The slippery blue fig tree fell over, and splashed into the water [of Hinchinbrook Channel].

15. *ban aɲḍa milbirmi bungili/ bala milbirmi miḍa/*
So that the milbirmi [sea] lay there; and the place [called] milbirmi.

16. *baŋum balagara wandin/ ḍabundaru/ bagurudawulu gariyaguru/ balaybalbu ɲinaygu miḍaŋga/*
Then the two [women] went up the coast, and along up the Tully River, right up to gariya [Tully Falls], to make their camp there, just downstream [from the Falls].

17. *miḍa baŋugara gadan/ aɲḍa damanḍaran baŋugaraɲu balay warayman/*
The two [women] made a camp [there]; and encountered their two sons there.

18. *balagara wayɲḍin/ bayimbamgu bagalɲaygu/*
The two women went uphill, to dig out grubs.

19. *bayi damanḍaran/ yuɽigu bagalɲaygu/*
The two sons [went] spearing kangaroos.

20. *aɲḍa ŋumandi mari/ gunimarigu/*
Then the father [mubuɲinmi] followed [his children's] tracks, looking [for them].

21. *muray baŋgul maŋgan/*
He picked up some hair.

22. *yaŋum yaŋum murayŋunu ŋaygu/ wiyaban baŋgugara/*
[and he said:] '[This is a piece] from my sons' hair. What have [those] two [daughters] done [to them]?'

23. *magaɽa baŋgul maŋgan/*
He picked up some skin.

24. *giɲa magaɽa/ guyimanḍu balagaraɲa/*
'This is [their] skin. The two of them must have been killed [by their sisters].'

25. *gayga baŋgul maŋgan/*
    He picked up an eye.

26. *giɲa giɲa midiɲu gayga/*
    'This is [my] small[er son's] eye.'

27. *baŋum wandin/ wumbugu maŋgalŋaygu/*
    [He] then went upriver, and picked up a head.

28. *giɲa bulganu wumbu/*
    'This is [my] big[ger son's] head.'

29. *balugali waymbarayaraɲu/ baguru baniɲu guɽawarabaḍanmiguru/*
    [He] began to go round the bend [in the river] and came to [the place called] guɽawarabaḍanmi.

The place name is descriptive: *guɽa* 'woman's sex organ', *wara* – a particle implying that the action involved an inappropriate topic, *baḍanmi* 'bite' in perfective relative clause inflection; literally 'the place where the man bit the woman's sex organ when he shouldn't have done so'. The name does not refer to anything in the present story.

30. *balay baŋgul magaɽa guga wumbu madalḍaɲu/*
    He threw all of the skin, head [and so on] away there.

31. *baŋum bayi aɲḍa wandinuga/ baguru gulbiɽguru/ bagu miḍagu buɽalŋaygu/*
    Then he continued up the river, along to gulbiɽ [the place where the two sisters had made their camp], and saw the camp.

-ga in the verb indicates that 'there is no going back'. That is, having found that his sons were murdered, the man went upriver, totally committed to avenging their death.

32. *bala baŋgul miḍa buɽan baŋugaraɲu/ yibiḍaranu/ aɲḍa balabawal buɽan yalŋgay/*
    He saw the camp of the two women, and, further off, the single men's camp.

33. *balay bayi miḍuriɲu/*
    He waited there.

34. *yibiḍaran ban ɲuɽbaɲu/ baŋgul ŋanban/*
    The two women came home, and he asked them:

35. *yaŋum wuɲḍiɲ ŋaygu/ galbinḍaran/*
    'Where are my two sons, who·should be here?'

yaŋum 'from here' seems in this instance to imply that this is the place the two sons should be found.

36. *yimba ŋali guyiman/ yugu ŋali bagan/ bagugaraɲangu guyimarigu/*
    'Nowhere. We killed them. We dug up [i.e. felled] a tree to kill the two of them.' [the women replied].

37. *bayindayi gilu ŋaygu ŋaliɲu damanḍaran ŋuɽbaɲ/*
    'Our two sons up the hill will be coming home soon.'

38. *ŋa/*
    [The father replied:] 'Yes.'

39. *baŋum/ balagara wayɲḍin bayimbamgu bagalŋaygu/*
    Then the two [women] went uphill to dig out grubs.

40. *damanḍaran baŋugaraŋu ŋuɽbaɲu/ bagul ḍaymbalŋaygu/*
    The two sons of the two [women] returned to find him there.

41. *ŋanban/*
    [The sons] asked [their grandfather]:

42. *ɲinda bayi wuɲḍaŋum/*
    'Where [have] you [come] from?'

43. *ŋaḍa marin/ yagun yabundigaraɲangu/*
    'I followed [the track of your] two mothers.' [he replied].

44. *ŋu/ giyi ŋinda yuɽi ḍanga/*
    'Oh, would you like to eat a piece of kangaroo?' [the sons asked].

45. *ŋu/*
    'Alright' [mubuɲinmi replied].

46. *baŋumdaya balagara ŋuɽbaɲu/ bayimbamgu bagalŋaɲu/*
    The two women returned from digging grubs uphill.

47. *baraymbaray/ balagara yanu/ damanḍaran/*
    The next day the two sons went out.

48. *aɲḍa balagara yabugara wayɲḍin/ bayimbamgu bagalŋaygu/*
    And the two mothers went uphill, to dig out grubs.

49. *aɲḍa bayi wayubi/ balayŋaru baŋgariɲu giḍarbin/ yamanibili/ mubuɲinmi buŋgaymarigu/ baŋum bayi ḍuɽan wayɲḍin/ ɲiyiŋgu bayali/*
    And he [the old man] started to transform himself; he painted

himself to make himself look pretty, just behind [the camp]
there; to become [i.e. to make himself into] a rainbow; and called
himself mubuɲinmi. Then he crawled uphill, his presence being
indicated by the noise the birds made.

50. *baŋgun gigan balan midi/ buɲali/*
The small[er sister] was told by the [bigger] one to go downhill.

51. *gaḍi ɲinda buɲa/ ŋagul miɲagu/ ɲiyiŋgu/ bayaɲugu/*
'Go on, you go downhill, to [see] what it is the birds are singing
about' [The elder sister said to the younger].

52. *ban midi buɲan/*
The small[er sister] went downhill [and said, talking to herself:]

53. *giyingiyi/ mubuɲinmi/*
'This here is mubuɲinmi.'

54. *ḍiŋgaliyaraɲu ban yuguba balgalɲaygu/ baliyalugalumban baŋgul
bulgaɲu/*
She started to run down with a stick, to hit him, but was swallowed
by him.

55. *bulgan ban ŋandaɲu/*
The big[ger woman] called out [to her sister:]

56. *ɲinda/*
'[Hey], you!'

57. *yimba/*
There was nothing [i.e. no reply].

58. *balanḍu ŋambaŋambariɲu buɲali/ ban buɲan duyginayaraygu yagul
ɲinaɲugu/*
She kept thinking about going down herself; [finally] she went
down and peeked at him sitting [there].

59. *giyingiyi mubuɲinmi/*
'This here is mubuɲinmi' [she said to herself].

60. *yugu banan/ ḍiŋgaliyarayman balgalmali/*
[She] broke off a stick, to run up with it and hit him with it.

61. *balan bulgaɲu/*
She was swallowed [by the rainbow-snake, mubuɲinmi].

62. *balagara ḍaymbalḍaymbalbariɲu balaygala bambaŋga/*
The two [sisters] met there in his stomach [and said to each other:]

63. *ɲinda/ ɲalina wayuman bulgaɲu/*
'You! [He] turned himself [into the rainbow-snake] and swallowed us,' [one said].

64. *ŋa/ bayi ŋalingu/ ŋuri/*
'Yes, he has got even with us' [the other rejoined].

65. *baŋum bayi ḍuɾan ŋuṛbaɲu/ miḍaguru/*
Then he crawled back to the camp.

66. *bayi/ damanḍaran ŋuṛbaɲu/*
The two sons returned home [and said to their grandfather:]

67. *ɲinda bayi miɲaɲunu maŋḍay/*
'What are you full up from [eating]?'

68. *ɲaḍa giɲan yabundigaraɲa bulgaɲu/*
'I've swallowed those two mothers [of yours]' [he replied].

69. *ŋaygu miḍa bulgan balubawal garḍu buɾa/*
[Go and] have a look out there for a big house for me!' [he continued].

70. *ŋu/ ŋali yanuŋura duyginḍarinaygu/*
'Alright, we'll go at once and have a look around' [the grandsons replied].

71. *balagara yanu/ waɾabadagu buɾalŋaygu yugugu/ bala – waymbaɲu balaygala balagara yugariga/ baŋum/ ŋuṛbaɲu balagara bagul buwanaygu/*
The two of them went out to look for a [hollow] turpentine tree. They walked round there at the hollow tree [i.e. having a good look at it, inside and out]. Then they returned to tell him:

72. *giɲa yalaydawu ŋali ɲinuna budili/ yugariga yubali/ ḍamiŋga bungili/*
'We'll carry you out there, to put you in the hollow tree, so that you'll sleep in that good [place].'

When this line was replayed the informant said it was ungrammatical as it stood: the initial *giɲa* should be omitted and *yalaydawu* replaced by *yalidawu* or *yaludawu*.

73. *ŋu/*
'Alright' [their grandfather replied].

74. *budin baŋgugara balaygala buybali/ baŋgugara ŋanban/*
   He was taken up there and put fully inside [the hollow tree] by
   the two of them, and then asked by the two of them:

75. *ŋindama yalay garḍa bungin/*
   'Are you alright lying here?'

76. *ŋa/ giɲa garḍa/ dinu ŋaḍa bungilmaɲ/*
   'Yes, it's fine here. Its [nice and] cool for me to sleep' [he replied].

77. *baŋum mulu aɲḍa ḍarbalḍaɲu baŋgugara/ baladayindu gulbalḍaɲu/
   maymbalḍaɲu baŋgu waɽabadagu/*
   Then the two of them plugged the [hole in the] end [of the log],
   and blocked in [the holes] in the top, plastering them all with
   turpentine tree gum.

78. *balagara ŋambaŋambariɲu/*
   The two [grandsons] had a think.

79. *ŋali/ḍidugu yanuli/*
   'We must go out for some ḍidu wood' [one of them said].

80. *bagul ɲaḍulmali/ ŋurigabun/*
   'To get even again by burning him with it' [he continued].

81. *balagara – gambilgubin mayin/ ḍidugu balay baɲilŋaygu/*
   The two of them went into the forest, to split ḍidu there.

82. *baygun baŋgugara/ muɲiman/ ḍidu aɲḍa bagan/ ŋangu yiŋgaɽman/*
   They broke [it] up very small, and sewed the ḍidu up so that it
   was [a long torch with a cone-shaped] mouth like a yiŋgaɽ-basket.

83. *ŋuɽbaɲu balagara balayguya ɲinaɲinaygu/*
   The two of them went back to wait a while on the other side of
   the river.

84. *bayi gigan midi/*
   The small[er brother] was told [by the other]:

85. *gaḍi buŋa/ buɽalŋaygu/*
   'Go on, go down and have a look!'

86. *bayi midi buŋan/ ŋanbalŋaygu/*
   The smaller one went down, to ask [the grandfather]:

87. *ŋindama bayi garḍa/*
   'Are you alright?'

88. *ŋa/ ŋaḍa giyi garḍa/*
    'Yes, I'm fine here' [the old man replied].

89. *bungi/*
    'Go to sleep [then]!' [the grandson told him].

90. *ŋuṛbayaraŋu/ muyŋgulgu buwanaygu/*
    [He] went back again, to tell the elder brother:

91. *ŋa/ bayinbayḍi garḍa bungi/ yiŋḍagayul/ warbal/*
    'Yes, he's lying down alright down there. But wait a while yet, he's still awake.'

92. *ɲinaŋu balagara/*
    The two of them sat [for a while].

93. *baŋum bayi bulgan buŋan/ ŋanbalŋaygu/*
    Then the bigger one went down to ask:

94. *ŋinda bayi garḍa/*
    'Are you alright?' [he asked his grandfather].

95. *yimbaḍu/*
    There was no [reply] at all.

96. *ŋinda bayi yalay garḍa bungi/*
    'Are you resting here alright?'

97. *yimbaḍu/ buŋguray gananganan/*
    There was no [reply] at all, just loud snores.

98. *ŋuṛbaŋu bayi buwanaygu midigu/*
    He returned to tell the small[er one]:

99. *ḍaŋḍa ḍagun/ buŋguray madan/*
    'He's asleep now, throwing out snores.'

100. *aŋḍariga/ ḍidu aŋḍa maba/*
     'Now we certainly must light the ḍidu [torches]!'

101. *ḍidu baŋgugara maban/ buŋalmali/*
     The two [men] lit the ḍidu [torches] and went downhill with them.

102. *ŋinda baliŋaru/*
     'You [go] behind' [one of the grandsons said to the other].

103. *ŋaḍa yali/*
     'I'll [go] here [in front].'

104. *waṟaynḍaran baŋgugara ḍidu buyban/ gandanaygu/ ŋamban bayi*
     muŋga biḍilbiḍilbariŋu bayingalandu/
     Each of them stuck his [burning] ḍidu [torch] right into [the
     hollow tree] to burn [the grandfather]. [They] heard the noise of
     him thumping away inside.

105. *buṟan balubawal/ garḍun/ buṟan bandayi garan mayiŋu/*
     [They] had a good look around, and saw smoke coming out from
     the top.

106. *ŋinda/ giyi/*
     'Hey, you!' [one grandson said to the other].

107. *giɲandayi garan mayin/*
     'Smoke's coming out up there.'

108. *baludayi wayɲḍiwayɲḍin/ balagara/*
     The two of them went up.

109. *ŋayingalu/*
     'There he goes!'

That is, half the rainbow-snake has escaped from the log and run off.

110. *balidayi balagara mugabaḍun/*
     The two of them took a short cut uphill.

111. *bayingalu bayi/*
     He was still in front [of them].

112. *balidayigu mugabaḍun/*
     Again [they] took a short cut uphill.

113. *bayingalu bayi/*
     He was still in front.

114. *balaydawu mugabaḍun/*
     They took a short cut upriver.

115. *bayingalu bayi/*
     He was still in front.

116. *baŋum aɲḍa/*
     And then [they said to each other]:

117. *aɲḍa ḍara galga/*
     'Let [him] go now!'

118. *ŋali aɲḍa ŋuṛba/*
    'We'll go home!'

119. *ḍina bala ŋuṛu galgayaraɲu/ ḍaran/*
    A heel print was left out there, where [the foot] was put down.

Lines 108–15 exhibit the phenomenon of two topic-chains proceeding 'leapfrog fashion' through a text. Thus 108, 110, 112, 114 make up one chain (topic 'the two grandsons') while 111, 113, 115 constitute a second chain (with topic 'the rainbow-snake'). Note also that a topic-chain can continue after a break for direct speech. Thus line 90 continues the chain begun in line 86 (and note that the topic NP has no realisation in 90).

Vocabulary

Only words occurring in the examples and texts above are listed here. Each root is specified for part of speech, and also transitivity (in the case of verbals) and noun class (in the case of nouns). The following abbreviations are used:

Vtr	transitive verb	*bayi*	class I noun
Vint	intransitive verb	*balan*	class II noun
Adtr	transitive adverbal	*balam*	class III noun
Adint	intransitive adverbal	*bala*	class IV noun
Time	time qualifier	Adj	adjective
Int	interjection		

No attempt has been made to cross-reference all 'fully grammatical' words – pronouns, noun and verb markers, and particles; however, some initial segments of roots are mentioned.

All loan words are clearly identified.

Since this vocabulary is intended solely to facilitate understanding of the grammatical examples and texts, it has not been thought appropriate to give a full statement of the 'meaning' of each item. Instead, entries are mostly confined to one or two English words that give some indication of the most 'central' meaning of the Dyirbal word.

All roots given occur in Guwal, unless Dyalŋuy is specifically indicated. All occur (to the best of the writer's knowledge) in the three dialects D, M and G unless otherwise indicated (i.e. by placing one or two of the dialect letters after the word, showing that it is restricted to this dialect(s)).

The alphabetical order followed is:

$$a, b, d, ḍ, g, i, l, m, n, ɲ, ŋ, r, ṛ, u, w, y$$

aɲḍa PARTICLE – 4.15.2

ba- for NOUN and VERB MARKERS see 3.2.2, 3.4.5, 6.5
babi(ɲḍa), *bayi/balan:* father's mother; (for female ego) son's children
babil, Vtr: slice, peel
babuligan, LOAN, *bala:* pub, publican
badibadi, *bayi:* a personal name
baḍal, Vtr: bite, chew
baḍigay, Vint: duck away
baḍinḍila D, *baḍinḍilaḍila* M, *balan:* satin bird

baḍiri M Guwal and D Dyalŋuy, *bayi:* water guana
baḍiy, Vint: fall (off, down)
bagal, Vtr: pierce, dig, spear
balagara, balamaŋgan – 3.3.2
balbal, Vtr: roll
balbaliy, Vint: roll (over)
balbulubil, Dyalŋuy, Vint: motion downriver
balbulumbal, Dyalŋuy, Vtr: wash downriver
balgal, Vtr: hit with long rigid implement, held in hand; kill

balgun, Adj: naked, out of cover

bamba, DM, *bala*: stomach

bambun, Adj: quite fat and healthy (when recovering from illness)

bana, DM, *balan*: fresh water

banagay, DG, Vint: return (home)

banal, Vtr: break (off)

bandagay, Time: many years ago

banday, Vint: burst (out)

bandubanal, Vtr: bend over

banḏal, Vtr: follow

banḏul, PARTICLE – 4.15.3

bangula, *balam*: wild cucumber

baniy, Vint: come

baɲil, Vtr: split (rotten log by bashing it on a tree, to obtain grubs)

baŋarmbal Dyalŋuy, Vtr: ask

baŋgal, Vtr: paint with finger, write

baŋgay, *balan*: spear

baŋguy DG, *bayi*: green frog

baray, Time: next week

baraymbaray, Time: dawn, morning

bargan, *bayi*: wallaby

bari, *bala*: stone tomahawk

barmba, *bala*: quartz

barmbiy, Vint: glitter, shine

barmil, Vtr: look back

barmiliy, Vint: look back

barɲan [PL -*mi*], *bayi*: youth

baṟa(y), Adj: held between legs

baṟal, Vtr: punch, drive in

baṟiɲbaṟiɲ, *bayi*: chicken hawk

bawalbil Dyalŋuy, Vint: go

bawalmbal Dyalŋuy, Vtr: lead

baya, *bala*: belongings, things

bayabay Dyalŋuy, *bayi*: man

bayal, Vtr: sing

bayḏubil Dyalŋuy, Vint: motion downhill

baygul, Vtr: shake, wave, bash

bayil, Vtr: turn round, stir, wring

bayimbam, *bayi*: grub sp.

bayŋguray Dyalŋuy, Vtr: sing

biḏamal M, Vtr: swive (have sexual intercourse with)

biḏil, Vtr: hit with rounded object; rain

bigay, *bala*: handle (of basket)

bigi, LOAN, *balan*: pig

bigin, *balan*: shield

biguɲ, *bala*: (finger/toe) nail

bilal, Vtr: send; give, involving motion

bilayŋgir, LOAN, *bala*: blanket

biliy, Vint: climb (tree)

bilmbal, Vtr: push

bilmbu, *bayi/balan*: widower/widow

bilŋgi, Adj: on lap, across legs

bima, *balan*: death-adder

bimu(nḏa), *bayi/balan*: father's elder brother/sister (and reciprocal)

binara, LOAN, *balam*: peanut

binḏiriɲ, *bayi*: small lizard

bingun, Adj: tired, unconscious

birgil, *bala*: frost, wintertime

biri PARTICLE – 4.15.3

biya PARTICLE – 4.15.3

biyilbiyil, *balan*: peewee

buba D Dyalŋuy, *bala*: body

bubil, Vtr: pull away from

bubunba, *balan*: pheasant

budil, Vtr: carry in hand

buḏa, Adj: not sweet enough (usually drink)

buḏaḏa, M Dyalŋuy, *balan*: (black) bird sp.

buḏay G, Vint: bathe

buḏubuyal M Dyalŋuy, Vtr: blow, puff

buḏur, *bala*: butt of tree

buga, Adj: stinking smell of dead man or animal, or rotten fruit

bula(y(i)), Adj: two

bulgan (PL: -*gay*), Adj: big

bulgay, Vtr: swallow

bulgu DG, *balan*: wife

buliḏiman ~ buliman, LOAN, *bayi*: policeman

bulmbiy, Vtr: be male progenitor of

bulu(nḏa), *bayi/balan*: father's father (and reciprocal)

bulugi, LOAN, *balan*: cattle

buluru, Time: very many years ago

bulwal, Vtr: expel breath in big gasps

bundalay, Vint: fight

bunday, Vint: break (e.g. string)

bundil, Vtr: take out

bundiɲ, *balan*, grasshopper

bunḍul, Vtr: hit with long flexible implement
bungil, Vint: lie down (to sleep)
buni DM, *balan:* fire
buṇḍal, Vtr: pull up
buṇḍan, *balam:* yellow walnut
buɲal, Vint: motion downhill
buŋgaymariy, Vint: call (a name)
buŋgu, *bala:* knee
buŋguray, *bala:* snore
burbil, Vtr: pick (fruit), pull off
burbula, *bayi:* a personal name
burgulburgul, *bayi/balan:* child that never matures
burguṛum, *bayi:* jumping ant
burira, LOAN, *balam:* potato
burubay, *bayi:* boil
buṛal, Vtr: see, look (at)
buṛba, *balan:* swamp
buṛbi, Adj: half-way
buṛɲḍal G, Vtr: eat (vegetables)
buṛula, Dyalŋuy, *balan:* fighting ground
buṛumba, *bala:* stump
buway, Vtr: tell
buwu, LOAN, *bala:* fork
buyal, Vtr: blow, puff
buybal, DM, Vtr: hide

dabaḍanay, Vint: duck down
dabil, Vtr: throw handful of solid bits at
daday, Vint: motion downriver
dagaral, D Dyalŋuy, Vtr: break
dagaray, Dyalŋuy, Vint: break
dagu, *bayi:* hammer bird
dalbi M, Adj: top (inside)
dali, LOAN, *bala:* Tully (a town)
daliy, Vtr: deliver blow to someone lying down
daman, *bayi/balan:* child (of female ego)
damba, LOAN, *balam:* damper
dambul, *bala:* lump at reverse of handle on shield
dambun, *balan*, mythical person – see text xxxi *b*
dandu D Dyalŋuy, *bala:* tree, wood

dangal, Vtr: wash downstream
daŋgil, *bala:* riverbank
daral, Adtr: do badly (object orientation)
darḍi DM, Int: its a good job it happened
darubal Dyalŋuy, Vtr: soak, immerse in water
darubay Dyalŋuy, Vint: bathe
dawulubil Dyalŋuy, Vint: motion up river
dawun, LOAN, *bala:* town
dayibul, LOAN, *bala:* table
dayubil Dyalŋuy, Vint: motion uphill
diban DM, *bala:* stone
digir M Dyalŋuy, *bala:* side of head between eye and ear
dimbay, Vtr: carry, other than in hand
dina, LOAN, Time: dinnertime
dindal Dyalŋuy, Vtr: stand
dinu, Adj: cool
diɲal Dyalŋuy, *bala:* eye
diɲalmali Dyalŋuy, *balam:* flour
diŋgal D, *bala:* head
dira, *bala:* tooth, name
diranayal, Vtr: threaten
diyi, LOAN, *bala:* tea
dudal, Vtr: mash with stone
duguy, *bala:* kauri pine
dulgubara, *bala:* a M horde
dumbal, Vtr: touch on sore place
dundu D, *balan:* bird (generic)
duɲanbara, *bala:* a place name
duŋgaray, Vint: cry, weep
durmal M Dyalŋuy, Vtr: cook, burn
duygiy M, Vtr: look in, look over

ḍaban, DM, *bayi:* eel
ḍabil, Vtr: stop [someone] doing something
ḍabu DG, *bayi:* fish (generic)
ḍabun, *balan:* Tully River
ḍada, Time: a few days time
ḍaḍa, *bayi/balan:* baby
ḍagal, *bala:* cheek
ḍagin G Dyalŋuy, Int: no, nothing
ḍagiɲ (PL: *-gay*) G, Adj: big

ḍagun, Adj: asleep; also used as noun, *bala:* a sleep, a night

ḍaguru, balam: umbrella palm

ḍala, Adj: shallow

ḍalnbil, Vint: dance (a jumping up and down style, mainly practised by women)

ḍalgi, LOAN, *bala:* dray, sulky

ḍalguṛ D, *bala:* meat

ḍalŋgal Dyalŋuy, Vtr: cut

ḍalŋgulay, bala: tongue

ḍalŋuy, bala: 'avoidance' or 'mother-in-law' language style

ḍami, Adj: fat

ḍamu, PARTICLE – 4.15.3

ḍana G, *bayi/balan/bala* (effectively plural third person pronoun): all

ḍanay, Vint: stand

ḍaṇḍa, Time: now

ḍaṇḍaru DG, Time: earlier on today

ḍaŋala, bala: a singing style (in DG)

ḍaŋali, balan: small stinging-tree

ḍaŋgay DM, Vtr: eat (vegetables)

ḍaral, Vtr: stand

ḍarbal, Vtr: join on, join together

ḍarḍi G, Int: its a good job it happened

ḍarga, balan: a personal name (text xv)

ḍaruḍa, LOAN, *bala:* trousers

ḍawuḍala, balan: (black) bird sp

ḍawun, bala: dilly-bag

ḍawunbara G, *bala:* English bee

ḍawuy, bala: steam

ḍaymbal, Vtr: find

ḍayŋul, Adtr: finish (object orientation)

ḍaywal, Vtr: catch fish by dragging net-like roll of grass through the water

ḍaywil Dyalŋuy, Vtr: = *ḍaywal*

ḍibanḍiban, bala: wart (espec. on cattle)

ḍidu, balan: tree sp; and lighted torch made from the tree

ḍidan D Guwal and M Dyalŋuy, *bayi:* water guana

ḍiḍuluruy, balan: blue-black forest kingfisher

ḍiga, LOAN, *balam:* cigarette

ḍigil DM, Adj: good

ḍigirḍigir, balan: a willy wagtail

ḍigubina, bayi: a legendary person, who can take the form of a falling star

ḍilbay, Adj: knowing how to do something; used to the work

ḍilbu DM Dyalŋuy, Int: no, nothing

ḍilmuray M Dyalŋuy, *bala:* (head) hair

ḍilŋgal, Vtr: throw or pour water

ḍilŋguwal, M Dyalŋuy, Vtr: = *ḍilŋgal*

ḍilwal, Vtr: kick, shove with knee

ḍina, bala: foot

ḍinaguda, bala: (softwood) tree sp.

ḍinaman, bala: boot, shoe

ḍinari, bala: root under water

ḍinbay M Dyalŋuy, *bala:* dirt, the ground

ḍinbil, Vint: jump (across – e.g. from rock to rock)

ḍindi, bala: chest

ḍiŋgaliy DM, Vint: run, play

ḍirbal, bala: a language

ḍirbalŋan, bala: tribal territory; *bayi/balan:* members of tribe

ḍirga, bayi: eel-spear

ḍiwunbay, Vint: call *ḍiwu*

ḍiwuṇu, balan: pink-chested kingfisher

ḍiyil, balan: starling

ḍubayga, LOAN, *balam:* tobacco

ḍubul, bayi: erection (of penis)

ḍubula, balam: black pine

ḍubumbal Dyalŋuy, Vtr: hit with rounded implement

ḍubuɲ Dyalŋuy, Adj: quiet

ḍuda, Adj: big(dilly-bag), long or bushy (hair)

ḍuḍaba, bayi: the first man (creator of animate and physical phenomena); the time of the creator

ḍudar G, *bala:* urine

ḍuḍaṛ DM, *bala:* urine

ḍudulu M, *balan:* brown pigeon

ḍuḍur G, *bala:* navel

ḍuḍuṛ DM, *bala:* navel

ḍuga, LOAN, *bala:* sugar

ḍugagayin, LOAN, *bala:* sugar-cane

ḍugi, Adj: big

ḍugumbil D, *balan:* woman

ḍuguṟ, *balam:* a wild yam

ḍulbun, *bayi/balan:* recently married person

ḍulbungan, *balan:* woman who entices her promised man

ḍulburuy, *bayi/balan:* married person

ḍulmal, Vtr: squeeze

ḍulu, *bala:* hip, rump, tree-spur sticking out into river; bottom corner of dilly-bag

ḍulun M, Adj: a lot

ḍuluḍulu, *bala:* Johnson hardwood tree

ḍulwal M Dyalŋuy, Vtr: get up, raise up

ḍumbuluʼ, *bayi:* a personal name

ḍungan, *bala:* bull oak

ḍunguru D Guwal and M Dyalŋuy, Adj: (done) hard

ḍuṇa, *bala:* leaves (or other rubbish) in water

ḍuṇḍurḍuṇḍur, *bala*, pink oak

ḍural, Vtr: wipe, rub

ḍurgay, Vtr: spear (when the spear is held on to, and the actor can see that which he is trying to spear)

ḍurgay, *bayi/balan:* sibling

ḍurma(n), *bala:* track

ḍurmaybal Dyalŋuy, Vtr: rub

ḍurŋay, Vtr: drink without stopping for breath

ḍuru D, Int: I don't know

ḍuṟal M, Vint: crawl

ḍuwa, LOAN, *bala:* shop, store

ḍuyal M Dyalŋuy, Vtr: peel, take clothes off

ḍuymal, Vint: crawl under [something]

gabal, *balan:* crane

gabal G, *bala:* sand

gabalngabal, *bala:* sandy ridge

gabay D Dyalŋuy, *balan:* girl

gabay D Dyalŋuy, *bala:* yamstick

gabiṟ Dyalŋuy, Adj: hungry

gabul, *balan:* forest carpet-snake

gadal M, Vtr: build camp; mend

gaḍal, Vtr: pass by without seeing

gaḍi, PARTICLE – 4.15.1

gaḍilmbay, Vint: prevaricate, pretend

gaḍin, *balan:* girl

gaḍin, *bala:* yamstick

gaḍiya [PL: *-mi*], *balan*, young girl

gagalum M, *bayi:* moon

gagilbara M Dyalŋuy, *bayi:* rainbow; *balan:* green pigeon; *bala:* blood-wood tree

gagiṟ Dyalŋuy, Adj: big

gala M, Time: earlier on today

galbabagal, Vtr: wash clothes

galbin, *bayi/balan:* child (of male ego)

galga, PARTICLE – 4.15.3, 4.12.2

galgal, Vtr: leave [it] be

gama DG, *bala:* a singing style

gama, M, *bala:* gun

gambal DM, *bayi:* rain

gambil, *bala:* mountains, tableland

gamu G, *balan*, water

gana, PARTICLE – 4.15.3

gana, Adj: front

gananganan, Adj: loud

ganba Dyalŋuy, Time: earlier/later on today

ganbil, Adtr: do badly (subject orientation)

ganday, Vtr: burn

gani DM, Adj: long way

ganibara D, *balan:* (wild) dingo

gaṇḍamal M Dyalŋuy, Vtr: follow

gaŋgiḍa ~ ŋaŋgiḍa, LOAN, *bala:* handkerchief

garan D, *bala:* smoke

garḍa, Adj: alright

garḍul, Adtr: do properly

gari, *balan:* sun

gari DG, *balan:* hairy mary grub

gariḍin, LOAN, *bala:* kerosene [tin]

garimal, *bala:* summer[time]

gariya, *balan:* Tully Falls

garmban M Dyalŋuy, *bala:* smoke, haze, mist, steam; *balam:* tobacco

garugaḍal, Vtr: pass by

gaṟbu DG, Adj: three; M, Adj: a good few

gawa, LOAN, *balan:* cow

gawu, PARTICLE – 4.15.1

gaya, bayi: mother's younger brother
gayambula, bayi: white cockatoo
gayga, bala: eye
gaygamali, balam: flour
gaygi, LOAN, *balam:* cake
gayṇḍal, Vint: break
gayu, bala: bark bag, basket or cradle
gi(ɲa)- for demonstrative NOUN MARK-
ERS see 3.2.2, 6.5
gibal, Vtr: scrape, scratch
gibaṛ, bala: a fig tree
gibaṛ, bala: mark on message stick
gibay, Vint: scrape, scratch
gidimbal, Vtr: tickle
giḍar, Adj: pretty
giḍiya, bayi: character in myth
gigal, Vtr: allow or tell [someone] to
do something
gigiba M Dyalŋuy, *balan:* shield,
peewee
gila- for NOUN and VERB MARKERS see
6.5
gilgariy M Dyalŋuy, Vint: jump
gilu, Time: later on today
gimbil, Vtr: [wind or cyclone] blow
ginagir, balan: mother or mother's
younger sister, and child(ren)
ginayṇḍaran Dyalŋuy, Adj: two
gindal, Vtr: look with a light
ginday, Vint: look with a light
gindimbal, Vtr: warn [of danger]
ginga D Dyalŋuy, *balan:* echidna, pig
giramay, bala: a language
giramaygan, bala: tribal territory;
bayi/balan: members of tribe
girḍibi, LOAN, Time: christmas[time]
giriŋgiriɲ, bala: sharp scream
giṛṇḍal, bala: honey
giwan, bala: bloodwood tree
giyara, balan: big softwood stinging
tree
gubaguba, bayi: type of stripy pearl
shell
gubal, Vtr: cover up
gubi, bayi: 'wise man'
gubila, Time: a few years ago
gubimbulu, bayi: 'very wise man'
gubu, bala: leaf

gububara, bayi: a spirit
gubungaṛa, balam: a palm tree
gubur, bala: a native bee
guda, balan: dog
gudaymbal D, Vtr: pass by
guḍagay D, *bayi:* alligator
guga, bala: skin
gugaṛ, bayi: black guana
gugayŋgugay, bayi: host of teenage
boys
gugu, balan: mopoke owl
gugula, balan: platypus
guguṛ, balam, young shoots of loya
cane
guguṛgay, Int: good job
guguwuɲ DG, *balan:* brown pigeon
guguwuy, Int: 'wait there'
gula M Dyalŋuy, *bala:* body
gulbal, Vtr: block, shut
gulbiṛ, bala: place name (on Tully
River, just below the Falls)
gulgiṛi, Adj: prettily painted (espec.
of man)
guli, Adj: strong, sharp, sweet
guliliɲ, M Dyalŋuy, *balan:* parrot
guliɲ, Adj: east
gulŋgal, Vtr: breastfeed
gulu, PARTICLE – 4.15.3
gulubu, bala: wind
gumbiyan, balan: echidna (= porcu-
pine)
gumbu, bayi/balan: mother's mother
(and reciprocal)
gumbu, Dyalŋuy, *bala:* bottom, arse,
tail of bird
gumbul G, *balan:* woman
gumburu, bala: mountain mist
gumuray D Dyalŋuy, *bala:* (head)
hair
guna, bala: faeces
gunbal, Vtr: cut
gunbay, bala: name of waterhole (on
Murray River)
gundal, Vtr: put in
gunga, Adj: raw, alive
guniy, Vtr: search for
guṇḍal, Vtr: drink
guṇḍil, Vtr: take skin, clothes off

guɲu, Adj: new
guŋgaga, *balan:* kookaburra
guŋgari, Adj: north
guŋgu, *bala:* red clay
guray, *bala:* red oak
gurbuṟu, *balan:* seven sisters (stars)
guriḍala, *bayi:* eagle-hawk
gurilnguril, *bayi:* a storm bird
gurugu, LOAN, *bala:* grog
guruŋgul, *bayi:* meat hawk
guruɲun M Dyalŋuy, *bala:* oak trees
guṟa, *bala:* vaginal opening
guṟur, *balan:* brolga
guwal DG, *bala:* everyday language style; voice
guwara D Dyalŋuy, Adj: three or more
guwu DM, *bala:* nose
guwugiɳḍu DG, *balan:* ibis
guwurmbal, Vtr: gather up
guwuy, *bayi:* spirit of a dead man
guya M, *bayi:* fish (generic)
guyabil Dyalŋuy, Vint: cross river
guyaŋgu, *bala:* water-gum tree
guyḍul Dyalŋuy, Vtr: bite
guyi, Adj: dead (of persons only)
guyibara, *balan:* curlew
guyimbara, *bayi:* murderer
guyŋgun, *balan:* spirit of a dead woman
guyŋguru, Adj: south

lada, LOAN, *bala:* ladder
landan, LOAN, *bala:* London (an established loan after the writer was called *bayi landanbara*)
laymun, LOAN, *balam:* lemon

mabal, Vtr: set light to; light
mabil, Vint: cross river
mabilŋgay M, Vint: cross river quickly
madal, Vtr: throw
maḍirabil Dyalŋuy, Vint: sit, stay
maḍirim, LOAN, Adj: mustering
maga, *balan:* a rat
magaṟa, *bala:* skin from dead human
magira, *bala:* yellow clay
magul, Time: 'meanwhile' – 4.14
magur M, *bala:* haze

mala, *bala:* hand
malayigara, *balan:* scorpion
mali, Int: exclamation of joy concerning food or drink
mambu D, *bala:* back
manbuṟu Dyalŋuy, *bala:* hand
manḍal, Vtr: point out
mani, LOAN, *bala:* money
manmay, Vint: move camp
maɲḍay DM, Vint: eat [vegetables] to appease hunger
maɲḍay DM, Adj: full up (with food)
maɲa DM, *bala:* ear
maŋgal, Vtr: pick up
maŋgay Dyalŋuy, Adj: no good
maraba M, *balan:* bird (generic)
marbay, Vtr: [ghost or spirit] frighten
margi, Adj: thin and emaciated [after illness]
margin, *bala:* gun
marigal, *balan:* chicken snake
maril, Vint: follow
maṟa, *bala:* snake or rat hole
maṟalu DM, *bala:* hollow log, shirt
maṟu, *bala:* mud
mawa, *balan:* shrimp
maya G, Int: no, nothing
mayaḍa M Dyalŋuy, *bayi:* grub
maybaḍa M, *bayi:* alligator
maybariy M Dyalŋuy, Vint: call out
mayi DM, *bala:* English bee
mayil, Vint: come out
mayilŋgay, Vint: D, come out forcibly; M, come out quickly
maymbal, Vtr: plaster
maymiy, Vint: visit [someone] to be given food or drink
midi, Adj: small
midin, *bayi:* possum
miḍa, *bala:* house, camp, camping-place
miḍiḍi DG, LOAN, *balan:* white woman, missus
miḍul, Vtr: take no notice of
mila, *bala:* clearing
milbir, *bala:* slippery blue fig tree
milbirmi, *bala:* Cardwell; *balan:* Hinchinbrook Channel

milgi, LOAN, *bala:* (cow's or goat's) milk

minbal, Vtr: hit with a long rigid implement, thrown; shoot

miɲa DM, 'what?' [see 3.2.4]

miɲaɲ, 'how many?' [see 3.2.4]

miɲay DM, *miɲi* G: 'when' [see 3.5]

mira, *bala:* front

miraɲ DM, *balam:* black bean

miyabuɽ, *bala:* black oak

miyanday, Vint: laugh

miyay, Adj: smiling

mubaɽay, *bayi:* large eel

mubuɲinmi, *bayi:* mythical man (text XXV)

muḍan, Adj: (fire or light) extinguished

muga M, Adj: half-way

mugay, *bayi:* grinding-stone

mugu, PARTICLE – see 4.15.3

mugu(ɲḍa), *bayi/balan:* mother's elder brother (and reciprocal)

mugulnba, Adj: whole, round

mugunan(ḍa), *bayi/balan:* mother's elder sister (and reciprocal)

muguru, Adj: quiet

muguy, Adj: too much

muguyŋgun D Dyalŋuy, *balan:* spirit of a dead woman

mulgu, *bayi/balan:* indistinct noise (e.g. talking some way off, when one is unable to make out who is speaking or what is being said)

mulmay, Vint: dive (into water)

mulu, *bala:* end (of log, road, swamp)

mulumdayman M Dyalŋuy, *bala:* message

mumba M Dyalŋuy, PARTICLE = *mugu* – see 4.15.3, 9

munay, Vint: vomit

mundal, Vtr: lead, take

mundi DG, Adj: a good few

mundu, Adj: offended

munilan, *balan:* chicken-snake

munu DM, *bala:* bottom, arse

munumadal DM, Vtr: give up, chuck [it] in

muɳḍal, Vint: divide

muɳḍu M Dyalŋuy, *balan:* woman

muɲi, Adj: smashed (into small pieces)

muɲa DG, Adj: a lot

muŋga, *bala:* loud noise

mura, *bala:* semen

muray, *bala:* head hair

muraynbila, *bayi/balan:* aboriginal person

murgan, *balan:* personal name (text XV)

muymbal, Vtr: extinguish (fire or light)

muyŋgul, *bayi/balan:* elder sibling

muyu G, *bala:* bottom, arse

muyumadal, G, Vtr: give up, chuck [it] in

nagay, Vint: bank of river breaks

nalɲil, Vtr: shake, sieve

naŋgalnaŋgal, *bayi:* small, stinging, black ants

nayi [PL: *-nba*], *balan:* young girl

nayŋul Dyalŋuy, Vtr: throw

nuba, *balan:* water-bag: tree from whose bark water-bags are made

nudil DG, Vtr: cut, sever

ɲaḍul DM, Vtr: cook, burn, light

ɲalmaru, Dyalŋuy, *bayi/balan:* child

ɲalŋga, *bayi/balan:* child

ɲambal, Vtr: paint with flat of hand

ɲamu, Adj: cooked

ɲanbal M Dyalŋuy, Vtr: pierce, dig, spear

ɲaɽa, *balam:* flame, bright light

ɲimal, Vtr: catch, hold, squeeze

ɲimbaɽ M Dyalŋuy, *balan:* dog; *bala:* (softwood) tree sp

ɲinay, Vint: sit, stay

ɲingal M Dyalŋuy, Adj: short

ɲiral, Vtr: poke [something sharp] into, pin

ɲiyi, *balan:* noise of birds, indicating that something is moving on the ground

ɲu- for PRONOUNS see 3.3, 6.2

ɲugay, Vtr: grind

ɲumbul, *bala:* beard

ɲunḍal, Vtr: kiss

ɲungul Dyalŋuy, Adj: one

ɲurɲu, Adj: too busy to notice

ɲuɽimal Dyalŋuy, Vtr: see, look at

ŋa- for NOUN MARKERS see 3.2.2, 6.5

ŋa- for PRONOUNS see 3.3, 6.2

ŋa, Int: yes

ŋabal DM, Vtr: immerse in water, soak

ŋabay DM, Vint: bathe

ŋaḍan, bala: a language

ŋaḍanḍi, bala: tribal territory; bayi/
balan: members of tribe

ŋaḍi, Adj: on shoulder, on horseback

ŋaḍil, D, Vtr: lose, take absolutely no
notice of, ignore

ŋaga, bala: leg

ŋagi(ŋḍa), bayi/balan: mother's father
(and reciprocal)

ŋalban, balan: father's younger sister

ŋalgal, Vtr: poke with stick

ŋalŋunda M Dyalŋuy, Adj: between
legs

ŋalŋunday M Dyalŋuy, Adj: on lap,
across legs

ŋama, balan: shield handle, trigger (on
gun)

ŋambal, Vtr: hear, listen to

ŋambiya DG, Adj and Noun: 'what's
it called?'

ŋami, bala: lap

ŋamiṟ, Adj: hungry

ŋamun, balan: breast, breastmilk

ŋanbal, Vtr: ask

ŋanday, Vint: call out

ŋangu, bala: mouth

ŋaɲum, DM, Int: I don't know

ŋaŋgiḍa ~ gaŋgiḍa, LOAN, bala: handkerchief

ŋargana Dyalŋuy, balan: light, flame

ŋariɲḍi, LOAN, balam: orange

ŋarmil D Dyalŋuy, Vtr: listen to, hear

ŋaru MG, PARTICLE – 4.15.3, 4.12.2

ŋaṟa, PARTICLE – 4.15.3

ŋaṟbal, DM, Vint: get a fright, jump
with fright

ŋaṟḍambay, Vint: plan some rather
difficult action

ŋaṟil, Vtr: answer

ŋaṟɲḍay, Vint: stare

ŋayan, LOAN, bala: iron

ŋayɲil DG, Adtr: do first/start doing
(subject orientation)

ŋi- for PRONOUNS see 3.3, 6.2

ŋi(ɲa)- G, for demonstrative NOUN
MARKERS see 3.3.2, 6.5

ŋilu M Dyalŋuy, Adj: cold

ŋiriwuɲal, balan: green pigeon

ŋirma M, bala: everyday language
style; voice

ŋu, Int: alright

ŋudaŋga DM, Time: the other day

ŋulga, Time: tomorrow

ŋuma(ndi), bayi: father, and father's
younger brother

ŋumbuŋga DM, Time: yesterday

ŋunbiṟal, Adtr: do first/start to do
(object orientation)

ŋunḍay, Vtr: blame

ŋunil D Dyalŋuy, Adtr: do first/start
to do

ŋunɲun Dyalŋuy, balan: breast, breast
milk etc.

ŋuɲaɲi D Dyalŋuy, bala: teeth, name,
seed

ŋuɲaɲuy M Dyalŋuy, bala: teeth
name, seed

ŋuri PARTICLE – 4.15.3

ŋurma PARTICLE – 4.15.3

ŋurɲḍi Dyalŋuy, PARTICLE: =ŋuri, see
4.15.3, 9

ŋuṟbay M, Vint: return (home)

ŋuṟbil D, Adtr: try, test

ŋuṟin, Adj: deep

ŋuṟu, bala: heel, heelmark

ŋuymal, Adtr: do properly

ṟala, bala: smaller of two sticks used
to accompany ḍaŋala-style singing

ṟaygi, LOAN, bala: rag

ṟubiy, Vint: eat (meat)

ṟudu, bala: top of vertical depression
at nape of neck, just below bone

ṟugal, Vtr: watch [someone] going

ṟugulu G, Time: the other day

ṟugulmba G, Time: yesterday

ṟugun [PL: -mi], bayi: youth

ṟulbal, Vtr: split (with tomahawk)

ṟulgu, bala: heart

ṟuwa, Adj: west

wabal, Vtr: look up at

wabu DM, *bala:* scrub

wabubara M, *balan:* (wild) dingo

wadam, bayi: snake (generic)

wadil D, Vtr: swive (have sexual intercourse with)

waḍa, bayi: crow

waga M, LOAN, Adj: work[ing]

wagay, Vtr: spear, holding onto the spear, when the actor cannot see what he is spearing

wagawa M, *balan:* blue scrub pigeon

wagi DG, LOAN, Adj: work[ing]

waguli, bala: blood

waguy DM, *bala:* sand

walagay Dyalŋuy, Vint: return (home)

walawalay, Vint: dance (shake-a-leg style)

walba Dyalŋuy, *bayi:* money

walgiy, Vtr: look over, in or round [something] at

walguy, bayi: brown snake

walmay, Vint: arise, get up

walmbil, Vtr: raise, lift, wake up

walŋa, bala: breath

walŋamu, bala: lung

wambal, Vtr: build mia-mia (cover frame with leaves etc.)

wamil, Vtr: watch someone without their being aware they are being watched

wandal, Vtr: hang up, scoop up

wandil, Vint: motion upriver

wanḍay, Vtr: call name [of]

wangawa D, *balan:* blue scrub pigeon

waɲ- for interrogative PRONOUNS see 3.3.3, 5.8.4, 6.6

waŋal DM, *bayi:* boomerang

waŋgagay, Vint: step over (e.g. log)

wara, PARTICLE – see 4.15.3

waraɲ M Dyalŋuy, Adj: three or more

waraɲuŋgul, M, Adj: three

warayi, balan: bony bream

waraymal, M, Vtr: find, meet

warbal, Adj: awake, can't get to sleep

warḍan, balan: rafter, raft, boat

wargiɲ G, *bayi:* boomerang

wariy M, Vint: fly

waruɲ Dyalŋuy, *bala:* sand, sugar

waṛabada M, *bala:* turpentine tree

waṛaynḍaran, Adj: each (of two) having his own

waṛu, Adj: crooked, bent

waway, Time: 'too soon' – see 4.14

wawul, Vtr: go (from here) to fetch someone (from there to here)

waybala, LOAN, *bayi:* white man

waymbaray, Vint: go round [something]

waymbay, Vint: go walkabout

waymin(ḍa), balan: mother-in-law

wayndil, Vint: motion uphill etc

wayndilŋgay M, Vint: motion uphill quickly

wayu, Adj: change[d] into something (e.g. text xxv)

windan, balan: yellow mountain bird

wiriɲḍila M, *bayi:* dragon fly

wirmban, Adj: thin [person], 'skin and bones'

wirŋgal Dyalŋuy, Vtr: scrape, scratch

wirŋgay Dyalŋuy, Vint: scrape, scratch

wiru, bayi: husband

wiyamay D Guwal and M Dyalŋuy, *wiyabay* M Guwal and D Dyalŋuy Adint; *wiyamal* D Guwal and M Dyalŋuy, *wiyabal* M Guwal and D Dyalŋuy, Adtr: do what/do how – see 3.4.4

wudu G, *bala:* nose

wudubalu, Adj: going straight on, blindly, without looking back

wuḍiy, Vint: grow up

wuḍu, balam: vegetable/fruit food (generic)

wugal, Vtr: give

wugiḍa, Adj: generous

wugiyam M, *balan:* firefly

wulay, Vint: vanish, get lost

wuma, bala: thick undergrowth

wumbu M, *bala:* head

wunay, Adj: slow

wundiy, Adint: do slowly

wuɲḍa- for interrogative NOUN and

VERB MARKERS see 3.2.4, 3.4.7, 6.5–6

wuṇḍirwuṇḍir, bayi: midges

wuṇḍurmbuyal D Dyalŋuy, Vtr: blow, puff

wura DM, Adj: little

wurawuragabunda, idiom [in locative case]: quite a lot

wurbay, Vint: say, speak, talk

wurbunurbun G, *bala:* tassel fern

wurgal Dyalŋuy, Adj: slow

wurmbu M Dyalŋuy, *balan:* crayfish, scorpion

wurmbur, bala: bone

wuygi, Adj: no good

wuyubal, Dyalŋuy, Vtr: tell

ya- for NOUN and VERB MARKERS see 3.2.2, 3.4.5, 6.5

yabala, bala: flat ground

yabu(ndi), balan: mother, and mother's younger sister

yaburi, Int: 'exclamation of terror'

yaḍa, PARTICLE – see 4.15.3

yaḍaṛ, bayi: stingaree

yagal, bala: pandamus tree

yagay, Int: exclamation to accompany some decisive action

yagi, Adj: broken, split, torn

yagin, bala: side of head between eye and ear

yalamay D Guwal and M Dyalŋuy, *yalabay* M Guwal and D Dyalŋuy, Adint; *yalamal* D Guwal and M Dyalŋuy, *yalabal* M Guwal and D Dyalŋuy, Adtr: 'do like this' – see 3.4.4

yalgay, bala: road, track

yalibin Dyalŋuy, Vint: come

yalŋgay, bayi: single man (beyond usual marrying age)

yalŋgayngan, balan: single woman (beyond usual marrying age)

yama, PARTICLE – see 4.15.3

yamani DM, *bayi:* rainbow

yamba, PARTICLE – see 4.15.3

yambil DG, Vint: fly

yanda, PARTICLE – see 4.15.3

yanu(l) ~ yana, Vint: go

yaŋgal, bayi: red bream

yaŋgu(n)bayḍigu, Time: next week

yara, bayi: fishing line

yaṛa, bayi: man

yaṛin, Adj: slim (of a woman)

yibay, Dyalŋuy, *balan:* fire

yibi M, *balan:* woman

yidiṛ, bala: grass

yiḍil, Vtr: *(gubi)* massages, rubs

yigam M Dyalŋuy, Adj: frightened

yigara, balan: crayfish

yilgil M Dyalŋuy, Adj: broken, split, torn

yilwul Dyalŋuy, Vtr: pull, take out

yimalimal, balan: welcome swallow

yimba DM, Int: no, nothing

yiṇḍa, Time: 'not yet' – see 4.14

yiŋari GM, *bala:* cave, hole

yiŋgaṛ, bala: long basket with cone-like mouth

yirguṇḍiy, Dyalŋuy, Vint: laugh

yiriṇḍila D, *bayi:* dragon-fly

yubal, Vtr: put down

yugaba, bayi: small brown rat

yugari MG, *bala:* hollow log

yugiyam D, *balan:* firefly

yugu, bala: tree, stick, wood (also G *balan:* fire)

yugubara, bayi: a spirit

yuguṛ M, *bayi:* barramundi

yulgara, Adj: leaning

yulmiy Dyalŋuy, Vtr: eat (meat or vegetables)

yulŋiy M Dyalŋuy, Vint: dance

yululumbal, Vtr: rock, nurse (baby)

yumal, bala: body

yunba, balan: water-python

yuŋaray, D, Vint: swim

yuŋga D Dyalŋuy, *bayi:* kangaroo, wallaby

yuŋgugan, Adj: another one

yuŋgul, Adj: one

yurmu, PARTICLE – see 4.15.3

yuṛal, Vtr: give through (e.g. window)

yuṛay, Adj: quiet

yuṛi, bayi: grey kangaroo

yuwur, PARTICLE – see 4.15.3

yuwuy, Int: 'that's right'

List of Dyirbal affixes

All allomorphs of grammatical suffixes are listed below, together with clitics. Forms *baɲuniɲ/baɲunday* (6.5.4) are omitted, as are plurals occurring with a single noun or adjective (6.1.8). The inserted *-n-* (7.5.1) is omitted. In each case reference is to the section(s) containing major discussion of the affix or clitic.

-a up; medium distance – 3.2.3, 6.5.7
-aru universal affix – 6.5.7, 6.7.1

-ba locative – 3.2.1, 6.1.5
-ba pronominal affix(?) – 6.2
-ba M extent(?) – 6.5.6
-baḍun 'really, very' – 6.1.1, 6.4
-(m)bal transitive verbaliser – 4.7.1
-(n)bal verbal aspect – 6.3
-balb- 'down, water' – 3.2.3, 6.5.7
-ban emphatic – 6.1.6
-bara 'someone/thing connected with – ' – 6.1.1
-baray M 'with a lot of – ' – 6.1.1
-bariy reciprocal – 4.8.2
-(m)bariy reflexive – 4.8.1
-baṛa comparative – 6.1.1, 6.4
-bawal 'long way' – 3.2.3
-bayḍ- 'down, non-water' – 3.2.3, 6.5.7
-bi universal affix – 6.7.3
-biday G 'without – ' – 6.1.1
-bil intransitive verbaliser – 4.7.1
-bila ~ -ba verbal inflection – 4.13.1
-bila ~ -ba 'with – ' – 6.1.1
-bu ergative/instrumental – 3.2.1, 7.6
-bu universal affix – 6.7.2

-da locative – 3.2.1, 6.1.5
-da pronominal affix(?) – 6.2
-daw- 'up, water' – 3.2.3, 6.5.7
-day- 'up, non-water' – 3.2.3, 6.5.7
-du ergative/instrumental – 3.2.1, 7.6

-ḍa locative – 3.2.1, 6.1.5
-ḍan(a) emphatic – 6.1.6
-ḍaran dual – 6.1.1
-ḍay G future tense – 3.4.3, 10.3.2
-ḍay verbal aspect – 6.3
-ḍilu ~ -ḍu emphatic – 6.1.1, 6.4
-(ɲ)ḍin catalytic affix with genitive – 4.11.1, 6.2
-ḍir kinship dual – 6.1.3
-ḍu ergative/instrumental – 3.2.1, 7.6

-ga locative – 3.2.1, 6.1.5, 6.5.3
-ga verbal inflection – 4.13.2, 10.3.2
-gabun 'another – ' – 6.1.1
-galiy verbal aspect – 6.3
-gali/a/u direction indicator – 3.2.3, 6.5.7
-gan feminine – 9.1.2, 2.4
-ganiy verbal aspect – 6.3
-gara 'one of a pair' – 3.3.2, 6.5.6, 6.1.1
-gayul 'the same' – 6.1.1, 6.1.4
-ginay participial – 4.6
-ginay 'covered with – ' – 6.1.1
-gir kinship dual – 6.1.3
-gira clitic – 4.16
-gu ergative/instrumental – 3.2.1, 7.6
-gu dative – 3.2, 4.4.1, 5.3.3–4, 6.1.5, 6.2
-gu allative – 3.2.1, 6.1.5
-gu ~ ŋgu time until – 3.5, 6.4
-gu purposive verbal inflection – 4.4.3, 5.3.3–4

guya 'across river' – 3.2.3

-*i* purposive verbal inflection – 4.4.3
-*i* down; short distance – 3.2.3, 6.5.7

-*l* noun class I – 3.2.2, 6.5, 8.4.4
-*li*, -*lu* – see -*ri*, -*ru*

-*m* DM negative imperative – 4.12.2, 10.3.2
-*m* noun class III – 3.2.2, 6.5, 8.4.4, 10.3.1
-*ma* interrogative clitic – 4.16
-*mal* ~ -*mbal* instrumentive, comitative – 4.9, 5.7
-*mal* ~ -(*m*)*bal* transitive verbaliser – 4.7.1
-*maŋgan* 'one of many' – 3.3.2, 6.5.6, 6.1.1
-*mariy* ~ (*m*) *bariy* reflexive – 4.8.1
-*mi* general genitive – 3.2.1, 4.11.2, 5.5.2, 10.3.2
-*mi* perfective relative clause – 4.10, 5.5.2, 10.3.2
-*mi* plural on 3 nouns – 6.1.8
-*mu* time since – 3.5, 6.4
-*mu* G negative imperative – 4.12.2, 10.3.2
-*mumbay* 'all of – ' – 6.1.1
-*muɲa* participial – 4.6

-*n* noun class II – 3.2.2, 6.5, 8.4.4
-*n* present-past tense – 3.4.3, 10.3.2
-*na* pronominal object – 6.2
-*nay* alternant of -*ŋay* – 4.4.2
-*nu* pronominal genitive – 6.2

-*ɲ* DM future tense – 3.4.3, 10.3.2
-*ɲa* nominal affix – 3.2.1, 5.8.3, 6.1.1, 6.2

-(*ɲ*)*ḏin* catalytic affix with genitive – 4.11.1, 6.2
-*ɲu* present-past tense – 3.4.3, 10.3.2

-*ŋaŋgay* DM 'without —' – 6.1.1
-*ŋara* G alternant of -*ŋura* – 4.5.5
-*ŋaru* M 'behind' – 3.2.3
-*ŋaru* 'is like a —' – 6.1.1
-*ŋay* verbal affix – 4.4.2
-*ŋga* locative – 3.2.1, 6.1.5
-*ŋgu* ergative/instrumental – 3.2.1, 7.6
-*ŋgu* ~ -*gu* time until – 3.5, 6.4
-*ŋu* simple genitive – 3.2, 4.11.1, 6.1.5, 6.2, 5.5.2
-*ŋu* relative clause – 4.10, 5.5.2
-*ŋum* ablative – 3.4.5, 6.5
-*ŋunda* 'somewhere' – 6.5.6
-*ŋunu* ablative – 3.2.1, 6.4
-*ŋunu* 'out of —' – 6.1.1
-*ŋura* DM verbal inflection – 4.5.5

-*ra* locative – 4.10
-*ri* motion(?) – 6.5, 3.4.5
-*riga* clitic – 4.16
-*riy* reflexive – 4.8.1, 7.7
-*ru* ergative/instrumental – 4.10
-*ru* motion – 3.4.6, 6.5, 7.7
-*ru* universal affix – 6.7.1, 6.1.7, 6.5.7, 7.7

-*ṛa* locative – 3.2.1, 6.1.5
-*ṛu* ergative/instrumental – 3.2.1, 7.6

-*u* simple genitive – 3.2.1, 4.11.1, 6.1.5
-*u* in front; long way – 3.2.3, 6.5.7

-*y* locative – 3.4.5, 6.5
-*yaray* verbal aspect – 6.3
-*yiríy* D reflexive – 4.8.1
-(*y*)*uŋgul* 'that's the one' – 6.5.6

References

Abercrombie, D. [1967]. *Elements of general phonetics.* (Edinburgh: University Press.)

Aguas, E. F. [1966]. *Unedited first drafts of Aboriginal languages collected February to March 1966 at Palm Island, North Queensland* [Typescript] (Canberra: Australian Institute of Aboriginal Studies.)

Allen, W. S. [1951]. 'A study in the analysis of Hindi sentence-structure' *Acta Linguistica* VI, 68–86.

Armstrong, M. and Murray, John [1886]. 'No. 118 – Hinchinbrook Island and the mainland adjacent', pp. 418–21 of *The Australian Race*, edited by Edward M. Curr (Melbourne and London), vol. II.

Banfield, E. J. [1908]. *The confessions of a beachcomber: scenes and incidents in the career of an unprofessional beachcomber in tropical Queensland.* (London: Fisher Unwin.)

[1911]. *My tropic isle.* (London: Fisher Unwin.)

[1918]. *Tropic days.* (London: Fisher Unwin.)

[1925]. *Last leaves from Dunk Island.* (Sydney: Angus and Robertson.)

Benveniste, E. [1948]. *Noms d'agent et noms d'action en Indo-Européen.* (Paris: Adrien-Maisonneuve.)

Birdsell, J. B. [1958]. 'Some population problems involving Pleistocene man'. *Cold Spring Harbor Symposia on Quantitative Biology* XXII, 47–69.

Blake, B. J. [1969]. *The Kalkatungu language: a brief description.* (Canberra: Australian Institute of Aboriginal Studies.)

Blake, B. J. and Breen, J. G. [1971]. The Pitta-pitta dialects. (Melbourne: Monash University Linguistic Communications.)

Bloch, B. and Trager, G. L. [1942]. *Outline of linguistic analysis.* (Baltimore: Linguistic Society of America at the Waverly Press.)

Boas, F. [1911]. *Handbook of American Indian languages, Part I.* (Washington: Smithsonian Institution.)

Bolton, G. C. [1963]. *A thousand miles away: a history of north Queensland to 1920.* (Brisbane: Jacaranda Press.)

Buchanan, F. J. [1900]. 'Aboriginal words and meanings [Eenawon tribe, N.S.W.]', *Science of Man* IV, 4, 64–5.

Capell, A. [1956]. *A new approach to Australian linguistics.* (Sydney: Oceania Linguistic Monographs.)

[1962a]. *Some linguistic types in Australia.* (Sydney: Oceania Linguistic Monographs.)

[1962b]. 'Language and social distinction in Aboriginal Australia', *Mankind* V, 514–22.

[1967]. 'Sound systems in Australia', *Phonetica* XVI, 85–110.

[411]

Capell, A. and Elkin, A. P. [1937]. 'The languages of the Kimberley division', *Oceania* VIII, 216–46.

Carron, W. [1849]. *Narrative of an expedition under the direction of the late Mr Assistant Surveyor E. B. Kennedy, for the exploration of the country lying between Rockingham Bay and Cape York.* (Sydney)

Chadwick, N. [1968]. *A descriptive study of the Djingili language, Northern Territory, Australia.* M.A. thesis (University of New England, Armidale); a revision will be published shortly by the Australian Institute of Aboriginal Studies, Canberra.

Chomsky, N. [1957]. *Syntactic structures.* (The Hague: Mouton.)

[1965]. *Aspects of the theory of syntax.* (Cambridge, Mass: MIT Press.)

[1971]. 'Deep structure, surface structure and semantic interpretation', in Steinberg and Jakobovits [1971].

Coate, H. H. J. and Oates, L. [1970]. *A grammar of Ngarinjin, Western Australia.* (Canberra: Australian Institute of Aboriginal Studies.)

Craig, B. F. [1967]. *Cape York* [Bibliography series, No. 2]. (Canberra: Australian Institute of Aboriginal Studies.)

Cunningham, M. C. (= M. C. Sharpe) [1969]. *A description of the Yugumbir dialect of Bandjalang.* (Brisbane: University of Queensland papers, Faculty of Arts, vol. 1, No. 8.)

Dixon, R. M. W. [1965]. *What is language?* (London: Longmans.)

[1968a]. *The Dyirbal language of North Queensland.* PhD thesis (University of London.)

[1968b]. 'Virgin birth', *Man* (n.s.) III, 653–4.

[1968c]. 'Noun classes', *Lingua* XXI, 104–25.

[1969]. 'Relative clauses and possessive phrases in two Australian languages'. *Language* XLV, 35–44.

[1970a]. 'Olgolo syllable structure and what they are doing about it', *Linguistic Inquiry* I, 273–6.

[1970b]. 'Languages of the Cairns rain forest region', pp. 651–87 of Wurm and Laycock [1970].

[1970c]. 'Syntactic orientation as a semantic property', pp. 1–22 of *Mathematical linguistics and automatic translation, Report NSF-24* (Cambridge, Mass: Harvard University Computation Laboratory.)

[1971]. 'A method of semantic description', pp. 436–71 of Steinberg and Jakobovits [1971].

[Forthcoming-a] 'The semantics of giving', to appear in Proceedings of the International Colloquium on Formalisation and Models of Language, held at Paris, 27–29 April 1970. (The Hague: Mouton).

[Forthcoming-b] 'Proto-Australian laminals', to appear in *Oceanic Linguistics* IX, pp. 79–103.

Douglas, A. Douglas [1900]. 'Vocabulary of the Kirrami tribe, Cardwell, Queensland', *Science of Man* III, 8–9.

Douglas, W. H. [1964]. *An introduction to the Western Desert Language*, revised edition. (Sydney: Oceania Linguistic Monographs.)

Elkin, A. P. [1954]. *The Australian Aborigines*, third edition. (Sydney: Angus and Robertson.)

Fillmore, C. J. [1968]. 'The case for case', pp. 1–88 of *Universals in linguistic theory*, edited by E. Bach and R. T. Harms. (New York: Holt, Rinehart and Winston.)

Glass, A. and Hackett, D. [1970]. *Pitjantjatjara grammar*. (Canberra: Australian Institute of Aboriginal Studies.)

Gunther, Rev. J. [1892]. 'Grammar and vocabulary of the Aboriginal dialect called Wirradhuri', pp. 56–120 of Appendix to Threlkeld [1892].

Hale, Horatio [1846]. 'The languages of Australia', pp. 479–531 of *Ethnography and philology* (United States Exploring Expedition, 1838–42; under the command of Charles Wilkes, U.S.N., vol. VI] (Philadelphia.)

Hale, Kenneth L. [1964]. 'Classification of the Northern Paman languages, Cape York Peninsula, Australia: a research report', *Oceanic Linguistics* III, 248–65.

[1970]. 'The passive and ergative in language change: the Australian case', pp. 757–83 of Wurm and Laycock [1970].

[1971]. 'A note on a Walbiri tradition of antonymy', in Steinberg and Jakobovits [1971].

[Mimeo-a] 'Language and kinship in Australia', to appear in *Word*.

[Mimeo-b] 'Walbiri conjugations'.

[Mimeo-c] 'Deep-structure canonical disparities in relation to analysis and change: an Australian example'.

Halliday, M. A. K. [1961]. 'Categories of the theory of grammar', *Word* XVII, 241–92.

[1967–8] 'Notes on transitivity and theme in English, parts 1–3', *Journal of Linguistics* III, 37–81 and 199–244; IV, 179–215.

Haviland, John B. [forthcoming] *A grammar of Guugu-Yimidhir*.

Henderson, E. J. A. [1966]. 'Towards a prosodic statement of Vietnamese syllable structure', pp. 163–97 of *In memory of J. R. Firth*, edited by C. E. Bazell et al. (London: Longmans.)

Henry, G. J. [1967]. *Girroo Gurrll, the first surveyor, and other aboriginal legends*. (Brisbane: Smith and Paterson.)

Hercus, L. A. [1966]. 'Some aspects of the form and use of the trial number in Victorian languages and in Arabana', *Mankind* VI, 335–7.

[1969]. *The languages of Victoria: a late survey* (2 parts). (Canberra: Australian Institute of Aboriginal Studies.)

Hershberger, Henry [1964]. 'Case-marking affixes in Gugu-Yalanji', pp. 73–82 of *Papers on the languages of the Australian Aborigines*, edited by Richard Pittman and Harland Kerr. (Canberra: Australian Institute of Aboriginal Studies.)

Hershberger, Henry and Pike, Eunice V. [1970]. 'Stress as related to the grammar of Gugu-Yalanji', pp. 791–810 of Wurm and Laycock [1970].

Hershberger, Ruth [1964a]. 'Personal pronouns in Gugu-Yalanji', pp. 55–68 of Pittman and Kerr, *op. cit.*

[1964b]. 'Notes on Gugu-Yalanji verbs', pp. 35–54 of Pittman and Kerr, *op. cit.*

Holmer, N. [1966]. *An attempt towards a comparative grammar of two Australian languages*. (Canberra: Australian Institute of Aboriginal Studies.)

[1967]. *An attempt towards a comparative grammar of two Australian languages*,

Part II – Indices and vocabularies of Kattang and Thangatti. (Canberra: Australian Institute of Aboriginal Studies.)

Holmes, W. R. [Constable Reg. No. 163]. [1898]. *Report to Inspector Fitzgerald, Townsville, dated 3rd April 1898.* (Queensland State Archives, col. 143.)

Jesperson, Otto [1924]. *The philosophy of grammar.* (London: Allen and Unwin.)

Kerr, Nora F. [1968]. *Preliminary report of fieldwork [on Nyigina]*, Part 1, mimeographed. (Canberra: Australian Institute of Aboriginal Studies.)

Kershaw, A. P. [1970]. 'A pollen diagram from Lake Euramoo, north-east Queensland, Australia', *New Phytol* LXIX, 785–805.

Kirton, Jean F. [1971]. *Papers in Australian linguistics No. 5.* (Canberra: Pacific Linguistics.)

Klokeid, T. J. [1969]. *Thargari phonology and morphology.* (Canberra: Pacific Linguistics.)

  [1970]. 'Relative clauses in Mabuiag', mimeographed (Cambridge, Mass: MIT.)

Kuryłowicz, Jerzy [1964]. *The inflectional categories of Indo-European.* (Heidelberg: Winter.)

Livingstone, H. [1892]. 'A short grammar and vocabulary of the dialect spoken by the Minyug people, on the north-east of New South Wales', pp. 3–27 of Appendix to Threlkeld [1892].

Longacre, R. E. [1964]. *Grammar discovery procedures.* (The Hague: Mouton.)

Love, J. R. B. [1931/2]. 'Introduction to the Worora language', *Journal of the Royal Society of West Australia* XVII, 53–69; XVIII, 13–22.

  [1938]. 'An outline of Worora grammar', pp. 112–24 of *Studies in Australian linguistics*, edited by A. P. Elkin (Sydney: Oceania Monographs.)

Lumholtz, Carl [1889]. *Among cannibals.* (London: Murray.)

Lyons, John [1963]. *Structural semantics.* (Oxford: Blackwell.)

  [1966]. 'Towards a "notional" theory of the "parts of speech"', *Journal o Linguistics* II, 209–36.

McCawley, J. D. [1968]. 'Concerning the base component of a transformational grammar', *Foundations of language* IV, 243–69.

McConnel, Ursula H. [1945]. 'Wikmunkan phonetics', *Oceania* XV, 353–75.

Mathew, John. [1910]. *Two representative tribes of Queensland.* (London.)

  [1926]. 'Vocabulary of the Kiramai language, Herbert River, Queensland', *Report of the Australian Association for the Advancement of Science* XVIII, 547–50.

Mathews, R. H. [1902]. 'The aboriginal languages of Victoria', *Journal and Proceedings of the Royal Society of N.S.W.* XXXVI, 71–106.

  [1903a]. 'Languages of the New England aborigines', *Proceedings of the American Philosophical Society* XLII, 249–63.

  [1903b]. 'Native languages of Victoria', *American Anthropologist* V, 380–2.

  [1904]. 'Language of the Wuddyawurru tribe, Victoria', *Zeitschrift für Ethnologie* XXXVI, 729–34.

Matthews, G. H. [1960]. 'The ergative relation in Hidatsa', pp. 184–7 of *Quarterly Progress Report of the Research Laboratory of Electronics*, MIT 15 January 1960.

  [1965]. *Hidatsa syntax.* (The Hague: Mouton.)

Matthews, W. K. [1953]. 'The ergative construction in modern Indo-Aryan', *Lingua* III, 391–406.

May, Sydney [1954]. 'List of words of the Mamu dialect' (Sydney: Mitchell Library Document 28.)

Milner, G. B. [1962]. 'Active, passive or perfective in Samoan: a fresh appraisal of the problem', *Journal of the Polynesian Society* LXXI, 151–61.

Nekes, Herman and Worms, E. A. [1953]. *Australian Languages*. (Fribourg: Micro-Bibliotheca Anthropos.)

Oates, Lynette [1964]. *A tentative grammar of the Gunwinggu language [of Western Arnhem Land]*. (Sydney: Oceania Linguistic Monographs.)

O'Grady, G. N. [1960]. 'More on lexicostatistics', *Current Anthropology* I, 338–9.

   [1964]. *Nyangumata grammar*. (Sydney: Oceania Linguistic Monographs.)

   [1966]. 'Proto-Ngayarda phonology', *Oceanic Linguistics* V, 71–130.

   [1970]. 'Nyangumardaconjugations', pp. 845–64 of Wurm and Laycock [1970.]

O'Grady, G. N. and Voegelin, C. F. and F. M. [1966]. *Languages of the world: Indo-Pacific Fascicle 6* [= *Anthropological Linguistics*, vol. VIII, No. 2].

Ray, S. H. [1907 a]. 'A grammar of the language spoken by the western islanders of the Torres Straits', pp. 6–48 of *Reports of the Cambridge Anthropological Expedition to the Torres Straits*, edited by A. C. Haddon, vol. III. (Cambridge: Cambridge University Press.)

   [1907 b]. 'The Yaraikana language of Cape York', pp. 271–6 of Haddon, *op. cit.*, vol. III.

   [1925]. 'Aboriginal languages', pp. 2–15 of *[Illustrated] Australian Encyclopaedia*, vol. I.

Reichman, W. J. [1964]. *Use and abuse of statistics*. (Harmonsworth: Penguin.)

Rosenbaum, P. S. [1967]. *The grammar of English predicate complement constructions*. (Cambridge, Mass: MIT Press.)

Ross, J. R. [1970]. 'Gapping and the order of constituents', in *Progress in linguistics*, edited by Bierwisch and Heidolph. (The Hague: Mouton.)

Roth, W. E. [1897]. *Ethnological studies among the north-west-central Queensland aborigines*. (Brisbane.)

   [1901–10]. *North Queensland Ethnography*. Bulletins 1–8 (Brisbane: Government Printer, 1901–5.); Bulletins 9–18 in *Records of the Australian Museum* VI–VIII, 1907–10.

   [1901 a]. *The structure of the Gugu-Yimidir language* (= NQE, Bulletin 2).

   [1901 b]. *Food, its search, capture and preparation* (= NQE, Bulletin 3).

   [1903]. *Superstition, magic and medicine* (= NQE, Bulletin 5).

   [1908]. 'Miscellaneous papers' (= NQE, Bulletin 11).

Samarin, W. J. [1967]. *Field linguistics*. (New York: Holt, Rinehart and Winston.)

Sapir, E. [1917]. Review of C. C. Uhlenbeck's 'Het Passieve Karaktur van het Verbum Transitivum of van het Verbum Actionis in Talen van Noord-Amerika'. *International Journal of American Linguistics* I, 82–6.

Schmidt, P. W. [1912]. 'Personal pronomina in den Australischen Sprachen', *Anthropos*.

   [1919]. *Die Gliederung der Australischen Sprachen*. (Vienna.)

Sharpe (*née* Cunningham), M.C. [forthcoming]. *Alawa phonology and grammar*. (Canberra: Australian Institute of Aboriginal Studies.)

Smythe, W. E. [1948/9]. *Elementary grammar of the Gumbaiŋgar language* (*North coast, N.S.W.*). (Sydney: Oceania Monograph 8, reprinted from *Oceania* XIX–XX.)

Staal, J. F. [1967]. *Word order in Sanskrit and universal grammar.* (Dordrecht: Reidel.)

Steinberg, D. D. and Jakobovits, L. A. [1971]. *Semantics, an interdisciplinary reader in philosophy, linguistics and psychology.* (Cambridge: Cambridge University Press.)

Strehlow, T. G. H. [1944]. *Aranda phonetics and grammar.* (Sydney: Oceania Monographs.)

Taplin, G. [1879]. *The folklore, manners, customs and languages of the South Australian Aborigines.* (Adelaide: Government Printer.)

[1880]. 'Grammar of the Narrinyeri tribe of Australian Aborigines', addendum to Taplin [1879].

Teichelmann, C. G. and Schürmann, C. W. [1840]. *Outlines of a grammar, vocabulary and phraseology of the aboriginal language of South Australia, spoken by the natives in and for some distance around Adelaide.* (Adelaide.)

Thomson, D. F. [1935]. 'The joking relationship and organised obscenity in North Queensland', *American Anthropologist* XXXVII, 460–90.

Threlkeld, L. E. [1892]. *An Australian language as spoken by the Awabakal, the people of Awaba or Lake MacQuarie (near Newcastle, New South Wales) being an account of their language, traditions and customs,* edited etc. by John Fraser. (Sydney: Government Printer.)

Tindale, N. B. [1940]. 'Distribution of Australian Aboriginal tribes', *Transactions of the Royal Society of South Australia* LXIV, 140–231.

Tindale, N. B. and Birdsell, J. B. [1941]. 'Tasmanoid tribes in North Queensland', *Records of the South Australian Museum* VII, 1–9.

Tompson, F. M. and Chatfield, William Jr. [1886], 'No. 131 – Natal Downs Station, Cape River', pp. 468–83 of *The Australian Race,* edited by Edward Curr (Melbourne and London), vol. II.

Trubetzkoy, N. S. [1969]. *Principles of phonology,* translated by C. A. M. Baltaxe. (Berkeley and Los Angeles: University of California Press.)

Trudinger, R. M. [1943]. 'Grammar of the Pitjantjatjara dialect, Central Australia', *Oceania* XIII, 205–23.

Voegelin, C. F. [1952], 'The Boas plan for the presentation of American Indian languages', *Proceedings of the American Philosophical Society* XCVI, 439–51.

Von Brandenstein, C. G. [1967]. 'The language situation in the Pilbara – past and present', pp. 1–20 of *Papers in Australian Linguistics No. 2,* edited by S. A. Wurm (Canberra: Pacific Linguistics.)

Watkins, C. [1963]. 'Preliminaries to a historical and comparative analysis of the syntax of the Old Irish verb', *Celtica* VI, 1–49.

[1967]. 'Remarks on the genitive', in *To honour Roman Jakobson* (The Hague: Mouton.)

[1970] *Indo Germansche Grammatik,* Band III, Teil I (Heidelberg: Winter).

Watson, F. J. [1944]. *Vocabularies of four representative tribes of South Eastern Queensland.* (Brisbane.)

Whitney, W. D. [1889]. *Sanskrit grammar.* (Leipzig.)

Worms, E. A. [1938]. 'Onomatopoeia in some Kimberley tribes of north-west Australia', *Oceania* VIII, 453–7.

Wurm, S. A. [1965]. 'Recent developments in Australian linguistics', *Lingua* XIV, 371–80.

    [1969]. 'Person marker sequences in Australian languages', pp. 51–69 of *Papers in Australian Linguistics No. 4*. (Canberra: Pacific Linguistics.)

    [forthcoming]. *Languages of Australia and Tasmania*. (The Hague: Mouton.)

Wurm, S. A. and Laycock, D. C. [1970]. *Pacific linguistics studies in honour of Arthur Capell*. (Canberra: Pacific Linguistics.)

Index of Australian Languages

Approximate locations of the Australian languages referred to are given in maps 1 and 2 (pages xxiv and 25). Reference below is to page numbers.